MACROECONOMICS

MACROECONOMICS
Theory and Policy

Anthony S. Campagna

University of Vermont

Houghton Mifflin   Boston

Atlanta   Dallas   Geneva, Illinois

Hopewell, New Jersey   Palo Alto   London

Printed in the U.S.A.

Library of Congress Catalog Card
Number: 73–9409

ISBN: 0–395–17085–0

To Ruth

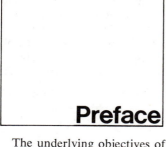

Preface

This book was written primarily for the student of intermediate macroeconomic theory. Accordingly, the discussion is kept on a plane rigorous enough to provide a solid foundation of theory and methodology, but not so advanced that the abstractions prevent an appreciation for this exciting subject. For this reason, mathematical expressions have been minimized and confined mainly to algebraic formulations. Furthermore, the amount of text allocated to policy questions should generate interest in the formal theoretical discussion.

The underlying objectives of this textbook are to provide the student with some awareness of the field of macroeconomics without unnecessary complexity, and to encourage critical analysis of traditional theory. It is hoped that this approach will stimulate both the understanding and refinement of traditional theory.

Part I contains the introduction to macroeconomic theory and methodology as well as national income accounting. The emphasis of NIA is on conceptual problems, interpretations, and social-philosophical implications; details are minimal, and the accounting techniques covered are only those which affect later work.

Part II is concerned with the development of traditional theory. The simple income-expenditure model is constructed, and successive complications are introduced until the general equilibrium model is reached. A classical macroeconomic model is presented in order to compare and contrast it with the Keynesian model.

Part III extends the general approach to macroeconomic policy. The policy tools are discussed and evaluated both in the abstract as well as in practical application. The discussion throughout this section may be more usefully labeled Political Economy, as socio-political issues are introduced to indicate their interactions with policy and theory. In addition, the critiques of Friedman, Galbraith, and Baran and Sweezy are included to provide the spectrum of dissent from the traditional theory presented earlier. In chapters 16 and 17 an impressionistic model is based partly on these and other numerous criticisms. An evaluation of market structure is pertinent to the discussion. Finally, economic growth is considered both in the traditional approach and with additional observations based upon criticisms and current concerns such as the growth vs. no-growth controversy.

One of the primary aims of this textbook has been to provide flexibility in use. Hopefully, the treatment of conventional theory is thorough enough to permit the selection of areas of concentration. Some chapters need not be covered sequentially, and others can be skipped entirely to accommodate the course's structure. Some instructors may wish to omit national income accounting or to cover it lightly, while others may wish to treat the policy chapters in this way. Whatever the emphasis of the course, the remainder of the book can be used as a reading supplement; in any case, experimentation is both possible and desirable.

Most of this book was written while I was on leave at Inter American University at San German, Puerto Rico. I would like to thank everyone associated with that institution for his cooperation and many kindnesses, and particularly Gerard

Latortue, whose efforts on my behalf made my stay there so enjoyable and productive.

Many others have contributed to the book's development, both prior to and during its manuscript stage, and many have influenced me both directly and indirectly. They are too numerous to mention, and footnotes are a rather inadequate manner in which to indicate indebtedness. However, the manuscript was reviewed and improved by the suggestions of Yukon Huang of the University of Virginia, Charles R. Britton of the University of Arkansas, and Joseph Chao of Wright State University. Their comments were extremely useful, and I would like to thank them for their help and absolve them from any errors that remain. Finally, a special note of gratitude to my wife, without whom there would be no book at all.

A. S. C.

Contents

Introduction

Interest in macroeconomics has increased greatly in recent years, and it might be thought that this branch of economics is relatively new. Actually, this is not the case, for since economics became a discipline, men have been concerned with macroeconomic issues. As the name implies, macroeconomics takes a broad view of the economic system and includes such areas as the measurement and determination of national income, the level of employment of labor and capital, the determinants and rate of economic growth, the price level, the effects of the public sector on the economy, and the effects of foreign trade on the domestic economy. Clearly, these are not new areas of interest but rather have occupied a central position in the development of economic thought.

What then accounts for the increased attention given to macroeconomics by economists, politicians, and laymen alike? Perhaps most of all it was the growing realization that some control over the economy is possible. As long as current economic conditions were regarded as immutable, only scholars were interested in examining market forces at work. However, as the belief that economic situations could be changed by conscious policy spread, the concern with macroeconomic problems became more general as well.

The acknowledgment of several existing economic options represents quite a departure from laissez-faire economic thinking, and consequently it has taken over a generation for this idea to gain acceptance, sometimes grudgingly. In the past it was held that the economy contained self-correcting mechanisms that could be expected to operate automatically. Given sufficient time, the economy would adjust to society's preferences as expressed in the marketplace. In the meantime, however, the community was forced to accept fluctuating economic conditions. Dissatisfaction and impatience with this state of affairs prompted a reexamination of traditional macroeconomic theory.

More than any other economist, past or present, it was John Maynard Keynes who redirected attention to the economic situation of today—the short run—from the economic situation of tomorrow—the long run.[1] His impatience with secular tendencies encouraged the change in attitudes necessary to permit the serious questioning of accepted doctrine.[2] He forced everyone to reexamine not only inherited economic doctrines but also the responsiveness of our economic, social, and political institutions to changing economic conditions. It is not our concern here to evaluate Keynes's ideas (a large part of this book is devoted to this endeavor) but to account for the increased attention given to the problems of macroeconomics with which he was mainly concerned. His influence in this entire field simply cannot be overstated.

---

[1] Witness his much-quoted remark, "In the long run we are all dead." Post-Keynesian economists, however, have not felt limited to the short run.

[2] This attitude seems to run through most of Keynes's work, the most influential of which is *The General Theory of Employment, Interest, and Money* (New York: Harcourt, Brace, 1936).

Microeconomics Versus Macroeconomics

A simple analogy may be helpful in differentiating the two principal areas of economic study: microeconomics and macroeconomics. Imagine the astronauts on a trip to the moon. As they wait on the launching pad, they have an excellent view of the surrounding area, the details are sharp and clear, and they can distinguish objects on the ground quite readily. Let us oversimplify and call this a pure microeconomic situation. Now, as they leave the earth, they cannot see many of the previously observed objects, and details get lost as the distance from the earth increases, but larger masses can now be distinguished: the entire coast of Florida, the southeast region of the United States, and so on. The merging of objects means that a process of aggregation has begun and that the world of pure microeconomics has been left behind. About halfway in the journey to the moon all details of the earth are gone, although large masses—the continents and oceans—may still be visible. Again oversimplifying, let us call this a macroeconomic situation.

The analogy has served the purpose of demonstrating that while the earth has remained the same, the viewpoint has changed. Much the same is true in economic methodology, which arbitrarily divides the study of economics into two broad categories so that different views of the same economy become possible. Macroeconomics relies on the aggregation of microeconomic information. Microeconomics is concerned with individual economic units—the household, the firm, the market for a good or service. From the study of an economic unit some principles of (optimizing) behavior are established and generalized to other, similar units; after a time a body of postulates is accumulated. The pricing and output policies of the firm and the utility-maximizing principles of the household are but two examples of this general approach.

As soon as units are aggregated into groups, firms into industries, households into consumers, and so on, the movement is away from microeconomics to macroeconomics. There is no sharp dividing line between the two, nor should there be. Thus, the movement from the price of oranges to citrus fruit prices, to fruit prices, to agricultural prices, to food prices, to the consumer price level represents a continuous, although divisible, spectrum. The process of aggregation from micro to macro of other economic variables is similar to that of price. Macroeconomics is not directly concerned with the consumption behavior of any one household or the investment behavior of any one firm but with total consumption and total investment. Yet while macroeconomics does not deal primarily with individual behavior, a knowledge of microeconomic theory is essential if a meaningful macroeconomic theory is to be constructed consistent with established microeconomic principles. As will be seen, this is no easy task.

Theory in Economics

Economics, and macroeconomics in particular, is a fascinating subject, dealing as it does with many intriguing problems of man's existence. There is a natural tendency on the part of students of economics to jump from the awareness of a problem to the formulation of immediate solutions. This tendency, while certainly understandable, should be avoided if rational solutions are to be obtained. It would be nice if it were possible to go immediately from problem to policy, but in the real world most problems do not respond to quick solutions based on superficial knowledge.

Reality is often confusing, even chaotic, but if one's goal is the interpretation of it, then some method must be found to reduce the complexity of reality to manageable proportions. It is necessary to find a description of reality that is simple and uncomplicated but still retains the essential features of its real-world counterpart. In brief, it is necessary to abstract from reality, to build a model of reality that helps one to understand and describe something without being confused by an overwhelming amount of detail and the resulting complexity.

Constructing a theory requires painstaking analysis and determination of which factors are essential and which may be safely omitted from the model. Only after one has acquired the knowledge of how an economy operates is it possible to think meaningfully about problems and proper policies. There is no justifiable way to skip the intermediate step between real-world problems and their alleviation—the difficult task of theorizing and model building. Economic theory is difficult, since it is necessarily abstract and calls for rigorous thinking, but it is also challenging and rewarding and essential for rational policy making.

In the chapters that follow the role of theory in economics will be examined at greater length. The topic is introduced briefly here only to indicate that one of the major aims of this book is to develop macroeconomic theory. Much of the book is concerned with the type of painstaking analysis so necessary in model building. The macroeconomic model is built up sector by sector in an incremental manner. Although the reader may experience some temporary confusion as a result, when all parts are brought together the logic of the model should become clear.

Once the model has been constructed and the tools of macroeconomic analysis have been developed, the discussion of policy questions will be undertaken. Policy alternatives are suggested throughout the text wherever appropriate, of course, but the systematic discussion of past economic policies and future possibilities is mainly concentrated in the last third of the book. With the introduction of political and social factors into the analysis, the economic model gains in realism and the value of patient development of the theory becomes evident.

Empiricism in Economics

Theory is essential for economic analysis, and the theory must be valid to permit prediction and viable policy. But what makes a good theory, and how is it distinguished from a bad theory? The obvious answer is that theory must be tested by the facts. If the empirical evidence supports or fits the theory, then the theory is retained; if the empirical evidence does not fit the theory, then either the theory is rejected or judgment is reserved until additional or better information is available.

A good theory, then, must explain behavior logically and also be consistent (or not inconsistent) with the facts. Naturally, the closer the relation between theory and data, the more confidence there is in its reliability and usefulness. The criteria for testing the relation are entrusted to the econometrician, who develops the necessary statistical and mathematical techniques to do the job.[3]

Furthermore, even good theory must be continually tested against the facts. In a dynamic economy established relations are likely to change, making old theories obsolete. All too often conventional wisdom retains its vigor long after its truths have been superseded. The point is that theories, good and bad, must be tested and

[3] It should be noted that with sound techniques one could go from facts to theory as well as vice versa, but the same logic and care in generalizing must be observed.

PART ONE

National income accounting, like other forms of accounting, is concerned with past events. Accountants generally do not make forecasts or value judgments. They simply record what happened in a system of accounts according to predetermined rules. Once the rules and the structure of accounts have been determined, accounting becomes a routine task. Changes in procedures are likely to be incremental and slow to come.

National income accountants have a much more demanding task than business accountants, and setting forth the procedures is a far from routine matter. This is because national income accountants determine in some manner the nature and extent of the economic activity that occurs in the nation over some time period. This would appear to be a straightforward assignment. That it is not is the subject of this part of the text.

The need for national income accounting scarcely requires extensive justification; a nation, like a firm, needs to know how it has performed and utilized the resources at its command. If the results are unsatisfactory and economic goals have not been achieved, corrective policies require objective data. The collection and presentation of this information is the job of the national income accountant, who employs statistics, accounting, and economic theory in order to carry out his assignment. A good deal of skill and effort are required to supply the necessary information.

Nevertheless, the study of the system of accounts and the set of rules formulated for national income accounting can get tedious at times. There is no way to overcome the prosaic nature of the subject matter. Therefore, in recognition of this potential obstacle, the discussion in this text will attempt to eschew undue details in favor of broader concepts. Details remain, of course, but the emphasis is clearly on concepts, problems, and interpretation. An explanation of what is included in national income accounting is required if one is to interpret the data rationally and use them wisely.

Accordingly, some basic knowledge of GNP is assumed, and the discussion is designed to elevate the level of analysis to the point where a better appreciation of the subject of national income accounting may be obtained. No one learns to be a national income accountant from a summary treatment in a textbook, but some awareness of the duties can be gained by considering the problems that must be dealt with, whether they are merely noted in skimming through these pages, in sampling them according to interest, or in delving into them industriously.

Issues
in
National
Income
Accounting

The Definition of Income

What is ultimately sought in national income accounting is some measure of the national income —the flow of goods and services from productive efforts over some time period. But what is income and how is it to be measured? Income is a flow variable,[1] but beyond this simple fact there is no set definition. The reason is that income in an economic sense must be defined in terms of satisfaction; income is the flow of satisfaction or the flow of benefits from consuming goods and services. Yet satisfaction is subjectively determined and consequently not subject to direct observation and measurement. Thus, the ideal index of the community's income must be abandoned in favor of a more pragmatic definition that permits quantification.[2]

Income must be measured, then, in value terms—in money terms—which means that a price must be attached to all transactions. Then all activities can be observed and measured, since they are expressed in the same units. Yet it is important to realize just what has been sacrificed in going from a satisfaction concept of income to the money valuation definition of income. The following constitutes only a partial discussion of this interesting question.

By using a money value of income—price times quantity—we have committed ourselves to counting only *currently* produced goods and services. There is nothing wrong with this approach, but the flow concept must be redefined so that for most

[1] A flow variable necessarily assumes its magnitude over time and is measured in that time period, that is, income per week, per month, per year; investment per quarter; and so on. See chapter 3.

[2] The difficulty of defining income is largely overlooked now, but it is appropriate to remind oneself occasionally of the problem. Note this statement: "Modern economic analysis recognizes that fundamentally income is a flow of satisfactions, of intangible psychological experiences. . . . A man strives for the satisfaction of his wants and desires and not for objects for their own sake." R. M. Haig, "The Concept of Income—Economic and Legal Aspects," in *Readings in the Economics of Taxation,* ed. R. A. Musgrave and Carl S. Shoup (Homewood, Ill.: Richard D. Irwin, 1959), p. 55. The income from a transistor radio, for instance, is found in the flow of benefits or satisfaction derived from it, not in its monetary value.

goods and services it must be stated for a definite period of time, after which the flow stops. Taking an extreme example for clarity, a transistor radio produced and purchased in the same period provides monetary income for those who produced it and satisfaction from ownership for the consumer. At the end of the accounting year the monetary income is duly registered and appears as income to the factors of production. However, the satisfaction received from production—the much broader concept of income—is understated, because although the radio lasts more than one accounting period, future accounting periods do not consider the satisfaction received from *past* production. The flow of income stops when the rewards of factors of production are recorded; the benefits received may go on for many more periods.

One possible method to correct the misrecording of income might be to accept the market value of the radio as a proxy for the satisfaction received[3] and then to prorate the value over the useful life of the radio. If the radio has an expected life of five years, then one fifth of the market value should be recorded as income in each of the five years. Surely, this is a better measure of income and satisfaction received than the alternative of assuming that the radio is completely used up in one time period and that all income and satisfaction stops after this time period.

For some consumer goods it makes no real difference which concept of income is used, since the good or service is consumed immediately and there is no carry-over into future accounting periods. There are many goods, however, particularly consumer durables such as stoves, automobiles, and refrigerators, that do last and yield satisfaction over many years. For these goods a distortion of the flow concept is inevitable. Its only justification is expediency. It would simply be too huge a task to estimate thousands of useful lives and then spread the value over future accounting periods. Perhaps in the case of goods such as automobiles or refrigerators it might be argued that the job would not be all that difficult and that it should be attempted. But remember goods such as hammers, birdbaths, kitchen utensils, and footstools also have useful lives of more than one period. Would it be worth the trouble to estimate these income flows? It then becomes a question of where to draw the line, and the easiest line to draw is the one that assumes all consumer goods (except housing) are used up in one period. This solves the problem in one stroke—the satisfaction definition of income is abandoned in favor of pragmatism. This is the course taken by the national income accountants, and it must be repeated that there is nothing wrong with it *if* one is aware of just what is involved in the decision. Economically, the focus is on current production and income flows are expressed in money value terms; philosophically, perhaps too much emphasis is placed on production and not enough on past accumulation. The available method of measurement, then, seriously affects the manner in which we view the performance of the economy and determine its success or failure.

It should be noted briefly here (elaborated later) that this treatment of consumer goods also applies to government purchases of goods and services but not to capital goods or producers' durables, which are in a different category. Capital goods are definitely used up in the productive process, and the national income

---

[3] Those familiar with traditional microeconomics will recognize this procedure as the assumed behavior of households going about maximizing utility by equating ratios of marginal utilities and prices of goods. Substitute market value for price and satisfaction for utility. Unfortunately, all the difficulties of utility analysis are retained in the substitution.

accountant does record the estimated use in an item called capital consumption allowance or, more familiarly, depreciation. The estimated unused value of the asset is carried forward to future periods.

The Meaning of Economic Activity

Broadly defined, any activity that uses up scarce resources can be considered economic in nature. If this is the case, then any activity that uses up scarce resources must lead to the creation of income, if there is some measure of satisfaction received in return. This must be the case for income defined in the larger sense, but for income defined in terms of money values, there must be some exchange, some transaction, whereby the value of the activity can be measured. Here is a problem. There are many activities that use up scarce resources and yield satisfaction (and hence income) but for which there is no observable transaction, no market exchange. Therefore, in order to employ the restricted definition of income, some definition of economic activity for purposes of national income accounting must be made.

The national income accountants have made a rather definite rule to simplify matters. All transactions that take place in the market are considered economic activity; all others (with some exceptions noted later) are not and are excluded from further consideration. Market transactions provide the value terms (P and Q) necessary for measurement and inclusion into income; nonmarket transactions do not.

This is a simple rule to apply, but it has some implications that go beyond the obvious violation of the meaning of economic activity. In particular, it excludes almost all activities that take place within the home: the housewife's services, home repairs, do-it-yourself activities, washing the car, chopping firewood, and so on. If these services were purchased in the marketplace, they would be included. Shine your own shoes, and the job is ignored; pay someone to shine them for you, and income is recorded. Clearly, the distinction is arbitrary and dictated by expediency and not principle, but who is going to estimate the value of these self-provided services and by what means? Furthermore, how can one distinguish the activities that are economic in character from those that are simply a part of living? Chopping wood, for example, may be a use of leisure time to keep physically fit and not primarily intended to be an economic activity at all. Too many activities in the home present these dilemmas, so it is simply easier to exclude them all.

One result of this rule is that it automatically labels the services of the housewife unproductive. All of her activities—cooking, sewing, cleaning, baby-sitting, budgeting—are excluded from national income. Again, if these services were purchased, they would be included. Thus, one of the nation's major activities is omitted and prompts the familiar but telling sarcasm that if an increase in national income is desired simply have housewives work for one another.

It is obvious that the national income accountants had a highly developed, market-oriented economy in mind when they determined the extent of economic activity. In such an economy most of the activities in the home would be minimal and could be ignored. Yet, as will be argued later, the absolute numbers for national income have sometimes become an end in themselves and have been used for purposes for which they were not intended by those who fail to appreciate the significance of the assumptions made in their development. Thus, it is misleading, if not absurd, to compare two or more economies by some number for national income, especially when these economies differ greatly in the number and variety of goods and services that appear in the marketplace. In many economies a great deal of economic activity still takes place within the home, and goods and services are produced at home and not purchased in the marketplace. The comparison of an advanced economy with an underdeveloped economy is simply not valid, although such comparisons occur frequently. In fact, it may be misleading to compare income data for different time periods within the same economy if, as has been often observed, a growing economy transfers more and more activities from the home to the marketplace. There will be an upward bias to the data, and an uncritical analysis could be unknowingly erroneous in estimating growth.

Market Transactions

To determine national income and product, there is, then, the general rule that only market transactions, with some exceptions, will be included in the measurements. We must now decide whether or not to break the general rule by excluding some market transactions and including some nonmarket transactions and, in any case, what price to use in valuing transactions.

Addressing the latter question first, it would appear natural to take the market price of a good or service as the proper price to use in recording transactions. The market price comprises all the costs (income) of the factors of production, including profit. If we are interested in the breakdown of national income by factor shares, market price should provide the necessary information. One problem arises immediately, since not all of the market price flows to factors of production; some part of the market price flows to government in the form of indirect business taxes—sales tax, excise tax, property tax, and so on. Shall we record the transaction net of taxes or not? If a transistor radio is sold for $10.00 with a 3 per cent sales tax, so that the consumer paid $10.30, what is the proper price to use? Students of public finance will recognize the problem as that of the incidence of taxation—who ultimately bears the burden of the tax, the buyer or seller or both? Economists have not been able to establish any general rules regarding the incidence of these indirect taxes, contending that there are too many factors involved and that each case must be examined independently before a judgment can be made. Since the national income accountants of the Department of Commerce are in no position to do this for each good, some simplifying assumptions had to be made. It was assumed that all indirect taxes are shifted forward to the consumer and that the price used to record the transaction should include them. In our example, $10.30 would appear as consumption expenditures. (The breakdown on the other side, the income side, is postponed for the present.)

The use of market prices as the yardstick to measure value transactions is not seriously contested any longer, although, as will be seen, there is disagreement when welfare implications are derived from market prices. For nonmarket transactions an estimate of the market price must be made, presumably that price which would have resulted if the transaction had been a market transaction. The word *presumably* indicates that the estimate is far easier to obtain theoretically than practically. In practice, the estimated price for nonmarket transactions is simply an actual market price for similar or related goods or transactions. This market price could be biased, however, since if the nonmarket transactions had actually occurred in the marketplace, the resulting price might have been different.

Excluded Market Transactions

Certain transactions that take place in the market are nevertheless excluded from measurements of national income, since they violate the general rule for the recognition of income: the good or service must be currently produced and must use up currently available scarce resources. Many transactions represent the transfer of wealth (or claims to wealth) or the exchange of commodities produced in some previous accounting period. To record these transactions would mean that the resulting total would reveal total money transactions,[4] while we are interested only in those transactions that lead to the creation of income from current production. Some examples of these transactions follow.

SECONDHAND SALES

The most obvious candidate for exclusion is secondhand sales. Here individual or economic units merely exchange ownership of an already existing good, and in the process no income from current production is created. Even if a profit is made, there is no income in the accounting sense, for the gain is offset by the recording of the good at the transaction price by the buyer. In short, the entire transaction is ignored, gain or loss, swindle or bargain.

If, however, a reward is offered to someone who brings the buyer and seller together, the reward is recorded as income. The function of creating a market is a legitimate economic activity, currently provided, and uses scarce resources, and hence the reward for this function is clearly income. The functions of the broker, used-car salesman, dealers of many kinds, auctioneers, are a few examples.

There is one exception to the generalization that all secondhand sales are ignored in the national income accounts. In a fairly recent change (August 1965) secondhand sales that involve more than one sector are recorded. The accounts are broken down into the following sectors by the national income accountants: the household sector, the government sector, the business sector, and the rest-of-the-world sector. The reason for the exception is to secure more accurate estimates of the capital stock by sector and also to make estimates of capital consumption allowances and investment more consistent.[5] For example, suppose an employee purchases a secondhand car from the company for which he works. Under the old procedures this transaction would have been ignored, and therefore the value of the car would have been carried as if it were still on the books of the company. It would have been carried as part of the capital stock of the business sector, and there would have been an estimate for depreciation recorded. The capital stock of business would thus have been overestimated, depreciation overestimated, net investment understated (gross I minus depreciation is equal to net I), and personal savings reduced. Under the new procedures personal consumption is increased and investment decreased to recognize the transfer of the capital item.

---

[4] This "flow of funds" accounting is a perfectly legitimate alternative to the scheme of the Department of Commerce; it simply measures different flows and is very useful for specific purposes.

[5] Although the actual accounts have not been introduced yet, it should be noted that they are also affected: The saving account reflecting personal saving and government surplus is adjusted to match the changes in investment, and therefore the totals of GNP are not affected by the exceptions but internal accounts are.

ILLEGAL ACTIVITIES

All unlawful activities, whether economic or not, are omitted from national income accounting. Here there is an admitted violation of income recognition by any definition of income. There is no justification for the exclusion of these activities if they otherwise meet the conditions imposed on any transaction. True, they are difficult to estimate, but that is not the reason for exclusion; rather it has simply been traditional to omit those activities that a society prohibits by law or in some sense considers undesirable. The definition of an undesirable activity changes, of course, from one generation to the next and from one society to another. Still, it is not the unwarranted comparisons or biased figures that deserve attention—these can be changed or accounted for. It is the larger issue of what constitutes desirable or socially useful activities that demands closer examination.

In a free market economy who is to say what is a socially desirable economic activity? What criteria are available by which to judge that one good is desirable and another is not, that one contributes to our well-being and another does not? If you think you could formulate a set of rules for evaluating activities, imagine the arguments that would arise over whether the following goods and services are socially useful or desirable and hence should be included in our national income: birth control pills, rifles, switchblades, gold-plated toothpicks, pet foods, liquor, tanks, tobacco products, motorcycles, greeting cards, embalming fluid, Phi Beta Kappa keys, prostitution, and gambling. Even a casual glance at these products would reveal the enormous potential for conflict over their utility. Indeed, it is not difficult to imagine arguments for the inclusion of some of these activities at a negative value—a subtraction from national income.

In the absence of any calculus to tell us which goods to include or exclude, most of the foregoing products are included in the national income aggregates. Again, no value judgments are made by the national income accountants, who simply record the market value of economic activities, excluding only those expressly forbidden by law. Their actions are understandable, but this exclusion must be kept in mind in interpreting the national income data. We will return to this subject in the critique of national income accounting.

CAPITAL GAINS AND LOSSES

All gains or losses caused by changes in the valuation of assets are excluded from the national income accounts. In a dynamic economy prices do change for a variety of reasons, some from the demand side and some from the supply side. Whatever the cause, changing prices mean that assets will be revalued and a gain or loss will result. A well-functioning market will revalue the assets automatically, in some cases rather quickly (as on an organized stock exchange), in others more slowly (as is true for private housing).

If no exchange or sale of the asset occurs, these gains or losses are so-called paper gains or losses. The individual is poorer or richer, but only on paper, since no gain or loss is actually realized. Obviously, then, these developments are ignored in accounting for the national income—no transaction occurs and no change in income is recorded.[6]

Even if a transaction does take place and a real gain or loss is realized, there is

---

[6] Without dwelling on this point, it should be clear that under certain definitions of income, a gain or loss would be recorded—briefly, the individual's economic power has surely changed.

still no recognition of the transaction for national income accounting purposes. We are interested in the flow of income from currently produced goods or services, not in the revaluation of past production. Therefore, the play of impersonal market forces that occurs continuously is not taken into account unless these forces affect current economic activity. These gains and losses could be considerable and could affect many economic decisions, some of which will be recorded by the national income accountants ultimately, but it must be remembered that we are interested in the flow of income, not in the flow of funds.

To repeat, all capital gains and losses are excluded from the national income accounts. Changes in the value of assets such as securities, personal assets, land, whether or not they result in realized gains or losses, are not a part of the currently produced collection of goods and services and are ignored.

TRANSFER PAYMENTS

Transfer payments, as the name implies, are income payments from one economic unit to another but not for current productive economic activity. They are transactions that transfer income without reference to the creation of income and hence must be excluded from national income accounts.

Government makes most of the transfer payments. It is, of course, in the best position to carry out redistribution of income schemes. Programs for welfare assistance, veterans' payments, social security, and direct relief are examples of transfer payments. In all of them the recipient does not perform any current productive activity or supply a service to the government in order to receive the payment, and the payments, while income to the recipient, are not recognized as income for national income accounting purposes.

A more controversial type of transfer payment is interest on the public debt. It is also excluded from the accounts but for different reasons. If the debt incurred could be traced directly to an asset, then the interest payment would be an income payment—a return—regarded just as any other interest payment. This can be done for some part of the public debt, but the major portion of the debt was incurred during World War II and subsequent wars, and the assets acquired can hardly be said to be yielding a return. Rather than try to apportion the part of interest payments that might be traced to assets, the national income accountants have decided to treat the whole amount as a transfer payment and exclude it from the accounts.[7]

Another type of transfer payment that does not affect the size of GNP but only its composition is the value of (net) gifts from persons to foreigners and (non-military) gifts and grants from government to foreigners. Prior to August 1965 such gifts were simply included in personal consumption and government expenditures. Now personal consumption and government expenditures are reduced by the amount of foreign transfers, shown separately in the accounts, and are offset by an increase in the net exports of goods and services. This treatment accords with the procedures used in the international balance-of-payments accounting.

Still another type of transfer payment is made by business in the form of bad debts, prizes, awards, scholarships, and similar nonfactor payments. These business transfer payments are not for currently produced goods or services, bear little or no relation to the output of the firm, and must therefore be excluded from the

[7] The treatment of interest on the public debt varies from country to country, and care should be taken when making comparisons.

accounts. (They are transfers of income, not payments made for services rendered.) Yet if these transfers were excluded, the accounts would not balance. Firms more than likely treat these items as costs that are passed along in higher selling prices. On the other side of the account, however, there would be no corresponding factor income recorded. For this reason business transfer payments are included as part of GNP but subtracted to arrive at national income, the sum of factor payments. (Of course, they are added back again to obtain personal income.)

Finally, there are other transfer payments that are excluded from the accounts because they are not currently produced goods or services. These include all gifts, inheritances, charity payments, and payments to nonprofit institutions.

FINAL VERSUS INTERMEDIATE GOODS

A good or service is considered final if it is not for resale or reprocessing, that is, it is in the hands of the final consumer. A good or service is considered intermediate if it will undergo further processing or marketing. The distinction is extremely important if one is to secure an accurate estimate of the value of the national product. Since we are considering excluded market transactions, it is appropriate to treat this item here, but only briefly, since it will be necessary to deal with it in more detail later.

All intermediate goods and services are excluded from national income accounting, even though they meet all the requirements for inclusion. The reason for exclusion is to avoid counting the same value—the same activity—twice. Most goods go through many stages of processing before they reach the ultimate user—from raw material to processing to marketing. To include the value of the good at each transaction would result in counting the same value more than once; this is because the value at these intermediate stages becomes a *cost* to the next stage and therefore will be included in the final value at the completion of this stage only to be passed on to the next stage, and so on. Only when the final user purchases the good is the proper value recorded.

Another way to look at the evolution of the final value is to note that only the value added (over cost of acquisition) at each intermediate stage may be correctly included, since incomes are created at each stage. Then if one totals the value added at each stage, the sum will be the value of the final product.

Included Nonmarket Transactions

As was noted, national income accounting is primarily concerned with recording market transactions and in the process recording incomes created in the production of the goods and services exchanged. But what if incomes created by current economic activity are not evidenced by a market transaction? To omit this type of income merely because there is no market record could seriously distort the value of the national product. Actually, there may be many income-creating activities of this kind, but only the more quantitatively important ones can be included. Since there is no market price recorded, estimates of the value of the activity must be made, and the task is difficult enough for the major items. Only those nonmarket transactions that materially affect factor incomes are included. Estimates of these items are made and then imputed to factor incomes and to the corresponding offset item of personal consumption to which they relate. Some of these major sources of nonmarket but income-creating transactions are discussed in the following sections.

INCOME IN KIND

In some industries part of the compensation paid to employees is in the form of food and lodging in addition to the more customary cash payment. To omit from compensation of employees (wages and salaries) that part of income received in kind would understate the factor incomes in those occupations where such payments are traditional (including food and shelter to members of the armed forces). The national income accountants therefore estimate the value of income in kind received (valued at the cost to the employer), add it to factor incomes (wages and salaries), and assume that the employees buy back the same items previously furnished "free" by the employer. In the accounts this means that wages and salaries are increased and personal consumption expenditures are increased by like amounts.

Although the procedure appears logical, there are some questions that arise. First, how accurate are the estimates? As with all estimates of nonmarket activities, the value placed on the transaction may be biased upward; this is even more likely in the case of income in kind. Imagine the problem in the estimation of housing income of the migrant worker. Second, national income accounting rules are violated: what is an intermediate good (cost of food and lodging) to the employer, normally excluded, now becomes a final good appearing as personal consumption (and wages) and is included. Apparently, the better estimate of factor incomes overrules the formal accounting procedure.

FARMERS' CONSUMPTION

Another imputation is necessary in the case of farmers who consume part of their own production of either food or fuel. To get an accurate measure of farm income, an estimate of farm-produced consumption must be made and added to income earned from sales. The estimated value of farm consumption is then added to personal consumption expenditures and to net profit on the income side. The other expenses connected with this production would be recorded in the proper categories, that is, depreciation, interest, and so on; hence the entry for *net* profit.

RENTAL INCOME OF PERSONS

This item, with its rather unfortunate label, has nothing to do with slavery but with another imputation made for the rental value of owner-occupied homes.

Recall the earlier discussion of income as a flow concept and specifically as a flow of benefits over some time period. We were forced to abandon the flow of satisfaction concept for pragmatic reasons and forced to regard all consumer goods as if they were used up in the period of purchase. This is true whether the item is an automobile or a hamburger, a durable or nondurable good. An exception to this practice is made in the case of housing services, because they are both quantitatively important and qualitatively different from other consumer durables in that the services rendered are more readily measurable and distinct from the question of ownership. A house yields essentially the same service whether it is occupied by its owner or by a tenant. Since the expenditure by tenants is included in the national product as a rental payment, it is necessary to impute a rental value in the case of owner-occupied homes as well or the flow of income from this important source would be understated.

In effect, the national income accountants treat the owner-occupied home as a business, with the housing service as the product that the owner buys from himself. As with any business, there are deductions from the estimated gross rental value, such as depreciation, mortgage interest, and property taxes, so that only the net rental value is included in the item "rental income of persons." The deductions or expenses are included in the appropriate places along with similar expenses of other businesses. Of course, on the other side of the account, the full amount is included in personal consumption expenditures.

OTHER IMPUTATIONS

More complex imputations are made for the activities of commercial banks, investment trusts, life insurance companies, and other financial intermediaries. To avoid unnecessary detail, only a brief description of these complicated procedures will be presented here—just enough to indicate their purpose.

In the case of commercial banks, the problem once again concerns the fact that not all of the banks' activities result in monetary payment; specifically, some part of the cost of providing services may be cancelled by the nonpayment of interest rather than indirect or direct charges to the customer. For instance, no interest is paid by the banks on demand deposits. Instead, the banks apply whatever income they derive from the use of the demand deposits to the costs of servicing customers' checking accounts and therefore can keep the service charge to customers low and at a fraction of the true administrative costs. Since this is a non-monetary allocation, there is no record of what actually happens, and therefore the value of the true service performed by banks is understated. To remedy this, an imputation is made to reflect the true costs of services rendered by the simple device of assuming that all interest earned by banks is paid out to depositors and then charging the full amount of the costs of services rendered. The end result is an increase in the income side for interest received, which is matched on the expenditure side by an increase in service charges—personal consumption expenditures.

Another type of problem occurs in the treatment of the activities of life insurance companies and similar institutions. Premiums for life insurance include elements of both current consumption expenditure and saving; similarly, receipts from insurance companies involve both capital transfers and current returns. There is no way to distinguish between the transactions in these areas that occur between insurance companies and policyholders. The national income accountants have decided not to try to distinguish but to resort to another simplifying device. In effect, insurance companies are treated as individuals, which means that all benefits and all premiums are disregarded as being mere transfers. All of the income of the insurance companies is imputed to policyholders (appearing as interest income), who then buy back the services of the insurance company at a value equal to the operating expenses of the companies (appearing as personal consumption expenditures), and any difference between income and expenses becomes simply personal saving. Thus, the issue of what part of insurance activity is consumption and what part saving is resolved.

Additional Problems in National Income Accounting

So far we have been concerned mainly with explaining definitions and developing the rules by which the national income and product data are to be collected. Once the rules have been determined, credibility requires that they be consistently followed and that any changes which do occur be planned and orderly. There are some problems, however, that go beyond the definitional ones and that are perhaps even more important. Primarily, these are interpretation problems caused by uncritical acceptance of the published data. Only a few of these issues can be discussed here.

PRICE CHANGES

In order to make comparisons over time, it is necessary to correct the current dollar magnitudes for changes in prices. GNP figures could rise without any real change in output if inflation had occurred, and conversely for falling prices. To make valid comparisons, prices must be kept constant by stating GNP data in terms of some base year prices. The matter is easily accomplished through the use of index numbers.

In practice, there is no one overall price index with which to deflate GNP. Consider all the components of GNP, and it will be obvious that no single price index could properly describe the movement of prices. In practice, then, a separate price index is calculated for as many series as is practical, that is, a separate price index for shoes, automobiles, furniture, medical services, and so on. Then each series is corrected for price changes independently. The result when summed is GNP in 1958 dollars (current base year), or better, GNP in constant dollars (since it is not strictly necessary that all series have the same base year). If one compares the two totals—GNP in current dollars with GNP in constant dollars—it will be clear in which direction prices have changed; division of the two totals results in what is called the implicit price index. Thus,

$$\frac{\text{GNP in current dollars}}{\text{GNP in constant dollars}} = \text{Implicit price index,}$$

or

$$\frac{\text{GNP in 1972 dollars}}{\text{GNP in 1958 dollars}} = \text{Implicit price index,}$$

or in actual numbers for 1972

$$\frac{\$1,155.2}{\$790.7} = 146.1$$

If the implicit price index exceeds 100, prices must have risen, and vice versa. The implicit price index can only be attained by this final division. It is the most general of all price indexes, including as it does consumption, investment, government, and foreign trade expenditures, but care must be used in its manipulation. It reflects not only changes in prices but also changes in the composition of GNP. Thus, the attempt to shift the base period by standard procedures is invalid, and even year-to-year comparisons could be misleading if significant changes in the composition of GNP occur.

Of course, all index numbers have their difficulties, and those used in deflating GNP are no exception. Still, corrections for price changes must be made and made easily to permit the ready comparison of real GNP over time. The attempt is worthwhile, but one should be aware of some shortcomings, which are merely stated here for the interested student to pursue: (a) the method of calculation of individual series price indexes generally imparts a bias to price movements;[8] (b) the whole area of quality changes is generally ignored; (c) changes in the composition of GNP—the different collection of goods available in different time periods—require that the base year be periodically changed to reflect the essentially different worlds being compared. There are many more interesting index number problems that could be mentioned—the point here is that care is needed in interpreting these numbers.

Index numbers are generally computed and interpreted as follows: Each commodity entering into GNP can be viewed as a value term derived from its price, P (an average), times the quantity, Q, exchanged. Thus,

$$P_i Q_i = \text{Value of Commodity } i.$$

The value must be corrected for price changes by deflating it to reflect base year prices. This is done by dividing each value term by a price relative, P_i/P_o. Thus,

$$\frac{P_i Q_i}{P_i/P_o} = P_o Q_i$$

where P_o is the price of this commodity in the base year. Dividing each series by the ratio of prices results in the desired expression: this year's quantity valued at base year prices. Changes in GNP that merely reflect changes in price are now eliminated, and only changes in quantities are registered—the so-called real changes, resulting in real GNP, or GNP in constant dollars. Adding each series, we obtain

$$P_{o1} Q_1 + P_{o2} Q_2 + P_{o3} Q_3 + \cdots + P_{on} Q_n = \Sigma P_{on} Q_n,$$

where each term has been corrected for price changes and the summation sign, Σ, indicates the mathematical shorthand notation for this addition. The subscript on the price term indicates that the prices are base year prices, and the second number identifies the commodity. It is the price term that appears in the denominator of the expression for the calculation of the implicit price index.

THE OVEREMPHASIS ON GNP

It is perhaps ill-advised to attach such importance to GNP to the exclusion of all other indicators. This number is quoted daily; its true meaning is sometimes overlooked. Is this a serious concern, or is it just a cavil of the specialist?

[8] The bias is the result of the widely used method of accounting for price changes, the Laspeyres method. According to this method, favored for computational considerations since the base remains constant, price changes are measured with reference to the base year values. Expenditures for a commodity in any given year, $Q_n P_n$, the "corrected" for price changes by restating the expenditure value to ascertain how much would have been spent if the quantity of the base period were purchased at current and base year prices. Thus, the index number is given by $Q_n P_n / Q_o P_o \times 100$, where Q and P stand for quantity and price and the subscripts are o for base year and n for the given year. If prices rise, the index is greater than 100. The question is, If prices had risen, would the original quantity have been purchased? If, as prices rise, quantity purchased falls (that is, normal demand curves), then the above expression overstates the price change by assuming quantity constant; hence the upward bias for rising prices and the downward bias for falling prices.

Increasingly economists and laymen have questioned both the validity and the interpretation of GNP. They accept the need for some measure of the nation's output, but deplore the uncritical acceptance of mere numbers as the sole indicators of the society's welfare. The citation of ever larger numbers, they contend, may conceal deterioration in society and postpone the recognition of some vital problems. In this section we can only touch upon a few of these areas, but the reader can easily extend the analysis to many instances where societal values and the economic system seem to conflict. It is hoped that the issues raised here will not be forgotten once this section is closed. Whether or not you agree with the arguments, you should not dismiss the significance of the effects on society of actions based on a particular view of that society, in this case, on the measure GNP.

THE OVEREMPHASIS ON THINGS

GNP measures the society's current production in the manner previously discussed. We are familiar with the criticism that national income accounting cannot measure all the economic activity that takes place. Also, the accounts do not recognize leisure time and activities. Yet much of what makes up the quality of life may be composed of just those activities that are not measured. Thus, more of everything, as measured by GNP, need not be better than less of everything. This viewpoint leads inevitably to the overexploitation of our physical resources, and it also obscures the social relationships of men. Marx called it "commodity fetishism" —the emphasis upon the production and exchange of things that blocks appreciation and understanding of the relationship between producer and laborer.[9] The social nature of production is forgotten, and abstract things are emphasized and take on independent lives, produced and exchanged in the marketplace. One need not be a Marxist to verify that national income accounting does not bring out the social interaction of men that is inherent in the production process. Yet these relationships must be examined before a society and its economic system can be judged and charges of exploitation of one group over another be resolved. The preoccupation with the numerical value of GNP results in an overemphasis on things and precludes the raising of these larger issues.

THE UNDEREMPHASIS ON COMPOSITION OF GNP

Again, if GNP measures things, which things are being measured? First, there are "frivolous" type goods, from early American toilet seats to fur-covered refrigerators; from electric manicure devices to his-and-her bathtubs. They tell us a good deal about our society, and every social philosopher has had his sport with the subject. Naturally, there are many value judgments involved in the categorization of goods, and the subject is left open to debate, with the reminder that the production of these goods results in additions to GNP.

Second, and of much greater concern, is the production of goods and services that may threaten the very survival of man. Until recently not much thought was devoted to the subject of how the production of man affected his environment. Goods were produced and their value added to GNP, which rose steadily higher. Some of these goods were endangering human life, but still many people delighted in the growing GNP figures, proclaiming improvement in the standard of living and boasting of the fruits of the economic system. Now that the environmental

[9] For a summary, see Paul M. Sweezy, *The Theory of Capitalist Development* (New York: Monthly Review Press, 1942), pp. 34–40.

issue is widely discussed, people tend to regard such thinking as fatuous, but it still persists to some degree. Hopefully, the harmful products can be identified and eliminated, but what of the highly valued, convenience items like nonreturnable bottles, plastics, and gadgets of all sorts? What can be done with factories that pollute the air and water with their waste products? Currently the national income accountants merely add the production of the plant into the accounts, thus increasing GNP by the market value of production and ignoring the harmful by-products of production.

What is the meaning of more production being better than less production? To avoid such thinking and to take account of environmental problems, we need an entirely new concept that would register a reduction in the national output in such cases. Kenneth Boulding has suggested that GNP be made into Gross National Cost to emphasize the using up of materials in the production and consumption processes.[10] Still other approaches are possible, all of which would properly discourage undue concentration on uncorrected production values.

ECONOMIC GROWTH AS A GOAL

Economists must share in the blame for overlooking environmental questions, since they have advocated economic growth as a goal without fully recognizing all the accompanying implications. Economic growth is a means of providing higher living standards and more jobs, of course, but there are costs involved as well. One of these costs is the overexploitation of resources and the environment. The question, Growth at what cost and for whom? was seldom asked.

Mere economic growth, reflected in rising GNP, is not enough. First, because there is no consensus on what types of goods will increase human welfare, and thus on which goods should be produced and which curtailed. Nor as yet is there any mechanism by which to make such decisions. Second, there has never been a thorough study of the ecological aspects of production—we do not know how our production of goods affects the environment. Third, it is not total GNP that must be increased to affect human welfare but per capita GNP, that is, GNP divided by population. The pressures of a growing population force production of more goods and services (influencing the numerator), which means even more exploitation of our resources and a diminishing quality of life for growing numbers of people. Economic growth concentrates largely on increasing national output. Yet the denominator is equally important. Economists must take a less sanguine view of economic growth as the way to provide for growing numbers and begin to warn of population pressures putting limits on our resources.

Even per capita economic growth must be qualified. Being an average, it can be misleading. Much more attention must be given to the distribution of the national output. Again, national income accounting is silent on this issue. Issues that may cause social unrest are not illuminated by the summary accounts.

It may be argued that national income accounting was never intended to cover these areas. Perhaps it is asking too much of the available data to seek from them both information and answers to social issues. Is it better to have completely objective and consistent data even with the shortcomings?

It is probable that most economists would agree that national income accounting should be free of values and should not be directed toward specific problems.

---

[10] Kenneth E. Boulding, *Economics as a Science* (New York: McGraw-Hill, 1970), p. 45.

Perhaps the main point of this section is that such a stand may no longer be tenable. GNP data are interpreted by many who do not appreciate the complexities involved in their determination. If social actions do result from use of the data, which they do, then the economist has the responsibility to ensure that the data provide the kinds of information necessary for rational action. If GNP data do conceal more than they reveal, the economist must find new approaches that better explain the existing conditions. It is easy for the economist to disown the erroneous interpretations placed on GNP data, but this ostrich-type behavior is inexcusable. For these are not just academic concerns, they are issues that involve the very survival of man as he goes on producing things, inferring human welfare from these things, and despoiling the environment in which he must live.

The National Income and Product Accounts

After our brief survey of what national income accounting measures, we are now ready to discuss the accounts themselves. Perhaps it is best to ask first where the national income originates and to look at the national output from the viewpoint of where it is created. In tracing the national income and product data to their sources, many of the conceptual problems of the last chapter become clearer. The distinction between business and nonbusiness economic activity, and the kinds of activities included in the national output, become apparent. These are important considerations, and although the income-originating accounts are no longer formally presented as they are in this chapter, some useful insights into the fundamentals of national income accounting are provided by beginning the analysis with this approach.

To segregate economic activity by origin, we follow the national income accountants in breaking down economic activity into four major sectors: the business sector, the personal sector, the government sector, and the foreign trade sector. Taking each in turn, we can measure each sector's contribution to the national product; summation of the sector results then yields the national income and product totals.

The Business Sector

By far the largest part of the national product originates in the business sector, and hence it would seem appropriate to begin the analysis here. Table 2.1 presents the national product originating in the business sector for the calendar year 1972.

Since GNP was $1,155.2 billion for the year 1972, more than 84 per cent can be traced to the business sector. That such a large proportion of GNP is accounted for by the business sector follows from the way in which the output (production) of the other sectors is valued and from the definition of economic activity. This

TABLE 2.1
NATIONAL INCOME AND PRODUCT ORIGINATING IN THE BUSINESS SECTOR, 1972

(Billions of Dollars)

1. Compensation of Employees	534.7	20. Sales:	
2. Wages and Salaries	471.4	To Consumers, Government, Rest-of-World	797.1
3. Supplements	63.3		
4. Corporate Profits and Inventory Valuation Adjustment	84.9	21. To Business (Capital Goods)	172.3
5. Profits Tax Liability	42.7		
6. Dividends	23.3	22. Change in Inventory	6.0
7. Undistributed Profits	25.8		
8. Inventory Valuation Adjustment	−6.9		
9. Net Interest	44.0		
10. Proprietors' Income	74.2		
11. Rental Income of Persons	24.2		
12. National Income Originating in Business Sector	762.0		
13. Business Transfer Payments	4.6		
14. Indirect Business Taxes	109.6		
15. Less:			
Subsidies Less Current Surplus of Govt. Enterprises	1.7		
16. Statistical Discrepancy	−1.5		
17. Charges Against Business Net Product	873.0		
18. Capital Consumption Allowances	102.4		
19. Charges Against Business Gross Product	975.4	23. Business Gross Product	975.4

will become evident as the other sectors are discussed. The business sector includes all corporate and noncorporate business firms and any other organization that produces goods or services for sale at a price designed to cover the approximate cost of production. Thus, in addition to the obvious business firms, the business sector includes farm units, professional practitioners, family businesses, real estate firms, financial institutions, cooperatives, lessees of real property, and government enterprises. Government enterprises include the U.S. Government Printing Office and TVA on the federal level as well as publicly owned enterprises like transit and water systems or electrical utilities at the local level.

Table 2.1 reveals the essence of accounting for national income (production). The right-hand side of the account shows the final production of the business sector that resulted in sales or additions (deletions) to the inventories maintained; the left-hand side of the account records the disposition of the receipts from productive activity into income created, taxes incurred, and other charges.

BUSINESS GROSS PRODUCT

Taking the right-hand side first, items 20 and 21 record the sales receipts. Item 20 shows the sales of *final* production to other sectors. (Notice the omission of sales to other business firms, which are intermediate products, of course, and excluded to avoid double counting.)[1] Item 21 shows sales of *capital goods* to other businesses, which are employed in the production of other goods and used up over time and are thus intermediate goods but are treated differently in the accounts. In effect, this procedure treats the sale of capital goods as final product without recognition of the capital stock used up in the current production of goods and services. The proper procedure, according to the rules of national income accounting, would be to eliminate the intermediate product—the part of the capital stock used in the current period (called depreciation or capital consumption), so that only the net addition to the capital stock would be recorded. Failure to make the necessary deductions for capital consumed obviously results in double counting, for it includes an intermediate product. Why is an exception made for capital goods sales and consumption?

To answer the question, one must appreciate the crucial role played by investment in the economy. This can be illustrated by using the following symbols, which will appear throughout this book. Let I_g be gross private domestic investment; D, depreciation, or capital consumption allowances; I_n, net investment; and K, capital stock. Then,

$$(2.1) \qquad I_g - D = I_n \quad \text{and} \quad I_n = \Delta K,$$

where the Greek letter delta (Δ) means change. Then $\Delta K = K_t - K_{t-1}$, or the change in capital stock from the beginning of the period, K_{t-1}, to the end of the period, K_t. For only one period the following outcomes are possible:

$$I_g - D > 0; \quad I_n > 0; \quad \Delta K > 0;$$

and productive capacity grows.

$$I_g - D = 0; \quad I_n = 0; \quad \Delta K = 0;$$

[1] The inclusion of sales to other firms would turn the account into a production statement resembling a profit-and-loss statement of a single firm. To balance the account, one would have to add an item to the left-hand side of the account called "purchases from other firms." This would raise the totals of the account without altering its composition.

and productive capacity remains constant, the economy simply replacing capital consumed.

$$I_g - D < 0; \qquad I_n < 0; \qquad \Delta K < 0;$$

and productive capacity declines as the economy fails to replace capital consumed.

Although this is not the place for a lengthy discussion of the economic importance of investment and capital stock, the above sketch should be sufficient to indicate it. Since these variables are so important, the data that measure them should be as accurate as possible. Here, then, is the rationale for treating sales of capital in an exceptional way, for the data on depreciation are not as reliable as the data for gross investment. There are various methods to calculate depreciation used by firms and recognized by the Internal Revenue System. All are designed to estimate the wear and tear of capital assets as well as to provide some protection against obsolescence. To estimate how much of a capital good is used up in any one period, its useful life, and changes in technology that may make it obsolete is obviously a difficult task, and the results can only be crude at best. In a dynamic economy where technological change is so rapid, obsolescence is always a threat, but how can it be forecast? In an economy where production schedules change and the use of the plant fluctuates, how can an accurate estimate of wear and tear be calculated? The answer is that these estimates cannot be accurate, and in practice some simplified arithmetic method is adopted that may or may not reflect the true capital consumption and that may be adopted more with an eye for its tax treatment than for its accuracy (replacement cost).

There are still other problems connected with this variable. While all other exchanges are valued at current market prices in the accounts, depreciation is based on historical cost and not on replacement cost. Furthermore, the dollar amounts of replacement investment do not reflect the probability that the new capital goods are likely to be more productive than the assets being replaced. If there has been a change in technology, it is likely to be embodied in the replacement asset.

Without belaboring the point, it is clear that depreciation is a highly complex variable and that the estimates for it are likely to be inaccurate. The Department of Commerce, however, has no recourse but to accept these estimates provided by the firms. Yet rather than reduce the accuracy for a reasonably good estimate for gross investment by subtracting an inaccurate estimate for depreciation, it has decided to double count (by including an intermediate good) in obtaining gross product. The national income accountants, therefore, leave intact the gross investment estimate and add back depreciation on the other side of the account in order to balance it.

If depreciation estimates were reliable, then the correct procedure would be to subtract it from gross investment on the right-hand side and adjust the profit figure accordingly. (The profit total is already determined net of depreciation; this is why depreciation must be added back in order to balance the account.) If depreciation estimates were accurate, there would be no need for a gross product and no reason to include an intermediate good. The emphasis would shift to the more meaningful net product.[2]

Continuing with the right-hand, or revenue, side of the business sector account, the final entry, item 22 in Table 2.1, is for the net change in inventory. The item

---

[2] It is worth recalling here that gross investment includes residential construction as well as the more usual capital assets but does not include government construction or capital assets, which are regarded as final goods and recorded under government purchases.

is necessary if currently produced goods and services are to be correctly measured, since there is no reason to expect current production to match current sales. If the net change is positive, current production exceeded current sales; if only current sales were entered in the national product accounts, not all of the production that took place or the incomes earned would be recorded. The fact that some production was unsold at year end does not affect the basic purpose of accounting for current production. Obviously, when current sales exceed current production, some of the goods must have come from the beginning inventory and hence have been produced last period. Therefore, the production of last period must be excluded from current output, and the net change in inventory would be negative.

The net change in inventory adjusts the sales items already recorded; the process is automatic in the accounting method and may be briefly sketched as follows:

INVENTORY ACCOUNT

Beginning Inventory	Q_{t-1}
Add: Production	P
Goods Available for Sale	
Less: Goods Sold	S
Ending Inventory	Q_t

For those who prefer symbolic language, the whole process can be summarized quite simply. Writing the accounting table

$$Q_{t-1} + P - S = Q_t,$$
$$P - S = Q_t - Q_{t-1},$$

if $P = S$;	$Q_t = Q_{t-1}$;	and Δ inventories $= 0$;
if $P > S$;	$Q_t > Q_{t-1}$;	and Δ inventories > 0;
if $P < S$;	$Q_t < Q_{t-1}$;	and Δ inventories < 0.

CHARGES AGAINST BUSINESS GROSS PRODUCT

If the right-hand side of the account records the receipts from sales (and unsold production), then the left-hand side must represent the expenditure or cost of sales (and unsold production). In the first section the amounts paid to the factors of production are recorded by type and, when aggregated, become the national income originating in the business sector. Most of the items are self-explanatory, so that only a brief description of each is necessary.

Compensation of employees (item 1 in Table 2.1) includes direct wage and salary disbursements together with other labor income and supplements, including employer contributions to social security, private pensions, health or welfare funds, compensations for injuries, and similar minor payments to labor.[3]

Profits originating in the corporate sector (item 4) are presented according to the distribution of those profits: a portion going to taxes, for the payment of dividends, or retained by the corporations. The only difficulty here is with the treatment of the corporate profits tax liability as a part of factor cost. It is assumed that the corporation income tax is not shifted but is borne by the stockholders. In effect,

[3] Note the treatment of the social security tax on employers. It is regarded as a labor cost and shifted forward, not backward.

this means that the tax and any changes in it do not affect other factors of production, their rewards, or product prices. Economists disagree over whether or not (and in which direction) the corporation income tax is shifted. In default of any consensus, the national income accountants have simply chosen the easy expedient.

Item 8 in Table 2.1—inventory valuation adjustment—requires some explanation. Generally, national income accounting attempts to remove all gains and losses due to price changes (recall the capital gains discussion). In the case of inventories, changing prices often result in profits or losses as a result of the various methods of valuing inventory transactions. The inventory valuation adjustment adjusts the profit account by the amount of such inventory profits or losses. For example, in a period of rising prices the inventory accounting method called FIFO (first in, first out, which assumes that goods are sold from stock in the order in which they were acquired) results in the overstatement of profits, while in periods of declining prices an understatement of profits results.[4]

The other items of factor costs are relatively straightforward or were previously discussed. Item 9, net interest paid, includes interest received minus interest paid by the business sector. Proprietors' income, item 10, is the return to all unincorporated enterprises. The total includes items more properly allocated to other types of factor rewards, such as labor income and interest on capital, but these enterprises seldom maintain their books to permit such a breakdown and thus the net income is treated as net profit. Finally, rental income of persons, item 11, includes imputed rental income of owner-occupied homes, which was discussed earlier, as well as rental income received by firms not normally doing business in real estate.

So much for factor income. We come now to payments made by the business sector that are nonfactor rewards but are a part of gross product. Business transfer payments (item 13) are payments made to persons for which no factor service is received in return. The transfers include gifts, prizes, awards, and the like as well as bad debt charges. These items are costs to the firms but not factor costs.

Indirect taxes (item 14) are those that are treated as costs by the firms and assumed to be reflected in the prices charged to consumers. Such levies as the excise, sales, and property taxes are regarded as shifted forward and are included

---

[4] For example, assume the following transactions and the FIFO method:

Beginning Inventory	1,000 units @ $3 =	$3,000
Purchases	500 units @ $5 =	2,500
Goods Available for Sale	1,500 units	$5,500
Less Sales	700 units @ $3 =	2,100
Ending Inventory	800 units	$3,400
Actual Change in Inventory	−200 units	$ 400

Obviously, it is illogical to record a positive change in value and a negative change in units. Therefore, inventory adjustments are in order:

(1) For Δ inventory (on right-hand side of account), the entry is for −$1,000 (−200 units @ $5, which is the result of the actual unit change × current price).

(2) The inventory valuation adjustment shows a gain of $1,400 (700 units @ $2, which measures the difference between book cost and replacement costs of inventories used up). The inventory valuation adjustment as it would appear in the accounts corrects the profit total by the entry for −$1,400, the overstatement of profits. The adjustment corrects profits for the difference between book costs of sales ($2,100) and their current replacement cost ($3,500).

On the other hand, LIFO (last in, first out) would be more appropriate for national income accounting purposes, since the goods acquired last would reflect current market prices, which are required by national accounting rules. In this connection, it should be noted that the net change in inventories on the other side of the account is stated in current market prices.

in the sales totals on the revenue side of the business account. Because, however, the tax receipts flow to government and not to business, a reconciling item is needed on the expenditure side to balance the account.

Subsidies (item 15) are grants by government to business and are usually thought necessary to induce more factor effort. Since the subsidy results in a lower sales price, the market value of the output (on the revenue side) would be less than the factor incomes recorded in producing it. Therefore, the subsidy that appears as factor income originating in the business sector must be subtracted from factor incomes in order for the account to balance. Thus, subsidies appear as a negative item on the expenditure side.

Combined with subsidies is the current surplus of government enterprises. The surplus can be regarded as analogous to profits of business, but certain differences must be noted. First, the surplus does not include depreciation, because the capital assets were never recorded as investment but as final purchases; second, the surplus does not include interest paid by government, since both profits and interest are not regarded as factor costs because it is too difficult to separate the functions of government enterprises as suppliers of goods and services from their subsidy operations. Under this somewhat arbitrary procedure, interest paid by government enterprises is included in the general government account, and capital asset expenditures are included in general government purchases. The surplus then is added to the expenditure side, not as a factor income but in order to balance the account, since the sales of government enterprises on the other side obviously include more (or less) than the expenses and incomes earned in their production. Finally, since both subsidies and surplus pose some thorny questions of proper treatment, and since they are sometimes interrelated, they are shown as one item in the business sector account.

In the estimation of GNP, the national income accountants obtain separate estimates of the two sides of the account. Inevitably errors will result; the statistical discrepancy (item 16) measures the extent of these errors and is traditionally recorded (plus or minus) as a reconciling item on the charges side of the business sector account. (As noted later, it also appears as an adjustment in the subsidiary gross savings and investment account. This assumes the error is in total saving or total investment but without specifying which component is in error.)

The Personal Sector

Table 2.2 shows the national income and product originating in the personal sector. The personal sector, it must be remembered, includes charitable institutions, universities, foundations, and similar organizations as well as its most appropriate component, households. The measurable economic activity that takes place in these institutions consists solely of wages and salaries (including imputations) and supplements. The nature of the production found in these institutions, largely services, transforms the product account into an income account. The measurement of the output of the personal sector is found by the costs of inputs or factor cost.[5]

---

[5] Note that prior to 1965 interest payments by the institutions of the personal sector to nonpersonal sector lenders were included as part of national income originating in the personal sector. Interest payments were considered to be the measure of productivity of the assets purchased by the personal sector and financed by outside lenders. In 1965 this procedure was changed, because it was thought that much of the households' borrowed funds were used to finance living expenses, and the relation between interest charges and real assets could no longer be supported.

TABLE 2.2

NATIONAL INCOME AND PRODUCT ORIGINATING IN THE PERSONAL SECTOR, 1972

(Billions of Dollars)

1. Compensation of Employees	36.8		
2. Wages and Salaries	34.5		
3. Supplements	2.3	5. Net and Gross	
4. Income Originating in Personal Sector	____ 36.8	Product Originating	____ 36.8

How else could one measure the output of a university professor, a maid, or a similar worker, which represents the personal sector's contribution to national product? The only market transaction is the payment for services rendered. Since all the output of this sector is considered to be final, regardless of obvious examples of intermediate product and despite the fact that the output is measured by income, the distinction between net, gross, final, intermediate, and total income and product is meaningless here. Output is measured by input—labor input.

The Government Sector

The same treatment is given to the production originating in the government sector, as can be seen in Table 2.3. Once again, all the activity that takes place in the government sector is considered to be final product, despite the fact that so large a part of governmental activity is clearly intermediary in character, for instance, law enforcement, justice, foreign relations, and so on. Furthermore, all activity is valued at factor cost—the labor cost of the government employees. Of course, there is no other way to value government services, since they are not sold on the market, nor do taxes act as a price for the services. Indeed, many services are assumed by government because a price cannot be charged for them. The good is indivisible, which means that individuals cannot (or would not) assign a value to the service from which they benefit, and therefore no price can be assigned. Taxes and the services rendered simply are not directly related.

In the absence of any sales value of government output, the national income accountant is forced to measure the output of government at factor cost. Factor cost, however, is limited to labor cost, since all capital costs are regarded as final purchases from business and interest charges cannot be related to asset returns.

TABLE 2.3

NATIONAL INCOME AND PRODUCT ORIGINATING IN THE GOVERNMENT SECTOR, 1972

(Billions of Dollars)

1. Compensation of Employees	135.4		
2. Wages and Salaries	121.3		
3. Supplements	14.1	5. Net and Gross	
4. Income Originating in Government Sector	____ 135.4	Product Originating	____ 135.4

The result of this procedure is that the cost of government grows with the growth of the services of labor and is thus readily apparent, but the productivity of government is never measured. If government services are labor-intensive, a biased view of the growth of government is inevitable. While this is true of other organizations as well, hospitals for instance, the controversy over the growth and cost of government is always a popular topic in the political arena, yet seldom is this concern understood in the light of the nature of government services or their valuation.

The Rest-of-the-World Sector

There are two approaches to the treatment of foreign trade in a system of national accounts: It is possible to regard national output in geographical terms and to record the output and the shares accruing to the factors of production from domestic production only; or it is possible to focus on domestic factor incomes regardless of where the actual production occurred. Our national accounts are based on the latter method.

Accordingly, the influence of foreign trade on factor incomes must be considered; thus, United States output accruing to foreign residents must be subtracted from the accounts; and output accruing to United States residents from foreign production must be added. These adjustments are made in the rest-of-the-world sector account, as shown in Table 2.4, by netting the international flows of factor incomes.

TABLE 2.4
NATIONAL INCOME AND PRODUCT ORIGINATING IN THE REST-OF-THE-WORLD SECTOR, 1972

(Billions of Dollars)

1. Compensation of Employees	*		
2. Corporate Profits and Dividends	6.3		
3. Net Interest	1.2		
4. Income Originating in the Rest-of-the-World Sector	7.2	5. Net and Gross Product Originating	7.5

* Less than $0.05 billion.

Of course, these factor incomes could be included under previous totals of factor incomes, and the rest-of-the-world sector could be eliminated. However, too much important information would be lost by this procedure, and it was thought preferable to make these data explicit.

Once again, since we are using factor incomes as the measure of production, the net and gross product originating are identical. It is clear (from the positive numbers) from Table 2.4 that United States residents received more factor payments than they paid out to foreigners.

Summary of National Income and Product by Origin

The four sector accounts can now be combined into one account, as in Table 2.5, which shows total national income and product by sector of origin. A glance at Table 2.5 reveals, first, that the account oversummarizes, and second, that the oversummarization is at the expense of the business sector, while the other sectors' totals are simply copied from the sector accounts. In short, not much is gained by this additional account. It is not surprising, therefore, that the Department of Commerce has decided to abandon the concept of national income and product by sector of origin and has restructured the same data to record which sector had command over or purchased the national output and which factors received the incomes from national production. The restricting definition of economic activity makes these accounts by origin much less useful. Naturally, the national income and product by origin can still be ascertained from supplementary information provided by the Department of Commerce, but the official accounts are no longer concerned with where the output originated. The emphasis now is on the distribution of the national product by sector and by factor rewards.

If we had a closed economy, the conceptual change from the origin of production to command over production would simply be recognized by rearranging the data. In our open economy some adjustments to the data must be made. Some of the currently produced domestic output will be sold to, given to, or earned by foreigners, and these goods will then not be available to domestic residents. On the other hand, goods imported from abroad and available for domestic use must be

TABLE 2.5

NATIONAL INCOME AND PRODUCT BY SECTOR OF ORIGIN, 1972

(Billions of Dollars)

1. National Income Originating in			8. Gross Product Originating		
Business Sector		762.0	in Business Sector		975.4
Personal Sector		36.8	9. Gross (and Net) Product		
Government Sector		135.4	Originating in		
Rest-of-the-World			Personal Sector		36.8
Sector		7.5	Government Sector		135.4
2. National Income		941.7	Rest-of-the-World Sector		7.5
3. Add: Adjustments*	1.6				
4. Add: Indirect					
Business Taxes	109.5	111.1			
5. Charges Against Net					
National Product		1,052.8			
6. Capital Consumption					
Allowances		102.4			
7. Gross National Product		1,155.2	10. Gross National Product		1,155.2

* Includes adjustments for business transfer payments, government subsidies and surplus, and statistical discrepancy.

accounted for if the proper flow of goods is to be recorded. At the same time, this procedure also makes the national income accounts for the foreign sector agree better with the traditional treatment in the balance-of-payments accounts.

Table 2.6 shows the new, broader classification of foreign trade into exports and imports. On the left-hand side of the account are shown the total receipts from foreigners. This label is somewhat misleading, since the total includes goods and services (including invisibles) sold to foreigners, the factor incomes earned in trade, transfer payments made to foreigners by government and by persons, and the new international monetary unit—special drawing rights. This procedure, however, does permit the "command over goods" interpretation desired in this account. Prior to 1965 government nonmilitary grants and personal remittances in cash and in kind were treated as part of government purchases and consumption expenditures, respectively. Since these transfer payments did make United States production available to foreigners, they must be treated as exports; on the other side of the account they are recorded as the means of payment by foreigners.

On the right-hand side of the account are shown the total payments to foreigners. Since the net foreign investment figure is negative, the United States paid more to foreigners than it earned from receipts from foreigners; it has become a debtor to the rest of the world. The foreign transaction account is highly summarized, and analysis of the trade position of the United States cannot be carried out much further. The details can be found in the balance-of-trade statements of the Department of Commerce.

The Official Accounts

It is now an easy matter to construct the national income and product account to conform with the new emphasis on the distribution of the national output and the factor incomes earned in its production. Account 1 of Table 2.7 is the official national income and product account as it appears in the July 1973 issue of the *Survey of Current Business,* pages 16–17. Most of the items appearing in the

TABLE 2.6

FOREIGN TRANSACTIONS ACCOUNT, 1972

(Billions of Dollars)

1. Exports of Goods and Services	73.5	4. Imports of Goods and Services	78.1
2. Capital Grants Received by United States	0.7	5. Transfer Payments (Net) from United States Government	2.7
		6. Personal Transfer Payments (Net)	1.0
		7. Net Foreign Investment	−7.6
3. Receipts from Foreigners	74.2	8. Payments to Foreigners	74.2

account have been discussed, and those that are new are largely self-explanatory. Note the numbers in parentheses, which indicate the counterentries in the other subsidiary accounts. The latter are sector accounts, but instead of showing income originating by sector, they show receipts and expenditures by sector. Since we are concerned here with the flow of incomes and expenditures, the sector accounts include items not found in the national income and product account (note the transfer payments, for instance). A few minutes spent studying these accounts and their interrelations would be time well utilized.

Of particular interest is account 5, the gross saving and investment account. While it is not a sector in the sense in which we have used the word, the importance of saving and investment in economic analysis warrants special treatment. Since both saving and investment measure the same thing—unconsumed output— the two sides of the account are *identically* equal. In accounting this must be the case, and no particular importance is attached to this conclusion. Later, in theoretical work, (intended) saving need not equal (intended) investment, but in national income accounting they must always be equal, because they are measured magnitudes—measured after the fact (ex post). Since this may be a source of some confusion, we will return to this issue later.

Account 5, then, brings together all items that pertain to saving and investment and that may affect capital formation. On the left-hand side of the account, the investment side, two items are shown: gross private domestic investment, which includes fixed investment, construction in progress (including residences), and the change in inventories; and net foreign investment. The meaning of gross private domestic investment is clear, and it is necessary only to call attention once again to the use of the gross value, which means that depreciation must be added to the other side of the account as a form of business saving. Net foreign investment is included here because, like other forms of investment, it represents goods not available for domestic consumption. Thus, if exports exceed imports, the goods shipped abroad are, like investment goods, not for current domestic consumption. Note the reverse situation for 1972.

On the right-hand side of the account are the sources of saving: personal saving; business saving, which includes undistributed corporate profits, corporate inventory valuation adjustment, and capital consumption allowances (sole proprietorship and partnership saving are included in personal saving); and government saving. The remaining item, statistical discrepancy, has been traditionally included as part of gross saving and represents the unaccounted-for error in separately measuring GNP by product flows and income flows. As a balancing item, it means that the error is deemed to exist in total saving and/or total investment and in one or more of their components.

Other Accounts

In addition to the summary accounts, the Department of Commerce publishes many other informative subsidiary tables and accounts. Among these are GNP by type of product; national income by industry; gross corporate product; gross farm product; personal consumption expenditures by type of product; federal and state and local receipts and expenditures. An hour spent in reviewing these accounts will be worthwhile.

TABLE 2.7
SUMMARY NATIONAL INCOME AND PRODUCT ACCOUNTS, 1972
(Billions of Dollars)

1. National Income and Product Account

1.	Compensation of Employees	707.1	24. Personal Consumption Expenditures (2–3)	726.5
2.	Wages and Salaries	627.3	25. Durable Goods	117.4
3.	Disbursements (2–7)	627.8	26. Nondurable Goods	299.9
4.	Wage Accruals Less Disbursements (3–7+5–4)	−0.5	27. Services	309.2
5.	Supplements to Wages and Salaries	79.7	28. Gross Private Domestic Investment (5–1)	178.3
6.	Employer Contributions for Social Insurance (3–15)	39.0	29. Fixed Investment	172.3
7.	Other Labor Income (2–8)	40.7	30. Nonresidential	118.2
8.	Proprietors' Income (2–9)	74.2	31. Structures	41.7
9.	Rental Income of Persons (2–10)	24.1	32. Producers' Durable Equipment	76.5
10.	Corporate Profits and Inventory Valuation Adjustment	91.1	33. Residential Structures	54.0
11.	Profits Before Tax	98.0	34. Change in Business Inventories	6.0
12.	Profits Tax Liability (3–12)	42.7	35. Net Exports of Goods and Services	−4.7
13.	Profits After Tax	55.4	36. Exports (4–1)	73.5
14.	Dividends (2–11)	26.0	37. Imports (4–3)	78.1
15.	Undistributed Profits (5–5)	29.3	38. Government Purchases of Goods and Services (3–1)	255.0
16.	Inventory Valuation Adjustment (5–6)	−6.9	39. Federal	104.4
17.	Net Interest (2–13)	45.2	40. National Defense	74.4
18.	National Income	941.8	41. Other	30.1
19.	Business Transfer Payments (2–17)	4.6	42. State and Local	150.5
20.	Indirect Business Tax and Nontax Liability (3–13)	109.5		
21.	Less: Subsidies Less Current Surplus of Government Enterprises (3–6)	1.7		
22.	Capital Consumption Allowances (5–7)	102.4		
23.	Statistical Discrepancy (5–10)	−1.5		
	Charges Against Gross National Product	1,155.2	Gross National Product	1,155.2

2. Personal Income and Outlay Account

1. Personal Tax and Nontax Payments (3–11)	142.2	7. Wage and Salary Disbursements (1–3)	627.8
2. Personal Outlays	747.2	8. Other Labor Income (1–7)	40.7
3. Personal Consumption Expenditures (1–24)	726.5	9. Proprietors' Income (1–8)	74.2
4. Interest Paid by Consumers (2–15)	19.7	10. Rental Income of Persons (1–9)	24.1
5. Personal Transfer Payments to Foreigners (Net) (4–5)	1.0	11. Dividends (1–14)	26.0
6. Personal Saving (5–3)	49.7	12. Personal Interest Income	78.0
		13. Net Interest (1–17)	45.2
		14. Net Interest Paid by Government (3–5)	13.0
		15. Interest Paid by Consumers (2–4)	19.7
		16. Transfer Payments to Persons	103.0
		17. From Business (1–19)	4.6
		18. From Government (3–3)	98.3
		19. Less: Personal Contributions for Social Insurance (3–16)	34.7
Personal Taxes, Outlays, and Saving	939.2	Personal Income	939.2

3. Government Receipts and Expenditures Account

1. Purchases of Goods and Services (1–38)	255.0	11. Personal Tax and Nontax Payments (2–1)	142.2
2. Transfer Payments	101.1	12. Corporate Profits Tax Liability (1–12)	42.7
3. To Persons (2–18)	98.3	13. Indirect Business Tax and Nontax Liability (1–20)	109.5
4. To Foreigners (Net) (4–4)	2.7	14. Contributions for Social Insurance	73.7
5. Net Interest Paid (2–14)	13.0	15. Employer (1–6)	39.0
6. Subsidies Less Current Surplus of Government Enterprises (1–21)	1.7	16. Personal (2–19)	34.7
7. Less: Wage Accruals Less Disbursements (1–4)	–0.2		
8. Surplus or Deficit (–), National Income and Product Accounts (5–8)	–2.8		
9. Federal	–15.9		
10. State and Local	13.1		
Government Expenditures and Surplus	368.2	Government Receipts	368.2

(Continued on next page)

TABLE 2.7 (Continued)
4. Foreign Transactions Account

1. Exports of Goods and Services (1–36)	73.5	3. Imports of Goods and Services (1–37)	78.1
2. Capital Grants Received by the United States (5–9)	0.7	4. Transfer Payments from U. S. Government to Foreigners (Net) (3–4)	2.7
		5. Personal Transfer Payments to Foreigners (Net) (2–5)	1.0
		6. Net Foreign Investment (5–2)	−7.6
Receipts from Foreigners	74.2	Payments to Foreigners	74.2

5. Gross Saving and Investment Account

1. Gross Private Domestic Investment (1–28)	178.3	3. Personal Saving (2–6)	49.7
2. Net Foreign Investment (4–6)	−7.6	4. Wage Accruals Less Disbursements (1–4)	−0.3
		5. Undistributed Corporate Profits (1–15)	29.3
		6. Corporate Inventory Valuation Adjustment (1–16)	−6.9
		7. Capital Consumption Allowances (1–22)	102.4
		8. Government Surplus or Deficit (−), National Income and Product Accounts (3–8)	−2.8
		9. Capital Grants Received by the United States (4–2)	0.7
		10. Statistical Discrepancy (1–23)	−1.5
Gross Investment	170.6	Gross Saving and Statistical Discrepancy	170.6

* Numbers in parentheses indicate accounts and counterentry in the accounts.

One very interesting table shows the relationship among gross national product, national income, and personal income (see Table 2.8).

If we expand Table 2.8 with information furnished from other tables, we obtain some aggregates important for later work (see Table 2.9).

The Use of National Income Accounting

As previously noted, accounting information reveals only past transactions, but this *ex post* information can be very useful in plotting future changes. In order to make rational policy, it is essential to have some idea of where the economy

TABLE 2.8

RELATION OF GROSS NATIONAL PRODUCT, NATIONAL INCOME,
AND PERSONAL INCOME, 1972

(Billions of Dollars)

Gross National Product	1,155.2
Less: Capital Consumption Allowances	102.4
Equals: Net National Product	1,052.8
Less: Indirect Business Tax	109.5
Business Transfer Payments	4.6
Statistical Discrepancy	−4.8
Plus: Subsidies Less Current Surplus of Governmental Enterprises	1.7
Equals: National Income	941.8
Less: Corporate Profits and Inventory Valuation Adjustment	91.1
Contributions for Social Insurance	73.7
Wage Accruals Less Disbursements	−0.5
Plus: Government Transfer Payments to Persons	98.3
Interest Paid by Government (Net) and by Consumers	32.7
Dividends	26.0
Business Transfer Payments	4.6
Equals: Personal Income	939.4

TABLE 2.9

THE DISPOSITION OF PERSONAL INCOME

(Billions of Dollars)

Personal Income		939.2
Less: Personal Tax and Nontax Payments		142.2
Equals: Disposable Personal Income		797.0
Less: Personal Outlays		747.2
Personal Consumption Expenditures	726.5	
Interest Paid by Consumers	19.7	
Personal Transfer Payments to Foreigners	1.0	
Equals: Personal Saving		60.9

TABLE 2.10

SUMMARY NATIONAL INCOME AND PRODUCT SERIES, 1929–1972

(Billions of Dollars)

A. Gross National Product

Year	GNP	Personal Consumption Expenditures				Gross Private Domestic Investment				Net Exports	Government Purchases of Goods and Services			Final Sales	GNP in 1958 Prices	GNP Implicit Price Deflator (Index Numbers, 1958=100)
		Total	Durable Goods	Nondurable Goods	Services	Total	Nonresidential Fixed Investment	Residential Structures	Change in Business Inventories		Total	Federal	State and Local			
1929	103.1	77.2	9.2	37.7	30.3	16.2	10.6	4.0	1.7	1.1	8.5	1.3	7.2	101.4	203.6	50.6
1930	90.4	69.9	7.2	34.0	28.7	10.3	8.3	2.3	−.4	1.0	9.2	1.4	7.8	90.7	183.5	49.3
1931	75.8	60.5	5.5	29.0	26.0	5.6	5.0	1.7	−1.1	.5	9.2	1.5	7.7	77.0	169.3	44.8
1932	58.0	48.6	3.6	22.7	22.2	1.0	2.7	.7	−2.5	.4	8.1	1.5	6.6	60.5	144.2	40.2
1933	55.6	45.8	3.5	22.3	20.1	1.4	2.4	.6	−1.6	.4	8.0	2.0	6.0	57.2	141.5	39.3
1934	65.1	51.3	4.2	26.7	20.4	3.3	3.2	.9	−.7	.6	9.8	3.0	6.8	65.8	154.3	42.2
1935	72.2	55.7	5.1	29.3	21.3	6.4	4.1	1.2	1.1	.1	10.0	2.9	7.1	71.2	169.5	42.6
1936	82.5	61.9	6.3	32.9	22.8	8.5	5.6	1.6	1.3	.1	12.0	4.9	7.0	81.2	193.0	42.7
1937	90.4	66.5	6.9	35.2	24.4	11.8	7.3	1.9	2.5	.3	11.9	4.7	7.2	87.9	203.2	44.5
1938	84.7	63.9	5.7	34.0	24.3	6.5	5.4	2.0	−.9	1.3	13.0	5.4	7.6	85.6	192.9	43.9
1939	90.5	66.8	6.7	35.1	25.0	9.3	5.9	2.9	.4	1.1	13.3	5.1	8.2	90.1	209.4	43.2
1940	99.7	70.8	7.8	37.0	26.0	13.1	7.5	3.4	2.2	1.7	14.0	6.0	8.0	97.5	227.2	43.9
1941	124.5	80.6	9.6	42.9	28.1	17.9	9.5	3.9	4.5	1.3	24.8	16.9	7.9	120.1	263.7	47.2
1942	157.9	88.5	6.9	50.8	30.8	9.8	6.0	2.1	1.8	.0	59.6	51.9	7.7	156.2	297.8	53.0
1943	191.6	99.3	6.6	58.6	34.2	5.7	5.0	1.4	−.6	−2.0	88.6	81.1	7.4	192.2	337.1	56.8
1944	210.1	108.3	6.7	64.3	37.2	7.1	6.8	1.3	−1.0	−1.8	96.5	89.0	7.5	211.1	361.3	58.2
1945	211.9	119.7	8.0	71.9	39.8	10.6	10.1	1.5	−1.0	−.6	82.3	74.2	8.1	213.0	355.2	59.7

Year																
1946	66.7	312.6	202.1	9.8	17.2	27.0	7.5	6.4	7.2	17.0	30.6	45.3	82.4	15.8	143.4	208.5
1947	74.6	309.9	231.8	12.6	12.5	25.1	11.5	—.5	11.1	23.4	34.0	49.8	90.5	20.4	160.7	231.3
1948	79.6	323.7	252.9	15.0	16.5	31.6	6.4	4.7	14.4	26.9	46.0	54.7	96.2	22.7	173.6	257.6
1949	79.1	324.1	259.6	17.7	20.1	37.8	6.1	—3.1	13.7	25.1	35.7	57.6	94.5	24.6	176.8	256.5
1950	80.2	355.3	278.0	19.5	18.4	37.9	1.8	6.8	19.4	27.9	54.1	62.4	98.1	30.5	191.0	284.8
1951	85.6	383.4	318.1	21.5	37.7	59.1	3.7	10.3	17.2	31.8	59.3	67.9	108.8	29.6	206.3	328.4
1952	87.5	395.1	342.4	22.9	51.8	74.7	2.2	3.1	17.2	31.6	51.9	73.4	114.0	29.3	216.7	345.5
1953	88.3	412.8	364.1	24.6	57.0	81.6	.4	.4	18.0	34.2	52.6	79.9	116.8	33.2	230.0	364.6
1954	89.6	407.0	366.4	27.4	47.4	74.8	1.8	—1.5	19.7	33.6	51.7	85.4	118.3	32.8	236.5	364.8
1955	90.9	438.0	392.0	30.1	44.1	74.2	2.0	6.0	23.3	38.1	67.4	91.4	123.3	39.6	254.4	398.0
1956	94.0	446.1	414.5	33.0	45.6	78.6	4.0	4.7	21.6	43.7	70.0	98.5	129.3	38.9	266.7	419.2
1957	97.5	452.5	439.8	36.6	49.5	86.1	5.7	1.3	20.2	46.4	67.9	105.0	135.6	40.8	281.4	441.1
1958	100.0	447.3	448.8	40.6	53.6	94.2	2.2	—1.5	20.8	41.6	60.9	112.0	140.2	37.9	290.1	447.3
1959	101.6	475.9	478.9	43.3	53.7	97.0	.1	4.8	25.5	45.1	75.3	120.3	146.6	44.3	311.2	483.7
1960	103.3	487.7	500.2	46.1	53.5	99.6	4.0	3.6	22.8	48.4	74.8	128.7	151.3	45.3	325.2	503.7
1961	104.6	497.2	518.1	50.2	57.4	107.6	5.6	2.0	22.6	47.0	71.7	135.1	155.9	44.2	335.2	520.1
1962	105.8	529.8	554.3	53.7	63.4	117.1	5.1	6.0	25.3	51.7	83.0	143.0	162.6	49.5	355.1	560.3
1963	107.2	551.0	584.6	58.2	64.2	122.5	5.9	5.9	27.0	54.3	87.1	152.4	168.6	53.9	375.0	590.5
1964	108.8	581.1	626.6	63.5	65.2	128.7	8.5	5.8	27.1	61.1	94.0	163.3	178.7	59.2	401.2	632.4
1965	110.9	617.8	675.3	70.1	66.9	137.0	6.9	9.6	27.2	71.3	108.1	175.5	191.1	66.3	432.8	684.9
1966	113.9	658.1	735.1	79.0	77.8	156.8	5.3	14.8	25.0	81.6	121.4	188.6	206.9	70.8	466.3	749.9
1967	117.6	675.2	785.7	89.4	90.7	180.1	5.2	8.2	25.1	83.3	116.6	204.0	215.0	73.1	492.1	793.9
1968	122.3	706.6	857.1	100.8	98.8	199.6	2.5	7.1	30.1	88.8	126.0	221.3	230.8	84.0	536.2	864.2
1969	128.2	725.6	922.5	111.2	98.8	210.0	1.9	7.8	32.6	98.5	139.0	242.7	245.9	90.8	579.5	930.3
1970	135.2	722.5	972.6	123.3	96.2	219.5	3.6	4.5	31.2	100.6	136.3	262.6	263.8	91.3	617.6	977.1
1971	141.6	745.4	1,049.4	136.2	98.1	234.3	.8	6.1	42.7	104.4	153.2	284.9	278.7	103.6	667.2	1,055.5
1972	146.1	790.7	1,149.1	150.5	104.4	255.0	—4.6	6.0	54.0	118.2	178.3	309.2	299.9	117.4	726.5	1,155.2

TABLE 2.10 (Continued)

B. National Income and Disposition of Personal Income

Year	National Income	Compensation of Employees	Proprietors' Income Business and Professional	Proprietors' Income Farm	Rental Income of Persons	Corporate Profits and IVA Total	Profits Before Tax	Profits After Tax	Net Interest	Personal Income	Less: Personal Tax and Nontax Payments	Equals: Disposable Personal Income	Less: Personal Outlays	Equals: Personal Saving	Personal Saving Rate* (Per Cent)	Disposable Personal Income in 1958 Prices
1929	86.8	51.1	9.0	6.2	5.4	10.5	10.0	8.6	4.7	85.9	2.6	83.3	79.1	4.2	5.0	150.6
1930	75.4	46.8	7.6	4.3	4.8	7.0	3.7	2.9	4.9	77.0	2.5	74.5	71.1	3.4	4.6	139.0
1931	59.7	39.8	5.8	3.4	3.8	2.0	−.4	−.9	5.0	65.9	1.9	64.0	61.4	2.6	4.1	133.7
1932	42.8	31.1	3.6	2.1	2.7	−1.3	−2.3	−2.7	4.6	50.2	1.5	48.7	49.3	−.6	−1.3	115.1
1933	40.3	29.5	3.3	2.6	2.0	−1.2	1.0	.4	4.1	47.0	1.5	45.5	46.5	−.9	−2.0	112.2
1934	49.5	34.3	4.7	3.0	1.7	1.7	2.3	1.6	4.1	54.0	1.6	52.4	52.0	.4	.7	120.4
1935	57.2	37.3	5.5	5.3	1.7	3.4	3.6	2.6	4.1	60.4	1.9	58.5	56.4	2.1	3.7	131.8
1936	65.0	42.9	6.7	4.3	1.8	5.6	6.3	4.9	3.8	68.6	2.3	66.3	62.7	3.6	5.4	148.4
1937	73.7	47.9	7.2	6.0	2.1	6.8	6.8	5.3	3.7	74.1	2.9	71.2	67.4	3.8	5.3	153.1
1938	67.4	45.0	6.9	4.4	2.6	4.9	4.0	2.9	3.6	68.3	2.9	65.5	64.8	.7	1.1	143.6
1939	72.6	48.1	7.4	4.4	2.7	6.3	7.0	5.6	3.5	72.8	2.4	70.3	67.7	2.6	3.7	155.9
1940	81.1	52.1	8.6	4.5	2.9	9.8	10.0	7.2	3.3	78.3	2.6	75.7	71.8	3.8	5.1	166.3
1941	104.2	64.8	11.1	6.4	3.5	15.2	17.7	10.1	3.2	96.0	3.3	92.7	81.7	11.0	11.8	190.3
1942	137.1	85.3	14.0	9.8	4.5	20.3	21.5	10.1	3.1	122.9	6.0	116.9	89.3	27.6	23.6	213.4
1943	170.3	109.5	17.0	11.7	5.1	24.4	25.1	11.1	2.7	151.3	17.8	133.5	100.1	33.4	25.0	222.8
1944	182.6	121.2	18.2	11.6	5.4	23.8	24.1	11.2	2.3	165.3	18.9	146.3	109.1	37.3	25.5	231.6
1945	181.5	123.1	19.2	12.2	5.6	19.2	19.7	9.0	2.2	171.1	20.9	150.2	120.7	29.6	19.7	229.7
1946	181.9	117.9	21.6	14.9	6.6	19.3	24.6	15.5	1.5	178.7	18.7	160.0	144.8	15.2	9.5	227.0
1947	199.0	128.9	20.3	15.2	7.1	25.6	31.5	20.2	1.9	191.3	21.4	169.8	162.5	7.3	4.3	218.0

1948	224.2	141.1	22.7	17.5	8.0	33.0	35.2	22.7	1.8	210.2	21.1	189.1	175.8	13.4	7.1	229.8
1949	217.5	141.0	22.6	12.7	8.4	30.8	28.9	18.5	1.9	207.2	18.6	188.6	179.2	9.4	5.0	230.8
1950	241.1	154.6	24.0	13.5	9.4	37.7	42.6	24.9	2.0	227.6	20.7	206.9	193.9	13.1	6.3	249.6
1951	278.0	180.7	26.1	15.8	10.3	42.7	43.9	21.6	2.3	255.6	29.0	226.6	209.3	17.3	7.6	255.7
1952	291.4	195.3	27.1	15.0	11.5	39.9	38.9	19.6	2.6	272.5	34.1	238.3	220.2	18.1	7.6	263.3
1953	304.7	209.1	27.5	13.0	12.7	39.6	40.6	20.4	2.8	288.2	35.6	252.6	234.3	18.3	7.2	275.4
1954	303.1	208.0	27.6	12.4	13.6	38.0	38.3	20.6	3.6	290.1	32.7	257.4	241.0	16.4	6.4	278.3
1955	331.0	224.5	30.3	11.4	13.9	46.9	48.6	27.0	4.1	310.9	35.5	275.3	259.5	15.8	5.7	296.7
1956	350.8	243.1	31.3	11.4	14.3	46.1	48.8	27.2	4.6	333.0	39.8	293.2	272.6	20.6	7.0	309.3
1957	366.1	256.0	32.8	11.3	14.8	45.6	47.2	26.0	5.6	351.1	42.6	308.5	287.8	20.7	6.7	315.8
1958	367.8	257.8	33.2	13.4	15.4	41.1	41.4	22.3	6.8	361.2	42.3	318.8	296.6	22.3	7.0	318.8
1959	400.0	279.1	35.1	11.4	15.6	51.7	52.1	28.5	7.1	383.5	46.2	337.3	318.3	19.1	5.6	333.0
1960	414.5	294.2	34.2	12.0	15.8	49.9	49.7	26.7	8.4	401.0	50.9	350.0	333.0	17.0	4.9	340.2
1961	427.3	302.6	35.6	12.8	16.0	50.3	50.3	27.2	10.0	416.8	52.4	364.4	343.3	21.2	5.8	350.7
1962	457.7	323.6	37.1	13.0	16.7	55.7	55.4	31.2	11.6	442.6	57.4	385.3	363.7	21.6	5.6	367.3
1963	481.9	341.0	37.9	13.1	17.1	58.9	59.4	33.1	13.8	465.5	60.9	404.6	384.7	19.9	4.9	381.3
1964	518.1	365.7	40.2	12.1	18.0	66.3	66.8	38.4	15.8	497.5	59.4	438.1	411.9	26.2	6.0	407.9
1965	564.3	393.8	42.4	14.8	19.0	76.1	77.8	46.5	18.2	538.9	65.7	473.2	444.8	28.4	6.0	435.0
1966	620.6	435.5	45.2	16.1	20.0	82.4	84.2	49.9	21.4	587.2	75.4	511.9	479.3	32.5	6.4	458.9
1967	653.6	467.2	47.3	14.8	21.1	78.7	79.8	46.6	24.4	629.3	83.0	546.3	506.0	40.4	7.4	477.5
1968	711.1	514.6	49.5	14.7	21.2	84.3	87.6	47.8	26.9	688.9	97.9	591.0	551.2	39.8	6.7	499.0
1969	766.0	566.0	50.5	16.7	22.6	79.8	84.9	44.8	30.5	750.9	116.5	634.4	596.2	38.2	6.0	513.6
1970	800.5	603.9	50.0	16.9	23.9	69.2	74.0	39.3	36.5	808.3	116.6	691.7	635.5	56.2	8.1	534.8
1971	859.4	644.1	51.9	16.8	24.5	80.1	85.1	47.6	42.0	863.5	117.5	746.0	658.8	60.2	8.1	554.9
1972	941.8	707.1	54.0	20.2	24.1	91.1	98.0	55.4	45.2	939.2	142.2	797.0	747.2	49.7	6.2	577.9

* Personal saving as a per cent of disposable personal income.

Source: *Survey of Current Business* 53 (July 1973): 52.

stands at present and where it is likely to go if left unmanipulated. Future trends can be forecast by examining the past and present data and establishing relations that can help explain the movements of the national income aggregates.

Out of these relations can come the knowledge of how to gain some control over the economy in the short run and how to influence the system to insure long-run growth. Historical perspectives are useful for both time horizons.

In addition to providing information for forecasting and management of the economy, the GNP data also delineate the results of the economy in operation. We can observe the distribution of the national output—who gets command over it: it is important to know which sector—consumers, investors, government— purchased the national output. Much of macroeconomic theory is connected to such knowledge, as will be noted shortly. In addition, the data give information on a wide variety of other issues: the distribution of income by factor shares, the distribution of output in terms of private versus public control, the origins of national output by sector and type of business organization, and many more breakdowns of the national income and product data that provide a good picture of all facets of the economic system. Indeed, the uses of the data are as many and diverse as the people who use them, and anyone not familiar with the information collected would be wise to consult a July issue of the *Survey of Current Business*. Whatever limitations the data may have, used with care they can provide many insights into the performance of the economic system.

PART TWO

Accounting is limited by its procedures to the world where things are true by definition. Working with accounting data would not provide a full understanding of how an economy operates, for they record what has already happened, not why or how the data came to be what they are.

It is the task of theory to ask these questions, and to do so, it employs the type of analysis that permits the inclusion of behavioral components. In mathematical terms, the movement is away from identity equations to conditional equations that can handle functional relationships. The use of conditional equations and causal relationships helps to establish the case for the necessity of theory, but the study of theory is often a major stumbling block in the study of economics. For this reason, chapter 3 is concerned with the justification for, and the tools of, macroeconomic theory.

Chapters 4 through 12 are concerned with the generally accepted macroeconomic theory of an advanced capitalist economic system. The theory is developed incrementally until chapter 12, where all parts are brought together in a general model of the economy.

Introduction to the Theory of Macroeconomics

3

If one looks at the national income accounts—at any item—and asks why this number is what it is, honesty requires an "I don't know" answer. Ask how the number may change or be expected to change, and again the number alone yields no clue. There is no way to understand economic relationships or changes in these relationships without first organizing the thought process so as to facilitate the handling of these questions. This is the task of theory; it cannot be escaped.

Still, the world is a complicated place. To attempt to account for all the influences that bear upon anything would be futile. In economics, especially, it is true that everything depends upon everything else. One can either throw up one's hands in despair, or try to isolate the most relevant factors, the most powerful influences, and discard the others. When certain factors are discarded, something less than a complete explanation is forced upon us, but only through the process of abstraction can any manageable explanation be made. Therefore, the first point to remember is that theory—the theory of anything— does not purport to provide a complete explanation.

To illustrate the meaning of theory and the methodology of partial equilibrium analysis, let us take a familiar example from microeconomics: the simple but elegant model of price determination in a market. The determinants of demand and supply functions are well known, so we may write,

(3.1) $\quad D = f(\text{price, income, number of consumers, expectations, taste, ...});$

(3.2) $\quad S = g(\text{price, resource prices, technology, number of sellers, expectations, ...}).$

The letters f and g in these expressions are functional notations and should be understood to stand for "is related to," "depends upon," or "is a function of" the items in the parentheses. The parentheses enclose the main determinants common to most markets, while the three dots indicate the possibility of other variables that may be pertinent in specific markets. Still, we never see demand and supply curves drawn from expressions like (3.1) and (3.2). The limitations imposed by two-dimensional surfaces require that the number of variables be reduced. This can be done if all variables except one in the parentheses are accounted for *and held constant*. Equations (3.1) and (3.2) then take the familiar form

(3.3) $$D = f(\text{price});$$
(3.4) $$S = f(\text{price});$$

and assuming an equilibrium position exists,

(3.5) $$D = S.$$

Now we have demand and supply as functions of price, with everything else held constant. This is the method of partial equilibrium analysis; other factors have been considered and held constant. In graphical terms, the other factors determine the *position* of the curve, and when they are changed, the entire curve shifts. On the other hand, changes in price cause movements along a stationary curve. The former changes are called changes in demand or supply, and the latter are called changes in the quantity demanded or supplied. These changes are illustrated in Figure 3.1.

The example given plainly illustrates the need for, and the construction of, theory. It is hoped that this brief exposure to the complexities of theory building will help the reader appreciate later that what may appear to be astonishingly simple theories were in fact difficult to formulate.

What can be said, then, of the dictum that practical men understand more about economic processes than do theorists, that men of action are better able to grapple with problems than are isolated abstractionists? Sayings such as these are really disputing the need for theory, but they miss the point. The practical man as well as the theorist is "theorizing." He, too, organizes material from various sources, reduces real events to manageable proportions, and concentrates on one or two facets of a many-sided problem in reaching a solution. The practical man may not be as rigorously logical as the theorist, but, explicitly or not, he employs similar techniques. The real question is whose "theory" will best fit reality? Is it beneficial to state theory explicitly, including the assumptions made and the methodology employed, so that the conclusions can be evaluated and tested? Most men who aspire to find solutions in the social sciences, where the object of study (behavior) is complex and ever-changing, would answer *yes*.

Macroeconomic Theory

Macroeconomics, as was noted, is concerned with aggregate quantities and relationships, such as total consumption, investment, and government expenditures. The practice of aggregation, which distinguishes this field from microeconomics, has advantages but also creates problems. A brief survey of these problems is required now, although a deeper appreciation of them must await the critical attitudes that can only develop with more exposure to the entire subject.

One difficulty is the complex area known as the aggregation problem—the classifying of widely varying goods or activities into one general category, which is

FIGURE 3.1

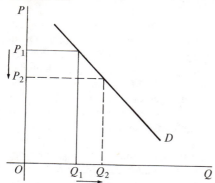

(a) Change in Quantity Demanded
Due to Change in Price

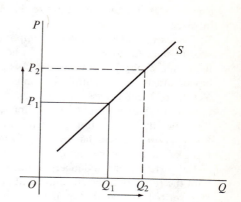

(b) Change in Quantity Supplied
Due to Change in Price

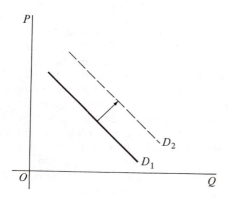

(c) Change in Demand Due to Change
in Factor Previously Held Constant

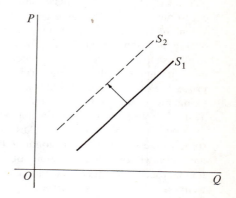

(d) Change in Supply Due to Change
in Factor Previously Held Constant

treated as a homogeneous variable. For example, under consumption expenditures are listed all goods and services consumed by households, from refrigerators to toothpaste, and under investment goods are listed all capital goods used by the business sector, from giant furnaces to candy showcases. In other words, by classifying such items together, we have obscured the composition of that particular aggregate. In many cases, the failure to recognize the separate components of these aggregates results in faulty and misleading work. Thus, to speak of changes in investment expenditures means that the total has changed, but it is clear that during any period some industries expand, some contract, and others remain stable, so that the change in the aggregate may not reflect accurately the structure and composition of the demand for investment goods. If deliberate policy were being constructed to affect the flow of investment spending, would it not be important to know which industries were expanding and which contracting, or which types of investment goods were being purchased and which not? Otherwise, policies designed to stimulate or stabilize investment spending could be ineffective or incorrect.

The same is true for the consumption aggregate. Consumption, as will be noted shortly, depends to a large extent on household or family income: $C = C(Y)$. Thus, if income changes, consumption changes. Aggregate theories of consumption behavior are based on simple relations and for many purposes are quite adequate. Yet there can be cases when even a prediction of the direction of change of consumption expenditures in relation to income changes can be wrong. This also illustrates the aggregation problem, for there are instances when it is important to know *whose* incomes have changed and how their consumption patterns resemble those of the rest of the sector.

In short, one of the dangers of macroeconomic theory is that of *overaggregation,* with the result that the structure and composition of the aggregate magnitudes may be overlooked and that policies designed to influence those aggregates may be ineffective or inefficient. One obvious remedy is to disaggregate to the extent necessary to avoid the problem. This is often done, particularly with factual information, but it must be remembered that the more disaggregation that takes place, the closer to microeconomics the analysis becomes. Then one might be confronted with the opposite concern.

One of the benefits of working with highly aggregated variables is that the very overaggregation just criticized does confer a high degree of stability to aggregate relations not otherwise found. Since the structure and composition of the aggregates are ignored, all extreme forms of activity tend to cancel out in the adding-up process. For instance, the consumption patterns of those engaged in communal living are offset by the consumption patterns of the status-seeking suburbanite. Thus, many relations found in macroeconomic theory and tested repeatedly tend to be highly stable, which makes successful prediction more feasible. Indeed, some would say that macroeconomic theory is made possible by this stability alone and that without this canceling of extremes, this balancing, averaging process, no macroeconomic theory would be possible. Although in the adding-up process the richness of variety is submerged in the whole, stability is a boon; when it is upset, there is a good chance that one of the aggregation problems is the cause.

Another problem in macroeconomic theory is the careless use of logic in going from the particular to the general. The inductive method of reasoning often leads to errors called the fallacy of composition: what is true for the part may not be true for the whole. Generalizing from particular cases is hazardous, as the following examples demonstrate.

Consider the farmer who wishes to increase his income. He increases the size of his crop, but if every farmer did the same, the price of the crop might fall, resulting in a decline in income, not an increase. Again, if workers in a particular plant decide to accept lower money wages in the attempt to increase employment, they might be successful for their particular plant, but if all workers agreed to accept lower money wages in order to increase total employment, it might happen that the level of employment would not change at all. We will come back to the latter example, which brought Keynes and his contemporaries into sharp conflict. This aggregation problem is the result of using partial equilibrium analysis in a general equilibrium situation.

There are also some difficulties in deciding which variables to aggregate and how to aggregate them. One can group data in a variety of ways, some meaningful and others not. The choice is often dictated by the availability of data and the nature of the analysis being performed. It makes quite a difference, for instance, whether one aggregates investment spending by industry, by product, across industries, and so on. The aggregate selected must be meaningful for the problem at hand and must be capable of being related to other aggregates, or the whole exercise may be futile.

There are other, somewhat more technical, problems in aggregating that are largely mathematical concerns. Discussion of these is better left to advanced work. Generally, they concern how the structure of the aggregate influences or could influence the ability to test hypotheses. In some cases, too much weight is given to a small portion of the total, yielding biased results; in other cases, this does not occur. In short, a changing situation could under some circumstances cause rejections of a theory when it is basically correct or acceptance of a theory that is suspect. Also, there are problems in deciding how to aggregate variables, whether linearly or with more complicated mathematical forms.[1]

Macroeconomic Variables

The variables of macroeconomic analysis have already been indicated as including consumption, investment, the money supply, the price level, the interest rate, and the wage rate. In one sense, these variables are self-explanatory, but closer scrutiny reveals the need to clarify them further so that they may be used properly and understood thoroughly.

The first distinction to be made among these variables is whether they are stock or flow variables. This distinction is necessary because of the time element present in all economic variables. A stock variable is one that has meaning only at a *specific point in time*. Thus, the capital stock of an economy only has meaning when expressed as a magnitude at a certain time—for instance, as of December 31, 1974, the capital stock of the nation was x billions of dollars. Other examples of stock variables are the money stock, inventory, savings, and population data. Accountants will recognize these as balance sheet items revealing values as of a certain date—the "still" picture of a firm. When added, the aggregates become macroeconomic stock variables.

In contrast, there are those variables, the flow ones, that cannot be meaningfully expressed except in terms of a *time period*. Thus, we speak of income per year, per quarter, or per week; investment, consumption, and saving per quarter or year. The time period must be considered explicitly when referring to these variables, or else it makes little sense to use them. One could not say that personal income was $800 billion without stating over what time period this amount of income was earned. It must read $800 billion for the year 1974. Nor does it make sense to refer to the stock of income being $800 billion as of December 31, 1974. The income was obviously earned during the course of the year, not on December 31st.

On the whole, the distinction between stock and flow variables is clear, although there are times when failure to remember it can lead to errors. For example, investment spending is a flow variable, and capital stock is a stock variable, but the relation between them is sometimes erroneously interpreted by the unwary. That is, positive net investment, I, adds to the stock of capital K, or subtracts

[1] For more on the mathematics of aggregation problems, see R. G. D. Allen, *Mathematical Economics* (London: Macmillan and Co., reprinted 1959), pp. 694–724.

from the stock of capital by another flow variable, depreciation, D, according to the following set of expressions already encountered:

$$I_g - D > 0; \qquad I_n > 0; \qquad \Delta K > 0;$$

capital stock grows.

$$I_g - D = 0; \qquad I_n = 0; \qquad \Delta K = 0;$$

capital stock remains constant.

$$I_g - D < 0; \qquad I_n < 0; \qquad \Delta K < 0;$$

capital stock declines.

The subscripts g and n refer to gross and net. The interaction between stock and flow variables is clearly illustrated by this example, which was selected because of its importance in macroeconomics.

Other relationships between stock and flow variables likely to cause some confusion arise when the two become mixed in mathematical operations. Dividing stock variables by stock variables or flow variables by flow variables causes no problems. Thus, the real wage, the money wage deflated by a price variable, W/P, or the proportion of wealth in the form of capital stock, K/W, are easy to interpret: the real wage rate is a flow variable, W, divided by another flow variable, P. In the case of K/W, both are stock variables. Intuitively these ratios make sense. But what of M/P, the real value of the money stock or Y/K, the output-capital ratio? In M/P the stock variable appears in the numerator and the flow variable in the denominator. For Y/K the reverse is true. In both cases, the time element does not cancel out and therefore must enter the analysis. It is necessary to exercise caution when using these ratios so that there will be no mistake about the time dimension used.

The Use of Variables in Macroeconomic Analysis

Variables, being unspecified entities, are capable of being manipulated in many ways. The choice of methods depends largely on the nature of the problem and the degree of sophistication required. Economists generally use some variant of two broad types of analysis—static and dynamic.

Static analysis is concerned with states of equilibrium, and static models inquire into the forces leading to, maintaining, and reestablishing, if necessary, the equilibrium condition. The market mechanism establishing an equilibrium price is a good, simple example of static analysis. The influences on the market are enumerated, and a model is built showing how the market establishes an equilibrium that clears the market. Yet the *exact* process by which the market forces act upon the model is left unexplored, and there is no particular emphasis given to the passage of time in the process. Static analysis is more interested in the basis for an equilibrium than in giving a detailed account of how the condition was established or how long it took to get there.

With a model in equilibrium any change in the variables will cause the model to react until a new equilibrium is reached. The comparison of these two equilibrium states is called comparative statics. Again, there is no exact accounting for how the new position was reached or how long it took to reach it.

FIGURE 3.2

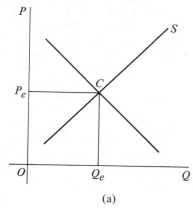

(a)

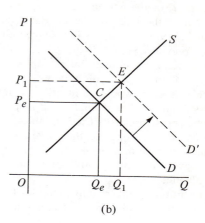

(b)

Figure 3.2 shows the concept of static analysis graphically. In Figure 3.2(a) an equilibrium price and quantity are established by the model of the market just discussed.

Point C is the equilibrium solution to the supply and demand equations. If one of the determinants of demand, say, income, changes, we have a change in demand, a shift in the curve, and a new equilibrium established at point E in Figure 3.2(b). We are not sure what path the variables took as they adjusted to the changed condition, nor do we know the time necessary for all adjustments to work themselves out. The model predicts that the new equilibrium will be established at point E, and it permits us to visualize the overall movement from C to E. Finally, the method of comparative statics is concerned with the examination of the states of equilibrium as they exist at points C and E. Comparison of the two equilibrium conditions is often of great use and reveals much about the working of the model.

If the analysis demands more precise delineation of how the model works at various stages, or if there is the possibility of a disequilibrium situation, the method that should be employed is dynamic analysis. Here, the path that the variables take to reach an equilibrium (or disequilibrium) can be made explicit by bringing in the time element. The variables take on values by time periods, and thus their movement and interaction can be studied. Naturally, the model becomes more explicit under dynamic scrutiny, but it also becomes more complex and mathematical. For this reason, most dynamic analysis is left for advanced work. However, one simple type of dynamic analysis, called period analysis or sequence analysis, can be handled quite readily and will be the only type used in this book.

Again, using the simple market model, we can modify the equations to illustrate dynamic analysis. Thus,

(3.6) $D_t = a - bP_t$
(3.7) $S_t = c + dP_{t-1}$
(3.8) $D_t = S_t$, which is the static, or equilibrium, solution.

Equation (3.6) is simply a restatement of a linear demand function. The subscript t refers to any arbitrary time period, and the equation reads that the demand for this commodity at time t, which is the current time period, is a function of price at period t, or the current price. Equation (3.7) says that supply at period t is a function of the price of the previous period, $t-1$. In this simple model sellers decide how much to supply in the current period based upon the price they received in the previous period (expecting, of course, to receive the same price in the current period). Agricultural examples come to mind, as crop decisions must be made well in advance of harvests. Equation (3.8) is an equilibrium condition, which *if it exists* would be identical with the one that would be reached by static analysis. The results of applying a model like this depend upon the values of the parameters (temporarily fixed variables) in the model—in this case, upon the values of b and d, the slopes of the curves. By assigning values to the parameters, it is possible to trace out various paths that the model would take. A diagram of these paths gives the name to this type of model—the cobweb—because of the apparent resemblance.

Substituting numbers into equations (3.6), (3.7), and (3.8) enables us to follow the workings of this type of dynamic analysis:

(3.6)′ $$D_t = 75 - 3P_t$$
(3.7)′ $$S_t = 50 + 2P_{t-1}.$$

In order to solve these equations, the lag in the supply equation must be dropped. This would establish an equilibrium price, for only in equilibrium would $P_t = P_{t-1} = P_{t-2} = P_{t+1} = \cdots$. By dropping the lagged response of supply to price, we can ignore time altogether and solve the equations in the same manner as in the static equilibrium case. Thus, setting $P = P_t = P_{t-1}$, we can equate (3.6)′ and (3.7)′ to get an equilibrium P as follows:

$$D_t = S_t$$
(3.8)′ $$75 - 3P = 50 + 2P$$
$$P = 5.$$

To find the equilibrium quantity, simply substitute the equilibrium price into equation (3.7)′ and solve. Then,

$$S_t = 50 + 2(5)$$
$$= 60.$$

The equilibrium solutions to the problem are $P = 5$ and $Q = 60$. While equilibrium solutions exist, there is no indication of whether they will ever be reached or how. This must be ascertained by allowing the model to develop over time, that is, by making it dynamic. In order to observe the working of the model, assume an initial price P_o. The only condition we impose is that $P_o \neq P_e$, the equilibrium price. Assume an initial price of $P_o = 10 = P_{t-1}$. Then, given P_{t-1}, we can substitute it into (3.7)′ and find the quantity that would be supplied in period 1:

$$S_t = S_1 = 50 + 2(10)$$
$$= 70.$$

We can now substitute the solution for the supply side into equation (3.6)′, remembering that $S = D$ in equilibrium and for every period, since the market must be cleared; that is, $D_t = S_t = a - bP_t$. Then,

$$S_1 = a - bP_1$$

$$70 = 75 - 3P$$
$$1.67 = P.$$

These values are the solutions for period 1, given the initial condition P_0. Now, given the price for period 1, the price that sellers will expect in the next period, we can substitute it into equation (3.7) and solve for period 2; for period 2, the price in period 1, P_1, becomes P_{t-1}:

$$S_2 = 50 + 2P_{t-1}$$
$$= 50 + 2(1.67)$$
$$= 53.34.$$

Once again, substituting this value into the demand equation gives,

$$53.34 = 75 - 3P_2$$
$$7.22 = P_2.$$

These values and those for subsequent periods are shown in Table 3.1 and Figure 3.3. The continuation of this process reveals the dynamic path and the time re-

TABLE 3.1

Period	S_t	P_t	$(P_o = 10)$
1	70.00	1.67	
2	53.34	7.22	
3	64.44	3.52	
4	57.04	5.99	
5	61.98	4.34	
6	58.68	5.44	
7	60.88	4.71	
8	59.42	5.19	
9	60.38	4.87	
10	59.74	5.09	
∞	60.00	5.00	

FIGURE 3.3

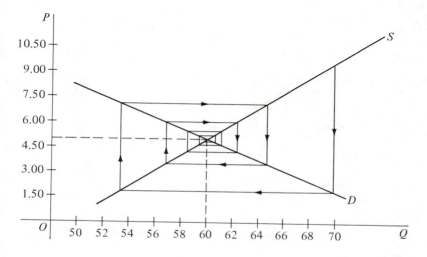

quired to reach an equilibrium that we already know from the static solution. In this case, the model converges to an equilibrium regardless of the initial condition P_o, and thus the model is called a stable one. If the model is once again disturbed, say by a change in D, the whole process starts all over again, but the model will converge to a new equilibrium and again exhibit its stability. This process is illustrated in Figure 3.4. Another way to examine the stability conditions is to compare the slopes of the curves. To achieve stability, the slope of the supply curve must be greater than the slope of the demand curve. In our example, $\frac{1}{2} > \frac{1}{3}$.

Before we turn to the unstable case, note the peculiar behavior postulated by this model—the producers never learn anything, never revise their expectations, but doggedly stick to the same expectations: they always expect the price in the current period to be equal to the price of the previous period. This is a rather simplistic notion of how expectations enter into the analysis, but it is typical of many economic models.[2] Expectations or more generally, uncertainties in economic theory have always been underemphasized.

If we retain the same basic model but change (switch) the coefficient of the price variables in equations (3.6)′ and (3.7)′, these equations would read

(3.6)″ $\qquad\qquad\qquad\qquad D_t = 75 - 2P_t$
(3.7)″ $\qquad\qquad\qquad\qquad S_t = 50 + 3P_{t-1}.$

As before, the static solution yielding equilibrium values can be found by equating the two equations and solving. Thus,

$$D_t = S_t$$
$$75 - 2P = 50 + 3P$$
$$5 = P,$$

which is the equilibrium price.

FIGURE 3.4
THE COBWEB MODEL: THE STABLE CASE

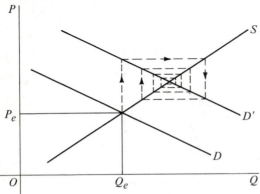

---

[2] See, however, Adolph Lowe, *On Economic Knowledge* (New York: Harper & Row, 1965).

Substituting into (3.7)'' for the equilibrium quantity gives,

$$S = 50 + 3(5)$$
$$= 65,$$

which is the equilibrium quantity.

These are equilibrium values, which *if ever reached* will be maintained as are any equilibrium values. The question in this case is, If the initial values are not the equilibrium ones, is the path toward or away from the equilibrium condition? Again, in order to start the model, we assume an initial price $P_o = 4 = P_{t-1}$. Substituting this original price into the supply equation (3.7)'' gives

$$S_t = 50 + 3(4)$$
$$= 62.$$

Setting this quantity equal to demand yields the corresponding price:

$$62 = 75 - 2P$$
$$6.50 = P.$$

Proceeding as before by substituting this price into the next period's supply equation (P_t becomes P_{t-1} in the next period) allows the model to work itself out. This time, however, the movement is away from equilibrium (explosive), which denotes an unstable model. Here the instability is caused by the slope of the demand curve ($\frac{1}{2}$) being greater than the slope of the supply curve ($\frac{1}{3}$). Figure 3.5 and Table 3.2 show the movements of the model. Note here that static analysis is incapable of describing this model, since it is confined to equilibrium conditions

TABLE 3.2

Period	S_t	P_t	$(P_o = 4)$
1	62.0	6.50	
2	69.5	2.75	
3	58.25	8.38	
4	75.14	−0.07	

FIGURE 3.5
THE COBWEB MODEL: THE UNSTABLE CASE

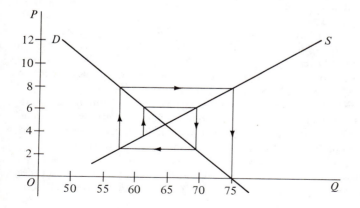

only. Obviously, dynamic analysis can be a powerful aid in the understanding of systems in various stages of disequilibrium.

Finally, for the sake of completeness it should be noted that there is a third possibility with the cobweb model, a continuous but constant path around the equilibrium point but neither converging toward nor diverging from that equilibrium point. Figure 3.6 shows this somewhat unlikely condition.

FIGURE 3.6
THE COBWEB MODEL: THE CONTINUOUS OSCILLATING CASE

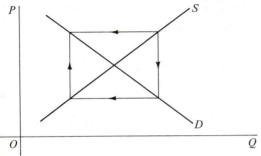

This continuous oscillation is the result of the slopes of the curves being equal. There is no possibility of an equilibrium in this case. The unreality of the expectations assumed in this model is obvious in this situation. It is difficult to support a hypothesis that no one learns from actual experience.

The Concept of Equilibrium

In parts of the preceding discussion the concept of an equilibrium was used somewhat imprecisely. By equilibrium was meant the balancing of opposing forces, a stabilizing process, where there is no tendency for change unless the balance is disturbed. The notion of an equilibrium in this sense is easily understood. It is now necessary to become a bit more exact in defining equilibrium, so that there will be no misunderstanding as to its meaning.

Time becomes once again important in a more explicit discussion of equilibrium concepts, not the actual chronological passage of time but a period of time in which certain changes can take place and certain changes cannot. Thus the short-run equilibrium is some arbitrary time period in which the capital stock of an economy is held constant—the number and size of firms is fixed. An economy can then be examined under this constraint, which emphasizes the utilization of existing resources and focuses upon the employment of existing factors of production. A short-run equilibrium assumes, often tacitly, that other variables both within and acting upon an economic system remain unchanged. Thus, demographic data, social and political attitudes, various legal and religious institutions, customs, traditions, and many other attitudes are assumed to remain constant, or nearly so, and permit the examination of the economy without serious disturbances. The short-run equilibrium concept is the one used throughout most of this book, since the primary emphasis is on income determination and employment of resources.

When one relaxes these assumptions, permitting capital stock to grow and some or all of the other variables to change, the long-run equilibrium concept takes effect. The long-run concept embodies economic growth and tries to deal with the type of variable that changes only slowly over time. Disturbances that occur to an economy in various short runs become smoothed out, and long sweeps or trends of the economy become apparent. The meaning of an equilibrium in this context is the analysis of the condition necessary for an economy to grow while maintaining some balance—an orderly growth utilizing available resources in some optimal way over time.

Another way to view these equilibrium concepts is to regard them in terms of stock and flow conditions. The short-run concept is satisfied when flow variables are in equilibrium. Since investment spending also occurs in the short run, to achieve a flow equilibrium, additions to the stock of capital as a result of current net investment must be ignored. In the short run the emphasis is on the demand side of investment spending. In the long run additions to capital stock cannot be ignored, and the long-run equilibrium can be viewed as stock equilibrium. In the long run the effects of investment spending on the productive capacity of the economy, the supply side, must be recognized. For an equilibrium growth over time, the growing capacity must be balanced by the growth on the demand side.

Thus, it is possible to have a short-run or flow equilibrium but not a long-run or stock equilibrium. Additions to capital stock disturb the long-run equilibrium. The analysis of how an economy adjusts to these disturbances received much attention from post-Keynesian scholars. On the other hand, it is not possible to have a long-run or stock equilibrium without having a flow equilibrium. When an economy reaches "full" equilibrium, both flow and stock equilibria must be attained, which means the economy has reached the stationary state. In the stationary state the additions to capital are balanced by an equal consumption of capital, so that the stock of capital remains fixed. Since the stationary state is obviously seldom, if ever, reached, any economic system is constantly reacting to the changes that occur in the short run. The structure of these changes and their effects upon the growth potential of an economic system have assumed enormous importance in a world struggling with the problem of economic development.

Mathematics in Economic Theory

It has been implicitly assumed in the preceding discussion that the analysis of many economic models requires some sophisticated techniques that include the use of mathematics. The notions that variables change, interact over time, are functionally related, and so on, and the clearly dynamic nature of the analysis of economic growth in the last section, all appear to demand rigorous expression if these processes are to be clarified or handled at all. Indeed, it is difficult to eschew the clarity of expression afforded by mathematics, for even if one were to shun the symbolic forms, one would still be forced to express the model in terms that largely follow the form of mathematical expressions and logic. It is now generally accepted that mathematics has an important role in the development of economic theory, and the need for it is seldom disputed. Many of the variables with which economics deals can be expressed quantitatively and measured. Economics lends itself to quantitative expression, and the data generally studied are available.

But many people have wondered whether the use of mathematics is not being overdone, so that instead of resulting in clarity it results in obscurity. The degree of mathematical sophistication required to work in economics is growing, without apparent benefits. Some of these complaints are registered by those who fail to appreciate the benefits derived. Others, however, sense some danger in the growing use of highly complex mathematical models.

There is first the concern that the use of complex mathematical models makes the science of economics appear to be too exact. Economics, after all, is a social science, which studies the behavior of men in the marketplace. Exact predictions of behavior may not be possible. A second, related criticism is that not all variables can be quantified and thus some are perhaps omitted from empirical work based on the abstract models. Social and political attitudes and other institutional, cultural, or traditional influences are ignored or relegated to the background and not related to economic motivations. This complaint has a long history, but it stubbornly persists despite the swing to the opposing view. Failure to recognize the limitations of the use of mathematics in economics has resulted in the economist becoming merely a social engineer, a technician who shuns making judgments. This last criticism has grown of late with the increasing use of econometrics, which attempts to test economic theory based on explicit mathematical formulations. Some feel that something is lost in the concentration on improving forecasts and developing elaborate models.

What can we conclude? Economists seem to be uncertain themselves in which direction the profession shall proceed—toward more or less use of mathematics. This much is clear: some use of mathematics will always be justified in economic theory, but the question remains, how much? The whole issue is raised here in order to alert the reader to a current controversy in the field and also to set forth the policy to be followed throughout this text. In general, mathematics will be used only as a shorthand method to express in another way the argument advanced in the written portion or as a device to help explain the text for those who prefer it. An attempt will be made to avoid explaining material only mathematically.

Methodological Concerns

Some of the problems of macroeconomic theory have been discussed. In this last section it will be useful to examine a few of the problems created by the methodology employed, that is, the methods or techniques used to formulate economic doctrines and principles. The manner in which one proceeds in creating a theory will frequently determine the usefulness of the entire undertaking.

Anyone can make up a theory. All that is needed is a condition calling for analysis, some conception of forces creating this condition, some perception of the motivations of those who find themselves in this condition, some awareness of an ideal situation that would allow this condition to be isolated and studied, and some ability to reason in a logical manner in order to reach conclusions that follow from the abstractions created by this process. In shorter terms, given a problem, one must abstract from reality by isolating the important influences on the problem, making some assumptions about possible behavior, and then reasoning through to some conclusion. We form some kind of hypothesis and then test the hypothesis and validate the results. The hypothesis can be put forward initially or after some direct empirical evidence has been gathered—either by pure conjecture or by direct observation.

Regardless of where the hypothesis originates, soon after the problem is delineated, some assumptions about behavior must be made, requiring some value judgments. It is recognized that some assumptions must be made to establish the conditions necessary for the analysis of the problem. But the existence of value judgments is not so readily admitted, although they frequently intrude, desired or not. Both assumptions and value judgments warrant further discussion, since they are the source of many problems and misunderstandings.

Assumptions are the basis of the whole theory-building procedure. They set the stage and govern the course of the analysis. Without them, no restrictions on reality are possible, and hence no theory. They delineate the world we wish to study, and they should be carefully stated so that others may evaluate the usefulness or applicability of the theory being formed and the conclusions reached. Some examples may help to explain this function. Many statements in economics begin (or should begin) with phrases like the following: "Let us assume perfect competition," "Let us assume full employment," and so on. These phrases alert the reader to any special conditions imposed at the outset, and he may then follow the reasoning with full knowledge of the limits of the model.

It is clear that assumptions play a major part in the development of a theory or model. Very often criticisms of theory are really criticisms of the assumptions made; the assumptions are either too restrictive or unrealistic or both. No matter how impeccable the logic, the analysis is useless because the world postulated by the theory does not exist. In one sense, this is an ill-founded objection, trivial since the purpose of theory is not to duplicate the real world. Perhaps "pure" theory is always defensible, that is, regardless of the realism of the assumptions, the task of the theorist is to deduce the consequences of his model. The model may be subsequently tested or modified by others, but a theory need not have direct application initially to be useful.

Yet in another way, the criticism is justified. Unrealistic assumptions lead to barren theories, which are often retained beyond their usefulness. A body of theoretical knowledge, once accepted, becomes what Galbraith calls "the conventional wisdom," and its uncritical acceptance allows only small refinements rather than productive revisions. Our view of the world is structured by this traditional knowledge, and we may fail to see the changes in the social fabric that require new theories to explain them. There is thus a danger in retaining assumptions about the structure of the world if they result in misleading conclusions and ineffective policies. Theories, then, become obsolete not because of faulty logic but because the abstractions have lost their meaning and are now too far removed from reality to permit correct prediction or policy making. Kenneth Boulding has described this tendency toward obsolescence as follows: "As science develops, it no longer merely investigates the world, it creates the world it is investigating."[3] Obsolete assumptions hinder the development of economics as a science and the possible alleviation of economic hardships that correct policies might prevent. In later chapters we will refer to this subject again as some of these assumptions come under question.

It follows from what has been said that the assumptions made in constructing a theory should be explicitly stated, so that they will be quite evident and there

---

[3] Kenneth E. Boulding, *Economics as a Science* (New York: McGraw-Hill, 1970), p. 121.

will be no question as to how they are used in the model. Value judgments, too, if they are to influence theory, should be clearly specified. There are still some, of course, who maintain that economics is a value-free subject and as objective as any other branch of science;[4] this is positive economics, which studies what is, as opposed to normative economics, which examines what ought to be. Yet it is difficult to avoid making value judgments in a social science, whether they become explicit or not. Probably the important requirement is that value judgments not be hidden. Consider a few judgments made by economists, and this requirement will become clearer. Is it a value judgment to assume that consumers, if they had all the knowledge needed, would purchase goods in such a way as to maximize utility? Why is this rational behavior, and not some other less organized method for spending income? What is there behind the assumption of the diminishing marginal utility of income but some value judgments? Do firms maximize profits or are other goals equally desirable? Why would profit maximization be deemed rational behavior when it remains invariant regardless of the economic situation or the economic condition of the firm or industry? Is not efficiency, inherent in maximizing principles, a value judgment itself?

In the final analysis, there is probably no way to escape making value judgments, since even in selecting problems for study we make judgments about what is important. Economic theorists are no more able to escape the society of which they are a part than are other scientists. Values creep in—social, political, and cultural —so that a value-free social science appears a utopian goal. It would be better to recognize these value judgments whenever they enter into the study and deal with them as openly as with the assumptions. The opposite tendency, the attempt to eliminate all values from the discipline, can only result in the economist becoming a mere technician who disavows his ability to state opinions based on imperfect information.

[4] Milton Friedman, *Essays in Positive Economics* (Chicago: University of Chicago Press, 1953), p. 4.

National Income Determination: The Simple Models

National income accounting measures economic activity that has taken place in a certain economy over a period of time, but the gathering and classification of data in a specified way does not reveal why the numbers are what they are. This "why" is the *raison d'être* of macroeconomic theory. The purpose of this chapter is to develop the tools for the initial study of how the national income is determined and how it changes. The models will be simple but capable of revealing much of the theoretical basis for modern thinking in macroeconomics. In order to keep the discussion on a simple level, the theory is presented rather dogmatically, with only occasional references to possible shortcomings. In later chapters more searching questions of the assumptions made and the methodology followed will be possible, and they will be more meaningful if some understanding of the whole area is established first. We turn first to a concept that many economists would agree was Keynes's major contribution to the body of economic theory—the consumption function.

The Consumption Function

Here is one of those concepts in economics about which one wonders why it was not thought of before, since it is so simple and (especially now) so obvious. It is the idea that the amount of the national product that goes to personal consumption is principally determined by the amount of income flowing to households. More particularly, the amount of disposable income—income after taxes—determines the amount of consumption expenditures.

Symbolically,

(4.1)
$$C = C(Y_d),$$

where C is the amount of consumption expenditure and Y_d is personal disposable income. Of course, there are other factors that may help to explain the volume of consumption, but disposable income is regarded as the most important independent variable, the major influence.

We must specify just how C and Y (we can drop the subscript d now) are related in order to elaborate on this general functional relation. The simplest assumption to make is that the relation is linear. Thus, we write

(4.2)
$$C = C_a + cY.$$

Equation (4.2) is an expression for a straight line and is to be interpreted as follows: mathematically, C_a is the y intercept in the positive quadrant, and economically, it measures the amount of consumption when income is zero. This means that in the short run, in which we are working, there is some minimum amount of consumption (from past savings) even when there is no income, and thus consumption never falls to zero. This amount of consumption is called autonomous consumption, since it is independent of the level of income.

Mathematically, c is the slope of the line, and economically, it measures the extent of the change in consumption with respect to a change in income. Keynes called it the marginal propensity to consume (MPC). It shows what portion of a change in income will be consumed. Thus,

$$c = \frac{\Delta C}{\Delta Y} \left(= \frac{dC}{dY} \right) = MPC.$$

Keynes believed the MPC to be positive but less than 1, which means that some portion of additional income will be spent but not all of it, and it follows that consumption cannot be unaffected by a change in income. Since we have assumed a linear relation, the MPC is a constant (the slope of a straight line is always a constant), and we have thus assumed that whatever the level of income of a community, any change from that level will be divided up into consumption and saving in the same fixed proportions. These statements can be summarized as follows:

$$MPC = c \text{ is always positive;}$$
$$\overline{MPC} = \bar{c} \text{ is a constant;}$$
$$0 < c < 1 = MPC \text{ lies between 0 and 1.}$$

The marginal propensity to consume relates to changes in consumption brought about (induced) by changes in income. If the aim instead is to discover what proportion of a given *level* of income is devoted to consumption, another concept, called the average propensity to consume, is needed. The average propensity to consume (APC) can be written as C/Y and derived by dividing both sides of equation (4.2) by Y:

(4.3)
$$\frac{C}{Y} = \frac{C_a}{Y} + c.$$

Since c is a positive constant, the following relationships between APC and MPC hold:

$$APC > MPC, \text{ since } \frac{C_a}{Y} + c > c;$$

and as Y increases,

$$APC \downarrow \text{ but } \overline{MPC}, \text{ since as } Y \uparrow, \frac{C_a}{Y} \downarrow.$$

The Saving Function

In deriving the consumption function, we automatically determined the saving function. This is because households are only permitted to do two things with their incomes—consume and save. Once one of these variables has been determined, the other is also. Thus, the saving equations are complements to the consumption equations. The saving function is written

(4.4) $$S = S(Y_d).$$

Again in linear form (like the consumption function) and after dropping the subscript d, equation (4.4) becomes

(4.5) $$S = -S_a + sY.$$

Here $-S_a$, which is equal to the amount of saving when income is zero (autonomous saving), is exactly equal to C_a, the corresponding amount of consumption. The autonomous consumption came about through spending of past saving, so that $-S_a$ measures the same amount of dissaving.

Analogous to the consumption function, s is called the marginal propensity to save (MPS) and measures that amount of a change in income which is saved. The marginal propensity to save is also a positive constant, which measures the slope of the saving function. Thus,

$$MPS = s \text{ is always positive;}$$
$$\overline{MPS} = \bar{s} \text{ is a constant;}$$
$$0 < s < 1 = MPS \text{ lies between 0 and 1.}$$

Again, the marginal propensity to save relates to changes in saving brought about by changes in income. If the amount of saving as a proportion of a given *level* of income is sought, then it is necessary to find the average propensity to save (APS), which is S/Y. Dividing both sides of equation (4.5) by Y gives the APS:

(4.6) $$\frac{S}{Y} = \frac{-S_a}{Y} + s.$$

Since s is a positive constant, the following relationships between the APS and the MPS hold:

$$MPS > APS, \text{ since } s > \frac{-S_a}{Y} + s;$$

and as Y increases,

$$APS \uparrow \text{ but } \overline{MPS}, \text{ since } \frac{-S_a}{Y} \uparrow \text{ as } Y \uparrow.$$

Now, since households can only split up their incomes into consumption and saving, the following relationships hold:

(4.7) $$Y = C + S;$$
(4.8) $$\Delta Y = \Delta C + \Delta S.$$

Any change in Y must be made up by $\Delta C + \Delta S$.

(4.9)
$$\frac{\Delta Y}{\Delta Y} = \frac{\Delta C}{\Delta Y} + \frac{\Delta S}{\Delta Y};$$
$$1 = MPC + MPS.$$

(4.10)
$$\frac{Y}{Y} = \frac{C}{Y} + \frac{S}{Y};$$
$$1 = APC + APS.$$

Any level of Y must be divided up into consumption plus saving.

The hypothesis relating consumption expenditures to disposable income is easily seen in graphical form once the relation has been specified. The schedule that shows the amount of consumption at various hypothetical income levels is called the propensity to consume schedule or, more simply, the consumption function. If we assign values to autonomous C and to the MPC, we can construct such a schedule. Assume that autonomous consumption is $20 billion and that the marginal propensity to consume is 0.8. Substituting these values into equation (4.2), $C = C_a + cY$, we can write the hypothetical relation

(4.2)' $C = 20 + 0.8Y.$

This equation is illustrated in Figure 4.1(a). The vertical axis measures real consumption, and the horizontal axis measures real disposable income. Note that both measures are in real terms, which means that they have been corrected for price changes—prices are not allowed to affect the analysis at this stage.

In Figure 4.1(a) the y intercept shows autonomous consumption at $20 and the MPC is shown as $\Delta C/\Delta Y = 80/100 = 0.8$, which is the slope of the consumption schedule. In this simple model there is only the household sector, and therefore consumption expenditures are the only source of demand.

The aggregate supply curve, Y, is shown as a 45-degree line bisecting the angle with a slope of 1. In graphical terms, this means that any point on this line is equidistant from the two axes, so that income can be read directly from it or with reference to either axis. It is a guide line by which to interpret the graph more readily. In economic terms, however, the 45-degree line represents the aggregate supply schedule, which shows the hypothetical supply that producers are willing to provide under the assumption that their willingness to supply goods is governed by their ability to sell the output. In other words, in the course of production suppliers incur costs in the form of wages, rents, interest, and profits, or what amounts to the same thing, they create incomes. This income plus nonfactor income and other adjustments leading to disposable income is represented on the horizontal axis. Obviously, the suppliers *expect* to sell the output or retain some for inventory. Since the Δ inventories is regarded as investment, this is not allowed in this first model, where only consumption takes place. Suppliers therefore supply what they think they can sell, and this amount is exactly matched by consumption. The 45-degree line indicates this fact governing aggregate supply; at any point on it, aggregate demand (C) equals aggregate supply (Y), and therefore the proceeds from sales equal the costs of production, and the supply conditions are fulfilled.

The curves intersect at only one point, which represents an equilibrium level of income. This point is at an income of $100, at which level all of the income is consumed—a kind of break-even point. At income levels to the left of $100 on

FIGURE 4.1

THE CONSUMPTION AND SAVING FUNCTIONS (in Real Terms)

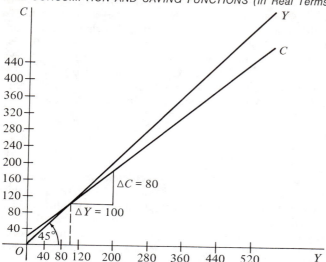

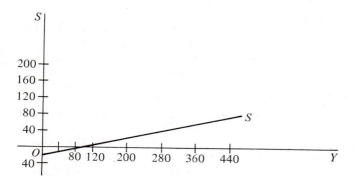

the curve, $C > Y$, consumers are spending more than they earn, and therefore dissaving occurs equal to the gap between C and Y. Producers, of course, would increase production, creating more incomes, and the economy would move toward the $100 level of income. To the right of the $100 level of income on the curve, $Y > C$, which means that consumers are saving part of their incomes and that costs are larger than sales proceeds, so that producers would reduce output.

The same information can be gathered from the graph of the saving function, Figure 4.1(b). Since the saving function is the complement to the consumption function, it becomes

$$S = -20 + 0.2Y,$$

where the −$20, or dissaving, represents the same amount as autonomous consumption and the *MPS* is 0.2 (= 1 − *MPC*). At the break-even, or equilibrium, level of income, $100, saving equals zero. To the left of this level saving is negative and to the right of it saving is positive. The amount of saving can be read directly from Figure 4.1(b) or indirectly from the consumption chart, Figure 4.1(a), as the difference between *Y* and *C* at any income level. They are clearly the same thing, since $Y = C + S$, or $Y − C = S$. Again, the slope of the line is the *MPS* and can be determined directly from the graph as given by $\Delta S/\Delta Y$. But once the *MPC* is given, so is the *MPS*, from the equation $1 = MPC + MPS$, or $1 − MPC = MPS$.

Expanding the Model: Simple Income Determination

In the previous section we evaded to some extent which concept of income was applicable. With some explicit assumptions this uncertainty can be removed. In this first model we can eliminate government and the foreign trade sector. Also we can assume that all firms are sole proprietorships and hence that the owners receive all the profits and pay taxes as individuals. Without government, without corporations, and without foreign trade, there are no taxes or retained earnings, and net national product, disposable income, and national income all become virtually the same and can be treated as identical. For the moment, which concept of income is employed is immaterial, and we may simply write *Y* for income.

Expanding the model to the two-sector economy admits the business sector into the model. The business sector, as a sector of final demand, buys investment goods that include machinery and equipment, construction, and the change in inventories. The investment demand function is quite a complicated matter, as will be noted, and not easily summarized in a simple equation. Nevertheless, it is necessary in the beginning to make an assumption in order to simplify. The simplest assumption, apparently favored by Keynes, is to regard all investment expenditures as autonomous, independent of the level of current income. This means that investment plans are fixed and geared to long-run expectations and are not influenced by current economic conditions. Investment is simply a constant regardless of the level of income. The fixed volume of investment is what firms would like to spend, anticipate spending ex ante rather than what they actually do spend. Thus, both *C* and *I* are ex ante or planned amounts, given the level of income; they are schedules of intentions. It is customary to assume that consumption plans are realized, while investment intentions may not be realized. As a first approximation, this is a viable assumption and will be retained until explicitly relaxed.

Under these assumptions the two-sector economy becomes

$$(4.11) \qquad\qquad Y = C + I,$$

where *I* equals autonomous investment and is assumed to be constant. Aggregate demand is made up of consumption and investment. On the other side, all income is paid out to individuals, and without government, personal income is equal to personal disposable income. Since consumers can only consume and/or save, we can write

$$(4.12) \qquad\qquad Y = C + S.$$

Since the two Ys in these equations are equal, we can equate (4.11) and (4.12) to find an equilibrium where aggregate demand equals aggregate supply:

(4.13) $$C + I = C + S$$

or we can write the same equilibrium in terms of income not consumed:

(4.14) $$I = S.$$

Equation (4.14) is always true for the national income accountant and should be written as $I \equiv S$. Only with an equilibrium level of income, however, is it true that $I = S$. This important conclusion is explained in the following discussion. In the following model Y is aggregate supply, and $C + I$ is aggregate demand. Rewriting the consumption function and the investment function,

(4.15) $$Y = C + I$$
(4.16) $$C = C_a + cY$$
(4.17) $$I = I_a,$$

where I_a is autonomous investment and is constant. Substituting equations (4.16) and (4.17) into (4.15), which is the equilibrium condition where aggregate demand equals aggregate supply, we obtain

(4.18) $$Y = C_a + cY + I_a,$$

or

$$Y = \frac{1}{1-c}(C_a + I_a).$$

Equation (4.18) simply restates the equilibrium condition, that aggregate demand equal aggregate supply. It shows the extent to which the autonomous elements in the system generate spending and incomes until they just balance the incomes created by production. This multiplier process will be explained presently in more detail. First it is necessary to grasp the mechanics of simple income determination.

Assume that $I_a = \$60$ billion, and the consumption function remains $C = 20 + 0.8Y$. Then the substitution into (4.16) and (4.17) gives

(4.19) $$Y = C + I$$
(4.16)' $$C = 20 + 0.8Y$$
(4.17)' $$I = 60.$$

To solve for the equilibrium level of income, substitute (4.16)' and (4.17)' into (4.19) and solve for Y, or somewhat easier, substitute directly into (4.18):

(4.18)' $$Y = \frac{1}{1 - 0.8}(20 + 60)$$
$$= 5(80)$$
$$= 400,$$

which is simply the result of the multiplying factor times the constants in the model. Let us be clear about why this is an equilibrium level of income. Recall that aggregate supply is that level of output that producers think they can sell over some time period. In the production of this output incomes are created that form the basis for the demand for the output. In our example producers expect a return flow in the form of sales proceeds equal to $400; if they receive this much, there is no tendency to change production plans; that is, an equilibrium exists.

Supply Side

Production = Disposable Incomes Created   = $400

Demand Side

Consumption = $C = 20 + 0.8(400) = \$340$
Investment   = $I = 60$ =   60
                                         _____
Aggregate Demand $400 = $400 Aggregate Supply

Producers expected to receive $400 in sales proceeds and they did; consumers expected to consume $340 out of their disposable incomes and they did; investors expected to spend $60 on investment goods and they did. Thus, all plans are realized and no one is frustrated, and therefore there is no incentive to revise the plans of the subsequent period.

Again, if this is a true equilibrium, equation (4.14) shows that it can be determined by equating saving and investment. Given the saving function

(4.20) $$S = -S_a + sY = -20 + 0.2Y,$$

and the investment function

(4.21) $$I = I_a = 60,$$

and the equilibrium condition $I = S$, it follows that

(4.22) $$\begin{aligned} -S_a + sY &= I_a \\ -20 + 0.2Y &= 60 \\ Y &= 400. \end{aligned}$$

That is, planned $S = -20 + 0.2(400) = \$60$ is equal to planned $I = \$60$. Therefore, all plans are realized; the unconsumed output is the same.

An equilibrium level of income is not likely in reality, but it is possible to study an equilibrium condition with the aim of understanding what forces move an economy. Now producers do not know what the equilibrium level of income is; so let us assume they produced output worth $300 and thus created a like amount of income.

Supply Side

Production = Disposable Incomes Created   = $300

Demand Side

Consumption = $C = 20 + 0.8(300) = \$260$
(Saving   = $S = 40$)
Investment   = I =   60
                                         _____
Aggregate Demand $320 > $300 Aggregate Supply

In this case, aggregate demand $(C + I)$ is larger than aggregate supply $(C + S)$, or in terms of saving and investment, planned I is larger than planned S. It appears that at an income level of $300 people plan to spend more than firms had anticipated, with the result that the firms underproduced. The only way for this excess demand to be satisfied is by the drawing down of past stocks, or $-\Delta$ inventories. But the change in inventories is by definition a part of investment demand. Therefore, investors drew down inventories, which they had not planned to do. The national income accountant dutifully records the information at the end of the period and observes that $I \equiv S$. The explanation for this is simple.

(ex ante)	Planned Investment	=	$60
	Unplanned Investment:		
	$-\Delta$ Inventories	=	-20
(ex post)	Realized Investment	=	$40 = Realized Saving

Recall that consumption plans, and hence saving plans, are always realized, and it follows that investment expenditures bear the frustration of unrealized plans. Yet the national income accountant records what actually happened, not what people hoped would happen when the period began. The ex post magnitudes are always equal $(I \equiv S)$; they have to be because we define them that way. Accountants always work with identities. Yet when plans are unrealized, the firms will take steps to correct the situation in the next period. In our example, with goods disappearing from the shelves, they will increase production and in the process increase incomes. This process will continue until all plans are realized, and this we have called the equilibrium output level.

Now suppose instead that firms had decided to produce output worth $500, expecting to receive back an equal amount.

Supply Side

   Production = DI Created   = $500

Demand Side

   Consumption   = $420
   (Saving = $80)
   Investment   =   60
   Aggregate Demand $480 < $500 Aggregate Supply

Here aggregate demand $(C + I)$ of $480 < $500 of aggregate supply, and $S > I$. At an income level of $500 people plan to spend less than firms had anticipated, with the result that inventories increase as the unsold output accumulates on the shelves. If the firms continued to produce at this level, the additions to inventories would continue, but since the Δ inventories was unplanned, the probable action is to reduce production, and of course, incomes, until there is no unintentional inventory accumulation. This is the case only at the equilibrium level of income. Again, the national income accountant merely observes what happened at the end of the period.

(ex ante)	Planned Investment	=	$60
	Unplanned Investment:		
	$+\Delta$ Inventories	=	$+20$
(ex post)	Realized Investment	=	$80 = Realized Saving

The ex post data are then recorded in the national income accounts. To repeat, only in equilibrium will saving and investment be equal ex post as well as ex ante; only then will plans be realized and result in no tendency for anyone to change his behavior.

The simple income determination model can also be shown graphically. Figure 4.2 presents the same information as has been given in the text. In part (a) of the figure, aggregate demand and aggregate supply schedules are plotted. The aggregate supply curve is the same as that of Figure 4.1, but the aggregate demand curve now includes investment demand in addition to consumption demand. To add the

FIGURE 4.2

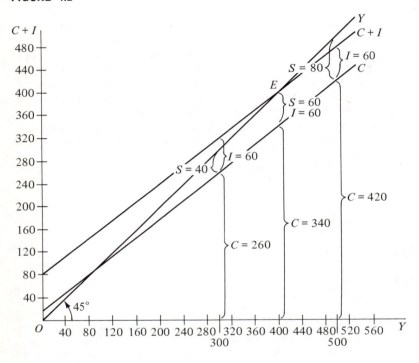

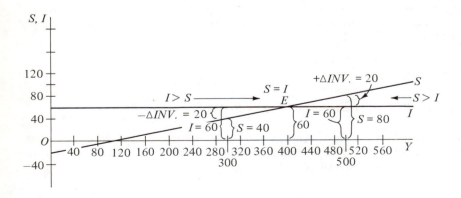

investment function to the consumption function is very simple if investment is a constant. The schedule shifts upward and parallel by the amount of investment spending; at each hypothetical level of income, aggregate demand is greater by the amount of I. As can easily be verified by inspection of Figure 4.2, the new schedule for aggregate demand, $C + I$, is exactly $60 greater than the consumption schedule, C, at every possible Y. The intersection of aggregate demand, $C + I$, and aggregate supply, Y, occurs at point E, which, as already noted, is the equilibrium level of income, $400: at point E, $C = \$340$, $S = \$60$, and $I = \$60$. The vertical distance between the $C + I$ curve and the C schedule measures I, and the vertical distance between $Y = C + S$ and the C schedule measures S. At point E these vertical distances are the same.

At points to the left of E, it is clear that $I > S$, which means that aggregate demand is larger than aggregate supply, and there will be a tendency for production, and hence incomes, to increase as $-\Delta$ inventories occurs. The movement stops at point E. At points to the right of E, $S > I$, that is, aggregate supply is larger than aggregate demand, and the opposite movement occurs. Thus, the forces making this a stable equilibrium are the plans of firms being frustrated and the subsequent actions taken; the expectations of firms are of the stabilizing type. It would also be well to recall here that prices do not change in this simple model despite the fact that inventories are being either accumulated or depleted. The analysis is still all in real terms.

Exactly the same information is given in Figure 4.2(b), where the analysis is in terms of saving and investment. Note the shape of the investment function. Investment, being an autonomous constant and independent of the level of income, is simply a horizontal line at the amount of the constant. Again, the S and I schedules intersect at point E, the same equilibrium level of income. Here, planned S of $60 is equal to planned I of $60.

To the left of point E, $I > S$, or planned I is larger than planned S, which means inventories are being drawn down, and to the right of point E, $S > I$, where the reverse occurs. Note that when $S \neq I$, it is the level of income that adjusts until they are equal. Production plans are altered, causing incomes to change as well. Later in the chapter we will consider if and how employment changes along with changes in income.

Note that the word *equilibrium* does not connote a desirable state of affairs in the sense that it is the "proper" one. All that it means is, given the conditions and assumptions stated in the model, there is some level of income where there is no tendency for change. An equilibrium level in this sense could mean 10 per cent unemployment. Only by accident, said Keynes, would the full employment level of income coincide with the equilibrium level.[1]

The Simple Multiplier

In the process of determining the equilibrium level of income, some notion of a multiplier mechanism was introduced briefly but without explanation in equation (4.18). It was evident in the numerical examples as the equilibrium level of income jumped from $100 with only consumption demand to $400 with the addition of

---

[1] One can argue over whether an economy could be in equilibrium with 10 per cent unemployment, since an economy that did stabilize at that level would be working improperly. See Gardner Ackley, *Macroeconomic Theory* (New York: Macmillan, 1961), p. 382, for a discussion of this point.

investment demand; that is, one component of aggregate demand, I_a, changed by $60 and the equilibrium level of income, Y, changed by $300. It is not readily apparent why this should be so, and hence the multiplier process requires more explanation. To make the multiplier process as straightforward and clear as possible, it is best to begin with static analysis and to deal only with income changes, although the process is naturally dynamic.

Rewriting the basic equation for the equilibrium level of income, we obtain,

$$(4.23) \qquad Y = C + I.$$

Any change from that level must be composed of ΔC and ΔI regardless of where the change originated. Altering equation (4.23) to recognize changes gives,

$$(4.24) \qquad Y + \Delta Y = C + \Delta C + I + \Delta I.$$

Since we are interested only in the changes from the old level of income, we must subtract the original Y from (4.24) to concentrate on the changes. Subtracting $Y = C + I$ from (4.24) yields,

$$(4.25) \qquad \Delta Y = \Delta C + \Delta I.$$

The ΔI presents no problem, for a change in a constant is simple to handle. The change in consumption, given the consumption function of $C = C_a + cY$, is

$$(4.26) \qquad \Delta C = c\Delta Y.$$

That is, assuming autonomous consumption, C_a, remains unchanged, any change in consumption must be induced by a change in income.[2] Substituting (4.26) into (4.25) gives

$$(4.27) \qquad \begin{aligned} \Delta Y &= c\Delta Y + \Delta I \\ &= c\Delta Y = \Delta I \\ &= \frac{1}{1-c}(\Delta I), \end{aligned}$$

or

$$\frac{\Delta Y}{\Delta I} = \frac{1}{1-c}.$$

The term $1/(1-c)$ is called the simple multiplier, the value of which depends solely on the marginal propensity to consume. The multiplier can be written as follows:

$$\frac{\Delta Y}{\Delta I} = \frac{1}{1-c} = \frac{1}{1-MPC} = \frac{1}{MPS} = \frac{1}{s}.$$

Recall the assumption made about the marginal propensity to consume, that $1 > MPC > 0$; it follows that the numerical value of the multiplier must be greater than 1. If the $MPC = 1$, the multiplier would be infinite, and if the $MPC = 0$, the

---

[2] If autonomous consumption did increase, then the change in expenditures would also initiate the multiplier process in the same manner as shown for changes in investment expenditures:

$$\Delta Y = \frac{1}{1-c}(\Delta C_a), \qquad \text{or} \qquad \frac{\Delta Y}{\Delta C_a} = \frac{1}{1-c}.$$

multiplier would equal 1. In the calculation of the value of the multiplier, it is easier to work with the *MPS*, for as is shown, the numerical value can readily be calculated as the reciprocal of the *MPS*.

In the numerical examples given, the $MPC = 0.8$ and the $MPS = 0.2$. Therefore, the value of the multiplier is 5:

$$\frac{1}{1 - c} = \frac{1}{1 - 0.8} = \frac{1}{2/10} = \frac{1}{1/5} = 5.$$

In the calculations it is easier to use $1/s$, which is seen as the last term, $1(1/5)$, in this expression.

It is now an easy matter to show mathematically why the equilibrium level of income jumped from \$100 to \$400 as investment spending was introduced into the model. There was no investment in the first model, $I = 0$, so that the entire amount of investment spending represented ΔI. Therefore, income changed as follows:

$$\Delta Y = \frac{1}{1 - c} (\Delta I)$$

$$= \frac{1}{1 - 0.8} (60)$$

$$= 5(60)$$

$$= 300.$$

To find the new equilibrium level of Y, it is necessary to add the changes to the old level of Y:

$$Y_{\text{old}} + \Delta Y = Y_{\text{new}},$$

or

$$\$100 + \$300 = \$400,$$

as already given. The value of the multiplier remains constant, of course, as long as the *MPC* remains unchanged. Thus, a further ΔI can quickly be calculated for its effect on Y by simply multiplying ΔI by 5. If $\Delta I = \$50$, then $\Delta Y = \$250$, and if $\Delta I = \$10$, then $\Delta Y = \$50$, and so on.

Another look at equation (4.18)$'$ will reveal how quickly the equilibrium level of income can be computed once the notion of the multiplier is clear. In the simple income determination models used here, the equilibrium level of Y when only consumption was permitted can be calculated easily as follows:

$$Y = C$$
$$C = C_a + cY = 20 + 0.8Y.$$

Substituting in the first equation gives

$$Y = \frac{1}{1 - c} (C_a)$$

$$= \frac{1}{1 - 0.8} (20)$$

$$= 100.$$

The same multiplier is used to determine the equilibrium level of income with only consumption expenditures. Then we added investment spending of $60 to the model:

$$Y = C_a + cY + I$$
$$= \frac{1}{1-c}(C_a + I)$$
$$= \frac{1}{1-0.8}(20 + 60)$$
$$= 5(20 + 60)$$
$$= 400.$$

These exercises in mathematics show how the value of the multiplier is calculated, but they do not explain economically what is happening in the model to bring about the observed results. Using the comparative static method of analysis, there is really no way to explain the multiplier process; in the explanation that follows, note the introduction of time, which makes the process dynamic. After this explanation the process can be made more rigorous.

Assume that firms decide to increase investment spending because of long-run anticipations. As they increase I, factor incomes in the capital goods industries increase. The income receivers will decide to spend and to save out of this additional income according to the MPC and MPS. As they spend a portion of their incomes, the incomes of the factors in the consumption goods industries increase. The additional incomes in the consumption goods industries also result in spending and saving and in the process create additional income for others, and so on. The respending of the additional increments of income, when added together, will result in the total change in income as observed earlier. At each round in this respending process the amount spent gets smaller and smaller and gradually becomes insignificant. This is because the MPC is smaller than 1 and not all of the increments in incomes are spent, but at each stage some of the income leaks off into saving. Income not spent, that is, saved, does not call forth the production decisions of firms to increase output, which was the cause of the increase in factor incomes. Thus, the additions to incomes become smaller and smaller until a new equilibrium level of income is reached. At this new equilibrium level the increase in income will result in a higher amount of saving just sufficient to equal the new level of investment spending.[3]

To speak of rounds of spending and respending obviously implies the passage of time, but static analysis cannot handle time and it appears as if the new equilibrium level of Y is reached instantaneously. This is impossible, of course, and therefore, to make the process a little more realistic, dynamic analysis is called for, even though it complicates matters.

The Multiplier Elaborated

A simple dynamic model can be obtained by using period or sequence analysis of the type previously used in the cobweb models. Assume for this model that the old equilibrium level of income remains in period 1 but that in period 2 firms decide to increase the level of investment spending. If we assume further that the

---

[3] It should be noted that the multiplier process works in reverse as well and that a decrease in investment spending will result in a reduction in the level of income by the same multiple.

capital goods industries are operating with excess capacity and can therefore supply the investment goods in the same period in which they are ordered, then the incomes of factors in the capital goods industries increase also in the same period. Finally, assume that there is a lag in the response of consumption to changes in income; that is, consumption in any period t is a function of the income of the previous period, $t - 1$. A one-period lag in the consumption adjustment to new levels of income is not at all unrealistic. As a matter of fact, additional lags could be postulated for both C and I, and the model could be extended, but our aim at this point is conceptual clarity.

These assumptions change our original model to account for the inclusion of time as follows:

(4.28) $$Y_t = C_t + I_t$$
(4.29) $$C_t = C_a + cY_{t-1}$$
(4.30) $$I_t = I_t.$$

The assumption that all investment is autonomous is retained, so that the only real change is to introduce a lag in the consumption function that forces the model to consider time explicitly. This is seen most clearly by substituting (4.29) and (4.30) into (4.28):

(4.31) $$Y_t = C_a + cY_{t-1} + I_t.$$

For the *static solution* of (4.31) to obtain the equilibrium level of income, it is necessary to drop the time lag in the consumption function and to recognize that in equilibrium, and only in equilibrium, $Y_t = Y_{t-1} = Y_{t+10} = Y_e = \cdots$. The substitution of Y_e for both Ys in equation (4.31) gives the same familiar equilibrium condition we obtained using comparative statics, since time is no longer relevant:

(4.32) $$Y_e = C_a + cY_e + I,$$

or

$$Y_e = \frac{1}{1-c}(C_a + I).$$

Returning to dynamic analysis, let us see how equation (4.31) works and how the new equilibrium level of income is reached. Again assume that there is no change in aggregate demand in period 1 but that in period 2 investment demand changes. As investment demand changes, so does income in period 2 for $\Delta I = \Delta Y$ by our assumption. In period 3 consumption changes, because income changed in period 2. The amount of the change in consumption is $\Delta C = c\Delta Y$, but since $\Delta Y = \Delta I$, the change in consumption can be written as $\Delta C = c\Delta I$. In period 3 income changes again by the amount of the new additional higher level of investment, ΔI, plus the incomes created by spending on consumption goods, $c\Delta I$. In period 4 the ΔI spending continues and income increases; also, the change in consumption spending is again $c\Delta I$ for ΔI in period 3; plus $c(c\Delta I) = c^2\Delta I$ change in consumption (income) caused by the respending of incomes created by consumption spending in period 3. This process continues indefinitely, since the multiplier never works itself out entirely—the number of periods is infinite. The whole process is perhaps better grasped if seen in tabular form, as shown in Table 4.1. In the table the initial equilibrium level of income is given by $Y = C + I$, and ΔI first occurs in period 2. The arrows indicate the subsequent ΔY caused by the

TABLE 4.1

Period		
1	Y	$= C + I$
2	$Y + \Delta Y = C + I + \Delta I$	
3	$Y + \Delta Y = C + I + \Delta I + c\Delta I$	
4	$Y + \Delta Y = C + I + \Delta I + c\Delta I + c^2\Delta I$	
5	$Y + \Delta Y = C + I + \Delta I + c\Delta I + c^2\Delta I + c^3\Delta I$	
6	$Y + \Delta Y = C + I + \Delta I + c\Delta I + c^2\Delta I + c^3\Delta I + c^4\Delta I$	
n	$Y + \Delta Y = C + I + \Delta I + c\Delta I + c^2\Delta I + c^3\Delta I + c^4\Delta I + \ldots + c^{n-2}\Delta I$	

change in consumption brought about as factor incomes earned in the capital goods industries are spent. Note that any ΔI induces ΔC, but that as time passes and these ΔYs are spent, the spending stream becomes smaller and smaller.

To see how the formula for the multiplier can be derived mathematically, subtract the original level of income, $Y = C + I$, from the expression for period n in the Table 4.1:

$$\Delta Y = \Delta I + c\Delta I + c^2\Delta I + c^3\Delta I + c^4\Delta I + \cdots + c^{n-2}\Delta I.$$

Factoring ΔI from the right-hand side, we obtain,

$$\Delta Y = \Delta I(1 + c + c^2 + c^3 + c^4 + c^5 + \cdots).$$

The expression in parentheses is a geometric progression. The formula for the sum of a geometric progression is,

$$S = \frac{a - ar^n}{1 - r},$$

where a is the first term in the series, r is the common ratio $(r \neq 1)$, and n is the number of terms in the series. For the multiplier, the number of terms (periods) is infinite, so that as $n \longrightarrow \infty$, $ar^n \longrightarrow 0$, r being a fraction. Then the entire expression becomes,

$$S = \frac{a}{1 - r}.$$

Substituting 1 for a, and c for r, gives,

$$S = \frac{1}{1 - c},$$

which when put into the geometric expression gives the formula for the calculation of the changes in the model:

$$\Delta Y = \Delta I\left(\frac{1}{1 - c}\right),$$

which is the formula for the multiplier given previously.

For those who prefer actual numbers to symbols, Table 4.2 follows the multiplier

TABLE 4.2

Period	Y	$+$	ΔY	$=$	C	$+$	I	$+ \Delta I$	$+ \Delta C$

Period	$Y + \Delta Y =$	$C + I + \Delta I + \Delta C$
1	400	$= 340 + 60$
2	$400 + 10$	$= 340 + 60 + 10$
3	$400 + 18$	$= 340 + 60 + 10 + 8$
4	$400 + 24.40$	$= 340 + 60 + 10 + 8 + 6.40$
5	$400 + 29.52$	$= 340 + 60 + 10 + 8 + 6.40 + 5.12$
6	$400 + 33.62$	$= 340 + 60 + 10 + 8 + 6.40 + 5.12 + 4.10 + \ldots$
n	$\underbrace{400 + 50}_{450}$	$= \underbrace{340 + 60 + 10 \quad + \quad 40}_{450}$

process from an equilibrium level of \$400, the old level, to a new level of \$450 caused by $\Delta I = \$10$. The form of Table 4.2 follows that of Table 4.1 to facilitate the understanding of both.

Recall that the $MPC = 0.8$ and hence the multiplier is 5. Since $\Delta I = \$10$, it follows that $\Delta Y = \$50$ and that the new equilibrium level of income is \$450. Table 4.2 reveals how the new equilibrium was reached. In period 2, $\Delta Y = \Delta I = \$10$; in period 3, $\Delta Y = \$18$, made up of $\Delta I = \$10$ and $\Delta C = c\Delta I = 0.8(10)$, brought about by the previous ΔY. The process continues period by period until the sum of the changes equals \$50, with $\Delta I = \$10$ and $\Delta C = \$40$. The arrows indicate the declining importance over time of any initial change in aggregate demand in its influence on the level of income.

Again the movement from one equilibrium to another can be looked at from the saving and investment equilibrium condition. Only when income has reached the level to generate the amount of saving necessary to equal investment will the change in income cease and an equilibrium exist. Table 4.3 shows the process of

TABLE 4.3

Period	$I + \Delta I = S + \Delta S$
1	$60 \qquad = 60$
2	$60 + 10 > 60$
3	$60 + 10 > 60 + 2.00$
4	$60 + 10 > 60 + 3.60$
5	$60 + 10 > 60 + 4.88$
6	$60 + 10 > 60 + 5.90$
n	$60 + 10 = 60 + 10$

TABLE 4.4

Period		
1	Y	$= C + I$
2	$Y + \Delta Y = C + I + \Delta I$	
3	$Y + \Delta Y = C + I$	$+ c\Delta I$
4	$Y + \Delta Y = C + I$	$+ c^2 \Delta I$
5	$Y + \Delta Y = C + I$	$+ c^3 \Delta I$
6	$Y + \Delta Y = C + I$	$+ c^4 \Delta I + \cdots$
.	.	. .
.	.	.
.	.	. .
n	Y	$= C + I$

bringing about the equality of saving and investment. It is left uncompleted and unexplained so that the reader can test his understanding of the mechanics under discussion.

The foregoing discussion on the multiplier process assumed that the change in aggregate demand, ΔI, was a *permanent* change, that producers had decided to spend an additional amount on investment goods. Suppose that the change in aggregate demand occurred in one period only and then returned to its previous level. How would the equilibrium level of income be affected? Table 4.4 follows the format of the other tables and shows what happens in this case.

It is apparent from Table 4.4 that with a single increase in aggregate demand, the level of income increases, but the increases get smaller and smaller until they approach zero and then the level of income returns to its previous level. Here the changes in consumption get smaller and smaller as the initial ΔY is respent and respent.

Again, the same process is shown numerically in Tables 4.5 and 4.6. By now they should require little in the way of explanation.

TABLE 4.5

Period	$Y +$	ΔY	$=$	$C +$	I	$+ \Delta I + \Delta C$
1	400					
2	400 +	10	=	340 +	60	+ 10
3	400 +	8	=	340 +	60	+ 8
4	400 +	6.40	=	340 +	60	+ 6.40
5	400 +	5.12	=	340 +	60	+ 5.12
6	400 +	4.10	=	340 +	60	+ 4.10 + $\cdots$
.	.			.	.	
.	.			.	.	
.	.			.	.	
n	400		=	340 +	60	

TABLE 4.6

Period	I	$+$	ΔI	$=$	S	$+$	ΔS
1	60			$=$	60		
2	60	$+$	10	$>$	60		
3	60			$<$	62		
4	60			$<$	61.6		
5	60			$<$	61.28		
6	60			$<$	61.02		
.	.				.		
.	.				.		
.	.				.		
n	60			$=$	60		

Finally, the multiplier process is depicted in Figures 4.3 and 4.4. Rather than plot actual numbers the figures merely suggest the general nature of the mechanism

FIGURE 4.3

THE MULTIPLIER PROCESS FOR A PERMANENT CHANGE IN AGGREGATE DEMAND

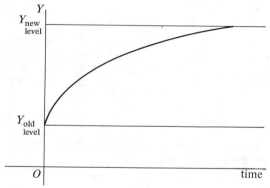

FIGURE 4.4

THE MULTIPLIER PROCESS FOR A SINGLE PERIOD CHANGE IN AGGREGATE DEMAND

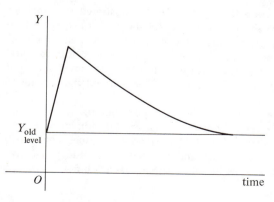

by smoothing out what would otherwise be a step function, that is, the movement would be represented by bars or steps erected at each period.

Income, Employment, and Aggregate Demand

In this last section the relationship between income, employment, and aggregate demand will be discussed. In the foregoing models, when aggregate demand and aggregate supply were not equal (or alternatively, when $S \neq I$), the level of income adjusted until they were. A logical question is, What happened to the level of employment as the level of income changed? What relation, if any, can be shown between the two variables?

Recall the assumptions made concerning an economy operating in the short run: fixed capital and hence fixed productive capacity of the capital stock, unchanging technology, fixed quality and quantity of the labor force, and given natural resources. With these assumptions the quantity of labor is free to fluctuate according to how much of the productive capacity in any period is utilized. Thus, the supply side is given by the quantity of factors and their productivity; the productive capacity of the economy is determined but, of course, need not all be utilized.

The aggregate production function summarizes this information:

$$O = f(N, K, R, T),$$

O is output capacity, N is the labor force, K is the stock of capital, R is the given natural resources, and T is technology. The production function merely states that output is a function of inputs and is analogous to the production function of a firm. What the short-run assumptions have done is to transform the production function as follows:

$$O = f(N, \overline{K}, \overline{R}, \overline{T}),$$

and output becomes a function of labor input, with everything else held constant. The short-run aggregate production function can then be written,

$$O = f(N) \qquad \text{or} \qquad O = Y = g(N).$$

Since the productivity of labor is largely determined by the productivity of capital and the state of technology, it follows that the amount of labor employed in any one period measures to some extent the amount of the productive capacity utilized during that period.

This one-factor production function, $Y = f(N)$, can be illustrated in a manner analogous to that for a firm in the short run. Figure 4.5 shows this aggregate production function. It shows a typical production curve under the assumption of diminishing returns. It also answers the question about the movement of output and employment in relation to each other: they move together. Since the level of output determines the amount of incomes created, the level of income and the volume of employment also move together.

Thus, if aggregate demand increases, we should expect output, income, and employment to increase, and vice versa. It is clear that in this simple model the emphasis is put on the demand side; the level of demand determines how much output and employment will be forthcoming and to what extent the productive capacity is utilized. The bias for stressing the demand side comes from the

FIGURE 4.5

THE AGGREGATE PRODUCTION FUNCTION

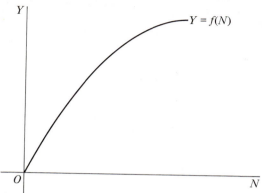

Keynesian model, which was the direct opposite of previous models that stressed the supply side. The importance of aggregate demand in this model helps to explain the policy conclusions that are deduced. An economy that fails to utilize its resources is suffering from a deficiency of aggregate demand, which can be corrected. Consumption expenditures or investment spending will have to be increased, or failing that, the public sector will have to step in and remedy the situation. The introduction of the public sector into the analysis is the subject of the next chapter.

Before turning to that fascinating subject, there is an opportunity here to illustrate some aggregation problems. Recall that assumptions made in the short run are legitimate as first approximations, but as time proceeds, they become less and less tenable. This is one source of error, not of the theory but of its use.

More important, we established the link between aggregate demand and employment—they varied directly, moved in the same direction. How close is this relationship? Could not an increase in aggregate demand lead to little or no change in employment? The answer is yes, for changes in employment depend upon the source of the change in demand. Different responses of employment to changes in demand are possible, depending upon whether the demand was for output in industries that are labor-intensive or for those items produced with little or no labor. Thus, the statement that demand and employment tend to move together must be qualified to be correct in a general sense, but the relationship must be examined for each particular case.

Also, in our models we have used real magnitudes. The relation between Y and N must be in real terms. It is obvious that an increase in money income need not be related to employment changes in the same manner. A study of this relation of inflation and employment is postponed until a later chapter.

In conclusion, aggregation problems are very much in evidence in the formulation of the aggregate production function. The structure and composition of industry or firm production functions are lost in the summation process. The subject is recapitulated here so that the limitations of our analysis will not be overlooked in the midst of the order and certainty of mathematical logic. In later chapters we will recall these limitations as we explore their impact on macroeconomic theory.

Government and the Economy

In the latter half of the twentieth century any economic model that omits the public sector is unrealistic; government plays such a large role in our lives, and particularly in our economic lives. It is the purpose of this chapter to introduce the public sector into the model, using the same introductory approach as with the household and investment sectors. Its purpose is to generate some appreciation for the impact of the government sector on the economy, leaving for later work the necessary elaboration.

Government Expenditures

When discussing the public sector it should be recalled that all levels of government are included, from the local school district to the federal government. Again the aggregation problem obscures some of the determinants of government expenditures, since various levels of government are guided by different sets of influences. At the very outset, then, there is a problem, for we must establish what determines the amount and type of government expenditures. We also need to know what is the economic impact of government expenditures—first by size and then by type. There will be no systematic attempt to find the answers at this stage. It is enough to indicate a few influences and thereby to justify the procedure actually followed in this chapter. Government expenditures, G, may be said to depend upon some or all of the following: population pressures, war versus peace, environmental concerns, political ideology, social and cultural attitudes, tradition, natural catastrophes, and so on. A glance at the list suggests that any attempt to explain government spending is bound to be complicated. To explain government spending requires an interdisciplinary approach, and the economist working alone is likely to be hampered by his inability to deal with some of these amorphous variables. It is not surprising, then, that economists have not developed an aggregate theory to explain government expenditures. Up to the present time it is customary in economics to treat government spending as being determined outside of and apart from the internal economic system. This type of variable is called an exogenous one, not determined by or influencing other economic variables in the system. It is therefore generally taken as given and included in the model without explanation. This procedure can be defended as a useful introductory expedient but represents a real lack as the models become more complex and the need to explain the interaction among sectors becomes more pressing.

All government spending is autonomous, according to what was assumed, and we may write $G = \overline{G}$. Our first model, with government as a sector of aggregate demand, then becomes

(5.1) $$Y = C + I + G$$
(5.2) $$C = C_a + cY$$
(5.3) $$I = \overline{I}$$
(5.4) $$G = \overline{G}.$$

Substituting (5.2), (5.3), and (5.4) into (5.1), the equation for the equilibrium level of income is

(5.5) $$Y = \frac{1}{1 - c}(C_a + I + G).$$

It is clear that government expenditures are analogous to autonomous investment. If we assign a numerical value to G and retain the same numerical values for the other components of aggregate demand, the model can be solved to find the new equilibrium level of income. Thus, we have

(5.2)′ $$C = 20 + 0.8Y$$
(5.3)′ $$I = 60$$
(5.4)′ $$G = 20$$

which when substituted into equation (5.5) yields the equilibrium level of income:

$$Y = \frac{1}{1 - 0.8}(20 + 60 + 20);$$
$$= 5(100);$$
$$= 500.$$

With the introduction of government expenditures of \$20 into the model, the level of income changed by \$100, from \$400 to \$500. Obviously, the same multiplier applies to government spending as to autonomous consumption and investment,

(5.6) $$\frac{\Delta Y}{\Delta G} = \frac{1}{1 - c},$$

and for the same reasons. A change in aggregate demand brings about a multiple change in the level of income. When government buys goods and services, it creates incomes that are respent and respent, and the multiplier mechanism proceeds as before.

The introduction of government into the model can be seen in Figure 5.1. Shown in part (a) is the equality of aggregate demand and aggregate supply. They become equal at the income level of \$500, as previously ascertained. Note that autonomous government expenditures are added to the old $C + I$ schedule, which shifts the curve parallel by the amount of G, which is \$20. The equilibrium level of income moves from point E to F, or by the amount of $100, which is G times the multiplier $= $20(5)$. (Exactly the same results would have occurred if investment had changed by $20.)

FIGURE 5.1
GOVERNMENT EXPENDITURES IN THE SIMPLE MODEL

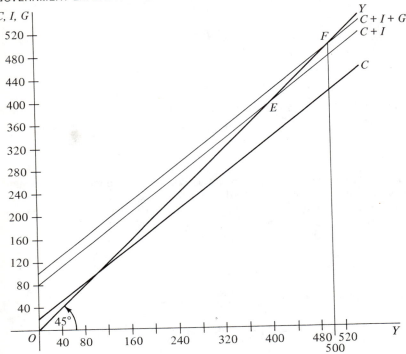

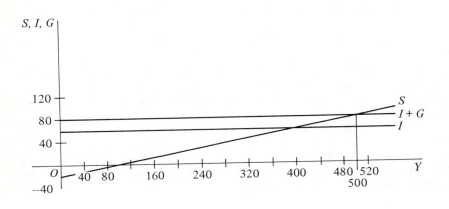

In Figure 5.1(b) the conditions for an equilibrium level of income in terms of saving and investment are shown, but now redefined to include government expenditures. The new equilibrium condition becomes

(5.7)
$$S = I + G,$$

and no longer must private saving be offset by private investment. With government in the model private S could exceed private I, the difference being made up by another offset to leakages from the spending stream, G. It has already been pointed out that autonomous G is analogous to autonomous I. This is easily seen in Figure 5.1(b) as government expenditures are added to the investment schedule, shifting the curve upward and parallel. Of course, the equilibrium level of income, $500, is the same as that reached before. Income must rise by enough ($100) to induce the additional saving ($20) to offset the additional government spending ($20), which is another way to determine when the multiplier stops. The equilibrium level of income could have been calculated directly from the following:

(5.8) $\qquad\qquad S = -S_a + sY = -20 + 0.2Y$
(5.9) $\qquad\qquad I = \overline{I} = 60$
(5.10) $\qquad\qquad G = \overline{G} = 20$

and from the equilibrium condition

(5.11)
$$S = I + G$$
$$-20 + 0.2Y = 60 + 20$$
$$Y = 500.$$

Government Taxes

A world without taxes might be a delightful place to live, but unfortunately such a state is hopelessly unrealistic. Taxes are a fact of life in every economy. In this section the simple models are extended to include taxes, but in keeping with the rest of the model the forms of taxation will be kept to the elemental ones. Again, as with government expenditures, the treatment of taxes concentrates on the impact of taxes on the economic system only from the viewpoint of their effect on the level of income, the fiscal policy aspect of taxation. For the present we are not concerned with questions of equity or justice in taxation or with any other facet of this fascinating subject. Furthermore, in keeping with our inability to determine the level of government expenditures there will be no attempt to discuss the determinants of taxation. In effect, this amounts to the rather simplistic notion that taxes are raised in order to pay for expenditures. Temporarily, this assumption will suffice, but it must be reexamined later in the discussion of fiscal policy.

The form of taxation most comparable to the assumption of autonomous government spending would be an autonomous amount of taxes; such a tax is a per capita or head tax (poll tax), since this form of taxation is independent of the level of income or the economic situation in general. It is simply a tax per person or household, and questions of equity aside (it would be a regressive tax), it is certainly an easy tax to understand and administer.

The assumption of autonomous taxes gives the following model:

(5.12) $$Y = C + I + G$$
(5.13) $$C = C_a + c(Y - T)$$
(5.14) $$I = \overline{I}$$
(5.15) $$G = \overline{G}$$
(5.16) $$T = \overline{T},$$

where equation (5.16) is the expression for autonomous taxes. Note that equation (5.13) for the consumption function must be altered to reflect explicitly the dependence of consumption upon disposable income, $Y - T$. Households, in effect, now must use their incomes in three ways: $C + S + T$; that is, some of the income that was previously controlled by households now flows to government. As a result, personal consumption is affected and less of income will be spent by the private sector, but on the other hand, government receipts are increased and spent by the public sector. The total leakages from the spending stream, saving plus taxes, are balanced in equilibrium by the spending of other sectors, investment and government. Thus, the new equilibrium condition can be written as

(5.17) $$S + T = I + G.[1]$$

The equilibrium level of income can be computed by substituting (5.13) − (5.15) into (5.12),

(5.18) $$Y = \frac{1}{1 - c}(C_a + I + G - cT).$$

Equation (5.18) is the same as (5.5) with the exception of the term for taxes, $-cT$. Taxes, of course, are deflationary, constituting a leakage from the income stream that reduces the incomes of the household sector. If we assign a value to the amount of taxation and retain the previous values for the other variables, the equilibrium level of income can be computed. Let $T = \$20$, which results in a balanced budget, since $G = \$20$. Substituting into equation (5.18) gives

(5.18)′ $$Y = \frac{1}{1 - 0.8}[20 + 60 + 20 - 0.8(20)]$$
$$= 5(84)$$
$$= 420.$$

With the introduction of taxes, the equilibrium level of income falls from $500 to $420. Recall that with the introduction of $G = \$20$ into the model, the level of income went from $400 to $500; now with an equal amount of taxes added ($T = \$20$), the level of income falls, but not back to the Y of $400, the level that existed before government entered the model. The reason for this is not immediately obvious but can be explained once the impact of government spending versus taxation on aggregate demand is made explicit. For government expenditures, the impact on aggregate demand is the full amount of the change ($\Delta G = \$20$, in

---

[1] It must be remembered that these conditions always hold in terms of national income accounting: $S + I \equiv I + G$. Only in equilibrium is it true that $S + I = I + G$. The aggregate income of households, $Y = C + S + T$, makes up the supply side and aggregate demand is $Y = C + I + G$. Equating the two yields the $S + T = I + G$ equilibrium condition.

our example) times the multiplier. The government spending created incomes for households equal to the full amount; then consumers respent some of this increment and saved the remainder, and so on. We noted that the aggregate demand schedule, $C + I + G$, shifted upward by the full amount of the government expenditure: Y increased from \$400 to \$500. On the other hand, taxes affect the level of aggregate demand through their immediate effect upon consumption, since taxes reduce disposable income. The question is, then, how much will consumption (and aggregate demand) be affected by the tax. Consumption will fall, not by the full amount of the tax but by the MPC times the tax. The remainder of the tax will be paid for by a reduction in saving, but saving was a leakage anyway. The reduction of income caused by the tax is thus divided up between $C + S$, just as an increase in income would have been. The consumption schedule (and the aggregate demand schedule) falls by the reduction in C, which is,

(5.19)
$$\Delta C = -c\Delta T.$$

Since c is a fraction, the fall in consumption is obviously less than the amount of the tax. The effect of taxes on the level of income can also be seen by comparing the various multipliers.

The tax multiplier is given by

(5.20)
$$\Delta Y = -\frac{1}{1-c}(c\Delta T),$$

or

$$\frac{\Delta Y}{\Delta T} = \frac{-c}{1-c}.$$

The numerator is a fraction $(-c)$, which means that the value of the multiplier is less than the value of the other multipliers, which are (assuming that $\Delta C_a = \Delta G = \Delta I$):

(5.21)
$$\Delta Y = \frac{1}{1-c}(\Delta G) = \frac{1}{1-c}(\Delta C_a) = \frac{1}{1-c}(\Delta I),$$

or

$$\frac{\Delta Y}{\Delta C_a} = \frac{\Delta Y}{\Delta G} = \frac{\Delta Y}{\Delta I} = \frac{1}{1-c}.$$

In terms of our numerical example the other multipliers are 5, but the tax multiplier is exactly 1 less, or 4, computed as follows:

$$\frac{-c}{1-c} = \frac{-0.8}{0.2} = (-)4.$$

With a tax multiplier of 4, it is easy to compute the change in income recorded earlier—income fell from \$500 to \$420, with taxes of \$20; the ΔY of \$80 = \$20(4).[2]

---

[2] Another way to grasp the difference between the multipliers is to view government as having $MPC = 1$, so that the income is spent at least once and the first term in the geometric series for the multiplier is 1. The tax affects C through the reduction in Y_d, but the initial reduction of C is not equal to 1 but to the MPC times the tax, which is less than 1. See also the mathematics in the text for the balanced budget multiplier.

The effect on the model with taxes added can also be seen in Figure 5.2. Part (a) shows the aggregate demand and supply data. The equilibrium level of Y before taxes was at point F, where $Y = \$500$. As the head tax of $20 is imposed,

FIGURE 5.2

GOVERNMENT EXPENDITURES PLUS AUTONOMOUS TAXES IN THE SIMPLE MODEL

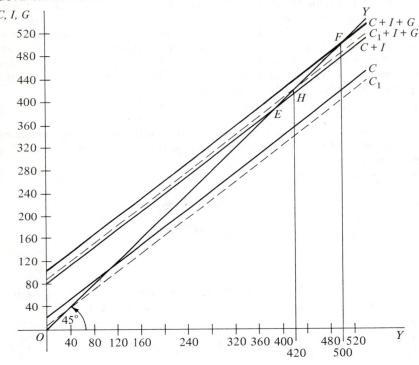

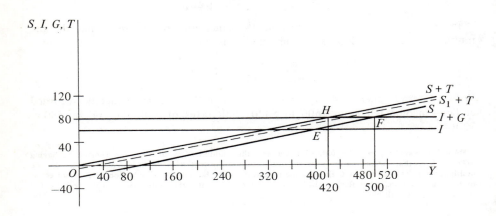

the consumption function falls by $MPC(\Delta T)$ or $0.8(\$20) = \$16$. The parallel downward shift is shown by the consumption function labeled C_1. This downward shift of the consumption function shifts the entire aggregate demand schedule down by the same amount, shown as $C_1 + I + G$. The new equilibrium occurs at point H, where $Y = \$420$ and the aggregate demand intersects the aggregate supply schedule.

In Figure 5.2(b) the alternative equilibrium condition is given. Note that taxes act as a leakage, and thus the amount of taxes is added on to the old saving curve, shifting the schedule upward and parallel as shown by the curve labeled $S + T$. This curve shows the full amount of taxes ($\$20$) and indicates that the level of income would fall to $\$400$. However, since some of the taxes would be paid for out of saving, this curve is not the amount of the *total* leakage. The proper shift of the $S + T$ curve is given by the schedule labeled $S_1 + T$. Here only that portion of the tax that represents the *additional* leakage is added to the old saving curve S. This amount is $\$16$, since $\$4$ of the tax comes out of saving; that is, MPS times the tax, or $0.2(\$20), = \$4$. Of course, the $S_1 + T$ schedule intersects the $I + G$ schedule at the equilibrium level of income of $\$420$. Taking the two parts of the figure together, it can readily be seen that the tax of $\$20$ is paid for by a reduction of C equal to $\$16$ and a reduction of saving equal to $\$4$. It is the latter reduction of saving that accounts for the less powerful tax multiplier.

The Balanced Budget Multiplier

The fact that the government expenditures multiplier is more powerful than the tax multiplier provides an interesting case in fiscal policy effects. If government expenditures are matched by the same amount of taxes so that the budget is balanced, what is the effect upon the level of income? Most people would probably say that government has no effect on the economic system, that it is neutral. In fact, even with a balanced budget, government is not neutral, but its actions are expansionary. The level of income will increase by the amount of the expenditures ($=$ taxes). This result is brought about by the working of the balanced budget, or "unit," multiplier. It is derived as follows. The effect of government expenditures on the level of income is given by the expenditures multiplier,

$$(5.22) \qquad \Delta Y = \frac{\Delta G}{1 - c},$$

and the effect of the tax multiplier on the level of income is given by

$$(5.23) \qquad \Delta Y = \frac{-c\Delta T}{1 - c}.$$

The net effect of the government budget can be seen by combining the multipliers of (5.22) and (5.23):

$$(5.24) \qquad \Delta Y = \frac{\Delta G}{1 - c} - \frac{c\Delta T}{1 - c}.$$

Since $\Delta G = \Delta T$ when the budget is balanced, we can substitute ΔG for ΔT in (5.24) and combine terms:

$$(5.25) \qquad \Delta Y = \frac{\Delta G - c\Delta G}{1 - c} = \frac{\Delta G(1 - c)}{1 - c} = \Delta G,$$

or

$$\Delta Y = \Delta G,$$

or dividing both sides by ΔG,

$$\frac{\Delta Y}{\Delta G} = 1.$$

Equation (5.25) shows that the change in the level of income is equal to the change in government expenditures (or taxes, of course). This is an important result, for not only does it show that the government impact is not neutral when the budget is balanced but it also means that the *level* at which the budget is balanced is also extremely important.

In our model when government is introduced, the budget is balanced. Before government was included, the equilibrium level of income was $400. With a balanced budget, $G = T = \$20$, and the level of income rose to $420, or by the amount of expenditures and taxes. In the calculation of the multipliers the expenditures multiplier was 5 and the tax multiplier was 4, and it is this difference that accounts for the unit multiplier. This result can also be visualized from Figure 5.2, where it is seen that with government expenditures alone, the equilibrium level of income rose from $400 to $500. With the introduction of taxes of $20 ($= G$ of $20), the level of income fell not to the original level of $400 but to $420.

It is clear from the foregoing that government expenditures and taxes affect the level of income differently. It would be too dogmatic to assert, however, that in reality the level of income will change by the amount of the budget totals. It is mathematically correct to state that the balanced budget multiplier is equal to 1, but is it economically sound? Only by accident is it likely to be unitary and work as described. It is better to say that the impact on the level of income is likely to be *positive* ($\Delta Y/\Delta G > 0$) and to avoid the exactness of the mathematics.[3] Actually, there are too many leakages from the income stream, and much depends upon what the expenditures were for, who received the incomes so generated, and who was taxed, for the lump sum tax in the model is scarcely realistic.[4] For the present it is better to stay with the very important conclusion that government spending is likely to have a greater impact on the level of income than is government taxation; the effect is likely to be expansionary even when the budget is balanced.

Transfer Payments

Transfer payments are one means by which a society may choose to redistribute income. As such they are frequently referred to as negative taxes. Poverty programs and welfare schemes utilize the concept of transfer payments as well as the more generally accepted programs of social security, veterans' payments, and unemployment compensation. Transfer payments were not included in GNP but are included in personal income and hence have some effect on the level of spending and income. In this section only the effect on the level of income is examined,

---

[3] For a recent discussion and estimation of the balanced budget multiplier, see Michael K. Evans, "Reconstruction and Estimation of the Balanced Budget Multiplier," *Review of Economics and Statistics* 51 (February 1969): 14–25.

[4] For an interesting discussion of this issue, see W. J. Baumol and M. H. Peston, "More on the Multiplier Effects of a Balanced Budget," *American Economic Review* 45 (March 1955): 140–148.

leaving aside for the time being all discussion of the merits of redistribution of income.

It is probably a simplifying assumption to regard transfer payments as autonomous and independent of the level of income. Some of them, such as unemployment compensation, vary (inversely) with the economic condition, falling with prosperity and rising with recession. The retirement decisions of individuals could also be affected by the state of the economy. Other transfer payments, such as veterans' payments, are unaffected by the economic situation. If in the short run we do assume that the transfer payments are autonomous, in the long run the assumption becomes less tenable. Over time, society's attitude toward redistribution and transfer payments is likely to change. Indeed, one of the consequences of economic growth may well be the lessening of resistance to redistribution schemes; it is easier to share when there is more to share.

For the present, the short-run assumption of autonomous transfer payments will be retained. The model then becomes:

$$(5.26) \qquad Y = C + I + G$$
$$(5.27) \qquad C = C_a + c(Y - T + R)$$
$$(5.28) \qquad I = \overline{I}$$
$$(5.29) \qquad G = \overline{G}$$
$$(5.30) \qquad T = \overline{T}$$
$$(5.31) \qquad R = \overline{R},$$

where R is autonomous transfer payments and the rest of the model is unaffected except for the consumption function, which now includes the additional source of income not included in Y. The substitution of (5.27), (5.28), and (5.29) into (5.26) yields the equation for the equilibrium level of income:

$$(5.32) \qquad Y = \frac{1}{1 - c}(C_a - cT + cR + I + G).$$

The equation for Y now includes the new source of spending, and the term cR measures the amount. Transfer payments are also divided up into additional consumption and saving, as shown by $\Delta C = c\Delta R$, and thus the effect on the level of income is,

$$(5.33) \qquad \Delta Y = \frac{c\Delta R}{1 - c},$$

which is the transfer payments multiplier. Again, since only a fraction of the transfer payments is spent, $c\Delta R$, it follows that the government expenditures multiplier is more powerful. That is,

$$(5.34) \qquad \frac{\Delta G}{1 - c} > \frac{c\Delta R}{1 - c}$$

for the same change in government spending ($\Delta G = \Delta R$). It also follows that a tax-financed change in transfer payments leaves the level of income unaffected. If $\Delta R = \Delta T$, the substitution into the tax multiplier and transfer payments multiplier gives

$$\Delta Y = \frac{-c\Delta T}{1 - c} + \frac{c\Delta R}{1 - c},$$

or

$$(5.35) \qquad \Delta Y = \frac{-c\Delta T + c\Delta T}{1 - c} = 0.$$

The tax-financed change in transfer payments mathematically renders the government policy neutral. This result, however, depends upon the assumption of a constant $MPC(c)$. It could easily be argued that those who pay the tax are likely to have a different MPC from those who receive the transfer payments. In all likelihood the MPC of the recipients of transfer payments would be close to 1, which means that the inequality of equation (5.34) is suspect. It is further possible that a tax-financed change in transfer payments is not neutral but expansionary if there is any plausibility to the idea that the MPCs of the groups are different. In short, one must be wary of unconditionally accepting conclusions based on equations (5.34) and (5.35); in reality more information is needed before one can measure the impact of transfer payments on the level of income.

The Income Tax

Taxes that either use income as a base or that tend to vary with the level of income are more appropriate and realistic tax functions than are autonomous taxes. Even property and sales taxes, which are not directly related to income, tend to move in the same direction as income—perhaps with a lag. In any case, income taxes are important in our tax structure, and it is necessary to include them in the model.

By far the simplest relation between taxes and income is the linear one, which is written

$$(5.36) \qquad T = T_a + tY,$$

where T_a represents autonomous taxes and t is the marginal propensity to tax $(MPT) = \Delta T / \Delta Y$. The terms in the expression are analogous to other linear functions—the consumption function, for example. Equation (5.36) allows for autonomous taxes as well as taxes based on income, and both T_a and t are constant. The fact that t, the MPT, is constant means a proportional income tax, one where the rate of taxation is unchanged regardless of the level of income. A tax structure in which everyone pays a fixed percentage of his income would be a proportional tax. In reality, the United States income tax, though progressive in rate structure, turns out to be roughly proportional in practice (at a rate of approximately 20 per cent). The progressivity of the tax has been eroded by exemptions, deductions, and the existence of various loopholes. It is therefore not too unrealistic to write the tax function based on income as a proportional tax for the economy as a whole. The model becomes

$$(5.37) \qquad Y = C + I + G$$
$$(5.38) \qquad C = C_a + c(Y - T_a - tY + R)$$
$$(5.39) \qquad I = \bar{I}$$
$$(5.40) \qquad G = \bar{G}$$
$$(5.41) \qquad T = T_a + tY$$
$$(5.42) \qquad R = \bar{R}.$$

Substituting and solving for the equilibrium level of income yields

(5.43)
$$Y = \frac{1}{1 - c + ct} (C_a - cT_a + cR + I + G),$$

or

$$Y = \frac{1}{1 - c(1 - t)} (C_a - cT_a + cR + I + G).$$

The difference between this expression for the equilibrium level of income and previous expressions is in the multiplier term. The value of the multiplier is reduced by the addition of the term ct because as income increases, so do tax collections. The leakages from the income stream increase with increases in income and do not, as before, remain constant. With a proportional tax the *amount* of taxes increases as Y increases; with a progressive tax the leakages would increase even more, since the *rate* of taxation would increase as well. Since taxes flow to government, consumption and hence aggregate demand are reduced, and it is this reduction that lowers the value of the multiplier. Rewriting the multipliers, it is clear that

$$\frac{1}{1 - c} > \frac{1}{1 - c + ct},$$

since additions to the denominator of a fraction lower the value of that fraction. If we assign a value of 25 per cent to the *MPT*, t, the calculations yield

$$\frac{1}{1 - 0.8} > \frac{1}{1 - 0.8 + 0.8(25)}, \quad \text{or} \quad 5 > 2.5.$$

The importance of income taxes in this model lies in the fiscal policy effects of government activity.[5] Since the multiplier is reduced, government expenditures are not as expansionary as before. As government expenditures increase, incomes rise,

[5] With the introduction of income taxes, graphical analysis becomes complex and may easily confuse rather than clarify. For the interested student, some suggestions concerning the changes necessitated by income taxes are outlined in this footnote. Income taxes affect disposable income and hence consumption, so that the change in presentation involves the change in aggregate demand through consumption function changes. The consumption function rotates as in the figure shown in this footnote, reflecting the fact that the slope of the schedule has changed from c to $c(1 - t)$. The original consumption function is C_0 and the new consumption function is C_1. The two consumption functions are not parallel as with autonomous taxes but diverge as the level of income increases. The yield of the tax, being proportional to income, increases as the level of income increases. Disposable income and consumption are also affected for the same reason. In fact, the vertical distance between the two consumption curves at every level of Y is given by $c(tY)$ or *MPC* times tax yield; this is how much c falls, for disposable income falls by the amount of the tax yield, $Y_d = (Y - tY)$. After calculating the effects of the tax on the consumption function and plotting C_1, it would be straightforward work to add the other autonomous components of aggregate demand and arrive at the new equilibrium level of income. The curve labeled $C_1 + I + G$ for aggregate demand gives the equilibrium level of income at Y_e.

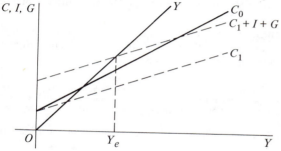

but disposable income does not rise by the full amount, since part of the additional income flows back to government in the form of higher taxes. Thus, if government spends $1, taxes are $0.25 (assuming a 25 per cent tax) so that disposable income increases by $0.75 and consumption by 0.8($0.75) = $0.60.

Thus, the effects of government activity are less destabilizing, and the consequent impact on the level of economic activity is less disrupting.

Proportional income taxes offer more stability than lump sum taxes, and progressive taxes offer more stability than proportional taxes. Income taxes are one of the built-in stabilizers, so called because they are part of the system and require no action by government—they work to stabilize the economy automatically. As incomes rise, so do tax receipts, and as income falls, taxes fall. Thus, income taxes tend to smooth out fluctuations in income as aggregate demand changes.[6]

Stability, of course, is not an unmixed blessing. If the government policy is to increase the level of income, then as income increases, the increasing taxes act as a brake to further expansion. On the other hand, a deficit-financed program to stimulate the economy will not require as large a deficit, since taxes flow back to offset the expenditures. Again, if changes in tax policy are to be used to stimulate the economy, they will not be as effective as government expenditures, since increases will reduce Y_d and C and hence, at the resulting lower level of income, taxes will be less than anticipated; reductions in taxes will increase Y_d and C and the level of income, so that more taxes return to the treasury. It is clear that the introduction of income taxes into the model requires more critical determination of government policy, since the effects on the budget and on the level of income must be evaluated if the impact on the economy is to be correctly gauged.

It can also be stated here, without proof, that the balanced budget multiplier would continue to work as it did with just autonomous taxes.[7] That is, if the tax yield were such as to equal the amount of government expenditure, the level of income would change by the amount of that level of expenditure and taxes.

Gap Analysis

A more thorough discussion and evaluation of fiscal policy will be undertaken later, but before leaving the public sector analysis, it might be useful to sketch the essence of fiscal policy through the use of the techniques already developed.

As seen earlier, an economy can be in equilibrium at less than the full employment level of income or at more than the *real* full employment level of income (of course, prices are no longer constant in this case). The amount by which an economy falls short of, or exceeds, the full employment level of output is called the gap, and aggregate demand is either too little or too great (by the amount of the gap).

Assuming that full employment and price stability are the goals of the economy, it is clear that something must be done about the level of aggregate demand. Figure 5.3 shows the need for some modifications of aggregate demand.

---

[6] Other built-in stabilizers include unemployment compensation, social security programs, farm price supports, the corporation income tax, and possibly corporations' dividend policies. These stabilizers tend to move in the opposite direction from the movement of income and thus help to dampen the fluctuations; they reduce the amplitude of the cycle.

[7] For proof, see Richard A. Musgrave, *The Theory of Public Finance* (New York: McGraw-Hill, 1959), ch. 18.

FIGURE 5.3

GAP ANALYSIS

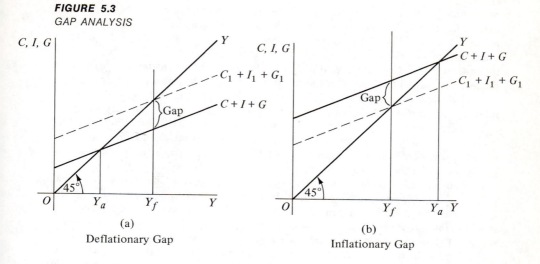

(a)
Deflationary Gap

(b)
Inflationary Gap

In both parts (a) and (b) the full employment level of income is designated Y_f and the actual level of income is given as Y_a. Of course, the $C + I + G$ curve is the aggregate demand schedule for this economy in this time period.

In part (a) the level of aggregate demand is not sufficiently high to employ all of the economy's resources. In order to reach full employment, aggregate demand would have to rise to the level indicated by $C_1 + I_1 + G_1$—enough to close the gap. Note that aggregate demand need not increase by the difference between Y_f and Y_a but only by the amount of the gap itself. This is because of the multiplier; the gap times multiplier would then equal the difference between Y_f and Y_a. In part (b) the productive capacity of the economy is given by Y_f, and no additional *real* *output* can be produced in the short run. If aggregate demand exceeds aggregate supply at this level, only *money* income can rise as a result of a rising price level. In short, pure inflation results from excess demand at the full employment level of income. Again, aggregate demand must be reduced by the amount of the gap in order to reach the full employment level of income at stable prices.

The question is how is aggregate demand to be affected? For purposes of this analysis, it does not matter which sector—C, I, or G—adjusts its demand, only that aggregate demand must be changed from its present level. There is no a priori reason to expect the household or business sectors to alter their spending plans, since these plans were formulated on the anticipation that the income level Y_a would prevail. Presumably, there are no reasons to expect the plans of the private sector to change, even if the equilibrium level of income turns out to be less than the full employment level.[8]

It follows that some type of public action is required. The public sector is the only one that can act in the national interest free of any constraints and without the shackles of fixed plans and commitments. The actions the government takes can be of two broad forms: it can attempt to influence the demand of the other sectors, or it can change its own portion of the aggregate demand to fit the needs of the eco-

[8] We will return to this assumption in later chapters.

nomic condition. In the former, government can change the cost of borrowing, that is, the rate of interest; fix other credit terms; use arguments of moral suasion, for instance, save more, buy bonds; alter depreciation rates and other rules; change other portions of the tax laws to give tax credits against the purchase cost of new investment goods, and so on. If it acts directly, government can increase or reduce the level of spending, G, or alter the tax yields, T, or both. From the foregoing it is clear how these actions would affect the level of income. It is likely that attempts to influence the private sector would be indirect and by no means certain to be effective. The greater the uncertainty, the better the case for direct government intervention. In a deflationary gap situation government would cut taxes or increase spending, or some combination of both. In an inflationary gap situation the proper policy would be the reverse—increase taxes or reduce spending, or both.

Of course, these models are simple, but they do capture the essence of fiscal policy as it is viewed today, and they do bring out two important facets of the problem of fiscal policy in general. First, there is the heavy reliance placed on government to keep the economy on an even keel, either through direct or indirect means. This raises questions with regard to the stability of the capitalist system and modifies the nature of capitalism to such an extent as to make the label "capitalism" deceiving. Second, the entire gap analysis focuses on the demand side —showing the Keynesian bias. The supply side is passive or ignored, and it is aggregate demand that is emphasized and that causes the economy to fluctuate. Some consequences of this emphasis will be investigated in the following chapters.

Foreign Trade and the Open Economy

6

So far we have treated the economy as if it were a closed economy having no interaction with other economies. Since all economies trade, we must gain some insight into how such trade affects the economic system. The extent to which an economy is affected by foreign trade depends, of course, on how much it depends on the production of others. For countries like Great Britain and Japan, foreign trade is vital, and a good deal of activity that occurs in these economies is directed toward foreign markets. Trade under these circumstances is necessary for survival. For other countries, such as the United States, foreign trade constitutes only a minor fraction of economic activity, something like 5 per cent of GNP. Despite the small magnitude of foreign trade, the importance of this sector has grown since the late 1950s, and of course, trade with the United States is important to foreign countries. The United States market, being so large, has tremendous impact on the other economies that trade with it. Five per cent of $1 trillion is $50 billion, larger than the GNP of many countries.

Foreign trade is important even for the United States, and in recent years the balance-of-payments problem has become a source of major concern. In fact, there are instances when the "proper" domestic policy has been overruled in favor of the "proper" foreign trade policy. Low interest rates to stimulate domestic borrowing and spending have been discouraged, since (money) capital might flow to other economies where the rate of return is higher. Furthermore, other types of commercial policy such as tariffs and quotas have been employed with material consequences for the domestic economy and have caused economic repercussions in other economies. No nation is immune from the effects of world trade, for no economy is self-sufficient to the point where it can insulate itself from the vicissitudes of international trade and exchange. In this chapter we explore the effects of trade with other economies on the economic model we have been developing.

Exports

Exports are a component of aggregate demand, but the source of the demand for the economy's production comes from residents of other countries. As part of aggregate demand, exports in the abstract are no different from the other components. In the production of goods and services for export, domestic factors of production gain incomes, out of which they consume or save or invest. The source of the income is immaterial. On the other hand, their production, since it is sold abroad, is not available for domestic consumption.[1] Thus, goods sold abroad increase domestic incomes without increasing domestic supply. The implications of this feature concerning the stimulus of exports on employment and income are self-evident and help to explain the export-expansion goal of many economies. The problems that such goals bring about are not always obvious, but we hope to develop some appreciation for them later.

What determines the volume of exports? What variables can help explain the demand for one economy's production by another? Some of the important determinants of the volume of exports are: incomes of the other economies; relative prices of commodities, the differences in prices of goods in one economy versus those in other economies; all types of commercial policies—tariffs, quotas, exchange restrictions, and so on; the availability of reserves or exchange—the currency acceptable in international markets; tastes; monopolistically produced goods —only one seller of the item; political factors and trading blocs; custom and tradition; natural resources, and so on.

A glance at these influences is sufficient to note that for the most part they are not determined by or in the domestic market; they are exogenous—external to the market under examination. In addition, some of the variables are slow to change and in the short run can be considered stable or constant. This means that exports can be taken as autonomous—independent of the *domestic* level of income. The assumption of autonomous exports is probably a reasonable one and makes the model appear as follows:

$$(6.1) \qquad Y = C + I + G + X$$

$$(6.2) \qquad C = C_a + c(Y - T + R)$$

$$(6.3) \qquad I = \bar{I}$$

$$(6.4) \qquad G = \bar{G}$$

$$(6.5) \qquad T = \bar{T}$$

$$(6.6) \qquad R = \bar{R}$$

$$(6.7) \qquad X = \bar{X}.$$

Here X equals autonomous exports, and for simplicity the model includes only autonomous taxes. Once again, the equilibrium level of income can be calculated by substituting (6.2), (6.3), (6.4), and (6.7) into equation (6.1):

$$(6.8) \qquad Y = \frac{1}{1 - c}(C_a - cT + cR + I + G + X).$$

---

[1] In this regard, exports resemble investment goods. In both cases the output is not available for consumption. In fact, the term "foreign investment" is used in national income accounting to describe exports. "Foreign disinvestment," then, refers to imports, and the term "net foreign investment or disinvestment" is used to indicate the overall balance.

The only new element in (6.8) is exports, X. It is clear that exports are also subject to the multiplier effect in the same manner as investment expenditures. For a change in exports, we can write,

$$(6.9) \qquad \Delta Y = \frac{1}{1 - c} (\Delta X),$$

for exports create domestic incomes that are respent and respent, causing the level of income to rise by some multiple.

Imports

Imports are the goods and services purchased from other economies by domestic residents. As such, they are a leakage from the income stream, for incomes earned from the production of these goods accrue to foreigners, and the sales receipts do not return to domestic producers but flow abroad. Therefore, like saving, they represent income not spent on domestic production. It is easy to see why nations sometimes go to extremes in attempting to limit the volume of imports. In fact, there are times when the prevailing mood seems to favor the old mercantilistic doctrine that a nation choosing to be strong must expand exports as much as possible and drastically curtail imports. No one bothered to ask what utility the accumulation of treasure was supposed to bring or what would happen if all nations pursued this goal simultaneously. Still, the notion persists.

In the foregoing model the aggregate demand given by $C + I + G + X$ represents domestic goods and services. As soon as an economy becomes an open economy and foreign trade is permitted, each sector of aggregate demand is likely to be involved in the purchasing of goods produced abroad; some of the goods will be purchased by consumers, some by investors, and some by government. A difficulty arises here, for the imports are added to the demand for domestic production with the result that the aggregate demand schedule becomes the demand schedule for both domestic and foreign production. Each component of aggregate demand includes the amount of domestic demand and the amount of foreign demand, because it is impossible in many cases to separate the purchases by the economy that produced them. Very often the good involved contains elements both of domestic and foreign production. Many goods are shipped as intermediate goods, requiring further processing or marketing. Parts of automobiles, for example, are produced abroad; foreign entertainers perform in establishments owned by domestic entrepreneurs; foreign wines, beverages, and tobacco, and so on, are resold in a variety of forms. The difficulty of separating economic activities by the economy where they take place forces the collection of data that measure both domestic and imported output—total C, total I, and total G.

Since we are interested in the aggregate demand for domestically produced output and the amount of output actually received by domestic residents, a subtraction of the amount of imports must be made; the subtraction cannot be made by sector, so that it is necessary to subtract the total in a lump sum. The subtraction is made from exports, which puts the transactions with the rest of the world on a net basis. The aggregate demand function becomes,

$$(6.10) \qquad Y = C + I + G + (X - M),$$

where M equals the value of the total imports in any given time period.

Before completing the model, it is necessary to examine the determinants of the import function to discover what accounts for the demand for foreign-produced goods and services. The variables in the import function resemble those for the export function with the exception that the influences relate to domestic residents. Some of these influences are: relative prices of similar, related products—prices at home versus those abroad; the level of income; tastes; foreign exchange; commercial policies; political and ideological concerns; cultural and traditional elements.

It is common to assume that most of these variables remain unchanged in the short run and to presume that many of the influences can be subsumed under the level of income variable. As income rises, tastes for foreign goods increase, travel increases, cultural contacts of all kinds increase, and so on. In addition, there are certain autonomous imports, independent of the level of income, which are typically critical raw materials and some farm produce. With these assumptions, the import function is reduced to

$$(6.11) \qquad M = M_a + mY,$$

where M_a is autonomous imports and m is the marginal propensity to import, $\Delta M / \Delta Y$, which gives the proportion of a change in income that affects the volume of imports. Some fraction, say, of an increase in income will be spent on goods produced abroad. The linear form of the function is simple and corresponds to that used in the consumption and tax functions. The entire model can now be written as follows:

$$(6.12) \qquad Y = C + I + G + (X - M)$$
$$(6.13) \qquad C = C_a + c(Y - T + R)$$
$$(6.14) \qquad I = \overline{I}$$
$$(6.15) \qquad G = \overline{G}$$
$$(6.16) \qquad T = \overline{T}$$
$$(6.17) \qquad R = \overline{R}$$
$$(6.18) \qquad X = \overline{X}$$
$$(6.19) \qquad M = M_a + mY.$$

The substitution of equations (6.13) through (6.19) into (6.12) permits the calculation of the equilibrium level of income:

$$(6.20) \qquad Y = \frac{1}{1 - c + m} (C_a - cT + cR + I + G + X - M_a).$$

Since imports depend upon the level of income, the value of the multiplier is reduced. As income increases, a portion of this increase, the marginal propensity to import, m, is spent on foreign goods and not respent on domestic production. Income not respent does not create domestic incomes, which are not respent, and so on. Imports are simply another leakage like saving and taxes. The condition for the equilibrium level of income could also be written

$$(6.21) \qquad I + G + X = S + T + M,$$

which shows that the total leakages, $S + T + M$, must be offset by the spending of the components of aggregate demand, $I + G + X$.

It is clear that the marginal propensity to import, m (or alternatively the *MPC* foreign goods), reduces the multiplier, since the denominator of the fraction is increased:

$$\frac{1}{1-c} > \frac{1}{1-c+m}.$$

If $m = 0.05$ and *MPC* $= 0.8$, the numerical values of the multipliers are:

$$\frac{1}{1-0.8} > \frac{1}{1-0.8+0.05} \quad \text{or} \quad 5 > 4.$$

Thus, any change in aggregate demand that previously would have expanded the level of income by a multiple of 5 would now, with imports in the model, increase income by less. Imports can have widespread repercussions in the economy beyond the immediate loss to the income stream. This is the first impression of the effect of foreign trade on the domestic economy, but it must be qualified later in the chapter.

Graphically, the linear import function and the autonomous export condition can easily be represented. Figure 6.1 shows the two functions and indicates the essence of the trade balance.

The horizontal line represents autonomous exports, and the upward sloping curve shows the import function, which depends on the level of income. The slope of the import schedule is the marginal propensity to import, $\Delta M / \Delta Y = m$. The two schedules intersect at a level of income Y_1, and at this level exports equal imports. At income levels to the left of Y_1, $X > M$ and there is a "favorable" balance of trade; at income levels to the right of Y_1, $M > X$ and there is an "unfavorable" balance of trade.

Although numerical examples and graphical analyses get a bit cumbersome with the introduction of more functions into the model, they are included here for the benefit of those who may profit from them. Assigning numerical values to the model gives

(6.22)	$Y = C + I + G + (X - M)$
(6.13)′	$C = 20 + 0.8(Y - 20 + 0)$
(6.14)′	$I = 60$
(6.15)′	$G = 20$
(6.16)′	$T = 20$
(6.17)′	$R = 0$, for simplicity
(6.18)′	$X = 20$
(6.19)′	$M = 4 + 0.05Y,$

where autonomous exports $X = \$20$, and autonomous imports $M = \$4$, and the marginal propensity to import $m = 0.05$. Substituting these values into equation (6.22), the equilibrium level of income becomes,

$$(6.20)' \quad Y = \frac{1}{1 - 0.8 + 0.05}[20 - 0.8(20) + 60 + 20 + 20 - 4]$$
$$= 4(100)$$
$$= 400.$$

FIGURE 6.1
EXPORT AND IMPORT FUNCTIONS

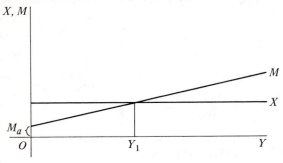

At the equilibrium level of income, $400, the following magnitudes result:

$$C = 324 \qquad X = 20$$
$$I = 60 \qquad M = 24$$
$$G = 20 \qquad S = 56$$
$$T = 20 \qquad R = 0.$$

Of course, the alternative conditions for the existence of an equilibrium level of income must be satisfied as well:

$$S + T + M = I + G + X$$
$$56 + 20 + 24 = 60 + 20 + 20$$
$$100 = 100$$

total leakages are offset by expenditures. It is not necessary for exports to offset imports exactly, or for saving to offset investment, or that the government balance its budget; the only thing required is that the *total* amount of leakages be offset by injections of expenditures of a like amount.

The additions to the model are included in Figure 6.2, which shows the effects of adding foreign trade to the model. The numerical model given earlier includes only autonomous taxes and assumes transfer payments are zero for the sake of simplicity. These assumptions take us back to the numerical model of chapter 5 [see equation (5.18)′] and to Figure 5.2. The equilibrium level of income at that stage was $420, as shown in Figure 6.2. With the introduction of autonomous exports of $20 and autonomous imports of $4, the y intercept changes from $84 to $100. Note that the intersection of aggregate demand and aggregate supply occurs at an income level of $400, which is $20 less than the original Y of $420. This is because at the equilibrium level of income imports are $24 and exports are $20, and the leakages—imports—exceed the injections—exports—by $4, which when multiplied by the new multiplier of 4 yields the fall in the level of income of $16 due to the adverse export balance. The remaining $4 of the fall in income is the result of the lower multiplier—the increase in income caused by the exports, $20(4) = $80, being actually $4 less than the fall in income as the other components of demand become subject to the new multiplier: $84(5) = $420 > $84(4) = $336 by $84.

The inclusion of imports as a function of income causes some graphic peculiarities. Note that at low levels of income $X > M$, and therefore the foreign trade sector contributes to the growth of income; the effect is positive. At an income level of \$320, $X = M$; and at income levels beyond \$320, $M > X$, and the leakages outweigh the positive effects of trade. This can be seen from Figure 6.2, as the $C + I + G + (X - M)$ schedule is below the $C + I + G$ curve after the intersection at \$320.

The fact that imports are greater than exports means that the level of income is unlikely to remain at the equilibrium level of \$400. Unless this economy has an

FIGURE 6.2

FOREIGN TRADE SECTOR ADDED TO THE MODEL

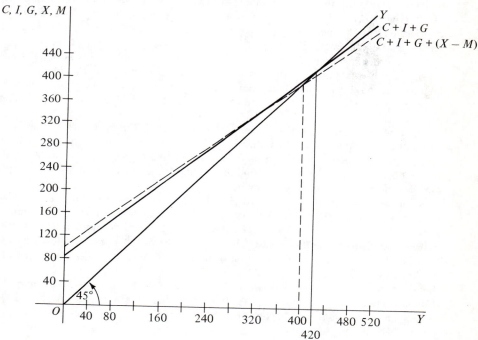

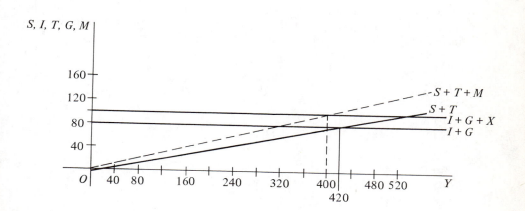

unlimited amount of gold and foreign exchange, or other countries are willing to finance the deficit by accumulating the domestic currency and securities, the imbalance of trade must sooner or later be corrected. For our import function, a lower level of income would solve the imbalance problem, but it is unlikely that any country will choose this solution. Lower incomes and unemployment would be unpalatable to most nations. The other variables in the import function could also be sources for the correction mechanism. Tariffs, import quotas, exchange restrictions, and so on, appear to offer immediate relief, although in the long run they may be self-defeating. An attempt to improve the terms of trade by deflationary policies could turn the relative price variable more to the domestic economy's favor. Higher taxes or reduced government spending might accomplish a reduction in prices or stop the increase in the price level, but this could entail the reduction of income and employment as well.

On the other hand, some attempts to increase exports could be explored. Export subsidies, more effective marketing and advertising techniques, manipulation of interest rates to lure capital to the domestic economy, tied-in aid agreements, and, in general, the plea for free trade and the removal of any barriers may help expand exports.

These remedies have all been tried at one time or another, and they are listed here not as desirable but only as illustrative. Any further discussion of the balance-of-payments problem would take us far afield, but the existence of a foreign trade sector does pose problems not found in a closed economy. Even in our simple model some of these problems are evident.

As in previous figures, part (b) of Figure 6.2 restates the equilibrium condition in terms of leakages from, and injections into, the income stream. Autonomous exports, X, are added onto the $I + G$ curve, shifting the curve upward and parallel by the amount of the exports, $20. The slope of the $S + T$ curve is altered by the fact that the imports are also a function of income; the curve rotates upward and to the left as this dependence is added. Again, at income levels below $320, $X > M$, that is, the vertical distance between $I + G + X$ and $I + G$ is greater than the distance between $S + T + M$ and $S + T$; income therefore increases. At $Y = \$320$ the distances are equal, and beyond that level $M > X$ until the equilibrium level of income of $400 is reached.

The Foreign Trade Model Expanded

Now that the numerical and graphical analyses have been completed for the simple model, it might be useful here to expand the model to include taxes as a function of income and transfer payments. The model becomes,

$$(6.23) \qquad Y = C + I + G + (X - M)$$
$$(6.24) \qquad C = C_a + c(Y - T_a - tY + R)$$
$$(6.25) \qquad I = \bar{I}$$
$$(6.26) \qquad G = \bar{G}$$
$$(6.27) \qquad T = T_a + tY$$
$$(6.28) \qquad R = \bar{R}$$
$$(6.29) \qquad X = \bar{X}$$
$$(6.30) \qquad M = M_a + mY.$$

The substitution into (6.23) to derive the equilibrium level of income yields

$$(6.31) \qquad Y = \frac{1}{1 - c + ct + m} (C_a - cT_a + cR + I + G + X - M_a).$$

With the introduction of income taxes, the multiplier is further reduced. As income increases, so do the leakages—taxes and imports. The original multiplier was 5. With $t = 0.25$ and $m = 0.05$, the value of the multiplier falls to

$$\frac{1}{1 - c + ct + m} = \frac{1}{1 - 0.8 + 0.8(0.25) + 0.05} \sim 2.2.$$

Foreign Trade and International Interdependence

It is not sufficient to study the effects of foreign trade upon an economy without considering the international repercussions that trade inevitably brings. One nation's exports are another's imports, and vice versa. Since imports and exports affect the level of income of any economy, it follows that economic fluctuations can be transmitted to other economies as trade rises and falls. Thus, an economy is never independent of the economic conditions of other economies.

The manner in which economies become interdependent is not difficult to understand. Say the level of income of a country, the United States, increases as a result of an increase in investment spending; the multiplier analysis has shown that the level of income grows by some multiple. As income increases, so do imports, since $M = f(Y)$. But the imports of the United States are exports of other countries, say, Japan. As exports increase in Japan, so does the level of income—again by the export multiplier. Now, if we postulate that imports depend upon income for the Japanese economy as well, then as income increases, so will imports into Japan. Some of these imports will be from the United States, and hence exports increase for the United States as does the level of income in the United States. As the United States income increases, so will imports, and so on, and the whole process continues, as with the usual multiplier analysis. Like the multiplier mechanism, however, the spending at each stage is smaller than the previous one, and thus the spending dwindles and the process ends for all intents and purposes after a time.

This international interdependence illustrates quite clearly what many fail to see: exports depend upon imports, too; one nation's exports are another's imports, and vice versa. A nation's restrictions on trade interrupt the flow of trade and disrupt the income and employment levels of all its trading partners, who in turn upset the levels of their trading partners, and so on. Thus, every nation has a vital stake in maintaining stable trade conditions and avoiding disrupting fluctuations in the economic condition of major economies. For the business cycle can be exported also, as the experience of the 1930s so dramatically proved. It is not surprising, then, that international organizations such as the International Monetary Fund and the General Agreement on Trade and Tariffs have been formed to oversee the affairs of international trade. Major economies have a particular responsibility to maintain stable trade conditions, since fluctuations in their income levels, and hence imports and exports, vitally affect the smaller economies; whereas the reverse is not likely to be true. The imports of the United States, for instance, are crucial to a smaller economy, say Colombia, but the imports of Colombia from the United States are not likely to affect the level of United States economic activity very much.

The discussion of the effects of foreign trade on an economy has been of necessity on an elementary level. Most of the major questions in this interesting area soon get too intricate and are better left to more advanced study. The problems of finance, balance of payments, gold, and exchange rates are so complex that it would be inappropriate to examine these concerns at this stage. In the later discussion of fiscal and monetary policy it will be necessary to return to the questions of foreign trade in order to explain how the foreign sector may affect the policies pursued, even though, as with the United States, the foreign trade sector is a minor part of the level of economic activity.

For the present it is only necessary to introduce trade into the model and to show how the level of income is affected. In addition, the interdependence of economies in world trade has been indicated so that a better perspective of the effects of trade can be gained.

Income, Employment, and the Price Level

In the foregoing chapters the determination of the equilibrium level of income emphasized the role played by aggregate demand. The supply side of the process was largely ignored. It is time to remove some of the assumptions made about aggregate supply, so that behavioral variables for producers can be more realistically included in the analysis. As the supply side becomes more explicit, it will also be necessary to examine a little more critically the relationship between output and employment. The link between output decisions and employment decisions must be established.

In the preceding models all variables were stated in real terms and prices were not permitted to affect the analysis in any important way. To assign a passive role to the price level variable cannot long be justified. The price level affects economic decisions and is affected by them. The passive role assigned to prices again reflects the Keynesian bias,[1] which must be modified if we are to develop a more realistic model. The connections between output, employment, and the price level are important, and it is too simplistic to constrain any one of the components of this network.

The interrelationships between output, employment, and the price level are so complex that no simple model can hope to delineate all the intricacies. The models that follow, therefore, are meant to be suggestive rather than rigorous and precise representations of reality. They are presented here for three reasons: first, the models help to bring out the relations between output, employment, and the price level in a clear manner; second, the models, imperfect though they may be, do capture what many people have in mind as representing the interrelations involved; third, the models offer a transition to later work regarding employment and infla-

[1] For a fascinating but sophisticated discussion of this subject, see Axel Leijonhufvud, *On Keynesian Economics and the Economics of Keynes* (New York: Oxford University Press, 1968).

tion. It is the second reason that prompts our warning about the nature of the models. Their limitations must be kept in mind, so that they may be put into the proper perspective.

We proceed, then, to explain very briefly the microeconomic basis for the macroeconomic relations that are needed. Since it is the supply side that must be modified, we must review the firm's behavior as it reacts to the conditions it faces. That is, what determines how much a firm will decide to supply in the short run, and how can these individual decisions be aggregated to give the aggregate supply curve of the economy?

The Supply Curve of the Firm

In the short run, when productive capacity is held constant, the production function of the firm is given by

$$(7.1) \qquad O = O(N, \overline{K}),$$

where O is output, N is labor input, and K is capital stock. Equation (7.1) restates the short-run condition that output depends upon labor input, with everything else equal; labor is the only variable input. It is also customary to assume that technology is constant and that natural resources and raw materials pose no problems for the firm. Under these conditions output varies directly with labor input.

It is also generally assumed that the law of diminishing returns is operative, and as a consequence, the way in which output varies with labor input is also specified. Recall that the law of diminishing returns states that successive equal increments of a variable factor of production added to fixed factors results in increasing output, but after some point the successive increases in output get smaller and smaller. A graph of equation (7.1) with the assumption of the law of diminishing returns (or the law of variable proportions, as it is sometimes called) is shown in Figure 7.1.

In Figure 7.1(a) the total product (TP) curve for a typical firm is given, showing increasing returns in the early stages of production and then diminishing returns (after point A). Output increases are smaller after point A until output reaches a maximum at point C. Thereafter, increments of labor subtract from total output as the curve bends the other way. The average product of labor (APP) is at a maximum at point B and then declines.

As in other areas of economics, it is the marginal, or extra, unit of labor that is significant. The marginal physical product of labor (MPP) is derived from the TP curve by calculating and plotting the slope at various points on the curve, $\Delta TP / \Delta N$, or more precisely, $d\,TP/d\,N$. The marginal product of labor is seen in Figure 7.1(b) to increase up to point A, where diminishing returns set in, and thereafter to decline to a value of zero (where total product is a maximum) and finally to become negative after point C. The average product of labor (APP) is derived from the TP curve by constructing rays from the origin to points on the TP curve, dropping perpendiculars from these points, and measuring the value of the tangent formed thereby ($TP/ON = APP$). These values, when plotted, yield the APP curve in Figure 7.1(b).[2] The rational range of operation for this firm

---

[2] This brief description is not intended as a comprehensive discussion of all facets of the short-run production function nor of the law of diminishing returns. It is a reminder to those who are already familiar with this area of study. Those to whom this and the following section are unfamiliar would profit by a reading of any number of texts in microeconomics. See Donald S. Watson, *Price Theory and Its Uses*, 3d ed. (Boston: Houghton Mifflin, 1972), part three.

FIGURE 7.1

TYPICAL FIRM'S SHORT-RUN PRODUCTION FUNCTION

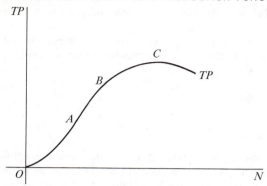

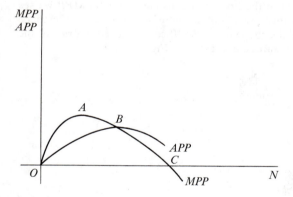

would be at output levels between *B* and *C*. To stop short of *B* would not recognize that the *APP* is still increasing, while to go beyond *C* is clearly irrational, since total product falls and *MPP* becomes negative. Just where the output would be optimal depends, of course, on the price of the factors of production being considered; the production function is a technical relation that cannot answer this question.

Since in the short run only labor is permitted to vary, it is only the price of labor that is of concern to the firm. Presumably, other factor prices are not affected by labor market operations. Labor being the only variable input, wages become the only variable cost, and additions of labor to the production process are the only changes in variable costs—that is, marginal cost (*MC*) is

$$(7.2) \qquad MC = \frac{\Delta TC}{\Delta Q} = \frac{\Delta \text{ Wage bill}}{MPP} = \frac{W}{MPP},$$

where *TC* is total cost, *Q* is quantity of product, and *W* is the money wage rate.

The fact that the change in the wage bill equals the money wage rate, W, implies that the labor market is a perfectly competitive one in which the firm can purchase all the labor it needs at the equilibrium wage rate, W, without affecting that wage rate.

If we further assume that the firm also sells in a perfectly competitive market and that its only goal is to maximize profits, then we can write the profit-maximizing condition as

(7.3)
$$MC = MR = P = \frac{W}{MPP},$$

or

(7.4)
$$W = P(MPP).$$

The left-hand side of (7.4) is the money wage rate (Δ wage bill), and the right-hand side is marginal revenue product (marginal product of the last unit of labor times what that product can be sold for). The firm hires units of labor up to the point where the last unit brings in as much revenue as it costs.

Putting everything together, it is easy to grasp the short-run behavior of a firm operating under conditions of pure competition. From equation (7.2) it is clear that as more units of labor are employed, the MPP falls, because of the law of diminishing returns; with W given to the firms and constant, from W/MPP we see that as the MPP falls, MC must increase as output increases. Therefore, the shape of the MC curve is the inverse of the shape of the MPP curve, since the price of the factor is constant. The marginal cost curve is given in Figure 7.2.[3]

FIGURE 7.2
THE SHORT-RUN MARGINAL COST CURVE

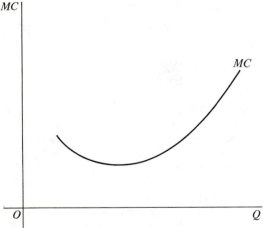

Again the law of diminishing returns is evident in the MC curve as costs fall in the early stages, reach some minimum, and then increase sharply.

[3] The average cost curve, not shown in Figure 7.2, would also be the inverse of the APP curve and would bear the same relationship to the MC curve as it did to the MPP curve.

Going back to equations (7.3) and (7.4), a firm faced with a rising *MC* curve and wishing to maximize profits must receive a higher price as output expands. The willingness of firms to produce more output as price increases transforms the *MC* curve into the firm's supply curve.

If we modify the firm's supply curve in order to bring in the shutdown price —minimum price at which the firm will operate in the short run (*P* = *AVC*, average variable cost)—the individual supply curves can be aggregated into an industry supply curve and by extension into the aggregate supply curve for the economy as a whole. Figure 7.3 sketches the aggregation process, ignoring the fact that the axis of each diagram shows a different *Q*.

Figure 7.3(c) shows the aggregate supply curve as an upward-sloping curve, which exhibits a degree of constancy at either end. In the beginning portion of the curve there is a horizontal portion representing some minimum price level to induce output or, alternatively, constant costs over some range of output. By the latter interpretation, *MPP* does not increase at the outset of production nor does it decrease until the output level has increased by enough to run into inefficiencies.

FIGURE 7.3
AGGREGATION TO THE AGGREGATE SUPPLY CURVE

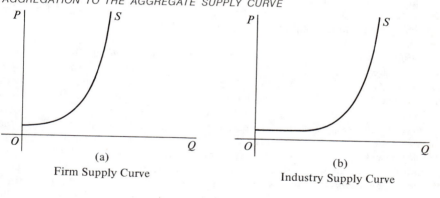

(a)
Firm Supply Curve

(b)
Industry Supply Curve

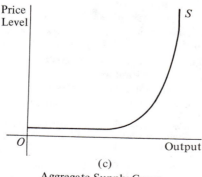

(c)
Aggregate Supply Curve

At the upper end the supply curve becomes vertical, indicating that no additional output is possible, since all resources are fully employed. The general shape of the curve will become clearer as the discussion proceeds.

The upward-sloping aggregate supply curve stands in sharp contrast to the 45-degree supply curve used in the previous models. Recall that the 45-degree curve was drawn with the axes referring to real magnitudes. With the introduction of prices into the analysis, more of the economic decision-making process is brought out, and producers take on a more active role in the determination of the national output. Furthermore, there appear to be limits to the production levels at either end of the range of possible outputs, but particularly at the upper end, where full employment is reached. It is now possible to show how employment is likely to vary with output and not assume, as was done previously, that somehow additional income meant a corresponding addition to employment. Before discussing these relations it would be appropriate to consider the connection between the previous aggregate supply curve and the one discussed in this chapter.

Aggregate Supply and Aggregate Demand Analysis from Different Perspectives

The curious will wonder about the relationship of the income determination model used previously (the so-called Keynesian cross), which employed the 45-degree line aggregate supply curve, and the present aggregate supply curve. Figure 7.4 helps to explain the transition from the former model to the present one, where prices are included explicitly.[4]

In Figure 7.4(a) the graph of the income determination model is the same as before: aggregate demand, D_1, D_2, and so on, intersect aggregate supply, the 45-degree line, and the level of income is determined. The entire analysis was conducted in real terms, which means that each component of aggregate demand was corrected, or deflated, by an appropriate price index. Alternatively, one could view the price level as stable during the period under consideration and transform the analysis into money terms. Money $C + I + G + X - M$, multiplied by current (stable) prices, equals goods and services produced at current (stable) prices; the amount of money spent equals what it is spent on. No one alters his plans because of price fluctuations—the adjustment comes in the form of a change in inventories. The abstraction from prices forces an adjustment to be made somewhere else in the system, and by our assumption producers were the group who came away frustrated whenever a disequilibrium situation existed.

Now consider what happens when prices are brought into the analysis, as in Figure 7.4(b). Of course, the amount supplied now varies with the price level, since producers must be compensated for increasing costs brought about as a result of diminishing returns. But how is the horizontal axis to be interpreted, since output consists of, say, oranges, chairs, and automobiles? What is the meaning of output as an aggregate? Here is an index number problem of great complexity, and once again the aggregation problem appears. About all that can be done is to relate each

---

[4] To illustrate this approach to the aggregate supply curve and subsequent income determination, the analysis follows that of Edward Shapiro, *Macroeconomic Analysis*, 2d ed. (New York: Harcourt, Brace & World, 1970), ch. 17, and Lester V. Chandler, *The Economics of Money and Banking*, 4th ed. (New York: Harper & Row, 1964), ch. 12. These two disparate sources offer some basis for the contention that this type of analysis is generally accepted. In the fifth edition Chandler no longer includes this section.

FIGURE 7.4

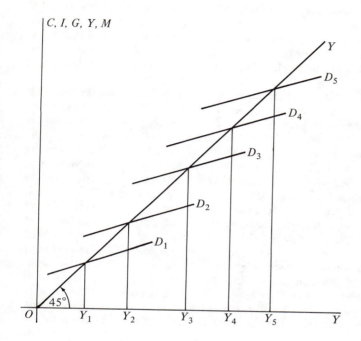

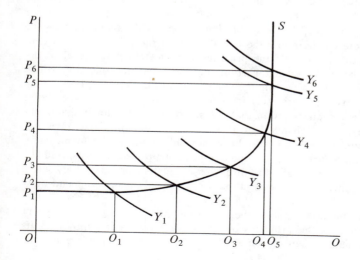

unit of output to some common basis, some *numéraire*. Each unit of output will have to be expressed in terms of the units that could have been purchased for $1 in some base period. Theoretically, it is possible to speak of a dollar's worth of oranges or a dollar's worth of chairs. A dollar's worth of national defense, however, staggers the imagination. The horizontal axis for output must remain a theoretical possibility, but it empirically poses a severe index number problem and an aggregation problem, which we will discuss later in order to qualify the theoretical deductions.

Consider now the aggregate demand curves as represented by the curves labeled Y in Figure 7.4(b). These demand curves show the familiar relationship between output and price such that lower levels of output can be expected to command higher prices and higher levels of output will be associated with lower price levels. Corresponding to D_1, there is Y_1; to D_2, Y_2, and so on. The aggregate demand spending as given by Figure 7.4(a) must now be reinterpreted in part (b) to determine which output and price levels are consistent with the level of spending. For the demand level of D_1, there is an output level of O_1 and a price level of P_1, and so on. As demand increases, prices rise as costs increase, while output increases get smaller (for equal change in aggregate demand). Finally, after Y_5, any increases in aggregate demand simply result in price level increases, because output is fixed by the full employment of resources. Thus, for Y_6, there is only a price level change as sectors of demand bid against each other for the fixed output. This is the condition of excess demand inflation called variously "true" or "pure" inflation. It is clear that the price level varies with the level of aggregate demand and the capacity of the economy. We can explore this further, but first we must take a closer look at what is assumed in the construction of demand curves of the type given by the Ys in Figure 7.4.

In order to move from the demand curves (Ds) of the 45-degree linear diagram to the demand curves (Ys) in part (b) of Figure 7.4, we must find some mechanism that will equate the volume of aggregate demand spending (D) with total spending including prices (Y), since by definition $D_1 = Y_1$ and $D_2 = Y_2$ and so on. The device used is the assumption that along any Y curve the total spending is constant: $\overline{PO}$. If $Y = PO$ for any point on the curve, this is a condition of unitary elasticity that states in words that the same total expenditure will be made for production regardless of the price level of that output. This assumption, while convenient, unfortunately undermines the introduction of the price level as a contributing variable in the analysis. If the price level cannot affect the level of demand, then little is gained by changing from the 45-degree line diagram, which could easily be made to bend, reflecting the law of diminishing returns. If the price level and the output level vary inversely in such a way that the total expenditure remains fixed, there is the presumption that the structure of demand remains unchanged and that price level changes are distributed in a manner that does not disturb the expenditure on individual products, not only along any demand curve but also for shifts in the curves. Again, the aggregation problem returns, and the simple models are unable to handle the problems of relative prices as they affect substitutions or complements. The aggregation problem is always present and must be kept in mind.

The contribution of the new supply curve is to bring into the analysis the concept of capacity utilization and the problems an economy faces as it approaches its capacity limits. The inefficiencies encountered are the result of assuming that the law of diminishing returns is operative and hence costs increase as output increases, "causing" the price level to rise. The price level remains a passive variable so far in this analysis, as the interdependent relations of the system are not explained. Some of these relations can be indicated with a few extensions of this model, but without the introduction of more variables (the entire money market) and more complex functions to help explain the aggregate demand components, the analysis must remain suggestive. Still, to many, the concept of the economic system is shaped by the type of model given here and to some extent by those that follow in this chapter.

Aggregate Supply, Aggregate Demand, and the Level of Employment

The relation between the level of employment and the level of income has not been made clear, nor is it a simple matter. We can explore the relation using the model of this chapter, and with some modifications of the model get some idea of how employment is likely to vary with income and output.

We begin by removing the assumption that the demand curve for output is a rectangular hyperbola, one of unitary elasticity where total expenditure is constant along any one demand curve. Substituted in its place is an aggregate demand curve that is downward-sloping, but little else is assumed in advance, and the elasticity at various points would have to be computed. The graph of the modified aggregate demand curves and the aggregate supply function is given in Figure 7.5(a).

As before, real output is measured on the horizontal axis and the price level on the vertical axis. The intersection of the supply and demand schedules gives the output that will be sold and the price level, or the average price per unit of output. (The index number problem still remains.) The money income of this economy can be calculated as PO and is equal to the area of the rectangle formed by dropping perpendiculars from the points of intersection of aggregate demand and aggregate supply.

In Figure 7.5(b) the employment side of economic activity is presented. The horizontal axis is the same as that used in part (a), so that the relationship between output and employment can be visualized directly. The supply curve of labor, N_s, is assumed to be perfectly elastic—a horizontal line, which means that the supply of labor offers no problems to this economy. All labor is homogeneous and equally productive; therefore, we may speak of units of labor or man-hours of labor interchangeably. These attributes of labor follow from the assumption of a perfectly competitive labor market. The important thing here is that labor of a given type or of equal productivity is available and willing to work.[5]

The demand for labor comes directly from its productivity, as we have already seen. The productivity of labor in the short run depends upon what is assumed

---

[5] Of course, the labor supply must be fixed in relation to some reward also. Keynes held that the supply of labor was a function of the money wage rate and that at the going rate the supply of labor was given to the economy. After full employment, however, the money wage would have to increase to entice additional labor into the market. As we will see, the classical economists reasoned that the supply of labor was a function of the real wage rate, W/P. In the Keynesian case, workers are subject to "money illusion," while in the classical case, workers are highly rational. For the present, we can forego a choice between the two, since we are interested in the availability of a *quantity* of labor with regard to output. As we proceed, however, some qualifying remarks must be made in the discussion of labor market repercussions.

FIGURE 7.5

AGGREGATE DEMAND, AGGREGATE SUPPLY, OUTPUT, AND EMPLOYMENT

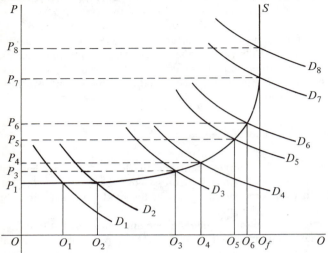

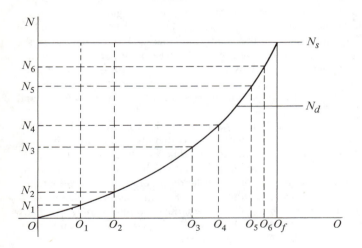

regarding returns to scale; productivity varies with the level of output. In previous chapters we assumed that the firms in the economy were all subject to the law of diminishing returns and that in the aggregate the same condition held. In the beginning stages of production one may assume either increasing or constant returns to scale. For simplicity, the latter is used here. The demand curve for labor, N_d, is shown in Figure 7.5(b) and follows the pattern dictated by the law of diminishing returns. In the beginning of the productive process equal increments of labor yield equal increments of output (constant returns); eventually, however, equal increments of labor input result in smaller and smaller increments of output (diminishing returns). Finally, at O_f, the full employment level of output, no further increments of output are possible, at least given the labor market conditions that prevailed at the outset of the period.

Connecting the two parts of Figure 7.5, it is now possible to understand how income, employment, output, and the price level are related. We want a general impression of the relationships without the qualifications to be introduced later in the discussion. In the early stages of the production process returns to scale were assumed constant. This assumption is now clear from Figure 7.5. As demand increases from D_1 to D_2 in this horizontal range of the aggregate supply curve, output increases from O_1 to O_2, but the price level remains constant at P_1. The explanation for the constant price level can be found in Figure 7.5(b). With constant returns to scale, the change in output from O_1 to O_2 required the same change in labor input, N_1 to N_2, as did all previous additions to output. All labor input is equal in efficiency, and the productivity of labor remains constant ($\overline{MPP}$) in this range. Since labor is the only variable cost, the marginal cost of production, MC, also remains constant. The competitive labor market yields a given, constant money wage, W, which when divided by the constant MPP—$\overline{W}/\overline{MPP}$—results in a constant MC. Firms in this competitive market equate MC and P to maximize profits; if MC is constant, there is no reason for P to change as output expands in this area of output. Note that in this range, where output and employment vary proportionally, there is a large amount of unemployed labor. The amount of unemployment is shown in Figure 7.5(b) as the difference between N_s and N_d at any level of output. It follows from this discussion that regardless of the goals of this economy, whether priority is given to full employment, price stability, economic growth, a more equitable distribution of income, or the maximization of economic freedom, anything that increases aggregate demand is desirable. Assuming these are equilibrium levels of output in the sense that there is no tendency for change in the private sector, the "proper" fiscal policy of government would be a cut in taxes or an increase in expenditures or both. A fiscal policy designed to increase aggregate demand would be successful in increasing output and employment, and any such policy would be likely to meet with a minimum of resistance from the political side or from the general public. These would be popular moves, and cries of encroachment of government and the loss of economic freedom would be muted. In the process the economy would move away from pure capitalism with its assumption of laissez-faire government. Both Adam Smith and Karl Marx would be nonplussed at this Keynesian prescription for a faltering economy. This rather crude fiscal policy, with its resulting beneficial effects, retains a powerful hold on the minds of many, who, even if they are willing to qualify the results, still retain this conception of the economic system.

A schematic presentation of the analysis of output, employment, and the price level is given in Table 7.1, so that the reader may recognize the changes that occur in these relationships as output changes. The table is for quick reference, however, and not a substitute for the deductive reasoning required for complete comprehension.

Now let us assume that a similar increase in aggregate demand occurs when the output is in the intermediate range of the aggregate supply curve. The demand changes from D_3 to D_4 in Figure 7.5. From part (a) it is evident that the change in output is smaller than the previous change and is accompanied by a change in the price level. From part (b) it is clear that diminishing returns have set in and now

it takes more labor input to get out a unit of output; for any constant increment of output, more labor input is required as the level of output expands. The productivity of labor falls in this range of output. As output expands from O_3 to O_4, the MPP falls, and with W constant, the MC of output increases, and the profit-maximizing firms will only supply the additional output at a higher price level. Increases in aggregate demand bring about output increases, but the price level rises also. Employment also rises, but the fall in productivity means that the real wage, W/P, also falls as the price level rises. Thus, the wage bill, N times W, increases and the level of money income increases, but the real gain to those previously employed is diminished by the fall in the productivity of these added units of labor causing a rising price level. If workers are subject to money illusion,[6] as we have assumed, they will continue to offer the same amount of labor for hire. (If they are not subject to money illusion, they realize that they have lost ground and will offer less or bargain for higher wages.) In effect, there is trade-off here; more employment at a fixed wage as against the loss in real income of the employed workers prior to the change. Without unions the response of the labor force to this situation is unclear and, as far as we are concerned, indeterminate. The response of the government with its fiscal policy tools is also indeterminate; much depends upon the extent of the rise in prices and upon value judgments concerning the other economic goals—in this case particularly the distribution of income concerns. Obviously, the goal of full employment is approached by the change in aggregate demand, and some degree of price instability is very likely to be tolerated without any governmental action. In fact, the change in demand could even have been precipitated by the increases in public expenditures. Again, Table 7.1 summarizes these changes.

Assume once more a similar increase in demand, this time in the near capacity range and designated in Figure 7.5 as the movement from D_5 to D_6. Now the output changes $(O_6 - O_5)$ are much smaller than previous ones, while the price level jumps substantially $(P_6 - P_5)$. The productivity of labor really falls in this range, as is clearly shown in part (b); the change in labor input required $(N_6 - N_5)$ to produce the output demanded $(O_6 - O_5)$ is much greater than was the case for previous additions to output. Naturally, MC increases substantially and is reflected in the increase in the price level. All that was true in the intermediate range becomes magnified now: the increase in money income, the fall in real wages and now real income as $\Delta P/P > \Delta O/O$, the declining productivity of labor, and the increase in employment (or the decrease in unemployment). In this first model all these conditions are caused basically by the law of diminishing returns, since the assumption of pure competition everywhere rules out other possible causative factors. Under these conditions a change in demand that occurs when an economy is approaching its limits of productive capacity will increase employment but will also run into strong inflationary pressure emanating from the demand side (supply in this simple model remains passive and independent of demand changes). If these are equilibrium levels of output, the trade-off between the rising price level and the amount of unemployment reappears to plague those who find the situation as depicted to be undesirable. Apparently, a stable price level and the movement toward full employment are incompatible, and some judgments must be made and

---

[6] Money illusion refers to the tendency to regard only changes in money values in making economic decisions; price changes or what money amounts will buy (real changes) are ignored.

priorities set. Policies designed to restrict demand will stabilize prices but increase unemployment, and policies to achieve full employment will force up the price level. Although officially the United States is committed to a policy of full employment through the Full Employment Act of 1946 (in which little attention is given to the price level), it has never vigorously pursued this goal, and price level concerns have limited its unqualified pursuit. Fiscal policy will therefore tend to vacillate in this area, as much subject to political and special interest pressures as to the economic implications. But the issues are too complex to be discussed within the context of this model, and it is better to defer discussion until the model is qualified. Table 7.1 shows the direction of change of the variables under consideration. All of the foregoing movements in the variables continue as the economy approaches its absolute short-run capacity. Eventually, let us assume, the changes in aggregate demand take the economy to its maximum output—the demand curve would be that labeled D_7 with a price level of P_7 at the full employment output of O_f. Any increase in demand, such as D_8, beyond this output will merely result in price level changes. Since output is fixed, any attempt by any group or sector to secure more of the nation's output will be futile and result only in bidding up prices. This is the classic case of excess demand inflation. In Figure 7.5(b), of course, there is full employment and $N_s = N_d$ at O_f. The MPP has also reached its limit and approaches zero. No additional output is possible, and the supply curve becomes a vertical line, indicating that the elasticity of supply with respect to the price level is zero. All changes beyond O_f are simply price changes, and while money income can expand, real income cannot; prices and money income vary proportionally ($Y_m = \overline{O}P$).

For the economy under examination, increases in demand beyond D_7 would clearly be undesirable. Some effort would have to be made to curb the pressures of excess demand. If the private sector were unwilling to give up any portion of its control over the nation's output, the public sector would have to surrender some of its share or force sectors of the private economy to surrender theirs. Thus, decreases in public spending or increases in taxes or both would serve to reduce demand pressures. Once more, as in the initial output stages, fiscal policy becomes clear, at least in the general sense. Furthermore, the fiscal policy measures would be popular and not likely to be seriously contested. Table 7.1 summarizes the situation at full capacity.

The model used here is rigid and simple, allowing only select changes to occur; other changes are excluded because of the assumptions made about the structure of the economy. The exclusion of some types of response and the omission of the interdependent relations that exist among the variables can only be justified as necessary for an initial approach to the problem. It is time to relax some of these rigid constraints.

The Interdependence of Supply and Demand: Both Schedules Shift

Aggregate demand and aggregate supply are not independent of each other, and hence changes in demand affect the supply of output. Changes in supply brought about by changes in demand were ignored in the previous model but must be recognized to make the analysis more realistic. In the course of the discussion some of the interdependent relations will become explicit, while others can only be suggested.

We begin the analysis by removing the assumption that the money wage rate is fixed, and we now assume that the labor market determines the going money wage as it responds to the current market conditions. The money wage rate becomes endogenous—determined by the current operations of the system. Both supply and demand for labor may fluctuate in response to current conditions, even in the short run.

We retain the assumptions that there is perfect competition in all markets; that diminishing returns are faced by each firm and by implication by the economy as a whole through the aggregate production function; that firms maximize profits; that both prices and wages are flexible upward and downward; and in general all those assumptions regularly made when dealing with short-run behavior.

With these alterations in the model, we must reconsider the deductions made using the simpler model. In order to present these adjustments clearly, we use the same analysis of changes and format as before. Figure 7.6, starting from Figure 7.5, incorporates the new revisions to be made in the model. The supply curve of labor, N_s, does require some additional interpretation. In previous analysis the money wage rate, W, was fixed, as if determined in some previous period. Now the money wage rate is free to vary according to labor market conditions. The horizontal supply curve for labor must mean, then, that whatever the money wage rate is, the supply of labor poses no problem to our analysis. It is perfectly elastic at *the going money wage rate,* not at some fixed money wage rate. The supply of labor adjusts to the prevailing money wage rate, but at all output levels there is never a shortage of labor.

Increases in demand that occur at low levels of output, intersecting the aggregate supply curve in the horizontal range, are not likely to alter the deductions or conclusions of the previous model. Recall the conditions that prevail over this range of output: the economy is operating under conditions of constant returns, and the *MPP* and *MC* are constant; the price level of output, matching *MC*, is also constant; in the labor market there is widespread unemployment, and real and money incomes are quite low. It would appear once again that changes in demand would increase employment and output without putting any pressure on wages and prices. There is too much unemployment for any pressure in the labor market, and in the absence of any change in wages, there is no pressure on prices ($\overline{MC}$ and $\overline{MPP}$). Of course, with perfect competition, there is no arbitrary price or wage increase with increases in demand. In short, there is no reason to alter the analysis that ignored the possible interdependent relations. The conclusions with regard to governmental policies also hold, and policies designed to increase demand would be equally effective and welcomed in this range of output. Changes in aggregate demand that occur in this range are not included in Figure 7.6 so as to avoid a cluttered diagram; refer to Figure 7.5 for this section.

Changes in demand that occur in the vertical section of the aggregate supply curve also do not seriously affect the conclusions of the previous model. Once again, output cannot be increased; therefore, any increase in demand results merely in price level changes and, *in this case, wage increases* as well. As aggregate demand increases, price levels rise as consumers bid for the limited supply. As prices rise, so do the money profits of firms, who now take steps to increase profits still more by expanding output. But all labor is employed ($MPP = 0$, of course), and any attempt to increase output by firms will merely result in bidding up money wages as firms attempt to lure workers away from where they are currently employed.

Also, if it is true that prices rise first, then real wages fall initially, and labor clamors for more, and with full employment and firms increasing their demands for labor, there is little resistance anywhere against the upward spiral of wages and prices. This is demand pull inflation (or excess demand, true, or pure inflation), which calls for a reduction in demand to halt the whole process. In general, the same conclusions hold as in the previous analysis and as summarized in Table 7.1. Note, however, that wages are no longer constant at some fixed money wage rate but follow along with the increase in prices. Thus, real wages may decline at first but eventually rise again, the money wage rate increasing as firms bid it up. Thus, admitting a possible lag, eventually wages catch up to profits, and in real terms neither profit takers nor wage earners are hurt by demand pull inflation. There are

FIGURE 7.6
INTERDEPENDENCE OF AGGREGATE DEMAND AND AGGREGATE SUPPLY

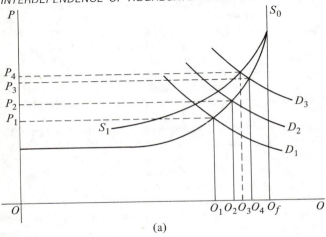

(a)

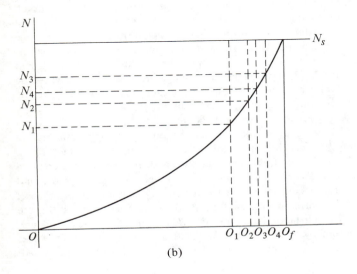

(b)

some groups, however, whose wages are "sticky" and tend to lag behind the general level: teachers, government employees, and some service workers. These groups are hurt to some extent, depending upon the lag involved. The real redistribution of incomes comes at the expense of fixed income groups and creditors. Fixed income groups, from bond coupon clippers to old-age pensioners, find their real income reduced as the price level rises and there is no way to "catch up." Creditors also find they are repaid with dollars of reduced purchasing power, and the sum they lent out will no longer command the same volume of goods and services. These groups are "taxed" in this indirect manner, and everyone is taxed more as they move into higher income tax brackets. The built-in stabilizer siphons off some of the increase in money income automatically. Further tax increases or reductions in public spending would also be acceptable fiscal policies under these conditions. This sketch of the inflationary process caused by excess demand is incomplete, since the money supply as a variable has not been included. Presumably, the monetary authorities play a passive role and go along with the process by supplying sufficient money to appear neutral. This one-sided view of demand pull inflation, still held by many, will have to be corrected and modified in later discussions.

The departure from previous work comes in the intermediate range of output from the level where there are no longer constant returns to scale up to the output levels immediately preceding capacity output. The aggregate supply curve, shown in Figure 7.6(a), bends in this region, indicating that output increases are accompanied by price level increases as well. This much is evident from the shape of the curve. What is not so evident is the fact that the supply curve could shift as demand increases, and instead of moving along a stationary supply curve, a new supply curve becomes appropriate.

Assume that aggregate demand shifts from D_2 to D_3 in Figure 7.6(a). With a stationary supply curve, the output would have increased from O_2 to O_3 and the price level would have risen from P_2 to P_3. These movements, however, ignore the interdependence of supply and demand and are likely to be checked by the interaction. As the schedules interact, the dynamic nature of the process by which the variables react becomes even more pronounced than in previous discussions. In the present model we are limited to comparative statics, but we can still indicate the essence of this complex interaction.

As aggregate demand increases, the first pressure is likely to be on prices; the closer to capacity, the greater the pressure. Firms benefit from this demand inflation as money profits increase. It is rational for firms to expect the price level to stabilize or even increase further, and hence they have the incentive to expand output. As they hire more labor to produce more output, they must incur rising marginal costs, for in this range of output the productivity of labor falls rapidly $(MPP \downarrow)$. Firms are willing to hire more labor, however, since each additional unit of labor also brings in more revenue as prices rise. But the increase in the demand for labor also brings with it an increase in the money wage rate as firms bid up the price of labor. As the wage rate increases, it is likely that the prices of other factors will rise also, since in the short run capital cannot be substituted for labor, and the price of existing capital is likely to reflect some recognition of this constraint.

If the price of all inputs rises, each level of output will only be produced at a higher price level, or else profits will not be maximized. Thus, the supply curve shifts upward and to the left, as given by the aggregate supply curve S_1 in Figure

7.6(a). The intersection of this supply curve, S_1, with the aggregate demand curve, D_3, reveals that output did not expand from O_2 to O_3 but only from O_2 to O_4 and the price level rose from P_2 to P_4. Not only do diminishing returns affect costs and hence prices but now the prices of the factors themselves increase, pulling up prices still further.

Here then, even with some rigid assumptions, is the major problem of many developed economies in recent years: how to achieve full employment and price stability simultaneously. The nearer the goal of full employment, the more elusive the goal of price stability, and vice versa. Furthermore, if this model is realistic at all, the inflation is likely to lead to bitter arguments over who was to blame. If the lag between rising prices and rising wages is not too long, then each side, business and labor, will accuse the other of "causing" inflation. Actually, the "cause" of inflation is difficult to locate in this system, but surely the pressure comes from the demand side, and as the system reacts, both prices and wages are pulled up as individual economic units acted rationally in the face of the situation confronting them. Yet labor may point to the high money profits, and firms will point to rising wages that increase costs of production, and so on. In the end certain groups are more vulnerable to inflation, and these are the ones who suffer, whatever the ultimate cause of the disturbance. Under these circumstances, it is unlikely that any spontaneous relief from these demand pressures and the subsequent controversy will come from the private sector.

Yet the "proper" government reaction is far from clear. A policy to reduce aggregate demand appears warranted, but will the economic system react by increasing output and reducing prices? Even with pure competition and the assumption of perfectly flexible wages and prices, the hoped-for conclusion probably would not follow. Reductions in aggregate demand may put some downward pressure on prices and therefore on the rate of money wages which firms will pay. If other input prices fall also, the aggregate supply curve may return to the original one, S_0. The real question is whether or not the level of aggregate demand will stay at D_3. If the wage bill, $W \times N$, is falling, so will the level of aggregate demand, and the unsold output at O_3 will soon command lower prices. In reality, the level of demand may fall back to the original level of D_2, which means output falls back to O_2 and employment falls back to N_2. Employment, which without interdependent relations would have risen to N_3, and with these relations to N_4, is now back at the original level. The period of deflation with W and P falling brings us back to where we started.[7] The government dilemma is obvious: to reduce demand brings price reductions but at the expense of employment; to do nothing encourages the inflationary process unless the increases in aggregate demand were only temporary. Still, in a period of rising prices the expectations of the continuation of this trend are likely to spur additional purchasing now before prices rise still further, and thus a reversal of demand pressures is not likely.

To quarrel over the proper government policy in these circumstances would not be very profitable, because the choice between unemployment and price stability is made even more complex once the assumption of perfect competition is removed. It is not necessary to rule out perfect competition entirely, since some sections of

---

[7] This discussion is a variant of the controversy between Keynes and the neoclassical school, in which the exchange focused on whether or not a reduction in the money wage would lead an economy to full employment from an underemployment "equilibrium." A more complete explanation of the arguments on both sides is postponed until after the classical model has been developed.

the economy still approximate the model. Yet, in an economy dominated by oligopolistic firms, administered pricing, and labor unions with a host of possible actions or motivations, the assumption of flexible wages and prices appears naive at best. It is unlikely, for instance, that the supply curve will fall back to S_0 as wages and prices of inputs fall. If demand should be reduced, it is much more likely that firms will attempt to retain their prices, and labor its wages, and therefore the adjustment is likely to be felt by reduced employment and output (the situation in Figure 7.6 where S_1 and D_2 intersect). Prices and wages have become "sticky" and inflexible in a downward direction as power has become institutionalized in a variety of ways.

In fact, the supply curve could have shifted upward as a result of the exercise of this power, even in the absence of pressure from the demand side. Unions pressing for wages beyond productivity considerations or firms setting prices without too much regard for demand could push up prices and the supply curve. This is called cost push inflation because the impetus comes from the cost side. The elimination of market power is not so easily attained by government policy.

Whatever the cause of inflation, prices are likely to be "sticky" downward. Prices and wages rise but seldom fall, and inflation becomes difficult to control. Efforts to control inflation from the demand side may succeed only in reducing output and employment; efforts to achieve full employment may result mainly in increasing prices and wages. The dilemma remains and gets worse. The questions and problems presented in this section will be treated at greater length in following chapters.

Shifts in the Supply Schedule

The impetus for change in an economy can also come about from changes on the supply side. Shifts in the supply curve can also cause some repercussions on the demand side. Unlike demand, however, most of the changes on the supply side can be traced to long-run influences and therefore are beyond our short-run concerns. Again, the emphasis on demand is seen here. Nevertheless, some indications of what these changes are and how they are likely to affect the analysis can be discussed here in an introductory manner. Recall that the aggregate supply curve was derived from the aggregate production function, which made some assumptions about the nature of production and business motivation: that is, aggregate supply is a function of labor, capital, natural resources, and technology, and in the short run everything is held constant except labor input. In addition, the law of diminishing returns was assumed and the firms were assumed to maximize profits. The economy also operated within a known and unvarying social and political milieu. These are basically long-run variables and were held constant to focus on the short run. To change the aggregate supply curve, therefore, one must remove one or more of these constants and observe what happens. As a long-run variable is permitted to change, there will be repercussions on the short-run variables as well as on other long-run variables. It will be possible to deal with only a few of these interactions here.

The supply curve that shifts upward and to the left was encountered earlier and was blamed on the exercise of market power. Either wage increases were granted beyond what productivity warranted, or firms sought to increase profits by charging prices beyond what costs of production warranted. Either or both of these conditions would push the supply curve upward, which means that every level of output will only be produced at a higher price level. This is cost push inflation, which can only occur if imperfect competition is widespread and the market power goes unchecked.

If the aggregate demand schedule remains unchanged, the result is a higher price level and lower output (see D_2, for instance, in Figure 7.6, as S_0 is pushed up to S_1). Employment falls as well as output, so some outcry is likely to be made. Once again, attempts to change the economic picture run into difficulties. Any government policy runs a risk of nonacceptance and may even be blamed for the situation it is attempting to combat. Thus, decreases in demand bring some pressure on the price level but they further reduce output and employment (see D_1 in Figure 7.6); increases in demand to relieve the unemployment problem will successfully increase output and increase the price level as well. Thus encouraged, employees or unions may seek another round of the same, receiving temporary benefits until others catch up, and the whole process continues.

So far, we are within the boundaries of the short run, since the push can occur in the short run. Other short-run policies might be taken—wage and price controls and some monetary measures.[8] Over a longer period other attempts to break up the market power could be undertaken: antitrust action, union control, or compulsory collective bargaining, and so on. Over a still longer period, firms could begin the substitution of capital for labor and seek to make labor more productive. Firms might export capital and produce abroad, where labor is less expensive. Labor unions might press for cost-of-living clauses in labor contracts, for guaranteed incomes, for enlarged fringe benefits, and for protection from foreign sources. Even the supply of labor could be affected over long periods of cost push inflation. All groups will search for the way out of the impasse, and all are likely to seek an answer in technological change—the panacea of the twentieth century. Technological change could moderate the inflationary pressures by permitting more output with the same input (or the same output with less input), and the increase in the productivity of inputs could forestall the rising costs of production.

Once technological change is introduced, there are many paths an economy can follow; much depends upon the nature of the technical change. Technology can be of various types: labor-saving, capital-using; labor-using, capital-saving; labor-saving, capital-saving. Little can be said a priori about which type will be predominant, but it is obvious that the link between output and employment is no longer as certain in the long run. We can only suggest a few cases.

Suppose the technological change was such as to preserve the existing labor-capital ratio used in production but in such a way that the average product of labor was increased. In the short run this would mean that the production function shifted upward and parallel, so that for every unit of labor input, there would be more output. The supply curve in this case would shift to the right, as shown in Figure 7.7.

The economy can now produce more, as shown by S_1, and firms would be willing to supply more at the same price level. The supply curve would also shift in this manner for an increase in the supply of labor or an increase in the capital stock (both inputs with the same productivity as previously existed). The produc-

---

[8] The economy might also suffer from adverse foreign trade developments, as inflation reduces exports and increases imports.

FIGURE 7.7
SUPPLY CURVE SHIFTS PARALLEL TO THE RIGHT

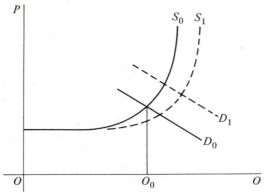

tive capacity of the economy has increased, but what happens on the demand side? If aggregate demand remains fixed, the price level will fall as the additional output is supplied. But the productive capacity will not be utilized; there will be unemployment of labor, capital, or both. Aggregate demand must grow also (see D_1) if the additional capacity is to be utilized. If we assume that money wages are inflexible downward (and therefore costs of production do not fall), a falling price level is not very encouraging to producers. If prices also are inflexible downward, then more of the capacity will go unused as demand changes little or not at all. A policy of increasing demand to match the growth on the supply side would appear to be necessary if the growth made possible by technological change is to be beneficial.

If the technological change affects the marginal product of labor (the production function shifts upward in a nonparallel way), and if as the productivity of labor is increased, the costs of production fall, the supply curve shifts to the right and downward. Figure 7.8 shows the new supply curve S_1, which indicates that

FIGURE 7.8
SUPPLY CURVE SHIFTS AS THE MARGINAL PRODUCTIVITY CHANGES

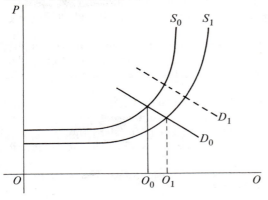

each level of output will be supplied at a lower price level, or more will be supplied at the old price level.

Of course, a change in the quality of labor or changes in the productivity of capital might also shift the curve in this manner. If money wages are inflexible downward, they are not inflexible upward, and increases in labor productivity will probably be followed by the demand for higher money wages. If granted, production costs do not fall, prices do not fall, and the additional output will not be supplied. The potential output will be higher than the actual output, and there will be unemployed labor and capital. If, however, aggregate demand increases, more of the capacity can be utilized as output and employment increase.[9]

The analysis could go on and on, but enough has been said of the problems of growth and the long-run issues. We shall return to some of these problems later. The interaction of the long run and the short run poses some peculiar problems. The short-run goals of full employment and price stability take on added complexity when they are put into the context of growth. Both goals appear more difficult to achieve as the balance of the growth of demand with the growth of supply also becomes a goal of the long-run economy. It is also more difficult to connect all this with the employment variable. Just how employment varies with the interaction of the long run and the short run, along with the changes in technology, is not clear. This is particularly true with labor-saving technological changes. For these reasons, even the concept of full employment needs some refinement. *Technological unemployment* becomes a nightmare to the labor union leader, and many have responded with job-protecting clauses or featherbedding provisions in labor contracts. Still, a man employed doing nothing (or underemployed) is an economic waste of a resource. What is the meaning of full employment if there are many in this category?

Is full employment possible in a dynamic economy? Presumably, as industries expand and contract there should also be an expansion or contraction in the demand for labor. Will the skills required by the expanding industries be those no longer needed by the contracting ones? They may not be at all related, in which case we have *structural unemployment*. In the foregoing models there was some direct relation between output and employment. Now this relation must be re-examined if increases in demand occur in industries using highly specialized labor. Changes or shifts in demand may lead to little or no change in employment or perhaps even to an increase in unemployment. Here is the aggregation problem again—what is the source of the demand, for which products, for which skills, and so on? Suppose the demand increased for output that is produced with little or no labor?

Again, the changes in demand may open up jobs in one area of the country, but unemployment may be located in quite other areas. A purely competitive labor market assumes that labor is mobile, but in reality there are many barriers to mobility, some noneconomic.

Increases in demand could also occur when firms are operating close to capacity or under conditions where labor and capital are used in fixed proportions, and therefore there is little opportunity to hire more labor in the short run.

Finally, there is so-called *frictional unemployment,* where men are voluntarily

---

[9] Each case presents a wide choice of possible actions and reactions. To pursue them all here is not feasible. It seems best to leave the analysis in this suggestive stage.

out of work seeking better or different positions. As a society becomes more affluent, more of this type of unemployment can be expected, since saving would tend to be higher. Whatever makes a man discontented with his job—lack of money, prestige, or power—makes for frictional unemployment. Since society places a value on these factors, frictional unemployment will vary. Generally, it is stable enough to permit some forecasting, but no one knows surely what proportion of the unemployment rate is frictional unemployment.

Thus, full employment may no longer be possible in the short run, and increases in aggregate demand cannot be regarded simplistically as the cure-all for unemployment. For Keynes, viewing massive unemployment, such concerns were irrelevant. But as an economy approaches full employment, as it grows in an era when technological change is rapid and sought after as a goal itself, it is no longer sufficient to advocate increases in aggregate demand to insure full employment. As shown even in our simple models, the goal of full employment is no longer compatible with the goal of price stability.

The definition of full employment, then, becomes an arbitrary matter and like all complex definitions satisfies no one. The Council of Economic Advisors in 1962 determined that employment of 96 per cent of the labor force constitutes full employment. Many others felt that a 4 per cent unemployment rate was too high and too complacent considering that other economies were operating at between 1 and 2 per cent rates. Also, definitions of who constitutes the labor force are open to controversy.[10] Full employment is an elusive concept—difficult to define and difficult to achieve.

Conclusions and Qualifications

This has been an important chapter, presenting some of the problems of an advanced economy: the relations among output, employment, income, and prices; the seeming incompatibility of the goals of full employment and price stability; the tendency toward an institutionalized inflationary bias; the problems of growth; and so on. The purpose has been to convey the essence of these problems. To many, the economic system works roughly as developed in these models. For these people, the analysis could end here. It would be possible to work within the framework of the economy provided by the models developed here.

This does not imply that the simple models are complete or precise. There are many additions and refinements that could be made. Still, they are fundamentally correct. The models are good analogies; they represent good theories. The analysis so far has avoided as many value judgments as possible and appears to be as objective as can be expected. There were many instances when further elaboration had to be postponed until more knowledge was acquired. Sometimes the simple models do not permit extensive discussion of problems and policies. Nevertheless, the essence of system remains.

The question naturally arises, How accurate is this vision of the economic system, and to what extent have we created the world we wish to study? Does our conception of the economic system lead us to make the assumptions that predetermine the conclusions? What are the consequences of our possibly faulty perception?

In the chapters that follow these questions must be answered insofar as possible.

[10] For a short nontechnical discussion of definitions and concepts, see Department of Labor, Bureau of Labor Statistics, *How the Government Measures Unemployment*. Report No. 312 (1967).

Some of the assumptions can be removed and the conclusions reexamined. In effect, we must create new models or modify the old ones according to the results of the inquiry.

First, however, we must elaborate on the simple models developed to this point. This should provide us with further insights into the working of the economic system and our view of how it operates. The models should become more realistic in the sense that some of the simple functional relations are amended to account for more influences and more appropriate assumptions regarding human behavior.

The following chapters develop the consumption and investment functions; introduce money and interest explicitly into the models; complete the Keynesian model and compare his system with the classical model; and discuss the problems, policies, issues, and other matters pertinent to the two descriptions of the economy. After discussing the Keynesian system, we shall return to the questions raised in this section and evaluate the theory. Some attempt will be made to develop new models or modify the old ones. Finally, the long-run theories of the problems of growth will be examined and evaluated.

The Consumption Function Elaborated

The linear consumption function used in the simple models, $C = C_a + cY$, where consumption depended upon the level of disposable income, was a very useful starting point in the study of this variable. The singling out of disposable income as the major determinant of the amount of consumption was certainly reasonable and made it possible to determine the equilibrium level of income easily. Still, the function is too simple and conceals the richness of this variable; it ignores the many facets of human behavior in the marketplace. Surely, other variables, influences, motivations, drives, must also help determine the amount of consumption expenditures, and it is to the enumeration and explanation of these that we now turn. In addition to augmenting the consumption function, we can ask how it is likely to be affected over time. But in the end we will still not be able to identify completely the variables that govern the consumption function, for consumption is one of the more tantalizing economic variables which invites continual reexamination. Before including new variables in the consumption function, however, it is necessary to review its principal determinant, income.

The Concept of Income

DISPOSABLE INCOME

There is little doubt that income plays a significant role in determining the volume of consumption expenditures. Yet like so many other economic variables, income must be defined more precisely before it can become operationally useful. As soon as one begins to examine the concept of income, what originally appeared to be a simple problem of definition soon becomes a disconcerting tangle of conflicting concepts. In this section we will discuss some of these concepts of income and indicate their effects upon the consumption function.

The concept of *disposable income* is relatively straightforward and was used in our simple models. Even here, however, it is necessary to elaborate: Is it *current* disposable income that influences consumption, or does it take time for consumers to adjust to changing income levels? Are there lags in the adjustment of consumption to income? Perhaps it would be better to write the consumption function in this manner:

$$(8.1) \qquad C_t = C_a + c_1 Y_t + c_2 Y_{t-1} + c_3 Y_{t-2} + \cdots,$$

which shows that current consumption, C_t, depends upon several different income levels. The strength of the relation is given by the value of the c's, which are the *MPC*s out of the different income levels. More than likely, the c's are all different in this formulation and probably would decline in value the farther they are from the current period.[1] Equation (8.1) recognizes that consumers adjust their spending decisions over time as they become accustomed to the new income levels. For those whose incomes fluctuate widely, the notion of an adjustment period is tenable. For those whose incomes are stable or change very slowly, the passage of time and an adjustment period are irrelevant. Naturally, much depends upon how the income period is defined. It makes a significant difference whether Y is income per month, income per quarter, or income per year. If we accept Y as income per year and the ΔY as a lump sum change as of a certain date, there may well be some adjustment period. Smaller and less dramatic increases at several intervals are less likely to require an adjustment period.

Moving to the economy as a whole, and aggregate Y and C, it may well be the case that there will be a lag in the response of a community to changes in income. But for a large portion of that community, the lag is likely to be small or non-existent. In general, those who tend to spend a large portion of their incomes on consumption will adjust rapidly to changing income levels. Empirically a lag is likely to occur, but theoretically it does not appear to be overly important, and the use of current disposable income as the main determinant of current consumption is not unrealistic or unwarranted, at least for simple models.[2]

The concept of disposable income is sometimes criticized as being an incorrectly chosen measure of the effect of income on consumption, since consumers do not base decisions on it but on income over which they have control. Thus, disposable income must be reduced by the amount of contractual payments—rent, car payments, and other fixed items in the household budget—and then the remainder can be used to measure the influence on consumption. This concept of income, called *discretionary income,* may be useful in some situations or for some purposes, but it does not appear to affect the theoretical case for using disposable income. Contractual payments are still consumption items and can be adjusted over time. It is better not to distinguish among consumer goods according to the method of payment but to continue to use the wider income concept.

ABSOLUTE VERSUS RELATIVE INCOME

In the previous models it was only the number of dollars of income that was important; the quantity of dollars determined the amount of consumption, both for the household and for the economy. All that mattered was the *absolute level of income.* The use of absolute income in the consumption function comes primarily

---

[1] In econometrics such a function is called a distributed lag. This very interesting device can be used with a number of variables. See L. M. Koyck, *Distributed Lags and Investment Analysis* (Amsterdam: North-Holland Publishing Co., 1954).

[2] For a comprehensive discussion of both the theory and empirical results of household behavior, see Robert Ferber, "Research on Household Behavior," *American Economic Review* 52 (March 1962): 19–63. The bibliography of this survey article is quite extensive.

from the theory of household demand. In microeconomic theory the individual consumer (or family) is rational, motivated by a desire to maximize utility given limited means for doing so. As the consumer enters the marketplace, he possesses full knowledge of all phases of that market, has fully developed tastes, acts independently of any other consumer unit, and is prepared to alter his consumption patterns by marginal shifts according to the conditions he faces. With this behavior in mind, it is not surprising that a similar process was postulated for consumers as a whole. The transition from individual units to consumption as a sector of demand was made easily, and along with it went all the assumptions made at the microeconomic level.

If the assumptions made for an individual consumer are changed, the aggregate consumption function will also be changed. Suppose instead of the usual assumptions about how a consumer makes choices among goods, we assume that consumers buy goods and services largely out of habit. Each consumer becomes accustomed to a certain collection of goods and services that gives him sufficient satisfaction so that he feels no compelling urge to change his habits. Further suppose that the habits of consumption are formed largely on the basis of the highest level of income attained by consumers (provided that the highest level was not the result of a sudden spurt).

Another assumption made (often tacitly) about individual household behavior is the independence of tastes and wants.[3] Each consumer determines his own consumption choices independently of anyone else's choices. Such a view of autonomous behavior does not conform very well with the observations of human behavior made by sociologists and psychologists. There is ample evidence that many of our wants are culturally determined and that tastes and wants are interdependent among consumers. Generally, consumers tend to emulate the consumption patterns of others, and more particularly, they are apt to emulate those in a higher social or economic class. If we accept these assumptions, a household forms its consumption pattern on the basis of its peak income and its position in the array of income distribution.

At any given time the higher income groups consume a smaller proportion of their incomes than do the lower income groups; the higher the percentile in the income distribution, the larger the proportion of income saved. Over time, as incomes of households increase while the distribution remains stable, the ratio of aggregate consumption to aggregate income will be constant. As long as households remain in the same percentiles, they will continue to consume and save the same proportions out of their growing absolute incomes. This is the *relative income hypothesis,* in which consumption depends upon the position of the household in the income scale and which recognizes the interdependence of consumption patterns among consumer units.

The relative income hypothesis can be expressed as

(8.2)
$$\frac{C}{Y} = a + b\left(\frac{Y}{Y_0}\right),$$

where Y_0 is peak income. Equation (8.2) shows that the *APC*, C/Y, will be higher during recession (when $Y_0 > Y$) than during expansions (when $Y > Y_0$). This result will be shown to be important shortly.

---

[3] The assumption of independent consumption patterns facilitates the aggregation of household behavior. When wants become interdependent, the aggregation problem is made extremely complex.

In the long run, as the level of income grows, each new Y becomes a peak and thus $Y_0 = Y_{t-1}$. In equation (8.2) the term Y/Y_0 becomes some constant value that includes the growth rate of income $1 + g$, and the whole expression for the APC is reduced to a constant value. The relative income hypothesis gives the long-run consumption function the following properties:

(8.3) $$C = cY.$$

The consumption function goes through the origin—there is no y intercept.

(8.4) $$\frac{C}{Y} = c.$$

$APC = MPC$, and both are constant ($\overline{APC} = \overline{MPC}$). Of course, $\overline{APS} = \overline{MPS}$.

The relative income hypothesis was introduced by J. S. Duesenberry in order to explain the conflicting empirical evidence following tests of the consumption function.[4] Early attempts to test the theory all appeared to yield results favorable to the consumption function as given by Keynes (the absolute income form). The initial tests of the consumption function were conducted using budget studies that gave cross-section family data. Plotting family income data by income class and the average consumption expenditures of families in that class invariably led to the verification of the Keynesian-type consumption function.[5] Unfortunately, as in all

[4] J. S. Duesenberry, *Income, Saving, and the Theory of Consumer Behavior* (Cambridge, Mass.: Harvard University Press, 1949). A very similar relation between C and Y was given by F. Modigliani, "Fluctuations in the Saving-Income Ratio: A Problem in Economic Forecasting," in *Studies in Income and Wealth* (New York: National Bureau of Economic Research, 1949), Vol. II. The relative income hypothesis bears a surface similarity to Veblen's notion of conspicuous consumption. However, for Veblen, the emulation process of consumers and the status-seeking consumption expenditures are wasteful of resources and represent irrational behavior. None of this is implied in the relative income hypothesis.

[5] A typical cross-section budget study would yield a diagram such as the following:

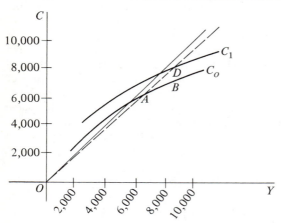

Obviously, the picture fits the description of the Keynesian consumption function: APC falls as Y rises (and MPC also falls, as Keynes suggested). With the schedule C_0, families that had an income of $6,000 would move from point A to B, with a $2,000 increase in income, assuming other families had a proportional change in income. They would consume little of the additional income. But if the relative income prevailed, the C schedule shifts to C_1, and these families continue to spend the same proportion of their incomes—the APC is constant, as shown by the ray from the origin (connecting A and D), along which the APC is constant. The families move from A to D on C_1. Other families would make a similar adjustment to C, and therefore the APC is unaffected by the change in incomes.

cross-section studies, the data were for a given point in time, and the results could not be extended to cover future time periods unless one were willing to make some assumptions. The results of cross-section studies are valid only for the period covered by the data; thus, cross-section data cannot deal with changes and are of little help in testing the MPC concept, which is based on changes; they cannot be used for the APC either, unless another assumption is made—that as income changes and consumers move into higher income classes, they will consume the same proportion of their new incomes as did the previous family that had that income. In short, they move along the consumption curve. This is exactly where the relative income hypothesis differs from the absolute income concept. According to the latter, as incomes increase, APC falls and APS rises; according to the relative income hypothesis, as incomes increase and the distribution is undisturbed, the APC remains constant, since consumers find new, superior goods to consume as they come into contact with different consumption patterns. The entire consumption function shifts upward to preserve APC constant. Budget studies cannot deal with such questions and are severely limited as a source of data with which to test the consumption function.

The empiricists soon turned to time series data, and using regression techniques, began getting results that are more appropriate for testing the validity of the consumption function. Time series data relate C and Y period by period, and from these data some measure of how these variables vary over time, how C changes as Y changes, can be observed directly. Again, there was general confirmation of the consumption hypothesis that C and Y do vary directly.

However, a new controversy developed when the results of using different time periods were compared. Over long periods of time the consumption function appeared to be proportional, that is, to go through the origin, where the $APC = MPC$ and both are constant.[6] In shorter time periods the data indicated a break in the relation, which can be accounted for if the consumption function had shifted upward over time. In these shorter period schedules there would be a y intercept, meaning a nonproportional consumption function of the type we have been using and where $APC \neq MPC$ and the APC falls as income increases. Obtaining different consumption functions for different time periods offers no comfort to the empiricists bent on upholding or refuting theoretical hypotheses. To explain the apparent contradiction in the form of the consumption function, some economists sought to find variables that might help to explain the upward shifting of the consumption function, while others sought an explanation in the redefinition of the concept of income used in the theory. Figure 8.1 shows the conflicting evidence that prompted the controversy.

The long-run consumption function, C_{LR}, goes through the origin and shows the expected relationship with income. The data on which it is constructed are annual averages of decade data, going all the way back to the last third of the nineteenth century. By using averages of annual consumption, one average for each decade, the short-run aberrations are canceled, and the smoothed data are felt to reflect the underlying relationship between C and Y.

Taking annual data on both C and Y also gives a relation that conforms to the general consumption function as used in our work. However, it was noticed that a better description of the data could be had by breaking up this long period (from

[6] The long-run consumption function was studied by Simon Kuznets, *Uses of National Income in Peace and War* (New York: National Bureau of Economic Research, 1942). See also his work *National Income: A Summary of Findings* (Princeton, N. J.: Princeton University Press, 1946), p. 53.

FIGURE 8.1
THE CONSUMPTION FUNCTION: LONG RUN VERSUS SHORT RUN

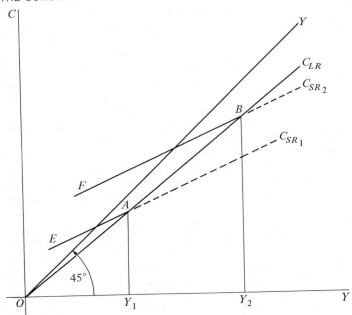

1929 to the 1960s) into two shorter periods. The scatter diagram that results from plotting annual data appeared to show two general cluster areas: one for the pre-World War II years and one for the postwar years. Thus, two consumption functions gave a better fit than did one schedule. The result is shown in Figure 8.1 in the two short-run consumption functions, C_{SR_1} and C_{SR_2}. The former is for the prewar years and the latter for the postwar years.[7] It appears as though the consumption function has shifted upward over time.

To reconcile this conflicting evidence, it is necessary to examine variables other than income that might have been responsible for shifting the consumption function upwards in the manner indicated. If these data do support this shift, then it can be argued that the long-run function fit to decade averages is misleading and that only by accident does it appear to be proportional and go through the origin. If, however, it is believed that the long-run function is basically correct, then it is necessary to show that the observed upward shift could not have resulted from changes in variables other than income and that there are other explanations for the apparent contradictory functions.

Arthur Smithies attempted a reconciliation of the data by looking at some of the variables that might help to explain the shift of the consumption function and thus justify the short-run function as the basic relation between C and Y.[8] According

[7] The war years are omitted from the analysis, since consumption expenditures were restricted during the war, and hence to include the experience of the war years would be misleading and inappropriate.

[8] Arthur Smithies, "Forecasting Postwar Demand: I.," *Econometrica* 13 (January 1945): 1–14. See also James Tobin, "Relative Income, Absolute Income, and Saving," in *Money, Trade, and Economic Growth, Essays in Honor of John Henry Williams* (New York: Macmillan, 1951), pp. 135–56.

to Smithies, the following variables had changed sufficiently to account for the fact that at each level of income households were spending a larger proportion on consumption (that is, the entire C schedule shifts upward): (1) wealth—with the accumulation of wealth, households spend a larger portion of their incomes; (2) new products—as new products appear on the market, the households quickly adapt to them and make them part of their consumption patterns; (3) geographical migration—the movement from the farm to the cities resulted in changing consumption at every income level, since the urban family tends to spend a larger proportion of its income than does the rural family.

Duesenberry, in addition to challenging the microeconomic theory of consumer demand, challenged the explanation for the shift. He found that plausible as these arguments were, changes in the variables just cited were simply not sufficient to account for the shift. He sought an alternative explanation by maintaining that the consumption function did not shift due to these factors but because income fluctuated during the course of the business cycle. Therefore, in the absence of the business cycle the basic relation between C and Y was proportional and would resemble the schedule as shown by the long-run function. His explanation for the different consumption functions by time period makes use of his theory of consumer behavior given earlier and expressed in equation (8.2). In Figure 8.1 assume a community has an income level of Y_1—the highest level of income this economy has attained. Therefore, consumption patterns are based on this level of income, and the distribution of income has been determined. The community, in moving to Y_1, continuously adjusted its consumption habits as higher income levels were reached; it moved along the long-run schedule C_{LR} where $\overline{APC} = \overline{MPC}$. Now, after Y_1 has been the level of income for a time, suppose a recession occurs. As incomes fall, consumers attempt to retain their consumption patterns, for they have formed habits that are not easily changed. They have grown accustomed to a certain collection of goods and services and are reluctant to give up or alter this collection. Households try to maintain their consumption habits, but with Y falling, they can only do this at the expense of saving. They therefore move from point A towards point E on the short-run curve C_{SR_1}. This movement registers the reaction of the consumers to the falling Y, since as they move along this curve, the APC increases and the APS decreases; as Y falls farther, some consumers must dissave. Thus, as incomes fall below peak levels, consumers do not move back along the long-run consumption function and thereby reduce C and S in the same proportions as they increased them when income was rising. Instead, the attempt to protect previous consumption habits forces them down the short-run curve, where a higher proportion of income is devoted to consumption.

As the economy recovers and income increases, consumers move back up the short-run schedule from E to A as they attempt to return to habits formed when income was at the peak level, Y_1. Of course, the movement from E to A means that the APC falls and the APS increases. If incomes continuously increase beyond Y_1, new consumption habits will be formed, since each new Y is a peak. The community moves along the long-run curve once again, dividing up the income levels and any additions to them in the same manner as they did at Y_1 (again $\overline{APC} = \overline{MPC}$). The distribution of income must remain fairly stable in this movement, since emulation plays a significant part in the behavioral justification of this hypothesis. As the income level rises, the amount of savings increases, which is consistent with the observed behavior of high-income groups.

Assume that when the peak income of Y_2 is reached, another recession occurs. Once again, consumers do not move back along the long-run curve but try to protect their consumption habits and therefore move down the short-run schedule, C_{SR_2}. The movement is from point B towards point F, and in the process the APC rises and the APS falls. If income recovers once more, the reverse movement would occur (F to B) until income returns to Y_2. Any increase in income beyond Y_2 will result in new peaks and therefore new habits, and once again the community moves along the long-run consumption function, C_{LR}.

According to this analysis, the long-run consumption function is the true schedule and represents the way in which consumers would really act in spending their incomes. From time to time, they are frustrated in their plans and are forced to make unwanted adjustments. The business cycle upsets the orderly process of forming consumption patterns and maintaining them. Therefore, in shorter time periods empirical consumption functions will appear to resemble the short-run schedules, which are nonproportional and in which the APC varies with income. Yet these are temporary disruptions to the otherwise methodical adjustments made with changing incomes. The long-run schedule represents the basic, underlying description of consumer behavior and is consistent with all data collected, once the effects of the business cycle are taken into account.

Duesenberry's explanation has some obvious appeal and appears to capture some elements of the psychological behavior of consumers. It is easier to adjust consumption habits while the level of income is rising, and it is not unrealistic to assume that these habits are formed through emulation and the desire for social acceptance and approval. Furthermore, reductions in income do pose problems for consumers, and the hypothesized behavior that they will try to retain the old habits for as long as possible is very plausible. It is not easy to break old habits, especially when one is asked to give up consuming goods to which one has grown accustomed. Duesenberry's reconciliation of the apparent contradiction of consumption functions is impressive, and his explanation of consumer behavior evokes a sympathetic response.[9] Right or wrong, he has altered our view of the simple consumption hypothesis, and his introduction of sociopsychological motivations counterbalances the mechanistic emphasis of less sophisticated models.

Other economists tried to reconcile the inconsistent empirical consumption functions, and their explanations led also to the conclusion that the long-run relation was the more basic, although their reasons differed somewhat from Duesenberry's.

One of these economists, Milton Friedman,[10] found the source of the conflict to be the improper definition and measurement of income. According to him, people base their consumption plans on *permanent income*. Permanent income can be loosely defined as that amount of income that could be consumed while leaving the amount of wealth intact. Money income actually received (or measured income) includes a transitory or unplanned component as well. Transitory income does not affect the consumption plans of households.

Consumption expenditures are also divided into a permanent component and a transitory one. The permanent part is a function of permanent income, while the

[9] Needless to say, the summary given in the text cannot do justice to the original work. The same statement can be made for the other theories and explanations that follow, and therefore detailed criticisms are also avoided.

[10] Milton Friedman, *A Theory of the Consumption Function* (Princeton, N. J.: Princeton University Press, 1957).

temporary part is not related to other variables and therefore is likely to be small or zero, with the remainder of transitory income going to saving. It is important to note here that consumption is defined in the physical sense—the using up of goods, the flow of services. This means that durable goods are considered to be saving, but the value of the services that flow from the use of durable goods is consumption.

The permanent income hypothesis can be summarized as follows:

(8.5)
$$Y_m = Y_p + Y_t$$
(8.6)
$$C_m = C_p + C_t,$$

where m, p, and t represent measured, permanent, and transitory components. Further, the consumption function is held to be proportional:

(8.7)
$$C_p = kY_p,$$

where k is the factor of proportionality and depends on the interest rate, i; the ratio of nonhuman to total wealth, w; and a catchall variable, u, which mainly reflects age and tastes [thus, $k = f(i, w, u)$]. These factors, and hence k, are independent of the level of permanent income.[11] These factors permit the APC to vary for individuals or to change over time. Nevertheless, the value of the APC is independent of the *level* of permanent income.

To grasp what the permanent income hypothesis suggests, let us oversimplify to some extent. The root of the problem is found in the transitory component of income. Empirical studies of the consumption function are not concerned with permanent income but with money income. The result is that consumption functions of the type we have used, $C = C_a + cY$, naturally use the observed money income for Y and thus cannot be relied upon to reflect the true income-consumption relation; the wrong income measure is employed.

For some groups of families the average of all transitory incomes equals zero, $Y_t = 0$; that is, the positive transitory incomes cancel the negative transitory incomes (of course, the same is true of transitory consumption). Also, it is possible that within this group of families, some will have a higher permanent income than others, but these also balance, so that the average Y_p can be used and related to average C_p.

For other, lower-income families, there will be a higher proportion that will be experiencing negative transitory incomes than will be getting temporary increases. For these families,

(8.8)
$$Y_m = Y_p - Y_t;$$

that is, money incomes fall below permanent levels. Yet these families continue to consume on the basis of their permanent incomes. They therefore consume a larger fraction of their money incomes, and the APC goes up. The APC of permanent income, however, is constant, as always.

For higher-income families,

(8.9)
$$Y_m = Y_p + Y_t,$$

and temporary windfalls, and so on, boost the money incomes above the permanent

[11] A more technical part of the permanent income hypothesis holds that transitory and permanent incomes, transitory and permanent consumption, and transitory income and consumption are uncorrelated. In effect, this alters the time horizon for decision making from current influences to lifetime expectations, for transitory fluctuations are not permitted to affect current actions.

levels. In this case, more families are receiving temporary gains than are experiencing losses. These families also base their consumption patterns on permanent incomes, and therefore, all of the temporary income will be saved. Here the *APC* of money income falls, but again, the *APC* of permanent income remains the same.

As a consequence of these temporary changes in income, the consumption function studies that use money *Y* and money *C* will look like the short-run curves of Figure 8.1. The consumption function will appear to be nonproportional, with the *APC* varying with income. But if the measure of income were the proper one, the permanent level on which consumption plans are based, then the consumption function would resemble the long-run curve and be proportional, and the *APC* would remain constant. Money income consumption functions show dissaving at low income levels and increasing saving as income increases. The observed relations conceal the true underlying consumption behavior, for families are consuming on the basis of permanent income and tend to consume the same proportion of this income.

In this brief summary of the permanent income hypothesis, it would appear that the theory is irrefutable in the sense that it cannot be tested directly. There is no way to obtain permanent income data, since there is no mechanism for consumers to reveal what they consider to be their permanent incomes. Even with some data only a portion of the population in certain occupations experiences income fluctuations large enough to affect the outcome of empirical tests. In its strict form the permanent income hypothesis probably could never be refuted or confirmed.

What determines when temporary income becomes permanent income? This would appear to be an empirical problem, but again where would the data come from? Friedman himself has suggested that a change in income that persists for three years be considered permanent. If this is the case, it is another way to say that it takes time for consumers to adjust to changes in income. If so, then the permanent income concept can be reduced to equation (8.1), where consumption depended upon several income periods via the lag mechanism.[12]

Perhaps the permanent income hypothesis poses some unnecessary constraints for empirical verification. A modified concept might be more useful—"normal" income might be a more general and less demanding concept than permanent income.[13] No doubt consumers do have some notion of what their normal income is and even how it is expected to change in the near future. Indeed, some form of expected income that affects current consumption is a very useful and plausible concept and a valuable contribution to the explanation of consumption expenditures.

The introduction of time into the analysis led some economists to consider an even broader horizon than the traditional short-run periods. Why not consider lifetime earnings, consumption, and saving? With a simplifying assumption over

---

[12] One of the more interesting exchanges on the permanent income hypothesis and on this area in particular can be found in H. S. Houthakker, "The Permanent Income Hypothesis," *American Economic Review* 48 (June 1958): 396–404, and the replies in the December 1958 issue of the same journal by R. Eisner, "The Permanent Income Hypothesis: Comment"; M. Friedman, "Comment"; and H. S. Houthakker, "Reply," pp. 972–93. Also with this modification the permanent income hypothesis appears to have been anticipated by T. M. Brown, "Habit Persistence and Lags in Consumer Behavior," *Econometrica* 20 (July 1952): 355–371.

[13] This point is well made by M. J. Farrell, "The New Theories of the Consumption Function," *Economic Journal* 69 (December 1959): 678–696. This article is a valuable source for the discussion of the "proportional" theories. The bibliography itself is useful for anyone wishing to pursue this topic.

an individual's lifetime, one such hypothesis held that an individual would consume all of his income over his lifetime and be left with no saving.[14] In a world free of uncertainty it would be possible to arrange one's affairs in this manner. A growing, young population would show positive saving; a stationary population no saving; and an aging population would show dissaving, since they will be living off past saving. Also, as real income per capita rises over time, the savers will be saving more as their lifetime earnings increase than will the dissavers, and aggregate saving will increase.

This rate of growth hypothesis states that the aggregate saving (consumption) is determined by population structure and the per capita real income. If these variables changed in a stable way over time, the relation between aggregate saving or consumption is one of proportionality to the rate of growth of aggregate real income. The assumption of the motivations for saving and the absence of uncertainty may be overly simplified, but there is no question that a longer horizon for consumption spending may help explain current behavior.

There are still more, slightly different concepts of income. But enough has been discussed at this stage to indicate that what began as a simple straightforward relation, consumption as a function of income, has become a rather complex one. Which income is to be used—absolute, relative, permanent, expected, lifetime— in the consumption function relation? More important, what happens to the stability of relations observed between C and Y, and how do we account for it? What can be said with confidence about short-run changes in C and Y—the MPC? Some of these points remain unanswered and others ignored. The short-run emphasis of Keynesian economics permits the assumption of stability to be realistic for most purposes. In the long run too many other factors, many outside the economic structure, may influence human behavior. Perhaps even the observed stability in any period can be traced to fortuitous factors—the canceling of extremes, the aggregation problem, and so on. Much remains to be uncovered in the relation between consumption and income, not to mention the effect of other variables that are discussed further on.

Before turning to other influences on consumption, let us return to the controversy that instigated all the concern over the proper definition of income. Is the consumption function proportional or nonproportional; does the APC fall as income increases, or does it remain constant? More important, why is it necessary to know which is correct?

Perhaps too much attention has been devoted to the discussion of proportional and nonproportional consumption functions. In the long run no economy can continue to dissave, so that the short-run curves are more unrealistic the longer the time period under consideration. Still, it is possible to use the nonproportional schedules for shorter periods. It is questionable how much of the conflicting evidence is simply the result of the time period involved and how much reflects genuine differences accounted for by the various hypotheses. How critical is the knowledge? The conclusion that the consumption function is proportional is not required of the various theories presented here; they would remain valid approaches to the explanation of consumption even without this result. In the end, these are empirical questions, and only empirical work can untangle the theoretical func-

[14] F. Modigliani and R. E. Brumberg, "Utility Analysis and the Consumption Function: An Interpretation of Cross-Section Data," in *Post-Keynesian Economics*, ed. K. K. Kurihara (New Brunswick, N. J.: Rutgers University Press, 1954).

tions. Evidence to test the theories will be difficult to obtain. In the meantime, the short-run schedules must be used for the immediate future periods.

In the long run it may well be possible that the *APC* is constant. This means that as income grows, a constant proportion will be devoted to consumption. If the short-run schedules were used for long-run analysis, this would imply that as income increases, less and less would be destined to be used for consumption purposes, as the *APC* would fall. If income is not to fall, the other sectors—*I*, *G*, or *X*—would have to increase their proportions of the growing income levels. We can speculate on the prospects of increased demand from these sectors. Investment probably would not be encouraged, since *C* would not be rising proportionally and since less investment may be needed over time as the capital stock becomes more productive. Exports may not expand, since all advanced economies may be faced with a similar condition. Expansion of demand, then, is likely to take the form of exports to economies under economic or political domination. Outright colonialism may be passé, but economic imperialism persists. There is certainly instability in going this way, and some far-reaching repercussions can be expected. The last resort would be an expansion of government demand to compensate for the lack of consumer demand. Increased government demand could arise from further development of the welfare state—public health schemes, housing, government-owned railroads and communications—and the nationalization of industries such as steel or national defense. In any case, the character of capitalism would be altered fundamentally, and the effects on society would be disrupting.

Yet these developments could take place without much of a change in the *APC* and, in fact, independent of any change. Whether or not the *APC* varies with income, considerations such as these become important, and the conflicting evidence over proportionality becomes relevant. The problem is that political and social forces must also be considered, and these may overshadow the importance of the economic issues discussed here. The longer the period of time, the more variable becomes all human behavior.

Other Determinants of Consumption Expenditures

PRICE VARIABLES

The Price Level

The influence of changes in the price level on aggregate demand, and particularly on consumption demand, is not at all clear despite the knowledge of how prices affect individual markets. There are aggregation and index number problems here; one must know to what extent consumers are able to substitute lower-priced goods for those whose prices have risen. For this it is necessary to know which prices have risen and the elasticity of demand for the products concerned. These are formidable obstacles, and it is not surprising that economists have few answers as to how price changes affect total consumption. Furthermore, consumption depends primarily on income, so that one must observe what happens to income as prices change. Thus, as prices rise or fall, disposable income could remain constant; could change in the same direction; or could change in the opposite direction. Income changes could also vary proportionally, more than proportionally, or less than proportionally with price changes.

In the United States economy price level changes and disposable income changes move in the same direction. (This is not uniformly true, since there may be a lag in income responses, but it is still a substantially correct statement.) In recent years prices in the United States economy have risen steadily and so has disposable income. So the real question is, Have the changes in prices and incomes been proportional or not, and what is the effect on consumption expenditures? If disposable income increases more than proportionally to the increase in the price level, we might expect consumption expenditures to increase, perhaps even more than proportionally to the price level changes.[15] If prices and incomes change proportionally, real income remains constant and presumably there should be no effect on consumption. If the change in prices is proportionally greater than the change in income, real income falls and consumption may be affected as consumers adjust to the new real income level. Whether or not consumption falls as real income falls would depend theoretically upon the consumption hypothesis: by the absolute income hypothesis, C should fall; by the relative or normal income hypothesis, C may not fall at all, and the impact may be entirely on saving.

These descriptions of consumer reactions to changing prices and incomes are predicated on the belief that there is no money illusion. Money illusion in this case refers to the failure of consumers to notice that both prices and incomes are changing; they see only prices changing or only incomes changing. Real income is given by

$$\frac{Y \text{ money}}{\text{Price level}},$$

which gives the command over goods and services of the money income received—the purchasing power of income. If consumers see only the numerator, Y, increasing, they may feel better off and spend more on consumption. Others may see only the denominator, P, increasing and feel worse off and reduce consumption expenditures. At any one time both groups will be reacting to changing conditions, and it is difficult to judge in what direction consumption expenditures are likely to vary. It is not known to what extent money illusion exists in the economy, but it is likely to be diminishing as mass media attempt to present economic information that could dispel some of the irrational behavior. We must be on guard, however, against making hasty judgments and calling some consumption expenditures or cutbacks irrational. Some individuals or groups may experience real income changes opposite to those felt by the majority. According to aggregated data, real income or even real income per capita could be falling, while for some consumers it could be increasing. The aggregation over all consumers, all incomes, and all prices conceals what happens in individual cases, and it does not deal with what happens to relative prices in the price structure. One must either disaggregate or consider the change in relative prices as a specific variable.

Relative Prices

Price level changes are not likely to be evenly distributed over all goods or groups of goods; the prices of some goods will change more than those of others. Consumers, by altering their consumption patterns, could spend more, the same, or less on consumption goods and thereby affect the aggregate consumption expenditure. Much depends upon the availability of substitute goods in those cases where

---

[15] This appears to be the case for the United States economy in the late 1960s. Whether or not this trend will continue into the 1970s is unknown at this writing, and in fact may never be known, as the wage and price controls changed the data, making them incomparable with earlier series.

price changes are greater than the average. The price changes of complementary goods will also alter the total consumption expenditure. In periods of prolonged inflation, say, it is not unreasonable to assume that consumers will become acutely aware of the relative prices of the goods they normally purchase as opposed to those goods that are infrequently purchased—steak versus chopped meat versus chicken, and so on. Consumers could stop buying some items altogether or buy them less frequently. These adjustments must affect aggregate consumption, but little is known concerning how.[16]

If consumers spend largely on the basis of habit, then little in the way of short-run adjustments can be expected. However, as time goes on and the inflation continues, more and more adjustments can be expected in consumer budgets. Breaking habits is not easy, but given time most habits will be scrutinized, and painful as the process may be, some surgery on the budget and consumption patterns will be undertaken. Some consumer resistance to change can probably be traced to feelings about the permanency of the changes and what future changes can be expected, a subject to which we now turn.

Price Expectations

How prices are expected to behave in the future can vitally affect the amount of current consumption. People acting on expected future conditions can play havoc with the attempt to analyze the current economic condition. Expectations, although recognized as important, are seldom permitted to enter the analysis in a significant manner.

One example of expectations in economics is the notion of expected, or normal, or permanent, income encountered in the last section. Consumers spending out of some expected income proved to be a valuable addition to the set of influences on consumption. It helps to explain the consumption behavior of many people (M.D.'s in residence, graduate students, those receiving temporary reduction in income), which is not otherwise explicable if only current income is used. So price expectations may also help explain additional consumption behavior not relevant to a world without uncertainty.

Many economic decisions that must be made currently are of necessity based on incomplete information. The future is always uncertain to some degree, and actions taken now may not be the appropriate ones if the future were known. Yet we are forced to act on our expectations of what the future holds. Economic theory has a difficult time with this variable, as it does with any subjective, unobservable one.[17] How consumers react in the face of uncertainty and, more important, how expectations of the future are formed are areas where much more information is needed, probably requiring an interdisciplinary approach.

Theoretically, if prices are expected to rise, consumers would buy more goods currently, and if prices are expected to fall, consumers would postpone some purchases. Naturally, these reactions are more germane to goods capable of delayed consumption—consumer durables, furniture, or luxury items. Of course, these are

---

[16] See, however, G. Ackley and D. B. Suits, "Relative Price Changes and Aggregate Consumer Demand," *American Economic Review* 40 (December 1950): 785–804.

[17] Attempts have been made to include expectations into the analysis, among which are J. R. Hicks, *Value and Capital* (Oxford: Oxford University Press, 1939), and recently, A. Lowe, *On Economic Knowledge* (New York: Harper & Row, 1965). See also the many works of G. Katona and his work at the Social Science Research Center at Michigan cited in the reference section at the end of the book.

also high-cost items in the household budget, and consumers can be expected to be more price conscious about them.

One problem with a variable like expectations is the possible self-fulfilling tendency if consumers act on the basis of those expectations. For example, at the beginning of the Korean War consumers, remembering the shortages of goods in World War II and fearing higher prices, rushed out and stocked up on certain items. In doing this, they brought about the shortage they had feared. Their expectations turned out to be correct, but in the absence of those expectations no such shortage would have existed.

One final problem to be discussed at this time is that expectations of people can be influenced by other people's forecasts of those expectations. Those who make economic forecasts of human behavior are predicting the actions, say, consumers will take. In the process of publishing these forecasts, they may influence the behavior of those people who were the subjects of the forecasts. Forecasts of a heavy consumer demand may influence consumers to spend more, and similarly with forecasts of future price changes or income changes. In an age of rapid global communication, who is to determine how vulnerable people are to news events and forecasts and how susceptible they are to manipulation, so that their views and expectations of the future are altered. The psychology of inflation is an excellent example of expectations feeding on themselves and being reinforced by almost daily pronouncements of price changes. Will wage and price controls break that conditioning and stop the scramble to stay ahead? Only time will tell, but one thing is certain—expectations will be a critical part in the process, but our knowledge of how to integrate them into the formal analysis is weak; economists have often worked in the realm of perfect foresight, and the absence of uncertainty has minimized the role played by expectations.

MONETARY VARIABLES

The Interest Rate

Prior to the appearance of Keynes's *General Theory,* there was a widely held belief that the rate of interest was one of the (if not the only) most powerful influences on consumption. This contention was based on the observation that people prefer goods now to goods later, and thus if people did forgo current consumption, there would have to be some reward for doing so. The rate of interest here permits the postponing of consumption now with the prospect of commanding more goods later; the rate of interest facilitates saving and allows people to express their "time preferences" for consumption over saving. The classical economists went further than this and assumed that excess cash balances, idle money, would be saved as long as the rate of interest was positive, and that as the rate of interest rose, more saving would occur. The rate of interest, then, became the main determinant of the division of income between consumption and saving; the higher the rate of interest, the greater the saving.[18]

The belief that the rate of interest plays such an important part in the consumption versus saving decision is no longer widely held. In fact, this entire chapter, which enumerates the many other influences, is sufficient to dispel such a simplistic idea. It is true that *some* people may well be affected by the rate of interest in their

---

[18] For a summary of pre-Keynesian interest theories and their effect upon consumption, see Joseph W. Conard, *An Introduction to the Theory of Interest* (Berkeley: University of California Press, 1959).

decision to save more as the rate of interest increases. There are others, however, who might save *less* as the interest rate rises, since they might have some specific goal in mind and the higher interest rate means higher income; thus, there would be no need to save as much to reach the goal. There are too many other motives for saving—retirement, consumption-spreading as given under the rate of growth income hypothesis, estate building, and so on—for much to be concluded about the relation between saving and the rate of interest. In the aggregate as the rate of interest increases, the people who save more may be balanced by those who save less. Even if this offsetting effect were not complete, it is still not believed that the rate of interest is a very influential variable; personal saving may be relatively interest-inelastic. Interest rates do not vary over a wide range and do not fluctuate rapidly, so that the necessary evidence to measure consumer response is inadequate. Perhaps changes in the interest rate of from five to ten points would be needed to test the relation. Such changes are not likely to occur over a short period, and in their absence most economists would agree that the rate of interest is not a particularly powerful variable in helping to explain consumption expenditures.

Credit

The availability of credit presents an interesting problem: does the time of payment affect the amount of consumption? Does credit permit consumers to obtain goods now instead of later, after the purchase price had been accumulated, but not affect the type of goods or the volume of goods purchased? Does the existence of credit make consumers less price conscious? Are they willing to pay, or be misled into paying, higher prices over and above what the cost of credit might add?

Credit as a variable did not bother economists very much until after World War II. The amount of credit and its availability were not extensive, and credit institutions were not developed. Over time the amount of credit has increased tremendously—by over 1,000 per cent in total since 1939 and by over 2,000 per cent in installment credit alone[19]—and the total amount of consumer credit is over $150 billion. While the proportion of GNP going to consumption has decreased over this period, credit as a proportion of consumption has doubled. Moreover, much of the growth of credit has taken place in the past decade or so. As the use of credit increased, so did the number and types of institutions dedicated in whole or in part to supplying it. Yet the availability of credit does not imply that consumption patterns were altered, and the use of credit does not mean that people were spending more of their incomes. Only the time of payment has been directly affected.

The terms of credit are probably equally as important as its availability. Down payment conditions, interest costs, and repayment periods are obviously important considerations to the credit users. Since the middle 1950s the terms of credit have been largely unregulated and the use of credit has expanded. During the Korean War the Federal Reserve regulated the terms of credit, and this regulation proved to be a powerful weapon to curb consumer spending, especially on consumer durables. Imagine what might occur in the automobile market if the Federal Reserve were again empowered to dictate the terms of credit and chose to require one half of the purchase price as a down payment with a one-year repayment period.

---

[19] See consumer credit series in any *Federal Reserve Bulletin*.

Congress, after many years of discussion, finally did take some action on the interest cost of credit with the Consumer Credit Protection Act of 1968. The law required full disclosure of the true interest cost of credit instead of the many confusing variants of interest charges in use for many years. Despite the apparent benefit to consumers, no one expected the use of credit to be significantly affected. Interest or finance charges were seldom important to the consumer; the availability of credit and the terms on which it was offered were regarded as more important considerations.

In the past the effects of credit on consumption were unclear. Surely, the availability of credit affected some, while to others it made little difference. In the aggregate no firm relation has been established. The terms of credit have been granted more importance to consumers than has the cost of credit. Yet credit terms change slowly, and consumers can be expected to adjust to them quickly and in a one-time manner. Consumption of consumer durables proved to be more controllable by adjusting the terms of credit than the availability of credit, since institutional arrangements may take control out of federal hands, and the Federal Reserve lacks jurisdiction over some financial intermediaries. To conclude, it is unclear whether or not credit results in people spending more of their incomes on consumption.

A new credit instrument may provide more direct evidence in the future. The widespread dissemination of the credit card has made credit instant and painless, lacking the formalities of applications, forms, and interviews. The easy access to credit may indicate some definite relation between this form of credit and consumption. The evidence is not in yet, but it may well be that this form of credit may show a positive relation with consumption. Much depends upon the rationality of the consumer—a quality that no one is sure of.

SOME STOCK VARIABLES

Stock of Consumer Durables

In our discussion of consumption expenditures in national income accounting, recall that all consumption goods were considered final product and were regarded as used up in the period in which they were purchased. Consumer durables such as automobiles, refrigerators, and washing machines are surely not used up in one period but may provide useful service over many years. Here is the problem with consumer durables: they resemble investment goods in that their useful life extends over several periods and then they must be replaced. Consumer durable purchases are likely to be similarly affected by time and depreciation.

If the stock of durable goods in the hands of households is high, there is likely to be little demand for additional goods, and vice versa. A year of heavy purchases of consumer durables may be followed by years of declining purchases. Thus, the purchase of consumer durables fluctuates, and this fluctuation can cause some problems in the explanation of consumption expenditures in any one period.

Other factors prevent a simple relation between consumer durables, consumption, and income. The age distribution of the population and the number of consumers who are in the marriageable age group will affect the amount spent on durable goods. Social attitudes, the identification of a houseful of consumer durables—all the latest models—as indicative of success, will obviously affect the demand for consumer durables. Some of these attitudes may have been fostered by the manufacturers of these goods as they practice the policy known as planned obsolescence. Since these goods are likely to require a large outlay, credit can be an important factor, as noted in the last section in the case of the automobile. These are also the kinds of goods in which the relative income hypothesis may be most applicable; as income rises and emulation takes place, these are the kinds of goods that would become part of the new consumption patterns formed.

Of course, these are also the kinds of goods whose purchase can be postponed. Also, the irregularity of purchase can make for instability in the economy, since the industries that produce consumer durables are very important in the economic structure. Furthermore, many satellite industries have grown up around the major industries to furnish complementary products or service. Just look at the automobile industry alone. On the one hand, the more cars on the road the more economic activity generated; on the other hand, fluctuations in the demand for automobiles is very likely to have widespread repercussions throughout the economy.

How then is total consumption affected by the existence of consumer durables? Are nondurable expenditures reduced when durables are purchased, or over time is the proportion of income used for consumption of consumer durables and nondurables relatively stable? That is, if the *services* of durables were spread out over their useful lives, would the amount of income devoted to consumer durables be fairly constant? The lack of data does not permit a ready answer to these questions, and no simple relationship has been established among consumption, income, and durable versus nondurable goods.[20] Each period would have to be studied to arrive at any conclusions, and generalizations are questionable.

Wealth

It would appear almost self-evident that wealth would affect consumption, but the relation is far from certain. The amount of current income need not be a constraint to consumption for those who have accumulated wealth. Presumably, the more wealth one has the more willing one would be to consume more of one's income and the less willing one is to accumulate more. The satisfaction or utility one derives from wealth diminishes the more wealth one has; therefore, the desire to save or accumulate more falls as wealth increases and the APC current income rises. It follows that two people with equal incomes but unequal wealth will consume differently; the wealthier one will have a higher APC. If the community as a whole becomes wealthier, it will have a higher APC—as was maintained by those who defended the absolute income hypothesis.

This discussion, although intuitively appealing, assumes that the marginal utility of wealth diminishes as wealth increases—the more wealth one has the less utility is derived from additional wealth. Yet it is just as plausible to say that the more wealth one has the more one is willing to accumulate. Additional weatlh may not bring diminishing satisfaction, since one's taste for wealth may change as the accumulation proceeds. If the latter is correct, then the APC may well remain constant or change very little.

For the community as a whole the distribution of wealth is so unequally divided that little additional consumption might be forthcoming with additions to wealth. Only a redistribution of wealth may stimulate consumption, and even then, the

---

[20] However, see Friedman's treatment of consumer durables in the permanent income hypothcsis discussed earlier.

stimulation may be short-lived if consumers adjust to their new economic situation rapidly. This reaction would be consistent with the relative income hypothesis.

The effect of wealth on consumption is not as obvious as it appears. One attempt to show a direct relation was made by A. C. Pigou.[21] Pigou sought to explain how an insufficiency of aggregate demand $(C + I)$ and thus a less-than-full employment level of income could have some self-correcting mechanism that would increase C, remove the lack of demand, and move the economy toward full employment.[22] Assuming that wages and prices are perfectly flexible, the existence of unemployment should force down wages and be followed by falling prices. Even if wages and prices fell proportionally (real wage, W/P, remains constant), the deflationary process could provide the mechanism needed. As prices fall, the real value of wealth, wealth$/p$, increases, and it was argued that the community would choose to spend more on current consumption. The increase in real wealth acts as a stimulant to consumption in the same manner as an addition to wealth. These are rational consumers with no money illusion.

However, for some forms of wealth, the numerator would fall as well, since the marketplace can be expected to revalue assets as prices fall. Wealth held in the form of land, buildings, stocks, inventories, or other goods would be revalued downward. No stimulus to consumption can be expected from these wealth-holders.

In addition, as prices fall, debtors are made worse off as the real value of their debts is increased. Debtors may well be forced to reduce consumption, balancing those creditors who are made better off and who may increase consumption.

The only type of wealth for which there is no offset is in the form of government obligations—money and near money in the form of government bonds. They have a fixed money value, and the debtor (government) need not curtail its expenditures as it becomes "worse off." People holding wealth in these highly liquid assets are made better off, or feel that way, and they may choose to spend more on current consumption. As C rises, the economy moves toward the full employment level of income. The effect upon consumption of falling prices is appropriately called the Pigou effect.

Pigou himself thought of this effect as a theoretical possibility but did not attach more importance to it as a practical policy for stimulating consumption. However, as we shall see, the concept has been revived in another form. The Pigou effect still relies upon the assumption of the diminishing marginal utility of wealth, which was criticized earlier. Furthermore, it ignores the possible destabilizing effects of expectations. As prices fall, expectations may develop that they will fall even farther, so that consumption is not increased—it may even fall. Even if the fall in prices worked, the extent of the fall in prices required to stimulate consumption appreciably may have to be so great as to result in severe disruptions to the economy.

As a practical policy, the Pigou effect leads to the conclusion that the way to cure unemployment is to make the wealthy wealthier. This is not likely to be a very popular strategy.

To conclude, the effects of wealth on consumption may be positive, but the strength of the relation still remains unclear. Wealth, in whatever form it is held,

---

[21] A. C. Pigou, "The Classical Stationary State," *Economic Journal* 53 (December 1943): 343–351. Also see his "Economic Progress in a Stable Environment," *Economica* 14 (August 1947): 180–188.

[22] Much of this discussion will be more meaningful after the classical system is discussed.

may influence consumption habits, but much depends upon attitudes toward wealth, the distribution of wealth, the rationality of consumers, and the social attitudes towards accumulated wealth.

SOCIAL, PSYCHOLOGICAL, AND PHILOSOPHICAL VARIABLES

Keynes grouped together many factors of this kind under the heading of subjective factors. According to Keynes, some of the motives for consumption that underlie his notion of the propensity to consume are "Enjoyment, Shortsightedness, Generosity, Miscalculation, Ostentation, and Extravagance." The motives for saving follow, of course, as "Precaution, Foresight, Calculation, Improvement, Independence, Enterprise, Pride, and Avarice."[23] Economists have sought to find more objective factors and have more or less drifted away from these vague, unquantifiable factors. The impatience of economists with these amorphous variables is understandable, but something of the richness of human behavior is also sacrificed. Perhaps the economist has for too long dealt with only rational behavior and is unable to handle a variable like avarice or generosity. Yet surely these motivations exist, and they have some influence on consumption, whether measurable or not. Not only do they exist but they are likely to change over time as social attitudes, mores, and cultural patterns change.

Consider the present generation conflict. On one side there are the suburbanites busy accumulating goods and gadgets, constantly searching for more goods, for more status to enrich their lives. Multiple cars and television sets are normal to this way of life. At the other extreme there are those living in communes, rejecting materialism, and seeking spiritual rejuvenation. Goods that make life comfortable are shunned. In between there are various shades of behavior as people confront their lives and sense the frustration of seeking satisfaction in the accumulation of material goods. Surely, these attitudes will affect consumption patterns, not only in the composition of consumer demand but also the proportion of income devoted to consumption. If, contrary to Duesenberry, people begin to emulate the consumption patterns of those whose needs are much simpler, the effect upon consumption would be enormous and would disrupt the workings of many of our institutions.

Take the institution of advertising, for example. One of the more important functions of advertising is to convince people to want more, to create a demand (or enlarge one) for more goods. The whole economy is geared to production and sales, to ever-increasing consumption necessary to purchase the growing productive output of our industries.[24] There are pressures for consumption from all sides, and many would argue that our lives are dominated by commercial considerations. What happens if all decide to consume less? What happens to our unused production if we remain unconvinced by the exhortations of Madison Avenue? While the answers are unknown (or too frightening to be mentioned), it is easily seen how attitudes can influence consumption and cannot be ignored, especially over long periods of time.

Some would take issue with the contention that advertising increases the demand for goods and services. People do not purchase more goods as a result of advertising; they only alter the composition of that demand. People may be persuaded

---

[23] J. M. Keynes, *The General Theory of Employment, Interest, and Money* (New York: Harcourt, Brace, 1936), p. 108.

[24] See the description of this relation in J. K. Galbraith, *The Affluent Society* (Boston: Houghton Mifflin, 1958).

to buy more of Brand X and less of Brand Y rather than more of both. Therefore, the proportion of income consumed, the *APC,* remains unaffected even if what is purchased is influenced.

Others would argue that total consumption is affected as well; that as a result of advertising, sales promotion schemes of all kinds, and other forms of nonprice competition, people spend a *higher proportion* of their incomes on current consumption (*APC* rises) and immediate gratification. Perhaps even tastes are formed by advertising, and these tastes require more goods for the enjoyment of life. Tastes are formed in a variety of ways, but there is no reason to deny some part to advertising and sales promotion. As might be expected, no real conclusions can be reached on the basis of available evidence. Some answers would be most welcome in view of the frequently heard complaint that advertising is wasteful and serves no useful purpose. Others have argued that advertising is necessary for capitalism to survive, not as Madison Avenue might imply, because consumption is increased, but in order to utilize the excess saving (surplus) generated by advanced capitalist systems.[25] To many intellectuals, the commercial dominance and the atmosphere created by the emphasis upon consumption have resulted in the deterioration of the quality of life. These grounds alone are sufficient to demand some more definitive answers as to the effects of advertising and other marketing techniques.

In an era of rapid technological change the introduction of new products can influence consumption as well. A new product, heralded by advertisers, can quickly be assimilated into the consumption patterns of consumers. The more dramatic the product—television, automobile, and so on—the more readily does it become part of the necessary collection of goods for the decent life. These goods, the dream of a marketing expert, can influence consumption expenditures as consumers become willing to consume a higher proportion of their incomes or even to dissave in order to acquire them. The availability of credit facilitates the fulfillment of these desires when current income is insufficient.

Psychological factors also play a part when income is unstable. Consumers with unstable incomes can be expected to save more than those whose incomes are fairly predictable. It has also been observed that in periods of much uncertainty people tend to save more of their incomes. In times of social unrest, perplexing world events, wars and reactions to them, uncertain price fluctuations, and so on, we can observe a higher *APS* than would have been the case in the absence of these disrupting events. Some of the increases in the *APS* during periods of the later 1960s have been attributed to the Vietnam War and the social unrest it created. Too many things appeared uncertain, and people saved more.

Having considered these psychological and philosophical variables, we now must enumerate other factors affecting consumption patterns even if their precise influence is unclear. They are important enough to warrant further investigation and can no longer be ignored.

LONG-RUN VARIABLES

Population

Population changes mean the number of consumers change; increases in population mean a greater demand for all consumer goods from diapers to automobiles. Population growth is one way to ensure that the growth in production will be

---

[25] For instance, see Paul A. Baran and Paul M. Sweezy, *Monopoly Capital* (New York: Monthly Review Press, 1966).

purchased. As an economy turns out more and more consumer goods (and if the growth is to continue), there must be more consumers or the existing population must purchase more. Advanced economies face a dilemma. Economic growth increases the productive capacity of the economy and provides more jobs, but the growth in population, which may be desirable in terms of the growth of the market, brings with it other problems: an inadequate food supply, depletion of energy sources, pollution, overcrowding, disease, lack of housing, and in general, a decline in the quality of life and the dignity of man.[26] For the less developed economies the problems are compounded, since the productive capacity of the economy may not be growing at all or growing too slowly relative to the growth in population.

The increasing concern over the problems that accompany population growth may not tolerate any longer the notion that more consumers are needed to purchase the additional output. Of what use are increasing goods if the planet is being destroyed by their production? The destruction of the environment and the rate of consumption of natural resources may be too high a price to pay for economic growth. When one considers what kinds of goods are being produced, other value judgments must be made. Population problems will be reintroduced in the long-run context of economic growth, but enough has been suggested here to point out the significance of population for consumption expenditures.

Age Distribution

Not only is the total population important but the age distribution of the population must also be considered. Both ends of the age distribution, the old and the young, tend to spend a higher proportion of their incomes than do those in the middle. A youthful or an aging population can be expected to spend more and save less, everything else being equal.

The age at which people marry can affect the amount of consumption. A youthful population in a society that encourages young marriage may tend to spend more than an aged population. Young families with children may also tend to spend more than those without children. Of course, the age distribution changes slowly over time, so that consumption estimates on a year-to-year basis are not affected. Still, consumption patterns will change as the age distribution of the population changes. Many of these changes will depend upon other cultural factors, as seen in the marriage age and attitudes towards children. Other changes can be traced to society's attitudes toward the aged—whether or not some retirement scheme is in effect, health care availability, welfare schemes, and so on.

Other Population Characteristics

Geographical location of the population plays some part in the consumption function. For many years there has been a migration from rural areas to urban areas. It has been observed that urban dwellers tend to spend a higher proportion of their incomes on consumption goods than do rural dwellers. Therefore, the migration has resulted in a higher *APC* for the community as a whole.

The occupational mix can affect consumption spending. Farmers save more than other groups. Probably the instability of income accounts for some of this, and perhaps even religious attitudes can be brought into the explanation. The amount

---

[26] An alarming view of these problems is given by P. Ehrlich, *The Population Bomb* (New York: Ballantine Books, 1968).

of education might help to explain some observed differences in consumption patterns. Income instability and cultural differences among races have been shown to account for some differences in the amount of consumption. The list could easily be extended and the population broken up in a number of different ways, but the effort may make the explanation of consumption too involved for our purposes.

Distribution of Income

Some recognition that the distribution of income affects consumption has already been encountered in the relative income hypothesis. The relative position in the income scale helped to determine consumption patterns and helped to explain the long-run constancy of the APC. If the distribution remains fairly constant, $\overline{APC} = \overline{MPC}$, and any change in income leaves the proportion of income consumed undisturbed. Also, any attempt to influence the level of consumption expenditures by redistributing income from higher income groups to lower income groups, who presumably would spend more, will not be successful. This method for increasing the level of income was justified frequently on these grounds. Of course, the social goal of redistribution of income often made the argument more palatable.

The argument for redistribution of income was based on Keynes's notion that the MPC also falls as income increases. (We have assumed it constant in our models.) If this were the case, then consumption would increase as income was redistributed from higher to lower income groups. Empirically, the marginal propensity to consume has been found to be fairly constant,[27] and many turned away from redistribution arguments with these findings.

The arguments were always clouded by confusion of the APC and the MPC. It is correct to state that lower income groups spend a higher *proportion* of their incomes. All the consumption theories in this chapter are consistent with this observation. If the MPC is constant (or nearly so), however, no change in the short run can be expected in consumption expenditures. Over time, if this shift of income is permanent, the APCs will be affected. For higher income groups, the APC may well *fall* as their incomes fall, and if lower income groups do emulate the upper income groups, they will have less compulsion to spend and more incentive to save. Thus, over time *consumption may fall* in the aggregate following redistribution that is regarded as permanent.

Confusing? Consumption could increase, decrease, or remain the same with a redistribution of income from higher to lower income groups. Actually, the confusion is the result of viewing the consumption function according to different theories—the absolute, relative, or permanent hypothesis. The conclusions may be indeterminate and perhaps can be left that way. For the redistribution of income is a goal by itself and need not become mixed with the goal of the stabilization of income. If redistribution of income is thought to be required by the principles of social justice, then it may well be pursued as a goal of public policy independent of other goals.

This is not to say that fiscal policy can ignore the effects of the redistribution on consumption expenditures and the level of income. Indeed, tax rates can be adjusted to obtain revenue and principles of equity can be embodied in the tax

---

[27] Harold Lubell, "Effects of Redistribution of Income on Consumers' Expenditures," *American Economic Review* 37 (March 1947): 157–170.

structure. Social justice and redistribution can be satisfied with an eye to the effects on consumption but not necessarily constrained by those effects. Of course, re-distribution can also be accomplished by government expenditures of the type that benefit the lower income groups more than other groups.

As a practical matter, the distribution of income has remained fairly stable for decades. Furthermore, tax reform proposals that might affect the tax burdens of income groups are generally resisted, so that little redistribution has taken place. Some government expenditure programs designed to benefit the lower income groups have also not been overly successful.

What has happened is that the level of income has grown over time, but it has not been more equally distributed. Many people have settled for income growth as the means for all to share the economic progress and have abandoned or sub-ordinated the goal of income equality.[28] Only partly can this be blamed on the uncertainty of the effects of redistribution on consumption expenditures.

Conclusion

What started out as a relatively straightforward explanation of consumption as depending largely on the level of disposable income has revealed consumption to be a complex function. We have an embarrassment of riches—too many influences and too many explanations. We can admit the theoretical possibilities in each case but are often left with some question over the importance of this variable or that. It is the task of the econometrician to answer the question of which variables should be considered the important ones. The econometrician soon finds that these vari-ables are not independent of each other, as might be found with the population variables or in the education, occupation, race combinations. To some extent, these variables are measuring the same thing, and thus some of them can be eliminated. Also, some have turned out to be insignificant in the explanation of consumption, such as the interest rate or the amount of liquid assets.

Still, the answers are not definite. Income, by some measurement, is still the most important variable, and thus we may credit Keynes with a major insight. The simple and direct function he had in mind still remains the basis for understanding aggregate consumption expenditures. The modifications introduced by others brought us closer to reality and deepened our appreciation for the complexity of this variable. If as a result some confusion remains, it may be the necessary price to pay for realism. All of the answers are not in, and not all the evidence examined nor theoretical formulations developed to permit an unqualified consumption func-tion. Meanwhile, one must keep all these modifications in mind when one deals with the consumption function.

---

[28] More of the effects of fiscal policy on income groups will be discussed in later chapters.

The Investment Function

Investment is one of the pivotal variables in any economic system, particularly when the decisions about it are made by the private sector and based on individual motivations. All economic systems must deal with capital formation, but the impetus for capital accumulation will probably differ in various economic systems. In a primarily capitalist system investment takes on added significance, for it has generally been one of the most unstable variables in the system. The movement of investment spending with GNP is an irregular one, in contrast to the relationship between consumption and GNP. Investment is an active variable, and consumption is a passive one.

The instability of investment is what makes this variable so crucial, for the instability causes fluctuations in the level of economic activity and employment. Investment spending plays a central part in most theories of the business cycle. As we will see, the variability of investment can be traced to many factors, but since investment decisions are largely private, any attempt to influence this variable will have to be indirect in nature. Since all advanced economies favor control over the business cycle, it is apparent that investment spending and the process of capital accumulation must be understood if severe economic fluctuations are to be avoided.

A good reason to study investment spending is to understand fluctuations in the level of economic activity. Another is to understand the critical part played by investment in the process of economic growth. The capital stock of an economy is a very important variable in the determination of the productive capacity of that economy. Positive net investment (gross investment minus depreciation) is an addition to the stock of capital and hence to the productive capacity. At least, when an economy is adding to its capital stock, it is capable of producing more, and economic growth is made possible. Whether or not this added productive capacity will be utilized depends to some extent on the amount of investment spending. Thus, investment spending is important on both sides of the growth process. On the demand side it constitutes a sector of aggregate demand that buys some of the output of the economy; on the supply side the added net investment contributes to the growth of the productive capacity of the economy. Investment is important in both the short run and the long run.

A third feature of investment is that in the process of investing in new capital goods an economy can register all the latest technological developments. Indeed, technological change is likely to reside mainly in the latest capital goods. To a large extent, this is how an economy recognizes and embodies technological advances. New capital goods that replace worn-out ones are likely to be superior technologically to those they replace.

There is no question that investment is a critical variable in the economic system, and it is a rather complex one. There are no simple relations here, no ready formulas to follow, and no easy solutions to the problems that arise in explaining investment. Perhaps the most difficult area to study in economics is investment and capital accumulation. Even more than consumption, investment remains an elusive variable, and no one theory has managed to explain the investment process fully or to everyone's satisfaction. As a preliminary, we must dispose of some difficulties that arise as soon as one begins to examine this variable.

Some Immediate Problems

In national income accounting investment was defined to include producers' durables (plant and equipment), the change in inventories, and construction in progress. Also recall that the owner-occupied home was treated as a business, which means that new home construction and major additions must be treated as investment. So the first problem arises in the possible confusion over which part of investment spending is referred to when the term *investment* is employed. There would be no problem if all parts of the investment total could be explained by the same set of influences. But there is no reason to expect the same motivations for investment in machinery as for new homes, nor could the change in inventories be explained in the same manner as the construction of a new plant. There is always an element of speculation in the inventory variable. When combined with production and scheduling decisions, this speculative feature places this variable in a special category requiring a separate explanation. Similarly, the housing industry and construction in general demand separate study, for they have their own peculiar problems. Thus, most people mean producers' durables in the form of machinery and other equipment when they use the term *investment,* and we will do the same in this chapter.

Types of Investment

Even with the concept of investment limited to producers' durables, there are categories of investment that must be considered separately if overgeneralization is to be avoided. There are different motivations for investment despite the common goal—profit. First, there is *autonomous investment,* which has been the type used so far in the analysis and which means that investment was undertaken regardless of the level of income. Investment appeared to be independent of current economic conditions and therefore based on future expected conditions. The disregard for the present may be a characteristic of certain investment projects: investment for a new product, for some innovation, or for some cost-saving device. Some investment of this type can always be expected to take place in a dynamic, technology-oriented economic system.

Other types of investment can be grouped temporarily under the general heading of *induced investment,* meaning that economic conditions and changes in those conditions do affect the volume of investment. As the level of income grows, more investment is needed to produce the higher level of output, and more investment may be undertaken in contemplation of further income growth. The dependence of investment upon income will be examined presently, but it is clear that there is a sharp distinction between induced investment and autonomous investment.

Replacement investment is another part of total investment for any one period. As plant and equipment wear out, they must be replaced if the firm is to continue operations. Obsolete equipment may be replaced even before it is worn out, so that technological change and replacement become even more entangled. Replacement investment does not technically add to the level of capital stock, but it may still add to the productive capacity of the economy if it is technologically superior.

Other motivations for investment include projects undertaken for *safety purposes;* for *modernization* of existing facilities; for *competitive reasons,* to keep up with competitors, domestic and foreign; and for *beautification, ecological,* or *environmental* concerns, whether undertaken voluntarily or under some compulsion.

The difficulty here is that data on investment do not distinguish one type of investment from another or separate the motivations that underlie the observed investment total. Yet the analysis of investment spending (not to mention the policies designed to influence it) would surely be different for each type. There is at the moment no choice but to accept the investment data in their present form with the knowledge that they group together various types of investment.

Two Investment Decisions

It is common to consider "the" investment decision as if there were only one irrevocable decision. In a practical sense, there are at least two investment decisions, and these are connected to the stock and flow variables in the process of capital accumulation. Most economists tend to view the whole process in terms of one decision—a view that may be permissible under some circumstances but inhibiting or misleading under others.

The first investment decision is whether or not to add to capital stock—let us call this the stock decision. As will be noted, many factors enter into this decision, but for the present all that is necessary is for the decision to be made using as much objective information as is available. Similarly, there is no need to specify which motivation for investment is predominant. For whatever reason, there is a decision to add to capital stock because the existing level or type will not do—the optimal level or combination has not been attained.

The second decision, let us call it the flow decision, is concerned with *when* to spend on investment in order to reach the optimum capital stock as determined by the first decision. It is a matter of timing. Generally, firms have some options in considering the proper time to fulfill investment plans.

The two decisions introduce time into the process, for they can be made in different time periods. The decision *to invest* can be made in one period, and the decision *to spend* can be made many periods later. In some cases, the two decisions are made simultaneously, and this is the case that is generally held to be the normal condition by those who see only one investment decision. In many other cases, the two decisions do not coincide, and more than likely this should be regarded as the normal situation. Only by accepting two investment decisions is it possible to account for the observed *postponement* of investment spending and the *canceling* of investment projects. An investment project could be approved but no funds allocated to it, and perhaps, as conditions change, the entire project is scrapped.

This kind of behavior is more applicable to the large firm, which can be expected to employ capital-budgeting techniques. Large firms do account for the bulk of investment expenditures, so that their behavior is the appropriate type to consider. Yet even the smaller firm with much less formal procedures probably acts similarly whenever large sums are involved. In either case, it is a way to record a commitment without incurring any obligation, for the first decision is an internal matter and only the second decision requires outside contracts. It can also be viewed as one way to postpone the crucial decision until more information becomes available. In practice, the larger the firm, the greater the bureaucracy that requires the formal distinction between the two decisions so that the responsibility for them can be more readily assigned.

If there are two investment decisions, then at any time there will be many investment projects that have been formally approved or are being considered but against which little or nothing has been spent. There is a backlog of possible investment projects. Over some period of time, some of these will be undertaken and investment spending will occur. Other projects will be postponed and some will be canceled. In any event, it will take time to complete an investment project, and there is no reason to expect investment *spending* to be spread out evenly over the life of the project.[1] Nor will it be readily apparent why some projects are undertaken and others canceled. The factors operating at the firm level may be unobservable at the aggregate level.

Postulating two separate investment decisions complicates matters somewhat. Still, it helps to clarify the relation between stocks and flows in the theory of investment. In our discussion of stocks and flows in chapter 3, we wrote the investment relation straightforwardly as

$$I_g - D \gtreqless 0; \qquad I_n \gtreqless 0; \qquad \Delta K \gtreqless 0,$$

which states that if gross investment minus depreciation is positive (negative), net investment is positive (negative), and the change in capital stock is positive (negative). In this context it is clear how the flow variable, investment, affects the stock variable, capital stock. The relationship holds by definition and occurs *after* investment spending has taken place.

With two investment decisions, the forgoing expression is turned around, so to speak; the capital stock decision is made first, followed (if at all) by later decisions to spend. Once the expenditure of funds has taken place, the above investment relationships are true, of course, but our problem is not to define but to explain the entire process of capital accumulation. It is therefore necessary to bring in behavioral variables wherever possible and to recognize the institutional framework within which investment decisions are made.

---

[1] See Shirley Almon, "The Distributed Lag Between Capital Appropriations and Expenditures," *Econometrica* 33 (January 1965): 178–196; and "Lags Between Investment Decisions and Their Causes," *Review of Economics and Statistics* 50 (May 1968): 193–206; and A. S. Campagna, "Capital Appropriations and the Investment Decision," *Review of Economics and Statistics* 50 (May 1968): 207–214.

The Investment Function

Like consumption, investment depends upon many things, some more important than others: there are objective factors and subjective ones, measurable and unmeasurable ones, and institutional and cultural ones. No one has been able to sort them out and develop a coherent investment function. A brief glance at some of these influences may reveal why the investment variable has proved so unmanageable.

$$\text{Investment} = f(\text{internal conditions, external factors,}$$
$$\text{and cultural and other institutional}$$
$$\text{influences}).$$

Under these general categories we can list some of the more important factors (see Table 9.1). The categories overlap, of course, and are used merely for convenience. The list is not complete, but it does reveal why investment is difficult to explain (though some of the more awkward issues that are problems for advanced work are not even included).

In general, we can identify the first investment decision, the stock one, with the external factors and the second investment decision, the flow one, with the internal factors. These are broad generalizations; some overlapping occurs, and both decisions are influenced by the third category of cultural and institutional factors. The external factors are beyond the control of the firm or industry, although they do exert some influence over the decision of whether or not to invest.[2] The internal

TABLE 9.1
INVESTMENT INFLUENCES

Internal Factors	External Factors	Cultural and Institutional Variables
Past Profits	Interest Rate	Attitudes Toward Risk
Depreciation Allowances	Government Policies (Fiscal and Monetary)	Attitudes Toward Profit and Success
Sales	Technological Change	Attitudes Toward Capital Accumulation and Power
Production Process (Possibility of Substituting K for N)	Level of Economic Activity and Changes in the Level	Religious Institutions
Other Financial Assets	Other Expectations and Forecasts	Permissive Political Structure
Expectations	Conditions in Capital Goods Industries (for Costs)	Education of Population
Age of Plant	War Versus Peace Conditions	Attitudes Toward Thrift
	Political Stability	
	Labor Force	
	Monetary Institutions	

---

[2] It is not necessary to view these external factors as identical with the type found in the assumption of perfect competition. Obviously, firms in imperfect competition can exercise some power over others external to them.

influences are generally financial variables and are thus more influential in the investment spending decision.

Firms, at least the successful ones, keep a watchful eye on the economy as a whole when they want to decide whether conditions warrant additional investment. While it is true that firms are interested in higher profits, they cannot view their operations as isolated from the surrounding economy. This makes the investment decision rather difficult, and the existence of two distinct investment decisions becomes more understandable. In the course of the discussion of investment and capital accumulation some of these variables will be examined at greater length as the relation between the two investment decisions is clarified. The purpose of this section has been to point out that investment is a complex variable, and to state that investment is undertaken for profit really begs the question.

The Theory of Capital

The first part of any investment decision is whether or not to invest at all; this we have called the first investment decision—the stock decision. We have noted that many influences continuously affect the process of capital accumulation, and we must therefore make some limiting assumptions in order to get started in the examination of this complex variable. Assume that all the internal factors mentioned earlier are considered somehow by the firms but for the moment are not of paramount importance. Assume, also, that all the institutional and cultural factors are constant or relatively stable and do not affect the investment decision at the time it is being made. Moreover, all the external factors, except for the cost of the capital good and the interest rate, are to be considered constant. What is left is a decision that is more clear-cut: whether or not an investment project is worthwhile, *everything else remaining equal.* The factors that enter into the decision are the cost of the capital good, the market rate of interest, and some estimate of the income to be derived if the investment were made. Under these conditions an investment decision is made possible.

On a microeconomic level no one firm has control over the prices of the capital goods it buys or over the market rate of interest. The prices of capital goods (given to the firm) are determined by the conditions in the capital goods industries, and the rate of interest is determined in the money market (both statements assume perfect competition in all markets). Once imperfect competition is admitted, large firms can possibly exert some leverage in these markets. For the moment, however, the assumption of perfect competition is retained in order to concentrate on the investment decision itself.

The rate of interest is the perfectly competitive rate determined in the money market and can be taken as equivalent to the rate on long-term government securities. Other interest rates fluctuate in the same direction as the long-term government bond rate, and this rate therefore serves as an average and is a good one to use as an abstraction of the market rate of interest. In a perfectly competitive money market all firms would be able to borrow at this going rate.

In recent years there has been a tendency for firms to use internal funds to finance investment projects. Retained earnings, profits, and depreciation allowances (cash flow) are available for use without the firm having to enter the money market. This may be partly because of the conservative attitude of businessmen who do not wish to be saddled with a fixed debt, as would be the case with borrowed funds. An investment project that fails is painfully visible on financial statements. The use of internal funds is also a way for firms to insulate themselves from shifts in the money markets that at times have caused a short supply of funds and thus barred the undertaking of fruitful investment projects. With the use of internal funds, stockholders do not receive all the profits, and the firms' customers furnish the investment funds, because they pay higher prices than would have been necessary had the firm turned to external sources for financing. With borrowed funds, the interest cost is tax deductible, and at first this would appear to offer the best avenue for investment financing. The growing use of internal funds is evidence that other factors are becoming more important than this tax consideration. Of course, the firm could finance its investment by floating new stock, but this route appears to be the least advantageous, since it dilutes control and offers no tax advantages. These options are readily available to the large firms but the smaller ones (or growing ones) may be limited to borrowing. Actually, then, the interest rate *as a cost* is a more critical consideration for the smaller firm than for the larger one, and the availability of funds is even more important. The larger firm faces no serious supply problem and can borrow at better rates or turn to its other options.

Still, if a firm does elect to use internal funds, it ought to charge itself a rate of interest. The use of these funds involves an opportunity cost, and this cost must enter the investment decision as an implicit cost to be considered in any calculation of profitability. Incidentally, this cost is not recognized for tax purposes, since it is an economic cost and not an out-of-pocket expense. Note, too, that even in a collective-type economy some implicit interest cost must be recognized, since there must be some method of differentiating among the possible competing projects. Therefore, some calculations of the profitability of investment projects must always be made in a manner similar to that which follows.

If we continue to assume perfect competition, the rate of interest is given to the firm, but if all firms demand more funds, the rate of interest is bound to be affected. For the economy as a whole, the rate of interest is a variable and must itself be determined. The determination of the interest rate and the money market will be the subject of later chapters.

The prices of capital goods can also be assumed to be known and given to the firm. They depend upon cost conditions in the capital goods industries, which are beyond the influence of a perfectly competitive firm. With imperfect competition, of course, the possibility again arises that large, oligopolistic firms can exert some power, even if they are dealing with other oligopolistic firms on the supply side.[3] The smaller firms would have no such opportunity and would be forced to accept the terms of the large capital goods suppliers.

Even if we continue to assume perfect competition, if *all* firms increase their demand for capital goods, the cost of capital goods is likely to change as the capital goods industries react to the demand pressures put on them. What happens in the capital goods industries is largely determined by the cost structures and the capacity utilization of the firms in those industries. In the short run demand pressures could result in increases in the prices of capital goods as firms attempt to increase output but run into inefficiencies. If, however, the firms are operating at far less than capacity (or the law of diminishing returns is not applicable), then prices need not increase significantly. Again, if imperfect competition is admitted, prices may not

---

[3] This is the familiar notion of countervailing power as introduced by J. K. Galbraith in his book *American Capitalism* (Boston: Houghton Mifflin, 1962).

increase for some time, because oligopolistic pricing policies may not permit much price flexibility and firms may simply accumulate and backlog orders.

Over a longer time span capacity utilization would still be important, but the cost structure of the industry would become equally critical. If the demand for new capital goods continues (or firms in the capital goods industries *expect* them to continue), production of capital goods will be increased. As production increases, firms could be faced with increasing costs, constant costs, or decreasing costs, depending upon the nature of the productive process. If inefficiencies enter in quickly, costs will begin to increase; if as production expands new cost-saving techniques are introduced, costs may actually decrease. Output could also be increased without any change in unit costs. Therefore, what happens to the prices of capital goods depends upon which long-run cost condition is appropriate. To complicate matters further, the capital goods industries, enjoying a boom, could decide to increase their productive capacity by investments of their own. The expectation of growing investment demand resulting in increased capacity to produce capital goods could change the cost structure of previous operations. That is, if demand pressures had forced firms to incur increasing costs with the old plant, the new investment that enlarges capacity could permit the firms to supply the additional capital goods without running into increasing costs.

What happens to the cost of capital goods is not easily determined, depending as it does on the cost structure of the industry, the degree of capacity utilization, the existence (or not) of imperfect competition, and the response of the firms in the capital goods industries to demand pressures. To determine which of these influences are most likely to occur, singly or in combination, is an empirical problem that cannot be resolved theoretically. Therefore, some assumption is necessary, and the most suitable one to make for the present is that the capital goods industries operate under conditions of constant costs (or what amounts to the same thing, that the industries always have excess capacity and can expand output without significant cost problems).[4]

With this assumption, the cost of capital goods can be said to be known to the firms. Since the rate of interest was also assumed known, all that is required now is to calculate the yield of the capital good and the elements of the first investment decision will be in hand. We must now determine the income that can be expected to flow from the operation of the capital good under consideration.

The trouble with capital goods is that they last a long time, and this alone makes the investment decision difficult. If a new machine is expected to last for twenty years, it is necessary, *for each year,* to estimate

1. the *expected output* of the machine (in units)
2. the *expected selling price* of these units of output
3. the *expected gross income* from the machine for each year—(1) times (2)
4. the *expected costs* associated with this machine year by year (maintenance and repair, and so on, but *not* the "sunk" costs of depreciation or interest costs)
5. the *expected net income* from the machine year by year for twenty years—(3) minus (4)

Note the words *expected* and *estimated* in this list. They imply barriers to action, for the longer the capital good is expected to last, the more difficult the decision

---

[4] Empirical cost functions are difficult to obtain, but the assumption of constant cost is at least not inconsistent with some of this work. See A. A. Walters, "Production and Cost Functions: An Econometric Survey," *Econometrica* 31 (January 1963): 1–66.

becomes. It would be natural to postpone the decision as long as possible until more information becomes available, but unfortunately there is never enough information, and eventually some action must be taken even with imperfect knowledge of the consequences. It would also be natural to try to make the decision easier by obtaining "objective" information. The management tool of systems analysis and mathematical techniques are designed to provide more objective data. But there is no way to eliminate completely the subjective expectations of those who are given the task of decision making; that is, some of the data, some of the input into the mathematical formulas, are not themselves objective but are based upon expectations and thus are subjective. Many probability statements are of this type. Keynes expressed his reservations about mathematical calculations of this type:

Most, probably, of our decisions to do something positive, the full consequences of which will be drawn out over many days to come, can only be taken as a result of animal spirits —of a spontaneous urge to action rather than inaction, and not as the outcome of a weighted average of quantitative benefits multiplied by quantitative probabilities. Enterprise only pretends to itself to be mainly actuated by the statements in its own prospectus, however candid and sincere. Only a little more than an expedition to the South Pole, is it based on an exact calculation of benefits to come. Thus if the animal spirits are dimmed and the spontaneous optimism falters, leaving us to depend on nothing but a mathematical expectation, enterprise will fade and die;—though fears of loss may have a basis no more reasonable than hopes of profit had before.[5]

The estimation of the income flow from the machine is difficult in an uncertain world. All that can be stated with confidence is that some estimates are made, but the process by which they are obtained might as well be called "animal spirits." Attempts to reduce uncertainty by formalizing the estimating process into mathematical expressions may help, but they cannot eliminate the fact that expectations play a vital part. So far, no one has provided a satisfactory explanation of how these expectations are formed.[6]

The Mathematics of the Investment Decision

Once the expected net earnings have been estimated for every year in which the machine will operate, some method must be found to reduce this income stream to its present worth. The income from this machine will accrue over many years, but the cost outlay to purchase it must be made now. What is needed is some procedure by which the current outlay and future returns can be compared. The mathematical method that permits such comparison is called *discounting;* the discounting of this future income stream to the present yields the *present value* of the income stream. The present value of the expected earnings can then be compared directly to the current (present) outlay for the piece of equipment. What the mathematical procedure recognizes is that a dollar tomorrow is not the same as a dollar today. (If it were, there would be no such thing as a rate of interest.)

The method used in discounting is the reverse of that used for compound interest calculations. Since compound interest is more familiar, our discussion can start

---

[5] J. M. Keynes, *The General Theory of Employment, Interest, and Money* (New York: Harcourt, Brace, 1936), pp. 161–162.

[6] In this connection, no better start could be made than by reading Keynes's thoughts contained in chapters 5 and 12 of *The General Theory.*

here. If one lends out \$1 at 5 per cent for one year, one would get back at the end of the year

$$\$1.00 + 0.05(\$1.00) = \$1.05.$$

If one relends the entire amount for the second year, one would get back at the end of the second year

$$\$1.05 + 0.05(\$1.05) = \$1.1025,$$

and so on, year after year. Here the interest was compounded annually, but more frequent compounding does not affect the analysis and the same conclusions emerge. We wish to generalize this method, so let us make the original principal $\$1.00 = P_0$ and the rate of interest i. The principal at the end of any period may be identified by the subscript attached to P. For the first year,

$$P_0 + i(P_0) = P_1,$$

or more generally, factoring P_0,

$$P_0(1 + i) = P_1$$
$$\$1.00(1 + 0.05) = \$1.05.$$

For the second year, the entire sum, P_1, was reloaned, so that the general formula gives

$$P_1(1 + i) = P_2$$
$$\$1.05(1 + 0.05) = \$1.1025.$$

However, since $P_1 = P_0(1 + i)$, this expression can be substituted in the second-year calculation to give

$$P_0(1 + i)\ (1 + i) = P_2,$$

or

$$P_0(1 + i)^2 = P_2.$$

In a similar way, the expression for the third year (assuming the entire amount P_2 was loaned out) would be

$$P_0(1 + i)^3 = P_3$$

and for the fourth year,

$$P_0(1 + i)^4 = P_4$$

and so on. In general terms, the expression for annual compound interest in which the accumulated interest is not withdrawn is

$$P_0(1 + i)^t = P_t,$$

where the subscript t stands for the year. The mathematical expression for compound interest answers the question, How much will \$1 invested today and compounded at a certain rate of interest grow to after some time period?

The process of discounting asks a different question: What sum is required *today* to grow to \$1 if the sum invested earns 5 per cent compounded annually? Obviously, the sum required today will be less than \$1. In general terms, what is required is to solve for P_0 in the expression for compound interest to get

$$P_0 = \frac{P_t}{(1 + i)^t};$$

that is, if one knows the amount one wants to receive after some time period, P_t, how much must one put up today so that this sum plus interest will accumulate to the desired or known goal? Similarly one could ask, given a sum payable or earned in the future, what is the *present value* of that sum? The present value of $1 after period 2 is

$$P_0 = \frac{P_2}{(1 + 0.05)^2} = \frac{\$1.00}{(1 + 0.05)^2} = \$0.907;$$

for one could invest $0.907 today at 5 per cent compound interest, and at the end of year two, this sum would grow to $1.

Additional examples may help to clarify this frequently confusing concept. Suppose a parent at the birth of a child wishes to ensure that the child will receive a college education, which he estimates will cost $20,000. How much must he invest *today* at an interest rate of 6 per cent so that the proper sum will be available after seventeen years? The answer is $7,420.[7]

Suppose a student received a negotiable claim (riskless) for $10,000, payable ten years hence. The student, however, wants the money now, not ten years from now. For how much could he sell this claim in the market if the rate of interest is 4 per cent? The answer is $6,760. No one would give him more than $6,760, because this is how much one must invest at 4 per cent to receive $10,000 at the end of ten years. Neither would the student accept less than $6,760 for the same reason. Note what happens to the amount as the rate of interest changes: If the interest rate rises to 6 per cent, the present value of the claim *falls* to $5,580. The rate of interest and the present value vary *inversely*. Now to receive $10,000 after ten years, it is only necessary to put up $5,580 because the interest rate has increased.[8]

Before returning to the investment decision, it is worthwhile to digress a little more in order to discuss the application of this concept to the bond market. The

---

[7] Present value tables are available in almost any book on business finance. These tables give the present value of $1 for various interest rates and for various time intervals. Of course, one could make one's own calculations, but the arithmetic gets tedious.

[8] The following table should help to explain the relation between the process of compounding and discounting.

| | Compound Amount of $1 | | | Present Value of $1 | |
| | At | At | | At | At |
Period	5%	10%	Period	5%	10%
0	1.0000	1.000	0	1.000	1.000
1	1.0500	1.100	1	0.952	0.909
2	1.1025	1.211	2	0.907	0.826
3	1.1570	1.332	3	0.864	0.751
4	1.2150	1.464	4	0.823	0.683
5	1.2760	1.610	5	0.784	0.621

From the table it can be seen that $1 will grow to $1.276 at 5 per cent and $1.610 at 10 per cent after five years. The left-hand side of the table is for the compound interest calculation. To see the relation between compounding and discounting, take the previous example, where after two periods the original $1 grew to $1.1025 at 5 per cent compound interest. Now, if a principal of $1 grew to $1.1025 in two years at 5 per cent, then a principal of $x will grow to $1.0000 in two years at 5 per cent and will be in the same proportion:

$$\frac{1}{1.1025} = \frac{x}{1.0000} = 0.907,$$

which is the reciprocal of 1.1025. On the right-hand side, the present value of $1 after two periods is equal to 0.907. This is the relation between compounding and discounting that we have been seeking: the present value is the reciprocal of the compound interest calculation. Further examples and discussion can be found in P. Hunt, C. M. Williams, and G. Donaldson, *Basic Business Finance* (Homewood, Ill.: Richard D. Irwin, 1971), ch. 8, on which the present discussion is based.

conclusions reached will prove very useful in subsequent work. Assume a bond pays a yearly return of $100 and all the holder must do to collect it is to present a coupon for payment. The bond reaches maturity after a period of six years, at which time the principal is also repaid. If the market rate of interest is 5 per cent and the bond price was $10,000, what is the present value of the bond?

The general formula for the calculation follows from the previous discussion, and each year's return must be discounted to the present as follows:

$$V_p = \frac{R_1}{(1+i)} + \frac{R_2}{(1+i)^2} + \frac{R_3}{(1+i)^3} + \frac{R_4}{(1+i)^4} + \frac{R_5}{(1+i)^5} + \frac{R_6}{(1+i)^6} + \frac{P}{(1+i)^6},$$

where V_p is the present value of the bond, R is the coupon amount, i is the market rate of interest, and P is the principal of the bond. Substituting into the formula,

$$V_p = \frac{100}{(1+0.05)} + \frac{100}{(1+0.05)^2} + \frac{100}{(1+0.05)^3} + \frac{100}{(1+0.05)^4} + \frac{100}{(1+0.05)^5}$$
$$+ \frac{100}{(1+0.05)^6} + \frac{10,000}{(1+0.05)^6},$$

which gives,

$$V_p = 95.20 + 90.70 + 86.40 + 82.30 + 78.40 + 74.60 + 7,460;$$
$$= 7,967.60.$$

The present value of the bond is $7,967.60, and the present value of just the six $100 payments is $507.60. This is just another example of discounting an income stream. What happens when the bond has no maturity date—a perpetual or consol bond? A bond that will not be redeemed reduces the general formula

$$V_p = \frac{R_1}{(1+i)} + \frac{R_2}{(1+i)^2} + \frac{R_3}{(1+i)^3} + \cdots + \frac{R_n}{(1+i)^n} + \frac{P}{(1+i)^n}$$

to

$$V_p = \frac{R}{i} \qquad \text{as } n \to \infty.\,[9]$$

[9] The expression for the calculation of present values is a geometric series, the sum of which is given by the same formula previously used in the multiplier:

$$S = \frac{a - ar^n}{1 - r},$$

where a is the first term in the series; r is the common fraction; and n is the number of periods. The substitution of the present value expression into the formula for the sum of a geometric series gives

$$V_p = \frac{\dfrac{R_1}{1+i} - \left[\dfrac{R_1}{1+i} \times \left(\dfrac{1}{1+i}\right)^n\right]}{1 - \dfrac{1}{1+i}} + \frac{P}{(1+i)^n}$$

$$= \frac{R}{i}\left[1 - \left(\frac{1}{1+i}\right)^n\right] + \frac{P}{(1+i)^n}.$$

As n gets very large or approaches infinity, this expression reduces to

$$V_p = \frac{R}{i}.$$

This same formula is used to "capitalize" an income stream that is perpetual. There are many applications of this concept, so that some effort to learn it will be rewarding for the many uses to which it can be put.

Thus, if the bond returned $100 per year and the market rate of interest were 5 per cent, the present value of the bond would be $100/0.05 = $2,000. If the market rate of interest fell to 2 per cent, the present value of the bond would rise to $5,000; and if the market rate of interest rose to 10 per cent, the present value of the bond would fall to $1,000. Thus, the value of the bond and the rate of interest vary inversely, and therefore bond prices and interest rates vary inversely also. This is an extremely important relation, and it is important to see why it holds.

The $100-per-year income stream at 5 per cent was capitalized to give the present value of the bond at $2,000. No one would pay more than $2,000 for this bond, because they could buy another security for $2,000 that at 5 per cent would yield the same return of $100. Similarly, no one would accept less than $2,000, since one would not be able to get a comparable return of $100 on the lower-priced security one would be forced to purchase. Thus, $2,000 would be the price of the bond in all trading transactions. Now, if the market rate of interest rose to 10 per cent, the value of the bond would fall to $1,000. Why? At the higher interest rate, to obtain a return of $100, it is only necessary to invest $1,000. Therefore, any security that yields only $100 will fall in value to that level where the rate of return matches the market rate, 10 per cent. Thus, the holders of the security of $2,000 now find it is worth only $1,000, and they have suffered a $1,000 capital loss. At an interest rate of 10 per cent, no one would be foolish enough to pay $2,000 for this bond to earn $100 when they can buy two $1,000 bonds and receive $200.

If the rate of interest falls, say, to 2 per cent, the value of the security would rise to $5,000. In order to obtain a return of $100 when $i = 2$ per cent, it is necessary to invest $5,000. The market will revalue all existing securities to reflect the change in interest rates, and the bond that was worth $2,000 at $i = 5$ per cent is now valued at $5,000 at $i = 2$ per cent. We will have many occasions to make use of the inverse relation between bond prices and interest rates when the money market is brought into the analysis explicitly. The whole concept and the mathematics fit into the present discussion, and hence this digression. In any case, it is well to be familiar with these relations even for the management of one's personal financial affairs.

The Marginal Efficiency of Capital

Now that some of the background mathematics has been reviewed, it is time to apply the discounting concept to the investment decision. We wish to obtain some guideline by which to determine the profitability of investment and hence whether or not the investment project should be undertaken. For an investment project, the income stream is represented by the expected net earnings; the present value of the income stream is represented by the cost of the capital good; and the discount rate, which makes the discounted value of the income stream just equal to the cost of the capital good, is known as the marginal efficiency of capital. Thus, the formula becomes

$$K_p = \frac{R_1}{(1+r)} + \frac{R_2}{(1+r)^2} + \frac{R_3}{(1+r)^3} + \frac{R_4}{(1+r)^4} + \cdots + \frac{R_n}{(1+r)^n} + \frac{S}{(1+r)^n},$$

where K_p is the cost (price) of the capital good; R is the expected net earnings from the capital good; S is the scrap value (if any) of the capital good; and r is the rate of discount, or the marginal efficiency of capital. From our previous assumptions, the price of the capital good, K_p, is given and the expected net income by year, R, has been estimated. If we ignore the scrap value of the asset, so that the last term disappears, what is left unknown is r, the marginal efficiency of capital (MEC). If we solve the expression for r, we arrive at one crucial element in the investment decision, the MEC, which is interpreted as the rate of return or the yield expected from the capital good.

For example, assume a machine that costs $421.20 will last for five years ($n = 5$) and each year will earn $100 net income and that after five years the machine is worthless even for scrap.[10] Substituting these data into the formula gives

$$421.20 = \frac{100}{(1 + r)} + \frac{100}{(1 + r)^2} + \frac{100}{(1 + r)^3} + \frac{100}{(1 + r)^4} + \frac{100}{(1 + r)^5}.$$

Solving this expression for r gives $r = 6$ per cent, which is the rate of return, an abstract number that Keynes called the marginal efficiency of capital:

. . . I define the marginal efficiency of capital as being equal to that rate of discount which would make the present value of the series of annuities given by the returns expected from the capital-asset during its life just equal to its supply price.[11]

Having calculated the MEC, the rate of return over cost, the firm is in a position to make the first investment decision. All that is necessary is to compare this rate of return with the (given) market rate of interest at which the firm could lend funds and receive a return:

$$\text{If } r = MEC > i,$$

the investment project is preferred to lending out funds, is profitable, and will be undertaken.

$$\text{If } r = MEC < i,$$

the investment project will not be undertaken and the firm may prefer to lend the funds.

$$\text{If } r = MEC = i,$$

the firm is indifferent as to which alternative it chooses.

The first investment decision is based on the comparison between the MEC and the rate of interest. The profitability of investment projects is easily compared, since the two numbers are both abstract.[12] Note that the rate of interest does not enter into the calculation of the MEC but is compared to it after the calculation has been made.

The MEC of investment projects can change as the elements that determine it

---

[10] The assumption that the returns from the machine are constant over its life ($= \$100$) is for arithmetic simplicity. In all likelihood, the net returns would decline as the machine aged and more maintenance and repairs became necessary. The assumption that the returns are all positive also simplifies the mathematics considerably.

[11] Keynes, *The General Theory*, p. 135.

[12] While the decision appears straightforward, there are obviously cases where the "wrong" decision would be made based on this criterion. A machine centrally located in a plant may have to be purchased or the plant would close down, for instance. Still, the general rule is useful for many other "marginal" projects. In addition, the point of indifference, $MEC = i$, if ever reached, would probably result in postponement or rejection of the project, since the calculation of the MEC involved several estimates. Businessmen who would reject such calculations often deal in rules of thumb that approach the formal process. See M. H. Spencer and L. Siegleman, *Managerial Economics*, rev. ed. (Homewood, Ill.: Richard D. Irwin, 1964), ch. 12.

change. If the cost of the capital increases, the *MEC* will fall, and as the cost of the capital good decreases, the *MEC* will rise, everything else equal. Similarly, if the expectations of future revenue or costs change, the *MEC* will change, too— in this case, the *MEC* will vary directly with changes in net expected income. Again, the market rate of interest may change, which will result in a reevaluation of projects previously rejected or, if possible, those previously accepted. Thus, some projects can be postponed and others canceled as conditions change. But other projects, once started, are difficult or impossible to stop.

There is some question of what rate of interest a firm would use as an implicit cost if it employed internal funds. If it uses the market rate of interest, there is no problem. If, however, it uses a lower rate than the market rate, more investment is likely to take place, since more projects will appear profitable. In reality, it may well be that with the level of interest rates prevailing in recent years most investment projects probably were far above them, so that the strict criterion may not be applicable in any case. It may well be the case that firms ignore the implicit cost involved in the use of internal funds, preferring to reason along accounting rather than economic lines. This may be especially so with smaller firms, since the larger firms can be expected to employ rather sophisticated capital-budgeting techniques.

The Marginal Efficiency of Capital and the First Investment Decision for the Firm

At any one time the firm may be contemplating several different investment projects, some perhaps fanciful musings and others carefully planned ones. Whatever the type of investment or the motivation for considering it, the investment projects can be expected to yield different rates of return, different *MEC*s. A ranking of these projects according to the expected rate of return would result in an *MEC* schedule as given in Figure 9.1.

The vertical axis measures the *MEC* and the rate of interest, and the horizontal axis measures the stock of capital associated with the rate of return given by the *MEC*s. It is important to note that the rate of return is for new capital stock and is unrelated to the yields on past capital goods and that the horizontal axis also

FIGURE 9.1
THE MEC SCHEDULE OF THE FIRM

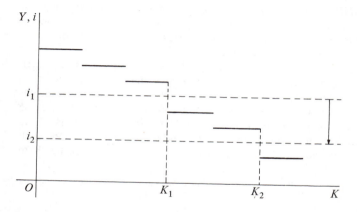

measures the new capital stock.[13] The investment projects are ranked from the highest rate of return to the lowest, since it is assumed that the firm would exploit the most profitable opportunity first.

Now, given a rate of interest i_1 the firm will consider undertaking the first three investment projects and thus would add OK_1 to its capital stock. The first three projects are profitable, because according to our rules, the rate of return expected from them exceeds the market rate of interest, that is, $MEC = r > i$ for all three projects. All other investment projects are unprofitable, since $i > r$ for these investment possibilities. If the market rate of interest fell to i_2, the next two investment projects would become profitable and if undertaken would increase the capital stock from OK_1 to OK_2. Still, the last project yields a rate of return less than the market rate of interest and would remain on the shelf.

Aggregating the Firms' MEC Schedules to the Economy as a Whole

The MEC schedule for the firm is direct and easily interpreted, since the firm considers only a specific *type* of asset used by it in the production process. Yields on assets used by the firm can be expected to vary as firms contemplate improvement projects, safety projects, and so on. Aggregation of firms' MEC schedules to the industry level also appears to be straightforward, and again similar types of assets are being considered. The meaning of a marginal asset, while perhaps somewhat indefinite, is still understandable as long as assets of a particular type or related to a particular process are assessed.

For macroeconomic purposes, the aggregation of such MEC schedules for the economy as a whole results in some interpretation problems, and the term *marginal* must be reconsidered. Once different types of capital goods are added together and ranked by yields, the meaning of the MEC schedule loses its clarity, for the MEC calculation relates only to a particular type of asset, not to assets in general. Aggregating the firms' MEC schedules (or industries') would smooth out the steplike schedules of firms, since rates of returns will be found to fill in the gaps. Ranking the MECs from highest to lowest would give the MEC schedule for the economy as a whole, as pictured in Figure 9.2.

The only interpretation that the aggregation process will support is that the economy will benefit most if investment projects with the highest yields are undertaken before those that are lower. To speak of the marginal efficiency of capital is to mean the highest MEC attainable by the economy. One more, or a marginal, unit of the asset with the highest MEC will confer the greatest return to the economy. The MEC schedule for the entire economy thus becomes a very abstract concept— a necessary result of the aggregation process.

In Figure 9.2, if the market rate of interest is i_0, all investment projects for which the MEC, r, exceeds this rate will be undertaken and the economy will accumulate, in time, OK_0 units of capital. The intersection of i_0 and the MEC curve indicates the point of equality, $i = r$, and the level at which additions to capital stock cease to be profitable for the economy. Investment projects below the current market rate of interest on the MEC schedule will be unprofitable and are not pursued. One such asset is indicated by R on the MEC schedule. If the market rate of interest falls to

---

[13] For a different and more critical view of the MEC schedule for a firm and for the economy, see G. Ackley, *Macroeconomic Theory* (New York: Macmillan, 1961), p. 472.

FIGURE 9.2
THE MARGINAL EFFICIENCY OF CAPITAL FOR THE ECONOMY

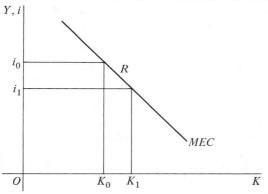

i_1, more investment projects become profitable, including R, and when they are completed they will bring the level of capital stock to the new desired level of OK_1.

In this manner, the *MEC* schedule becomes a demand curve for capital stock, and on this schedule the demand for capital goods has been considered an inverse function of the rate of interest. The *MEC* schedule also determines the *optimum* or *desired level* of capital stock for the economy. The optimum level of capital stock is determined when the *MEC* is equal to *i*, the market rate of interest. Capital stock with yields in excess of this rate should presumably be undertaken, for the rate of return to the economy exceeds the normal rate of return on all assets, real and monetary. Assets with less than the going rate of interest are not worthwhile, and the economy would be underutilizing its resources if these projects were undertaken. The optimal stock of capital is given where the rate of return is everywhere the same in the economy.

The first investment decision is, then, the determination of the optimum level of capital stock: the amount of capital stock desired by the community will determine how much of the economy's resources will be devoted to the production of implements and how much to the "roundabout" process of capital goods production, which entails the sacrifice of (consumer) goods now for more goods later.

Having determined the optimum level of capital stock, we must examine how the economy moves toward this desired level; that is, once the capital *stock* level has been determined, it is necessary to explain the *flow* side, thus completing the explanation of the entire process of capital accumulation.

The Theory of Investment and the Accumulation of Capital

The second investment decision in the process of capital accumulation is concerned with *when* to make the actual investment expenditure. The first decision was made in the stock part of the process, where the desired level of capital stock was determined. How we reach that desired level of capital stock is the flow decision, the second decision. Investment spending is likely to be more influenced by financial concerns than the stock decision; past profits, depreciation accruals, other assets, and so on, become important variables in the consideration of when to spend and at what rate. In the initial discussion of investment spending these financial variables will play a secondary role and the rate of interest will continue to represent the main financial determinant. Other parts of the second investment decision that tend to complicate matters—such as the possibility of postponing or canceling investment projects—are similarly ignored.

The attention then shifts to the *dynamic* consideration of investment spending. We want to know the *time* it takes to move from one level of capital stock to the new desirable level; the path by which the gap is closed; and the rate of spending and any change in that rate.

The time and path of investment spending in closing the gap between actual and desired capital stock depends to a large extent upon the capital goods industries. In the discussion of the cost of capital goods the supply conditions of these industries were examined at some length. Recall the assumption that the capital goods industries were operating under constant cost conditions. Therefore, *the only limit to the rate of investment spending is the physical capacity of the capital goods industries* to supply the goods ordered.

With this assumption, it is possible to get a simple overall view of the process of capital accumulation. The operation and interaction of the two investment decisions are shown in Figure 9.3.[14] In Figure 9.3(a) is shown the first investment decision—the stock part—where the optimum or desired level of capital stock is determined. At the interest rate of i_0 the equality $i_0 = r_0 = MEC$ gives the desired level of capital stock, K_0. Once this level of capital stock is reached, and if the rate of interest remains unchanged at i_0, there will be no further capital accumulation; the level of capital stock is in equilibrium where the desired level equals the actual level, and only replacement investment takes place in this situation.

In Figure 9.3(b) the second investment decision is shown. The flow part of capital accumulation shows the time and path by which investment spending closes the gap between actual and desired levels of capital stock. At the interest rate of

FIGURE 9.3

THE TWO INVESTMENT DECISIONS AND CAPITAL ACCUMULATION

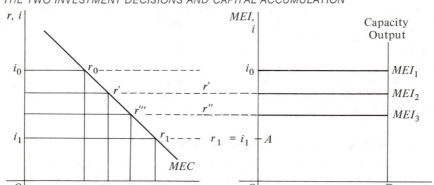

[14] Much of this discussion is based upon the work of Ackley, *Macroeconomic Theory,* and A. P. Lerner, *The Economics of Control* (New York: Macmillan, 1944), ch. 25. Lerner's work, particularly, helped to clarify the theory of capital.

i_0 there is no (net) investment spending, $I_n = 0$, since the capital stock is in equilibrium, having adjusted to that interest rate.

Now suppose the rate of interest falls to i_1. The intersection of i_1 and the MEC schedule produces a higher desired level of capital stock, as shown by K^*. Some of those assets previously considered unprofitable at the interest rate of i_0 now become profitable at the lower interest rate of i_1. The stock decision thus results in a gap equal to $K^* - K_0$; the desired level of capital stock exceeds the actual level.

Additions to the stock of capital, that is, positive net investment, is called for in order to close the gap. Figure 9.3(b) shows how investment spending takes place. At the interest rate of i_0 we have $I_n = 0$, but now with the fall in the rate of interest to i_1, net investment becomes positive. How much investment spending takes place in each period? The limit to investment spending is given by the physical capacity (costs are constant) of the capital goods industry, shown as $\bar{I}$ in Figure 9.3(b). Thus, in period 1, $\bar{I}$ amount of investment takes place, given by the horizontal line labeled MEI_1. This schedule (MEI) is called the marginal efficiency of investment schedule and shows the amount of investment that occurs in each time period at each rate of interest. Under our assumptions, the *rate of investment spending is constant*.

Period 1 investment, when added to the stock of capital of part (a), adds an amount of capital equal to $K_1 - K_0$ $(I_n = \Delta K = K_1 - K_0)$. The additional capital stock moves the economy down the MEC schedule, where, of course, the yields are lower as less profitable projects are undertaken. Still, the rate of return, as shown by point r' on the MEC schedule, exceeds the market rate of interest, i_1. Therefore, more investment spending is desired. In period 2 the same amount of investment spending occurs, MEI_2, as was the case in period 1. The rate of investment spending is constant and equal to the capacity output of the capital goods industries. Period 2 investment spending adds an amount of capital stock equal to $K_2 - K_1$ $(= K_1 - K_0)$. As before, the additional capital stock moves the economy farther along the MEC schedule, where yields are even lower. Yet as long as the rate of return, r'' now, exceeds the rate of interest, i_1, investment spending will continue. Thus, in period 3 investment expenditures equal to MEI_3 will be made, and so on, until investment spending adds sufficient capital to reach the optimum or desired level of K^*. When the desired level of capital stock is reached, $i_1 = r_1$, and no further investment will be made. In Figure 9.3(b), $I_n = 0$, as shown by point A on the vertical axis. The economy will be in equilibrium until something disturbs it: either a change in the rate of interest or a change in the variables previously held constant in the construction of the MEC schedule. (Situations given by points r', r'', and so on, on the MEC schedule represent points of temporary equilibrium that cannot persist for long, since more capital stock is desired as long as $r > i$.)

What happens to the process of capital accumulation if the assumption of constant costs in the capital goods industries is removed? If the capital goods industries did experience increasing costs as they expanded output, the rising costs of the capital assets would force down the yields and the temporary equilibrium position would be reached much sooner—that is, *the rate of investment spending* would fall in each period. The rising costs reduce yields, which when equated with the rate of interest result in less and less investment spending per period, fewer and fewer additions to capital stock, and consequently, a longer time period required to reach the desired level of capital stock. In view of the earlier discussion about the nature of the capital goods industries, the additional complications in the theory of capital accumulation brought about by introducing increasing costs do not appear to be justified.[15]

Shifts in the *MEC* Schedule

The process of capital accumulation just outlined occurred in direct response to a change in the market rate of interest; the economy moved *along* a stationary *MEC* schedule. The impetus for further capital accumulation could also come from *shifts* in the *MEC* schedule. Such shifts result from the removal of the "other things being equal" condition that determined the position of the curve. A look back at the variables in the investment function reveals the numerous factors that could change and thereby shift the *MEC* curve. Indeed, these factors may be more important in the explanation of investment expenditures than the change in interest rates. Interest rates may not change by amounts sufficient to affect investment, or the trend toward internal financing may have robbed the rate of interest of its former explanatory power. The rate of interest may still be important to the smaller (growing) firm, which may have no alternative method of financing, or to indus-

[15] We can, however, briefly indicate the differences between the earlier analysis and the analysis with the assumption of increasing costs. The footnote figure is like Figure 9.3 except for the different limitations on investment spending—not physical capacity but cost conditions limit the rate of investment spending. Again, as the rate of interest falls to i_1, net investment occurs. This time, however, as investment spending proceeds, the capital goods industries incur increasing costs. As the asset costs go up, the yields go down. Therefore, net investment is curtailed somewhat, as in each period the spending proceeds until the (falling) yields, r, are equal to the rate of interest, i_1. Thus, in period 1 the

CAPITAL ACCUMULATION WITH INCREASING COSTS OF CAPITAL GOODS

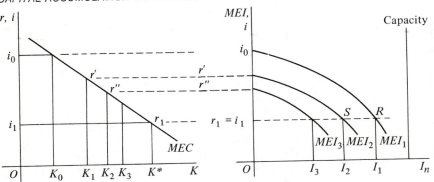

equating of the yield and the rate of interest occurs at point R and investment spending stops at this point. To go beyond would mean that $i > r$. The shape of the *MEI* curve is derived from the supply curve of the capital goods industries, which is now the familiar upward sloping supply curve and not the horizontal one used before. The *MEI* is the mirror image of this supply curve—the rate of investment spending now falls as the yields of assets decline as costs increase. Adding period 1 investment to the capital stock again moves the economy down the *MEC* curve, but since $r' > i_1$ (as before), investment again is called for; but the amount of investment is now less than period 1, as the new temporary equilibrium at S is more quickly reached. Adding I_2 to the level of capital stock begins the process of accumulation once more until K^* is finally reached. Thus, the main difference in the entire operation is *the rate of investment spending*. With rising costs in the capital goods industries, the rate of spending declines period by period; with constant cost, the rate of investment spending is also constant.

tries that rely upon long-term financing in order to survive. The construction industry and the utilities are the best examples of industries to which the interest rate remains important. For other firms and industries, the interest rate may not be as critical. Many empirical results confirm the declining importance of the rate of interest for the investment decision.[16] For some firms, this may mean that the yield on marginal capital assets is far above the rate of interest, so that the barrier to investment is not seen as the cost of funds and is dismissed. For other firms and industries, the other variables in the investment decision overshadow the rate of interest. In these cases, investment becomes relatively more interest-inelastic, and the *MEC* schedule looks more like that in Figure 9.4(b).

It is clear that the same change in the interest rate evokes a much greater response in the desirability of capital stock in part (a), where the demand is relatively elastic, than in part (b), where the demand is relatively inelastic. If this is the case, then factors other than the rate of interest assume more importance in the explanation of past capital accumulation. Probably most economists would agree that the rate of interest is no longer of *primary* importance in the majority of investment decisions, although they are not likely to agree on the factors that have supplanted the rate of interest. Some of these factors will be discussed, but first we must explore the mechanics of capital accumulation as the *MEC* schedule shifts and then inquire into which factors are most likely to account for the shift.

The mechanics of the process need not delay us too long, for they are essentially the same as that for movements along the curve. Figure 9.5 shows the process of

FIGURE 9.4

THE ELASTICITY OF THE MEC SCHEDULE

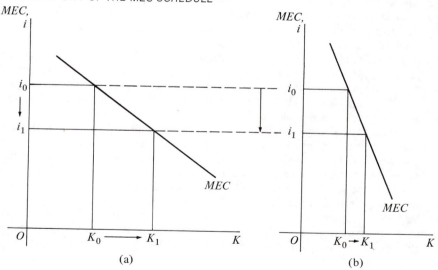

(a)   (b)

---

[16] J. R. Meyer and E. Kuh, *The Investment Decision* (Cambridge, Mass.: Harvard University Press, 1957). See also M. K. Evans, *Macroeconomic Activity* (New York: Harper & Row, 1969), ch. 5, for a somewhat different view. When surveyed, firms generally downgrade the importance of interest rates. A recent example can be found in Jean Crockett, Irwin Friend, and Henry Shavell, "The Impact of Monetary Stringency on Business Investment," *Survey of Current Business* 47 (August 1967): 10–27.

FIGURE 9.5

SHIFTS IN THE MEC SCHEDULE AND THE PROCESS OF CAPITAL ACCUMULATION

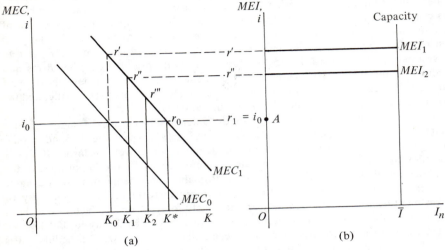

capital accumulation as the *MEC* schedule shifts (now drawn with slightly less interest elasticity).

Assume that for some reason the *MEC* schedule shifts from MEC_0 to MEC_1. With the shift in the schedule, more capital stock is desired at each rate of interest. More particularly, at the ruling interest rate, i_0, the desired level of capital stock changes from K_0 to K^*. The process of moving to this new desired level of capital stock differs slightly from the previous cases. After the *MEC* schedule shifts, the rate of return, r', at the original level of capital stock, K_0, exceeds the market rate of interest, i_0. As usual when $r > i$, investment is called for and justified; now all investment projects along the new *MEC* schedule that exceed the rate of interest are profitable, and as they are undertaken, the economy approaches K^*. The rate of investment spending is shown in Figure 9.5(b), which continues the assumption of a constant rate of investment spending. In the first period investment projects that yield r' will be undertaken, which when added to the capital stock level move the amount of capital from K_0 to K_1. In the second period the investment spending is given by MEI_2, which again is constant at the reduced yield level of r''. The new investment of period 2 increases the capital stock to K_2. This process of capital accumulation continues until the stock of capital reaches the optimum level of K^*. At this level of capital stock the rate of return, r_0, returns to the original rate and is once again equal to the rate of interest, i_0. Net investment is now zero (point A), and the economy is once again in equilibrium with regard to its capital stock.

Sources of Shifts in the *MEC* Schedule

THE AMORPHOUS VARIABLES

In listing the variables that influence the investment decision, there were many nonquantifiable ones that may enter into the functional relations in ways that escape direct observation. Even those variables that are observable are not easily analyzed, because they interact with each other and with other variables in many subtle and often unknown ways. Some of these variables reflect the attitudes of society towards risk taking, towards accumulation and power, towards profit taking and success, and so on. Even a permissive political philosophy and structure could affect the accumulation of capital.[17] These cultural or institutional variables can play a significant part in any attempt to explain past capital accumulation. Since they are unquantifiable, they are frequently overlooked in favor of more objective factors. Yet men—and it is men who make investment decisions—cannot be divorced from the society of which they are a part, and as the mores and values of that society change, men eventually adapt to them. In advanced capitalist societies industrial leaders are seldom leaders in social innovation, and they are generally on the defensive when the changes are far-reaching. Yet over time the resistance is overcome and new initiatives become readily accepted. Such was the case with workmen's compensation, social insurance, and many other schemes reflecting changed attitudes that were eventually accepted by all.

There is no reason to expect that attitudes towards the accumulation of wealth and power are immune to change or that businessmen would not respond to these changes. The only justification for omitting these from the analysis is that they change so slowly over time that it is safe to ignore them in the short run. In the long run the social attitudes and institutional framework in which an economic system operates should not be ignored.

Other variables in this general category are more directly observable but still lack precision in their explanatory power to account for capital accumulation. Surely, political stability and an orderly government encourage investment, which extends into the future. So also would a society that set up adequate "rules of the game"—a monetary and judicial system, for instance—and lived by them. Stability in all these institutional arrangements is probably necessary for investment, but this is more easily stated than proved.

Other factors in this group that are more susceptible to direct observation and quantification could be brought into the analysis. Certainly, government budgetary policies affect the investment outlook; expenditure and taxation plans affect all members of society, and business leaders can be expected to attempt to gauge their impact. Naturally, if the impact is more immediate—taxes on business or depreciation policies—the situation would be more carefully considered. Government policies have tried to influence the volume of investment spending: such policies as the investment tax credit or the liberalization of depreciation rules were made with this purpose in mind.

Similarly, the assessment of the international situation can affect investment spending and capital accumulation. Not only war versus peace considerations would apply but also the commercial policies of nations and their tendencies toward change. In addition, in recent years firms have increasingly been engaged in investment abroad. Corporations have gone "multinational" in the search for markets, for less costly labor, or for better treatment on taxes, tariffs, and so on. Thus, the anticipated effects of political stability, trading blocs, and experimentation with new political and economic institutions, both regional and international, become extremely important in the investment decision.

---

[17] See R. H. Tawney, *Religion and the Rise of Capitalism* (New York: Harcourt, Brace, 1926). For some further insights, see George Dalton (ed.), *Tribal and Peasant Economies* (New York: Natural History Press, 1967).

The variables discussed here are meant to suggest the kinds of influences that bear upon the investment decision. Just how they affect the process of capital accumulation is not quite clear. But they do enter into the decision somehow and thus affect the demand for capital goods and change the position of the *MEC* schedule. They may not be capable of shifting the curve directly, but they alter people's views of the world and cause them to adjust their plans accordingly. Expectations based on these and other variables should be given adequate consideration in any explanation of the investment decision.

EXPECTATIONS

Capital goods last a long time, and the decision to buy them involves some estimate of future conditions, necessarily based on incomplete information and uncertainty. The expectations involved in the calculation of the *MEC* have been stressed before: the expected future revenue, the expected future operating costs, the expected future demand, and so on.

What determines these expectations and how they change is by no means clear. Some of the variables in the previous section may be included as influences as well as many other subjective factors like the decision maker's state of health on the day of the decision, his mental state, his stubbornness, his personal prestige, power plays, his whims, his ego, and so on; and since the decision is often made by more than one man, all sorts of conflicts become possible.

Still, there will most likely be an attempt to make the decision as objective as possible, and for that purpose, all kinds of information are gathered to facilitate the decision-making process. Accounting, legal, financial, sales, production, and other data may be considered in the process of reaching a decision. But these data are often only forecasts, also based on expectations, so that the information may not be so objective after all.

The decision makers could turn to outside forecasts made by government agencies, independent research organizations, newspapers, and similar organizations to secure a general view and then ascertain how the firm or industry might be affected. This is frequently done, but there are some drawbacks to the method. First, the forecasts were made for the industry or the economy as a whole, *including* the firm or industry contemplating action. If the firm reacts to the forecasts and others do also, the forecasts may turn out to be wrong: the subjects of the forecast were influenced by the forecast. This brings us to the second drawback. If the firms do react to forecasts, or if they are heavily influenced by the actions of other firms, it is possible to get swings of optimism or swings of pessimism sweeping through the economy, reinforcing a trend and making for fluctuations in the level of economic activity.[18] The fluctuations may not have resulted at all or might have been less severe if the waves of optimism or pessimism had not brought them about. It is evident that expectations are not independent of other expectations and forecasts, so that people are guided not only by their own views of the future but by others' views as well. The degree of acceptance depends upon how much faith people have in whoever is making the forecast. The chairman of the board of the Federal Reserve making a forecast about future interest rates would be much more influential than a newspaper editor on the same issue.

[18] A theory of the business cycle along these lines was developed by A. C. Pigou, *Industrial Fluctuations*, 2d ed. (New York: Macmillan, 1929).

No one knows how expectations are formed or how they are changed, even if they are acknowledged as an important variable in the system. One consequence of infectious expectations may be the overreaction to waves of optimism or pessimism. In periods of optimism firms may order too many capital goods, building excess capacity in the expectation of continued boom conditions. For a time their expectations may be self-fulfilling, since as they order new investment goods they create incomes in the capital goods industries, which gives a multiplier effect, and so on. Then, when the new investment goods begin to supply additional output and they begin to pile up in the warehouse, the misplaced optimism is realized.[19] Now firms are saddled with excess capacity, making a future recovery more difficult, since the excess capacity must be worked off before new investment goods are ordered and economic conditions improve. Expectations here result in instability, always a specter of capital accumulation. The unprofitable investment ventures may make the decision maker more wary the next time, or even swing the situation to one of pessimism, even though the basis for such expectations is unrealistic.

Feelings of optimism create expectations favorable to investment, and hence the *MEC* schedule shifts upward and to the right, as shown in Figure 9.5. Adverse expectations would, of course, shift the schedule in the opposite direction. If the expectations are fulfilled, the economy moves toward some kind of equilibrium, not necessarily at a desired level. If the expectations are not fulfilled, then the economy is left with idle plants and excess capacity or a shortage of plant and pressures on supply and the price level. Excess plant is reduced only through the slow process of depreciation, while the plant shortage is limited by the capacity of the capital goods industries. The instability of an already unstable sector is compounded if the capital goods industries also get caught up in the waves of optimism or pessimism. They may also overbuild their capacity in anticipation of continued demand or else fail to enlarge their capacity because of undue pessimism.

In a world of perfect foresight the variable expectations would be meaningless. In our uncertain world, however, expectations become a legitimate variable, capable of creating instability and havoc. It is probably a more important variable than is generally recognized. The discussion in this section hopefully indicated some of the reasons for this statement.

TECHNOLOGICAL CHANGE AND INNOVATION

In our earlier work the production function was found to be the relation between factor inputs and output. An important part of that function is the way in which the inputs are combined in the production process. In general, this is the meaning of technology in the production function. The existing technical knowledge, the "state of the arts," determines how the inputs will be combined in the production process in order to obtain the production possibilities open to the firm. This engineering function, when combined with the factor costs, would then determine the production possibility that is the most efficient and the least costly.

Technological *change* occurs when the same output can be produced with fewer inputs or when a greater output is possible with the same inputs. Technological change can shift the total product curves and thus postpone the effects of the law of diminishing returns. Small wonder, then, that it has received so much attention

---

[19] The same result from a different source can be found in situations where firms order more capital than is immediately necessary in order to take advantage of discounts or other economies.

over the years. In the present context we are interested in the effects of technological change on the process of capital accumulation, and for the present we ignore the source of technological change or its effects in areas other than the economic one.[20]

Contrary to what might be imagined at first, the impact of technological change on the demand for capital goods is not at all certain. Some changes in technology economize on the use of capital stock and may thus decrease the demand for capital stock. The *MEC* schedule in this case shifts downward and to the left to reflect the decrease in demand. Such changes in technology are called capital-saving. It sometimes happens that one machine replaces and does the job that several machines did before. Other technological changes result in more capital stock being used in the production process, and these changes would increase the demand for capital stock, thus resulting in a shift of the *MEC* schedule upward and to the right. These technological changes are called capital-using. Of course, it is possible that some changes in technology leave the proportion of capital stock unchanged, and these changes are neutral insofar as capital is concerned.

While we are concerned here only with the effect of technological change on the demand for capital, it is useful to point out that labor is affected in a like manner. Some technological changes would be labor-saving, some labor-using, and others neutral. When the two factors are considered together, various combinations emerge: technological changes can be capital-using, labor-saving; capital-saving, labor-using; or both capital-saving and labor-saving.

In the aggregate it is not clear which type of technological change has occurred or is likely to prevail in the future. Too many other factors cloud the picture.[21] This is partly because technological change is embodied in new capital goods and partly because new capital goods are frequently the result of an innovation of some kind, so that isolating the change in technology for its effect on the demand for capital is made extremely difficult.

The effect of innovations on the demand for capital goods is somewhat clearer. Innovations refer to new products, new industries, new techniques or processes (technological change?), and so on, and are likely to call for more capital goods. In fact, innovations can play a very important part in the development of an economy, for as they are introduced they affect the level of economic activity.[22] The more dramatic the innovation, the more far-reaching the consequences. Such innovations as the railroad or the automobile are examples of the type of product that can drastically alter the course and character of an economic system. Still, even less dramatic innovations are likely to affect the economy, and particularly the demand for new capital stock. Innovations are likely to increase the demand for capital stock (although not necessarily for labor—the computer, for example) and push the *MEC* schedule to the right.

---

[20] A good summary of the meaning and effects of technological change can be found in E. Mansfield, *The Economics of Technological Change* (New York: W. W. Norton, 1968). For the effects of technology on mankind from a social or philosophic view, see the works of H. Marcuse, among which is *One Dimensional Man* (Boston: Beacon Press, 1964).

[21] Some estimates have been made, however. See E. F. Denison, *The Sources of Economic Growth in the United States*. Supplementary Paper No. 13 (New York: Committee for Economic Development, 1962).

[22] Innovations play a significant part in J. A. Schumpeter's theory of economic development and the business cycle, *The Theory of Economic Development* (Cambridge, Mass.: Harvard University Press, 1934).

It is impossible to separate investment spending into that caused by techno-logical change and that caused by innovations by inspection of investment data. It is not easy to separate the two even on a theoretical basis. Nor is it possible to forecast future technological change or future innovations. There is no way to forecast whether future changes will be capital-saving or capital-using, and we are left with rather unsatisfactory answers to the question of how technological change affects or will affect investment decisions.

Similarly, innovations cannot be forecast, but at least it is probable that the influences on investment spending will generally be positive. While future innova-tions may not be as consequential as the automobile, they may still be dramatic enough to have some real impact on the economic system. The space industry offers an example of this type. Other innovations may not be as significant, but their cumulative effects could be important. Still, whether these innovations will be ultimately capital-using or capital-saving cannot be anticipated, and the effect on *total* investment spending (beyond the initial impact) is again impossible to predict.

INVESTMENT AS A FUNCTION OF INCOME

In previous models investment was assumed to be autonomous—independent of the level of income. This simplifying assumption was useful and permitted us to concentrate on other aspects of the model, but it is too simple for more detailed work, for it presumes investment spending will be constant regardless of the level of income and output. An assumption of constant investment expenditures, whether the economy is in a recession or a boom, does not conform well to reality.

A step towards a more realistic model is to make investment vary with the income level. In one sense, this relation is merely technical, that is, to produce higher levels of output, more capital stock is required. Thus, investment is *induced* by *changes* in the level of income. The relation is given by the expression

$$(9.1) \qquad\qquad I = I_a + dY,$$

where I_a is the autonomous part of investment spending, which continues as before to be independent of the level of income, and d is the marginal propensity to invest, $\Delta I / \Delta Y$. This investment function is perfectly analogous to other linear functions used in the previous models.

The autonomous part, I_a, can be regarded as being the innovational type of investment spending, while the other part, dY, or the induced portion, is brought about by the requirements of higher output levels. It is not sufficient, however, to rely on the technical explanation of induced investment, particularly after our discussion of the behavior attitudes involved in the decision-making process. The explanation, as might be expected, is found in the profits of investment spending. Generally, income and profits vary directly, and profits increase more than wages in initial spurts of income. Therefore, using income as the inducement for more investment spending is a recognition of this relationship, and income serves as a proxy for a profit variable. In addition, the larger profits also furnish the means to finance the investment expenditures internally. Again, increases in income can generate expectations of a continuing trend, making investment spending appear appropriate.

Putting equation (9.1) into a simple model to bring out the essence of this function gives

(9.2) $Y = C + I$
(9.3) $C = C_a + cY$
(9.4) $I = I_a + dY.$

Substituting equations (9.3) and (9.4) into (9.2) gives the equilibrium level of income as

(9.5) $Y = \dfrac{1}{1 - c - d}(C_a + I_a).$

The only change from the very simple model is found in the expression for the multiplier. The introduction of induced investment increases the multiplier, since

$$\frac{1}{1 - c - d} > \frac{1}{1 - c},$$

and in fact, the new multiplier is often called the *super multiplier*. It is clear that a reduction in the denominator of a fraction increases the value of the fraction. Economically, the multiplier is larger, because as income increases not only is consumption induced by the *MPC* but investment is induced as well. The spending and responding stream is made larger in the same way as an increase in the *MPC* would have provided. As Y increases, C increases, but now I increases as well, which further increases Y and C and I until the new level of capital stock is sufficient to produce the higher level of income. Any change in the autonomous components of aggregate demand, C_a or I_a, will result in a change in income given by the super multiplier:

(9.6) $\Delta Y = \dfrac{1}{1 - c - d}(\Delta C_a \text{ or } \Delta I_a).$

If we assign a value of 0.1 to the marginal propensity to invest, d, and retain the same value of $MPC = 0.8$, then a change, say, in investment spending of $10 will increase the level of income as follows:

$$\Delta Y = \frac{1}{1 - 0.8 - 0.1}(10),$$
$$= 10(10),$$
$$= 100.$$

The multiplier has increased to 10 from the simple multiplier of 5, which was the case considering only autonomous investment.

Figure 9.6 illustrates income determination with induced investment. In part (a) are shown the familiar aggregate demand and aggregate supply data, and as before, the intersection of the two schedules results in the equilibrium level of income. Adding induced investment to the previous aggregate demand schedule rotates the schedule, for now the slope of the investment curve is not zero but a positive constant ($d = \Delta I / \Delta Y$). Thus, as Y increases, more investment is induced, and the gap between the two curves reflects this condition. The only reason the two demand curves diverge is because of induced investment. The change in the investment function moves the economy from income level Y_0 to Y_1, a greater change than would have occurred with autonomous investment. (With an income level of Y_0, a change in investment equal to the difference between Y_0 and the new I curve would have increased the level of income only to something like that given by point A.)

In part (b) the saving and investment data are presented. Again, the upward-sloping investment curve reflects induced investment, and the intersection with the saving schedule yields the equilibrium level of income. The same equilibrium condition must be met, of course, and planned saving and investment must be equal

FIGURE 9.6
INCOME DETERMINATION WITH INDUCED INVESTMENT

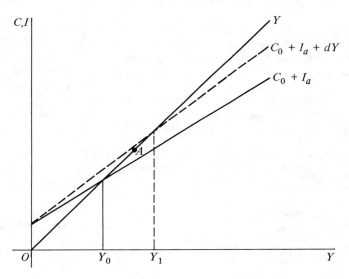

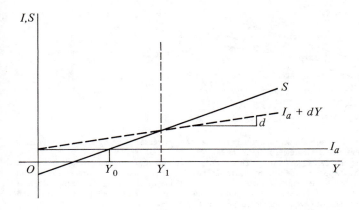

for the level of income to be in equilibrium. The super multiplier can also be seen here as a direct result of induced investment.[23]

Adding induced investment to the model is an improvement over the autonomous investment assumption made earlier, but there are some shortcomings of this function that should be mentioned. Despite the behavioral justification discussed earlier, there still remains a strong technical flavor to this function: investment increases by a constant amount, d, of any change in the level of output regardless of how high or low the original output level. The response is too automatic, too certain.

More important, it is *changes* in the level of income that induce additional investment, and the function should read

$$(9.7) \qquad\qquad I = I_a + f(\Delta Y).$$

That is, net investment is zero at the original output level (Y_0 in Figure 9.6), and the change in output (Y_1) induces positive net investment. Once sufficient capital has been accumulated to produce Y_1, net investment again falls to zero. Thus, net investment is independent of the absolute level of income, and a function that makes investment depend upon income is rather circular. A better formulation would consider how *changes* in income affect investment spending more explicitly; this is done in the next section. For those interested, appendix A presents the models developed earlier with induced investment added to them.

---

[23] An interesting result of this model has been called the *paradox of thrift*. Attempts by a community to save more out of a given income level will be self-defeating, and it may actually end in saving less. This is just an example of the fallacy of composition—one individual could succeed in saving more, but if all individuals attempted to save more, the level of income would fall, and they would end up saving

THE PARADOX OF THRIFT

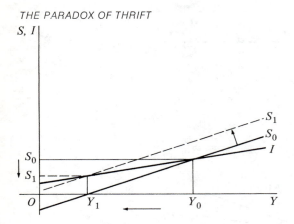

less collectively. The footnote figure shows this result. As the *APC* increases from S_0 to S_1, Y falls from Y_0 to Y_1, so that the amount of saving falls from S_0 to S_1.

The super multiplier is the cause, of course. The paradox is more amusing than significant, for it poses a problem for those who always preach thrift. Keynes had great sport with this paradox and quoted gleefully from passages of Bernard Mandeville's book *A Fable of the Bees,* an allegorical poem which scandalously (for its day) portrayed what would happen if everyone decided to save more and consume less and in effect practice what was often preached.

The Accelerator

The theory of investment that is concerned with investment stimulated by changes in the level of output is known as the accelerator theory. Changes in the level of income, from whatever source, change the amount of capital stock required to produce the new level of output and hence the amount of net investment necessary to reach the new required level of capital stock. The *MEC* schedule shifts as a result of changes in the level of income, and the optimum level of capital stock is changed also. This is the essence of the accelerator, although some qualifications are discussed later. It is perhaps easier to understand the concept with the use of symbols and techniques developed earlier.

The capital stock required to produce a given level of output is given by the expression

$$(9.8) \qquad K = vY,$$

where v, or K/Y, is the capital-output ratio that shows the average amount of capital stock required to produce a unit of income. For advanced economies, the capital-output ratio is relatively low, about 3 or so. If $v = 3$, it takes \$3 worth of capital stock to produce \$1 worth of income. For less developed economies, which are characteristically less efficient, the capital-output ratio is three or four times that of the developed economies.

If we assume v is constant (technology is constant, and of course, $K/Y = \Delta K/\Delta Y$, the average and marginal capital-output ratios are equal), then for any period t the amount of capital stock required is given by

$$(9.9) \qquad K_t = vY_t.$$

Assuming a constant v, any change in income will require the same proportional change in the required capital stock. Thus,

$$K_{t+1} = vY_{t+1}; \qquad \text{or } K_{t+6} = vY_{t+6}; \qquad \text{or } K_{t+n} = vY_{t+n};$$

that is, the desired level of capital stock changes by the same ratio. Assuming that income in the next period, Y_{t+1}, increases, the capital stock must also increase, as shown by

$$(9.10) \qquad K_{t+1} = vY_{t+1}.$$

In terms of *changes*, the move from period t to period $t + 1$ can be stated explicitly as

$$(9.11) \qquad \begin{aligned} K_{t+1} - K_t &= vY_{t+1} - vY_t \\ &= v(Y_{t+1} - Y_t). \end{aligned}$$

But $K_{t+1} - K_t = I_t$, which when substituted into (9.11) gives the accelerator form of investment:

$$(9.12) \qquad I_t = v(Y_{t+1} - Y_t),$$

where I_t is net investment and v is the accelerator. Investment is a function of the change in the level of income,[24] so the following relations hold:

---

[24] To be strictly correct, the accelerator theory calls for investment as a function of the *rate of change* of income and would be expressed as $I_t = f(dY/dt)$. The more rigorous form of the accelerator can be seen in the numerical example in the text.

If Y is increasing,

$$Y_{t+1} > Y_t \quad \text{and} \quad I_t > 0;$$

net investment is positive.

If Y is decreasing,

$$Y_{t+1} < Y_t \quad \text{and} \quad I_t < 0;$$

net investment is negative.

If Y is unchanging,

$$Y_{t+1} = Y_t \quad \text{and} \quad I_t = 0.$$

Before examining the plausibility of the accelerator theory, it might be useful to gain some insight into how it is supposed to operate by working through a numerical example. Table 9.2 traces out the accelerator mechanism under the following simplifying assumptions:

1. The capital-output ratio, v, is constant and is equal to 3.
2. Depreciation accurately measures the amount of capital consumption and is equal to one fifth of the level of capital stock at the end of the previous period.

With these assumptions, it is fairly easy to grasp the meaning of the accelerator theory.

In Table 9.2 we begin with the assumption that output was at a level of $500 for several periods. Therefore, the required capital stock is equal to $1,500: $K = vY$; $1,500 = 3(500)$. Capital consumption in period t is equal to $300, which is ⅕ (1,500), the previous period's capital stock level. Since the output level was unchanged, there is no need for new capital stock; net investment is zero, and gross investment is $300, that is, replacement investment equals the capital consumption.

Now suppose that an increase in government spending or autonomous investment results in an output level of $510 in the next period, $t + 1$. The required level of capital stock increases to $1,530: $K = 3(510)$. Capital consumption is still $300, based on one fifth of the capital stock of period t, and of course, replacement in-

TABLE 9.2

THE ACCELERATOR

Period	Output	Required K	Capital Consumption	Investment Replacement	Net	Gross
t	500	1,500	300	300	0	300
$t + 1$	510	1,530	300	300	30	330
$t + 2$	525	1,575	306	306	45	351
$t + 3$	550	1,650	315	315	75	390
$t + 4$	575	1,725	330	330	75	405
$t + 5$	575	1,725	345	345	0	345
$t + 6$	560	1,680	345	345	−45	300
$t + 7$	550	1,650	336	336	−30	306
$t + 8$	500	1,500	330	330	−150	180
$t + 9$	400	1,200	300	300	−300	0
$t + 10$	400	1,200	240	240	0	240

vestment is also unchanged. However, to produce the output level of $510, capital stock of $1,530 is required, which means that additional capital stock is required over and above that being replaced. Therefore, net investment of $30 takes place, and with the replacement investment of $300, makes gross investment equal to $330. Another way to look at the process is to realize that $1,530 worth of capital stock is needed to produce the output level of $510. At the beginning of period $t + 1$, $300 worth of capital stock is used up, leaving a level of $1,200. Therefore, gross investment must make up the required difference of $1,530 − $1,200 = $330, of which $300 represents merely replacement investment and $30 represents additional investment.

Suppose further that in the next period, $t + 2$, the output level once again increases, to $525. By the same process, required capital stock increases to $1,575, calling for net investment of $45 to bring the capital stock level up to the required amount. In period $t + 3$ the output level further increases, and the net investment expenditures rise to $75 to reach the required level of capital of $1,650.

In period $t + 4$ the output level further increases to $575, but the additional net investment required remains at $75. The reason for this brings out the essence of the accelerator. The changes in the level of output were as follows:

$$\text{from } t \text{ to } t + 1: \quad \$510 - \$500 = \$10 = 2.0 \text{ per cent;}$$
$$\text{from } t + 1 \text{ to } t + 2: \$525 - \$510 = \$15 = 2.9 \text{ per cent;}$$
$$\text{from } t + 2 \text{ to } t + 3: \$550 - \$525 = \$25 = 4.8 \text{ per cent;}$$
$$\text{from } t + 3 \text{ to } t + 4: \$575 - \$550 = \$25 = 4.5 \text{ per cent.}$$

Note that income increased by increasing amounts and at increasing rates up to $t + 4$, but the change from $t + 3$ to $t + 4$ was the same and at approximately the same rate as was the previous change from $t + 2$ to $t + 3$. The accelerator affects net investment on the basis of *the rate of change of income* and not the absolute change. If the rate of change of income remains constant, net investment will remain constant, and if the rate of change increases or decreases, the amount of net investment increases or decreases.

It is already clear that the accelerator can cause some instability, since any change in output is magnified in the investment sector as it responds to needed capital requirements. In our example, any change in income affects the capital stock requirement by a multiple of 3. Going on with the example, income remains unchanged in period $t + 5$, and thus no net investment is required, but gross investment *falls* as replacement investment falls because of the failure in previous periods to increase the rate of investment spending. In period $t + 6$ the output level falls by $15, requiring less capital stock than the previous period. Thus, net investment becomes negative (−$45) by three times the fall in income. Gross investment indicates that not all of the capital consumed ($345) is replaced. In period $t + 7$ income again falls *at a decreasing rate,* and thus the fall in net investment (−$30) is not as great as in the previous period (−$45). In period $t + 8$ income again falls at an *increasing rate,* with the expected result on investment spending. In period $t + 9$ the fall in income is so great that there is no replacement investment, and gross investment falls to zero (it cannot go lower). Finally, a new equilibrium level is assumed to be reached at $400, and once again net investment is zero and only replacement spending occurs.

The simple model of Table 9.2 brings out the essential feature of the accelerator principle. The basic instability introduced by the technological requirements of capital stock accumulation in response to output changes is clearly illustrated. Also, the importance of capital goods production in the explanation of economic fluctuation becomes apparent. Recall that investment also changes the level of income; adding the accelerator makes investment respond to changes in the level of income, and the potential for instability is increased. The interaction of the multiplier and the accelerator is given in appendix B.

Before concluding that the model presents some upsetting possibilities, it is necessary to qualify it a good deal by scrutinizing the assumptions upon which it is based.

1. There is the assumed behavior of decision makers, which is at odds with the behavior discussed earlier. Instead of hesitant, calculating behavior, there is a rather mechanistic, reflexive action; people appear to react to conditions in an automatic way.

2. Producers must expect the changes in output to be permanent, and they rush out to accumulate capital. Surely, this is unrealistic, and a lagged response is called for until the observed changes appear to be permanent rather than temporary changes. Reflexive expectations are hardly expectations at all.

3. In some sense, the accelerator appears to be a truism: of course, more capital goods are needed to produce larger outputs. Behavior according to (1) and (2) lends support to this criticism. Actually, in the short run the accelerator *is* a truism, and only in the long run does it become pertinent in the analysis.

4. The assumption of a constant technology making v constant can only be justified in the short run as a simplification. Over time, in a dynamic economy where technology is so revered, the assumption becomes less and less tenable.

5. The working of the model along the lines of Table 9.2 assumes that the economy is operating at full capacity. With all capital goods being used in production, any attempt to increase output is futile, so that new capital stock is mandatory to supply the output. This may be true at times, but most firms and industries operate at less than capacity, so that increases in demand can be met with existing facilities. There is no immediate need to hurry out and buy more capital stock; the old capital stock would be utilized to capacity first while the producer is given time to evaluate the permanence of the increase in demand.

6. It is also assumed that the capital goods industries are able to supply the ordered capital stock in a relatively short time. These are off-the-shelf types of capital goods. Ordinarily, one can expect delays between order, delivery, and installation of the capital goods.

7. Once convinced of the permanence of demand changes, the producer is assumed to order only as much capital stock as is necessary to meet the additional output. Actually, many producers will decide to order more capital stock than is immediately necessary in order to build in excess capacity anticipating future demand conditions or to realize some economies in ordering in quantity. Even the capital goods industries may expand their capacity, with the result that future demand change will be met from this excess capacity and little impact will be made on further capital accumulation. Income changes in the future may well be delayed as this excess capacity is worked off.

For these and other reasons, the accelerator principle is far less definite than is postulated in the preceding example.[25] There is no doubt that the concept does

---

[25] For a summary of the accelerator literature, see A. D. Knox, "The Acceleration Principle and the Theory of Investment: A Survey," *Economica* 19 (New Series) (August 1952): 269–297.

explain some of the motivations for investment spending, but its strict application does not appear to be warranted. In the short run, particularly, it is apt to be less useful than in the long run, where it may be more applicable. The accelerator will be discussed further in the theory of economic growth, where it becomes an important factor.

Conclusion

In discussing the process of capital accumulation, we have barely touched upon the many problems inherent in it. It remains one of the most complex parts of economic analysis, and at this stage many parts must be omitted. The discussion has shown that capital theory is still very complex despite all efforts to simplify.

It is hoped that some appreciation for the technical aspects of capital theory, such as the calculation of yields, has been gained as well as some understanding of the behavioral part of the decision-making process. By emphasizing the fact that there are two investment decisions, some automatic behavior that has been attributed to capital accumulation has been questioned: decisions are not always irrevocable nor are they instantaneous.

It is clear that there is no one theory or one completely coherent explanation of investment spending. From Smith to Marx to Keynes, the interest in the process of capital accumulation has been apparent, and the explanations of the process have been as diverse as the writers who expressed them.

Pre-Keynesian
Macroeconomics
and
the
Introduction
of
the
Money
Market

There is no coherent body of knowledge that can be referred to as pre-Keynesian macroeconomics. No writer before Keynes had a complete model that can be considered representative of accumulated thought. Another name for pre-Keynesian writers frequently used is *classical,* which covers everyone from Smith to the neoclassical writers of the twentieth century. The best known of the neoclassical economists is A. C. Pigou, an outstanding British economist who best described the economic thought of his time and whose work was thus used by Keynes as he compared and contrasted previous macroeconomic principles.

The classical economists (so first called by Marx) included men of varying interests from various backgrounds: Adam Smith, David Ricardo, Thomas R. Malthus, John Stuart Mill, James Mill. The neoclassical economists included F. Y. Edgeworth, Alfred Marshall, and A. C. Pigou, who refined and extended the classical precepts. It is difficult to generalize the thought of such a diverse group of men, but some comments can be made to indicate their general philosophy, their assumptions, and their approach to economic problems. Some appreciation for their vision of the world must be gained if their contributions to economic doctrine are to be properly evaluated.[1]

In general, they placed great faith in the ability of human reason to analyze and solve problems. If men were presented with the necessary information and alternatives, they could be relied upon to make rational choices. These economists

---

[1] There are a number of texts that cover the history of economic thought and trace the development of economic doctrines. The interested reader will find a few of these listed in the reference section at the end of the book.

believed that men were rational, and out of this grew their trust in the individual. They were realists, on the whole, but remained committed to the belief that ultimately the rationality of individuals could cope with most of man's problems.

It follows that they found government intervention of any kind to be unnecessary, if not harmful; laissez-faire government was the desired goal—that government governs best that governs least. Government should set the rules of the game —determine and control the monetary and judicial systems—but otherwise keep its hands off the economy. They reached this conclusion by viewing the economy as composed of small, independent (atomistic) firms operating in free and open markets. They assumed pure competition in all markets. If pure competition were the case, then the basic tenet of capitalism, self-interest, would be regulated and controlled by the working of competitive markets. It is always necessary to temper one's demands (for higher wages, greater profits) in trying to maximize one's rewards, which is the expression of self-interest, because there are always many others attempting to do the same thing. Thus, an "invisible hand," according to Smith, regulates the marketplace, and no government intervention is necessary.

Methodologically, the classical economists were primarily interested in the determination of value (price, wage rate, interest rate), and the distribution of the output (wages, rents, interest, profits). Thus, they tended to use partial equilibrium analysis, concentrating on one market while holding everything else equal. Of extreme importance was their proclivity to work in terms of the long run. They were interested in how things worked out over time, free from short-run aberrations. Despite the emphasis on the long run, however, their views on economic growth were extremely shortsighted. With the exception of Marx (himself now considered classical), they failed to see the effects of the Industrial Revolution on economic development. Indeed, their prognosis for human progress was depressing and led Carlyle to dub economics "the dismal science." They felt that progress was possible but extremely difficult, and their limited visions left little hope for most of mankind. Their views on economic progress are best left to the discussion of economic growth, where consideration of the long run is more appropriate.

It is very important, however, to keep in mind the classical emphasis on the long run, for it helps to explain some of their preoccupations and conclusions. It is also important to remember the long-run emphasis when the classical "model" is compared to Keynes's model, which is basically short-run in nature. The comparison is often invalid, yet some contrast is almost inevitable, and Keynes himself stressed the differences in analysis and in the conclusions reached. Keynes and post-Keynesians themselves set up a classical "model" along the following lines in order to be able to compare it with, and thus to assess, the model of Keynes.

The Classical Model

THE LABOR MARKET

In chapter 7 we reviewed the profit-maximizing condition for a firm operating under pure competition. The necessary condition for profit maximization was found to be the output level where $MC = MR$. Since in the short run labor is the only variable input, the MC was found to be

$$MC = \frac{W}{MPP},$$

where W is the money wage rate and MPP is the marginal physical product. Recall that in a perfectly competitive labor market W is the money wage rate at which all firms can hire labor. As they do so, they add a constant amount to total costs for each increment; hence W is the change in total costs, or the change in the wage bill, the numerator of the expression for MC. The denominator is the change in quantity per increment of labor.

Under pure competition price can be substituted for marginal revenue (MR), and the profit-maximizing condition becomes

$$MR = P = MC = \frac{W}{MPP},$$

or

$$P = \frac{W}{MPP},$$

or

$$MPP = \frac{W}{P}.$$

All these expressions give the short-run, profit-maximizing condition for a firm and, by extension, for the economy; labor is hired up to the point where the last unit contributes in revenue what it costs. It is the last expression that shows most directly the derived demand for labor: labor will be demanded according to its productivity, its contribution. The productivity of labor is determined by the production function as it is combined with other factors. In fact, the slope of the production function gives the MPP of labor, since labor alone varies; therefore, the MPP curve of stage II becomes the demand curve for labor. Since $MR = (MPP)(P)$, and P is a constant, the shape of the curve is determined by the productivity of labor. Thus, the demand for labor can be expressed by substituting N_d for MPP and writing the preceding expression in functional terms as

$$(10.1) \qquad N_d = N_d\left(\frac{W}{P}\right),$$

which states that the demand for labor is a function of the real wage rate, and when labor is hired "correctly," profits will be maximized.

The supply of labor is also a function of the real wage rate and can be written as

$$(10.2) \qquad N_s = N_s\left(\frac{W}{P}\right).$$

The supply of labor as a function of the real wage rate was justified by classical economists in terms of the disutility of work. Since work involves disutility, men have to be compensated in order to induce them to provide the work effort; presumably, the greater the compensation, the more effort is induced. Either men work longer hours or additional labor is enticed into the work force as the reward increases.[2] Note the reward is not higher *money* wages but higher *real* wages.

---

[2] The classical economists did not postulate the possibility of a backward-bending supply curve of labor. That is, as the real wage rose up to some point, more labor was offered, and the substitution effect (substituting income for leisure) was greater than the income effect. After some real wage rate

Remember these are highly rational men, who are not fooled by rising money wages that are accompanied by rising prices, leaving them no better off than before. Only if real wages are rising will additional labor be forthcoming. In a word, workers suffer *no money illusion.* The supply curve of labor was thus generally regarded as upward-sloping to the right, as is the general case for supply curves. Under these assumptions, the labor market can be pictured as in Figure 10.1.

The labor supply and demand schedules are made linear for simplicity, and at their intersection an equilibrium real wage rate, $(W/P)_e$, is determined. For the classical model, this real wage rate is more than just an equilibrium rate—it also coincides with the full employment real wage rate, because anyone willing and able to work can find employment at this going rate.

Anyone not willing to accept this wage rate has priced himself out of the market and is *voluntarily* unemployed. And, of course, there is no need for anyone to work for less than the going real wage rate, since all labor is homogeneous. An examination of Figure 10.1 should reveal the labor market mechanisms at work to ensure the equilibrium conditions. If for some reason the real wage rate $(W/P)_1$ were established, it is clear that the demand for labor would exceed the supply—shown by the distance AB. At this low wage rate firms would attempt to increase output to increase profits, but as they attempted to secure the necessary labor, their efforts would be frustrated, since at the low real wage rate the supply of labor would be relatively small. Accordingly, competition among firms for the available labor supply would result in the bidding up of the real wage rate until the equilibrium rate, $(W/P)_e$, was restored. Similarly, if the real wage rate, $(W/P)_2$, were established, a surplus of labor—unemployment—equal to the distance CD would develop. This relatively high real wage rate cannot persist, and if we continue to assume that prices remain stable, the only way to restore the equilibrium real wage rate and full employment is for workers to accept a reduction in the money wage, so that the real wage falls. This time, the surplus labor competes for the available jobs by forcing down the money wage. In the absence of any price changes (which will be introduced later), money wages adjust to the equilibrium real wage rate by the automatic, self-correcting forces of pure competition. The end result of the analysis is that the only equilibrium that can be sustained is the real wage rate that

---

the reverse might take place, where the income effect becomes greater than the substitution effect and workers prefer more leisure to more income. With a higher real wage it is necessary to work fewer hours to accumulate the amount of income desired. The supply curve of labor becomes backward bending as in the figure.

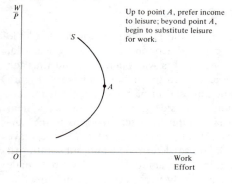

Up to point A, prefer income to leisure; beyond point A, begin to substitute leisure for work.

FIGURE 10.1
THE CLASSICAL MODEL OF THE LABOR MARKET

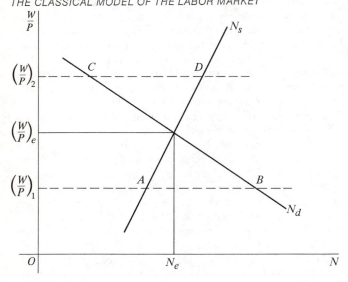

guarantees full employment, N_e. No other level of employment can last, and certainly no other level can be called an equilibrium; involuntary unemployment is impossible. It is clear why Keynes writing in the 1930s would have had some difficulty accepting this conclusion. The classical model was for the long run, however, and the conclusion is better stated as a *tendency* toward full employment over time.

THE PRODUCTION FUNCTION

In order to express the production function of the classical model, it is necessary either to ignore the long-run emphasis or to work with some artificial economy, as many of the classical economists did—that is, the "stationary state" where capital accumulation stops and the stock of capital remains fixed (only replacement investment is permitted). It seems preferable to state the production function in contemporary short-run terms:

$$(10.3) \qquad\qquad Y = Y(N, \overline{K}, \ldots),$$

where, as before, labor is the only variable input and all other determinants of the production function are held constant. The classical economists, following Ricardo, generally assumed that the law of diminishing returns was operative, and thus the production function in this model is the same as used throughout our work. Figure 10.2(a) shows the resulting production function, and in part (b) the labor market is reproduced. The figure depicts how the "real side" of the economic system operates. In the labor market the only variable input is determined, as is the corresponding real wage rate. Thus equations (10.1) and (10.2) of the model have been solved. Now taking the quantity of labor so determined and substituting it into the production function (10.3) determines the amount of real output made possible by the labor input. In Figure 10.2 it is only necessary to extend upwards the full employment quantity of labor, N_e, until the intersection with the production function. The full employment level of output, Y, is thus determined. Everything else being equal (technology, labor force, and so on), no other output level is possible in the short run.

In this manner the interaction of the labor market and the aggregate production function determines the real wage rate, the quantity of labor, and the output level. The sequence runs from the determination of the level of employment, and then given N, to the determination of the level of output with this labor input. The real side of the economy has been resolved; we say real side because the decisions are primarily production ones and those involved in the choice between work and

FIGURE 10.2
OUTPUT AND EMPLOYMENT DETERMINATION IN THE CLASSICAL MODEL

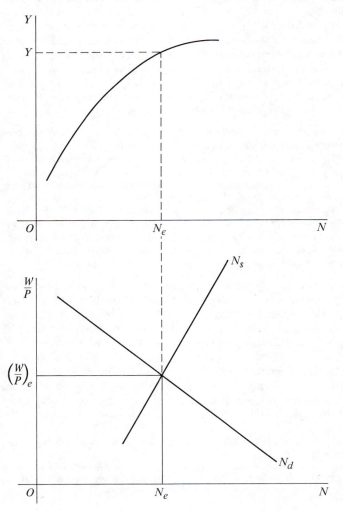

leisure, utility and disutility. Value terms have been omitted or are inappropriate. It is therefore necessary to find the means to value the output and determine the rewards to labor. For this we need a monetary system and a theory of price determination; we must add the monetary side to the real side for a more comprehensive model.

SOME BACKGROUND—SAY'S LAW

Jean Baptiste Say popularized and spread the work of Adam Smith and in the process added a concept that has come to be known as Say's Law. It is often bluntly stated as "supply creates its own demand." This expression is a summary phrase for his belief that in the long run there is a tendency towards equality of aggregate supply and aggregate demand, and thus a general oversupply or glut is not possible. In Keynesian terminology, there would be no lack of effective demand, no insufficiency of demand, and thus no need to be concerned about the very thing that Keynes took great pains to emphasize. Say, of course, did work with long-run tendencies, but it is still useful to ask how this desirable state was to come about.

It all stems from the real decision concerning work versus leisure. Since work involves disutility, no one will produce more than he has to in order to sell it and buy the goods and services he desires. A producer of chairs will produce a certain number of chairs per period, which when he sells them will provide him with the income he needs to demand the goods of others. No one produces except with a view to consumption. Here is John Stuart Mill's famous statement of the concept:

Is it . . . possible that there should be a deficiency of demand for all commodities, for want of means of payment? Those who think so cannot have considered what it is which constitutes the means of payment for commodities. *It is simply commodities.* Each person's means of paying for the productions of other people consists of those which he himself possesses. All sellers are inevitably and *ex vi termini* ["by the meaning of the word"] buyers. Could we suddenly double the productive powers of the country we should double the supply of commodities in every market, but we should by the same stroke double the purchasing power. Every one would bring a double demand as well as supply: everybody would be able to buy twice as much because everybody would have twice as much to offer in exchange. It is a sheer absurdity that all things should fall in value and that all producers should, in consequence, be insufficiently remunerated.[3]

Say's Law was seldom as explicitly stated, but there is no doubt that some notion of production creating demand was carried over into classical analysis.[4] In general, an oversupply of all goods was not possible, but there is the possibility of a glut or oversupply in any one market. A producer could miscalculate the rewards from his production. An oversupply in one market will result in a falling price (and income), but this is just the proper signal in free markets for those producing this good to produce less or transfer their resources to the production of some other good.

Note that this interpretation of Say's Law appears to be applicable to a barter economy. Does the introduction of money make a difference? Not to the classical economists, who held that money is a veil over the real economy and that no sub-

---

[3] John Stuart Mill, *The Principles of Political Economy* (1848; reprinted New York: D. Appleton, 1872), vol. II (ch. 14, p. 107).

[4] In the text we are concerned with only one interpretation of Say's Law. According to Schumpeter, Say, responding to critics, restated his concept, so that several interpretations are possible (including one that comes close to national income accounting identities). See J. Schumpeter, *History of Economic Analysis* (New York: Oxford University Press, 1954), pp. 615–625.

stantial modifications are necessary with its introduction. For those who believed in the rationality of man, production for money income should make no difference, and the proceeds from production would be respent on other goods. Money was just a medium of exchange that facilitated trade but did not affect it. After all, work for money income still involved disutility, so why work more than necessary, accumulating idle money? There are no Silas Marners in this society. No one derives pleasure from holding or hoarding idle balances of money. The importance of Say's Law comes from the fact that it enters the classical model via the quantity theory of money to help explain the valuation of goods and services.

THE QUANTITY THEORY OF MONEY

There is no single quantity theory of money just as there is no single classical model. All that can be stated with certainty is that as the name implies, the quantity of money is a crucial variable in the system. The best place to begin the discussion may be with Irving Fisher's equation of exchange, which can be written as

$$MV = PT,$$

where M is the stock of money; V is the velocity of money, which means the number of times each unit of the money supply is used during a given period; P is the price level; and T is the volume of transactions that take place in the period. Fisher's equation of exchange might better be written as a truism, $MV \equiv PT$, since it says that the amount of money in existence times the number of times it is used is equal to what it purchased. The equation of exchange is a tautology in which the money expenditures made (MV) are identically equal to the value of the goods and services exchanged against them. Useful as the equation of exchange may be in categorizing the sectors involved, it cannot be a theory because it is true by definition.

To turn the equation of exchange into a theory, it is necessary to postulate that a change in one of the variables induces systematic and predictable changes in the other variables. Then the equation of exchange would no longer be a truism, since it would no longer be true by definition but could be refuted by appealing to empirical evidence. This statement of the quantity theory transforms the equation of exchange into a theory of price level determination. We rewrite the equation of exchange as

(10.4) $$MV = PY,$$

where Y is the physical output of the period, and not total transactions, which include all exchanges. Y is closer in definition to national income accounting concepts. It is assumed that Y and T bear some fixed relation to each other, so that no serious distortion is created by the substitution. The reason for using Y instead of T in the equation is to direct attention towards physical output and the employment relation, since employment is one of the key variables in the short-run analysis.

Here is where Say's Law makes its contribution, for its operation always results in full employment. If there were unemployment (involuntary), all that would be needed would be to increase production to put these resources to work. Since the output would always be sold (supply creating markets), there would be no reason why unemployment should ever exist. Therefore, the tendency is always towards full employment. The crude quantity theory, therefore, took Y as given and fixed and equal to the full employment level of output. In addition, it assumed that V was constant as well. The determinants of the velocity of money, V, were assumed stable enough not to be affected once full employment was reached. The determinants of the velocity of money include the pay period, credit institutions and practices, the amount and extent of vertical integration of firms, or anything that affects the rate of circulation of the money supply.

Now, if both V and Y are fixed, it follows that any change in the quantity of money affects the price level in the same direction and by the same proportion. This is the essence of the crude quantity theory. From $MV = PY$, it follows that if the money supply increases by 5 per cent, the price level increases by 5 per cent, and so on. The assumption of a constant V and Y is essential for this conclusion. Also necessary, but not stated, is the attitude toward money balances found in moving from Say's Law in a barter economy to its operation in a money economy. That is, no one desires to hold idle money balances, and money is simply used as a medium of exchange. Thus, with output Y fixed, any additional M will mean an excess of money available for exchange purposes. As people divest themselves of their excess money balances and attempt to spend them, they only succeed in bidding up the price level, because output is fixed. P rises until all excess money balances have been eliminated. M and P vary proportionally and P is flexible upwards. Similarly, a reduction in the money supply would force people to reduce spending in order to retain the same amount of money balances for exchange purposes as they held before. But the reduction in spending means unsold goods, so that producers (operating in pure competition) reduce prices to sell their output. Thus, as M falls, P falls proportionally and prices are flexible downward as well.

The quantity theory as given here becomes a theory of aggregate demand, for changes in the money supply affect the volume of spending, which affects the volume of output. Of course, it is necessary to relax the crude quantity theory of money to permit unemployment and to restate the hypothesis to show the influence of M on PY, and not M on P alone.

Now an increase in M will result in excess money balances, which with V constant will increase money income, PY. Prices will probably rise in the same direction but not necessarily proportionally, and if unemployment exists, both output and employment can be increased by the stimulation of a change in M. Once full employment is reached, however, the old quantity theory takes over, and any change in M will affect only P and proportionally.[5]

With the introduction of the quantity theory of money, the classical model becomes:

$$(10.5) \qquad N_d = N_d \left(\frac{W}{P}\right)$$

$$(10.6) \qquad N_s = N_s \left(\frac{W}{P}\right)$$

$$(10.7) \qquad Y = Y(N)$$

$$(10.8) \qquad MV = PY.$$

[5] If the change in M is rapid or very large, V is likely to change as well, and the crude quantity theory breaks down. In hyperinflation the changes in price level are greater than the changes in MV with Y constant.

It works as follows: equations (10.5) and (10.6), the labor market, determine the volume of employment, N, and the real wage rate, W/P; once N is known, the output level, Y, is determined from the production function, (10.7); the substitution of Y into (10.8), together with the assumptions that V is constant and that M is controlled (and given) by the monetary authorities, permits the quantity theory to determine the absolute price level, P; given P, the money wage rate, W, can be determined from (10.5) or (10.6), since W/P is known. This classical model is both internally consistent and complete as far as it goes.

GRAPHICAL ANALYSIS

It may be easier to understand the classical model if it is presented in graphical form, as in Figure 10.3. In part (a) the labor market, as described by equations

FIGURE 10.3
THE CLASSICAL MODEL

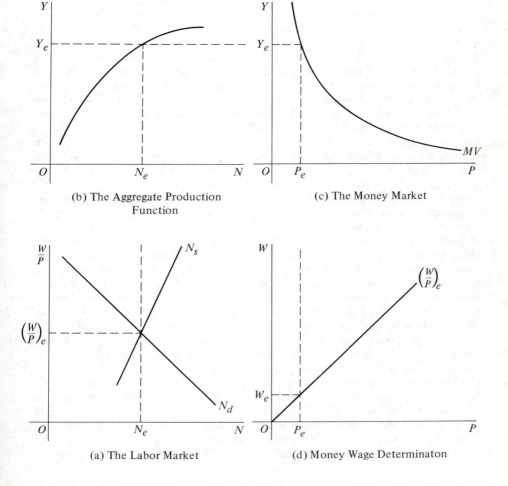

(b) The Aggregate Production
Function

(c) The Money Market

(a) The Labor Market

(d) Money Wage Determinaton

Sequence	Equation	Diagram Part	Description	Determines	Given or Assumed
1	$N_d = N_d\left(\dfrac{W}{P}\right)$ $N_s = N_s\left(\dfrac{W}{P}\right)$	(a)	Labor Market	$N, \dfrac{W}{P}$	Labor Force—Population Society's Attitudes Toward Work Versus Leisure
2	$Y = Y(N)$	(b)	Production Function	Y	N from Labor Market
3	$MV = PY$	(c)	Quantity Theory	P	M from Monetary Authority V Constant by Assumption Y from Production Function
4	—	(d)	Money Wage Determination	W	P from Money Market $\dfrac{W}{P}$ from Labor Market

(10.5) and (10.6), is given. In part (b) is shown the aggregate production function of equation (10.7). These two parts merely reproduce the "real" side of the marketplace, already discussed with Figure 10.2. The money market is shown in part (c), where as before, M is determined by the monetary authorities, V is assumed constant, and Y is given from part (b). Under these conditions the quantity theory determines the price level, P. The shape of the MV curve comes from the assumption that with the given money supply and its velocity, MV, a certain level of money income, PY, can be supported. If $M = \$200$ and $V = 3$, a money income of $600 can be supported. If $PY > \$600$, people could not hold the transaction money balances they had become accustomed to holding at existing prices. As they decreased spending to recapture these cash balances, goods would go unsold, and competition among sellers would force the price level down until the supportable level of money income was again reached. Similarly, if $PY < \$600$, the money balances of the public in excess of those needed for transaction purposes would cause people to spend, driving up the price level until the equilibrium level of money income were restored. In the money market of part (c) the MV curve is a rectangular hyperbola, meaning that with MV equal to PY and with MV constant, money market equilibrium is possible with a high Y and low P or with a low Y and a high P. Y and P must vary inversely and equal the constant MV in amount. A moment's reflection will reveal that if Y were high, the output could only be sold at a low price level, since the money market can only support a given money income. When Y is low, the smaller output can be sold at a larger price level, as people bid up the price level of the limited output.

Thus, in part (c), once Y is known from the aggregate production function, the price level, P, is determined, as shown on the horizontal axis from the intersection of Y and the MV curve. Finally, in part (d) the money wage can be determined once the price level is given from part (c). The line W/P from the origin measures a constant real wage rate; the slope of the line is equal to W/P. A higher real wage would appear as a new line from the origin to the left of the one shown (the slope would be greater), and a lower real wage would appear as a line to the right (and the slope would be lower). Note that the real wage is a ratio, W/P, which means that to measure the change, it is necessary to look at both the denominator and the numerator. For instance, the real wage rate could increase if the numerator, W, rose while the denominator, P, remained constant; or if W and P rose but the increase in W was proportionally greater than the increase in P; or if W remained constant while P decreased; or if W and P decreased but the decrease in P was proportionally greater than the decrease in W.

In Figure 10.3, starting with part (a) and proceeding to (b), (c), and (d), it is possible to trace the working of the classical model. The results are given with the subscript e, and the process is summarized below the figure. In mathematical terms, there are four equations and four unknowns—N, W/P, Y, P—with M and V given and W determined afterwards. The system is therefore correctly determined and consistent, and a solution is possible. (Note, however, the tacit assumption that there is always an equilibrium in the labor market, $N_d = N_s$, at some real wage.)

To increase the understanding of the classical model and its mechanics, it might be useful to examine the model in operation as it reacts and responds to changes. Only a few of the more important changes will be considered here, and the reader is encouraged to work out some of the other possible changes on his own.

Consider first a change in the supply of money, the origin of which is left unspecified. Suppose the supply of money increases. How will the system react? The first indication of the change occurs, of course, in the money market, as shown in Figure 10.4(c). For an increase in M, the MV curve shifts upward and to the right, meaning that the new money supply will support a higher level of money income. But with no response from the real side and with Y already at the full employment level, the price level rises as people spend the excess money balances. Output being fixed, the increase in spending merely drives up the price level. As prices rise, there is a repercussion in the labor market, since the rise in prices reduces the real wage. The fall in real wages is shown in Figure 10.4(a) and indicated by $(W/P)_1$. It is clear that at this lower real wage rate the demand for labor exceeds the supply, because firms could profitably use more labor. As firms attempt to increase output, they face a labor shortage at the real wage, $(W/P)_1$, and competition among them forces them to bid up the money wage. As long as the labor shortage exists, they continue to bid up the money wage until the shortage is eliminated. This occurs at the old equilibrium real wage, $(W/P)_e$. It follows that an increase in M does not affect the "real" side of the economy, only the money side. The increase in M resulted in an equal increase in W and P to keep the real wage constant [see part (d)]. All that the change in M accomplished was a proportional change in the price level, exactly what the quantity theory would predict for a change in M at full employment with everything else equal. The change in M brought about inflation as both wages and prices increased. The results are summarized below Figure 10.4.

Consider next a shift in the production function, as shown in Figure 10.5. Assume that technical change shifts the production function upward in a non-parallel way, so that both the average and marginal products of labor are increased. The shift in Figure 10.5(b) is of this kind. The shift in the production function makes labor more productive and thus increases the demand for labor to N_{d_1}. Recall also that the demand curve for labor is derived from the slope of the production function (marginal productivity of labor), and now that the slope of the

FIGURE 10.4
THE CLASSICAL MODEL: CHANGE IN THE MONEY SUPPLY

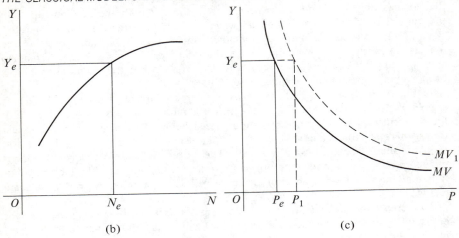

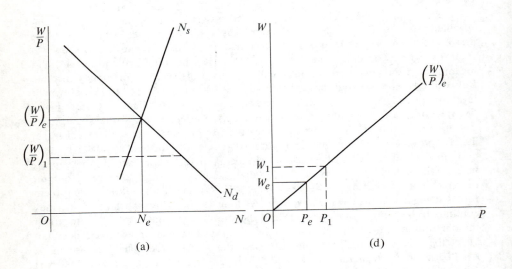

Sequence	Equation	Diagram Part	Change	Initial Reaction	Final Results
1	$MV = PY$	(c)	$+\Delta M$	$P\uparrow$	$+\Delta M$; $+\Delta P$ Proportionally
2	$N = f\left(\dfrac{W}{P}\right)$	(a)	—	$\dfrac{W}{P}\downarrow$ as $P\uparrow$	—
3	$N = f\left(\dfrac{W}{P}\right)$	(a)	—	$N_d > N_s$; $W\uparrow$	$+\Delta W$ Proportional to ΔP $\dfrac{W}{P}$ Remains the Same

production function has been changed, a new derived demand curve is necessary. In any case, firms demand more labor now that it is more productive, because at the old prices more profit can be made as output expands. The firms soon find, however, that with the supply of labor fixed, they must pay a higher real wage, $(W/P)_1$, in order to induce the additional labor required, $N_1 - N_e$, to work. Output expands as shown in part (b), both because more labor is employed, N_1, and because all labor is more productive. With the new higher level of output, Y_1, the price level must fall to P_1. This is because nothing else has changed in the money market, and with a constant M (and V), the additional output can only be sold at a lower price level. The given money supply can only support a certain

FIGURE 10.5
THE CLASSICAL MODEL: SHIFT IN THE PRODUCTION FUNCTION

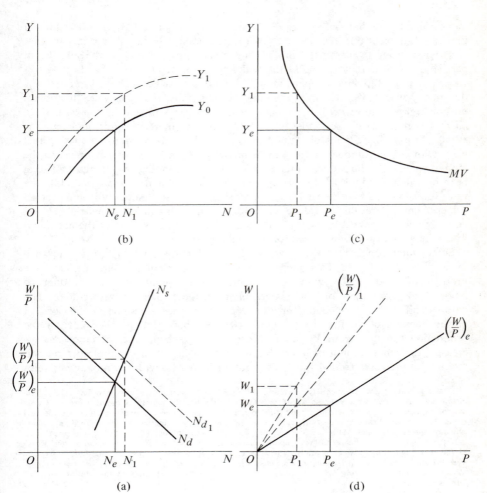

Sequence	Equation	Diagram Part	Change	Initial Reaction	Final Results
1	$Y = Y(N)$	(b)	Δ Technology	Shifts Function Upward, Nonparallel	$Y \uparrow$
2	$N = N\left(\dfrac{W}{P}\right)$	(a)	—	Demand Curve Increases	$N \uparrow; \dfrac{W}{P} \uparrow$
3	$MV = PY$	(c)	—	$P \downarrow$ as $Y \uparrow$ $M + V$ Constant	$P \downarrow$
4	—	(d)	—	$\dfrac{W}{P} \uparrow$ as $P \downarrow$ ΔW Uncertain	ΔW Uncertain (Could Rise, Fall, or Remain Constant) $\dfrac{W}{P}$ must $\uparrow$.

money income, so that as Y increases, P must fall. In Figure 10.5(d) it is clear that the real wage must rise in order to draw the additional labor as shown in part (a).

The real wage ray from the origin thus rotates upward and to the left. From part (c) it is clear that as P falls, the real wage rate increases, so that in part (d) we are interested in what happens to W, the money wage. As depicted in part (d), the money wage, W_1, also increases, and since P falls, the real wage unambiguously increases. However, it is possible for money wages to remain constant, since all that is required in the model is for real wages to increase, and this occurs as P falls. In part (d) the middle (unlabeled) ray shows this possibility: a rising real wage with constant money wage. In this model it is not clear what happens to the money wage. It is no wonder that the benefits of technological change had long been heralded, for look at the results: output and employment increase, while the price level falls, so that the real wage of workers increases. Actually it is not at all evident that the results would be so certain or unambiguously beneficial.[6] Note, however, that a change on the real side does affect the money side of the economy. The results are again summarized following the figure.

Some interesting results follow if the production function shifts upward in a parallel manner. This kind of technological change alters the average product of labor (AP) without changing the marginal physical product of labor (MPP), and therefore there is no change in the demand curve for labor. The parallel shift of the production function does not change the slope or the position of the demand curve for labor. Figure 10.6(b) shows the parallel shift in the production function from Y_0 to Y_1. Since the average product of labor has increased, the same amount of labor, N_e, is now capable of producing more output, and output increases from Y_e to Y_1. As output increases, with the money variables

---

[6] The classical economists themselves realized that the results were not always beneficial. They predicted that as the real wage rose, so would population and hence the supply of labor. Thus, *over time* the supply curve of labor would increase (shift to the right), which would once again reduce the real wage. This rather dismal prospect of a constant (although slowly increasing) level of living made economic progress difficult. This would occur despite the rise in output and the fall in the price level.

If the supply of labor increased without any change in demand, the situation becomes even worse as the real (and money) wage actually falls. The classical economists, especially Malthus, of course, were especially interested in the *long-run* problem of population growth and its effect on the economy. Modern economists are being forced to return to this variable for more study as the Malthusian devil refuses to die.

constant, the price level of the output, Y_1, must fall. In part (c) the price level falls to P_1, since the money supply can only support a given money income. As the price level falls, the real wage increases, say, to $(W/P)_1$. The rising real wage, if maintained, would lead to unemployment equal to the distance RS in part (a). In part (d) the real wage is shown as increasing because of the fall in the price level, with the money wage, W, remaining constant; the real wage is thus $(W/P)_1$.

According to classical precepts, competition among the unemployed would drive the money wage, W, down, restoring the old real wage and eliminating the unemployment [W_e to W_1 in Figure 10.6(d), restoring $(W/P)_e$]. Contrary to a strict

FIGURE 10.6
*THE CLASSICAL MODEL: SHIFT IN THE PRODUCTION FUNCTION.
CASE 2. A PARALLEL SHIFT*

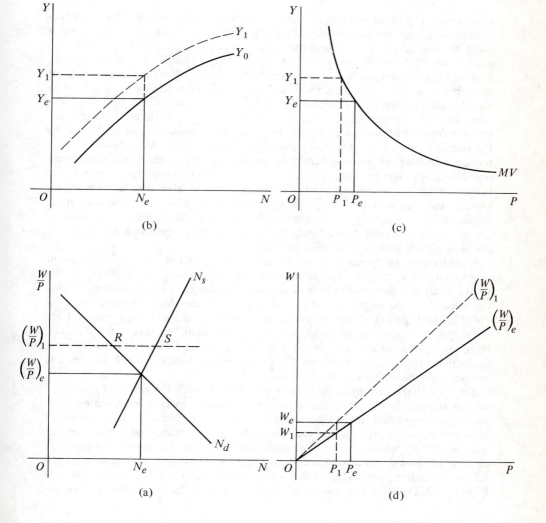

(b)

(c)

(a)

(d)

Sequence	Equation	Diagram Part	Change	Initial Reaction	Final Results
1	$Y = Y(N)$	(b)	Δ Technology	Shifts Function Upward, Parallel $Y \uparrow$	$Y \uparrow$
2	$MV = PY$	(c)		$P \downarrow$ as $Y \uparrow$ $M + V$ Constant $P \downarrow$	$P \downarrow$
3	$N = N\left(\dfrac{W}{P}\right)$	(a)		$\dfrac{W}{P} \uparrow$ as $P \downarrow$ Unemployment Results	$W \downarrow$ to Restore Original $\dfrac{W}{P}$ and Eliminate Unemployment
4		(d)		$W \downarrow$ as $P \downarrow$	

interpretation of classical analysis, labor is unlikely to be content with this situation for very long: the productivity of labor is increasing, but the *real wage remains constant*. True, the level of output has increased and the price level has fallen, but workers are unlikely to feel better off unless they suffer from money illusion. Neither are they likely to be very concerned with the source of the increase in labor productivity, even if the increase was solely the result of better capital stock introduced in the production process. On the contrary, it is not unrealistic to assume that labor would try to maintain the higher real wage, $(W/P)_1$, if necessary combining in some form of organization to gain the power to do so, an action prohibited by the classical view of an atomistic competitive labor market. After all, those who remain employed are made better off by the higher real wage, even though some unemployment must be suffered. Moreover, it is not unreasonable to assume that labor would pay more attention to the average product of labor than to the marginal product and thus would see its productivity increasing. Firms might also be more cognizant of the average productivity change than the marginal productivity change, since productivity is difficult to measure in either case and marginal productivity almost impossible to measure in many cases.

With these assumptions in mind, let us examine the only admissible cause of unemployment in the classical system—*the rigid money wage*. In Figure 10.6 this would mean that competition fails to develop (for the preceding reasons) and that the money wage does not fall, and as a consequence, unemployment develops, RS at $(W/P)_1$. In Figure 10.7 the effects of an arbitrarily imposed rigid money wage are shown; the money wage demanded, say, is "too high," so that at the high real wage unemployment develops. If there is no competition in the labor market or if competition fails, *then in both cases*, labor has priced itself out of the market and any unemployment that ensues is voluntary.

This is an important situation in classical analysis. With the help of Figure 10.7 we can analyze the effects on the economic system of a market imperfection. Suppose that competition in the labor market is severely reduced by the existence of some organization, say, a union that demands a money wage that pushes the real wage to $(W/P)_1$ which is above the equilibrium real wage. Of course, this arbitrary exercise of market power makes full employment impossible. Unemployment develops (voluntary, according to classical analysis) equal to EF, or $N_2 - N_1$, in Figure 10.7(a). With a real wage of $(W/P)_1$, only N_1 units of labor will be demanded by firms, which still want to maximize profits. Without any change in the price level, firms must reduce the profit-maximizing labor input to N_1, which means [from part (b)] that output also falls to Y_1. As output, Y, falls, the price level will rise, assuming that M and V remain constant. The price level must rise as the limited output is competed for, but the rise in the price level must be less than the rise in the money wage, because the real wage must increase [from part (a)]. Therefore, both P and W increase but the $\Delta W > \Delta P$ to ensure that the real wage increases. In part (d) it is clear that wages increase proportionally more than prices.

Since we began with the assumption of an imperfect labor market where wages are flexible or rigid downward, there is no self-correcting mechanism that can

FIGURE 10.7
THE CLASSICAL MODEL: EFFECTS OF A RIGID WAGE

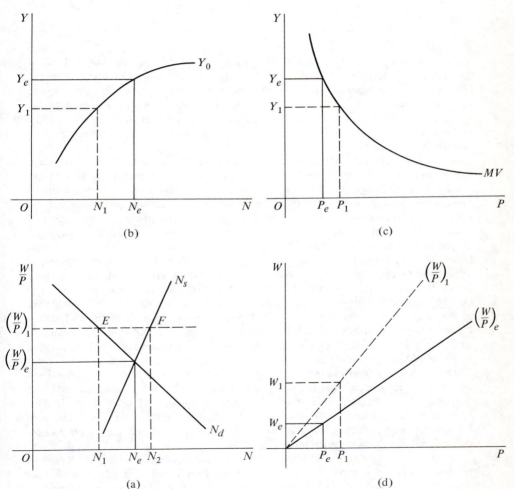

Sequence	Equation	Diagram Part	Change	Initial Reaction	Final Results
1	$N = N\left(\dfrac{W}{P}\right)$	(a)	ΔW	Arbitrary ΔW Increases $\dfrac{W}{P}$	$N \downarrow$, Unemployment of $N_2 - N_1$, and $\dfrac{W}{P} \uparrow$
2	$Y = Y(N)$	(b)	—	Demand for Labor Falls as $W \uparrow$	$Y \downarrow$ as $N \downarrow$
3	$MV = PY$	(c)	—	$P \uparrow$ as Output Falls	$P \uparrow$
4	—	(d)	—	Since $P \uparrow$, $W \uparrow$ More to Make $\dfrac{W}{P} \uparrow$	$W \uparrow$ $\Delta W > \Delta P$

restore full employment. Without competition money wages do not fall when unemployment develops. Therefore, the conditions remain—unemployment in the labor market and consequently a reduced output at increased prices. True again, those who are employed are better off, since their real wage has risen despite the fall in output and the increase in the price level. The lesson is clear: Without competition a rigid money wage leads to unemployment, and that unemployment is essentially voluntary.

It is called voluntary unemployment because all that labor has to do to return the economy to full employment is to agree to reduce the money wage so that the equilibrium real wage will be restored. In the classical model this conclusion is inescapable, and no level of output other than the full employment level can be regarded as an equilibrium level. With flexible wages and prices, competition will move the economy toward the full employment of resources and the maximum output consistent with the free choices of the community regarding work versus leisure. If something gets in the way of the smooth functioning of the system, if imperfections develop, then, of course, the conclusions are altered. One of these imperfections, a rigid or inflexible money wage, results in unemployment. The classical economists argued that a reduction in the money wage (or something akin to the restoration of competition) would eliminate the unemployment and return the economy to its former equilibrium position. It is well to examine this argument, since the policy of voluntary wage cuts to reach full employment is still advocated by some as a proper and feasible policy.

The question is, can money wages be reduced without affecting the price level by the same amount, so that the real wage can fall and employment increase? For the classical economists, the answer is *yes,* since their view of price determination rests with the quantity theory, whereby the money supply determines the price level. Costs of production, of which wages are the major part, play no role in determining the absolute price level.

In one sense, the classical argument (using partial equilibrium analysis) involved the fallacy of composition—what is true for one firm is not necessarily true for all firms. If the workers in one firm agree to accept lower money wages, it is true that this firm could increase employment, expecting to receive the same price for its output; thus, the real wage falls and employment increases. Workers in this firm do not affect the price of the output they help to produce, since they do not affect the demand for their production. But if all workers agree to accept a lower money wage, what will happen to the price level? If the price level falls, there will be a movement back to the original real wage and thus to the original employment level. What happens to the price level depends upon what happens to aggregate demand as money wages fall.

Assume that as money wages fall, employment and output increase, so that *total* wages paid in the economy increase.[7] Output expands as the reduction in money wages reduces the cost of production, and firms that maximize profits will increase output and employment. The question is, will the additional output be sold at the expected prices?[8]

The consumption component of aggregate demand is likely to be affected adversely. Even if the *MPC* of the additional workers is equal to that of the previously employed workers, the *MPC* would still be less than 1, so that the workers would not buy back all of the output. Furthermore, as money wages were cut, there would be a redistribution of income from workers to profit takers. (This fact alone raises all sorts of questions about the social justice involved in this policy.) If, as Keynes believed, the *MPC* of nonwage groups is lower than the *MPC* of wage groups, then the redistribution would result in a decrease in consumption and an increase in saving. In any event, the additional output would not be consumed and inventory accumulation would take place. If this inventory change were unintended, competition would force down prices until the excess was depleted. As prices fell, the real wage would increase and firms would cut back on output and hence employment. These movements would continue until the original real wage, output, and employment levels were reached, and the only result of the cut in money wages would be a period of deflation. Falling prices might affect consumption via the Pigou effect, but as previously discussed, it may not be powerful enough to affect the conclusion that consumption would be adversely affected by the reduction in money wages.

If consumption demand is insufficient to purchase the additional output, investment demand must increase in order to prevent the sequence of falling prices, output, and employment. How, then, can investment demand be expected to react to the reduction in the money wage? In Keynesian terminology, what happens to the marginal efficiency of capital, both for shifts in the curve and movements along the curve? Probably the only determinant that would shift the curve in the appropriate direction would be expectations. Businessmen might gain a sense of confidence in the future as money wages were cut. They might even wish to take advantage of the cut in money wages to invest right away, with the expectation that wages would go up again. On the other hand, they might react by postponing investment projects, expecting that wages would fall even farther. On balance, with wages falling and the effects of aggregate demand uncertain, the latter expectation is more likely. Businessmen are not likely to be encouraged by deflation and widespread feelings of uncertainty.

[7] This says that the demand for labor is elastic with respect to the money wage $(\bar{P})$; $(\% \Delta N)/(\% \Delta W) > 1$, so that total wages paid to workers increase. If the demand for labor were inelastic, the total wage bill would fall, and surely, aggregate demand would fall, and most of the classical argument is lost immediately.

[8] The classical economists rather ignored their own major contribution to microeconomic theory. If under competition production is extended to where $MC = P$, then as wages fall, MC falls, and presumably prices should fall as well. Prices, however, were related to the quantity of money.

The process of deflation, as wages and possibly prices fall, could serve to reduce the rate of interest and thus possibly spur investment spending. During deflation not as much money is needed to make transactions and exchanges, and the excess money balances will be used to buy securities. As the demand for securities increases, their prices rise and the interest rate falls. This possibility was recognized by Keynes but rejected in favor of a more direct monetary policy. Much depends upon the interest elasticity of the demand for investment goods. If the investment demand is relatively interest-inelastic, then not much can be expected from the falling interest rate via deflation—the so-called Keynes effect.

Other aspects of investment spending appear even less likely to increase in response to falling wages. It is unlikely that inventory accumulation would take place as long as the prospect of falling prices remained viable. Construction activity appears to face the same expectational possibilities as the demand for producers' durable goods. Foreign trade might be stimulated by the reduction in wages and the additional exports might increase investment. Still, other countries are bound to retaliate and remove the favorable trade advantages.

If investment cannot be relied upon to ensure an adequate level of demand, then prices will have to fall for the unsold output. Again as prices fall, the real wage increases and firms cut back output and employment. The process continues until the original levels of output and employment are reached and the original real wage is restored. The reduction in wages would not work to push the economy toward full employment.

This analysis of a cut in money wages can be illustrative only, because it is conducted along static lines with many things held constant or ignored (technology, *MPC,* rate of substitution of labor for capital in the production process, and so on). But to pursue the matter any further would be unproductive, since the policy of reducing money wages to cure unemployment is not feasible in the current institutional setting of most economies. Most economies rely upon monetary and fiscal policies to influence employment because of the existence of institutions not found in the classical model—unions, imperfect competition of all kinds, large government, and so on.

Even in the classical model a government could use monetary policy to control employment. See again Figures 10.6 and 10.7, where unemployment develops because the real wage is "too high." The monetary authorities could increase the supply of money, thus increasing the price level to lower the real wage and return the economy to the full employment level of output. Why, asked Keynes, go through an agonizing period of deflation with all its uncertainties when monetary policy could do the job?

SAVING AND INVESTMENT AND THE ROLE OF THE RATE OF INTEREST

As has been noted, the classical model reaches conclusions based upon the belief that there could never be a lack of aggregate demand and therefore unemployment. Say's Law and the assumed flexibility of wages and prices operate to clear all markets, so that the equilibrium full employment level of output is maintained. Still, the model does not explicitly allow for saving; might not saving result in an insufficiency of aggregate demand and thus upset such comfortable conclusions? The classical economists had another instrument to ensure that there would never be a lack of demand—the flexible rate of interest.

If saving occurs, the investment sector would borrow the funds and spend them on investment projects, thus making up for the possible insufficiency of aggregate demand. The mechanism that regulates the flow of funds is the market rate of interest. There would always be some rate of interest that would equate saving and investment. We can formalize these statements by adding a few equations to the classical model:

(10.9) $$S = S(i)$$
(10.10) $$I = I(i)$$
(10.11) $$S = I.$$

Equation (10.9) is the classical saving function, where saving is made to depend upon the rate of interest; they are positively related—the higher the rate of interest, the more saving takes place. Of extreme importance is the idea that any saving that occurs is done in such a way that the funds become available to someone else to spend. There is no hoarding of funds in cigar boxes or under mattresses. This follows from Say's Law. No one is foolish enough to hold idle balances over and above those needed for transaction purposes. If there are excess balances, they would be put to work to earn a rate of return and not held idle or hoarded. No matter how small the rate of return, some reward is better than none. Remember the classical economists presupposed rational men, and rational men prefer goods now to goods later. To make people forgo present consumption, there must be some compensation paid. Some of the theories of interest get rather mystical and abstruse, but the major point is clear—any saving that occurs is made available for someone else to spend. The rate of interest (without justifying its existence) is some kind of reward and, whatever its value, is better than nothing. Furthermore, if the rate of interest rises, more saving occurs as the reward for postponing consumption increases.[9]

Equation (10.10) is the investment demand function. Investment varies inversely with the rate of interest. It bears some resemblance to the marginal efficiency of investment function encountered earlier. For our purposes, the function can be regarded as equivalent to the *MEI* schedule, but it would not be so in a strict interpretation of classical writings. The classical economists regarded the demand function as being based on the productivity of capital. In fact, the same type of analysis was carried over to capital as was used in deriving the demand curve for labor. The return to capital declined as more capital was employed and the profit-maximizing level of capital stock was found by equating the productivity of capital to its "price" —the rate of interest. It was Abba Lerner who in discussing the flaws in this argument developed the *MEI* concept.[10] There is no need to elaborate on that argument here, but the reader should realize that we are substituting the *MEI* function for the classical investment demand function.

Equation (10.11) guarantees that there is some equilibrium rate of interest that makes saving equal to investment; some rate of interest clears the market to ensure that all saving is invested and that an insufficiency of aggregate demand never de-

[9] See Joseph W. Conard, *An Introduction to the Theory of Interest* (Berkeley: University of California Press, 1959) for a discussion of interest rate theories.

[10] A. P. Lerner, "On the Marginal Productivity of Capital and Marginal Efficiency of Investment," *Journal of Political Economy* 61 (February 1953): 1–14. See also his *The Economics of Control* (New York: Macmillan, 1944).

velops. Figure 10.8 depicts the saving and investment segment of the classical model. With the introduction of equations (10.9) through (10.11), aggregate demand can now be broken up into its two components, consumption and investment.

Figure 10.8 is drawn on the classical assumption that both S and I are interest-elastic. Furthermore, the intersection of the schedules always occurs in the positive quadrant; that is, the rate of interest is always positive and no matter how low, would equate saving and investment. The classical economists did not contemplate a capital-rich economy that might drive the rate of interest down to zero or even to a negative figure before saving could be made equal to investment.

The capital market was also assumed to be competitive and to work like any other market. For instance, at i_1, $S > I$ and competition among savers would drive the interest rate down (again some return is better than nothing). The surplus saving is eliminated with no threat to aggregate demand. At i_2, $I > S$ and the shortage of funds would cause investors to bid up the rate of interest, and the market would ration the available funds. In much the same way, the market would adjust to changes in the saving and investment schedules.

Finally, note the "real" emphasis of the rate of interest in the classical model on both the demand and supply sides. The monetary aspects of the rate of interest are pushed into the background. This is consistent with the quantity theory and the assumptions made there.

To sum up the conclusions of the classical model: There is always a tendency toward full employment as perfectly competitive markets work through flexible wages, prices, and interest rates to ensure that aggregate demand is always sufficient to purchase the full employment output. Rigidities in the system alter the results but not the fundamental perception of the working of the economic system. For some, the classical model retains much of its explanatory power. Indeed, we have

FIGURE 10.8
THE CLASSICAL MODEL: SAVING AND INVESTMENT

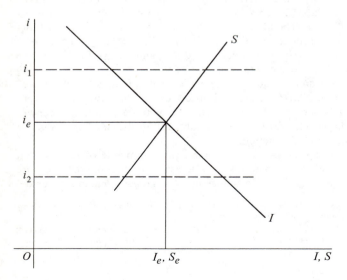

discussed the classical model in such detail because many people believe the essentials of the model to be valid even today, and therefore some appreciation of it indispensable.

The Money Market in the Keynesian Model

The monetary theory generally accepted at the time Keynes wrote *The General Theory* was some variant of the quantity theory. The central assumption of the quantity theory is that people hold a certain amount of cash balances to make transactions but do not hold idle balances that could be used for the production of income. The amount of cash balances might change as the price level changed or with changes in V or Y. Since both V and Y are assumed fixed, most variants of the quantity theory postulate a direct link between the money supply and the price level. Under the quantity theory, money functions as a medium of exchange, merely facilitating trade. No one holds idle money. As has been noted, this assumption comes from Say's Law, according to which all income is spent. Keynes was interested in demonstrating that there is a possibility of an insufficiency of aggregate demand, and therefore he had to attack the classical model at one of its most central points. He had to show that it might be quite rational for men to hold money balances in excess of those needed for exchange purposes. If this could be shown, then idle money balances mean that not all income returns to producers— that is, aggregate demand could be insufficient. To demonstrate this possibility, Keynes formulated the liquidity preference theory of the demand for money and interest rate determination.

THE DEMAND FOR MONEY

In the quantity theory the demand for money is only for exchange purposes, but this is not easily seen in the formulation $MV = PY$. Alfred Marshall[11] developed what has come to be known as the Cambridge version of the quantity theory, which emphasizes the demand for money to hold. It can be written as

$$M = \frac{PY}{V},$$

or more simply,

(10.12) $$M = kY,$$

where $k = 1/V$ and $PY = Y$, money income.

Equation (10.12) recognizes that people tend to hold a certain portion, k, of their money incomes in the form of cash in order to make transactions. The Marshallian k would be a fraction, say, one-fourth or one-eighth; thus, if the national income were $800 and $k = \frac{1}{4}$, a money supply of $200 would be needed for exchange purposes. On the average, $200 of cash balances would be held if the level of income were $800; $250 if the level of income rose to $1,000, and so on. Thus, the Cambridge approach emphasizes the amount of money being *held* at any moment, while the early version of the quantity theory stressed the velocity or the rate at which money was being *spent* on the average. Algebraically, they amount to the same thing, for k and V are reciprocals:

$$MV = PY; \qquad M = \frac{PY}{V}; \qquad M = kY; \qquad MV = Y.$$

[11] Alfred Marshall, *Money, Credit, and Commerce* (New York: Macmillan, 1923), pp. 44–45.

According to the velocity approach, the average dollar is spent four times per period ($V = 4$), and according to the cash balance approach, one fourth of the national income is not being spent at any one moment but is being held in the form of cash balances ($k = \frac{1}{4}$). The change in emphasis is not so critical for the quantity theory, but it does become important as it is taken up by Keynes in his emphasis on the demand for money to hold as cash balances. The demand for money was ascribed to three motives: the transaction, the precautionary, and the speculative motives.

THE TRANSACTION DEMAND FOR MONEY

The transaction demand for money is virtually the same as the Cambridge quantity theory of the demand for cash balances. In both cases, a certain amount of money is held to make ordinary transactions. It is clear that the same determinants of V will help explain k, and in both cases, it is money as a medium of exchange that is stressed.

The need for transaction money follows from the fact that there is a time difference between the receipt of income and its disbursement. Both for individuals and for businesses, the receipt of income, no matter how regular, is never exactly matched by the requirements imposed by routine transactions. Generally, income is received in periodic payments while disbursements may be spread out over the entire period. Thus, there is a need to retain some portion of income in order to make these transactions. Anyone who has ever received a paycheck knows that some of his pay is spent immediately and the rest is spent as the bills are received. In between, some portion of income is held idle in the form of cash balances against these future transactions.

How much is held in transactions balances? In general, individuals and businessmen will learn by trial and error how much transaction money is needed to last until the next pay period or receipt of income. Similarly, the community in the aggregate will choose to hold a certain proportion of the national income in the form of cash balances. If we select some time period and assume that disbursements are made fairly evenly throughout the period, we can get an average of how much cash is held for transaction purposes—this is the value of k. If we further assume that k is stable and linear, we can represent the transaction demand for money as in Figure 10.9 and symbolically as

$$(10.13) \qquad\qquad L_t = kY,$$

where L_t is the demand for money for transaction purposes; Y is the level of income; and k is the fraction of income held as cash balances. Since we have assumed a linear relation between L_t and Y, k is also the slope of the line that describes that relation.

In Figure 10.9 the relation is drawn under the assumption that k is equal to one-fourth ($k_0 = \frac{1}{4}$), for if $Y = \$1,000$, then $L_t = \$250$, and so on. If the community decided to hold a larger fraction for transaction purposes, k would rise, say, to $k_1 = \frac{1}{3}$. Similarly, if the community chose to hold less, k would fall to $k_2 = \frac{1}{5}$. If we continue to assume, however, that k is stable for the period under consideration, we can ignore such shifts and work with a constant and given value of k.

Post-Keynesian economists have questioned the constancy of k as the rate of interest increases. Transaction balances, being idle, do not yield any return. Perhaps

FIGURE 10.9

THE TRANSACTION DEMAND FOR MONEY

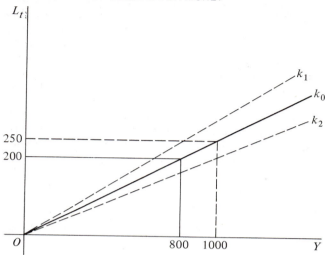

at some rate of interest people will find ways to economize on the use of cash balances, even those held for transaction purposes. At low interest rates the sacrifice of a return is not great and must be balanced against the cost and inconvenience of holding these funds in other, interest-bearing instruments. Still, as the rate of interest rises, the return sacrificed may begin to overshadow all the barriers, so that it will become reasonable to cut down on the amount of cash balances held for transaction purposes. If this were the case, the demand for transaction balances would be written as $L_t = f(Y, i)$, with perhaps some minimum i at which the function for i becomes active.

This behavior is witnessed frequently in corporation activity as treasurers of large firms invest temporary excess cash balances in United States government obligations rather than hold them idle. Sometimes they invest the funds over a weekend to take advantage of the existence of a market for these otherwise idle balances. Individuals may also avail themselves of the opportunity to put idle balances to work, but the practice is much less advantageous. Banks or other financial institutions may not pay interest on short-term deposits, and even when they do, the cost and trouble of making these transactions may not be worth all the effort. Still, if the return becomes high enough, people will probably begin to hold less in the way of transaction balances and seek outlets for the idle balances (such as the everyday interest type of saving deposits). In short, the theoretical possibility that the demand for transaction balances is an inverse function of the rate of interest must be recognized. We will, however, continue to assume that the relation can be ignored by assuming that any changes in behavior take place over a longer period of time than is under consideration and that people have adapted their habits to fit the current conditions and are slow to change. The transaction demand, then, is retained as $L_t = kY$.

THE PRECAUTIONARY DEMAND FOR MONEY

The precautionary motive for holding money is based on the need to hold cash in excess of transaction balances in order to meet contingencies of all kinds and to take advantage of unusual buying opportunities. Unforeseen circumstances may arise and prevent people from pursuing their normal routines in the marketplace. Unforeseen problems are often associated with traveling, when "just in case something happens" money balances are common.

With the widespread acceptance of the credit card, the demand for money to hold as a precaution is probably diminishing more each year. There is much less need to carry cash when a credit card will do; the fear of unforeseen contingencies is greatly reduced, and the desire for security that is so large a part of the precautionary motive is greatly satisfied by the existence of instant credit. Furthermore, the precautionary demand for money is likely to be even more sensitive to the interest rate and the foregone reward than is the case for transaction balances. Why carry cash when credit cards can be used for just about anything? The return sacrificed by holding idle funds is much more evident in this case with no loss of convenience. For these reasons, the precautionary demand for money is diminishing and can justifiably be included with the transaction demand and, for simplicity, also made a function of the level of income:

$$(10.14) \qquad L_p = f(Y),$$

where L_p is the precautionary demand for money. Presumably, as the level of income increases, there is more business activity, more traveling, and so on, and therefore more demand for money to hold to meet unforeseen contingencies. To the extent that some of this motive remains, it is easy to include it as part of the transaction demand and write

$$L_t + L_p = f(Y),$$

or simply,

$$(10.15) \qquad L_t = f(Y) = kY.$$

THE SPECULATIVE DEMAND FOR MONEY

It is with the concept of the speculative demand for money that Keynes attacked the monetary theory derived from Say's Law. The formulation of a speculative demand for money recognized a situation specifically denied by Say's Law and classical thought—the demand for money *as an asset,* the "store of value" function of money. The transaction and precautionary demands can easily be incorporated into the classical model under the general heading of money held for exchanges. The speculative demand for money to hold, over and above that needed for transaction purposes, implies that there are times when it is rational to hold money idle as an asset rather than to seek some rate of return, however small. If money is held as an asset, (a) it is not spent or lent to others, and therefore an insufficiency of aggregate demand is possible; (b) V, the velocity of money, cannot be regarded as constant but must be subject to fluctuation as the demand for money fluctuates; and (c) money must be a more complicated variable than envisioned by the classical economists and must be functionally related to other variables in the system. These issues should become clear as the speculative demand for money is examined in more detail.

In order to refute the classical premise that it is irrational to hold money idle, Keynes had to supply an explanation that would justify such behavior. He maintained that in the act of investing in securities an individual is automatically speculating whether he wants to or not; there must therefore be times when the speculation involves a loss. It follows that the "some return, however small" attitude of the classical economists with regard to excess cash balances is somewhat naive—surely, in the case of a loss it would have been preferable to hold idle cash. Keynes then set about to explain the conditions under which it is more rational to prefer *liquidity* than an interest-bearing security. The highest form of liquidity is cash, so that the demand for money to hold is translated into the speculative demand for money as an asset.

The conditions under which it may be more rational to hold cash than a security are easily demonstrated. Recall the discussion in chapter 9 pertaining to the calculation of present value. It was found that for a perpetual or consol type of bond, which never matures (or for a bond of very long term), the present or capitalized value can be found from the expression

$$V_p = \frac{R}{i},$$

where V_p is the present or capitalized value of the bond, R is the earnings from the bond, and i is the market rate of interest. The market value of the bond can be computed once the earnings from it and the market rate of interest are known. For example, if the bond yielded $40 per period and the market rate of interest were 4 per cent, the market value of the bond would be $1,000:

$$V_p = \frac{\$40}{0.04} = \$1,000.$$

If the market rate of interest fell to 2 per cent, the market value of this same bond would increase to $2,000:

$$V_p = \frac{\$40}{0.02} = \$2,000.$$

Similarly, if the market rate of interest rose to 8 per cent, the market value of this bond would fall to $500:

$$V_p = \frac{\$40}{0.08} = \$500.$$

These examples show that *the market value of the bond and the market rate of interest vary inversely*. In order to earn $40 when the market rate of interest is 4 per cent, one must lay out $1,000; to earn the same return of $40 when the interest rate is 2 per cent, one must lay out $2,000. Therefore, anyone holding a bond yielding a $40-per-period return can sell that security for $2,000 when the interest rate is 2 per cent. No one would buy the bond for more than $2,000, since he could buy another security for $2,000, which at 2 per cent would yield $40. Similarly, the seller would not accept less than $2,000, since he knows that for the buyer to get a return of $40 when $i = 2$ per cent he must put up $2,000 in the marketplace. Therefore, $2,000 is the capitalized value of this $40-per-period income stream, and the market will value equally all securities that yield this amount. Now, if the market rate of interest rose to 8 per cent, it would only be necessary to put up $500 in order to get a return of $40. Anyone holding the original $1,000 bond now finds it is worth only $500. No one would pay more for it, since he could buy another security for $500 and earn $40.

The fact that the market value of the bond and the market rate of interest vary inversely means that whenever one buys a security, one is speculating about future changes in bond prices and interest rates. If interest rates fall (and bond prices rise), there is a capital gain; if interest rates rise (and bond prices fall), there is a capital loss. If one expects interest rates to fall, it would be wise to buy bonds and utilize any excess cash balances. On the other hand, if one expects interest rates to rise, it might be judicious to hold cash rather than to suffer the loss as bond prices fall. In other words, the capital loss on the fall in the price of the bond may well offset the interest income from the bond. How much would the interest rate have to increase in order to wipe out the gain from interest income? The rate need rise only by the square of itself to erase the gain. In our original example, if the rate of interest rose by 0.0016, which is $(0.04)^2$, the interest income would be canceled by the capital loss on the bond. The value of the bond becomes

$$V_p = \frac{\$40}{0.0416} = \$961.78,$$

and the capital loss on the bond, $\$1,000 - \$961.78 = \$38.22$, is approximately equal to the return of $40 earned from the bond. Since an increase in the rate of interest by the square of itself is not large (for instance, 0.0016), the gain from the bond could be quickly canceled and a loss could follow. Therefore, some speculation is inevitable in buying securities, and contrary to the classical notion, there may be times when it is wiser to hold cash rather than a security even if the return is positive. Thus, Say's Law and the quantity theory derived from it are upset, and the conclusions deduced from them made uncertain. Money held as an asset over and beyond that needed for exchange purposes is possible and is made a function of the rate of interest. The speculative demand for money is written as

(10.16) $$L_s = L(i),$$

where L_s is the speculative demand for money, which varies inversely with the market rate of interest, i.

Note that the speculative demand for money is a function of the *expected* interest rate, and any changes are *expected* changes. It could be surmised that the speculative demand for money would be dynamic and relatively unstable. Furthermore, since expectations are seldom observed directly, changes in the demand could not be readily explained or even understood. However, some very simple forms of expectational behavior can be outlined, so that this concept can be studied more effectively.

For simplicity, then, it is necessary to postulate that those in the bond market grow accustomed to a "normal" interest rate, or better, some normal range of interest rates.[12] What is normal is presumably determined by recent experience. Since interest rates change slowly and in rather small amounts, the concept of what is normal also changes in a similar manner. A normal range might be, for example, from 5 to 7 per cent. Accordingly, a 10 per cent rate would be regarded as "high" and a 3 per cent rate as "low". The important point is that the majority of investors

---

[12] Also for simplicity, bonds are the only type of security considered for the present, and the choice is only between bonds and holding money.

expect the rate of interest to return to the normal range whenever it goes beyond the expected normal limits. As they react to this information, they affect the speculative demand for money. Just how they react can better be understood with the aid of a figure. Figure 10.10 shows the speculative demand for money.

In Figure 10.10 it is assumed that investors have become accustomed to interest rate fluctuations between 4 and 7 per cent and regard interest rates in this range as normal. Interest rates above 7 per cent are regarded as high, and interest rates below 4 per cent are regarded as low. The curvature of the relation comes from the assumption that not everyone in the marketplace holds identical expectations. The shape of the curve is derived from the assumed behavior of security buyers as follows. If the rate of interest were for some time in the normal range and for some reason rose above that range, say to 8 per cent, some people would immediately feel that this rate was high and would soon fall back to a level in the normal range. They buy bonds and reduce their speculative balances. Recall that if the rate of interest falls, bond prices rise and a capital gain is realized. If the rate of interest rose even further, more people would hold these expectations (of a falling i), and therefore more bonds would be purchased and fewer speculative balances held. Again, if the rate of interest is expected to fall back to the normal range, investors eye the capital gain and the attractive (even if temporary) high rate of return. At some very high rate of interest, say 12 per cent, everyone agrees that this rate is too high and will soon fall, and therefore everyone switches to bonds and the speculative demand for money approaches zero. The lesson is clear: at higher than normal interest rates, expectations of a future fall in the interest rate cause investors to prefer bonds to speculative cash balances; they expect capital gains as the interest rate falls (bond prices rise), and they earn a temporary high reward besides.

If interest rates fall below the normal range, the opposite expectations are generated. If the interest rate fell to 3 per cent, the expectation would be that it would soon rise (bond prices fall) back to the old range. Anyone who holds bonds at this low rate stands to suffer a capital loss as bond prices fall. Obviously, there would be a preference for cash rather than bonds (recall how little i must increase to

FIGURE 10.10
THE SPECULATIVE DEMAND FOR MONEY

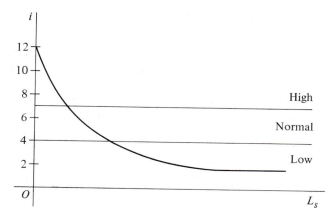

cancel any gain), and the speculative demand for money increases. As the interest rate falls even farther, more people will begin to expect that it will rise again, and therefore the speculative demand for money grows as more people shun bonds. Finally, the rate of interest might fall to the level at which everybody agrees that it can go no lower. There is some institutional rate of interest, say 2 per cent, below which the banking system could not function in the short run. This is the *liquidity trap,* at which point everyone prefers cash to bonds, since the expectations are uniform—interest rates are bound to rise; they cannot fall farther. The speculative demand for money is infinite—the curve becomes horizontal—and perfectly elastic with respect to this low rate of interest.

Within the normal range there is still some curvature to the relation between L_s and i, because not everyone in the market holds identical expectations. If the rate of interest were, say, 6 per cent, some would expect it to fall and some would expect it to rise. Beyond this generality, however, little can be inferred about behavior in the normal range. Again, what is considered normal is based on past experience, and it is plausible to expect that the normal range itself would change as investors grew accustomed to either higher or lower rates with the passage of time.

THE TOTAL DEMAND FOR MONEY

Combining the three motives for demanding money, the expression for the total demand for money becomes

$$(10.17) \qquad L_t + L_s = kY + L(i),$$

where some portion of the demand, L_t, depends upon the level of income, Y, and the speculative portion depends on the rate of interest. In many situations equation (10.17) can be written more directly as

$$(10.18) \qquad L = kY + L(i),$$

which again shows the total demand for money, L.

The total demand for money is illustrated in Figure 10.11. Part (a) shows the transaction demand for money. For a given level of money income, Y, the amount of transaction balances is constant, from the expression $L_t = kY$. Once k is known, then the level of income determines how much money will be demanded for transaction purposes. Since we have assumed that money held for transactions is unaffected by the rate of interest, the transaction demand is depicted as a vertical straight line.

Figure 10.11(b) shows the speculative demand for money. Since the speculative demand for money, L_s, is a decreasing function of the rate of interest, the curve exhibits the reactions of investors to expectations about the interest rate. At either extreme the expectations appear to coincide.

Finally, in Figure 10.11(c), the total demand for money, $L_t + L_s$, is shown, derived from the sum of parts (a) and (b). Adding the two curves together is easily done graphically and can be explained by selecting various interest rates to see how the relations operate.

Assuming throughout that the level of income remains constant (a very important assumption), then when the rate of interest is i_0, L_{t_0} will be demanded for transaction purposes and L_{s_0} for speculative purposes. The total demand for money can be read from the curve in part (c): $L = L_{t_0} + L_{s_0}$ which can be derived

FIGURE 10.11

THE TOTAL DEMAND FOR MONEY

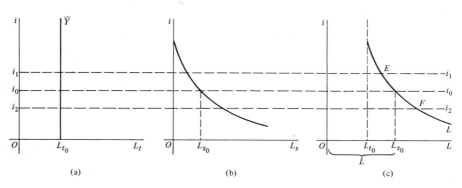

      (a)   (b)   (c)

from the intersection of i_0 and the curve. If the rate of interest changes from i_0 to i_1 or i_2, the transaction demand for money remains the same and equals L_{t_0}. The speculative demand for money does change, however, and thus the total demand for money changes.

At an interest rate of i_1 (relatively high) the total demand for money to hold falls; the community expectations are that the rate will soon fall and bond prices rise; therefore, the lure of capital gains and a good return induces the holding of bonds and the reduction of idle balances. Thus, the total demand for money falls, as can be seen in part (c) by the intersection of i_1 and the curve, which occurs at point E, to the left of the original intersection. If the interest rate falls to i_2, the opposite reaction takes place. Again, the transaction demand is unaffected, but at this lower rate of interest more people prefer to hold cash balances. At this lower rate the fear of capital loss that would accompany the expected increase in future interest rates (bond prices fall), combined with the low rate of return, prompts people to hold more speculative balances than the original amount. The increase in the total demand for money can be seen by the intersection of i_2 and the demand curve, which occurs at point F, to the right of the original intersection. In both cases the total demand for money is affected by changes in the speculative demand for money, with the level of income assumed constant. Note that as interest rates changed, the movement was along the curve, the shape of which is determined by the speculative demand for money.

THE MONEY MARKET AND THE DETERMINATION OF THE RATE OF INTEREST

If we continue to assume that the monetary authorities can control the money supply, we can construct the market for the supply and demand for money. Figure 10.12 adds the supply of money, M, to the demand for money to depict both sides of the market. If we assume that the supply of money is not influenced by the rate of interest, the supply side of the money market is simply represented by a vertical straight line. The amount of money, then, is determined by the monetary

FIGURE 10.12

THE MONEY MARKET AND THE DETERMINATION OF THE RATE OF INTEREST

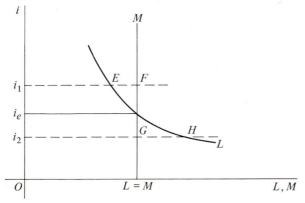

authorities and for present purposes is taken as given and independent of other variables.

The intersection of the supply of money, M, and the demand for money, L, determines the equilibrium rate of interest, i_e. At the equilibrium rate of interest, i_e,

$$M = L = kY + L(i),$$

and the demand for money is just equal to the supply of money. At an interest rate of i_1 the supply of money is greater than the demand for money, $M > L$, by the distance EF. As in all markets, the inequality between supply and demand must set in motion the forces necessary to correct the disequilibrium situation. At the interest rate i_1 people would prefer to hold bonds and reduce their holdings of cash. Expectations are that the rate of interest will fall and bond prices rise—a situation favorable to the holding of bonds. Therefore, the excess money supply will not long remain idle as people take these balances and buy bonds. As the demand for bonds increases, the price of bonds is driven up, and thus the market rate of interest must fall. As long as there is an excess money supply, this activity will continue until bond prices are bid up to the point where the market rate of interest falls to the equilibrium level, i_e, at which point people will be content to hold a larger amount in speculative balances. Equilibrium in the market is restored.

If the market rate of interest fell to i_2, the demand for money would exceed the supply, $L > M$, by the distance GH. At this lower rate of interest, people prefer cash to bonds, since they expect interest rates to rise in the future. There would thus be a tendency for people to get rid of their bonds and hold cash until interest rates had recovered. They attempt to avoid the capital loss when interest rates rebound, and besides, bond prices will fall and become a better buy. So they sell bonds, but in the process, bond prices are reduced as the supply of bonds increases, and of course, interest rates rise. This process continues until bond prices have fallen sufficiently and the interest rate has risen, so that there is no longer any excess demand for money balances. Equilibrium is restored and the demand for money has adjusted to the supply.

In this manner, the static equilibrium rate of interest is determined from

(10.19)
$$M = kY + L(i).$$

The supply of money equals the demand for it. Any other rate of interest cannot persist as people react to the changing conditions. As they buy and sell securities, they bring the market back towards the equilibrium state. Note that the determination of the equilibrium rate of interest in this Keynesian treatment emphasizes the monetary aspect of the rate of interest in contrast to the real emphasis of the classical school. It is the demand for, and supply of, money that interact to determine the rate of interest—the same kind of price determination as is found in any other market; the interest rate is a price like any other.

MONEY MARKET RESPONSES TO CHANGES IN VARIABLES

To complete the discussion of the money market and to reinforce the understanding of how it functions, it is appropriate to explain how the market reacts to changes in the variables of which it is composed.

Demand Changes

A change in the level of income, whatever the source, will change the demand for money as it affects the transaction demand. The transaction demand for money rises and falls as the level of income rises and falls. This is clear from the relation assumed: $L_t = kY$, with k constant. It is the process by which an economy shifts money to transaction balances that is of concern to us.

In Figure 10.13 the economy begins with an equilibrium condition indicated by the subscript zero; the level of income is Y_0, the transaction balances are L_{t_0}, and the rate of interest is i_0. Let the level of income increase to Y_1. This means a shift to the right for higher levels of income and the same shift for transaction balances (from L_{t_0} to L_{t_1}). In fact, assuming no change in the speculative motive, the entire demand for money curve, L, shifts to the right, with the same values at either extreme—a parallel shift. Now, assuming no change in the supply of money, where do the additional transaction balances come from? They must come from balances previously held for speculative purposes. But people will not be willing to give up speculative balances unless they think it is to their advantage to do so. We know that only at higher interest rates would people willingly decide to hold less speculative balances. In Figure 10.13 this is what happens as the new demand for money curve intersects the supply of money curve at i_1, and thus speculative balances have been reduced from $M - L_{t_0}$ to $M - L_{t_1}$, and transaction balances have been increased a like amount.

How does all this come about? As Y increases and more money is required for transaction purposes, people begin to sell their securities to obtain the needed cash. As they sell securities, they depress their price and increase the market rate of interest. As long as additional transaction balances are required, this operation continues. Finally, enough transaction balances are secured and the rate of interest has risen to the level at which people are content to hold less in speculative balances.

What occurs as income falls can be traced by assuming an initial level of Y_1 and letting income fall back to Y_0. The leftward shift in the demand for money results in less transaction balances, more speculative balances, and a lower rate of interest. The process by which transaction balances are transferred to speculative balances is similar to the preceding transfer in the other direction. As in-

FIGURE 10.13

CHANGE IN THE LEVEL OF INCOME

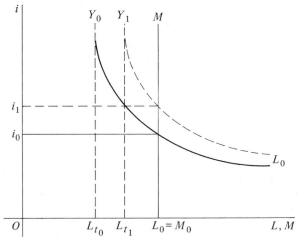

come falls and less money is needed for transaction purposes, people use the excess cash balances in order to buy securities (their only alternative by assumption). As they buy securities, they bid up their price and reduce the yield on them. As long as excess transaction balances exist, the process continues until they are depleted and the rate of interest has fallen to the level sufficient to induce people to hold more in speculative balances. As the rate of interest falls, more people begin to expect that it will increase in the future and are willing to hold more idle cash in that anticipation.

The adjustment process can also be viewed from the supply and demand mechanism. When income increased from Y_0 to Y_1, the demand for money exceeded the supply *at the original interest rate, i_0; $L > M$* at i_0. Therefore, the process just outlined occurred to bring about the equality of M and L once again. Similarly, as income fell from Y_1 to Y_0, $M > L$ at i_1 and again set in action the forces necessary to restore equilibrium in the market.

Change in the Speculative Demand

The speculative demand for money can change as well, since it is based on some concept of normal interest rates, and what constitutes normality is itself subject to change. If, as we have assumed, expectations are formed on the basis of recent past experience, the definition of normality may well change with that experience. For instance, if interest rates rose above what was previously considered normal and stayed at the higher level for some time, it is likely that people would come to consider the higher rates as the new normal range. The same would be true after interest rates had been depressed for some time. It is probable, then, that the speculative demand for money will change over time as expectations change. In graphical terms, this implies a shift in the entire curve. Even the shape of the curve can change over time. If more and more people come to have the same expectations and the market appears to react in unison, then the curve begins to approach a straight line. If expectations diverge over time, the curve bends even more.

Static analysis is not well suited for the analysis of how expectations found in the theory of liquidity preference are formed or changed. Indeed, one criticism of the theory is its presumption of the stability of expectations that permits one to draw a schedule. In addition, the postulated "all or nothing" kind of behavior— either cash or bonds—is rather naive. The essence of the theory, however, remains valid, as shown by post-Keynesian economists.[13] It is better for the present to retain the simple version of the theory of liquidity preference and the notion of expectations incorporated in it. This means that the speculative demand for money may well change, but we may not be able to explain why.

A brief illustration will suffice, just to see what is involved. Suppose after a period of inflation, with its attendant high interest rates, people had grown accustomed to these higher rates and accordingly had adjusted their concept of normal rates upward. Instead of the previous normal range, say 4 to 7 per cent, they expect the normal range in the future to be from 6 to 9 per cent. This means that at the old rates of interest more money will be demanded for speculative purposes, since the old rates will be regarded as too low. The entire schedule shifts to the right, as shown in Figure 10.14—more money will be demanded for speculative purposes at each interest rate.

With the money supply fixed, the excess demand for money will start the adjustment mechanism working. At the old interest rates the fear of loss is enhanced by the new expectations. People sell securities, depressing bond prices and increasing interest rates until they enter the new normal range. In short, the interest rates rise because people expected them to and acted on these expectations. The same could be said for the expectations of falling normal rates.

FIGURE 10.14

CHANGE IN THE SPECULATIVE DEMAND FOR MONEY

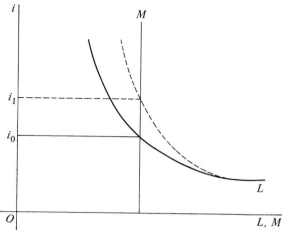

[13] J. Tobin, "Liquidity Preference as Behavior Towards Risk," *Review of Economic Studies* 25 (February 1958): 65–86.

There is something of a self-fulfilling prophecy at work here as people act on their expectations. These expectations could be unwarranted or based on solid evidence, but they are still unexplained. Monetary authorities could influence expectations just by casual remarks or hints in formal speeches. Interest rates of other countries could affect expectations of domestic reactions. The possible influences are too many to mention.

Changes on the Supply Side

A reaction in the money market can also be brought about by changes on the supply side. According to our assumptions, the monetary authorities have control over the money supply and can increase it or decrease it at will. In the United States the Federal Reserve is the monetary authority, and for the time being, we will retain the assumption that it has complete control over the money supply.

The Federal Reserve changes the supply of money through its authority to buy and sell government securities in the marketplace—its open market operations. If it wishes to increase the money supply, it will *purchase* government securities on the open market. It will be buying these securities from commercial banks and the general public. As it buys the securities, it pays for them with a check drawn on itself. These receipts of the general public are deposited in banks, in which case securities have been traded for money balances. The commercial banks are paid for their securities by the Federal Reserve increasing the banks' reserve balances, which it holds. Now, if the commercial banks are required to keep a certain minimum legal reserve against deposits, say of 20 per cent, then through a process analogous to the multiplier, the amount of money created by the banking system will be some multiple of the original Federal Reserve purchase. The banks, as they put the excess reserve balances to work by lending them out, create more money in the process. The bank expansion of the money supply would be by a multiple of five in the very simple case.[14]

If the Federal Reserve wishes to decrease the money supply, it will *sell* securities. In order to pay for the securities, the banks and the general public will draw down their reserves and money balances and thus trade money balances for securities. Again, the contraction of the money supply may be by some multiple of the original reduction of money balances. It should be recalled that the Federal Reserve System is under no compulsion to earn a "profit" on its security transactions and thus can buy and sell at whatever terms are required in order to induce the banks and the public to trade.

Effects of the Change in Money Supply on the Money Market

The change in the money supply will affect the money market largely through its effect upon the rate of interest. In general, an increase in the money supply can be expected to reduce the rate of interest, and a decrease in the money supply can be expected to increase the rate of interest; the rate of interest and the money supply tend to vary inversely. This can be seen in Figure 10.15, where changes in the money supply are illustrated.

In Figure 10.15 the intersection of the money supply, M_0, with the demand for money, L_0, determines a rate of interest that equates the two, i_0. Now suppose that

---

[14] There is no attempt here to discuss in detail the operation of the banking system. Anyone who cannot follow this summary is advised to consult a text in money and banking or even a good principles text.

the Federal Reserve decides to decrease the supply of money, say to M_1. It does so by selling securities, and in the process the increase in the supply of securities depresses their price and increases the yield on them. Since all interest rates move in concert with the bond yield, this is equivalent to saying that the market rate of interest will rise. At the higher interest rate people are willing to acquire securities and reduce their money balances.

If the Federal Reserve decides to increase the supply of money, the opposite reaction occurs. To increase the supply of money, the monetary authorities purchase securities, and as the demand increases, the price of securities rises and the rate of interest falls. As interest rates fall, people are more willing to hold money balances and possibly realize a gain on the sale of securities to the Federal Reserve. More and more people begin to hold the expectation that the interest rate will soon increase again. This is the case as the money supply increases to M_2 and to M_3. If the money supply increases to M_4 and beyond, however, a new situation occurs— a situation that Keynes called the liquidity trap. The liquidity trap means that everyone prefers to hold money and shun securities. (Money, of course, is the most liquid of assets.) That is, expectations in the marketplace begin to converge, and everyone expects the same developments. They simply expect that the rate of interest will increase, *since it can go no lower*. There exists some institutional rate of interest that is regarded as an absolute minimum, and once this minimum is reached, no one feels it will go any lower. The best policy under these circumstances is to hold idle cash, because of the fear of loss when interest rates finally do increase (and bond prices fall). Besides, with such a low interest rate, not much of a return is being sacrificed anyway.

The liquidity trap is not of particular interest in periods of prosperity, when interest rates are likely to be well above the institutional minimum. In periods of severe depression, however, its likelihood is increased considerably. This is what concerned Keynes at the time he was writing. Recall that the classical economists

FIGURE 10.15
CHANGES IN THE SUPPLY OF MONEY

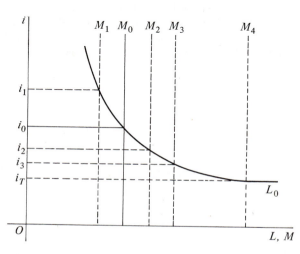

postulated a flexible interest rate in order to equate saving and investment. The importance of the liquidity trap is that it allows the possibility that the required interest rate to equate S and I may well be too low—the trap is encountered before the interest rates can fall to the level needed. Of course, if the interest rate is too high, so that $S > I$, then not all of income is spent. Aggregate demand could be insufficient, unemployment could develop, and so on. Keynes attacked the classical conclusion of an economy tending towards full employment by identifying the liquidity trap as a possible barrier. Therefore, even if wages and prices were flexible, the interest rate could still fail to equate saving and investment and a lack of demand could ensue and unemployment could develop.

Monetary policy could be successful in increasing the rate of interest but might have difficulty decreasing the rate of interest below some minimum. Monetary policy could be used, for instance, in a period of depression to reduce the rate of interest in order to stimulate investment and dampen saving. As bonds were purchased, the interest rate would fall but would finally run into the trap rate—i_T in Figure 10.15. Attempts by the monetary authorities to reduce the rate further would be unsuccessful. The Federal Reserve could buy the securities, of course, since people would be quite willing, even anxious, to sell, but the proceeds from the sales would all flow into idle balances, and the money would be held for speculative purposes. At the trap rate of interest the demand for money is perfectly elastic—infinite—since all expectations are identical.

Some Concluding Remarks

The foregoing analysis of the money market is rather simple and was intended only to suggest its essential operation. Many qualifications and additions could be made and the analysis extended. For instance, the demand for money remained unaffected by changes in the money supply in the previous section. This is obviously suspect. Moreover, post-Keynesian economists have modified the work of Keynes and added to his original analysis. Some of these are listed in the references, but they will not be discussed explicitly here.

In the next chapter we retain the simple view of the money market and combine it with the goods market in order to get a general equilibrium model. To view markets, for either goods or money, in isolation, is not realistic, since all markets are interdependent and interact to some extent. We need a broader view of what these interactions are and how they are likely to affect the economic system.

The General Equilibrium Model

In economics everything depends upon everything else—that is the essence of general equilibrium analysis. In the models used so far this fundamental insight was set aside in favor of the orderly development of theory. We must now take account of the interdependence of markets by a very simple but clarifying approach.[1] More formal models of general equilibrium require much more sophisticated mathematical techniques.

To begin the study of general equilibrium analysis, first consider the income determination model developed earlier in terms of the saving and investment criteria:

(11.1) $S = S(Y)$ (the saving function)
(11.2) $I = I(i)$ (the investment function)
(11.3) $S = I$ (the equilibrium condition).

Note that in this simple model there are three equations and four unknowns—S, I, Y, i—which means that mathematically there can be no unique solution to the model; in fact, the number of solutions is infinite. The mathematician states that the system is indeterminate (number of variables is larger than number of equations) in the sense that the variables can take on infinite sets of values. Still, in our earlier work we did determine a unique equilibrium level of income. How was this possible? It was made possible by assuming away one of the variables (interest, i) by making it constant, and by ignoring the money market. If i is considered constant, then in the model given by equations (11.1) through (11.3) there are three equations and three unknowns, S, I, Y. The system becomes determinate, but the rate of interest is not permitted to affect the analysis directly.

Similarly, when the money market was discussed, we derived the expression

(11.4) $M = kY + L(i),$

[1] This approach was developed by J. R. Hicks, "Mr. Keynes and the Classics: A Suggested Interpretation," *Econometrica* 5 (April 1937): 147–159, and reprinted in many collections on the subject of macroeconomics.

which gives the equilibrium condition in the money market. Here again, the number of variables exceeds the number of equations, so that there is no unique set of values that would yield a solution. There are two variables, Y and i, and one equation; M and k were assumed given or constant. A unique solution to (11.4) was found by assuming that the level of income, Y, was also given, which reduces the number of unknowns to one.

Thus, the goods market determined Y, *given i*, and the money market determined i, *given Y*. A general equilibrium model would have to determine both Y and i as the two markets are brought together. The interdependence then becomes apparent. Substituting (11.1) and (11.2) into (11.3), we can express the equilibrium condition in functional form as

(11.5) $$S(Y) = I(i).$$

Reproducing the money market equation gives

(11.6) $$M = kY + L(i).$$

We now have two equations and two unknowns, Y and i (with M and k constant), which could yield unique values for Y and i if solved simultaneously. Here is how equations (11.5) and (11.6) are to be interpreted:

(11.5) There are an infinite number of combinations of Y and i that make $S = I$; there is no unique set. In fact, this is the familiar concept of a schedule.

(11.6) There are an infinite number of combinations of Y and i that make $M = L$ (supply is equal to the demand for money); there is no unique set, and again this is a schedule.

If equations (11.5) and (11.6) are solved simultaneously, it is possible to find a unique set out of the combinations of Y and i that satisfies both markets. The system becomes determinate, and a unique set of values of the variables can be found. In graphical terms, the two schedules intersect and thus yield a solution for Y and i that satisfies both markets. There is only one combination of Y and i that can satisfy both markets at the same time.

This mathematical discussion can be transformed into diagrams quite readily, as is subsequently done. This chapter is concerned with depicting these relationships and elaborating the model to facilitate analysis.

The Goods Market

The goods market is represented in Figure 11.1. In part (a) the marginal efficiency of investment function is reproduced; investment spending and the rate of interest vary inversely. For simplicity, all curves in this chapter are drawn as linear ones—straight lines are easier to handle. Part (b) shows the necessary condition for an equilibrium level of income; the level of investment determined in part (a) must be matched by an equal amount of saving. Therefore, the 45-degree line in part (b) acts as a guideline, showing the equality of S and I for any point on the line. Part (c) brings in the saving function, which will show what level of income is necessary to call forth the saving determined in part (b). Finally, part (d) shows the goods market equilibrium and illustrates the infinite combinations of Y and i that are possible equilibrium values. It is best to explain how this system works by deriving the IS schedule from the beginning.

Select a rate of interest, say i_0, and in Figure 11.1(a), once the rate of interest is given, the amount of investment spending, I_0, is obtained directly from the *MEI* schedule. Once the level of investment is known, part (b) indicates the amount of saving, S_0, necessary to secure an equilibrium level of income. The intersection of the investment total with the 45-degree line ensures this result: $I_0 = S_0$. Now, once

FIGURE 11.1
THE GOODS MARKET (IN REAL TERMS)

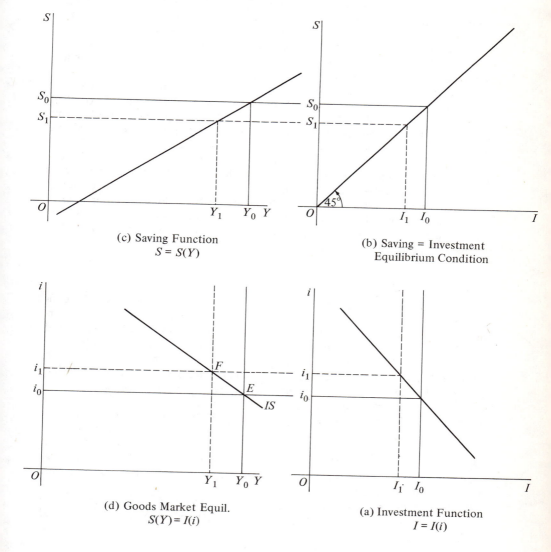

(c) Saving Function
$S = S(Y)$

(b) Saving = Investment
Equilibrium Condition

(d) Goods Market Equil.
$S(Y) = I(i)$

(a) Investment Function
$I = I(i)$

the amount of saving is known, it is an easy matter to ascertain the level of income, Y_0, required to generate this level of saving. The intersection of the saving level of part (b) with the saving function of part (c) determines the necessary income level, Y_0. Now extend the income level from part (c) downward to part (d), and extend the interest rate from part (a) to part (d), and a goods market equilibrium is made possible. The two extensions intersect at point E, which represents one combination (out of an infinite number) of Y and i that makes S equal to I and satisfies the necessary condition for an equilibrium level of income.

Now select another rate of interest, say i_1; in Figure 11.1(a) the level of investment spending, I_1, can be determined. At the higher rate of interest the amount of investment spending declines, as we would expect. From part (b) the amount of saving required to match the new level of investment spending is found to be S_1, less, of course, than at the previous level. In part (c) the decline in the required amount of saving means that the level of income required to produce this lower saving is also lower, and this is verified by the new income level of Y_1. In part (d) the extensions of the lower income level and the increased rate of interest intersect at point F, which represents another combination of Y and i that makes S equal to I and permits an equilibrium level of income.

Continuing to select various interest rates and tracing them through the system formed by these relations will result in points of intersection in Figure 11.1(d) that all lie on a schedule called the *IS* curve. That is, the *IS* curve connects all points in the plane that represent possible combinations of Y and i that make S equal to I and that give equilibrium income levels. The number of combinations of Y and i is infinite, as mentioned in the mathematical analysis, and of course, this is also the meaning of a schedule, which we have now derived. Note that Y and i vary *inversely*. When interest rates are relatively high, investment spending is relatively low, meaning that the level of income would be relatively low. At lower interest rates investment spending increases, which increases the level of income. Saving (and consumption) are seen to be passive in this analysis, as was the case in earlier discussions of income determination.

Changes in the *IS* Curve

The *IS* curve can change by changing the determinants that create it. The position of the investment schedule is determined by many factors, and as these factors change, the entire schedule shifts. The same is true for the saving schedule. A brief look at these changes and their effects on the *IS* curve may prove helpful later.

The investment demand curve is changed by factors that affect the *MEC* schedule. Suppose that expectations or technology changes so as to make investment spending appear more profitable. The investment schedule of part (a) will shift to the right, indicating that at each rate of interest more investment spending will take place. With everything else equal, this will shift the *IS* curve in the same direction. As investment increases, saving must increase, and this occurs only at a higher level of income. More investment spending means higher income levels at each rate of interest; the *IS* schedule shifts to the right. Similarly, anything that depresses investment will shift the investment schedule to the left and also shift the *IS* curve to the left.

The saving function can shift in a like manner. If the *APS* of the community increases, the saving function shifts upward (parallel) and to the left. At each level of income more will be saved. If this is the case, then the level of income required to match S and I is also affected. For instance, an increase in I will call for an increase in S, but with the higher APS, income does not have to increase by as much in order to call forth the additional saving. Therefore, an increase in the saving function will shift the IS curve downward and to the left. If the APS were to fall instead, the shift in the IS curve would be to the right. In this case, higher levels of income would be required to induce the same amount of saving as before.

Perhaps the best way to understand these changes is to sketch the changes and follow them through the system. The interested reader can do this himself and incidentally learn a great deal about the system and how it operates. A summary of these changes outlined is given in Figure 11.2, which is presented only to suggest the direction of change of the IS curve as it responds to changes in the variables.

The Money Market

Equilibrium in the money market is determined by a process similar to that in the goods market. By calculating the total demand for money at various interest rates and equating this demand to the supply of money, it is possible to analyze the equilibrium conditions. Figure 11.3 illustrates the money market and its operation.

In part (a) the speculative demand for money is shown. Once the rate of interest is known, the amount of money to hold to satisfy the speculative demand can be determined. In part (b) the supply of money is represented by the straight line connecting the two axes. What this constant money supply line means is that the entire money supply can be used for transaction purposes (intersection with vertical axis), or for speculative balances (intersection with the horizontal axis), or any combination of both (points on the line). Once the speculative balances have been determined in part (a), the remainder of the money supply must be available to

FIGURE 11.2
CHANGES IN THE IS CURVE

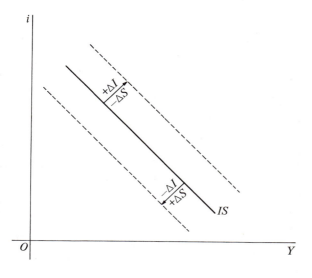

meet the transaction demand $(M - L_s = L_t)$. With the transaction balances known, the level of income that these balances will support is also determined from $L_t = kY$. Assuming that k is constant, the relation is given by the straight line in part (c). Once the level of income is known, it can be extended down to part (d), where a money market equilibrium is determined by the intersection with the extension of the interest rate from part (a).

To see the system in operation, select rates of interest for Figure 11.3(a) and follow the preceding procedure. At the interest rate of i_0 the amount of speculative balances demanded is L_{s_0}. Extending the speculative balances up to part (b), the

FIGURE 11.3
THE MONEY MARKET (IN REAL TERMS)

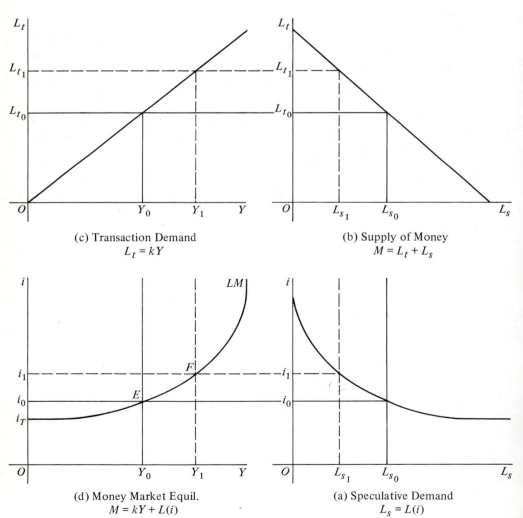

(c) Transaction Demand
$L_t = kY$

(b) Supply of Money
$M = L_t + L_s$

(d) Money Market Equil.
$M = kY + L(i)$

(a) Speculative Demand
$L_s = L(i)$

intersection with the money supply line indicates that there is L_{t_0} amount of money remaining to meet transactions. The transaction balances, together with the constant k, give us the level of income these balances can support. The transaction balances extension from part (b) and the extension of transaction balances and income from part (c) intersect at the income level Y_0. The income level Y_0 and the interest rate are brought together in part (d), where they intersect at point E. Point E represents one combination of Y and i that makes the demand for money, L, equal to the supply of money, M. This particular combination of Y and i is just one out of an infinite number that permit a money market equilibrium.

Choose another (higher) interest rate, say i_1. At this higher interest rate less of speculative balances are demanded (L_{s_1}). More people begin to hold the expectation that the rate of interest may fall and bond prices rise, and thus there is a movement to bonds and away from cash. With less money demanded for speculative balances, there is more available for transaction purposes, as seen by L_{t_1}. These larger transaction balances will support a higher level of income, as given by Y_1. Finally, the higher income Y_1 and the higher interest rate i_1 intersect at point F in Figure 11.3(d), which is to be interpreted as another combination of Y and i that permits a money market equilibrium by making M equal to L.

Continue the process of selecting rates of interest arbitrarily and trace the results through the system; the points of intersection in part (d) will all lie on a schedule called the *LM* curve. That is, the *LM* curve connects all points in the plane that represent combinations of Y and i that make M equal to L and that are money market equilibrium positions. The schedule simply connects the infinite number of these combinations.

Note that in the money market Y and i vary *directly*. When interest rates are high, speculative balances diminish, leaving more money for transaction purposes, which when spent increases the level of income. Conversely, when interest rates are low, more money is held idle in speculative balances and not spent, and it thus inhibits income growth. In addition, the *LM* curve has two extremes at which it becomes a straight line. At some low institutionally determined rate of interest, there is the liquidity trap. At this low rate, i_T, in Figure 11.3, the demand for money becomes perfectly elastic, as everyone's expectations concerning the course of future interest rate movements begin to converge. At the other extreme there is the theoretical possibility that at some high rate of interest the speculative demand for money may well disappear as the opposite expectations develop. With no speculative demand, all of the money supply is used for transaction purposes. As these balances are spent, income grows until resources are fully employed. Thus, *real income* is fixed by the limitation of resources. The *LM* curve becomes vertical at that point, showing zero elasticity with respect to changes in the rate of interest. We will return to these extremes later in the chapter.

Changes in the *LM* Curve

The *LM* curve also shifts in response to changes in the variables previously held constant during its construction. A study of these changes and how they affect the system may prove helpful in explaining the working of the model.

Suppose the concept of what constitutes a normal range of interest rate variation changes as wealthholders grow accustomed to higher rates and expect them to continue. These expectations shift the speculative balances curve to the right; at each interest rate more money will be demanded to satisfy the speculative motive. This means that at every interest rate less of the money supply will be available for transaction purposes. Therefore, the level of income must fall. If the level of income falls at each interest rate, this results in a shift in the *LM* curve to the left. A decrease in the demand for speculative balances shifts the *LM* curve to the right. Now at each interest rate more money is available for transaction purposes, and the level of income rises as these balances are spent.

The latter result (*LM* curve shifts to the right) can also be attained by increasing the supply of money. In Figure 11.3(b) an increase in the supply of money shifts the curve rightward, so that more money is available to satisfy both motives for demanding it. If the money supply increases while the speculative demand remains unchanged, then (as in the preceding case) more money is available for transaction demand and the level of income increases at each interest rate—the *LM* curve shifts to the right. A decrease in the money supply must, of course, have the opposite effects.

Finally, the proportion of income held in the form of cash balances, k, can also change over time and affect the *LM* curve. An increase in k [which is an increase in the slope of the line in Figure 11.3(c)] rotates the schedule to the left, and a decrease in k rotates the schedule to the right. If k increases, people hold more money idle and do not spend it as quickly; a decrease in k brings about the reverse. If k increases, the *LM* curve shifts to the left; if k decreases, the *LM* curve shifts to the right. The explanation of these shifts is left to the reader.

These changes in the *LM* curve are summarized in Figure 11.4, which merely suggests changes in the direction of the curve and is not intended to explain in detail what brings these shifts about.

It should be noted that in the next section the four-quadrant diagram, as represented by Figures 11.1 and 11.3, is replaced by a figure showing only part (d) for both sides of the market. Since only the *IS* or *LM* curve will be shown, the reader must recall the other details and explanations of Figures 11.1 and 11.3 mentally.

FIGURE 11.4
CHANGES IN THE LM CURVE

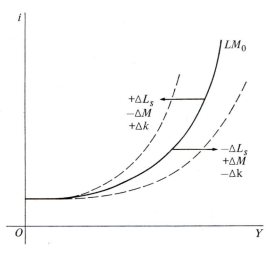

Also, changes in the *IS* and *LM* curves and how they come about must be remembered. Figures 11.2 and 11.4 will not by themselves suffice for subsequent work.

General Equilibrium

Both the *IS* and *LM* curves describe a relation between various combinations of Y and i. Certain combinations of Y and i are consistent with goods market equilibrium, where $S = I$, and certain combinations of Y and i permit a money market equilibrium, where $L = M$. Only one combination of Y and i permits an equilibrium in both markets simultaneously, and this is the general equilibrium condition. Mathematically, this unique combination of Y and i can be obtained by solving the two equations simultaneously; graphically, the identical solution is reached when the two curves intersect in the same plane. Figures 11.5 and 11.6 bring together the *IS* and *LM* curves to achieve the graphical solution to a general equilibrium. Figure 11.5 also shows a case of a goods market equilibrium and a money market disequilibrium, while Figure 11.6 also shows a case of the reverse.

The intersection of the *IS* and *LM* curves in Figure 11.5 gives the unique combination Y_e and i_e that satisfies the equilibrium condition in both markets, and thus a general equilibrium condition is reached. If this is true, any other combination of Y and i should set in motion market forces that will return the economy to the original equilibrium given by Y_e and i_e.

For example, suppose that interest rate i_1 was somehow established in the marketplace. At this high rate of interest, there would be equilibrium in the goods market, $S = I$, but disequilibrium in the money market. In the goods market Y and i vary inversely; thus, at this high rate of interest investment would be small, saving would be small, and the level of income would be small, as shown by Y_1 in Figure 11.5. As far as the goods market is concerned, this high rate of interest is entirely consistent. But in the money market, where Y and i vary directly, this high rate of interest i_1 and the *low* level of income Y_1 are contradictory. (The level of income for money market equilibrium can be found by dropping a perpendicular from point *B*.) Since at i_1, $S = I$ but $L \neq M$, something has to change in the money market. The supply of money is greater than the demand for it, $M > L$. At a high i less is demanded for speculative balances, and at the low level of Y less is demanded in transaction balances as well (compared, of course, to i_e and Y_e). These excess money balances, not needed for transactions, will begin to flow to the securities market. Bond prices are driven up and interest rates fall. As interest rates fall, investment increases (S increases) and Y begins to increase, moving down the *IS* curve. This process continues until the excess money balances are absorbed, for as Y increases so does L_t, and this requirement for higher transaction balances reverses the flow of funds and puts a brake on the falling interest rate.

This can be seen if one postulates that the economy went too far and that the interest rate fell to i_2. Again $I = S$ at i_2 and Y_2, but there is disequilibrium in the money market. The level of income Y_2 is inconsistent with money market equilibrium (the perpendicular from point *C*). At this higher level of income, Y_2, more money is required for transaction balances than at income level Y_e. Now the demand for money is greater than the supply of money, $L > M$. In order to support the income level Y_2, people would have to sell securities in order to obtain transaction balances. By so doing, they depress bond prices and increase interest rates.

FIGURE 11.5
*GENERAL EQUILIBRIUM; AND GOODS MARKET EQUILIBRIUM, MONEY MARKET
DISEQUILIBRIUM, AND THE ADJUSTMENT TO THE GENERAL EQUILIBRIUM CONDITION*

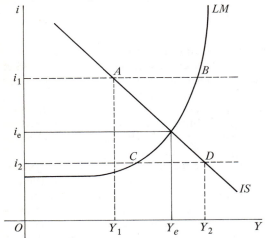

But as i increases, I falls and so does Y. The fall in Y requires less in transaction
balances, so that the flow of funds is stemmed. The movement is once again toward
the general equilibrium values of i_e and Y_e, the only combination of Y and i consistent with equilibrium in both markets.

In Figure 11.6 the reverse case is presented: conditions that make for equi-

FIGURE 11.6
*GENERAL EQUILIBRIUM; AND MONEY MARKET EQUILIBRIUM, GOODS MARKET
DISEQUILIBRIUM, AND THE ADJUSTMENT TO THE GENERAL EQUILIBRIUM CONDITION*

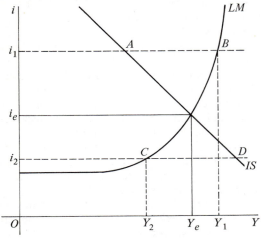

librium in the money market and disequilibrium in the goods market. Of course, as before, there is only one combination, i_e and Y_e, that satisfies both markets. We are only concerned with other combinations here to show the adjustment process.

Again assume a high interest rate i_1, which we now know is entirely consistent with an equilibrium in the money market provided the level of income is Y_1. At i_1 and Y_1, $L = M$, but there is disequilibrium in the goods market and $S \neq I$. In the goods market a high interest rate is consistent only with a low Y (see Y_1 in Figure 11.5 or drop a perpendicular from point A). Therefore, at i_1 and Y_1, $S > I$, for at income level Y_1 saving would be high, but at interest rate i_1 investment would be low. The adjustment process in the goods market then would proceed as follows. Since at i_1 and Y_1, $S > I$, the level of income would soon fall and would continue to fall at every interest rate greater than i_e. Meanwhile, as Y falls, less money is needed for transaction purposes, and the excess spills over into speculative balances. Bond prices are bid up and interest rates fall. The movement is down along the LM curve. Moreover, as interest rates fall, investment is stimulated (and L_t again increases) and thus puts a brake on the falling i and Y. Investment need not take up the entire burden of adjustment, since as Y fell, S also fell, and less investment was required to match the falling S. In this manner, the S and I equality is brought into being at lower levels of i and Y; the money market adjusts by the transfer of funds from transaction balances to speculative balances, which reduces i. Both reactions force down the rate of interest and the level of income to the general equilibrium values, i_e and Y_e.

Once again, if the movement overshot the mark and the interest rate i_2 were established, there would be money market equilibrium, $L = M$, but goods market disequilibrium, $S \neq I$. In this case, $I > S$, for at this lower rate of interest, i_2, investment would be high and income would be high (see Y_2 in Figure 11.5 or drop a perpendicular from point D). But where $L = M$ at Y_2, S would be low. As usual, when $I > S$, the level of income increases and continues to increase as long as $I > S$. As Y increases, so does the need for transaction balances, L_t. People sell securities, depressing bond prices and raising interest rates. The movement is up along the LM curve. Reaction in both markets thus serves to push the economy toward the only sustainable combination of Y and i, given by i_e and Y_e. As i increases, I falls and Y falls, and the adjustment process to match the lower S is made easier. Thus, the rate of interest and the level of income are increased until no further adjustments are necessary, resulting in the general equilibrium condition.

The markets thus exhibit stability and provide the mechanisms to reach or restore the general equilibrium values. Note, however, the inherent dynamic aspects of the adjustment process as funds flow and income changes over time. To analyze a dynamic model within the framework of a static model is extremely difficult. The adjustment processes worked out here are complex for this reason. But much can be learned about these markets if one is willing to trace the adjustment processes through patiently and systematically. Once an understanding of what is taking place is achieved, the analysis will appear much more intelligible.

Changes in the General Equilibrium

The general equilibrium, once attained, is also subject to change as the elements that compose it change. Other things do not remain equal for very long, and shifts in the schedules bring about movements towards a new equilibrium position. We are concerned here with how the system responds to these changes, but the only changes to be considered are those that are important, are likely to occur in the short run, and are subject to manipulation by the conscious action of public intervention.

A CHANGE IN INVESTMENT

Assume that investment changes for some reason. What happens to the system and how does it react? Figure 11.7 shows what happens to the model from the static view.

Consider first an increase in investment that shifts the IS curve from IS_0 to IS_1. It is almost axiomatic that an increase in I will increase Y, and it is true here as Y increases from Y_0 to Y_1. The intersection of the new IS curve with the old LM curve yields the higher income level but also results in a higher interest rate, i_1. This is new, for by the previous analysis an increase in I would have increased Y by some multiple, everything else being equal. The interaction with the money market means that other things do not remain equal, and as a consequence, the multiplier is affected; the simple multiplier is reduced. In Figure 11.7, without any repercussions in the money market, the level of income would have risen from Y_0 out to point A. With the money market interaction, the income growth is only from Y_0 to Y_1.

The reason is simple: the rate of interest increases, which chokes off some investment projects and thereby inhibits income growth. With no change in the money supply, an increase in investment stimulates income growth. As Y increases, more money for transaction balances is required. People sell securities, depressing bond prices and raising interest rates until enough money has been transferred for exchange purposes. As i increases, investment tapers off, and the system stabilizes in the new general equilibrium position given by i_1 and Y_1. The rise in investment spending is checked by the rising interest rate.

FIGURE 11.7
THE IS–LM *MODEL WITH A CHANGE IN INVESTMENT*

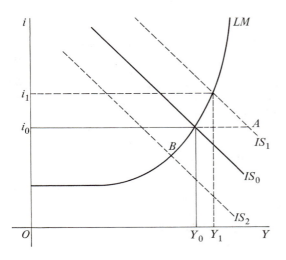

Of course, a fall in investment spending reduces the level of income, but the decline in income is cushioned by a fall in the rate of interest. In Figure 11.7, if *I* fell so that the new *IS* curve became IS_2, it is clear from the intersection with the *LM* curve at point *B* that both *Y* and *i* would be lower.

As *I* falls, the level of income would fall by some multiple, but with the interaction of the money market, the fall in income is not as great as with the simple multiplier used previously. Now, as *Y* falls, less money is demanded for transaction purposes. The excess flows to purchase securities, and bond prices rise and interest rates fall. As *i* falls, some investment projects become profitable, and so on, until the new equilibrium position is established. Once again the previous multiplier analysis must be qualified as money markets are allowed to affect the analysis.

A CHANGE IN SAVING

A change in the *APS* affects the model in much the same manner as a change in investment. It is useful to examine the change in the saving ratio, if only briefly, to promote understanding later of its role in economic growth and appreciation of the consequences of changes that have occurred in the past few years in the United States economy. Figure 11.8 shows the effect on the model of changes in the *APS*.

In recent years the *APS* has been *increasing,* resulting in a shift in the *IS* curve, such as the one shown as IS_2 in Figure 11.8. As saving increases and consumption (*APC*) falls, there would be a tendency for income to fall. With the simple multiplier, the fall in income would be out to point *A*, but with money market interaction, the level of income falls only to Y_2 (determined by the intersection of IS_2 and the *LM* curve). Once again, as income falls, less money is demanded for transaction purposes, and the flow of excess balances to security markets increases bond prices and reduces interest rates. As *i* falls, some investment is stimulated, and this cushions the fall in *Y* and *i*. Whether an increase in investment can be

FIGURE 11.8

THE IS–LM *MODEL WITH A CHANGE IN SAVING*

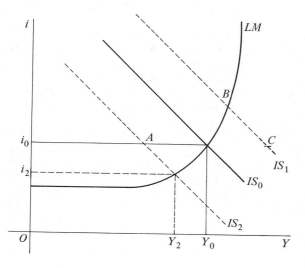

counted on in reality is a subject to which we will return in part III. In this model, with only $I = I(i)$, the theory is consistent with the stabilizing process.

For a decrease in the *APS,* we should expect the opposite. The lower saving increases income, but the larger transaction balances required also increase the rate of interest. The intersection of the new *IS* curve, IS_1, with the *LM* curve at point *B* indicates that this is indeed the case. Again, the fall in saving does not result in as large an increase as might be expected from the simple multiplier analysis (point *C*) because of the interest rate increase that accompanies it. Of course, this also assumes that investment is discouraged by the rising interest rate.

CHANGES IN THE MONEY SUPPLY

The money supply is a controllable variable, so that the monetary authorities can influence the system by deliberate action. In this section we are concerned with the possible effects on the economy of changes in the money supply only. The entire subject of monetary policy will be discussed in more detail in a later chapter.

Consider first an increase in the supply of money. A monetary policy that makes more money available would shift the *LM* curve to the right, as shown in Figure 11.9. The new static equilibrium occurs at the intersection of the new LM_1 curve and the *IS* curve, giving the new combination i_1 and Y_1.

An increase in *M* with no change in the speculative demand means that the initial impact would be an increase in the transaction balances. As people spend these excess balances, the level of real income increases, if there were unemployed resources to begin with and if *P* remains stable. The ΔY can come about if people change their consumption habits, or more directly, if investment spending increases. But for *I* to increase, there must be a fall in the rate of interest, for *i* is the only determinant of *I* in this model. But for *i* to fall, some of the ΔM must spill over into speculative balances, so that bond prices rise and interest rates fall. In this manner, the original ΔM is divided into transaction balances and speculative balances. The flow of money stabilizes the economy and finally stops when the increase in *Y* absorbs enough of the ΔM in transaction balances. The effects of an increase in *M,* and particularly the increase in real *Y,* are straightforward enough, but the assumptions upon which they rest will have to be reexamined again when applied to real world conditions.

A decrease in the money supply would shift the *LM* curve to the left, as shown by LM_2 in Figure 11.9. From the intersection of LM_2 with the *IS* curve at point *A,* it is clear that the result would be a higher interest rate and a lower income level. A decrease in *M,* everything else being equal, would in the first instance send people to the securities markets to sell their bonds in order to recoup lost transaction balances for income level Y_0. As they sell bonds, the interest rate rises and some investment is discouraged. As the amount of *I* falls, *Y* falls and eventually the system stabilizes, and the fall in *Y* requires less in transaction balances.

The ΔM in this adjustment process appears to be the type where the monetary authorities simply resort to the printing press to increase the money supply or to the furnace to decrease it. Open market operations make the process more direct, although people would still have to adjust their holdings of money for various purposes. To increase *M,* the Federal Reserve would purchase securities in the open market, thus driving up bond prices and reducing interest rates directly. To decrease *M,* the Federal Reserve would sell securities, and interest rates would tend to rise. The former is called a "loose" and the latter a "tight" monetary policy.

FIGURE 11.9

THE IS–LM *MODEL WITH CHANGES IN THE MONEY SUPPLY*

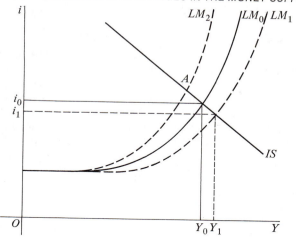

Some immediate applications of monetary policy appear with the simple *IS–LM* model. For instance, when investment increased (see Figure 11.7), the growth in income was checked by an increase in the rate of interest. People had to sell securities in order to gain transaction balances. If, as Y increased, the monetary authorities increased the supply of money, there would be no need for people to seek funds from the securities market; the increase in M would supply the needed transaction balances. With this monetary policy, the rate of interest would remain unchanged, and the growth of income would be comparable to that predicted by the simple multiplier (out to point A in Figure 11.7).

Similarly, a decline in investment and hence income could be cushioned by an increase in the money supply. Such an action would reduce interest rates and check the fall in I and Y. Other changes could also be modified by monetary policy, but any further discussion should await the introduction of the government sector into the model.

The *IS–LM* Model with Government

In adding the public sector to the model we follow the analysis used earlier when this sector was introduced. If we assume that government expenditures (G) and taxes (T) are autonomous, the addition of the public sector is quite simple. In Figure 11.10 it is necessary to change the axes to reflect the new equilibrium conditions. The total spending is now $I + G$, which is now matched by the total leakages $S + T$. The new equilibrium condition can be seen in part (b), where the 45-degree line now equates $I + G$ to $S + T$.

First let us introduce government spending. The additional component of aggregate demand, G, can be added to the other component, I, in part (a). The investment curve shifts parallel by the amount of *autonomous* G and is analogous to an increase in investment. The new $I + G$ schedule, when traced through the system, results in the new IS curve, labeled IS_1 in part (d). With everything else equal, an increase in spending can be expected to shift the IS curve to the right.

The result of the new government spending is a higher level of income, Y_1, and a higher rate of interest, i_1. The simple government expenditures multiplier has to be modified as the fiscal operation interacts with the monetary sphere. With the simple multiplier, the income growth would have been larger [out to point A in Figure 11.10(d)], but the actual growth in Y is limited by the increase in the rate of interest. Without taxes, the government expenditures must be financed by borrowing from the public. As it sells bonds, the price of bonds is depressed and interest rates rise. Furthermore, as people swap demand deposits for government securities there is no immediate net change in M from the deficit-financed expendi-

FIGURE 11.10
THE IS–LM MODEL WITH GOVERNMENT

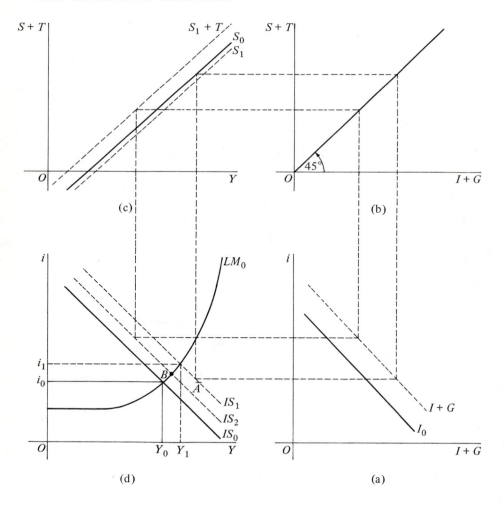

tures, but as Y increases, there may be some attempts to secure additional transaction balances, and this action reinforces the upward movement of the rate of interest. The increase in i does not affect G, of course, but it does affect I. That is, the increase in public spending reduces private spending. Whether or not this is desirable is not the issue here, only that the income growth is contracted.

To prevent the contraction in Y, an increase in M is needed to prevent the rate of interest from rising. This can be accomplished by deliberate monetary policy via the purchase of securities on the open market. An increase in M could also be obtained by selling the bonds to the Federal Reserve System instead of to the general public. The sale of bonds to the Federal Reserve has no offset and thus results in an increase in M; the same result could be had, of course, if the method of financing was through the printing press in the Treasury. Whatever the impetus, an increase in M would shift the LM curve to the right, forestall any change in i, and permit income to grow without this constraint.

Consider now the imposition of a lump sum tax, the amount of which is just sufficient to balance the budget. In the model the first reaction to the tax is in the reduction of the saving function—the APS falls. Recall that the tax affects disposable income and the consumption function shifts downward. Similarly, the saving function shifts downward (to S_1 in Figure 11.10), meaning that at each and every level of Y, less S will take place; thus part of the tax comes out of saving, and the shift in the curve reflects this reaction. To find the total leakages in the system, it is necessary to add the amount of the tax to the amount of saving at each income level. The (constant) tax, T, is added to the new saving function, S_1, to arrive at the new schedule for total leakages, $S_1 + T$ in Figure 11.10. Now, if we select various rates of interest and trace the operation of the system from the $I + G$ curve in part (a) to (b) to the intersection with the $S_1 + T$ curve in part (c), we will obtain a new IS curve that includes taxes as well as government spending —the IS curve labeled IS_2 in part (d).

Taxes, as we might expect, reduce the level of income, and along with it, the rate of interest. The intersection of the IS_2 and the LM_0 schedules at point B shows these results. Note that while the income level fell, it did not fall back to the original level, Y_0, which existed before the introduction of the public sector. This is the result of the balanced budget multiplier. However, with the inclusion of the money market, it is no longer possible to state that the balanced budget multiplier is equal to 1. With the rate of interest permitted to vary, some part of private spending might be affected, I perhaps. The size of the balanced budget multiplier would probably be less than 1, but the exact magnitude depends on a number of factors—the MPS, the interest elasticity of I, the method of financing G, the type of tax, the groups affected by the actions of the public sector, and so on. The entire matter of the balanced budget multiplier is best handled by stating that it is likely to be positive and simply turning it over to the empiricists.

Of course, the effects of the tax can be offset by monetary policy. An increase in M concurrent with the imposition of the tax could reduce interest rates and thus stimulate I. Income would not fall at all or as much, depending upon the size of the increase in M.

This is a simple model, yet it becomes evident that monetary and fiscal policies have repercussions throughout the system. Obviously, the two types of policies ought to be coordinated, but curiously enough, in the institutional setting of the United States, the two policies are not always coordinated and may even work at cross-purposes. In later discussion of monetary and fiscal policies we will take a look at this problem and point out instances of contradictory policies.

Elasticity of the *IS* and *LM* Schedules

A closer look at the *IS–LM* model is required if we are to judge it as a viable model. Specifically, we need to know more about the responsiveness of the model to changes in the variables—that is, the elasticity of the *IS* and *LM* curves must be examined as well as the general shape of the curves.

Looking at the *IS* schedule first, it is clear that the main determinant of its elasticity is the responsiveness of I to the rate of interest, i. Of course, the saving function also influences the elasticity (largely through the effects of the multiplier), but S has been treated as passive so far in the analysis and can be so regarded here as well. All we should recognize is that the lower the MPS, the higher the multiplier, so that any change in I will have a greater effect on Y.

As previously mentioned, the elasticity of investment with respect to the rate of interest is a more intriguing and uncertain question. The classical economists assumed that investment was interest-elastic, while Keynes and post-Keynesian economists have looked upon the investment function as being relatively interest-inelastic. For post-Keynesian economists other determinants of I may swamp in importance the rate of interest. The two views of interest elasticity of I are illustrated in Figure 11.11.

The shape of the *IS* curve follows directly from the shape of the I curve in Figure 11.11. Which one is "correct" and used in the analysis does have significance when the question becomes one of the efficacy of policy measures on the system. Before asking such questions, we need to reexamine the *LM* curve as well.

The *LM* curve has several ranges of elasticity with respect to the rate of interest. At one extreme the curve becomes perfectly elastic, and at the other extreme it becomes perfectly inelastic, and in between, it exhibits some degree of responsiveness. These ranges have been labeled the Keynesian, classical, and intermediate ranges, respectively, although the labels do not correspond to the actual beliefs of the Keynesians or classical economists. It has become traditional, however, to

FIGURE 11.11
THE INTEREST ELASTICITY OF INVESTMENT

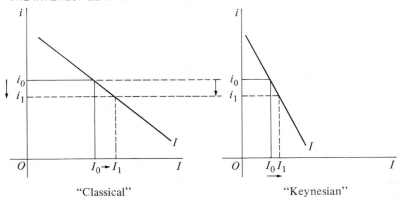

"Classical"   "Keynesian"

label these portions of the *LM* curve in this manner, and no harm is done if we keep in mind that these are only labels of convenience. Figure 11.12 shows the *LM* curve with these ranges identified.

In the Keynesian range the *LM* function is perfectly elastic with respect to the rate of interest. This is the liquidity trap, where some minimum interest rate exists that everyone recognizes as a minimum rate, thus preferring liquidity (cash) to securities. The demand for speculative balances approaches infinity at this rate of interest.

At the other extreme the *LM* function approaches zero elasticity with respect to the rate of interest. At some high rate of interest the demand for speculative balances may well disappear and with it the demand for money as a function of the rate of interest ($L_s = 0$). All *M* is used for transaction purposes, which, as may be recalled, is consistent with the classical assumptions.

Between these ranges the *LM* function shows some positive degree of elasticity —the so-called intermediate range. In this range both the transaction and speculative demands for money exist, depending upon the rate of interest and the level of income. The elasticities of these ranges are indicated in Figure 11.12 by the symbol *E*.

Monetary and Fiscal Policy

The effectiveness of monetary and fiscal policy will vary according to the elasticity of the *IS* and the *LM* function when the policy is initiated. For our purposes, policy actions are confined to control over the money supply and the manipulation of government expenditures and taxes. Figure 11.13 shows the effects of deliberate governmental policies.

FISCAL POLICY

Figure 11.13(a) is concerned with fiscal policy. In the pure Keynesian range of the *LM* curve, where the liquidity trap exists and the level of income is low, fiscal policy is seen to be very effective in increasing the level of income. An increase in

FIGURE 11.12
THE ELASTICITY OF THE LM *SCHEDULE*

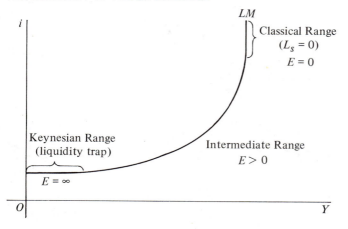

G or a reduction in T or both shifts the IS curve from IS_1 to IS_2, and Y moves from Y_1 to Y_2. To finance the increase in G, it is necessary to borrow from the public (since we are holding M constant). Presumably, there are enough specula-

FIGURE 11.13
THE IS–LM *MODEL AND FISCAL AND MONETARY POLICY*

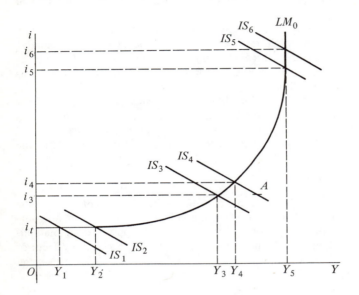

(a) Fiscal Policy

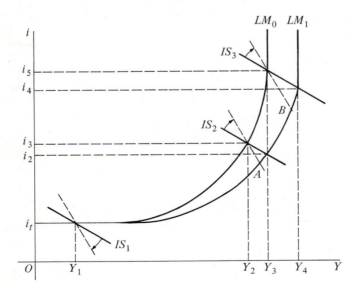

(b) Monetary Policy

tive balances around, and the trap has existed for some time, so that people are willing to lend these idle balances to the government. As G increases, Y increases by the full amount of the simple multiplier. In the liquidity trap i is constant, and therefore, investment spending is not affected by this "pure" fiscal policy measure. Fiscal policy is very effective in the trap region and was, of course, favored by Keynes, who had lost faith in the ability of the monetary authorities to act decisively.

If the IS curve intersects the LM curve in the intermediate range, fiscal policy is effective in increasing the level of income but not as effective as in the Keynesian range. If the increase in G is again financed by the sale of bonds to the public, there will be an increase in the rate of interest, because people had adjusted to the old rate, i_3, and would insist on a higher rate before they gave up their speculative balances. Therefore, as G increases, i increases along with it, and investment spending is adversely affected. The IS curve moves from IS_3 to IS_4, and Y moves from Y_3 to Y_4, an increase that is less than the increase in the trap. If taxes were cut, the same conclusions would apply, although the adjustments are more roundabout. As T is reduced, C is increased, and the increase in Y follows via the multiplier. But as Y increases, the need for transaction balances increases, and these can only come (M being constant) from speculative balances. Again wealthholders would only give up these balances if the rate of interest increased, and so on. The conclusions are the same whichever fiscal policy tool or mix is used—the policy is effective in increasing Y but not as effective as when the economy was more depressed in the trap.

A fiscal policy promulgated when the economy is operating in the classical range is not effective at all. The fiscal policy that shifts the IS curve from IS_5 to IS_6 has no effect on the level of income, which remains Y_5. In the classical range there are no speculative balances, and thus the only way for the government to borrow the funds to increase G is for it to sell bonds at such advantageous terms that the market rate of interest rises by enough so that the public finds it more profitable to lend these funds than to invest in capital goods. Obviously, an increase in G matched by an equal decrease in I leaves the level of income unaffected. Only the interest rate rises from i_5 to i_6, and the composition of aggregate demand is altered. Once again, a tax cut would lead to similar conclusions. Fiscal policy in the classical range is completely ineffective.

MONETARY POLICY

Looking at monetary policy alone leads us to the opposite conclusions with respect to the efficacy of policy in the various ranges.

In the Keynesian range of the LM curve, monetary policy is completely ineffective in changing the level of income. In Figure 11.13(b), as long as the economy is in the liquidity trap, the increase in the money supply will all go to idle hoards. People are quite willing to sell securities to the Federal Reserve as it attempts to increase M. However, the sales proceeds all go into idle balances because of the expectations of a rising i—the consensus of expectations at this low rate of interest. Thus, the ΔM is not spent and has no effect upon the level of income.

If the economy is operating in the intermediate range, monetary policy is effective in increasing the level of income; in Figure 11.13(b) the increase in M shifts the LM curve from LM_0 to LM_1, and the level of income changes from Y_2 to Y_3. In order for the ΔM to increase Y, it must affect I through a reduction in the rate of interest. As M increases, some of the increase must flow to the securities markets, where bond prices are bid up and interest rates fall. As i falls, investment is stimulated and Y begins to increase, but as Y increases, more money is needed for transaction purposes and the money flows stabilize after a time. Thus, some of the ΔM flows to speculative balances and is not spent against goods. This means that although monetary policy is effective in the intermediate range, the change in Y is not as great as it might have been if there were no speculative motive. With the speculative demand for money, idle balances increase when the interest rate falls, as it must to affect I. These idle balances limit the growth of income.

In the classical range monetary policy is completely effective. An increase in M shifts the LM curve from LM_0 to LM_1 and moves the level of income from Y_3 to Y_4. The growth in income is greater than that found in the intermediate range. As the Federal Reserve purchases securities, it bids up the price of these bonds and reduces the rate of interest. Wealthholders willingly sell the bonds for the profit but then look around for ways to invest the sales proceeds. *There being no idle funds,* people buy other securities or find that lending to those who wish to buy capital goods is now profitable. As i falls, investment projects become profitable, and the buyers of capital goods become more willing to borrow funds to finance I. The Federal Reserve can continue to increase M until all of the balances are absorbed into transaction balances needed, as I and hence Y increase. This result could have been expected from the quantity theory, where $M = kY$ and $\Delta M = k\Delta Y$. The change in income is given by $\Delta Y = \Delta M / k$, since all the ΔM must be absorbed into transaction balances. In the classical model the level of income thus grows by some multiple, k, which can be predicted, as is the case with the Keynesian multiplier. Thus, monetary policy is entirely effective in changing the level of income in the classical range, whereas fiscal policy is completely ineffective.

In the Keynesian range fiscal policy is effective, while monetary policy is useless. Between these extremes both fiscal and monetary policies are effective but not quite as powerful as in either extreme case.

MONETARY POLICY AND INVESTMENT DEMAND

From the foregoing it is clear that monetary policy is effective in changing Y but that it must influence investment through a decline in the rate of interest. What happens to monetary policy if we change the assumptions according to which its efficacy was judged?

Suppose, first, that investment spending and the rate of interest are not functionally related: the elasticity of I with respect to i is zero. Then attempts by the monetary authorities to drive down the rate of interest to stimulate I will be frustrated and useless. (It is assumed that all other components of aggregate demand are also independent of the rate of interest—a not unreasonable assumption.) Monetary policy would simply drive the interest rate down until finally the liquidity trap was reached. Clearly, the economy would be seriously disrupted, so that all kinds of expectations and fears would be generated by this blind policy. It is of little use to draw conclusions based on other things remaining equal in this case.

A more realistic assumption is to permit a functional relation between I and i but to assume that the relation is not very strong. This is the post-Keynesian assumption that investment is relatively inelastic with respect to the rate of interest. The effect would be to make monetary policy much less effective even under the best of circumstances.

In Figure 11.13(b) the dotted IS curves are drawn on the assumption of relative inelasticity. From the new IS curves it is clear that monetary policy is less powerful. In the classical range the new IS curve intersects the new LM curve at point B, indicating a lower income level than resulted earlier—Y_4. Note that the rate of interest must fall by a great deal even to induce this income growth. A fall in i of this magnitude would be most disruptive to the economic system. Similarly, in the intermediate range the new IS curve indicates a change in income out to point A rather than to Y_3. In the Keynesian range, the horizontal portion of the LM curve, the elasticity of the IS curve is irrelevant, as shown by the new IS curve replacing IS_1.

Some Remarks on the *IS–LM* Model

For many reasons, some of which will become apparent as we go on, it is not advisable to go much further with the analysis of the economy utilizing the $IS–LM$ model. The extremes of the model do not permit much flexibility and are unlikely situations as presented. Liquidity traps of the type pictured here are not likely to occur with regularity and become a pressing problem for policy makers. As useful as the concept is, it is not likely to be more than a theoretical possibility for advanced economies.

The classical portion of the model is also not well suited for critical analysis. The term *classical* in this connection is clearly a misnomer, for the classical economists postulated an economy that tended toward full employment. If real Y is fixed in the vertical range of the LM curve, how can monetary policy change the level of income? If all resources are not fully employed, and real Y is not fixed, how is this a classical condition? The entire policy of working with real income is awkward and limiting.

Furthermore, the either/or approach to policy—either fiscal policy or monetary policy—is both too simple and unnecessarily restrictive. It is too simple in the sense that there are few examples of "pure" monetary or "pure" fiscal policies. They are bound to interact as the two spheres—the goods and money markets—interact. It is too restrictive because the two policies are not permitted to work together. An expansionary fiscal policy can be accompanied by a facilitating monetary policy, so that the growth of income need not be constrained. For instance, in the intermediate range of 11.13(a) an increase in M could have permitted income to grow out to point A rather than to Y_4, as indicated by the intersection of IS_4 with the LM_0 curve.

However, to pursue all of these ramifications would be unproductive, since the model itself imposes restrictions that limit the analysis and circumscribe the vision of the world it is supposed to resemble. Nevertheless, we will have several occasions to review the model and make some changes in it.

The $IS–LM$ model is an excellent way of summarizing the Keynesian model. It helps to condense the analysis to essentials and permits a ready comprehension of what is involved. Whatever its shortcomings, it has proved a useful device for the understanding of Keynesian concepts. In this regard it was a major contribution. Before making any detailed criticism of the models used so far, it would be useful to review briefly the classical and Keynesian models, so that some comparisons of them can be made and some evaluations tentatively expressed.

Summary of Models and Conclusions

Using the *IS–LM* model for the analysis of the economic system captures most of the essentials of Keynes's model. Some have charged that his model is most applicable to an economy in a depressed state, and it must be admitted that there is some truth in this. The classical model can be criticized for just the opposite bias. In a real sense, then, the two models are complements rather than substitutes. The worlds they attempt to describe are quite different, and given the assumptions that they utilize, they are adequate. In part III some of these assumptions are re-examined, and a further evaluation of the models will be given. For the present it may prove useful to review the models in a formal manner in order to prepare the way for the more detailed critique.

The models are shown as they were developed in earlier work. Presenting them side by side may facilitate the comparison.

	Classical Model		Keynesian Model
(1c)	$N_d = N_d \left(\dfrac{W}{P} \right)$	(1k)	
(2c)	$N_s = N_s \left(\dfrac{W}{P} \right)$	(2k)	
(3c)	$Y = Y(N)$	(3k)	$Y = Y(N)$
(4c)	$MV = PY$	(4k)	$M = kY + L(i)$
(5c)	$S = S(i)$	(5k)	$S = S(Y)$
(6c)	$I = I(i)$	(6k)	$I = I(i)$
(7c)	$S = I.$	(7k)	$S = I.$

As soon as the Keynesian model is presented in the formal manner it is evident that the *IS–LM* model covers only equations (4k) through (7k) and that the factor markets are excluded.[2] Equation (3k), the production function, can be added without much discussion—it is the typical, one-factor, short-run production function. What of the labor market? Keynes accepted the microeconomic theory of the classical school and along with it the profit-maximization behavior of firms. Accordingly, the demand for labor can be written unhesitatingly as

$$(1k) \qquad N_d = N_d \left(\frac{W}{P} \right).$$

The supply curve of labor, however, poses a problem. If we accept the classical supply curve, we also accept the notion of an economy tending toward full employment (since Keynes also accepted the assumption of perfect competition in all markets). Furthermore, if we did accept the classical labor supply function, there would be no way to determine the price level. One way out would be to assume a constant price level, but this would surely confine us to very special conditions. The other way, stressed by Keynes, is to assume a rigid money wage and write the supply curve as

$$(2k) \qquad N_s = N_s \left(\frac{\overline{W}}{P} \right),$$

where $\overline{W}$ is the rigid money wage. This means that the supply of labor is fixed at the *given* money wage and that the supply schedule of labor is a horizontal line up to the level of full employment. Workers supply all the needed labor at the going money wage rate. This means, of course, that workers suffer from money illusion and that wages are inflexible downward. Of course, this assumption also permits an unemployment equilibrium, since it is the demand for labor that determines the volume of employment.[3]

Since we have assumed a rigid money wage, the demand for labor function becomes

(1k)
$$N_d = N_d\left(\frac{W}{P}\right).$$

The entire Keynesian system is then represented as follows:

(1k)
$$N_d = N_d\left(\frac{W}{P}\right)$$

(2k)
$$N_s = N_s\left(\frac{W}{P}\right)$$

(3k)
$$Y = Y(N)$$

(4k)
$$M = kY + L(i)$$

(5k)
$$S = S(Y)$$

(6k)
$$I = I(i)$$

(7k)
$$S = I$$

(8k)
$$W = \overline{W}.$$

Equations (4k) through (7k) determine the level of income, the rate of interest, the levels of consumption, saving, and investment, and from (4k) the division of

[3] The labor market can be represented as follows (Where N_f is full employment):

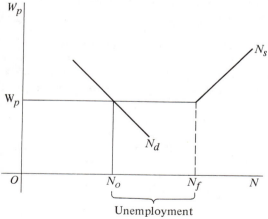

Unemployment

the money supply between transaction and speculative balances; given Y, the production function, (3k), determines the volume of employment (N); given N and W, the labor market determines the price level. Note that the solution of equations (4k) through (7k) *requires a stable price level*. Recall that we could have approached the analysis by another method—with the explicit assumption that prices were stable.

Whichever approach is used, the determination of the price level remains unconvincing, and one is left vaguely uneasy about the clever ways used to dodge the issue. In the next chapter we pursue this topic. It is important to note that the system works first to determine Y and then N. If N is found to be less than N_f, the system points to a policy that will change Y.

The classical model works in reverse, as follows: The labor market (1c) and (2c) determines the volume of employment, N, and the real wage, W/P. Given N, the production function, (3c), determines Y, which is always the full employment level, Y_f; given Y and assuming V constant, the money supply from (4c) determines the price level; finally, the product market of (5c) through (7c) determines the rate of interest and the levels of saving, investment, and consumption.

The formal differences between the models are readily apparent: the Keynesian model includes the speculative demand for money as a function of the rate of interest, the introduction of the consumption function, and the new supply curve of labor that assumes a rigid money wage and permits an unemployment equilibrium to exist. One can disagree over the extent of Keynes's contributions, and many have done so, but the formal models do not adequately reveal the major revolution that occurred in economic analysis after the appearance of *The General Theory*. Keynes made everyone rethink and reexamine his own beliefs and assumptions, so that an explosion of new developments followed his work in rapid succession. In recent years the explosion has subsided as economists have come to tinker with details and refinements. Keynes's real contribution may turn out to be an attitude—that men need no longer be content or complacent about the state of the economy, and hence activism is encouraged.

Still, the classical tradition lingers, and there are echoes of its philosophy heard frequently. The dispute is much more refined now, as the rigid models developed in this chapter have been modified and refined. In subsequent chapters the current debates originating from these models will occupy us often, and we will also be concerned with the shortcomings of the models and suggestions for improvements.

PART THREE

The abstract models of macroeconomic theory developed throughout part II are more or less generally accepted. In Professor Galbraith's happy phrase, they have become part of the "conventional wisdom." In developing the theory it was often necessary to be dogmatic and formal. The occasional brief criticisms aside, the intent of the discussion was to present traditional macroeconomic theory in an orderly way.

Having examined that portion of macroeconomic theory applicable to capitalist systems, it is appropriate to ask how pertinent it is to the current functioning of them. Both the classical economists and Keynes attempted to describe the economic system as they observed it. There is no reason to expect that economic systems remain stable enough to be described adequately by past models. As political and social conditions change, economic institutions and behavior do also. It is necessary, then, particularly in the social sciences, to reexamine continually the perceptions of the reality being studied. This is easier said than done, for it is easier to cling to traditional habits of thought than to deal with disquieting and disrupting challenges to acquired knowledge.

For example, the Keynesian and Marxian revolutions were so thorough that their visions of the world still persist in the thinking of people in all professions in all parts of the world, despite corrections and refinements that have been made to their work. Their ideas have passed into the realm of conventional wisdom; the irony of seeing their views staunchly defended would not have escaped them.

It is the purpose of part III to continue the rather large task of reexamining the theoretical models and the visions of reality they represent to determine their current applicability. It is not detailed criticism that is needed here, either of the original models or refinements made to them. Rather it is the broader question of the changing economic structure and its institutions that will occupy us in order to help us judge the usefulness of existing models. To do this, it may be necessary to sacrifice the mathematical elegance of formal models in favor of descriptive narrative, which may often turn out to be sketchy and incomplete. Some vagueness may well be the price of attaining a better description of current reality.

Thus, the examination of economic behavior in a fixed social and political milieu must give way to the description of economic institutions and behavior as they function in, and are influenced by, the society they serve. In brief, to alter macroeconomic theory (if that proves necessary) may require first the description of reality that can best be achieved by the principles of political economy—the original concept of the discipline. It is necessary to compare theory, policies, and results not only against the conditions they attempt to describe and influence but against changing mores and values as well. In this regard, the discussion of part III becomes more polemical and, of course, controversial. There is more room for disagreement with the criticism of past theory and the analysis of past and present policies; more value judgments creep in as well. It is hoped that the resulting intellectual stimulation will be worth whatever sacrifices this entails.

In part III some attempt will be made to use the principles of political economy to examine past theories, policies, and results and to construct a crude model based on the observations of the changing economic structure. In chapter 12 the theory of the price level is discussed; in chapters 13 and 14 the tools of macroeconomic policy and their use in recent years are examined; in chapters 15 and 16 an impressionistic model is developed; and finally, in chapter 18 the emphasis shifts to the long run and economic growth.

The
Price
Level

The determination of the price level has always been a problem in macroeconomics. The integration of the price theory of microeconomics and the macroeconomic concept of the price level has seldom been accomplished to everyone's satisfaction.[1] In fact, the need for a separate chapter on the price level *after* the main body of macroeconomic thought has been presented attests to the failure of our models to handle this important variable meaningfully. In this chapter we will review the models developed earlier and introduce the price level more explicitly. In later chapters a more critical appraisal of these models can be attempted.

At the outset it must be admitted that the emphasis of this chapter is on inflation rather than on deflation. The stress on inflation follows from the recognition of the circumstances found in the United States economy during the last generation. Ever since the Great Depression there has been a more widespread fear of deflation than of inflation. As long as those in authority have this memory and remain in power, policies designed to combat deflation can be expected without serious opposition. Thus, an inflationary bias is built into the United States economy. Both the programs of the public sector and the actions of the private sector are to blame for the drift towards inflation. Pragmatically, then, it is more fruitful to study these current trends than to study the past, when periods of deflation were more likely to occur. Some of the reasons for the inflationary bias will be pointed out, and afterwards we will assess the extent of the bias.

Prices in the Depressed Economy

To examine the nature of prices in a depressed economy, it is necessary to introduce prices into the *IS–LM* model.[2] In the previous discussion of the *IS–LM* model, prices were assumed to be stable and thus did not affect the analysis directly. Once prices are allowed to vary, the schedules can shift solely because of price changes, and the adjustment process is made more complex but also more realistic.

---

[1] For one of the more comprehensive attempts, see D. Patinkin, *Money, Interest, and Prices,* 2nd ed. (New York: Harper & Row, 1965).

[2] The introduction of prices into the highly aggregated *IS–LM* model still does not solve the problem.

The notion of stable prices is probably more defensible when the economy is operating at a low level of output. That is, in the area most identified with Keynes—the liquidity trap—the assumption of stable prices may be justifiable. Thus, in Figure 12.1, as the IS schedule shifts from IS_0 to IS_1, the level of real income moves from Y_0 to Y_1, with the price level constant. There is no need to alter any of the conclusions reached in the last chapter. Recall that as aggregate demand increases in the trap, the rate of interest remains constant, and therefore no part of private spending is discouraged. Of course, hidden from view is the resource market, where at this low level of output a large amount of unemployment exists. Hence, labor (of equal quality) can be hired at the going wage rate, is equally productive, and does not raise the cost of production. With competition, therefore, there are no reasons for prices to rise as output expands. In short, there are no supply limitations, only an inadequacy of aggregate demand. Naturally, an increase in the money supply has no effect on prices (contrary to classical thought), since all of the ΔM goes into idle hoards. It is already apparent that the IS–LM model is not well suited to the analysis of price changes, since it is still necessary to seek explanations from outside the model.

Nevertheless, let us suppose that an economy is stagnating at a level of output below the full employment level of Y_f. In Figure 12.1 the output level of Y_2 given by the intersection of IS_2 and LM_0 is such a level of output. Now let us resurrect the classical prescription for the remedy; since the real wage is too high, a reduction in money wages would restore full employment. Assuming everything else equal, the reduction in money wages eventually results in falling prices. Keynes argued that the fall in P would be proportional to the fall in W, leaving the real wage and the level of employment unchanged. Still, may not the process of deflation act as a stimulus to the economy?

FIGURE 12.1
THE DEPRESSED ECONOMY AND DEFLATION

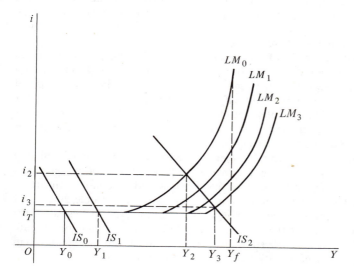

In order to see how this result is possible, it is necessary to list the assumptions upon which it rests. If we can assume a permanent money wage cut (no series of downward rounds); no reaction of consumers, investors, government (no changes in their plans or expectations); no money illusions; uniform wage cuts throughout the economy; and so on, then the following analysis is possible.

The downward flexibility of wages and prices in this deflationary period means that the real value of the money supply, M/P, increases. As prices fall, the given money supply will purchase more goods and services, and less money is needed for transaction purposes. In effect, falling prices act as an increase in the money supply, and the LM curve shifts to the right. With reduced prices, the need for transaction balances decreases, and the excess balances flow to the securities markets, where bond prices rise and interest rates fall. As the rate of interest falls, investment spending is stimulated and the level of income increases. Thus, deflation through this so-called Keynes effect brings about an increase in output and employment.

Using the speculative demand for money, the classical prescription is made feasible by the interest rate reduction. The economy moves along a stationary (by assumption) IS curve, and if necessary, further periods of deflation would push the economy closer to Y_f. In Figure 12.1 the income level moves from Y_2 to Y_3 as the LM curve shifts further to the right.

Still, there is the trap, and if the rate of interest necessary to restore full employment is less than the rate of interest in the trap, no amount of deflation can restore the full employment level of output. In Figure 12.1 it is not possible to reach full employment via deflation.

Of course, the Keynes effect rests on many assumptions, some quite unrealistic. Keynes himself, while admitting the possibility of increasing output and employment through deflation, rejected the idea, because the same results (i decreases) can be had directly by way of monetary policy. Why risk severe economic disruption when an existing economic institution can accomplish the same policy without difficulty?

What about falling prices and the Pigou effect? The falling price level increases real wealth and real money balances, and thus people increase consumption, which can increase Y, and so on. As previously suggested, however, the Pigou effect may not be very powerful, and besides it rests on a number of assumptions of its own. As a policy, deflation is not highly recommended.

There are other indirect effects of a period of deflation. Falling wages and prices will result in a redistribution of income from lower to higher levels. Depending on the MPC of income groups, the effect may well be to reduce aggregate demand if consumption falls. Deflation may help offset the fall in aggregate demand as tax liabilities fall, as money income falls, and as the real value of transfer payments increases. In addition, exports may be stimulated, as the falling price level makes for an improvement in the terms of trade.

It might be possible to argue over whether, on balance, the process of deflation is stimulating to income growth or not. However, a policy of voluntary wage cuts is not likely nor is it realistic. To suppose that labor would voluntarily undertake such a program in the public interest is to assume away the whole history of organized labor and the union as an economic organization. Add to this all of the other assumptions made about the economic structure and the behavior of individual units within it, and the suggestion of a wage cut to restore full employment is reduced to a theoretical possibility and is not a practical solution.

Prices in the Full Employment Economy

Before turning to the subject of inflation, which will occupy us for the remainder of the chapter, it might prove instructive if we analyze price changes when the economy is operating at the level of full employment. Let us define the pure classical case as one in which an economy is operating at full employment and when the rate of interest is so high that the speculative demand for money disappears. Graphically, this is the situation when the vertical portion of the LM curve coincides with the full employment level of income. In Figure 12.2 the LM_0 curve and Y_f identify this conjunction. For this case, the economy is at full employment, as indicated by the intersection of the IS_0 and LM_0 schedules. The rate of interest is i_0, which is frequently referred to as the natural rate of interest, that is, the rate at which $I = S$ at full employment.

Assume an increase in the money supply that shifts the LM curve to LM_1 and lowers the market rate of interest to i_1. As the monetary authorities increase M and drive down the rate of interest, investment is stimulated. But the demand for new investment goods cannot be satisfied, since all resources are fully employed. Unless consumption or government expenditures are reduced, the demand for investment goods sets up a competition among the C, I, and G sectors for the available resources. In technical terms, there is excess demand (given by the distance from Y_f to point A). The competition results in a bidding up of wages and prices until the real value of M falls. As more money is needed for transaction purposes, M/P falls and the LM curve shifts to the left. As long as excess demand exists, prices are bid up until the old equilibrium at LM_0 and i_0 is restored. (If we admit the speculative demand for money into the analysis, the adjustment process is hastened as people sell securities to obtain transaction balances.)

FIGURE 12.2
CHANGES IN THE FULL EMPLOYMENT ECONOMY

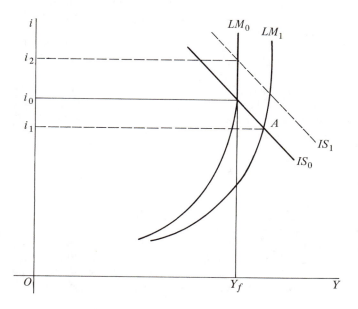

The result of the ΔM is a proportional change in P—the result of the usual quantity theory at full employment; at Y_f any ΔM will simply bring about inflation. The source of the inflation is *excess demand,* the only type recognized in the classical world.

Note also that the natural rate of interest is restored in the adjustment process. The market rate of interest must increase to discourage I, which was stimulated by the initial fall. It follows that as long as the natural rate of interest exceeds the market rate, there will be excess demand and inflation. If the monetary system continued to create (lend out) money at the interest rate of i_1, the inflation would continue.

Next assume an increase in aggregate demand, say, by optimistic expectations that shift the MEC schedule. The IS schedule shifts to IS_1, and the natural rate of interest rises to i_2. Once again, as I increases, we have a situation of excess demand unless G or C release the necessary resources to satisfy I. If not, the excess demand must result in rising prices. Without a speculative demand for money, the excess demand continues and inflation continues until the banking system stops feeding the inflation by lending out funds at the old natural rate, i_0, and begins to recognize that the natural rate of interest has risen to i_2. The interest rate must rise to discourage I. (Again, if we admit a speculative demand for money, the rising price level leads to the sale of securities to obtain transaction balances, with a subsequent rise in the market rate of interest.) In either case, the inflation is caused by excess demand at full employment. With the speculative demand, however, we have the unclassical result that the rise in the price level need not be accompanied by a ΔM.

Once more, Keynes's contribution of the liquidity trap and the speculative demand for money is evident. Yet the conclusions of the classical world are not seriously questioned. An economy operating at the full employment level of output will respond to changes in M or in $C + I + G$ largely by changes in the price level. It would be difficult to argue otherwise. Keynes or post-Keynesians would agree that an increase in aggregate demand at full employment will result in inflation— "true" or "pure" inflation. A different view of this type of inflation is given later in the chapter as the so-called demand pull model.

To conclude this section, it is only necessary to observe that the introduction of the price level into the IS–LM model certainly makes it more realistic. It has been a useful exercise. Still, the price adjustments are hidden from view, and the marketplace is still a competitive one in which the market system works most efficiently. The macroeconomics of this model cannot take us much further, and so it is time to turn to a new and more useful model where prices are introduced directly. First, however, we must define inflation more specifically.

The Definition of Inflation

For most people the definition of inflation is quite simple—it means rising prices. If pressed, they might add that the rise in prices is general and takes place over time. For many uses, this definition of inflation may be quite adequate. In fact, this is the meaning that we have given to the concept until now and that we may use again to prevent having to define the word every time it is used. Still, students of economics should be aware that many problems enter into its definition. Some of these are discussed here so that the word *inflation* will no longer call forth merely the simple definition but will encourage a more thoughtful and sober approach to this interesting economic problem.[3]

The first question is how to measure the change in prices and which prices to measure. In the United States there are three major price indexes: the consumer price index (CPI), the wholesale price index (WPI), and the implicit price index of GNP accounting. There is some overlapping of items included in these indexes, but they purport to measure different things. At times they have moved in different directions, making the movement of prices quite unclear. Which index should be used in order to determine whether or not inflation exists? Is it prices to the consumer; to the retailer or distributor; or a combination of all prices including government, investment goods, construction, and so on, as given by the implicit price index? The implicit price index is gaining favor, but the others are equally valid. Even if there were no question as to which index to use, there would still be the difficulty of computing the index number properly. There are a host of statistical problems inherent in the computation of any index number.[4]

Given the many statistical problems—selection of a base period and method of calculation, bias, the collection of the data, weighting problems, omission of quality changes, and other technical questions—even the most conscientious statistician can do no more than indicate some price patterns and movements. Economists have long been familiar with index number problems and the caution required in their interpretation. Still the newspapers and television broadcasters proclaim the latest change in some price index referring to monthly or quarterly changes of 0.1 per cent or 0.3 per cent. Not only are monthly or quarterly data incomplete but this kind of accuracy is not possible. If the monthly price index rises from 129.2 to 129.4, how is one to interpret such a change? The problem is compounded by the projection of the monthly change to an annual change: at this rate of month x, the annual rate would be 2.4 per cent per year, down (or up) from the 2.3 per cent of last month. This is simply a misuse of economic statistics. To some extent, economists are themselves to blame, since they publicize their own data. In recent years such pronouncements have served political ends as well and not economic principles.

The misuse of economic data has fostered all kinds of expectations and uncertainties, created money illusion, played on the fears of many, and brought about an inflationary psychology. Too many people when hearing that the price index rose by 0.2 per cent consider themselves to be worse off. If they expect the trend to continue and take actions to protect themselves, they may indeed bring on the further inflation they feared; if the process continues, an inflationary psychology develops and spreads rapidly.

Are people worse off if P increases by 0.2 per cent? They may be—or they may be better off, or even unaffected; the proper answer is, it depends. The price level is a *macroeconomic* measure and does not purport to measure the economic well-being of individuals. A certain collection of goods and services is examined and the price changes measured. If an individual consumes the exact goods in the exact proportion that the statistician has examined, then he can make some statement

---

[3] In the analysis of inflation, the best place to begin is with the outstanding article by M. Bronfenbrenner and F. D. Holzman, "Survey of Inflation Theory," *American Economic Review* 53 (September 1963): 593–661.

[4] The student unfamiliar with index number construction would do well to consult a text in statistical methods.

about his economic well-being. This would be rare indeed. For most people, the collection of goods and services consumed is far different from that measured by the statisticians. Suppose the price index rose by 0.5 per cent in one month, primarily because of an increase in the price of new cars, medical and health care, domestic help services, and the cost of meals in restaurants. A 0.5 per cent monthly price increase (approximately a 6.0 per cent annual rate) may be upsetting, but if an individual does not buy a new car, is not sick, does not employ a domestic servant, or does not dine out, how can he be worse off? He may well be unaffected by the current price movements, or better off if he is one of the income earners from the goods and services whose prices increased or if the goods he consumes fall in price, and so on.

Yet commonly people are made to feel worse off by the announced price change. There is no way for an individual to make this judgment short of a detailed examination of the data, keeping in mind that price changes vary geographically as well. One of the costs of the cost-of-living index (a rather inane title), or CPI, is the cost of considering how one is affected by it. It is much more than a problem of misinterpretation, because people act on the expectations they form from various sources, and they may create self-fulfilling prophecies of inflation.

A second decision to be made after selecting a price index and acknowledging the problems inherent in its construction is how large an increase in this index shall be called inflation. Is a 2 per cent increase in the price level inflationary? 5 per cent? 10 per cent? Who is to decide?

For some, any change in the price level is inflationary and, of course, bad, and there is a demand for policies to combat it. Others feel that a small, gradual (sometimes called creeping, but this has assumed a derogatory connotation) rise in the price level is desirable, since it fosters optimism and encourages economic growth. In August 1971, when the annual rate of inflation was about 5 per cent, the United States adopted wage and price controls. In Brazil, there was rejoicing when, at the same time, the rate of price change fell below 20 per cent.

There is no way to decide objectively that a certain percentage increase in the price level is inflationary and another rate is not. Nor is there any institutional setup to make the determination. Still, like the normal range of interest rate fluctuation, some consensus does develop of what rate is tolerable. Other rates of price change become intolerable—too large or too serious, and so on. In the end, as we will argue, it is not the absolute number that is important but how the society is affected. Who benefits and who loses and with what result?

A third problem is the time factor—how long must the ΔP last to be called inflation? Must the change in the price level always be in the same direction, or can inflation embrace periods of falling prices as well? Changes in the price level obey economic forces and do not correspond to neat calendar divisions. A "continuous," "steady," "persistent" rise in prices—these words are used to describe inflation, but they are vague and imprecise and further definitions are required. Data are published on monthly, quarterly, and annual bases, and these help us to focus on periodic price movements, but they do not necessarily define the proper period for the determination of price trends.

A fourth problem, which really belongs under index number problems, is the entire subject of changes in the *quality* of goods. Although this does present an index number problem, it is too important to be listed there. Economists have never been comfortable with the fact that the quality of goods can and does vary. The assumption of pure competition requires that goods be homogeneous—of equal quality—and most principles textbooks faithfully reproduce diagrams of the corn, wheat, and potato markets. For most goods, however, there are qualitative differences between like goods at any one moment, and there are certainly qualitative changes in goods and services over time. The index numbers that use the base period good as the weight fail to capture any change in the quality of the good. If the base period is 1967, then a chair for that year is compared to a chair in 1968 and in 1972. If the price of the chair has risen in 1972, the entire price change is recorded simply as a price change. Perhaps a new superior fabric was responsible for the price rise, and perhaps consumers were quite willing to pay a higher price for it. Still, in the index number it will appear as a pure price change. Similarly, for all kinds of goods, qualitative changes are made over time that may well justify a higher price. It would be an extremely difficult job, of course, to account for quality, but the index numbers are misleading. The farther away from the base period, the more acute the problem becomes.

Individuals may make some mental calculations in regard to separate goods they purchase, but the price index covers all goods, and few would stop to make similar adjustments in their reasoning with regard to all goods. Economists have had some fun out of this issue by proposing the following situation: given x dollars, would consumers elect to spend them out of a 1967 catalog or the current catalog (presumably with higher prices). The choice of the current catalog reveals a good deal about the problem of quality changes.

Unfortunately, the resolution of this problem is seldom so simple. There are cases where quality may have improved but the price change was more than warranted. These cases are difficult to demonstrate. The automobile industry routinely introduces optional equipment or safety items and increases the price of the car by some multiple of the cost. Such a pricing policy, if widespread, makes the observation of the inflation process very difficult.[5]

An even more interesting case is found when quality actually deteriorates. If the quality falls and price remains constant is that inflation? Since P is the same, the index number does not record it as having risen—it would be ignored. Yet the consumer is worse off, contrary to the signal given by the constant price index. Everyone knows of products whose prices have remained the same (or even increased) while the quality of the goods has fallen. Some examples are the candy bar of shrinking size, the substitution of plastic for chrome in household appliances, the substitution of imitation ingredients in countless products from the plastics in toys to imitation leather in shoes. Are these instances of unobserved inflation? Can economic well-being be inferred from price indexes?

Some economists have asserted that most of the observed price changes can be accounted for by improvements in the quality of goods. Thus, according to them, there has been little, if any, inflation.[6] Many consumers, to judge by the growing consumer movement, would reach quite the opposite conclusion. Waving their repair bills, they might point to the planned obsolescence strategy and the shoddi-

---

[5] This markup policy indicates a "target rate of return" policy, discussed later, and also helps to explain the profit push type of cost push inflation.

[6] Richard and Nancy Ruggles, "Prices, Costs, Demand, and Output in the United States, 1947–57," in *The Relationship of Prices to Economic Stability and Growth. Joint Economic Committee. U.S. Congress* (Washington, D.C.: Government Printing Office, 1958), pp. 297–308.

ness of many goods. The point of all this is that we cannot seek help from an index number. How to handle quality changes is a problem that will preoccupy the economist and the statistician for a long time to come.[7]

A fifth problem in defining inflation occurs with changes in technology. The results of technological change could be similar to those stemming from quality deterioration if the change in technology results in reduced costs but prices remain constant. Should the failure of prices, wages, and profits to fall be called inflationary? Should not technological change benefit society through falling prices? Technological change, like quality change, poses a difficult problem for economists; no one knows just how the benefits should be distributed to members of the society. In the world of pure competition there is no problem, for changes initiated by one firm are soon copied by all, and any excess profits are eliminated as costs and prices fall to the minimum level. In a world of widespread imperfect competition there is little left to this mechanism for ensuring that the benefits of technology and innovation are passed on to society.

The problem of technological change is only compounded when the knowledge that brought it about comes from government initiatives. Public spending that results in technological advances, whether they were supported directly or are spin-offs from research on defense or space, must be accounted for to determine the extent of private versus social benefit. Some of these technological advances made at public expense are even protected by patents. Patents help to shield market power, result in higher prices perhaps, and thus contribute to inflation. The relation between technological change and inflation may appear remote, but this may be because little work has been done in this area.

A somewhat peculiar problem arises in the definition of inflation when wage and price controls are administered. The conscious policy of government to control prices has been called a type of inflation—*repressed*, or *suppressed*, *inflation*. Inflationary pressures continue to exist, but prices are prevented from rising by governmental decree. Wage and price controls are common during periods of war, when resources are shifted from the private to the public sphere. In this case, excess demand for private goods would create inflation unless some controls were applied. The wage and price controls may be accompanied by a system of rationing and are frequently accompanied by the appearance of a black market.

In the United States the first major attempt to control wages and prices when the nation was not fully mobilized for war was in August 1971, when the Nixon administration imposed some direct controls over the economy. It is important to note that it was not a period of excess demand, so that suppressed inflation should not be identified with demand-caused inflation alone. Later in this chapter and again in the next chapter we will return to this policy for a closer appraisal. The problem with direct controls has always been the spurt in prices once the controls are removed. All historical examples indicate that this happens. Once the source of suppression is removed, the inflationary pressures are free to erupt.

In the article referred to earlier Bronfenbrenner and Holzman list some additional problems in defining inflation that are worthy of mention. How should the following be regarded:

---

[7] For an interesting discussion on the automobile, see Z. Griliches, "Hedonic Price Indexes for Automobiles: An Econometric Analysis of Quality Change," in *Government Price Statistics*. Joint Economic Committee. U.S. Congress (Washington, D.C.: Government Printing Office, 1961), pp. 173–96.

1. Commodity taxes and subsidies that affect price
2. The price increases that occur when supply is reduced following disruptions to the economy such as floods, hurricanes, war
3. Anticipations with regard to price level changes

Thus, we have seen that there are many problems connected with defining and measuring inflation. There simply is no one definition of inflation that solves all of these difficulties. Neither is there an index that can measure all of the changes in the price level with accuracy. The answer is not to throw out the price indexes and to despair over the proper definition of inflation. Rather, these indexes should be used properly and all their shortcomings recognized. With this knowledge the word *inflation* would be used with care. Moreover, after having gained a thorough understanding of the concept, it is possible to use a loose definition of inflation— such as a period of generally rising prices—to avoid having to make all the qualifications necessary for a rigorous definition.

Demand Pull Inflation

We have already been introduced to inflation that originates on the demand side. Indeed, excess demand inflation was the sole recognized source of inflation until fairly recently, and for some economists continues to be the only way in which inflation can occur.[8] Excess demand inflation may appear under various names, some of which will be mentioned as the analysis proceeds, but the important thing to remember is that the impetus comes from the demand side and is excess to the extent that the demand is too great relative to supply at existing prices.

In the discussion that follows, we shall assume that we can concentrate solely on the demand side without any repercussions on the supply side. Actually, there is no such thing as pure demand inflation of the type described here—a fact we shall have to reconsider later in the chapter. To help in the discussion of demand pull inflation, the aggregate supply curve, derived earlier, is employed. Figure 12.3 reproduces the familiar aggregate supply schedule. We can quickly review the results of demand changes on the stationary supply curve.

In the initial stages of the aggregate supply curve, when output and employment are at low levels, increases in demand result in the expansion of output (and employment) without affecting the price level. In this section of the supply curve the assumption of constant returns to scale means that additional labor is equally efficient, and since wages are constant, marginal costs do not rise. If MC is constant, there is no reason for prices to rise, and thus the profit-maximizing output ($MC = MR = P$ under pure competition) expands without inflation. The situation is shown in Figure 12.3 by the demand curves D_1 and D_2; the output levels O_1 and O_2; and the constant price level P_1.

Eventually, however, as demand grows, diminishing returns are encountered and MC begins to rise. As MC increases, the profit-maximizing firms must increase P. In Figure 12.3 the increase in demand from D_3 to D_4 pulls up the price level from P_3 to P_4. The output level increases also, but the increase in O, from O_3 to O_4, is less than would have occurred in earlier stages of the supply curve. This range of price and output changes is frequently referred to as *bottleneck inflation*.

---

[8] See, for instance, Milton Friedman, *Dollars and Deficits* (Englewood Cliffs, N.J.: Prentice-Hall, 1968).

As demand increases, all kinds of shortages and delays occur, and there are pressures on the prices of these scarcities. There are skilled labor shortages, raw material shortages, delays in delivery of capital goods, inventory shortages, and so on. As demand grows, the increases in price become greater than the increases in output. The closer the economy approaches to full employment, the greater the pressures on the price level.

Finally, the economy may find itself operating at full employment where real output is fixed. Any increase in demand will merely result in price level changes. Such is the case with the demand curves D_5 and D_6. Recall that this situation has been called "true" or "pure" inflation. At full employment, with the supply fixed, any attempt by one or all of the sectors of aggregate demand to secure more goods can only result in their bidding against each other and thus driving or pulling up the price level.

The process of excess demand or demand pull inflation is only sketched in here, since it is already familiar from previous discussion. It is more appropriate to ask now whether or not this type of inflation can continue and under what conditions it can be contained. For as prices and wages increase, *money* incomes (*PO*) can rise, but real incomes are fixed, since output is fixed. The aggregate supply curve is not well suited to show the changes in money income that occur as prices increase. To show the movements in income, the 45-degree diagram or the "Keynesian cross" diagram can be used, but unfortunately the direct observation of price movements must be sacrificed.

In Figure 12.4 the traditional 45-degree diagram is drawn with the income axis showing *money* income, and assuming that demand pull inflation has created an inflationary gap equal to *AB*, the full employment level of real income is indicated by Y_f. Any income level greater than Y_f, such as Y_1, can only exist as a higher

FIGURE 12.3
DEMAND PULL INFLATION

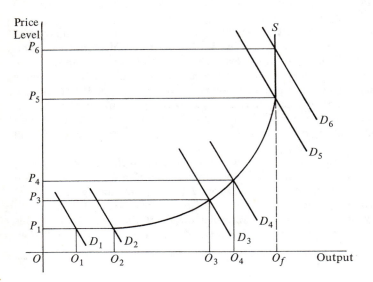

level of money income, which means that prices have risen after the Y_f level of output has been reached. The inflationary gap of AB originates with the desire of some or all components of aggregate demand, C, I, G, or $X–M$, to secure a larger share of the national product. Since output is fixed, this is impossible unless one or more sectors are willing to give up some of their share. It may well be that some sector may have to be forced to relinquish part of its share. In any case, the question now is whether the gap gets closed and the inflationary pressures abate as the economy moves to an equilibrium level of money income, such as shown by point D and Y_e, or whether the economy takes off in the direction of point E and the inflation continues without ever reaching an equilibrium level of income. How is aggregate demand affected by inflation? Are there any inherent limits to the growth of real demand?

Assume that no sector of aggregate demand is willing to give up any of its share of the national output and that the monetary authorities do nothing, that is, M is kept constant.

With M constant, the increase in wages and prices will result in a scramble for transaction balances. People sell securities to obtain cash, but as they do so, they depress bond prices and raise interest rates. As i increases, investment spending falls, and the fall in I reduces money income, perhaps by some multiple. Thus, there is a tendency for inflation to be checked with M constant, and it is held that the Keynesian system is equally capable of handling inflation or deflation. The economy *could* move toward an equilibrium at D.

But suppose I is not seriously affected by the increase in i, that I is relatively interest-inelastic. Inflation would continue until all of the money supply was

FIGURE 12.4

EXCESS DEMAND AND THE INFLATIONARY GAP

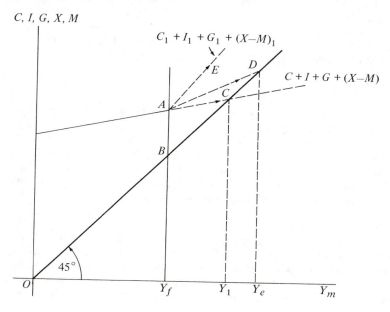

C, I, G, X, M

absorbed into transaction balances. Perhaps after that the economy might pause in its expansionary movement, but if expectations remain that future I will be profitable, the search for better and more efficient ways to use the available M would surely follow. New financial arrangements could affect V, the velocity of money, and the financial community might devise all sorts of ingenious schemes to economize on the use of money. As V increases, as the rate of spending increases, the price changes could begin to accelerate, leading the economy towards hyperinflation. As prices change rapidly, V increases rapidly, and soon no one wishes to hold money, preferring to hold goods. Eventually, of course, if allowed to continue unchecked, hyperinflation would lead to a breakdown in the entire monetary economy and leave in its wake the barter economy.

Thus, even with M constant, there is the chance that the inflation would not slacken but accelerate. Hyperinflation is usually the result of the aftermath of war, as in the German experience after both world wars. Sooner or later, the monetary authorities would have to step in and put a halt to the entire process. If inflation were permitted to continue for some time, an entirely new currency might be required.

Why did not the monetary authorities take steps to control the money supply when the inflationary pressures first became evident? A reduction in M would have increased the rate of interest and put a brake on inflation at the outset. As we shall see in the evaluation of monetary policy, it is not easy to decide when to restrict M or by how much. There are many lags to consider, and there is always the danger of applying the brakes too soon, so that the expansionary movement would be reversed before full employment were reached. The initial actions of the monetary authorities could set in motion all kinds of expectations that would be damaging to the process of capital accumulation.

What the monetary authorities do as inflation develops is obviously important, although the ultimate results of monetary action or inaction are not absolutely certain. Putting aside the monetary factor again, are there not other effects of the economic system that would modify the real demand of the sectors of aggregate demand? Thus, with M constant or with a slightly restrictive monetary policy, are there any indirect effects operating in the economic system to slacken inflation?

INDIRECT EFFECTS

Pigou Effect

Inflation reduces real balances, M/P, and real wealth, W/P. To the extent that wealthholders attempt to restore their old real balances or preserve the real value of their wealth, they may begin to save more and consume less. If C falls, there is a positive reduction of inflationary pressures. In earlier discussions of the Pigou effect there was some question about the size of the increase in P that would be necessary to bring about the reduction in C. Too large an increase in P may be too disrupting. If it works, however, the Pigou effect would mitigate inflation.

Effects on the Distribution of Income

Inflation may affect certain income groups in the economy differently, with some possible repercussions on aggregate demand. Inflation hurts fixed income groups, both pensioners and bond coupon clippers. Those living on fixed pensions or social security would soon find their real incomes shrinking and their real consumption demand reduced. High-income groups may also be living on fixed incomes, and for these wealthholders consumption may not be affected at all. On balance, it would appear that real C would fall, thereby releasing resources to the other sectors.

Also, if wages lag behind profits, C may fall if the MPC of wage earners is greater than the MPC of profit takers. The effect may be temporary if wages eventually catch up to former differentials.

Taxes and Transfer Payments

The built-in stabilizers help to reduce inflationary pressures. As prices rise, money incomes grow, pushing people into higher income-tax brackets. Inflation forces more saving as a larger part of income flows to the government sector and away from private spending. Transfer payments also affect aggregate demand, since they are paid in fixed dollar amounts and the real value of these payments falls and real C is reduced. These built-in stabilizers can be expected to work against inflation, but the effects of some other built-in stabilizers, such as farm price supports or the corporation income tax, are less certain.

Foreign Trade Effects

Rising prices can be expected to hurt exports and thus relieve some inflationary pressures from the foreign trade sector. The strength of this effect depends upon the importance of the export sector in the economy as well as the rate of inflation of trading partners. Foreign trade frequently depends upon relative prices, not just on price levels.

If domestic prices are rising faster than those of other economies, exports will tend to fall and imports rise. Of course, nations could react by changing their commercial policies—tariffs, quotas, exchange restrictions, and so on. Everything else being equal, inflation is reduced by foreign trade effects, but much depends upon the existing conditions of world trade and attitudes towards existing commercial policies and economic nationalism.

Price Expectations

Expectations of future price changes can either mitigate or aggravate inflationary tendencies. If the increases in the price level are regarded as temporary, the reaction of all buyers might be to postpone spending until prices had fallen to previous levels. It is simple for consumers to postpone consumption expenditures, particularly for durable goods. The investment sector could similarly postpone orders, and even government agencies may hold off on current purchases. These reductions in aggregate demand help to ease inflation.

However, if the price changes are expected to be permanent, little is gained by postponing expenditures. More than likely, the expectation might be for continued price increases, in which case it is smart to buy now before prices rise even farther. Consumption expenditures can be stepped up, investment orders rushed, inventories can be stockpiled, and so on. These current increases in aggregate demand merely add fuel to the inflationary fire.

On balance, not much can be concluded concerning the changes in aggregate demand, given our limited knowledge of how expectations are formed. In recent years, despite an inflationary psychology, the saving ratio has *increased*. True, other things enter into the determination of the saving ratio, but still this development contradicts the a priori theory of price expectations. Much more study of expectations as a variable must be undertaken before anything conclusive can be said about price expectations and aggregate demand.

Money Illusion

If consumers pay more attention to the increase in their money incomes than to changes in the price level, they are subject to money illusion. They may well spend a larger portion of their money incomes, and C would increase. The increase in the APC would tend to encourage further inflation.

Still, price changes are broadcast quite widely and appear in every medium. Even if misunderstood, price changes are not ignored. In fact, a case can be made that price changes are overemphasized as a result of people's exposure to information from all sources regarding the price level changes and price index numbers. Consumers could feel worse off and reduce consumption and increase saving. This reaction could be the cause of the contradictory result obtained for price expectations versus the observed increase in the APS. Just how money illusion would affect aggregate demand is not clear, therefore, and it may not be as important a determinant now as it may have been in the past.

To sum up, there are some indirect effects that would help ease inflationary pressures and some that pull in the opposite direction. In addition, some effects are rather uncertain in direction, and little can be determined intuitively. Thus, one cannot be sure that these indirect effects will halt inflation or even seriously weaken it. To control inflation, some conscious policy must be followed, even if that policy is to do nothing, as is the case when the monetary authorities keep the money supply constant.

EASY MONEY POLICY

Now suppose that the monetary authorities allow M to increase as P increases and thus furnish the money needed to finance the larger money income. In this case, there is no scramble for transaction demands as the monetary authorities purchase bonds and depress the interest rate. As M increases, i falls or remains constant and no private spending is discouraged. Aggregate demand does not fall and inflation continues unless abated by the indirect effects. There is no certainty that the indirect effects will operate to curb inflation; they may, in fact, merely aggravate the situation. Inflation will continue, and in terms of Figure 12.4, the economy could well move in the direction indicated by the path towards E.

If monetary policy only permits M to grow at a slower rate, the system need not explode into hyperinflation but move along a path of slow but steady inflation. In reality, monetary policy has seldom been consistently easy or tight, so that the economy may respond by spurts and retreats in price level adjustments. The effects of monetary policy are difficult to trace in any case, since there are numerous lags in practice. In addition, fiscal policy must be considered for its contribution to the curbing of the inflationary process.

FISCAL POLICY AND DEMAND PULL INFLATION

Since excess demand is the problem, government could reduce its demand and relieve the inflationary movements. A reduction in government expenditures will release resources to the production of goods and services to help satisfy the demands of the other sectors. Men and machines not engaged in the production of tanks can be utilized to produce washing machines. There are problems of mobility, of course, but at least theoretically, the resources could be shifted to produce other goods. Postponing the evaluation of fiscal policy until the next chapter, we can say that a reduction in G would appear to be a feasible policy to help fight inflation originating from the demand side.

The government could also increase taxes to reduce the demand of the private sector. This is a more indirect route but could be successful in combating inflation. An increase in personal income taxes should be deflationary, since it reduces $C,$ and an increase in business taxes should help reduce I. The reduction in G may have more powerful effects than the increase in $T,$ as may be recalled from the multiplier discussion. Of course, there is nothing to prevent a joint policy of a reduction in G and an increase in T.

Attempts by government to appeal to the private sector to consider the national interest in its actions are likely to go unheeded. Government could appeal to consumers to save more and buy bonds, but except in times of national emergencies, not much reaction can be expected. Similarly, appeals to business to postpone I are seldom heeded. In fact, a reduction in I may well be self-defeating, since additional I could very well increase the productivity of the economy and thus help reduce inflation.

Another method of controlling private expenditures is to give some government body (the Federal Reserve in the experience of the early 1950s) the power to determine credit terms. A large down payment and short repayment periods can be very effective in controlling installment purchases.

SUMMARY

To control inflation—demand pull or excess demand inflation—aggregate demand must be reduced. Rising prices do result in some indirect effects that operate in the economic system automatically and not as a result of conscious policy. Yet the overall impact of these indirect effects in halting or curbing inflation is far from certain. They probably cannot be relied upon to do the job of stopping inflation without more direct help. Those who argue otherwise are probably underestimating the expectations variable.

The correct monetary policy to curb inflation appears to be a restrictive policy: careful control over the money supply. The correct fiscal policy would be the reduction of government expenditures or an increase in taxes or both. Aggregate demand must be controlled. Of the other, secondary policies, appeals to the private sector —moral suasion—probably will be futile except in rare instances. Using governmental agencies to control credit conditions would be far more effective.

Cost Push Inflation

While not exactly new, inflation coming from the supply side was never considered significant or even likely to occur until the late 1950s. Contrary to previous experience, there was an *insufficiency* of aggregate demand, unemployed resources, excess capacity, and still prices were rising. Excess demand could not be blamed, and economists were forced to seek other explanations. They found it in sellers' inflation, or more commonly, cost push inflation. "Pure" cost push inflation, as described here, is unlikely to exist in practice, nor is it possible to isolate and distinguish it from inflation from the demand side. But it is possible to treat the types of inflation as theoretically distinct.

To analyze cost push inflation, we need an aggregate supply and demand diagram such as Figure 12.5. Suppose the intersection of the initial aggregate supply schedule, S_0, and the aggregate demand curve, D_0, occurs near the full employment level of output O_0. The analysis could begin at the full employment level of output just as well, but it is more realistic to assume a level near full employment, where the amount of unemployment is considered somehow tolerable. Now, with sellers' or cost push inflation, costs of production are made to increase, and the increase in costs shifts the supply curve upward and to the left, as in S_1; the same output, O_0, will now only be supplied at a higher price level—point A on S_1. A higher price is necessary for each output, and the shift in the supply curve results. The intersection of the new supply curve, S_1, and the demand curve, D_0 (constant by assumption), results in less output, O_1, with less employment and a higher price level, P_1. The costs are pushed by the exercise of economic power either by labor or by imperfect competitors. Cost push inflation explicitly recognizes the existence of imperfect competition, which may account for its having been so long neglected in formal economic models.

If market power is again exercised, the supply curve will shift in the manner indicated by S_2. Again the price level rises while output and employment fall. With demand constant, any further shifts in the supply curve must lead to these results.

IMPERFECT LABOR MARKETS

Cost push inflation requires market power, which means some degree of market imperfection has developed. There is no way that cost push inflation can occur if markets are purely competitive. An imperfect labor market can result in one type of sellers' inflation—often called wage push inflation.

FIGURE 12.5
COST PUSH INFLATION

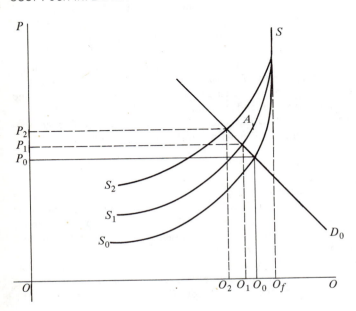

The breakdown of purely competitive labor markets began a long time ago, at the time of the guilds. Today one finds large unions, representing about a third of the labor force, forming a source of great potential market power. It is extremely important to note that most of the key industries have been unionized. For most of the important products—steel, autos, machinery as well as most of the important services, labor has been organized.

One must keep this condition in mind, because for wage push inflation to occur, it is not necessary for the entire labor force to be organized or have market power. It is only required that the market power be concentrated in industries whose output is essential to the smooth functioning of the economy.

How do sellers, in this case wage earners, manage to cause inflation? Armed with the market power gained through combination, the unions in some or all of these key industries must demand an increase in wages that is greater than their productivity warrants. For costs to rise and the supply curve to shift, wages must rise faster than productivity. If the change in W is larger than the change in productivity, costs rise and eventually prices rise to reflect the new cost conditions. In this manner, prices are pushed up from the supply side.

For pure wage push inflation to take place, there must be no excess demand for labor coming from employers who, seeking to hire additional labor, are willing to offer higher and higher wage rates. In fact, the best clue to the existence of wage push inflation is an increase in wages that exceeds productivity changes when unemployment exists. The money wage demand must be somewhat arbitrary.

To account for the ability of organized labor to exert market power, we must examine some of the institutional changes that have occurred over time that have accommodated the application of that power. After all, unions have been in existence for some time, and market power is not something novel. It should prove instructive, then, to list some of the institutional changes that have facilitated the rise of market power, or at least have not inhibited its exertion. The following modifications have been made to the economic structure or to the institutions that compose it, which have made wage push inflation more likely.

1. The labor unions have become stronger. The merger of the AFL and CIO served to promote strength through the pooling of information and financial resources and through fostering a sense of power and solidarity.

2. The growing power of the labor movement could have resulted in labor's resisting efforts to substitute capital for labor as the price of labor rose.

3. The practice of industry-wide collective bargaining has reduced the resistance of employers to wage demands. Particularly for oligopolists whose prices tend to be sticky, multi-employer bargaining by large unions has lessened the fears of each employer, since each firm is faced with similar cost changes and can raise prices without fearing the reaction of rivals.

4. As a corollary to (3), the resistance of employers is also reduced in periods of prosperity, when profits are increasing. Strikes at such times could be expensive in terms of profits and sales and the possible loss of markets. Of course, in sluggish periods the employers' will to resist wage demands may be stiffened.

5. Implicit in the foregoing statements is the condition that firms have some control over price. With imperfect competition, firms can pass on the wage increase in the form of higher prices. Firms that gain some control over prices can "administer" them without much concern for demand and supply conditions, since they control the markets they serve. Such power on the product side could result in

"excess" profits and be viewed by labor as a target when pursuing wage demands (whether or not such profits can be justified).

6. The goals of the union as an economic institution have changed. If the union wishes to maximize the benefits to its members regardless of the consequences (including the unemployment of some of its members), then it may act aggressively even if conditions do not indicate that the action is appropriate. *Pattern bargaining* is one example of how this is done: unions in one industry attempt to bargain for a lucrative contract earned in another industry, even if the economic conditions are adverse to such a contract. Similar results follow the attempt of unions to eliminate wage differentials among industries or among job classifications, and so on. Union rivalries can also result in a push for higher wages to demonstrate superiority.

7. The union push for higher wages is aided by the apparent immobility of labor. This is one way for a union to take advantage of the lack of a perfect labor market to press its demands. Organized labor gains more control over the supply of labor if labor does not readily move about and thus compete for the jobs in the high-wage industries. The workers' feelings of helplessness may themselves engender the need for compensation in the form of higher wages.

8. Where technology has made inroads into industries and has made operations routine and automatic, workers may feel demeaned and enraged by the monotony of boring routine tasks. In frustration they may demand to be compensated for their loss of dignity and sense of purpose.

9. Of course, the observed callousness of labor that pursues goals that could increase unemployment must be set off against the attitude of society toward unemployment. No longer will unemployment be tolerated with equanimity, and the government has pledged to use its power to see that full employment is maintained. The lesson is not lost on organized labor.

10. In periods of prosperity unions simply may become more militant. The closer to full employment the economy is, the more apt is a union to show its strength. Militancy can take the form of demanding a larger share of the national income at the expense of profits. The labor movement in the United States is not particularly ideological, so that militancy is often reduced to the demand for higher wages. Even if price increases follow, temporary gains are sufficient to induce the demands. Of course, union leadership changes and could seek different goals, but higher wages is still the most appealing goal.

11. The arbitrary push for higher wages is made easier if nonunion wages are tied to union wages. If employers of nonunion workers grant nearly matching wage increases to forestall unionization or strikes or to retain skilled personnel, there is no competition to hold down union demands. This is true even if there is a lag between the wage hikes of union workers and nonunion workers.

12. Government intervention in collective bargaining disagreements to avert a strike in industries or services regarded as strategic to the public interest often results in higher wages than would have been effected without intervention. In the national interest government mediators are called in and often "split the difference" between offers and demands. With this knowledge, the demands are boosted even higher, since the unions may anticipate the arbitrator's decision.

This list could probably be extended, but enough has been said to suggest the source of labor power. With the demise of the purely competitive labor market, the comforting tendency toward full employment is buried. Also gone, so it seems, is the Keynesian world of the rigid money wage and the assumption of money illusion. To the extent that competitive conditions remain or that money illusion persists, they are not to be found in the important industries, which have been unionized. The emergence of market power in the key sectors of the economy makes the theoretical models of the labor market presented earlier appear unrealistic and dated.

SELLERS' INFLATION AND ADMINISTERED PRICES

It is common to blame cost push inflation entirely upon the unreasonable demands of labor unions. Thus, the helpless business sector must go along with the blackmail and try to remain competitive. This view might be popular with the National Association of Manufacturers, but it deserves careful scrutiny.

Sellers' inflation, or cost push inflation, is also likely to originate from oligopolistic industries in the form of the so-called profit push. Attempts by these large firms to increase prices in order to increase profits or profit margins can also result in inflation from the supply side. Again, market power must exist for firms to accomplish these ends. To raise prices in the absence of any demand pressure requires a good deal of market power. These firms are able to set prices and keep them in force regardless of demand and supply changes; prices are administered.

The firms in these industries have an additional advantage over labor unions in being able to mask their exercise of market power. They often increase prices immediately following a wage settlement and then blame the increase in price on the higher wages. This is reasonable on the surface, but what if wages increased by, say, 7 per cent and prices increased by 10 per cent? Many of these firms produce various products and could increase prices on some goods and not others, but in a manner calculated to increase profits, meanwhile placing all the blame on labor. In addition, changes in the productivity of labor are seldom mentioned—what happens to the unit cost of production?

With a high degree of concentration in many key industries and with trends toward diversification and conglomeration, the possibilities for profit push inflation to occur are ample and may be increasing. The practice of price leadership in some of the more mature oligopolistic industries like steel removes the fear of price retaliation by rivals. More and more, oligopolistic firms "compete" by matching the price changes of their rivals; if the leader raises its price, others follow regardless of cost conditions or demand forces.

Given the fact that profit push is possible, are there any differences between profit push and wage push? It is held that profit push would be smaller, since profits are a smaller percentage of price than are wages. In addition, the push is likely to take place at widely separated intervals and then with an eye towards sales volume. Moreover, there may not be much rivalry among industries for profit margins and no pattern type of push as with wages. Finally, high profits would not necessarily increase aggregate demand as much as higher wages, which would affect consumption directly. The tendency toward a continuous spiral of wages and prices might be more probable from a wage push than from a profit push because of some restraints that limit the latter. For instance, if the fear of losing sales to rivals within the industry is eliminated, there may still be the fear of losing sales to other industries where substitute goods are available. Restraints on wage demands are much less direct. Still, once inflation starts and continues, most of the restraints become inoperative, as self-protection becomes the guideline for action.

SOME POLICY ISSUES

Recall that the appropriate policy to control excess demand inflation was to restrict aggregate demand by a tight monetary policy and to reduce the components of aggregate demand. Suppose these policies were initiated when the cause of inflation came from the supply side? How would the economy be affected? Figure 12.6 shows the typical case of sellers' inflation.

Given the initial demand curve D_0, the initial supply curve S_0, and the initial output level O_0, assume that cost push inflation shifted the supply curve to S_1. With demand unchanged, the intersection of D_0 and S_1 indicates that output falls to O_1; employment falls also and the price level rises to P_1. These are the expected consequences of cost push inflation. Now suppose that monetary and fiscal policies are successful in reducing aggregate demand to that shown by D_1. The result of this "wrong" policy mix is to reduce the price level to P_2 but at the expense of further reductions in output and employment (O falls to O_2). With the fall in aggregate demand, profits fall as output falls and employers begin to resist wage demands or temper price increases. Unions may feel some restraints as unemployment develops.

The burden of price stability falls on employment and output, however, and this burden may be intolerable. To solve one problem, price instability, it appears necessary to intensify another, unemployment. Further reduction in demand would simply continue to increase unemployment. If full employment is the first goal, then reductions in demand to fight cost push inflation appear to make matters worse. What happens on the monetary side? As D falls, O falls and P falls, making money income, Y_m, fall (from $Y_m = PO$). If money income falls, less money will be required for transaction balances ($\bar{k}$). If the fall in Y_m is accompanied by an appropriate fall in M, the conclusions just reached remain correct.

FIGURE 12.6

COST PUSH INFLATION AND CHANGES IN AGGREGATE DEMAND

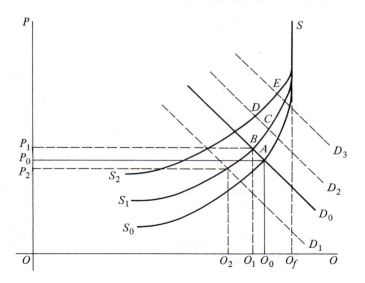

If M is held constant, the excess money supply must flow to securities markets, where interest rates will fall. As i falls, I may be stimulated, causing aggregate demand to increase again, and the movement might once again generate inflationary pressures. As Y_m increases, P increases, causing the excess money balance to flow back to transaction needs, and the economy returns to its former position. It would appear that the reduction in aggregate demand via a fiscal policy, say by a cut in G, will be unsuccessful unless accompanied by a fall in M. However, this conclusion is based on two very suspect assumptions: first, that investment is interest-elastic; and second, that firms will undertake investment projects when aggregate demand is *falling*. It is not likely that the expectations of businessmen would encourage I in the face of a conscious government policy of deflation. Thus, we continue to assume that a reduction in aggregate demand will decrease P and O and increase unemployment.

Now assume that nothing is done. That is, M is held constant and there is no policy attempt to reduce aggregate demand. Following the push, the supply curve is S_1, and with the original demand curve D_0, the price level rises (P_1), output falls (O_1), and unemployment increases. A government that let unemployment develop would soon be criticized. The question here is whether demand would remain unchanged at D_0. As the push occurs, with D constant, O falls and P increases, but the effect upon money income and real income is indeterminate, depending upon the elasticities of O and P. If Y_m remains unchanged, the foregoing results stand. If Y_m increases, then more money is needed for transaction purposes. In the scramble for more cash, interest rates rise, choking off some I. If the increase in Y_m was largely in wages, then the increase in C is offset by the fall in I, and again the economy returns to its former position. Aggregate demand cannot increase without a change in M. Of course, it is necessary once again to assume that I is interest-elastic and that businessmen are discouraged from I when aggregate demand, via the increase in C, is rising. These would be peculiar expectations.

It would appear that cost push inflation will terminate unless sanctioned by monetary policy. Yet, it appears to be just as unlikely that the push will be a once-and-for-all increase as it was for a once-and-for-all money wage cut. The initial push conferring temporary benefits on the activators will be followed after some time lag by other union and nonunion workers. To stay ahead requires another push by the original workers, and so on. An additional push to supply curve S_2 can be expected. Restrictive monetary and fiscal policies might halt the spiral, but the cost is an increase in unemployment.

It is therefore likely that the government policy will be expansionary in order to forestall unemployment increases, which become more and more unacceptable. Accordingly, as the push proceeds and unemployment develops, fiscal policy might well be to *increase* demand, say to D_2. If the increase in demand is an automatic policy whenever unemployment occurs, then a ratchet effect is the result: the government policy merely ratifies the price increases caused by the push. In Figure 12.6 the sequence is as follows: From the original position at A, the push moves the economy toward B; the increase in demand puts the economy back to the original output and employment level at C, but prices rise still more; another push moves us to point D, and demand increases to E, and so on.

Government fiscal and monetary policies sanction the use of market power and encourage its further use—all in order to preserve employment at some socially acceptable level. Furthermore, inflationary psychology is reinforced, and private demands are not reduced as the government sector expands. If the increase in *G* is financed by borrowing from the Federal Reserve or via the printing press, the money supply increases to facilitate the expansion of money income. Yet even a restrictive monetary policy may not dampen the inflationary psychology, and even further ingenious methods to economize on the use of *M* by new institutions, which in effect alter *V*, can be expected by the financial community. The spiral can continue amidst bitter arguments over who is to blame for it. To complicate matters even more, elements of demand pull can be expected to appear, so that it is impossible to fix blame or identify the source of inflation. Which came first—wage increases, price increases, government spending, and so on?

One conclusion emerges if we consider only the "pure" case of cost push inflation. If the government pursues policies more correctly aimed at excess demand inflation, there is bound to be trouble. In effect, the government is damned if it does something and damned if it does not. The dilemma is caused by the goal of full employment being incompatible with the existence of large blocs of economic power. A policy that responds to the exercise of that power is doomed to failure. Treating sellers' inflation with the tools appropriate for demand pull inflation simply will not work. The ordinary tools of monetary and fiscal policy cannot begin to cope with inflation generated by forces that have insulated themselves against the working of the marketplace.

Indeed, the restriction of aggregate demand could be self-defeating. To discourage investment spending will certainly curtail economic growth, which could increase output and reduce price pressures. More goods and services available to an economy reduces the scramble for more at the expense of the other fellow. Moreover, new investment can increase the productivity of labor and capital and forestall the need to push for a larger share of the nation's output. Real incomes can rise for more people.

Since cost push inflation originates out of the exercise of market power, one policy would be to attack the market power directly. Antitrust legislation is available to break up the centers of power. If the present laws are deemed inadequate, new ones could be passed to do the job. The application of antitrust laws, however, depends as much on political as on economic considerations. It is easy to see why. To advocate the breakup of large corporations into smaller, competitive ones or to advocate the dismantling of conglomerates is to be labeled antibusiness or worse, anticapitalist. Campaign funds often come from these sources, and congressmen often have financial interests in them. Indeed, government often draws upon the business sector for some of its leaders; corporate executives move back and forth between industry and government (including the military establishment). The government needs industry to provide the goods for the national defense. In short, there may not be much to be expected from government attacking market power. There may even be a tendency in the opposite direction. Whenever regulation of business is proposed or corporate abuses uncovered, the legal consequences amount to mere wrist-slapping. Business is also favored in tax treatment, as the Nixon administration demonstrated in August 1971. Recall the trends in protectionism, the oil import quotas (in fact, the entire oil industry can serve as an example of government encouragement of market power), the accelerated depreciation measures, and the investment tax credit. The multitude of examples from the defense industries would justify a book on the subject of government favoritism toward business.

The existing antitrust laws are not applicable against labor unions. The Taft-Hartley Act was designed to remedy this deliberate omission. The existing laws could be amended or new ones instituted to bring labor under control of legislation aimed at restraints of trade. But the likelihood of such actions appears to be remote. The labor vote, if there is such a thing, is far too important to risk alienating labor leaders.

If the breaking up of market power does not appear to be imminent, is there some other means to temper its use? One method sometimes proposed is compulsory arbitration in all key bargaining negotiations. Some governmental unit would sit in on the proceedings to protect the national interest. In some forms of this proposal, a representative for the consumers would sit in also to protect the interests of the weakest sector of society. Over time, this idea will probably gain in appeal, given the growing consumer movement and the public's irritation over strikes in essential services. We may, as we often do, back into it as a policy.

To the extent that the immobility of labor is responsible for the labor power that can be employed to push for extravagant wage demands, policies that help to increase the mobility of labor would be appropriate. A comprehensive national labor exchange that would make job vacancies known to all would certainly help. Very often the jobs available are not in the same geographical areas as the unemployed. Ignorance prevents the matching of openings and men. Incredibly, the United States is just beginning to work toward such a program despite the existing Labor Department bureaucracy and the volumes of data it collects. If the increase in mobility is to become a reality, more than just information is needed. Retraining programs may have to be strengthened and upgraded, which means a greater commitment to the problem is required. In addition, it may be necessary to begin a program of subsidizing the moving expenses of workers who relocate. Scandinavian countries have long practiced such a policy, but it has found little favor in the United States. There are pulls in the opposite direction, like welfare schemes that emphasize work without providing any jobs or alternatives.

Antidiscrimination laws in hiring might also break the hold of some labor power. This is particularly true in construction trades, where organized labor has successfully instituted all kinds of barriers to entry. Providing for some protection against the loss of pensions would free some men from remaining in the geographical area in which they became unemployed, hoping to be rehired. Without fear of losing their pensions, men would be more willing to move. These are only a few schemes to promote the greater mobility of labor. Other programs might be equally effective, and worthy of experimentation. There is little justification for the cant about unemployment and welfare unless some of these programs have been tried and some serious commitment to the solution of these problems has been made.

Another method to expose and control the application of market power is through some national incomes policy. Types of incomes policy have been used in Western Europe and the Scandinavian countries with varying success, although critical evaluations are rather difficult. Generally, they call for government guidelines for wage and price changes. Voluntary wage restraints and price guidelines that are consistent with the national interest are requested by a government board that oversees the program. Lacking sanctions, this voluntary policy breaks down easily once it is cracked. Guidelines were established in the United States and constituted a form of incomes policy. The Council of Economic Advisors determined the rate of wage increase that would match the rate of productivity increase. If the annual increase in wages amounted to 3.2 per cent (1962), it would equal the average rate of change of productivity and would not, therefore, increase costs and prices. The wage increase would be justified and noninflationary. In industries where the change in productivity exceeded 3.2 per cent, the price was supposed to fall, and in industries where the productivity fell short of 3.2 per cent, the price was allowed to rise. These price changes assume that all labor received the 3.2 per cent increase in wages. It is difficult to evaluate the success of the program, since the increase in wages in the absence of governmental intervention is, of course, unknown.[9] The program did not last very long in any case. There were no sanctions against those who failed to comply except for the accusing finger of government officials. Whether this "spotlight effect" was effective is open to question. Some people like to point to President Kennedy's confrontation with the steel industry in 1963 as evidence of success. The steel companies had raised the price of steel after the steel workers had agreed to limit their wage demands. President Kennedy berated the steel companies publicly (and their executives personally), and the price increase was rescinded. However, a few months later, away from the glare of the spotlight, prices were again raised. There were no teeth in the program. In effect, it asked economic units to reject one of the hallmarks of capitalism— the pursuit of self-interest. Which firm and which union will be concerned for very long with the national interest? Should they even be asked to minimize or restrict their rewards?

To ask these questions is to question the efficacy of voluntary programs. They may be more palatable politically but not very effective economically. In the end, a system for the regulation of wages and prices in the form of direct wage and price controls may be necessary. This medicine is strong and is resisted by everyone, doctors and patients alike. In war time direct controls are accepted, reluctantly but as necessary for the war effort. In other periods this anticapitalist scheme is rejected, since it interferes with the price system and the allocation of resources. Also, it is criticized for its accompanying bureaucracy, the nuisances of compliance and enforcement, the black markets that may emerge, and the failure of controls to control everybody, for some can evade the controls while others lack the means to do so. Thus, wages are more controllable than profits, and prices more controllable than quality and service deterioration, and so on. There are obviously justifications for these complaints but with the existence of sellers' inflation and an inflation psychology, this drastic step may be essential if reasonable price stability is the goal. In the following chapters the wage and price control program is considered again, both in theory and in practice.

The Phillips Curve

The structural conditions in an economy that result in the incompatibility of the goals of full employment and price stability are nicely illustrated by what has become known as the Phillips curve, after its originator.[10] The Phillips curve concentrates on wages and unemployment rather than on prices and unemploy-

---

[9] See G. P. Shultz and R. Z. Aliber (eds.), *Guidelines, Informal Controls, and the Market Place* (Chicago: University of Chicago Press, 1966).

[10] A. W. Phillips, "The Relation Between Unemployment and the Rate of Change in Money Wage Rates in the United Kingdom, 1862–1957," *Economica* 25 (November 1958): 283–299.

ment, since wages compose the major part of costs and price. The assumption made here is that wages and prices move together.

The curve itself is empirically derived and comes from plotting the relation between the rate of money wage increase and the rate of unemployment. It is based on the hypothesis that the rate of change of money wages can be explained by the level of unemployment and the rate of change of unemployment. The hypothesis is based primarily on the demand for labor: (a) When the demand for labor is high and unemployment low, money wage rates can be expected to be bid up by competing firms; when the demand for labor is low and unemployment high, money wages rates do not fall or fall very slowly; (b) when the *rate of change* of the demand for labor is increasing and the rate of unemployment decreasing, money wage increases will be larger than those granted when the rate of increase in the demand for labor is constant. Naturally, if the demand for labor were decreasing and unemployment increasing, the workers would be in a weak position to press for higher wages, and the employers' will to resist would be stiffened.

The hypothesis simply recognizes that the labor market and price system respond differently to wage increases than to wage decreases and that the power of workers to make wage demands depends upon the amount of unemployment. The unsymmetrical response to wage increases versus wage decreases will make the relation nonlinear, and this is confirmed by the curve based on Phillips's work, as shown in Figure 12.7. Plotting the percentage of wage increase against the percentage of unemployment over time and constructing a curve to describe the points, one would obtain relations like those in Figure 12.7. The inverse relationship between the rate of wage increase and unemployment is easily seen from the curves labeled P_1 and P_2.

FIGURE 12.7
THE PHILLIPS CURVE

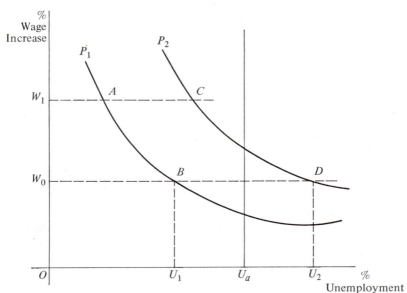

The value of this curve is not that it answers a lot of questions about inflation—in fact, it raises more questions than it answers—but that it makes one of the main problems in the control of inflation so vivid. There is a trade-off between wage (and price) stability and unemployment. The goals of price stability and full employment appear to be incompatible, and thus someone must set the priority goal, with its attendant social consequences, to be discussed later.

To illustrate the problem, let us assume that some rate of unemployment, U_a in Figure 12.7, has been deemed to be socially acceptable. Who determines the rate? In the 1960s the Council of Economic Advisors somewhat arbitrarily set the rate at 4 per cent. Why this number became so acceptable is a mystery and points to an institutional lag, because no other mechanism exists to establish such an important goal, which should reflect a general consensus and not an arbitrary judgment. In any case, the rate of 4 per cent became acceptable, probably through repetition. Assume further that some average rate of change of the productivity of labor has been determined, 3.2 per cent in the 1962 guideposts; if labor were granted an increase in wages of 3.2 per cent, there would be no inflationary pressures. If the percentage of change in W equals the percentage of change in productivity, costs and hence prices need not rise. In Figure 12.7 this noninflationary wage rate change is indicated by W_0.

Now let us suppose that the demand for labor is such that there is a tendency for wage rates to rise to W_1—an inflationary rate by definition. The higher wage demands need not be limited to wage push conditions but could reflect excess demand conditions where wage rates are pulled up by competing firms. Whatever the cause, what options are open to control the inflationary tendencies? If the Phillips curve for the economy were P_1, then monetary and fiscal policies that restrain demand are appropriate. We know that inflation is dampened by cutting aggregate demand but that unemployment increases—that is the unfortunate trade-off. But if the rate of unemployment "necessary" to halt inflation is less than the socially acceptable rate, the policy of reducing demand appears feasible. In Figure 12.7 such a policy might move the economy along P_1 from A to B, with a consequent increase in unemployment to U_1 $(< U_a)$. If, however, P_2 better described the relationships in the economy, similar monetary and fiscal policies to reduce demand may push the economy to an unemployment rate that is considered intolerable. In Figure 12.7 the movement is along P_2 from C to D and unemployment increases to U_2 $(> U_a)$.

The question is what determines the position of the Phillips curve? Obviously, this is important to know, since it governs the efficacy of traditional monetary and fiscal policy measures. The position of the Phillips curve is determined by all those factors discussed earlier under institutional changes that made wage push more possible over time—the immobility of labor, union growth and strength, and so on. These structural things determine the relation between the rate of change of wages and employment and the actual position of the curve. It follows that policies that move the Phillips curve to the left will make inflation control easier and more palatable. Some of these policies have already been suggested.

It follows also that the Phillips curve can shift over time as the structural changes take place, and an economy that had P_1 could find itself with P_2. Phillips's studies for the United Kingdom indicated that if wages were limited to the rate of change of productivity at between 2 and 3 per cent, the rate of unemployment necessary would be about 2.5 per cent. This may or may not be an intolerable rate, but the determination is not ours to make.

However, Samuelson and Solow, making a similar study for the United States, reached some rather discouraging conclusions.[11] They found that even if wages were to be limited to the growth in productivity of 2.5 per cent per year, the unemployment rate would have to be something like 5 or 6 per cent of the labor force. If an acceptable unemployment rate were at 3 per cent, the rate of inflation would be something like 4 to 5 per cent per year. In short, the United States appears to have a Phillips curve like P_2 in Figure 12.7, although the authors hasten to add that the position of the curve need not remain stable for all time. The United Kingdom, however, appears to be in a better position to combat inflation, although the reasons for the difference in the positions of the Phillips curves are unclear.

Demand Pull Versus Cost Push, and Mixed Inflation

So far, we have treated demand pull and cost push inflations as separate and distinct phenomena. This procedure may be valid for theoretical purposes, but once an attempt is made to identify the real causes of inflation, one runs into all kinds of difficulties. In practice it is virtually impossible to isolate the causes of inflation, and appeals to price data mainly prove frustrating.

Wages can be pulled up as excess demand pressures force firms to bid up wages even to the point where the increase exceeds productivity change. Wages can also be pushed up by the exercise of market power, the increase exceeding productivity changes. How can these be distinguished from data on wages, prices, and productivity (also difficult to measure)? Add to this the existence of lags of wage demands to price and profit changes, and the situation becomes most confusing. Most labor contracts run for several periods, and what may appear to be wage push increases are in reality a lagged response to demand pull conditions, and vice versa.

Similarly, prices can be pulled up by excess demand or pushed up by administered prices, and again there is no known method for distinguishing between the forces at work. The timing of price increases (or wage increases) does not help, because there are lags involved and because there is no way to determine which came first—the price increase or the wage increase. There is no base period from which to start to measure pushes or pulls and to distinguish between the causes.

In short, most economists would agree somewhat regretfully with the conclusion that to distinguish between demand-induced inflation and supply-induced inflation is not possible at this time. The empirical problems are simply too great to overcome with our present knowledge. We are forced to return to our initial statements about inflation, which indicated that macroeconomic analysis is not comfortable with the price variable, and to suggest that more rewarding research might be possible with disaggregation.[12]

---

[11] Paul A. Samuelson and Robert M. Solow, "Analytical Aspects of Anti-Inflation Policy," *American Economic Review* 50 (May 1960): 177–194. This is a very valuable source as well for an understanding of the problems in identifying the source of inflation and of the methodological problems that must be confronted.

[12] See the views on these problems of Samuelson and Solow, "Analytical Aspects of Anti-Inflation Policy."

More recent work on inflation has recognized both the existence and the interaction of demand pull and cost push elements. These are mixed inflation theories, one of which is the demand shift, or sectoral, inflation model of C. L. Schultze.[13]

Suppose the composition of aggregate demand changes; some industries experience an increase in demand for their output while others face a declining demand. In the industries where demand increases, an attempt to increase output can be expected, perhaps accompanied by an increase in price and hence profits. In trying to increase output, firms may have to compete for labor (in a tight labor market) or face rising wage demands of its existing work force (eyeing profits) with the result that wages quite likely will rise. Strikes and labor trouble would be costly here and employers' resistance fades. It is not unreasonable to suppose that for industries experiencing an increase in demand, prices, wages, and perhaps profits might increase. The higher wages are paid out of increased profits and might even exceed productivity changes. So far, these results are entirely consistent with the operations of the market system.

However, in industries faced with a declining demand, prices and wages do not fall and may even increase. Prices and wages are inflexible downward. Workers in these industries may try to secure a wage increase similar to that earned in the other industries. Thus, there is a wage push in these industries, leading to a price increase, and the shift in demand does not succeed in altering relative prices and wages. Obviously, market power is required for the push, and these results would appear strange with a purely competitive model. The spread of inflation can continue even further, and there is a general upward drift of prices and wages.

The situation is made even more realistic if the original industry that increased price produces a product that enters into the production function of numerous other industries. Steel is a good example of such a product, since it is used in the production of many other products.

The demand shift model does show the interaction between demand pull and cost push forces and does provide a reasonable explanation of how inflation can be spread throughout the economy. Price and wage increases in one sector may be justified by economic conditions, but in other sectors the market power created by imperfect competition prevents the indicated price adjustments from taking place and may even move prices and wages in the opposite direction. If monetary and fiscal policy validates these changes, the economy has experienced another round of inflation. The demand shift model is a vivid reminder that the ultimate causes of inflation will be difficult to ascertain if this type of interaction is commonplace. The proper policy mix to combat this type of inflation is just as uncertain as the one for sellers' inflation. Restraining demand may not be the answer either if unacceptable levels of unemployment develop.

The Inflationary Bias

In the introduction to the topic of inflation it was noted that inflation appears to be preferable to deflation. Too many people recall the downward spiral of wages and prices that occurred in the 1930s, and until that memory fades, deflation will

---

[13] C. L. Schultze, "Recent Inflation in the United States," in *Employment, Growth, and Price Levels.* Study Paper No. 1. Joint Economic Committee. U.S. Congress (Washington, D.C.: Government Printing Office, 1959).

be resisted. Indeed, that depressions of the type that occurred in the 1930s will no longer be tolerated testifies to the influence of Keynes and the widespread acceptance of public intervention in the economic system. The fear of depression and deflation helps to account for the acceptance of some degree of inflation. Thus, the tendencies toward inflation discussed in succeeding sections are allowed to operate in a climate of tolerance that might otherwise not have existed.

As an example of this bias, scant recognition is given to price stability in the Full Employment Act of 1946. Full employment is selected as the top priority goal for the United States economy, and there is the tacit assumption that the price level will have to adjust to accommodate that goal. It has been shown that the government's concern for full employment can aggravate an inflationary spiral. If cost push inflation results in reduced output and employment, an expansionary fiscal policy to increase employment will simply validate the cost push inflation and intensify it. To state this tendency is not to condemn the government's action—quite the contrary—but to point out a possible source of inflationary bias.

Other government programs operate more directly to ensure a built-in inflationary bias. Price supports for agricultural commodities and subsidies to the merchant marine, the airlines, and so on, are examples of programs that foster inflation. The same can be said about government regulatory agencies that fail to regulate. Higher prices can be expected from ignored inefficiencies and mismanagement. The entire preferential treatment given by government to the oil industry, with the assignment of quotas within the United States and the limiting of oil imports from outside the United States, is an example of a program that fosters inflation. An unparalleled case of governmental inconsistency in this area can be found in the Fair Trade Laws, which actually operate to stabilize prices and prevent price competition. Price reductions to increase sales were not allowed—no one was concerned about price increases. All government programs that set minimum fees, guarantee prices, subsidize sectors or groups, and so on, facilitate the upward movements in the price level. Also, tariffs, duties, and quotas, which help to restrict foreign competition, reduce price competition.

Minimum wage legislation can sanction inflation that has occurred and can stimulate a new round as workers attempt to maintain the differentials of the past. If the lowest level is increased, all higher levels want an increase to preserve the hierarchy of rewards. Other government policies designed to ensure the supply of some good, be it milk or oil, frequently end by stabilizing prices and curtailing competition.

Government procurement policies can also encourage inflation. Contracts awarded on a cost-plus basis are an open invitation to inefficiency and higher prices. Particularly damaging are noncompetitive contracts awarded to the leaders in the national defense industries. The huge cost overruns are accepted without question in the name of national security. The high rewards of the defense industries become a source of envy for others. Areas in which these firms are located find the boom conditions created both welcome and disquieting; they certainly see rising prices of housing and land. To appreciate what could happen, recall the demand shift model; it makes little difference to the model where the increase in demand originated.

Another example of government policy that contributes to the inflationary bias is the payment of the highest wages earned in an area where a government construction project is undertaken. Union construction wages, already relatively high, become the wages that must be paid on government-sponsored construction projects.

There are undoubtedly many other instances of government policies that contribute toward the inflationary bias. The foregoing examples are meant to suggest the types of policies involved and not to enumerate all the possible contributing programs. In this connection, it is necessary to repeat that the programs are not evaluated for their merit but are mentioned here only for their inflation bias. As we will see, fiscal policy in general might be said to have an inflationary bias, because politically it is popular to spend and unpopular to reduce spending or to increase taxes. Inflation adds to the coffers of the treasury as taxes increase out of rising money incomes. The transfer of resources to the public sector makes government expenditures easier to undertake. Congressmen learn the game of pork-barreling quickly and the vote-getting potential of government funds spent in their home constituencies.

In the private sector the tendency to built-in inflation is found in such practices as the escalator clause in labor contracts. These clauses provide for an automatic wage adjustment whenever the cost-of-living index rises by a stipulated amount. Consider the case of the United Auto Workers—whenever the cost-of-living index rises by the contracted amount, they are granted a wage increase; the wage increase will be passed on with the price of the automobile, which raises the cost-of-living index, which eventually raises the wage rates, and so on, in a reinforcing spiral. As more workers opt for such escalator clauses, this built-in inflationary bias will be strengthened.

The trend toward more and newer forms of imperfect competition has meant much less reliance upon price competition and more reliance on nonprice forms of competition. Prices do not fall in response to demand reduction; output and employment fall. Prices are sticky and inflexible downward. The results are the familiar oligopolistic practices of price leadership, outright collusion, shared market schemes, nonprice competition, and so on—all of which result in prices being flexible upward only and in reduced prices seldom being used to increase sales. If prices do not fall, inflation is clearly inevitable. At times, oligopolies faced with falling sales and profits *increase* prices in order to preserve profit margins or profit levels.

The Social Aspects of Inflation

The problems of inflation are difficult enough without the addition of social problems. The fact is, however, that inflation does not affect everyone to the same extent, and some groups lose more in inflationary periods than others. For these groups, inflation represents a harsh and seemingly arbitrary tax that only they are forced to pay.

We have already discussed some of these problems, but they are important enough to bear repetition. Inflation hits the fixed income groups very hard. Those who are retired and living on a fixed pension, social security, or even past savings are hurt because their money income is relatively constant. As prices rise, their real incomes fall and they command less of the nation's output. They are taxed as the redistribution of income proceeds by transferring income to groups that can protect themselves by demanding larger money incomes. Society had already cast them aside as being no longer productive, and now they find the meager income they were given is dwindling. The loss of dignity is made complete. Many of these people are sad and lonely people who feel betrayed and cheated. Many live alone, and their bitterness is borne in silence. Others who retired with a house and pension find they can no longer afford to pay the rising property taxes, which are irrationally tied to education expenditures. Forced to sell their houses and retreat to relatives, old-age homes, and perhaps public charity, they must wonder about a society that worships youth and condemns the old to live out their remaining years in bitterness and frustration. As their health declines, they find themselves spending most of their incomes on medical care and drugs to keep alive and little for food. For most, it is a private kind of hell.

Sometimes pensions are adjusted and social security payments increased, but always too little and too late. Attempts at reform are debated endlessly, and various welfare schemes are proposed, talked about, and shelved. There are also tax relief provisions for the elderly at both the federal and local levels. It is not as if nothing is being done, but what is done is simply not sufficient to overcome the damaging effects of inflation.

Others who live on fixed incomes—bond coupon clippers or rent receivers—are also hurt by inflation, but little sympathy is evoked for them. The lack of concern for this group extends far back in the history of economic thought.

Similarly, creditors are hurt by inflation while debtors benefit by paying off their debts in cheaper dollars. A creditor who lends $1,000 will be paid back $500 worth of goods and services if the price level doubles. The lesson is not lost on bankers, who in inflationary periods build some protection into their lending agreements as they anticipate further price increases. Their interest rates climb, and they hesitate to offer long-term financing without a bonus; mortgage rates rise and the terms become more stringent. But as interest rates rise and mortgage rates climb, it is the small fellow who is squeezed out of the money market. The people who need homes the most are the least able to pay the premiums. The small firm, which does not have access to organized money markets, is also damaged by its inability to borrow to finance operations.

Inflation also redistributes wealth. Any asset whose price remains fixed as prices increase loses value, while other assets whose price increases along with other prices retain their value. Bonds, mortgages, insurance policies are examples of the losers, while real estate and stock are examples of possible gainers. Governments are, of course, debtors, and so they benefit from inflation. But all government bonds lose value. This is particularly hard on small bondholders, who hold their savings in the form of small-denomination savings bonds. Encouraged to save by government, they find themselves subject to a special tax for their reward. In general, savings deposits of all types are reduced in purchasing power by inflation. Many small savers who hold their excess money balances in the saving accounts of banks or in building and loan shares find the rate of inflation may even outrun the rate of return on these assets.

Inflation may also redistribute income. In the early stages of inflation profits may rise more rapidly than wages, and the income is redistributed toward property income from labor income. Wages may catch up for a time only to face a new surge in profits, and so on. Also, union wages will tend to rise faster than non-union wages, which will respond after a lag. Other incomes lag, too—wages and profits in the service industries lag behind those in the manufacturing sector.

Salaries tend to lag behind wage increases. Salaries of teachers, public servants, military forces, and government workers all remain behind others in the inflationary race. Government employees frequently find they have to bear the brunt of government fiscal policy measures to reduce expenditures. It would almost seem that every government official believed that government salaries cause inflation, so senseless is their preoccupation with cutting expenditures in this way. The results of some of these inflation-induced income lags are just starting to be felt: the unionization of police forces, firemen, teachers, and hospital workers, and the work stoppages of these groups, who resent the loss of income and sometimes status as well. The chaos of strikes in these essential services is profound, but the irony of being considered essential but underpaid is not lost on these groups. Apparently, essential services call for self-sacrifice. It may be difficult to generalize on the movement of money wages versus real wages, but it is clear that some groups lag far behind, others keep pace, and still others keep ahead as inflation proceeds. This is true of profit as well. Still, redistribution of income (and wealth) does take place, and in times when inflation proceeds unchecked for long periods the effects of inflation become more apparent to all, and the knowledge is bound to cause social unrest and group conflicts.

Foreign trade is also affected by inflation. As previously noted, exports are hurt by the rising prices while imports appear more attractive. Assuming the rate of inflation to be less for our trading partners, the terms of trade move against us and the balance of payments is adversely affected. There are always calls for protective tariffs and all manner of import restrictions, and in times of inflation these are intensified. Ironically, the cries for protection come largely from those industries, such as textiles and apparel, which suffer from the importation of low-cost goods from abroad—the goods which the lower-income groups consume to escape the effects of domestic inflation.

Inflation is seldom confined to one country but rather spreads throughout the world. Inflation is partly responsible for the strains put upon international finances, as the gold supply and reserve currencies can no longer support the growing volume of trade. The International Monetary Fund had to seek a partial remedy in the new international money—the special drawing rights. The United States was forced to devalue the dollar twice, and massive realignment of exchange rates had to be undertaken. Nations were made unhappy, allies became disgruntled, and uncertainty over the future was heightened by these actions, whose cause can be traced partly to inflation. Thus, even foreign relations can be affected by inflation.

Political power is also redistributed by prolonged inflation. State and local governments surrender power to the central government. State and local revenues do not grow as fast as federal revenues. Forced to rely on sales taxes and property taxes, the local treasuries grow slowly. There has been an increase in the demand for state and local services—education, highways and roads, welfare, sewers, lighting, police protection, garbage disposal—but the revenues to provide these services lag behind. Unable to cope with these problems, local governments have turned to the federal government for help, and in the process they are weakened. Revenue sharing has been enacted to correct the situation and to assuage the angry and overburdened local taxpayer, who is revolting against the ever-increasing burden of the property tax and other local levies. In addition, local governments are constantly faced with an inadequate supply of able leadership, and cases of inefficient and corrupt leaders are many. Yet the higher salaries paid by industry attract the most able, and local governments are hard put to retain their best men. All these problems (and more) are magnified in periods of inflation.

The transfer of power to the central government has many roots—inflation is just one of the causes. In fact, fiscal and monetary policies to influence the economy have been responsible for some of the shift in power, since these policies are best initiated and implemented at the national level. It is natural, then, to look to the federal government for the proper policies to combat inflation. Yet government actions are often perverse and aggravate the many social problems brought about by inflation. Frequently, reductions in government expenditures taken in the name of inflation control are made at the expense of the groups who suffer most and are the most disadvantaged groups in society. How often are programs for schools, hospitals, libraries, job training, welfare, and housing cut in the name of fighting inflation? How often are cuts made in the foreign aid program (no votes lost there) that alienate friends abroad? Other government programs are left undisturbed—national defense, subsidies, and so on. Why is a dollar spent on education inflationary and a dollar spent on national defense not inflationary? All too often, government reductions in spending aggravate social problems.

On the taxation side inflation again has some impact—more people pay taxes and more move into higher tax brackets. Government revenues grow and so does the government influence over society. Higher taxes mean more grumbling; more grumbling means a keener awareness of what the other fellow is paying. Soon inequities are brought to light—inflation appears to benefit the high-income groups. There is special treatment accorded to gains that result when assets are revalued upward, as through inflation. These capital gains are taxed at a much lower rate than wages, and those who have capital gains—largely higher-income groups— benefit from inflation. So do wealthholders who hold their wealth in the form of state and local bonds. The interest on these bonds is tax free, and in periods of inflation these interest rates rise, giving a bonanza to those who need it least. These and other features of the tax code make it possible to benefit from inflation, and the benefits accrue to those who can avail themselves of them—the knowledgeable higher-income groups. The cry for tax reform stirs interest and expectations and then is lost in the cacophony of self-interest and political pressure.

Moreover, when inflation strikes hardest at the small man and the defenseless groups, it may be made worse by government action or inaction. Fiscal and monetary policies are carried out largely at the expense of those on the bottom. If there is a trade-off as indicated by the Phillips curve, the policy of pursuing price stability must result in a high level of unemployment. Who will be unemployed? The black and other minority groups, the unskilled, the teenager, the older workers, the handicapped, and so on. In short, those who are least able to take care of themselves are the ones who fall into the category of "socially acceptable" unemployed. Who needs a list of the social problems and the social unrest created by unemployment—unemployment tolerated by conscious policy?

It is clear that inflation is turning into more than just an economic phenomenon and that it involves struggles between groups, between governments, and between nations. As Bronfenbrenner and Holzman[14] remind us, if the distribution of income were determined in *real* terms, these struggles would become open and there would be open strife. Inflation acts as the great "social mollifier," allowing

[14] Bronfenbrenner and Holzman, "Survey of Inflation Theory," p. 626.

various groups to raise their money incomes without reducing other groups' incomes. However, the passive groups lose to the active groups, and among the passive groups can be found those at the bottom of society. They may not be mollified for long.

Economic growth, of course, can allow everyone's income to grow and thus eliminate the struggle over income shares. It is not clear, however, whether the passive groups would share in the growth process. Still, making the national output larger is at least superficially a good argument for alleviating the evils of inflation.

In the final analysis it may well be that the groups who benefit from inflation prefer it to any other state and are therefore reluctant to pursue vigorous policies to combat it. The central government receives additional revenues and additional power, and its debt burden is reduced. Firms find their money sales and profits increasing, and they can boast of increasing profits per share in glossy annual reports. Inflation makes every manager look good, because everything increases and increases. The stock market reflects inflation in the higher values of shares and the consequent prospects of future capital gains. Unions appear powerful in securing large wage increases. Real estate interests watch property values rise, bankers record higher and higher earnings, and large farmers get their price supports. Everyone's expectations appear to coincide after some period of inflation, and the expectations help to promote economic growth. Even the groups that do not keep pace with the rising price level are told to wait a bit longer to share in the growth. The effect on consumers is unclear, for they may both benefit from inflation in income gains and lose as buyers of lower-quality goods. If power groups like inflation, and if some inflation creates expectations favorable to economic growth, then people will learn to live with it, adjusting their affairs to protect themselves and taking advantage of opportunities to exploit the situation. It follows that one of the causes of inflation is inflation itself.

Monetary and Fiscal Policy

This chapter is concerned with a brief review of the tools of macroeconomic policy. The conclusion to be drawn from Keynes's analysis of advanced capitalism is that an active government is necessary to rescue the economic system from its inherent instability. This conclusion, once thought radical, has come to be more or less accepted, although reluctantly by many. Despite rhetoric to the contrary, most people consider it the duty of government to intervene whenever market forces fail.

Still, it is possible to accept the principle of government intervention without agreeing on the extent or frequency of that intervention. There is still controversy over how much government is enough, and what kinds of intervention are justifiable and likely to be successful. This is so partly because acceptance of government intervention has come about only recently, and partly because changes in the economic structure no longer permit the ready solutions that were once enthusiastically embraced.

The Keynesian revolution was also instrumental in altering the course of economics as a discipline. To allow active government intervention in the economic system, it is necessary to know more precisely what the economic conditions are and what they are likely to become. Many more economic data become essential for this closer scrutiny of the economy and for forecasts. It is clear that the quantitative side of the discipline was given a boost, and a wholly new branch called econometrics emerged. Combining statistics, mathematics, and economic theory, econometrics attempts to test economic theory and sharpen the tools of forecasting. Prediction of the future course of the economic system is required if the intervention is to be timely. The use of mathematical techniques in economics was not new, of course, but they became much more important as specific answers rather than theoretical descriptions were demanded. Sophisticated techniques were developed to improve accuracy and prediction, and soon the computer was needed to help solve complex systems of equations. Relations among economic variables had to be made much more specific, and in this process a better understanding of the economic structure became possible. We must be careful not to attribute too much of this to Keynesian analysis, since the Russian economists also turned to mathematics and the computer to help them solve the structural relations for better planning. Whatever the impetus, macroeconomic policy requires quantitative analysis and forecasting, but the real world is a complicated place, making the job of the econometrician far from easy.

Many policies can be included under the heading of macroeconomic policy—from debt management to revenue sharing. It is impossible to deal with all of them in one chapter; therefore, the emphasis will be on broad monetary and fiscal policies. We will describe the traditional tools and explain how they can be, and have been, used. If they are judged to be insufficient, we will suggest alternative or new policies that may be needed. First, however, we must ask what these tools are to be used for—what goals do we wish to attain?

Economic Goals

Most economists would agree with the following listing of economic goals, although they would not necessarily agree on the order: (1) full employment, (2) reasonable price stability, (3) an acceptable rate of economic growth, (4) an equitable distribution of income, (5) a high degree of economic freedom, (6) the provision for economic security, and (7) stability in trade relations and a balance-of-payments equilibrium. This is a formidable list, which would be challenging enough to fulfill as it stands but is made even more so because some of the goals may be conflicting. We have already mentioned the seeming incompatibility of full employment and price stability. Consider the possible conflicts between (3) and (4) and between (4) and (5). Add to these conflicts among *economic* goals the possible conflicts with goals from other areas of life—environmental, population, religious, sociological—and the controversy over which goals are to be satisfied and in what order is not surprising.

The problem is that no institutional arrangement exists to establish national priorities. Sometimes the executive branch of government has taken the lead, while at other times the legislative branch has been able to reach a consensus. In some areas even the courts have emphasized one goal over another. Perhaps the system of checks and balances operates against the setting of priorities. In a democracy, setting priorities may always be a question of compromise, of pragmatism in the face of changing conditions and national moods. Striking balances and making compromises unfortunately invite dissent, since no one is completely happy over the final decisions. Over time, priorities change as the strength of the opposing factions changes and as power shifts. Personalities also play their part; dynamic and colorful leaders in all phases of public life can help sway public opinion by promoting their views of the better society. Men like Franklin D. Roosevelt can lead an entire nation toward new goals.

Still, the establishment of national priorities is haphazard and left too much to chance. The political process is slow to adapt to changing attitudes, and these larger issues are seldom dealt with by candidates for public office. It is usually good political strategy to avoid controversial issues, and the issues themselves are vague. What exactly does full employment or price stability mean? What is an equitable distribution of income and how much economic freedom is desirable? How much economic growth and for what? How much security is enough? These are penetrating questions whose answers have been left vague and ill-defined by everyone but especially by those in public life. The issues may defy precise definitions, but they ought to be examined and thrashed out in public debate. To restrict the discussion because the issues are difficult is to relegate these important questions to the operation of chance. It is clear that some institutional innovations are called for and sharper political discussion required. As more people become better educated, perhaps disillusionment with the old political formulas will force the necessary changes.

Aware of the issues, we can now discuss an example of the determination of a national priority—the Employment Act of 1946. The act declared:

> The Congress hereby declares that it is the continuing policy and responsibility of the Federal Government to use all practicable means consistent with its needs and obligations and other essential considerations of national policy, with the assistance and cooperation of industry, agriculture, labor, and State and local governments, to coordinate and utilize all its plans, functions, and resources for the purpose of creating and maintaining, in a manner calculated to foster and promote free competitive enterprise and the general welfare, conditions under which there will be afforded useful employment opportunities, including self employment, for those able, willing, and seeking work, and to promote maximum employment, production, and purchasing power.

In thus declaring full employment a top priority goal, Congress touched all bases and, by inserting qualifying clauses, invited confusion and, what is worse, avenues for escaping rigorous definitions. The act is too vague and represents an intention of Congress rather than a real commitment. This is not to say that a strict definition by a body such as the United States Congress was possible or even desirable. However, some institution could have been set up to work toward more precise definitions. As the quotation shows, according to the definition by Congress one could define full employment in any way one wished. So the Employment Act turns out not to set a goal nor to establish any priority (note the qualifying clauses again) but rather to give a loose statement of national policy. What the socially acceptable rate of unemployment is will have to be determined elsewhere.

The Employment Act also created the Council of Economic Advisors. Composed of three members and supported by a staff, the council is supposed to provide the President with economic data and help him interpret the economic conditions. While it is not stipulated in the act, the members of the council have come largely from the academic world—noted professors on leave from prestigious institutions. In their annual *Economic Report of the President*, they often discuss the economic issues facing the nation. In their 1962 report the full employment rate was set at 96 per cent of the labor force; an unemployment rate of 4 per cent was considered "reasonable."[1] The number has stuck, and 4 per cent unemployment is still regarded as reasonable, despite changing conditions. This is certainly a questionable way to set national priorities.[2]

However, the Council of Economic Advisors (CEA) is an example of an institutional innovation that has served to disseminate information and to examine some of the crucial economic conditions of the country. In raising these larger issues, it

---

[1] *Economic Report of the President* (1962), p. 46.

[2] For an excellent discussion of the operation of the Council of Economic Advisors, see W. W. Heller, *New Dimensions of Political Economy* (New York: W. W. Norton, 1967).

has helped to elevate the discussion of economic problems. The CEA is not without criticism, however, and one of the more telling ones is the unspecified relationship between presumably independent economists and the President, who is understandably political. How independent is the CEA to interpret the economic situation, and how much allegiance is owed the President? The credibility of the council rests on the answers. The composition of the CEA has also been a source of criticism, since of late it has been composed of professors from similar educational institutions. It is argued that viewpoints from different backgrounds (business, labor, and so on) would add to the council's analysis and interpretation of economic conditions.

Conflicting goals and institutional lags are not new problems, either to economics or to politics. What may contribute to our present difficulties is the accelerated pace of change in the past generation or so. The faster conditions change, the less tolerance there may be for institutional lags, especially if the institutional lags interfere with the shifting of goals, no matter how vaguely stated. To pursue this line of reasoning is beyond the scope of this book, but some knowledge of what the goals are and how they are determined is necessary if macroeconomic policy is to be evaluated in perspective.

Monetary Policy

THE TOOLS OF MONETARY POLICY

The most important functions of the Federal Reserve System are the regulation of the money supply and the control of the cost and availability of credit. Monetary policy, therefore, is directed primarily to the performance of these tasks through the use of deliberate and discretionary actions. The Federal Reserve has three main instruments of control over money and credit: (1) open market operations, (2) changes in the reserve requirement, (3) changes in the discount rate. In addition, it has several selective controls over specific markets, among which are the margin requirement (which sets the credit terms on security transactions) and the ceiling on the interest rate commercial banks can pay on savings or time deposits (Regulation Q).

Recall briefly how these main instruments work to influence money markets. The fractional reserve system is a convenient way to gain control over the money supply. By requiring banks to maintain a stated percentage of their deposits as reserves, it limits the ability of banks to lend out funds and thus their ability to create money (by some multiple of deposits). It follows that the prime target of Federal Reserve policy will be the level of bank reserves, and the most potent weapon to influence reserves is the required reserve ratio. Lower the reserve ratio, and more funds are made available for loans; raise it, and less funds are available. However, being such a powerful tool, it is seldom used, since the effects of altering the ratio can be very disrupting to the banking system (particularly for increases).

Open market operations are the buying and selling of government bonds in order to influence indirectly the reserve position of banks. If the Federal Reserve buys bonds, the effects will be an increase in bank reserves, a possible increase in the money supply, and a possible fall in interest rates. These effects are potential stimulants to economic activity. Of course, sales of government securities result in the opposite effects. Open market operations constitute the most frequently used weapon of monetary policy, and since the Federal Reserve does not announce its policies or intentions, expectations of future monetary policy and monetary conditions are formed largely on the observed actions in the government bond market.

The Federal Reserve can also exert some indirect control over member bank reserves by its willingness or unwillingness to lend to member banks. Banks may find themselves in difficulty from time to time, either because they are violating or close to violating the reserve requirements or are faced with unforeseen local conditions that threaten to disrupt the operations of the bank. They may either liquidate some assets to meet the situation or borrow from the Federal Reserve. If they borrow from the Federal Reserve, they may do so by "discounting" some of their customers' obligations or by securing an advance of funds secured by appropriate collateral. In either case, there is a charge for borrowing, set by conscious Federal Reserve policy called the *discount rate*. By lowering or raising the discount rate, the Federal Reserve can encourage or discourage such advances and thus affect the level of reserves. In addition, the Federal Reserve can openly announce its intentions to be receptive or not to requests for loans and advances. In practice, the discount rate has served more as a signal of Federal Reserve policy than as a control device, but again, expectations of future monetary conditions are created by changes in the rate.

In any given situation, these three instruments of monetary policy can be used singly or in combination. They need not all be used in every case, but their use must be coordinated to achieve the maximum results. Without proper coordination the controls can work at cross-purposes. For instance, if the Federal Reserve wished to pursue a tight policy and restrict credit, it would raise the reserve requirements, sell securities, increase the discount rate, or use some combination of the three, depending upon the severity of the situation.

Suppose, for instance, the economy for some reason began to boom and inflationary pressures appeared. If the Federal Reserve were slow to respond or were to refrain from interfering, the marketplace would make its own adjustments to squeeze out all the credit available to exploit the booming conditions. Idle funds would be utilized and the velocity of money increased; banks would use up all of their excess balances; interest rates would rise, and so on. When the banks reached the maximum of their lending ability, they might turn to the Federal Reserve for loans. If the loans were granted, the money supply would increase further, and the banks would enjoy a bonanza as market rates of interest soared while the discount rate remained constant. Clearly, this could not continue or inflation would proceed without monetary restraint.

When the Federal Reserve does take action, it usually does so through open market operations, that is, sales of securities to reduce bank reserves.[3] As a result, interest rates rise still farther. Banks lose reserves, but their customers may still be demanding funds. Faced with declining loanable funds and rising demand for them, the banks begin to search for methods that will allow them to take advantage of the situation. They may refuse some customers or reduce the amount of loans to them. Small borrowers are squeezed out first, as well as those who cannot afford the higher interest rates. Banks can also be expected to attempt to gain reserves in order to lend them out. If they sell assets, say bonds, they will depress bond prices

---

[3] It is probably useful to recall at this point that the Federal Reserve is under no obligation to earn a profit and thus can offer advantageous terms to accomplish its aims.

and increase interest rates. If they turn to the Federal Reserve for loans, they may or may not be welcome. If the discount rate remains unchanged, the banks will find it profitable to borrow heavily. However, a coordinated Federal Reserve policy will have increased the discount rate as the market rate of interest rose. As a consequence, the banks find the sources of funds drying up and the boom is dampened. Of course, the Federal Reserve could have increased reserve requirements as well, but such a step is usually kept for a last resort, since it is so disrupting. In periods of recession, we might expect the reverse to happen. In either case, the use of monetary policy tools calls for coordination; otherwise they work at cross-purposes. The fact that power over the management of money and credit is concentrated in the hands of a few men may facilitate coordinated actions. At times, warnings from these officials are sufficient to reverse some mild trends. Appeals by these officials to the banking community to refrain from this action or that—so-called moral suasion—are not likely to be as effective as direct action. Still, their pronouncements and speeches do generate expectations, and these may affect actions. Little is known on this score, however.

SOME PROBLEMS IN MONETARY POLICY

The instruments of monetary management presented in the preceding sections appear to be straightforward and easy to apply. However, in describing them, many complicating factors were omitted; monetary policy is not without its problems or critics. It would be wise to examine some of these problems before looking at the use of monetary policy in the post-Keynesian era. We will have to be content with a summary of these problems, since a full-scale treatment would go beyond the text.

The first problem in the conduct of monetary policy is timing. In the preceding discussion there was no mention of time, but in a dynamic economy time cannot be ignored. The fact is that there are many lags in the conduct of monetary policy. The existence of lags in monetary policy is no longer seriously questioned, but the determination of how long and how important they are remains subject to considerable uncertainty and controversy.

The lags in the effects of monetary policy can be divided into two broad classifications: inside lags and outside lags. Inside lags refer to all the steps and time it takes to go from the first recognition that a problem exists to the point where the policy begins to affect the economy by its impact on aggregate demand and output. The lags can be subdivided in a number of ways, but the important part of inside lags is the knowledge that it takes time for monetary authorities to take action. They must first recognize the problem, meet to discuss the problem, and finally reach some accord as to what policy is to be followed. More lags occur until the action is carried out, and still more time elapses as the policy begins to affect the money markets. Thus, even though monetary policy is entrusted to a small group, which can be expected to reach decisions rather quickly, there are still lags. Despite the obvious flexibility of monetary policy, that policy is not and cannot be instantaneous.

Outside lags, on the other hand, are concerned with the response of the economy to the changed monetary conditions resulting from the monetary policy. Monetary authorities may react to a situation by altering money market conditions, but it is other economic units in the economy—consumers, firms, government—that must alter their plans in the face of the changed conditions. This outside lag is of considerable importance, for until these economic units change their behavior the economy will not be materially affected, and monetary policy to that extent would be ineffectual.

The length of the outside lags (as well as other lags) is crucial for the proper conduct of monetary policy, for it may well be that the duration of the lags may determine the effectiveness of monetary policy. If the lags are short, monetary policy can be used effectively as a stabilization tool; if they are long, monetary policy may help to increase instability and make matters worse. If the lags are short, then the Federal Reserve, armed with the knowledge of the current situation and forecasts of what the future holds, can initiate a policy with some confidence as to the results. If reaction to monetary policy is swift, then a policy initiated at the inception of a recession will probably help restore economic activity in a timely manner. If, on the other hand, the lag is long, say over a year, then policies begun in a recession and appropriate to that condition may become effective at a time when the economy has recovered; the time lag may result in the worsening of the economic condition, since an inappropriate policy is in effect.

Untimeliness is one of the risks of the operation of monetary policy, and that risk is increased the longer the lag between policy and response. The uncertainty thus created in the conduct of monetary policy is aggravated by the imprecise art of forecasting. At any point in time it is difficult to know just where the economy is operating in terms of the business cycle. Very often conflicting evidence is gathered—part of the economy is expanding and another part contracting—and the conflicting signals tend to confuse and forestall action until more evidence becomes available. If we cannot always determine where we are at the present, how much more difficult it is to predict where we will be in the future. The art of forecasting is certainly not perfected, and it is hoped that recent advances in econometrics will improve the state of the art.

Still, no one has given economists a crystal ball, and the uncertainties and risks involved in monetary policy have led some economists to question its use. If there are lags of uncertain duration at work and if the forecasts on which policy is based have not been overly reliable, then perhaps it might be preferable to revise our notions of a stabilizing and flexible monetary policy and pursue a different path. Led by Milton Friedman, some economists favor a set of rules for the Federal Reserve to follow regardless of the state of the economy.[4] They concentrate on the growth of the monetary supply as the key money variable and advocate that the Federal Reserve simply expand the money supply at the same annual rate as the long-run growth of the economy. Letting M grow at, say, 5 per cent per year is better than attempting to regulate M according to economic conditions. They argue that Federal Reserve monetary policy has been destabilizing in the past because of the long lags involved. At times the ΔM has been too great, and at times the ΔM has been too small. Thus, the ΔM and the timing of the policy have been upsetting to the economy. It is better to have rules than to rely on flexible policy; a steady growth in the stock of money is a superior policy to discretionary policy tools.

[4] Milton Friedman and his followers have expounded these arguments in many places. For recent summaries of them, see his articles "The Role of Monetary Policy," *American Economic Review* 58 (March 1968): 1–17; and "A Theoretical Framework for Monetary Analysis," *Journal of Political Economy* 78 (March–April 1970): 193–238. His statistical analysis can be found in M. Friedman and Anna Schwartz, *A Monetary History of the United States, 1867–1960* (Princeton, N.J.: Princeton University Press, 1963).

Some economists have been converted to this rule, and many more have resisted its appealing simplicity. For the latter group monetary policy may not be perfect, but deliberate, flexible policies are better than strict automatic rules. If the economy is to be guided by rules, what use is economic analysis? It is better to seek a deeper understanding of the economy than to rely on the rulebook. The questions of lags and errors in forecasting are serious ones, and the appeals for improvements in our knowledge are certainly justified. Friedman's conclusions are based upon empirical evidence, which itself has been questioned for accuracy and interpretation. Much more evidence, it seems, will be required before discretionary monetary policy will be abandoned. Friedman's view is consistent with the conservative philosophy, which distrusts the attempts of people to improve their lot and which prefers immutable laws to do the job.[5]

The concentration by the monetarists on the stock of money as the key monetary variable presumes that the velocity of the money will not change in a disrupting manner. That is, the velocity of money is held to be constant or nearly so and can be safely ignored as far as monetary policy is concerned. Such a sanguine view may underestimate the ingenuity of the financial community. The issue is a crucial one for monetary policy, for if the Federal Reserve pursues a tight money policy and restricts the growth of money and credit, it is important to know if the velocity of money will change and help subvert the policy of restraint. If ways can be found to economize on the use of the available money supply, then spending can continue unabated at least for a while. The effectiveness of monetary policy is thereby reduced, whether that policy involves the use of traditional weapons or of a fixed growth in the money supply.

This is a complex issue, involving as it does many other variables not explicitly considered in simple formulations—the price level, interest rates, expectations, and the effects on these and other monetary variables of new or changing institutions. Even the definition of money is subject to different interpretations. Some definitions of money include only currency plus demand deposits (M_1); other definitions add time deposits (M_2); some include government bonds. Still other definitions are possible; one of these (M_3) includes the deposits of nonbank thrift institutions (discussed later). What, then, is the money supply, and how shall its velocity be measured—against which definition of national income? Does inflation result in higher interest rates (just another price), or do high interest rates have some causal connection with inflation, and what of the consequent changes in velocity as the interest rate changes?

Until these and other questions are answered, the effectiveness of monetary policy will remain uncertain and controversial. There is no attempt here to examine these issues in detail. Instead we observe some data to get some impression of velocity changes and suggest some of the means by which the economy and the financial community economize on the use of the money supply and thus affect the velocity of money and complicate monetary policy.

The data on the income velocity of money indicate a secular increase in velocity (see appendix C). As V increases, less money is required to finance the growing income. A constant increase in M would not be a wise policy to follow under these conditions. Also, it is clear that the income velocity fluctuates according to the

[5] The "monetarist" view is pursued in chapter 15.

business cycle, rising in periods of expansion and falling during contractionary periods.

It is not the actual numbers that are our primary concern; we want to indicate more generally that the velocity of money can change and, to the extent that it does, that monetary policy will have to take it into account. Whatever causes the velocity of money to change, then, becomes another source of problems for the Federal Reserve and the operation of monetary policy.

Financial Intermediaries

One of the sources of problems for the Federal Reserve can be found in what are called financial intermediaries. These institutions—saving and loan associations, mutual savings banks, insurance companies, and pension funds—deal in "near money," the highly liquid deposits of the public. The financial intermediaries cannot create money like commercial banks but can affect the money supply indirectly through their actions, over which the Federal Reserve has little or no control.[6]

Here is how the financial community may respond to a tight money policy of the Federal Reserve and thus affect monetary policy. If the Federal Reserve mops up the excess reserves of the banking sector, the ability to make loans and increase the money supply is curtailed. As the Federal Reserve sells securities, the market rate of interest rises. The banking sector, faced with demands for loans, will seek to satisfy them and earn a high rate of return. Some banks will sell government bonds to obtain funds (even if it means a capital loss, as long as the interest rate is high enough and expected to remain high or increase further) and thus drive the interest rate up still higher. These funds are then loaned out to those whose investment opportunities warrant paying the high interest charges. There is nothing new here, as we have met this situation before. However, the velocity of money can be affected if the borrowers of the funds spend them rather quickly (which seems likely) and the purchasers of the bonds use funds that would have remained idle anyway. The banking sector has managed to transfer funds from idle hoards to active balances.

Meanwhile, as interest rates rise, the financial intermediaries switch their holdings from government bonds to assets that yield a higher return. In addition, they attempt to increase funds by increasing the rate of interest they will pay on deposits held with them. Savers are attracted by the higher reward and the ease with which they can convert these deposits to cash if necessary. Again, what is happening is that the financial intermediaries attract idle funds and convert them into active balances as they lend them out for mortgages and higher-yielding assets. Velocity increases accordingly.

In many ways, people and institutions scramble to economize on the use of money. Households reduce their demand deposits and shift funds to interest-earning deposits. They may begin to use credit and credit cards more extensively and spread out cash payments. Corporate treasurers find ways to economize on cash holdings by acquiring highly liquid assets and by lending out cash balances for short periods. The banking sector seeks to secure scarce reserves by participating in the Federal funds market more actively. Large banks pool their resources to provide loans to favored customers. Quite simply, banks lacking in reserves go out and acquire them—by pooling or borrowing another bank's excess reserves. Banks

---

[6] The role of financial intermediaries was stressed by J. G. Gurley and E. S. Shaw, "Financial Aspects of Economic Development," *American Economic Review* 45 (September 1955): 515–538.

have accommodated the corporate treasurer's wish for a highly liquid asset by inventing the Certificate of Deposit (CD), which is essentially a new short-term savings account paying a higher return. Firms buying on account pay the bills at the latest date possible, and some firms have permitted the payment period to be extended without penalty. In other areas, collection procedures are tightened to make use of these funds. Security dealers have initiated repurchase agreements whereby a customer can sell securities to the dealer for funds and agree to buy them back after a short time.

Government agencies have helped ease tight money conditions by buying up some assets (FHA loans, and so on), backing payment for others (VA loans), and in general supporting some markets and easing the strain of tight money on others.

All of these developments, and others not discussed, help to offset the Federal Reserve's tight money policy by increasing the velocity of money. The power of monetary policy is reduced. It is not clear how a policy of a constant annual rate of growth in the money supply would be an improvement. Many have suggested that the financial intermediaries be brought under the control of the Federal Reserve. Others advocate erasing the distinction between commercial banks and financial intermediaries by making the functions of both nearly identical. If financial intermediaries could accept demand deposits, and so on, their actions via reserves required could be controlled more readily by the Federal Reserve. These are possible remedies to the weakening of monetary policy by existing institutions.

Problems with Other Markets and Institutions

Even if the velocity does change, could not monetary policy be made tight enough to overcome the weakening effects? Probably a sufficiently tight monetary policy could offset the changes in velocity at some point, but such a policy of restraint may have severe repercussions in other markets. The destabilization of money markets is a kind of trade-off with effective monetary policy.

First it is necessary to recall the institutional relation between the Federal Reserve and the Treasury. The Federal Reserve is committed to help the Treasury manage its huge and growing debt. Naturally, the Treasury is interested in low interest rates (high selling prices) in order to minimize the interest payments on the national debt. In fact, from March 1942 to March 1951 the Federal Reserve was preoccupied with promoting Treasury bond operations to the extent that it controlled the bond market to ensure satisfactory selling prices and low yields. The bond prices were controlled—"pegged"—by the Federal Reserve, and interest rates were kept low. The Federal Reserve used its open market operations not to stabilize the economy but to maintain the sales price and yields of government bonds. In the now famous accord of March 1952 this pegging policy was abandoned, and finally, the open market operations could be conducted with a view toward stabilization. With interest rates pegged at a low rate, there was no hope of combating inflation, and in the early 1950s inflation was the problem.

Still, the Treasury has to manage a high federal debt of about $450 billion and interest charges of over $20 billion. The Treasury is periodically in the bond market, either to refund a portion of the debt that is coming due or to raise new funds to finance current deficits. In a period of inflation the Treasury would like to borrow at low interest rates, while the Federal Reserve may be pursuing a monetary policy that is attempting to increase interest rates and limit spending. Obviously, there is a conflict of interests, and the Federal Reserve may feel compelled to retrench on its stringent policies in order to support the Treasury's operations. Thus, this institutional arrangement may prevent the Federal Reserve from applying the restraining measures it may feel are warranted.

At times, however, the Federal Reserve has pursued a severe policy of restraint, for instance, during 1966—the so-called credit crunch—and again in 1969–1970. In both these periods monetary policy was called upon to stabilize the economy. The results in both periods, and particularly the earlier one, were confusion, uncertainty, and much consternation throughout the financial community. As interest rates rose, security prices fell, and the banking community scrambled for funds, for there was no lack of potential borrowers. It was a most upsetting period, and all of the effects of this severe policy are still not known. What has been learned, perhaps, is that reliance upon monetary policy alone to do the job of stabilization is asking too much of it. But we will pass over this discussion until later.

What also becomes apparent as monetary policy becomes more restrictive is the unequal impact it has on various markets and groups. While many people may be upset by stringent monetary policies and face extreme uncertainties, some markets and groups are hurt more than others. The housing and construction industry in general virtually collapses as interest rates climb. Many construction companies are small and rely upon loans to finance operations, and houses must be financed by mortgages. As funds dry up, these markets are hit hard. Similarly, all industries with a high level of fixed capital—railroads and public utilities—are hit, since they finance their capital stock acquisitions largely through long-term bonds. Once again, small business is hurt by high interest rates and, more particularly, the unavailability of funds. Many small firms rely upon short-term loans to finance current operations or inventories. They have no access to the money markets and cannot issue bonds or gain funds through equity financing. They generally turn to commercial banks for funds, and when the banks do not have funds (or prefer to lend them elsewhere), these firms are damaged. Since the bank officials and the firms' managers are likely to be well acquainted, some strained personal relations develop as well. The smaller community may feel the loss keenly. If the borrower is at all risky, he is completely prevented from borrowing. Some risky firms may well be the growing and dynamic ones, and again, all suffer from the growth obstacle of the lack of funds. The large corporations face no such obstacle. They either have sufficient internal funds to draw upon or they can borrow easily from a variety of sources. It is difficult to imagine General Motors strapped for funds, and in fact, the loan rate to large corporations—the prime rate—is lower because of their preferred position.

Another market hit by a severely restrictive money policy is the market for state and local bonds. Lacking revenue, the states and localities are forced to borrow, particularly for capital outlays. As interest rates rise, the burden becomes greater, and many states and localities cut back on capital expenditures with the result that much-needed projects go unfunded. Witness the reduction in capital expenditures for schools, for instance. As a side effect, since interest paid on state and local bonds is exempt from income taxes, those high interest rates are a nice source of income for those who can afford to hold these bonds—namely, the wealthy.

We will return to the effects of monetary policy later; it is sufficient to indicate that policies of restraint do not fall evenly on markets or groups. The tighter the policy, the greater the inequities. Since these effects are well known, the Federal

Reserve has been criticized a good deal for its policies during these periods, and it may respond to these criticisms by not pursuing its policies to the limit.

Fiscal Policy

THE BUDGET

It is natural to think of fiscal policy first in terms of the national budget. The manipulation of the budget to help achieve stabilization, a policy that has come to be known as compensatory finance, is familiar to us from the simple Keynesian models developed earlier. The simple models gave us an unambiguous policy prescription: when the economy is in a depressed state, it needs stimulation by government in the form of increased government spending, reduced taxes, or both; when the economy is booming and inflation threatens, it needs to be dampened by government increasing taxes, reducing expenditures, or both. These policies may throw the budget into a deficit or surplus, but this is permissible and represents just the natural outcome of compensatory finance. As with monetary policy, these guidelines seem simple and straightforward; that they are not will become apparent after they have been discussed in more detail, together with the problems of fiscal policy.

For many people, fiscal policy is only the simple budget manipulation called for by the goal of stabilization. As we will see, acceptance of an active fiscal policy took a long time to develop, and now that it has been achieved to some extent, it embraces only the superficial idea of changing levels of government expenditures or taxes. It is necessary to extend the conception of what is meant by fiscal policy by inquiring into the following: (a) which budget is to be manipulated; (b) what is meant by a deficit or surplus; (c) how is the deficit to be financed or surplus used; and (d) what in general can be said concerning budgetary philosophies? After we have examined these issues, a much clearer idea of fiscal policy and budget control will be possible.

To use the budget as a stabilization tool, it is necessary to know the impact of government activity on the economy. Yet measuring the impact of such activity is not as easy as it sounds. There is not just a single budget but four budgets, each measuring a different thing. Until recently, the analyst was free to choose whichever budget he wanted in order to stress whatever he wished to conclude. The situation has improved to some extent, although unanimity on which budget is most appropriate will be unlikely for some time. Until 1968 the *administrative budget* received the most attention, since it covers only those agencies that Congress controls directly through the appropriation process.[7] While it provides a useful measure of activity by specific agency or branch of government, the administrative budget omits trust funds (such as Social Security) and agencies not under the direct jurisdiction of Congress (such as the Federal Home Loan Banks) and includes the accounting practice of adding intergovernmental transfers to the totals by agency. Yet these omissions surely have some impact on the economy and should be considered.

The *cash budget* does include the trust funds and government-sponsored agencies, but as the name implies, only cash transactions are recorded. The administrative

---

[7] For a summary of budgets and budgetary process, see J. Scherer, "A Primer on Federal Budgets," Federal Reserve Bank of New York, *Monthly Review* (April 1965): 79–88.

budget treats some items on an accrual basis. The accrual items record the transaction in the period in which the exchange took place, not when it was paid for. Furthermore, the cash budget (and other budgets as well) frequently "nets" the activity of some agencies (their impact is lost in the process) and eliminates some transactions between government agencies. Still, the cash budget is useful for many purposes for which the administrative budget would be unsuitable.

The *consolidated cash budget* shows cash receipts and payments to the public and is a useful source for determining the cash position of the Treasury. The operations of the Treasury are furnished in frequent intervals, and government debt operations can be obtained quite readily. Still, there are accounting differences with other budgets, and the Treasury may be in the bond markets for a variety of purposes, each with a different impact on the economic system.

Yet another budget can be gleaned from the national income accounts—the *national income accounts budget*. The national income accounts budget is concerned primarily with *current* output and activity. Accordingly, it ignores all government activity directed toward previous years' output (such as capital items) and all financial transactions (bonds, loans, and so on). Furthermore, the GNP budget records an item when it is delivered, not when payment is made, and it also records corporate taxes on an accrual basis, not when payment is made. Other timing differences complicate the comparison of this budget with the others and also complicate the differential measure of government impact on the economy.

With all these budgets in existence, the confusion created in the minds of the public and the experts alike was inevitable. Not only was it difficult to measure the impact of government on the economy but people debated issues using different numbers from different budgets, leaving everyone bewildered. The opportunities for demagoguery and manipulation were considerable.

Accordingly, President Johnson appointed a commission to study the matter and propose a solution to the problem of budget choice. The commission came up with a recommendation that a new budget be adopted that would combine the features of the others. Thus, the *unified budget* was proposed and adopted by the Johnson administration for the fiscal year 1969 and thereafter.[8] Unlike the administrative budget, it includes the trust funds and the quasipublic agencies whose activities are supported by government lending programs. It is closer to the cash budgets in its recognition of expenditures and payments, but there are still many timing differences that must be considered.[9]

These budget differences soon get rather intricate and need not concern us here, for our main point has been to reveal the difficulty of obtaining reliable data on the impact of government on the economy. None of these budgets does the entire job, and few people are happy with the results. These budgets are well suited to answer specific needs, but as general measures of economic activity of the public sector, they are not wholly defensible.

Thus, one of the first problems in the examination of fiscal policy is the inaccuracy of measuring government impact by reference to budgets. The overall impact of government is usually considered only in terms of budgetary *totals*.

[8] *Report of the President's Commission on Budget Concepts* (Washington, D.C.: Government Printing Office, 1967).

[9] The annual reconciliation of the unified budget with the national income accounts budget can be found in the July issue of *Survey of Current Business,* which features the national income statistics.

Little is known about the impact of specific programs. Surely some programs have a greater impact on the economy than others, but the global budget would not reveal it—only a disaggregated approach might suggest the differential impact. Furthermore, the impact of government is largely viewed in terms of the overall net balance, a deficit being considered expansionary and a surplus contractionary. This has been called the *cross-section view,* which emphasizes only one period's results. A *time series approach* would view the net balance over time. For instance, a $2 billion surplus might be considered contractionary according to the cross-section view, but what if the surplus followed a period when the surplus was even larger—say $10 billion? Similarly, a $2 billion deficit might be considered expansionary if viewed by itself, but what if it followed a $10 billion deficit? Obviously, the time series approach gives a more comprehensive meaning to the words *expansionary* and *contractionary.*

Finally, the traditional budgets fail to recognize that while the government has some impact on the economy, it is also influenced by the economy. The state of the economy can throw the budget into a deficit or surplus depending upon the level of economic activity in the private sector. Tax collections and some expenditures depend upon the level of economic activity, so that a balanced budget at the beginning of the year may end up as a deficit with a depressed economy and a surplus with a booming economy. This would follow even if taxes remained unchanged and expenditures proceeded as planned.

For these and other reasons, an abstract budget is required to eliminate the effects of the state of the economy in attempting to measure the impact of the government budget on that economy. A reference base is required from which to measure the actual impact. Accordingly, the *full employment budget* surplus was developed to indicate whether the current budget is expansionary or contractionary under the assumptions that full employment exists and the price level is stable.[10]

The concept of the full employment surplus is easily grasped once the paradoxical features of it are explained. The impact of any government budget and the resulting surplus or deficit actually realized depends upon two things: the budget program itself, and the state of the economy. The budget program establishes the planned expenditures and planned revenues. But the actual expenditures and revenues depend upon the level of economic activity. Most tax collections depend upon the level of economic activity, and some expenditures vary *automatically* with economic activity.[11] Unemployment compensation is an example of an expenditure that varies with the level of economic activity. If we want the impact of a budget on the economy, the automatic changes must be separated from the discretionary actions of government. Furthermore, to compare one budget against another for their economic impact, it is necessary to eliminate from consideration changes that occur automatically. Therefore, one must establish some reference point that will both give a better picture of the actual impact of the government program finally adopted and permit the comparison of different budget programs for their economic significance. One possible bench mark would be obtained by calculating the surplus or deficit of each budget program at some fixed level of economic activity—the full employment level is the natural candidate for a variety of reasons. Only then can one budget be called more expansionary or con-

---

[10] The concept of the full employment surplus was expounded in the *Annual Report of the CEA* (1962), pp. 77–81.

[11] These are, of course, the familiar built-in stabilizers discussed earlier and reexamined later.

tractionary than another, and only then does the budget impact reflecting fiscal policy decisions become meaningful. An illustration might be useful here before any further explanation of this new abstraction is given.

Figure 13.1 depicts the concept of the full employment surplus. The horizontal axis measures actual GNP as a per cent of potential GNP (the measurement of which is discussed later).[12] The vertical axis shows the federal surplus or deficit as a per cent of potential GNP. Ignoring the dashed lines for the moment, the solid line labeled "Fiscal Program X" represents the results of the calculation showing the budget surplus or deficit that would have occurred at the various levels of economic activity with the tax structure and rates and the expenditure programs in year X. Thus, the *position* of the curve is determined by the expenditures and tax programs in the budget; the movement *along* the curve is the result of the *automatic* changes that occur as the level of economic activity changes. Thus, for fiscal program X, the budget would be balanced if the economy operated at 96 per cent of its potential GNP (point *A*) and would have a surplus of approximately 0.8 per cent of potential GNP if the economy operated at 98 per cent of its potential (point *B*). If full employment had been achieved, a surplus of approximately 1.6 per cent of potential GNP would have been realized.

Suppose now that the economy in year X actually operated at 94 per cent of its potential GNP and had a deficit, therefore, of approximately 0.8 per cent of

FIGURE 13.1

THE EFFECT OF THE LEVEL OF ECONOMIC ACTIVITY ON THE FEDERAL SURPLUS OR DEFICIT

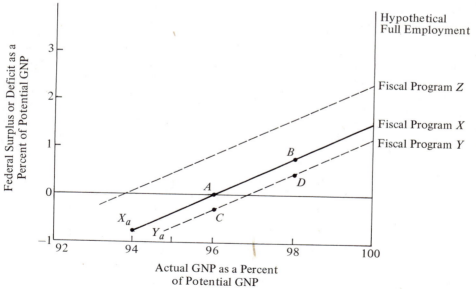

potential GNP. The full employment surplus concept as a tool of analysis shows that one reason the economy operated at 94 per cent of its potential was because the federal budget actually exerted a contractionary effect on the economy. The federal program projected to full employment clearly shows that a substantial surplus would have resulted had full employment been realized. The full employment surplus means that the government fiscal program must bear some of the responsibility for the failure to realize the potential output level and to achieve full employment. The fact is that tax collections were too large or expenditures too small to stimulate the economy to full employment; the government fiscal program was too restrictive, *even though an actual deficit occurred for the year,* making government policy appear expansionary. The deficit could have occurred despite (not because of) the fiscal program adopted. There is the apparent paradox: the deficit realized (and the low level of economic activity that resulted) did not mean the fiscal program was expansionary; rather it appears the program was not expansionary enough.

Now let us assume this lesson is not lost on policy makers, so that in the next fiscal program introduces some conscious changes: increased expenditures or reduced taxes or increased transfer payments, or some combination of these. The important point is that the new fiscal program results in a *lower full employment surplus.* The entire line shifts in Figure 13.1, as is the case with the downward shift to fiscal program Y. Now, if the economy operated at 98 per cent of potential (point D), a much smaller surplus would be realized, and if the economy operated at 96 per cent of potential (point C), a deficit would result. It is the height of the line that reflects the budget program, the more restrictive program being the higher. If in year Y the economy operated at 95 per cent of potential (point Y_a), there would be a deficit again of about 0.8 per cent. Once again the deficit could superficially be regarded as the result of an expansionary fiscal program, whereas it is again apparent that the fiscal program was not expansionary enough to reach full employment. Nevertheless, the discretionary fiscal policy changes were successful in providing a stimulus, as the movements from A to C and from X_a to Y_a show. Fiscal policies that result in upward shifts, such as fiscal program Z in Figure 13.1, are clearly more restrictive and contractionary than the other fiscal programs shown. The larger full employment surplus is the sign of restrictive policies, and reductions in the full employment surplus indicate expansionary moves.

To review, the full employment surplus concept recognizes that with any given budget program a whole range of actual surpluses or deficits is possible, depending upon the actual level of economic activity. Accordingly, calculations are made using the given budget program to show the federal surpluses that would result if the economy were operating at full employment and prices were stable. Full employment has been chosen as the reference point from which to measure the budget impact and indicate the directional changes of alternative budget programs.

The measurement of the impact of the budget is judged with this concept on the *size* of the surplus. Yet the size of the surplus cannot be calculated until *potential GNP* is determined. The calculation of potential GNP is quite a difficult task, involving estimates for all inputs, productivity, and other production function variables—a large job indeed.[13] The current method of calculating potential GNP

---

[13] The Department of Commerce is attempting to get better estimates with the use of input-output techniques. See the discussion by Beatrice N. Vaccara, "An Input-Output Method for Long-Range Economic Projections," *Survey of Current Business* 51 (July 1971): 47–56.

is rather crude. It was developed by Arthur Okun and has come to be known as Okun's Law.[14] The formula is:

$$\frac{GNP^* - GNP}{GNP} = 3.2(u - 0.04),$$

where GNP* is potential GNP; 3.2 is the average annual rate of growth of real GNP; u is the actual unemployment rate; and the figure 0.04 represents the assumption that employment is defined as full when 4 per cent of the labor force is unemployed. The potential GNP is related directly to employment data, as the formula shows. For every percentage point decline in the unemployment rate (say, from $u = 0.06$ to $u = 0.05$), the right side of the equation indicates that GNP would grow by 3.2 per cent in real terms. Thus, it is possible to measure the gap between potential GNP and actual GNP by referring only to the unemployment rate; the greater the difference between the actual unemployment rate and the 4 per cent rate, the greater the gap between potential GNP and actual GNP. Figure 13.2 shows the relation between potential and actual GNP using the method described here. Note the changes in the rate of growth of potential GNP and the revision in unemployment rate from 4 per cent to 3.8 per cent as of 1970.

FIGURE 13.2
ACTUAL VERSUS POTENTIAL GNP (IN 1958 PRICES)

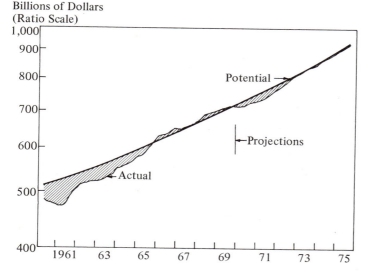

Source: *Economic Report of the President* (1970), p. 85.

The trend line of 3.2 per cent is through the middle of 1955 to 1962 IV quarter, 3.75 per cent from 1962 IV to 1965 IV, 4 per cent from 1965 IV to 1969 IV, 4.3 per cent from 1969 IV to 1970 IV, 4.4 per cent from 1970 IV to 1971 IV, and 4.3 per cent from 1971 IV to 1975 IV.

[14] A. M. Okun, "Potential GNP: Its Measurement and Significance," *Proceedings of the American Statistical Association, Business and Economic Statistics Section* (1962), pp. 98–104.

There is no pretense that this calculation is very accurate. Neither should the potential GNP growth indicated be interpreted as desirable or optimal. Figure 13.2 merely shows the crude estimate of the loss of output because of failure to employ the available labor force (at 96 per cent utilization rate). The output is lost forever, for a man-hour lost cannot be reclaimed. Billions of dollars of output were sacrificed while men were unemployed. This is waste—of men, output, and resources.

The concept of potential GNP is not without its difficulties with respect to the manner of its calculation. Refinements can be expected as acceptance of it grows. The use of potential GNP can also be seen in the calculation of the full employment surplus as given in Figure 13.3. The acceptance of the full employment surplus as the proper measure of the impact of the federal budget is growing yearly. In his budget message to Congress for fiscal year 1973 President Nixon stated:

The full-employment budget concept is central to the budget policy of this Administration. Except in emergency conditions, expenditures should not exceed the level at which the budget would be balanced under conditions of full employment. . . . We have planned the 1973 expenditures to adhere to the full-employment budget concept. . . .

The full employment surplus concept is being accepted, but much confusion over what it is still is widespread, probably because of its paradoxical elements referred to earlier.

Figure 13.3 shows the past record of the federal budget surplus calculations along with the actual surpluses or deficits. We do not intend to enter into discussions

FIGURE 13.3
FEDERAL BUDGET SURPLUS OR DEFICIT: ACTUAL AND FULL EMPLOYMENT ESTIMATES, NATIONAL INCOME ACCOUNTS BASIS

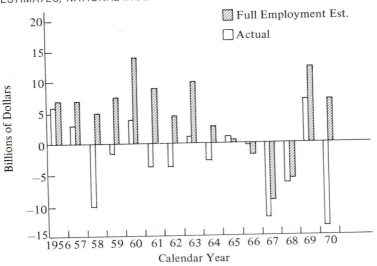

Source: *Economic Report of the President,* various years.

of fiscal policy measures actually taken—this will follow the discussion of the tools of policy and their problems. However, it is logical to include the figure here and to note the many years in which the budget programs resulted in a full employment surplus. It should be clear from this that fiscal policy has not been utilized wisely or even at all, but we will return to these questions and this figure in the next chapter.

SEVERAL BUDGET PHILOSOPHIES

It would appear from the discussion on budgets that government manipulation of the budget to achieve some end—full employment—is completely accepted. The budget program must be adjusted to whatever goals are being promoted— compensatory finance in one sense or another. Not everyone subscribes to this view of government behavior, nor was it always as acceptable as it now appears to be in political circles. It may be useful here to review briefly the different budget philosophies, so that a fuller appreciation of President Nixon's statement will be gained and a better understanding of fiscal policy obtained.

The Annually Balanced Budget

Many people continue to believe that government ought to balance its budget annually, that is, expenditures ought to match tax receipts. Erroneously equating this policy to neutrality of the government sector (or worse, likening the government to a household), conservatives and others disapprove of compensatory finance and disavow the need for stabilization policies.

The truth is that not only is government not neutral but also there is a fiscal policy associated with the annually balanced budget—a perverse one in its effect upon the economy. The effects are *pro cyclical:* if the economy is in a recession, tax receipts (based on declining incomes) fall. If expenditures are reduced to match the declining tax receipts, the economy will decline still further and tax receipts will fall still further, inducing further expenditure cuts, and so on. The reverse is true for an expanding economy.

Another rationale for the annually balanced budget is the fear of deficit financing with its attendant public debt. If government borrows in order to finance expenditures, the debt and interest payments on these funds will constitute a burden on future generations. If the fears are justified (the issue will be taken up shortly), the balanced budget philosophy at least becomes understandable if not supportable.

The Cyclically Balanced Budget

If economic conditions do not conform to neat fiscal year divisions, why not balance the budget over the course of the business cycle, which could run over many years. This "Swedish budget," so called after its originators, allows for conscious fiscal policy for stabilization purposes and tolerates deficits and surpluses as required but stipulates that over the course of the cycle the deficits will balance out the surpluses. This philosophy is certainly more appealing than the annually balanced budget, but some reservations quickly come to mind. It would only be fortuitous if the deficits and surpluses just balanced out. In the United States experience, for instance, the deficits have been much larger than the surpluses of late, despite the lack of an active fiscal policy for the most part. Furthermore, how could the relative size of business cycle swings be forecast in advance so that planned deficits and surpluses would balance? What if the duration of the downswings were far greater than the modest recoveries—the deficits incurred and the consequent borrowing would exceed the surpluses and the consequent repayment of the debt. In short, the cyclically balanced budget is intellectually more appealing than the annually balanced budget, for it does permit countercyclical activity of government fiscal policy. Nevertheless, in operation its usefulness could well be nullified by the unsymmetrical swings of the business cycles and our inability to forecast the cycles accurately enough.

The Budget of the Committee for Economic Development

A newer variant of the cyclical budget is found in the CED budget proposal.[15] The CED budget relies primarily on automatic stabilizers for countercyclical influences. Its program calls for the government to "set tax rates to balance the budget and provide a surplus for debt retirement at an agreed high level of employment and national income. Having set these rates, leave them alone unless there is some major change in national policy or condition of national life."[16]

Like the cyclical budget, the CED proposal appeals to many because of its rational views about budget balancing—deficits and surpluses occur when necessary, automatically through the built-in stabilizers. Fixed tax rates and advance expenditure programs impose on government the need for efficiency and economy and offer the possibility of debt reduction.[17]

However, the CED budget shares with the cyclical budget the shortcoming that deficits and surpluses will not balance out over a reasonable period of time. A more important criticism is the inability of the built-in stabilizers to do the whole job of stabilization; they simply are not that powerful. They can dampen the business cycle—reduce the fluctuations—but they cannot by themselves stabilize the economy. They reduce the swings of economic activity, but they cannot reverse the trends.[18] To bring a recession to a halt and *reverse* the direction of change of economic activity requires fiscal policy actions by government in addition to the automatic stabilizers.

The CED proposal, relying as it does on automatic responses of government, does avoid the political process, which can be time-consuming and subject to non-economic concerns. If it worked, there would be much to commend the CED proposal on that score alone. On balance, however, it would appear that the CED budget proposal is overly cautious and optimistic about the stability of the economy.

Formula Flexibility

To overcome the objection that built-in stabilizers are too weak, and at the same time to take advantage of their automatic features, the concept of formula flexibility

---

[15] The Committee for Economic Development is a nonprofit, nonpartisan, and nonpolitical organization of businessmen and scholars. See their report *Taxes and the Budget* (New York, 1947).

[16] Ibid., p. 22.

[17] There is also an equity problem, which is avoided by fixed tax rates: that is, if government revises tax rates too frequently, then the same money income is subject to different tax rates in different years, with the result that some people may be taxed more or less than others over time.

[18] R. A. Musgrave and M. H. Miller estimate that the built-in stabilizers reduce the fluctuations in income by about one third. See their articles "Built-in Flexibility," *American Economic Review* 38 (March 1948): 122–128.

was developed.[19] To give added power to the automatic stabilizers, which are not powerful enough by themselves to turn the economy around, tax *rates* should be adjusted downward as well. The tax rate adjustment would be automatic and would be tied to some index of economic activity; the unemployment rate or the index of industrial production of the Federal Reserve has been suggested. When the unemployment rate reached some specified number—say 6 per cent—the tax rates would be lowered. The Commission on Money and Credit recommended that the President be empowered to adjust the tax rate on the first tax bracket by up to 5 percentage points.[20] Presidents Kennedy and Johnson endorsed the proposal to give the executive branch the added power, but Congress has been decidedly cool to the idea and quite reluctant to give up any power over the purse strings.

Congressional resistance is one obstacle to formula flexibility schemes, and they are thereby probably doomed. Also, the reliability of an index or a single indicator as the signal for action can be questioned. Indexes are not always reliable, nor can changes in the number always be attributed to the same causes, calling for the same policy actions. Yet this is what formula flexibility assumes and requires. Better data would probably be the prerequisite for any formula scheme.

Functional Finance

The last budget philosophy to be discussed here is called functional finance.[21] There are no rules to follow, only a general set of policy prescriptions designed to achieve the goal of stabilization at the full employment level of income. Central to this philosophy is that government actions should be judged only by their results, not by established traditional doctrines. If full employment is the goal, government policies to reach it must be judged by how close they come to achieving it. It is the job of the government to maintain total spending, and it does so by regulating its own spending directly or by regulating private spending indirectly through taxes. But government spending must never be regulated by tax collections—taxes are simply the method of reducing private demand whenever excess demand threatens. Government can always print money if necessary to finance its expenditures; if inflation threatens as a result, taxes can be raised. The printing of money would not likely be required in near inflationary periods anyway, since money was printed to enable government to spend in order to reach higher employment levels.

The government should borrow or lend money when it wishes to control the rate of interest and hence investment. It need not borrow simply to finance current operations. It can print money when necessary or destroy it according to circumstances. The policies must be judged according to their results.

But one of the objections to the cyclical budget was the possibility that an economic system would require continuous deficits over time in order to keep the economy stabilized at high employment levels. This would imply that government would have to borrow to finance its deficit (if the printing press were resisted), and thus there is the prospect of a growing national debt. Would the national debt place some kind of limitation on government policies because of its adverse effects?

---

[19] See, for instance, *Money and Credit. Report of the Commission on Money and Credit* (Englewood Cliffs, N.J.: 1961).

[20] Ibid., p. 137.

[21] A. P. Lerner, "Functional Finance and the Federal Debt," *Social Research* (February 1943): 38–51. Also see his "The Burden of the National Debt," in *Income, Employment, and Public Policy: Essays in Honor of Alvin H. Hansen* (New York: W. W. Norton, 1948), pp. 255–275.

The Burden of the Debt

No such limitation is recognized by the principles of functional finance, and no real adverse effects or burdens are acknowledged either. There is no ceiling to the national debt nor any problem in paying the interest charges on it. As long as the public is willing to lend, it is trading one kind of government obligation (money) for another (bonds). If the public balks at further lending, it must either hoard or spend the money it holds. If the public hoards its money, the government will have to print money in order to finance its operations and pay its interest obligations. If the public spends its money holdings, there is no need for government to borrow, since it only wished to borrow to increase total spending and now it does not have to. If the spending gets too large and inflation threatens, government can increase taxes to reduce the inflationary pressure and perhaps repay some of the debt. This approach to debt management represents an extreme opposite philosophy to that of the budget balancers, who fear deficit financing and the increasing national debt. There are still cries of anguish over the size of the debt and the burden it creates, and there are still predictions of national bankruptcy.

Those who worry about the national debt fail to consider that the interest payments on it merely involve a transfer of funds from taxpayer to bondholder (for internally held debt). This may entail an adverse redistribution from low-income taxpayers to high-income bondholders, but this effect can be overcome by other government programs. Those who worry about burdening future generations fail to consider that they will inherit the bonds as well as the service charges.

Only if government squanders real resources is there a possible burden, since these resources are not available to satisfy private demands. Still the debt was accumulated to combat recessions, to finance public investment, and to finance war and war-related activities. The real losses caused by unemployment, which can never be recovered, are far greater than any burden caused by the transfer of funds between groups. The public investment in social overhead capital results in a debt because of the failure to finance these projects through a capital budget, and the expenditures are treated as part of operating expenses rather than as capital acquisitions. A large portion of the debt is accounted for by war. How is one to speak of a burden here? If the foreign policy moves were sanctioned by the electorate, the sacrifice of real resources seems to be warranted; if not, there is something wrong with the political process and the economic issues take second place. Recent frustration with Vietnam war policy appears to reflect political impotence more than dissatisfaction over the economic costs. Charges of waste of resources for war and defense spending are frequently made, and arguments over spending priorities abound, but seldom is the possible burden of the resource consumption on future generations mentioned. Perhaps the present generation finds it difficult to conceive of future generations sacrificing consumption; perhaps technological change will make the concept of sacrifice meaningless anyway. In the end, it can always be claimed that present wars preserve the future for these unborn generations.

Congress has not rushed to embrace the principles of functional finance and, in fact, goes through a yearly exercise of boosting the ceiling on the debt limit. According to many people, this yearly charade merely offers a platform for politicians to voice their concern over increased government spending and to preach thrift and economy. It is a charade because Congress then votes the spending appropriations that raise the debt level. To followers of functional finance, there is no such thing as an arbitrary debt ceiling. They would claim that the increasing public debt may gradually reach some kind of equilibrium level, where growth in the debt would stop. This would come about from an indirect effect on consumption. As the public accumulates government bonds, the additions to wealth would finally reach some point where no new additions would be desired and people therefore would increase consumption. But the increase in private spending would make it less necessary for government to spend and hence to borrow, and so on.

Aside from the problems of the possible redistribution of income as the debt is repaid, there are some problems in the conduct of monetary policy. A large public debt makes monetary policy practicable in the form of open market operations, but there have been times when it has worked against stabilization. We have already seen the effects of the Federal Reserve policy of "pegging" selling prices of bonds and their yields. The Federal Reserve is still constrained at times by its commitment to the Treasury to help in debt management. Also, the government bonds are highly liquid, "near money," and thus pose a potential inflationary threat. They are easily exchanged for cash. Proponents of functional finance would dismiss the problem of pegging as a departure from reason, and the latter problem would be met by increasing taxes—that is what changing tax policies are supposed to do.

DISCRETIONARY VERSUS AUTOMATIC FISCAL POLICIES AND THEIR PROBLEMS

In the foregoing discussion of fiscal policy deliberate policy actions have been distinguished from those that occur automatically. We have described the philosophical attitudes that favor both types of action. In this section an elaboration of these fiscal policy measures is necessary in order to give a deeper insight into the differences between discretionary and automatic policies and the problems involved in their use.

Discretionary Fiscal Policy

The naive models clearly indicate the proper fiscal policy whenever the levels of output and employment are different from the desired levels. If an economy needs stimulation, an increase in government expenditures or a decrease in taxes or both are called for; if an economy is experiencing inflationary pressures, it needs to be restrained, and the reverse fiscal policy is appropriate. Discontent with the current economic situation is supposed to move men of reason to examine the feasibility of changing unsatisfactory conditions. To gain some control over the economic system and to escape from servitude to the laws of chance is the very essence of all discretionary policy, be it monetary or fiscal. The intent is clear and the means are available; now it is time to inquire into the practical side of discretionary fiscal policy, beginning first with the expenditures side of the budget.

Government Expenditures

The first problem with altering government expenditures to achieve some goal is rather irksome though seemingly inescapable: *there is no valid and acceptable theory of government expenditures.* Without an economic theory of government expenditures to serve as a guide, the entire arena is left open to the tug of war of politics and compromise. Some unfortunate consequences follow from this fact that tend to diminish the value of discretionary action.

The first of these is the existence of lags. Fiscal policy tends to be inflexible, and much time elapses between the recognition of a problem (after some lag), consideration of options (more lags), enacted policy measures, and impact on the economy. These lags are analogous to the inside and outside lags of monetary policy. With the existing institutional practices of the United States Congress, they are virtually inevitable. The budgetary process is a nightmare of bureaucratic confusion. The budget is chopped up into areas of interest and sent off to subcommittees. Hearings are held, experts testify, and amendments are made. Both houses of Congress go through similar processes—from subcommittee to full committee to the house at large for each portion of the budget. After each bill has the general approval of both houses, the same procedure is followed all over again to get the funds allocated in the authorization bill, that is, an appropriations bill is necessary for each section of the budget. Much time is consumed in the process; everyone gets lost in the budget details; and few can grasp the significance of the budget as a whole, much less attempt to gauge its impact on the economy. This procedure is simply routine—imagine trying to institute drastic changes in the budget or experiment with new programs.

Congressional hearings offer a forum for political ploys of all kinds, from partisan political cant, to breast beating for economy, logrolling, porkbarreling, Christmas tree bill making, and in the end, disavowal of the results since everyone is unhappy. Thus, the budget that originates in the executive branch and is sent to Congress in January is first fragmented into many bills and then runs a tortuous, time-consuming path to final enactment many months later. The budgetary process is a complicated one and does not admit change easily, because the control exercised over sectors—agriculture, HEW, and so on—is jealously guarded by committees and their chairmen. To change the budget to meet current economic conditions appears to be incompatible with the slow institutional response dictated by tradition. The budgetary process has always been subject to criticism because of the time it takes and its failure to deal with budget totals. Rapidly changing economic conditions cannot be dealt with by this cumbersome system, and until reforms are made, lags of all kinds will make fiscal policy inflexible, unresponsive, and untimely.

Even if the lags were not so severe, the lack of a theory of government expenditures means that there is essentially no economic guide to indicate which expenditures are to be altered. Again, the field is abandoned to politics. As a result, there is a natural bias for expenditures to grow, since it is always easier and more popular to spend funds than it is to cut them. Thus, in reality it is easier to stimulate an economy through increased expenditures than to restrain the economy through reductions in spending. This bias is strong despite the pleas heard in both chambers for economy in government, balanced budgets, and the like. Of course, the effectiveness of discretionary fiscal policy is thus reduced.

Acknowledging the bias towards spending when change is contemplated, we may still ask which programs should be augmented or reduced? Without a theory, economists are forced to make value judgments like everyone else. Actually, the ability to alter spending is limited by several conditions: a large part of the budget, estimated at over 60 per cent, is made up of contractual items, which cannot be altered, and much of the budget is concerned with war and war-related activities, which Congress usually will not alter. The possibilities for discretionary action are thus severely reduced.

Generally, when reductions are contemplated, the nondefense portion of the budget is sacrificed. Social programs of all kinds—education, housing, welfare, job training, poverty programs, protection and development of natural resources, and so on—always seem to be slashed in the name of inflation control. Over time, social problems have become more visible and the national conscience has been aroused, and there is a growing resistance (not by all, to be sure) to cuts in these social programs. If the defenders of social programs and the defenders of defense spending are equally successful in resisting cuts, where can the spending cuts be made, and how much room is there for expenditure cuts as an instrument of discretionary fiscal policy?

In earlier times expenditures on public works played an important part in stabilization plans. Expenditures on government capital items—dams, roads, buildings, parks—were to be altered as economic conditions warranted. Desirable as the construction of public works may be, they are too inflexible for stabilization purposes and probably ought to be decided upon on grounds other than stabilization. One traditional criticism leveled at government investment or government spending in general is that private spending will be adversely affected by public spending, and because the reduction in private spending will offset the increase in public spending, the purposes of stabilization are not served. There is scant evidence of this kind of behavior, particularly if government spends on public investment projects that do not compete with private investment. Indeed, it would appear that the argument can be turned around to say that private spending is *encouraged* by public spending and by the government's commitment to stabilize aggregate demand.[22] Both the public and the private sectors have an interest in keeping the levels of output and employment as high and as stable as possible.

These obstinate problems in the conduct of fiscal policy insofar as expenditures are concerned—the lags, the lack of an expenditures theory which results in a bias to spend and squabbles among pressure groups and special-interest groups, the cumbersome budgetary process, the political process in general, and the fact that a large portion of the budget is made up of contractual obligations—render adjustment attempts inflexible and severely reduce the efficacy of fiscal policy in general.

Transfer Payments

Transfer payments offer more flexibility, or so it would seem, but they create similar problems and thus offer no real solutions. Whatever their merit for other purposes, transfer payments used as a device for stabilization run into similar difficulties as do the other expenditure adjustments that are part of discretionary fiscal policy.

Again there is the spending bias—it is easy to increase payments for disability, Social Security, retirement, medical payments, veterans' benefits, and so on, and such payments would, no doubt, have beneficial effects on aggregate demand. Yet such increases usually become permanent, in fact, contractual, and when the time comes to reduce them, it is impossible or undesirable to do so. Transfer payments are mostly used for achieving other goals—fighting poverty, providing incomes to the disadvantaged, and so on. They should not be employed to achieve stabilization as well, since their apparent flexibility is illusory.

Taxes

The alternative to adjusting expenditures to achieve stabilization is, of course, to manipulate tax receipts. As will be noted, in recent years taxes have more often

---

[22] This is one of the arguments of J. K. Galbraith in *The New Industrial State* (Boston: Houghton Mifflin, 1967).

been manipulated than expenditures. Unfortunately, tax changes present problems as well, some new and some already familiar.

Again there are lags. The political process precludes swift action, and like expenditure lags, tax changes may come too late to apply to the conditions that prompted them. For instance, the tax cut of 1964 took almost two years to enact, and the tax increase of 1968 took almost as long.

Once again, there is a possible bias owing to political realities: it is more popular to reduce taxes than it is to increase them. It is difficult to tell constituents that their taxes were increased in the national interest. The crowds are not pleased by such statements, however truthful. How much better it is to point to reduced taxes and more take-home pay. The bias is obvious, perhaps, but no less damaging to the conduct of a rational fiscal policy. The principles of taxation have received much more attention from economists than have expenditures, so that more is known about the impact of taxation upon the economy and upon various groups within it. Still, tax collections can be changed in a variety of ways: change the rates on existing taxes, change the tax structure or basis for taxation, introduce or discard a tax scheme, change some taxes (either rates or basis) while leaving others alone, and so on. Which change to employ would seem to be dictated by what goals are to be accomplished, but the matter is not all that easy. Nor is it particularly useful to note that, in general, increases in taxes tend to be deflationary and decreases, expansionary. Again, there are conflicting goals, like stabilization, growth, and equity, and these complicate efforts to achieve a sound tax policy.

For stabilization, the choice of which taxes to change and how depends upon the source of the trouble with regard to aggregate demand and upon the revenue effects of various taxes. If overall demand is high (or low), then increases (decreases) in both the personal income tax and the corporate income tax may be warranted. The income taxes are both responsive and powerful, and their effects on revenue collection are quickly calculated. There are, however, problems of equity between the two. Many economists contend that the corporation income tax is simply passed on to consumers in the form of higher prices. The incidence or burden of the tax is shifted forward, the effect being analogous to a sales tax, especially when the tax is increased, for prices seldom fall. If corporate plans for investment expenditures are not affected by tax changes, then the burden of stabilization falls to consumers. This may or may not be desirable, but it must be considered in drawing up a tax strategy. Similarly, in a recession period the granting of a tax credit to business to stimulate investment may have no effect on investment at all but merely represent a tax break for corporations. Not only economic effects must be considered but the equity effects as well. Though we temporarily leave the discussion of taxes now, the summary statements should serve as a warning that changes in taxes are not as simple as might appear.

Other federal taxes are not as powerful or as responsive as the income tax. Excise taxes, now mostly eliminated, might affect consumption through price changes. But estate and gift taxes as well as import taxes and all other revenue-producing fees are simply not useful for stabilization purposes.

State and Local Government Finance

In the foregoing discussion of fiscal policy only national expenditures and taxes were considered. Since states and localities also collect taxes and spend the receipts, they have fiscal policies, too, although they may not be explicit.

Most states are prohibited from deficit financing by their constitutions and must balance their budgets annually. Thus, the states and localities often work at cross-purposes to national fiscal policy and reduce the effectiveness of that national policy. When the federal government is attempting to stimulate the economy, the states and localities, faced with declining tax receipts, are reducing expenditures. In boom times the anti-inflationary policies at the federal level are offset by local governments, which are increasing expenditures.

Intergovernmental relations are complicated even further by the kinds of taxes promulgated by each branch of the public sector. Briefly, the state and local governments were constitutionally assigned to have authority over public goods for which the demand has now increased along with the increase in affluence—education, roads and highways, welfare, sanitary systems, and so on. The constant pressure for more expenditures on these items precludes spending reductions for fiscal policy purposes. The only possible change for local expenditures is upward.

However, the taxes imposed by state and local governments, primarily the sales and property taxes, are not as responsive to changing economic conditions as a tax based on those conditions—the income tax. Thus, tax collections do not rise as rapidly as changes in income, are not as easily changed, and thus are not as effective for stabilization purposes. The dilemma is that the demand for expenditures increases but the tax collections lag behind, so that the local governments are continuously strapped for funds. It follows, of course, that state and local actions are not very useful, and may be harmful, in the conduct of fiscal policy. More reliance on income taxes is required, either directly in some scheme with the federal government or indirectly with a revenue sharing scheme. Even then, it will probably still be true that fiscal policy decisions are best made at the national level and best implemented with national expenditures and taxes.

Expenditures Versus Tax Changes

A discretionary fiscal policy can involve changes in expenditures or taxes, but which should be changed is a question that we have not seriously discussed. From the section on the balanced budget multiplier it is clear that changes in expenditures are more potent than changes in taxes, but aside from this, the choice of which tool to use seems arbitrary. Many of the same problems attend the changing of expenditures and taxes. There are lags with each, as well as political considerations and problems of justice, which restrict either path towards a rational discretionary fiscal policy. In the past decade or so, changes in taxes have been favored over changes in expenditures, perhaps because fewer questions are asked concerning the uses to which taxes will be put. Many expenditures programs are controversial enough to preclude timely changes in them. Taxes are easier to explain, to control, and to manipulate.

The question is further complicated by the different philosophies that accompany the advocacy of one policy or the other. In the United States there has been a traditional fear of the centralization of power and possible conflict with one of the country's most cherished economic goals—the maximization of economic freedom. Fear of the power and the growth of government has always been a hallmark of an economic conservative. Thus, when the economy requires stimulation, the conservative responds by advocating a reduction in taxes rather than an increase in expenditures. A tax cut returns income to the private sector, which then makes private decisions to spend or save on essentially private goods. Government control over the economy is decreased. For one of liberal views, the need for more public goods makes such a policy unacceptable. The liberal prefers to increase expenditures on social goods while keeping revenues intact. Of course, the same dichotomy exists when a policy of restraint is required. The conservative advocates a decrease in expenditures, while the liberal advocates an increase in taxes.

These are generalities, of course, but they do serve to illustrate the political and social problems connected with the choice of policy tools. There being no adequate theory of public expenditures, the door is opened to conflict and to value judgments.

Automatic Stabilizers

It has been suggested that the conservative philosophy favors a reduction in government intervention into the economy. It is not surprising, then, to find the conservative bias for automatic or built-in stabilizers as opposed to discretionary policies. This conservative tradition was met before, favoring rules for the Federal Reserve to follow rather than discretionary policies. (In fact, the Federal Reserve System itself is a manifestation of the conservative tradition in that it is a quasi-public, private institution, responsible to Congress, and not really a central bank as in other countries.)

The automatic stabilizers vary inversely with the level of economic activity and thus exert a countercyclical influence. Unemployment compensation and the personal income tax structure are the main ones, but others are also stabilizing to a lesser extent—the corporation income tax, corporation dividend policies, and farm price supports. The automatic feature of these programs removes politics from the picture, as well as all other problems associated with discretionary fiscal actions. Automatic programs have wide appeal among liberals and conservatives both, but as already suggested, they may not be powerful enough to reverse the direction of the economy and must be assisted by deliberate policy actions. Little would be served by reiterating our analysis of built-in stabilizers in the overall fiscal policy plans. Instead, we turn to the effects of the automatic stabilizers on the full employment surplus.

Through the operation of the automatic stabilizers and through the growth of potential GNP, the amount of tax revenues grows year by year even with no change in the tax rates. Of course, the full employment surplus also rises year by year and, if left undisturbed, will act as a contractionary influence over the economy. The rising tax revenues act as a brake on the growth of economic activity and may prevent the attainment of full employment. This phenomenon has come to be known as *fiscal drag.*

To eliminate the drag on the economy, either government expenditures must rise to match the additional revenues or taxes must be reduced. Since taxes increase more than proportionally with increases in GNP, government expenditures must increase more than proportionally with GNP in order to match the tax receipts. Mere increases in government expenditures are not sufficient. Failure to increase expenditures or reduce taxes by the proper amount means that the surplus will develop and grow and full employment will not be reached or, if once attained, cannot be maintained. How to use this surplus depends on one's philosophy of government, as mentioned earlier. Conservatives would advocate tax reductions, and liberals, expenditure increases. It is clear that fiscal drag is a real problem in management of the economy via the full employment surplus concept. The job of stabilization is made easier but more exacting with the existence of the automatic stabilizers.

Macroeconomic Policy in Practice

The aim of chapter 13 was to review the tools and problems of deliberate macroeconomic policies. Some additional problems will be pointed out as the record is reviewed. Before turning to the discussion of past policies, we must reiterate a warning: discretionary stabilization policies are not always easily identified or traced to deliberate countercyclical actions; all too often other goals are being pursued simultaneously, and these goals may often be more influential than stabilization.

The budget is a complex document, reflecting as it does not only economic but political and social goals as well. At times, administrations have favored policies that could be justified on other grounds in addition to satisfying stabilization ends. Thus, economic difficulties can be shrouded in the cloak of other concerns on which a broader consensus exists. Governments have been loathe to admit economic setbacks and to apply the corrective policies indicated. Campaign pledges, party platforms, and past ideology frequently inhibit rational and timely actions. If a politician has pledged to lower taxes, it is unlikely that he would later welcome the suggestion to increase them, even if this policy is evidently the correct one.

Thus, actions that would have taken place anyway are sometimes attributed to stabilization policies. Increases in expenditures—say for national defense—can be defended on several grounds, one of which is the boost such spending gives to the economy. In addition, most programs receive more scrutiny during periods of recession or inflation, and long-term programs that have long been debated are then suddenly modified with an eye to the economic condition. It is almost impossible to separate the true countercyclical actions from these interactions and overlappings of programs and goals. One must inquire into the motives of each policy, and even then political rhetoric can often mask the true intent of the proposed action.

Unfortunately, anyone who examines the record of deliberate policy must confront these political realities, and some obvious examples will be provided later that illustrate the nature of the obstacles to the proper evaluation of macroeconomic policy. It is sufficient in this introduction to suggest the difficulty of judging policy actions.[1]

We begin by examining the economic fluctuations that have occurred in the post-World War II era. By hindsight, we can determine the policies appropriate for the period under consideration. We can then turn to the policies actually adopted and attempt to judge them for effectiveness in achieving stabilization. The effects of macroeconomic policies on society can then be examined to point out the frequently omitted social consequences of macroeconomic policy.

The Post-World War II Business Cycle

For understanding the discussion of the actual policies followed in the past several decades, some familiarity with the economic conditions that prevailed during the period is necessary. Since we are interested primarily in discretionary actions used to combat the cycle, it is appropriate to study the policies followed during the phases of the cycle. What is required first, then, is some acceptable measure of the business cycle and some acceptable method for determining the turning points of the cycles.

The work of the National Bureau of Economic Research (NBER) in analyzing the business cycle is one of the methods generally accepted and widely known. For our purposes, their definition of the business cycle will be more than adequate. The methodology of the NBER has been adopted by the Bureau of the Census in its monthly publication *Business Conditions Digest* (*BCD*), formerly called *Business Cycle Developments.*

Briefly, the methodology was derived from the painstaking scrutiny of many series of economic data, and from this examination emerged the identification of turning points in economic activity that, of course, define the business cycle.[2] Through repeated testing against the actual data, some of these series have been identified as roughly coinciding with the trend of general economic activity; other series tended to lag behind, while others appeared to lead. These leading series have been used as a forecasting tool, since they begin to show declines or improvements before the economy as a whole registers the changes in direction. We are not interested in the use of these data for forecasting purposes but only in the delineation of business cycle dates—the turning points when the economy was judged to have changed direction in the overall level of economic activity.[3] Table 14.1 lists the post-World War II business cycles and identifies the peaks and troughs of economic activity.

Figure 14.1 shows the same business cycle data in the form traditionally associated with this type of analysis. The movement of GNP, a coincident series, is traced over the period in relation to the cycles identified by the NBER. Note that

[1] For a fuller discussion of these points, see Wilfred Lewis, Jr., *Federal Fiscal Policy in the Postwar Recession* (Washington, D.C.: Brookings Institution, 1962). For a concise record of monetary policy, see L. V. Chandler, *The Economics of Money and Banking,* 5th ed. (New York: Harper & Row, 1969).

[2] For more detailed explanations, see the many publications of the NBER, particularly those of G. H. Moore (ed.), *Business Cycle Indicators* (Princeton, N.J.: Princeton University Press, 1961), vols. I and II.

[3] For a list of the economic series classified by leading, coincident, and lagging series, see any issue of *Business Conditions Digest.* The use of the leading series as a forecasting tool—the so-called barometric forecasting method—has been criticized for its shortcomings by many students of the art of forecasting.

TABLE 14.1

POST-WORLD WAR II BUSINESS CYCLES

Complete Cycle			Duration in Months	
Trough	Peak	Trough	Expansion	Contraction
Oct. 1945	Nov. 1948	Oct. 1949	37	11
Oct. 1949	July 1953	Aug. 1954	45	13
Aug. 1954	July 1957	Apr. 1958	35	9
Apr. 1958	May 1960	Feb. 1961	25	9
Feb. 1961	Nov. 1969	Nov. 1970	105	12
Nov. 1970				

Source: *Business Conditions Digest.*

the shaded areas show the periods of contraction and the unshaded areas show the periods of expansion.[4]

Pre-World War II Monetary and Fiscal Policy

Monetary and fiscal policies to stabilize the economy were barely evident in the pre-World War II years. Monetary policy was influenced more by the gold flows than by stabilization goals. The "correct" monetary policy might have been pursued but for entirely different reasons. Easy money policies in the 1920s, designed to stop the flow of gold to the United States and promote United States lending abroad, ended up by encouraging speculation, which was to prove disastrous in 1929. At times, the easy money policies actually may have helped to combat recessions, but the policies were too strong for the mild recessions and thus must be attributed to other pressures. When the stock market crash did come, the Federal Reserve, having no control over margin requirements, was bewildered and confused about what to do. It hesitated and then pursued tight money and credit policies that were too late and only made the nonspeculative sectors of the economy vulnerable. The end result is history—the Great Depression.

Monetary policy in the early years of the depression resembled past policies and was clearly inappropriate. The Federal Reserve was tardy in its actions, and when it finally acted to ease money market conditions, it was timid. The easy money policies employed in the early 1930s were too little and too late, and soon the bank panic of 1933 occurred and the gold standard broke down. Monetary policy became more aggressive after 1934, but by then the banks were swamped with excess reserves and monetary policy was severely limited. The banking sector had its own version of "liquidity preference," as interest rates were so low that banks were not eager to lend. In short, monetary policy up to the beginning of the Second World War was not particularly enlightened, but lessons had been learned and the Federal Reserve's power was enhanced to some extent by legal reforms.

The record of fiscal policy is even worse. Little was known of the expansionary

---

[4] Since the shaded areas of Figure 14.1 show contractionary periods, it follows that a *leading* series ideally should reach its peak before the shaded area and reach its trough within the shaded area. A lagging series would peak within the shaded area and reach a trough after the shaded area. Of course, a coincident series ought to reach its peak and trough on the boundaries of the shaded areas.

effects of government expenditures, and even if they had been realized, the prevailing philosophical views of government held by the Hoover administration, together with the small share of the national output allocated to the public sector, probably would have forestalled the deliberate expansionary policies on the scale required.

FIGURE 14.1

GROSS NATIONAL PRODUCT

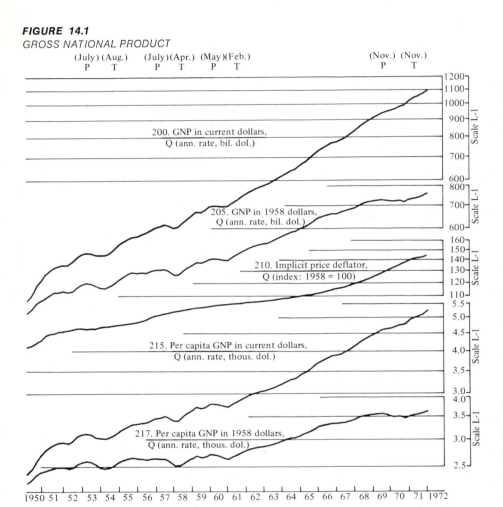

Source: *Business Conditions Digest.*

President Roosevelt took office championing balanced budgets but soon reversed himself and embarked on programs of public works, transfer payments, and other New Deal measures. Keynes had come to the United States to explain his multiplier theory to Roosevelt but was unsuccessful. Roosevelt did not understand him. Yet the New Deal did promote government spending for humanitarian reasons if not for logical fiscal concerns. Still, the actions were too little and too late and were actually offset at times by rising taxes.

Most economists would agree, therefore, that monetary and fiscal policies were not responsible for bailing the United States out of the Great Depression—World War II managed that. Pre-World War II macroeconomic policies must be judged as being too ill-conceived and haphazard to be considered under the heading of deliberate policy actions designed to stabilize the economic system.[5]

Economic Policy in the World War II Years

War, we are told, is an unnatural state, and policies undertaken in the war years cannot legitimately be judged by the same criteria used in peacetime. There is much to this argument, but in order to understand the postwar problems, it is necessary to review the economic policies that were pursued during the war years, for many of those policies had repercussions long after the conflict had ceased.

A nation mobilizing for a full-scale war must transfer resources to the public sector. Steel to make tanks must replace steel for automobiles, and a large part of the labor supply must be transferred to the armed forces. How are these resources to be transferred and still provide the new mixture of goods and services? Obviously, government expenditures must grow, and both private consumption and private investment must be curtailed. Thus, both consumers' and producers' durables were not produced at all in the war years. There were no new automobiles or refrigerators and few private investment goods permitted. Other consumer goods—meat, sugar, gasoline, and so on—were rationed to the general public. Direct wage and price controls were also imposed to prevent the bidding up of prices for the limited supply of all goods and services. In short, private demand was restrained, and real resources were transferred to the public sector to produce war goods.

The labor force was also involved in sweeping changes. The armed forces grew from 450,000 in 1940 to over 12 million in 1945. Who produced the war goods? In the mobilization process the unemployed were put to work; the blacks found discrimination eased; women were employed in all manner of jobs previously denied them for one reason or another; and many of the old prejudices against segments of the labor force were dropped. Unemployment as a percentage of the civilian labor force dropped from 17.2 per cent in 1939 to 1.2 per cent in 1944. At least part of the Keynesian vision had been verified, and idle resources were put to work by deliberate actions of government. The lesson was to be soon forgotten.

GNP (in current dollars) grew as well, from $99.7 billion in 1940 to over $210 billion in 1944, an increase of over 110 per cent. Much of the increase came from expenditures on national defense, which rose from $1.2 billion in 1939 to $87.4 billion in 1944, an increase of over 7,183 per cent. How were these government purchases financed?

---

[5] This extremely brief discussion can easily be supplemented by reading one or more books on this era. Two of these are J. K. Galbraith, *The Great Crash* (Boston: Houghton Mifflin, 1961), and L. V. Chandler, *America's Greatest Depression, 1929–1941* (New York: Harper & Row, 1970).

Early in the war effort this problem of fiscal policy had to be squarely faced, and the decisions made then are still affecting the United States economy. It was decided that the private sector was already making a large sacrifice in working long hours and doing without so many consumer goods. Perhaps fearing to test the limits of patriotism, the government decided that additional expenditures could not be financed by increased taxes on the overburdened private sector. Although taxes were increased, the major share of public financing was effected through borrowing.

Thus, the government deficit (on the national income accounts basis) went from $0.7 billion in 1940 to $51.8 billion in 1944. By borrowing rather than taxing to finance its expenditures, government avoided private unrest and, more important, sopped up much of the incomes earned by consumers, who could not spend them anyway. The policy, however, merely postponed some major problems. Over the duration of the war the Treasury had to borrow close to $200 billion in order to cover its deficits. Despite the efforts of big bond campaigns, movie star promotions, and payroll deduction plans, the general public did not buy all the bonds—the banking system had to take up the remainder.

The wartime monetary policy was to be severely restricted. In March 1942 the Federal Reserve and the Treasury reached an agreement that the price of government securities should not be allowed to fall or interest rates to rise (pegging policy). The Federal Reserve pledged to use the banking system to support the Treasury's operations. To do this, the instructions of the open market committee were simple—buy all securities offered for sale in order to guarantee prices and yields.

This open market policy of buying securities from all sellers resulted in the monetization of government securities, and the money supply increased tremendously—by nearly 200 per cent over the war's duration. Anyone could exchange a government security for money by presenting the bond to the Federal Reserve. In addition to increases in the money supply, the actions of the Federal Reserve kept interest rates from rising and thus insured a ready supply of credit for private use. It became necessary to empower the Federal Reserve to control credit terms over consumer loans, and the power over these selective credit controls remained in effect until the early 1950s.

These monetary and fiscal policies resulted in the United States economy emerging from the war with the following conditions: (1) repressed inflation brought about by direct controls over prices and the lack of consumer goods; (2) a huge accumulation of private savings held in the form of highly liquid assets —money and government securities; (3) a large government debt, which had to be serviced; and (4) the task of reconversion ahead.

Post-World War II Policies

Despite these facts, when the war ended in 1945 there were predictions that the United States economy would be plunged into a severe depression with massive unemployment. The reduction of government expenditures, combined with the problems of reconversion to a peacetime economy, were expected to result in the crippling of the economic system.

The forecasts of depression instigated some monetary and fiscal policies that must be explained with these fears in mind. First, most of the wartime price and wage controls were removed quickly and by mid-1946 were nearly all gone. Second, the Federal Reserve continued its policy of pegging, which means that interest rates were kept low as the Federal Reserve continued to support the Treasury's operations. These policies designed to forestall depression only served to aggravate the real postwar economic problem—inflation.

At the conclusion of the war the private sector, replete with money balances and highly liquid securities, was eager to spend these balances on goods and services unobtainable during the war. Consumers were eager to restore their old levels of living and even to elevate them by acquiring all kinds of consumer goods. The business sector was eager to rebuild and remodel its plants in order to seize upon the opportunities that the reconversion offered. With these excess demands and excess money balances, inflation was virtually inevitable. Prices increased from 1945 to 1946 by 5 points in the CPI and 7 points in the implicit price index, and after 1946 prices spurted from 68.0 in 1946 to 77.8 in 1947 (1957–1959 = 100) in the CPI and from 66.7 in 1946 to 74.6 in 1947 in the implicit price index (1958 = 100). Further increases followed in 1948 until the first postwar recession halted the process. Consumer prices had risen by over 30 points from the first war year to 1948, with two thirds of the increase coming after the war.

The postwar unemployment rate was rather low, less than 4 per cent, considering the nature of the reconversion program, and it remained at this level until the recession year of 1949, when it climbed to 6 per cent and over.

In view of these developments, the Federal Reserve's monetary policy seems perverse or ineffective at best. The policy of pegging merely fueled the inflation, and with the removal of the selective controls, little restraint came from the monetary side. The Federal Reserve did increase the discount rate several times after 1946 and set high member bank reserve requirements in this period. These policies were ineffective in restraining inflation, since banks could escape both restrictions by selling Treasury bonds to the Federal Reserve, which was obligated to buy them—liquidity was not the problem. Some people felt that monetary policy was ineffective anyway and that even the best monetary actions would not have been effective. Still others, looking back, feel that the postwar inflation was essentially inevitable and a natural consequence of war.

It appears that the only bright spot in postwar monetary policy was the concession forced by the Federal Reserve from the Treasury to discontinue the practice of supporting the short-term instrument—the Treasury bills and certificates. The Federal Reserve would continue to support the yields on new issues but would not be obligated to peg the yields on outstanding securities. The long-term yields were still maintained until March 1951.

The first postwar business cycle peaked in November 1948, and the contraction continued throughout most of 1949. The Federal Reserve reduced its reserve requirements in the second and third quarters of 1949. The Treasury reduced its interest rates on new issues, and of course, the Federal Reserve supported these lower rates. Again, the effectiveness of the policy is obscured by the outbreak of the Korean War.

The record of fiscal policy in this period is not much more enlightened. Naturally, government expenditures fell drastically after the war was concluded. National defense expenditures, accounting for most of the decline, fell by almost $60 billion from 1945 to 1946. Still, consumption increased by $23 billion and investment by $20 billion from 1945 to 1946. GNP in current dollars declined by only $3 billion from 1945 to 1946 (GNP in 1958 prices declined by $43 billion, however) and thereafter increased rapidly as the private sector demand continued strong while public demand remained relatively stable.

While it is true that government expenditures declined in the immediate postwar period, it is not possible to attribute the decline to deliberate fiscal policy action to combat inflation. National defense expenditures were no longer required. Similarly, taxes were not increased to restrain the inflationary pressures, so that the boom continued into 1948 unchecked by deliberate policy actions.

The economy expanded throughout most of 1948, with unemployment averaging 3.8 per cent and with manufacturing operating at approximately 92 per cent of capacity. Towards the end of 1948 (and through most of 1949) the economy reversed direction and entered into a recessionary period. The cause has been attributed to the overaccumulation of inventories in 1948. Whatever the cause, unemployment rose to over 6 per cent, manufacturing capacity fell to 82 per cent, and prices remained *rather constant,* as did the level of GNP.

Despite the fact that the Employment Act of 1946 was now history, deliberate fiscal policy measures were not employed to combat the recession. There was a tax cut in 1948 (passed in April and retroactive to January), but the purpose was *not* to combat recession, because the recession had not yet begun. The tax cut did, however, help to halt the recession and make it a mild one. Indeed, the balanced budget philosophy was still strongly followed in principle. Also acting as a stimulus to the economy, although whether or not deliberately is still somewhat controversial, was the Marshall Plan program of aid begun in late 1948. Clearly, the United States economy benefited from orders coming in from the rebuilding European economies.

In conclusion, it appears that deliberate macroeconomic policies to influence the first postwar cycle were either nonexistent or ineffective. Despite the debate over the Employment Act of 1946 and the educational process that might have been expected to result from the prolonged exchange of views, deliberate countercyclical measures were not employed in the first real test to which they could have been put. Once again, the military orders associated with the buildup for the Korean War probably were responsible for keeping the recession as mild as it turned out to be.

The Korean War and the Second Postwar Recession, 1953–1954

The Korean War began in June 1950 and immediately touched off a wave of expectations that shook the economy, which was just emerging from a recession. Consumers expected the same shortages of goods and services, the same rationing schemes, and so on, which existed in World War II. Similarly, the investment sector expected to be limited to its physical plant and thus to present output levels. The expectations were acted upon, and consumers rushed out to stock up on consumer goods and hoard them. Businesses added to inventories to insure supply. Naturally, such actions brought about the conditions feared—the shortage of goods. The prophesy was self-fulfilling.

The spurt in demand also brought about inflationary pressures. Between 1950 and early 1951 the implicit price index rose by nearly 6 points, the CPI rose by nearly 7 points, and the WPI by 10 points. Manufacturing plants used much more of their capacity, and GNP grew by over 11 per cent, with most of the rise accounted for by the private sector. Unemployment, however, remained high. The demand was financed by an increase in the money supply, an increase in velocity, the sale of liquid assets, and an increase in credit of all kinds.

The initial wave of hysteria began to subside by the second quarter of 1951, and the economy entered into an expansionary period until mid-1953. Money GNP increased by over 40 per cent from 1949 to 1953, and unemployment fell to under 3 per cent. After the initial spurt in inflation, prices were remarkably stable for the next several years—an extraordinary result, viewed in retrospect. Manufacturers were utilizing 96 per cent of capacity as both private and public demand expanded. National defense expenditures alone went from $13 billion in 1949 to over $48 billion in 1953. The money supply rose by over 16 per cent, and the velocity of money rose by 24 per cent in this period. Further financing came from large increases in credit. The public debt increased from $217 billion to $227 billion, but the private debt increased over $114 billion from 1949 to 1953.

The Korean War ended in July 1953, and soon afterward the United States economy headed into another recession. The peak of the expansionary period was July 1953, and the contractionary period extended to August 1954. In the downturn money GNP was hardly affected and neither was the price level, reflecting the mild nature of the decline. Real GNP, however, declined by some $6.5 billion. Manufacturing capacity utilization fell by over 10 percentage points, however, and unemployment again rose to over 5 per cent. In addition, the money supply and income velocity were fairly constant in the contraction. This second postwar recession has been blamed on the reduction in military spending, which was on the order of $11 billion from mid-1953 to mid-1954.

The foregoing brief description of the second postwar recession, from the trough in October 1949 to the trough in August 1954, can now be viewed with respect to macroeconomic policies that were associated with it. Taking monetary policy first, we know that the Federal Reserve had broken away from the shackles of having to support the Treasury's operation by the famous accord of March 1951. (The Federal Reserve was now free to act to stabilize the economy but had little experience on which to draw for guidelines.) The Federal Reserve, desiring the money market to return to free market forces, shifted its aim from providing an orderly market through pegging to preventing a disorderly market through more modest intervention. It chose also to deal only in short-term obligations of the Treasury (the "bills' only" doctrine), leaving the long-term obligations to follow market forces. It also decided not to buy new Treasury issues or deal in obligations that had similar maturity dates. Nor would it attempt to influence yields by swapping one type of obligation for another. The Federal Reserve remained fairly faithful to these principles over the entire period.

As for deliberate policy actions, the Federal Reserve did little to restrain the inflationary pressures of the early part of the period. It did act in early 1953 to combat inflation, even though the price level was very stable. The Federal Reserve feared inflation was the upcoming problem; therefore, it pursued a tight money policy. Some of its policies reduced member bank reserves indirectly, and the discount rate was increased. The tight money policy did not last very long, since it soon became evident that recession, not inflation, was the problem.

Once the true issue was recognized, the Federal Reserve set about to use its powers to reverse the downward trend. In May 1953 it began to buy securities and so increase bank reserves. In July 1953 the reserve requirements were lowered, and in February 1954 the discount rate was lowered. In the summer of 1954 it again lowered reserve requirements. In short, the Federal Reserve pursued an active monetary policy designed to ease the money market conditions: interest rates fell, the money supply increased, and some investment spending was stimulated. No doubt the Federal Reserve was now on the right path, but whether or not it was very successful in combating the recession is still debatable, as will be noted later. (No one attributed the decline to the tight money policies it pursued incorrectly.)

Fiscal policy, in the form of spending reductions on national defense, has been blamed for causing the recession. Once begun, the recession was not fought with fiscal policy tools. What made the recession a mild one was a tax cut, which was unrelated to the state of the economy. In early 1954 the excess profits tax was repealed, and a short time later excise taxes were reduced. In addition, the Internal Revenue Code was given a major revision, and the reforms involved resulted in tax cuts for both individuals and corporations. These tax reductions were about $7 billion but were partially offset by increased contributions to OASI (approximately $1.4 billion). Yet, the tax cuts came at the right time and, together with the easy money conditions, helped to make the recession a mild one.

Still, the tax cuts were too late to avert the recession altogether, a possibility readily admitted in retrospect. As the CEA put it, "The tax cuts took effect 6 months after expenditures began to fall. As it was, fiscal policy, taken as a whole, was contractionary in this period and was a major cause of the recession."[6]

After that judgment, there is little left to discuss concerning fiscal policy in this period. It is well known that the Eisenhower administration continued to cling to the balanced budget philosophy, even if the belief was not publicly stated. The first Republican administration in twenty years was not likely to risk another economic disaster nor even talk of one. Fortunately for it, the recovery came before the conflict was put to the test.[7]

The Third Postwar Recession of 1957–1958

The second postwar recession ended in August 1954, and for the next three years the economy was on the upswing, until July 1957. This expansionary period is very interesting in that it came about largely by changes in the private sector and primarily through changes in investment spending. In the period from 1954 first quarter to 1957 third quarter, gross private domestic investment increased by $22 billion, with fixed investment increasing by $16 billion and the change in inventories by $6 billion. In percentage terms, these increases are 45 per cent for total investment, 30 per cent for fixed investment (includes a 17 per cent increase for residential structures), and a 228 per cent increase in inventories. The boom in the investment sector was over, however, by early 1957, although the economy continued to expand until July 1957. Investment spending generally leads the general level of economic activity, and the multiplier effect postponed the downturn for the economy as a whole.

---

[6] *Annual Report of the CEA* (1963), p. 70.

[7] For an interesting insight into the formation of policy (and inside lags of fiscal policy), see the description of the Eisenhower administration in action during this period in Robert J. Donovan, *Eisenhower: The Inside Story* (New York: Harper & Row, 1956), a portion of which is reprinted in A. M. Okun (ed.), *The Battle Against Unemployment* (New York: W. W. Norton, 1965), pp. 126–134.

Money GNP in this expansionary period increased from $364.7 billion to $446.3 billion, representing a 22 per cent increase. Unemployment, however, did not decline so extensively, going from 6.0 per cent to 4.2 per cent. The price level rose as well, and the period of relative price stability appeared to be over. The implicit price index climbed to 98.0 from 89.5, the CPI rose to 98.5 from 93.7, and the WPI rose to 99.3 from 93.0. (Both the CPI and WPI have the base of 1957–1959 = 100; the implicit price index has 1958 = 100.) The price increases were small at first but became larger as the boom continued. The use of capacity by manufacturing firms rose rapidly in 1955 to 90.0 per cent and actually declined in 1956 to 88.2 per cent and further declined in 1957. Never since then has the utilization of capacity rate reached the levels of 1953. This expansionary period begins to record changes in the structure of the United States economy: note the rising price level, the sticky unemployment rate, and the decline of the manufacturing sector's use of its capacity. It is also interesting to note that while GNP increased by over 22 per cent, the money supply increased by only 4 or 5 per cent, with the income velocity of money increasing by over 17 per cent to finance the increase in income. Interest rates rose to their highest levels in decades, and corporate profits before taxes increased by approximately 21 per cent.

This remarkable boom came to an end in July 1957. Investment spending had declined earlier, in the first quarter of 1956. The reversal of spending for gross private domestic investment was dramatic. While fixed investment spending went from $67.2 billion to $62.7 billion from the third quarter of 1957 to the first quarter of 1958, the change in business inventories was a phenomenal −$5.4 billion from +$3.2 billion in the same period. Apparently, business optimism faltered and stocks were allowed to decline. Of course, capacity utilization fell even farther, to 73 per cent by the second quarter of 1958. Unemployment rates climbed back up to 7.4 per cent and remained well above 5 per cent until the mid-1960s. Money GNP rose to a level of $446.3 billion in the third quarter of 1957 and fell to a level of $438.3 billion when the contraction came to an end in the second quarter of 1958 (in April).

Still, prices continued to rise, with the implicit price index increasing by 2 points, the CPI by 2 points, and the WPI by 1 point. The money supply was held stable during the contractionary period, and the income velocity of money declined slightly.

Monetary policy during this complete cycle has been described as defensive. As already noted, the Federal Reserve elected to keep the money supply stable, so that the boom had to be financed by increases in velocity. In general, this represented a tight money policy, and with investors clamoring for funds, interest rates inevitably shot up to very high levels. In addition, the Federal Reserve increased the discount rate several times, to a high of 3.5 per cent in August 1957.

Despite these actions, the boom continued. In the face of high interest rates, investment spending continued, raising GNP and the price level. Apparently, the demand schedule for investment goods (*MEC*) had shifted to the right, making the rise in interest rates ineffective in slowing the demand. Furthermore, inventory changes were dramatic and not nearly so influenced by interest rate changes. Also, with no change in the money supply, all sectors were forced to economize on their money balances in order to finance the changes in income. During the boom, then, the Federal Reserve actions were weak and, if anything, helped to work against the expansion. It was not successful in halting the expansion, which may say more about the efficacy of monetary policy than against the policies pursued.

Following some confusing signals from the economy—rising prices and rising GNP—the Federal Reserve did not act to ease money conditions until October 1957, when it began to expand bank reserves by its open market operations. Shortly thereafter it lowered the discount rate to 3 per cent and early in 1958 lowered reserve requirements. The easing of credit conditions allowed interest rates in general to fall, but the effect was more pronounced in the short-term interest rates. During the contraction, then, monetary policy was more orthodox in application, although the lags in action were still apparent.

The same cannot be said of fiscal policy, however, as the Eisenhower administration continued to cling to balanced budgets and public thrift. The federal budget did register surpluses in 1955, 1956, and 1957 of $4.0, $5.7, and $2.1 billion, respectively, on a national income accounts basis (while state and local governments had deficits of $1.3, $0.9, and $1.4 billion for the same years). However, according to the full employment surplus, the restraining effect of the federal budget is quite obvious from the surpluses registered for 1956 and 1957 (see Figure 13.3). The economic role of government was limited, and primary reliance for the smooth operation of the economy was placed on the private sector. No serious efforts were made to fight the inflation or to deal with the rising unemployment that accompanied it. Fiscal policy actions were virtually nonexistent in this entire period.

The Fourth Postwar Recession of 1960–1961

In the recession of 1957–1958 money GNP went from $446.3 billion in July 1957 to $438.3 billion in April 1958, a decrease of 1.8 per cent. For the same period, real GNP (in 1958 prices) fell from $455.2 billion to $439.5 billion, a decline of 3.4 per cent. By April 1958 most of the inventory imbalances seem to have been adjusted, and the excess capacity created in the capital goods boom appears to have been more than just a temporary phenomenon. The decline of gross private domestic investment was sharp—some $14.7 billion, or 21 per cent—but again was on the increase by the third quarter of 1958. In the upswing, from April 1958 to May 1960, gross private domestic investment increased by $20.3 billion, or 36 per cent. In this same period government expenditures increased as well, not at the federal government level but at the state and local levels. These government units increased their expenditures by $6 billion, or over 6 per cent.

The recovery was brief, however, and the trends observed in the previous cycle were again evident in this one; the problems of the United States economy were changing, and shifts and conversions became more apparent and were to cause problems of interpretation that still exist. A description of the developments in this period, both economic and political, will reveal the nature of these persistent problems.

First, let us review the economic data. In the brief expansionary period of about two years GNP in current prices rose by $66.4 billion, or 15 per cent. GNP in 1958 dollars increased by $50.2 billion, or 11 per cent. The unemployment rate declined from its recession peak of 7.5 per cent in July 1958 to 5.0 per cent in June 1959 but soon rose again and hovered around 5.5 per cent for the remainder of the expansionary period. The failure of the unemployment rate to fall during an expansionary period is one of the problems of the United States economy to surface in this cycle. Such a high unemployment rate had previously been associated with the recessionary phases of the cycle, as was the case in the first two postwar cycles. In the 1957–1958 recession the unemployment rate had remained relatively high, and this development continued in this cycle at even higher rates.

Also noteworthy was the rather exceptional stability of prices as the upswing continued. Consumer prices rose on the order of 1.5 per cent, while wholesale prices remained quite stable. The same modest price changes are recorded by the implicit price index over the period. The stability in prices has been attributed to the "softness" or incompleteness of the recovery from the previous recession. Under these circumstances one would think that the inflationary psychology (a new notion at the time) would be positively affected and inflation made less fearful. However, this was not the case, and creeping inflation (another relatively new phrase) was feared, since prices had not declined in the previous recession. This extraordinary price stability, combined with the unusual reactions to it, point to a second problem emerging in the United States economy—inexplicable price behavior.

Capacity utilization by manufacturing firms is still another problem that appears again in this cycle. Manufacturing firms had operated at a low of 72.5 per cent of capacity in the previous downturn. The utilization of capacity rose in the expansionary period to 84.4 per cent in the second quarter of 1959 but then fell to 81.2 per cent in the second quarter of 1960, which was the peak of the cycle. The utilization of capacity was not to recover to the levels of the mid-1950s until the Vietnam build-up. Excess capacity appeared to be a normal state of affairs.

Once again, the increases in GNP were financed by changes in the velocity of money rather than by changes in the money supply. While GNP increased by over 15 per cent, the money supply increased only by something like 5 per cent. In the subsequent downturn little change was recorded in any of these variables (see Table C.1, appendix C).

Another problem became more serious in this period and has persisted to the present time—the balance of payments. Throughout most of the postwar period the United States had run a deficit in its balance of payments. Such deficits helped to provide liquid reserves to the rest of the world as the dollar became a key currency in the gold exchange standard. Yet in this period the deficit increased, from approximately $1 billion to over $3 billion in 1958 and to almost $4 billion in 1959 and 1960. Suddenly the rest of the world had too many dollars and some countries were demanding gold. The gold stock declined from the postwar high of over $24 billion in 1949 to over $19 billion in 1959. To add to these conditions, imports increased in this period while exports remained stable, and net exports of goods and services (national income accounts basis) declined from $5.7 billion in 1957 to $0.1 billion in 1959. These developments called attention to the movements of capital as short-term capital took flight to earn higher rewards abroad. No longer could interest rates be manipulated to serve only domestic considerations of output and employment, but now a watchful eye had to be kept on international financial markets as well. This new development shocked a nation that had considered itself immune from the vagaries of international trade. The shock waves still persist, and as we will see, there were some attempts to deal with this new phenomenon. The United States position in world trade was complicated by the newly created European Common Market. Long-term foreign investment, mostly to Europeans, increased from under $1 billion to over $2.5 billion in the decade of the 1950s. The United States government also contributed to the balance-of-payment woes as foreign economic and military aid increased over the same period. Military expenditures alone increased from $0.5 billion in 1950 to over $3 billion per year in the late 1950s. These and other developments created much confusion in the United States and in the international community in general. The existence of many current international difficulties attests to the fact that much confusion and indecision still remain.

The cycle reached its peak in May 1960, and the downturn began, lasting until February 1961. The recession was brief in duration and fairly mild in magnitude. Real GNP fell by only 1.4 per cent, and disposable personal income remained stable. Unemployment, however, climbed from the May 1960 low of 5.1 per cent to well over 6.0 per cent by the end of the year—an election year. High unemployment rates continued for several more years, never falling below 5 per cent and usually being well above that figure. The price level continued to rise—"creep" became popular usage—and by the end of the contractionary period the implicit price index had risen by 1.2 points, the CPI had risen by 1.0 points, and the WPI had remained stable.

The change in inventories turned the economy around as they fell from +$3.9 billion to −$3.5 billion in the period from the second quarter of 1960 to the first quarter of 1961. As might be expected, capacity utilization fell from 81.2 per cent to 74.2 per cent, and the stagnation of the economy became more visible and disturbing. In the monetary sphere most variables remained stable, as was true in the previous postwar recessions.

Before examining the macroeconomic policies pursued to combat this recession, it is necessary to broaden our review to include other areas and events that may have influenced those policies. The calm and cautious 1950s were giving way to the turbulent 1960s. Economic policies did not operate in a vacuum but were influenced by the changes taking place and were guided to some extent by those changes, which they themselves helped to create. While this mutual influence is always present, it becomes magnified in periods such as this one, in which the pace of change appears to have accelerated.

A major event that helped to shape the direction of change was the launching by the Russians of an earth-orbiting satellite in 1957. The Western world was shocked. Suddenly the mood of the Cold War changed, and in the United States there was widespread fear that the West lagged behind the Russians in space technology. Soon it was realized that Russian technology was also capable of matching United States know-how in weaponry as well. The United States seemed to be losing the battle for technological supremacy on all fronts. Naturally, the Cold War rhetoric intensified, and John F. Kennedy campaigned on the technological lag and the missile gap.

The technological lag was blamed on the educational establishment, and all kinds of introspective analyses were made, many financed by the federal government. Science courses and mathematics courses were overhauled, and soon the reading ability of students and graduates was questioned. There was a tremendous amount of interest in education at all levels, and the federal government became more active in this field. The National Defense Education Act, which was passed in September 1958, awarded funds for the study of mathematics, science, and foreign languages and also to increase the supply of teachers at the college level. Federal grants-in-aid to state and local governments for education increased from $345 million in 1950 to $727 million in 1960. The rush was on to close the education gap.

Social problems were also becoming more visible, Michael Harrington drew attention to the problems of poverty[8] and J. K. Galbraith wrote of the social imbalance of private affluence and public squalor.[9] The blacks were beginning to coalesce into an organized movement toward the end of this period, and soon Rachel Carson was to dramatize the environmental concerns so familiar today.[10] The lull of the Eisenhower years was over.

In the economic realm the Cold War rhetoric focused on another race—the rate of growth of the economy. The growth rate of the United States economy in the 1950s was about 3 per cent, while that of the Soviet economy was 6.5 per cent. It being necessary to establish capitalism's "superiority," there were demands that economic growth be accelerated. Recent growth rates did not differ from long-term averages but the growth rate was too low to provide for the additional jobs needed as the labor force expanded and the productivity of labor increased. While GNP increased, unemployment remained high and excess capacity was widespread. The price level was stable at first and then began to increase slowly. Also, international trade problems added to the troubles in the domestic economy. Somehow, these economic concerns were all to be solved by an adequate rate of growth.

Another economic problem, still with us, began to command attention in this era. The merger movement was on the increase, and the trend towards the concentration of industries continued. Market power of large firms was increased not only *within* industries but *across* industry boundaries as well. The conglomerate movement merely exaggerated the trend towards diversification that had begun earlier. Fewer and fewer firms were gaining control over the United States market, and the problems of this concentrated power were becoming evident.

The presidential campaign of 1960 reflected all of these concerns, but Mr. Nixon judged that economic issues had cost him the election and blamed the Eisenhower economic policies for his defeat.

In the expansionary phase of the cycle monetary policy tended to be restrictive as the Federal Reserve continued its policy of "leaning against the wind." That is, the Federal Reserve did not seek to reduce the money supply but acted to prevent the money supply from increasing. Interest rates rose dramatically, and the Federal Reserve did raise the discount rate several times until it reached 4 per cent by September 1959. Many have argued that monetary policy was tighter than need be in this period and blame the policy on inflationary fears.

The inflation subsided in early 1960, and it became apparent that the problem would once again be recession. This time the Federal Reserve acted to ease monetary conditions, although the response was not strong and perhaps a little late. Bank reserves were increased by open market operations. The reserve requirements were lowered, and the discount rate was lowered by 0.5 per cent in June 1960 and by another 0.5 per cent in August 1960. Interest rates fell at first as these monetary policies became effective, but soon the short-term interest rates were pushed up by deliberate policy.

With unemployment still very high, the short-term interest rates were allowed to rise. This was new to the United States economic policy mix. The Federal Reserve had become concerned over the balance-of-payments problem and particularly

---

[8] Michael Harrington, *The Other America* (Baltimore: Penguin Books, 1963).

[9] J. K. Galbraith, *The Affluent Society* (Boston: Houghton Mifflin, 1958).

[10] Rachel Carson, *The Silent Spring* (Boston: Houghton Mifflin, 1962).

over the movement of short-term capital outflows. The Federal Reserve attempted to discourage such capital outflows by keeping short-term interest rates high and long-term interest rates low to prevent adverse reactions for investment at home. Thus, it bought long-term obligations and sold short-term ones—a maneuver called "operation twist." The small foreign trade sector (in relation to GNP) was thus able to dictate monetary policy, and monetary conditions could not be eased further despite the high unemployment rate. A new constraint was added to the effectiveness of monetary policy.

Another outgrowth of this general problem was the abandonment of the "bills only" doctrine, since the Federal Reserve was forced to deal in long-run securities as well. Monetary policy was forced to recognize its own dilemma with regard to interest rates. High short-term rates may discourage domestic investment and low rates may encourage capital outflows. However, long-term rates could have the same effect, so that "operation twist" could only attack one element of the problem. How effective monetary policy was in this period cannot be judged with certainty. Too much depends upon the power of interest rates to affect behavior both for investment and for capital flows. If interest rates have little effect on domestic investment, then the Federal Reserve was too timid in stopping the capital outflows. At the same time, however, it did not pay enough attention to the domestic economy and the high unemployment. Perhaps too much was (and is) expected of monetary policy anyway, as this period may well demonstrate.

Fiscal policy was also not stimulating enough to battle the sluggishness in the economy. The Eisenhower administration still clung to the limited government, balanced budget philosophy. The full employment surplus shows the restrictiveness of the federal budget. In 1959 the full employment surplus was something like $6 billion, and for the year 1960 the surplus more than doubled, to about $13 billion. Despite the budget philosophy prevailing, the actual budget (national income accounts basis) showed a deficit of $10.2 billion for the calendar year 1958, the largest deficit ever. In 1959 the deficit fell to $1.2 billion, and in the recession year of 1960 the budget showed a *surplus* of $3.5 billion.

Aside from increased grants-in-aid to states for highway construction (going from some $0.4 billion in 1950 to over $2.8 billion in 1960, with the large increases occurring after 1971), little can be said of deliberate fiscal policy action by the Eisenhower administration. Indeed, the shock of the 1959 budget deficit caused a basic *reduction* in (administration budget) expenditures and an *increase* in taxes in 1960. Whatever policies were undertaken in response to the recession were small and made with great reservations by the administration.

Summary

The record of the first four postwar recessions with regard to deliberate fiscal and monetary policy is not very distinguished. For the most part, the tools of macroeconomic policy were seldom used, and if used, were employed timidly and too late. Deliberate monetary policy actions were at least attempted. Deliberate fiscal policy actions to control the business cycle simply were not undertaken. Whatever effects changes in the budget had upon the economic system were fortuitous at best and sometimes perverse. In summary, monetary and fiscal policies were either not employed or not well employed, and the record of deliberate macroeconomic policies up to the beginning of the 1960s was unsatisfactory. The gap between economic knowledge and political acceptance of that knowledge was still great.

The Prosperity of the 1960s, Ending in the Recession of 1969–1970

According to Walter Heller, when John F. Kennedy took office his knowledge of modern economics was not significantly greater than that of previous presidents. Balanced budgets were still considered sound, and prudent financial policies and frugality in government spending were still held to be virtues. Kennedy, however, was to reverse himself, and with the help of the CEA, he finally embraced the principles of the new economics.[11] His conversion, however, was not shared by many in Congress, and he was never to see the results of the theoretical possibilities in which he had come to believe. This will become evident as we resume the description of the economic and political situation in his administration.

The recovery following the trough of February 1961 was to last throughout the 1960s—it was one of the longest periods of prosperity. Still, it was a strange period, and many events influenced and overshadowed the economic situation. The structural problems that had begun to plague the United States economy in the 1950s continued into the 1960s and brought still more confusion to an expanding economy unprepared to deal with them. The entire decade is so packed with events—extraneous and pertinent to the economic system—that it is best to break up the period in order to discuss it intelligently. Naturally, any conclusions reached about such turbulent periods as this one must remain tentative and somewhat debatable.

THE ECONOMIC POLICIES OF THE KENNEDY ADMINISTRATION

John F. Kennedy assumed office in January 1961. It was not a happy time, and economic woes contributed to the general mood of unease. The recession, however, was waning and, as we know in retrospect, was to come to an end the following month. Kennedy took office with the promise to get the economy and the country moving again toward new frontiers of progress and growth. The promise of change may well have been sufficient to stimulate the expectations and hopes of many who had wrestled with the pervasive uncertainty. This was an important, although unmeasurable, factor in the economic recovery that followed shortly thereafter and should be kept in mind as we recount the economic conditions facing the new administration.

In January 1961 the unemployment rate stood at 6.6 per cent, the manufacturing sector's use of capacity stood at 74 per cent, and the national output was falling slowly. In the second quarter of 1961 this picture began to change as GNP (in current prices) increased by 9.3 per cent at annual rates and by the end of the year to 10.7 per cent. Unemployment, however, remained high and by year's end was still 6 per cent of the labor force. Capacity utilization increased a little, to 80 per cent, but the existence of slack in the economy could not be denied, and the idle resources became a national concern. Prices continued stable throughout 1961, while the money supply grew at the modest rate of around 3 per cent.

Clearly, the recovery had begun, but in a modest way and largely from the impetus in the private sector. Again it was the change in the inventories component of investment spending that was largely responsible for the reversal of economic trends. The change in inventories went from −$3.5 billion in the first quarter of 1961 to +$2.1 billion in the second quarter of 1961—a $5.6 billion change. The other sectors lagged behind, but by the end of the year consumption expenditures

---

[11] See the section on the education of presidents in Walter W. Heller, *New Dimensions of Political Economy* (Cambridge, Mass.: Harvard University Press, 1966), pp. 29–41.

had increased by 4.5 per cent, fixed investment by 7.1 per cent, and government expenditures by 6.7 per cent; net exports *fell* by almost 20 per cent.

It was a slow recovery and not much of it could be attributed to direct government actions. The automatic stabilizers did most of the work, and the real changes came from the private sector. Direct actions of government were more concerned with improved and enlarged transfer payments, accelerated public works programs, increased farm price supports, and similar actions. On the monetary side, the Federal Reserve pursued a relatively easy money policy and continued operation twist, designed to keep long-term interest rates low and short-term rates high.

There were, however, some interesting developments in this period, whose influence may never fully be known. One of these was the investment tax credit against new investment. The tax break, it was thought, would stimulate investment spending, boost the economy, and at the same time foster greater economic growth and productivity. The business community was suspicious of this Democratic initiative, and Congress postponed action on the matter. Both groups were later to change their minds, but for the present period only a nebulous result can be traced to this tax proposal—diminished hostility between business and government.

A second proposal that has proved to be quite influential was contained in the *Economic Report of the President* for 1962—the wage and price guideposts.[12] Just how the guideposts were supposed to work is already familiar to us and need not be discussed again. The important point is that the proposal was made at all. At a time when unemployment was so high and prices so stable, it should have seemed inappropriate to consider even voluntary restraints on wage and price decisions. Yet in the discussions that ensued, who is to measure the impact of these concepts on the minds of those affected? Which actions were undertaken as a consequence and which ones postponed?

The economy continued to expand in 1962 as GNP in current dollars increased by 7.7 per cent, to $560.3 billion; GNP in 1958 dollars increased by 6.6 per cent, to $529.8 billion. Unemployment fell, but only to 5.5 per cent of the labor force. The expansion was not vigorous enough and actually had begun to slow down. Capacity utilization increased somewhat, but the rate of utilization still hovered around 81 per cent. Prices continued relatively stable as output and employment increased.

The Federal Reserve permitted the money supply—demand deposits plus currency—to grow by only 1.5 per cent. However, in permitting member banks to increase the rate of interest payable on time deposits, the amount of time deposits grew by over 15 per cent, so that the broader concept of the money supply increased by over 7 per cent. The income velocity of money thus remained fairly stable at approximately 3.8 for 1961 and 1962. The Federal Reserve continued to use monetary policy to combat capital outflows and thus attempted to keep long-term rates low.

The slowdown in the rate of expansion was blamed primarily on the investment sector. The rate of increase in investment spending had declined. Two important proposals in this area were offered by the administration and accepted by Congress. Both would presumably stimulate investment and economic growth. In July the

[12] The *Economic Report of the President* for 1962 stands as a far-sighted, stimulating document that provoked many economic discussions and educated many, including the president. It contained discussions on the full employment surplus concept, economic growth, the trade problems, and the wage-price dilemma—all leading issues of the era. Economics was becoming respectable.

Treasury announced new depreciation schedules for tax purposes: rates were increased and quicker write-offs of capital goods allowed. In October, Congress passed the investment tax credit, which made investment projects more profitable. The impact of these measures would be felt, if at all, in the next period.

The slowdown in the rate of expansion resulted in a deficit in the federal budget of $3.8 billion (national income accounts basis). Revenues simply failed to grow as expected. In the midst of this slowdown President Kennedy pledged a tax reduction to stimulate the economy. This was a remarkable proposal—to reduce taxes when the budget was already registering a deficit. (This was a long way from the balanced budget philosophy.)

Accordingly, the administration's tax program for 1963 honored the pledge made earlier. Both individual and corporate taxes were to be reduced, with the reduction to individuals being around $8 billion and to corporations around $2.5 billion. Most of the reduction was to be the result of lower tax rates, but some reform measures were incorporated as well. The fate of this proposal was stormy, as we will see, and marked a peculiar turning point in political economy.

One final action deserves mention in this brief summary. In response to continued balance-of-payments problems and the lagging growth of exports, the Kennedy administration pushed for and received in the Trade Expansion Act of 1962 the power to negotiate tariff reductions. As the Common Market grew in power, many feared its tariff policy would severely injure the United States ability to export. The Trade Expansion Act of 1962 envisioned freer world trade by world wide reduction in tariff and trade barriers. The act gave the president the power to bargain for tariff reduction. The rather sweeping authority reflected the perilous state of United States trade and balance-of-payments problems.

Any discussion of the year 1962 would be incomplete without mention of two vastly different confrontations that occurred. The first of these was the clash between the president and the steel companies over violation of the wage-price guideposts. The United Steelworkers had announced that the union would abide by the guideposts in its wage demands. Administration pressure had succeeded, but in April the U.S. Steel Corporation announced a $6-a-ton price increase. As customary, other steel firms followed quickly with comparable price increases. Kennedy publicly denounced the price hike as selfish and irresponsible and made some threats of antitrust action and closer examination of government procurement policies. The steel companies relented and rolled back the price increase, but Congress and Wall Street were quite upset over the entire episode. In the public spotlight the steel companies chose to retreat, but not for long. In time, the anger of Congress and the frustrations of Wall Street subsided, but the lesson was not forgotten by those who were watching the emerging relationship between business and government.

The other confrontation of 1962 was a terrifying one. In October 1962 the Kennedy administration challenged the Russians over their Cuban missile deployment. The world seemed to stop. How many lives were changed and how many plans were altered as a result will never be known, of course, nor will economic data reveal the response of economic units to the events of this period. The newly instituted investment tax credit must have seemed trivial in comparison to possible annihilation.

The increasing insecurity continued into 1963, and the Cold War began to take on a new dimension—the space race. Men were now regularly orbiting the earth and looking at the moon. Federal expenditures for space research and technology, which had been $0.5 billion in 1960, had increased to $3.4 billion (national income accounts basis) in 1963.

Still the economy was sluggish, and GNP grew by only 5.4 per cent (4.0 per cent in real terms), to $590.5 billion. Unemployment continued high, at around 5.6 per cent, while manufacturers operated at 83 per cent of capacity. The economy was advancing too slowly, and one result of this was the prospect of another federal deficit, as tax receipts were much less than anticipated.

With these conditions in mind, the Kennedy administration once again pressed for a tax cut in order to stimulate the economy. The intriguing part of this fiscal action was that the proposed tax cut was also accompanied by large *increases* in expenditures (not to mention tax reforms, which were quickly thrown out). This proved too much for fiscal conservatives, and they delayed action on the tax bill and began cutting the expenditures. The Kennedy program was wrecked, and his fiscal policy initiatives are still being examined for their effectiveness. The investment tax credit has been said to have stimulated some several billions in investment expenditures, while the effectiveness of the wage-price guideposts may never be known, although it is endlessly debated. What new directions his fiscal action might have taken and what compromises he might have been willing to live with also will never be known, for he was dead in November 1963.

THE ECONOMIC POLICIES OF THE JOHNSON ADMINISTRATION

Lyndon B. Johnson took office immediately, and the Kennedy economic initiatives were continued. President Johnson was noted for his ability to persuade and to manipulate, and his politics of consensus soon resulted in the enactment of the tax cut bill (by promising to cut expenditures and be frugal); the Economic Opportunity Act of 1964 (by reducing expenditures on national defense); and other domestic legislation such as the mass transit bill, the interest equalization tax on foreign securities, and new farm legislation. The relationship of the president with Congress during this period is a fascinating one, which will occupy historians and political scientists for some time to come. So, too, will economists be interested in the economic results of the fiscal actions taken.

The major fiscal action was, of course, the tax cut. The bill provided for over $11 billion in tax reductions—$9 billion for individuals and over $2 billion for corporations. The effects of the tax cut have been debated, Walter Heller maintaining that it was a complete success and that it wiped out a full employment surplus of a like amount,[13] and Milton Friedman claiming that it has not been shown to be successful and that any credit must go to monetary policy.[14] It is generally conceded, however, that the tax cut worked, and for the time being, the debate over monetary versus fiscal policy can be set aside.

The tax bill was signed into law in February 1964 and was designed to affect the economy quickly by providing for the immediate reduction in withholding rates to match the new lower tax rates. GNP increased by 8.1 per cent from the last quarter of 1963 to the first quarter of 1964, and the remaining quarterly increases (at annual rates) were 6.8, 7.1, and 3.9. For the year, GNP increased by 7.1 per cent, to $632.4 billion; GNP in 1958 dollars increased by 5.4 per cent. All

[13] See Heller, *New Dimensions of Political Economy*, p. 70.

[14] See, for instance, M. Friedman in a dialogue with W. Heller in *Monetary Versus Fiscal Policy* (New York: W. W. Norton, 1969), p. 56.

components of GNP increased: consumption by 7 per cent, investment by 8 per cent, net exports by 44 per cent, and government demand by 5 per cent. Prices increased moderately, with the implicit price index climbing by 1.6 points, the CPI by 1.4 points, and the WPI by 0.2 points. Unemployment began to fall somewhat, to 5.0 per cent in the summer and to 4.9 by year's end. Greater use was also found for manufacturing capacity, and the utilization rate climbed to over 85 per cent. The money supply increased at the modest rate of about 3.8 per cent over the year and interest rates remained stable. Net exports rose in this period as exports grew, but the balance of payments still showed a deficit as private capital outflow continued. It appeared as if the economy were progressing nicely—according to the textbook, said Walter Heller—but events in the Bay of Tonkin were to change all that and forever becloud the issue of just how effective the fiscal actions were.

The analysis of the economy and actions to influence its direction becomes increasingly difficult from the mid-1960s to the present. This is partly because it is too recent a time period for final judgments, but beyond this, the changes in all areas of life became more rapid, more intertwined, and more subtle in their interaction with the economic system. Here, for instance, are a few events to illustrate the problems of analysis: the political campaign of 1964 saw the nation polarized and upset by the starkly contrasting views of conservatism versus liberalism; the Chinese had exploded a nuclear bomb; in early 1965 North Vietnam was bombed and the public was uninformed of what was happening (in fact, many believe, misled); the universities experienced further activism and unrest; Martin Luther King was to lead a civil rights march in Selma, Alabama; the poor expected much from the war on poverty, which turned out to be more like a skirmish; promises were made but did not dispel an incipient sense of unease.

Our inability to link these developments directly with the economic system should not prevent us from looking at the economy's performance in this period. The first half of 1965 made economists look good, and the textbook case seemed verified. GNP was growing at an annual rate of between 8 and 10 per cent, with relative price stability. The unemployment rate declined slowly to 4.5 per cent by summer, while capacity utilization climbed to a rate of over 88 per cent. Monetary policy continued accommodating as the slow growth in the money stock (M_1) was bolstered by a more rapid increase in time deposits. Interest rates were stable; some confidence was returning as gross investment climbed by 8 per cent in the first quarter of 1965.

In the summer of 1965 Johnson asked for additional funds for national defense and warned of further requests in the next budget. The United States economy was disturbed for years following this build-up in defense spending. Gone was the steady expansion and stability. Money GNP increased at a rate of over 10 per cent and real GNP by over 8 per cent in the last half of 1965. The economy began to heat up as the unemployment rate declined further, to 4.1 per cent at year's end, and capacity utilization rose to over 89 per cent. The implicit price index rose by 1.5 points and the CPI by 2 points and the WPI by 3 points from the beginning of the year. It was clear (in retrospect) that some restraining action would be required.[15] Either taxes would have to be increased, nondefense expenditures cut, or monetary restraints instituted. The signals were there and apparently recognized by the CEA in its warnings to the president.

[15] One of the more illuminating accounts of this period is found in Arthur Okun's book *The Political Economy of Prosperity* (New York: W. W. Norton, 1970).

Politics, however, got in the way, and no tax increase was proposed in 1965 or for 1966. A war tax would be difficult to defend before Congress and the public. Nondefense expenditures were not cut either—we would have guns and butter. In fact, excise taxes were *reduced* in 1965 and Social Security benefits *increased* (the added tax to begin in 1966) and made retroactive to January 1st. Fiscal restraints were out.

Monetary authorities, sensing danger all year long, increased the discount rate in December from 4.0 to 4.5 per cent to combat inflationary pressures. In June, W. M. Martin, chairman of the board of the Federal Reserve, had made a speech condemning current stock market speculation as having "disquieting similarities" with the 1929 situation, and now the Federal Reserve was applying monetary brakes to the longest boom in history. Johnson and the CEA were irate and insisted that the action should have awaited the new budget. Once again, the peculiar institutional arrangements of the Federal Reserve system came under attack. The independent nature of the United States central bank had been attacked for a long time, and the battle simply heated up. The antagonism quieted down soon after it became apparent that the Federal Reserve was correct in its assessment and as soon as the Johnson administration realized that its own failure to provide fiscal restraint meant that it could hide behind its arguments while gratefully watching the monetary authorities take action.

Meanwhile, the guideposts, still ostensibly in force, gradually gave way to mere jawbone control, as the administration lost its credibility and as inflationary pressures began to force price and wage decisions. As 1965 came to an end, the unemployment rate was falling; GNP was increasing; profits were rising; prices were rising; interest rates were rising; and everyone appeared to be enjoying the boom and looking to 1966 to see how long it would last.

The year 1966 saw a continuation of these trends. Fiscal policy continued to be ignored in favor of monetary policy. The suspension of the investment tax credit late in 1966 proved to be the only major fiscal policy action. True, nondefense programs of the "Great Society" were probably held down in the anti-inflationary budget and thus may have constituted some form of fiscal restraint, but reductions in these programs, in the opinion of many, hurt the country in subsequent years. Meanwhile, expenditures on national defense surged ahead as the Vietnam War escalated. National defense spending increased by over $10 billion, or 21 per cent, over 1965. Private sector demand continued strong as investment rose by over 12 per cent and consumption by over 7 per cent. Only the foreign trade sector continued its decline.

Accordingly, GNP rose to $749.9 billion in 1966, 9.5 per cent over 1965 (6.5 per cent in real terms). The size of the increase fooled many who had predicted a much smaller increase. Prices also continued their upward spiral as the implicit price index rose by 3.0 points, the CPI by 3.2 points, and the WPI by 3.4 points. All indexes showed signs of steady increases. Unemployment declined still further, to an annual average of 3.8 per cent, while capacity utilization increased to over 91 per cent.

The story of this period, however, is concerned mainly with monetary policy. Monetary policy was the only restraining force, and the monetary authorities became the culprits standing in the way of the boom. But as Okun put it, "In this episode, the Federal Reserve's independence proved to be a valuable national asset. It permitted the President and his administration to assume a passive role, tolerating an unpopular tight money policy silently without explicitly approving or endorsing it."[16]

The Federal Reserve restrained the economy rather selectively, as monetary policy simply could not do the job alone. The growth in the (simple) money supply fell to 2 per cent, and in the latter half of the year to zero, although time deposits continued to grow at 8 per cent. Although the discount rate remained constant, interest rates shot up to their highest levels since the 1920s. Yet the "credit crunch" hit the economy unevenly as the housing market virtually collapsed, with new housing starts falling from over 1.4 million units at the beginning of the year to 0.9 million units at the end. Mortgage interest rates rose close to 7 per cent on FHA loans, and even the prime rate of interest climbed to 6 per cent. Still, recent studies have shown that this credit squeeze had little importance to business spending on investment or on inventory accumulation.[17] This evidence is extremely important as further confirmation of the relative unimportance of the rate of interest as a determinant in the investment decision.

As implied in the growth of time deposits, personal saving as a percentage of disposable income had been increasing since 1965, and this trend accelerated toward the end of 1966. Some have attributed the increase to monetary policy and to higher interest rates. Others have noted that in times of extreme uncertainty people tend to save more. This was such a period, with the administration threatening a tax increase and the war taking on added importance.

Whatever the reason, consumption began to decline and the repeal of investment tax credit may have helped to slow the growth in capital spending. Toward the end of 1966 it appeared as if the economy were headed for a recession. Accordingly, monetary policy became less stringent and congressional critics less vociferous in the attack on the Federal Reserve System. The economic outlook for 1967 was much debated. There was little agreement among forecasters, businessmen, and politicians—they could only disclose by their contrary opinions both the uncertainty of the economic future and the precariousness of the art of forecasting. Talk of recession was contradicted by forecasts of an inflationary boom.

The record shows that the economy did experience a slowdown in early 1967. Money GNP rose by only 0.5 per cent from the fourth quarter of 1966 to the first quarter of 1967 and by 1.3 per cent in the next quarter. In 1958 dollars, GNP *fell* by 0.2 per cent and rose by 0.8 per cent in the same time period. In the latter half of the year the growth in GNP returned to the higher levels of preceding years. For the year, money GNP increased by 5.9 per cent, to $793.9 billion, while real GNP increased by only 2.6 per cent.

Other signs were mixed. Investment in capital goods fell off in the first half of 1967; the unemployment rate continued below 4 per cent; the capacity utilization rate fell by several percentage points; prices were moving upward, mostly in the CPI; and new housing starts rebounded in 1967 as monetary restraint was relaxed. The performance of the economy was mixed and gave confusing signals.

Faced with these developments, the administration decided that a tax increase

---

[16] Ibid., p. 81.

[17] See Jean Crockett, Irwin Friend, and Henry Shavell, "The Impact of Monetary Stringency on Business Investment," *Survey of Current Business* 47 (August 1967): 10–27. Further evidence can be found in a followup work by Henry Shavell and John T. Woodward, "The Impact of the 1969–70 Monetary Stringency on Business Investment," *Survey of Current Business* 51 (December 1971): 19–32.

would be wise to head off the inflationary boom it saw in the guns-and-butter philosophy. Congress and others saw no particular signs that a tax increase was necessary at this time and fought the administration tax surcharge proposal. Congress based its decision on current facts despite repeated efforts by the CEA to look ahead at the forecasts of the economy without a tax increase. Congress remained adamant and no tax bill was passed in 1967.

In defense of this congressional reluctance to comply with the wishes of the administration, it must be admitted that the economic picture was most unclear, with so many of the problems we have noted in previous cycles entering in at the same time and interacting to create confusion. Wilbur Mills, chairman of the House Ways and Means Committee, argued that no signs of *demand pull* inflation appeared to justify a tax increase, and his voice carried much weight.

As if to justify Mills's position, the administration's second major fiscal policy action was to restore the investment tax credit in May 1967, after it became apparent that the level of investment spending was falling in early 1967. Why a tax increase now? Was cost push inflation the problem anyway?

Monetary policy continued expansionary, the money supply increasing by over 7 per cent and time deposits by over 15 per cent. In April the Federal Reserve reduced the discount rate to 4 per cent; bank reserves rose at a rapid rate; deposits grew in thrift institutions; and in general, monetary policy was quite accommodating. Still, interest rates rose to new highs, reflecting a variety of situations and culminating in some puzzling reactions in financial markets. All levels of government were borrowing heavily, as were corporations that had been stung by the credit squeeze of 1966. Perhaps *expecting interest rates to rise still higher*, corporations borrowed, thus driving the rates up. The expectations were based on the uncertain tax changes and the fear that monetary restraints would again be relied upon.

The tax bill was not enacted in 1967, and the federal deficit soared to over $12 billion, largely because of the increase in national defense expenditures. With private demand increasing as well, the pressures on the price level grew. The implicit price index rose by 2.6 points in the last half of 1967, the CPI rose by 2.2 points in six months, and the WPI held stable. Under the stimulus of defense expenditures, the economy was pushing ahead without restraint or prospects of deliberate action to cool it off. The public was told the war would soon be over, and plans were aired for the peacetime economy.

The international trade situation offered no solace as the balance of payments again registered a large deficit. United States government grants and private capital outflows were larger than the net positive balance of goods and services. Indeed, the international community was upset over the trade situation in Britain and the United States. There were calls to put these houses in order. In November 1967 Britain devalued the pound from $2.80 to $2.40, and the Federal Reserve responded by increasing the discount rate back to 4.5 per cent to signal that the United States would defend the exchange rates vis-à-vis the dollar.

The United States had experienced a continuing deficit in trade transactions since the late 1950s. In the 1960s the trend worsened as imports grew in the inflationary period following 1965. Private capital outflow, including direct investment abroad, also increased from the mid-1960s. Finally, the Vietnam War and defense activities also contributed to the imbalance as government grants and loans grew. The situation was getting serious, and the calls for reform of the International Monetary Fund and trading policies increased. In September 1967 the IMF staff met in Rio de Janeiro to deal with the problems of diminishing reserves and other trade practices.

The administration's response to the worsening trade situation was to impose the interest equalization tax and to reduce the duty-free quotas of tourists. In addition, the private sector was asked to control voluntarily the amount of travel and investment abroad.

The international situation should not be underestimated, as can be seen in this astonishing statement by Arthur Okun: "The pleas and threats, the cajolery and rebukes of central bankers around the World had a major impact on our political process. . . . Without the World bankers, I seriously doubt that we would have enacted the fiscal program that was so urgently needed for our own good."[18] This statement reflects the prevailing political mood of the country and acknowledges that something had to be done. Meanwhile, the Vietnam War continued to drain the country of its strength, unity, and pride, and now a new confrontation in the spring of 1967 in the Middle East threatened to explode into a worldwide crisis. Despair in the ghettos resulted in riots in Newark and Detroit in the hot summer; and in October there was a massive peace march in Washington—the Pentagon was besieged. The year 1967 gave way to 1968 in an uncertain, insecure, and unpromising mood.

Events in early 1968 shook the nation still further: the U.S.S. *Pueblo* was seized by the North Koreans in January; the Tet offensive upset the military predictions that the war would end; the ghetto riots were blamed on white racism by the Kerner Commission; President Johnson announced he would not seek reelection after the New Hampshire primary results; Martin Luther King was assassinated in April and Robert Kennedy in June; Vietnam peace talks began in Paris on May 10th.

It is against this background that the economic actions of this period must ultimately be weighed. The long-sought tax increase was finally enacted and signed into law in June but made retroactive to April 1st. It provided for a 10 per cent surcharge on individual and corporate incomes. The tax increase was *officially* proposed in January 1967, although talk of tax increases had been going on for months prior to that date. The tax increase was to prove too little and too late—it had already been absorbed into the plans of economic units, and the actual impact of the tax was slight because of this prior discounting.

The tax increase could not match mounting government expenditures, despite the coercing actions of Congress to put a ceiling on them. Johnson was forced to accept a $6 billion reduction in his expenditures budget in return for the tax increase. Still, defense expenditures were exempted from any spending ceiling and expenditures in Vietnam alone climbed to $25 billion per year. Continued inflation was assured.

GNP in current dollars rose by 8.9 per cent, but real GNP rose by only 4.7 per cent over the 1967 level. The price level advances were ominous as the implicit price index rose by 4.7 points, the CPI by 4.2 points, and the WPI by 2.5 points (now both indexes have 1967 = 100), and there was no additional restraining force in sight.

The expected decline in private spending did not materialize, and both consumption and investment spending continued strong. Writing of this period, Okun admits the failure of economists to appreciate fully the moving forces in the

---

[18] Okun, *The Political Economy of Prosperity,* p. 89.

economic system or to explain their interaction. Expectations must have played a large part in the puzzling reactions in the private sector, and he states, "We would have to learn the paradoxical lesson that uncertainty about the nature of a policy of restraint may temporarily have a restraining effect even greater than that of the actual restraining measures."[19] And even more bluntly:

The difficulties of explaining the movements of private demand and the responses to public policy during 1968–69 remind us of how much economists have to learn. They also remind us that changes in attitudes in the private economy can at times swamp decisions of public policy. They argue for humility in our discussions of the economic outlook and for flexibility in the making of policy.[20]

The tax increase did not work as expected but just why remained obscure. Was it buoyant expectations, an inflationary psychology, or a reversal of reactions to a "peace scare"? Monetary policy fared no better. The Federal Reserve raised the discount rate in April to 5.5 per cent, but the rising interest rates did not stem spending. The money supply grew at over 7 per cent and time deposits by over 11 per cent as higher interest rates were permitted on savings accounts. In the latter half of 1968 the restrictive policies moved again towards accommodation as high interest rates and fiscal policy actions led to the belief that monetary policy would be too restrictive. The change in policy was only to make matters worse, for as we have seen, the boom was not restrained by fiscal actions.

Capacity utilization continued stable, and the unemployment rate stayed below the 4 per cent mark. Unit labor costs, however, rose by over 4 per cent as money wages began to rise at a faster rate in 1968.

In the latter half of 1968 world events continued to shatter complacency: there was the crisis in Biafra and the Russian invasion of Czechoslovakia; the Democratic convention in Chicago was a battleground and millions looked on in horror and disbelief at the spectacle of violence and bloodshed. It was a year in which the Pope banned all methods of birth control while Paul Ehrlich published the influential book *The Population Bomb* (Ballantine Books), which warned of the dangers of population growth. It was a strange year—men flew around the moon, and Richard M. Nixon was elected President of the United States.

Economic Conditions Under the Nixon Administration

President Johnson left office proposing a budget that would shift to a surplus balance to bring some restraint from the fiscal side. He also proposed that the surcharge be extended from its original expiration date of June 30, 1969, to June 30, 1970. President Nixon accepted these proposals and pledged to restore stability to the economy and to rely primarily on the free market to do the job—there were to be no guideposts, no jawboning, no moral judgments.

It soon became apparent that the expansion was not over as GNP advanced rapidly in the first and second quarters of 1969. Both quarters showed an increase at an annual rate of 7 per cent. However, prices also soared, and the inflationary pressures felt earlier were not subsiding. The implicit and CPI price indexes were rising at an annual rate of over 5.0 per cent, and the WPI index was rising by 3.9 per cent. Capacity utilization and the unemployment rate held stable in this period.

Accordingly, the new administration asked for the repeal of the investment tax

[19] Ibid., p. 95.

[20] Ibid., p. 96.

credit, since investment spending appeared strong enough not to require it. At the same time, April 1969, the administration also proposed that the tax surcharge rate be *reduced* to 5 per cent on January 1, 1970, and be ended entirely on June 30th. Since consumer demand was strong, there was considerable debate on this tax reduction, but it was finally passed. Social Security taxes went up as of January 1, 1969, and there was some cancellation of the tax relief.

Again, monetary policy was asked to provide most of the restraint. The growth of the money supply fell to under 4.5 per cent (at annual rates) in the first half of 1969, and in the second half the growth rate fell to under 1.0 per cent at annual rates. Time deposits *fell* by about 5 per cent for the year as interest rates rose on alternative assets. Interest rates had risen to their highest levels, and by May three-month Treasury bills were yielding 6.1 per cent, high-grade corporate bonds close to 7.0 per cent, and municipal bonds 5.5 per cent; the prime rate was 7.4 per cent; and the FHA mortgage yield was over 8 per cent. In April the Federal Reserve raised the discount rate to 6 per cent and increased the reserve requirement by 0.5 per cent.

Still investment spending surged on, and only the housing market was seriously affected by the high and rising interest rates. Consumer spending also continued strong, and only towards the end of the period did consumption begin to fall off and saving increase. The rate of growth of GNP began to slow down in the last quarter of 1969 to an annual rate of under 4 per cent. For the year, GNP in current dollars had increased by 7.6 per cent, 2.7 per cent in real terms.

Prices rose throughout 1969, and interest rates rose still further—the prime rate stood at close to 9 per cent and tax-free bonds at close to 7 per cent.

Unemployment crept down to around 3.5 per cent, as did the utilization of capacity, which fell to below 85 per cent in the fourth quarter and to 86 per cent for the year. Output per man-hour showed little change from the previous year, although wage increases continued. But the CEA saw signs that the anti-inflation policy was beginning to be effective and predicted that the situation would improve in 1970.

The Nixon administration began withdrawing ground troops from Vietnam in the summer of 1969, but what effect this policy had upon the expectations of people and economic units was, and still is, unclear. The United States trade position continued to worsen, and the new administration was soon to approach our trading partners for concessions. The rest of the world was helping to underwrite United States foreign policies and the United States inflationary boom—some friction was inevitable.

The economic situation at the end of 1969 was ambiguous, with the growth rate of GNP declining, unemployment stable, and prices rising rapidly. The administration, fearful of making inflation worse but concerned over a possible slump, decided to pursue a policy of moderation. Fiscal and monetary policies would be employed in moderation to restore stability, even if the time horizon had to be lengthened by a policy of "gradualism." In its review of Johnson's 1970 budget, the administration proposed to cut government expenditures by $4.0 billion and pledged to hold expenditures down to $192.9 billion for fiscal 1970.

The economy failed to respond to the policies adopted by the Nixon administration. In fact, the economic condition worsened. Current dollar GNP for the year rose by only 5.0 per cent, with the middle quarters pushing up the growth rates of the first and last quarters. GNP in 1958 dollars actually *fell* by 0.4 per cent from

1969, the first break in an expansion that began in 1961. The economy was sluggish; demand failed to grow, and the situation was only aggravated by an auto strike in the last quarter of 1970.

The administration's plan was to get the economy moving by a moderate stimulus in policy. The Federal Reserve increased the rate of growth of the money supply early in 1970, and for the year the growth rate was around 5.5 per cent. Still, interest rates did not fall significantly in the first half of 1970, but very likely investment spending would have collapsed anyway if it was based more on expectations and physical capacity than on monetary considerations. The Federal Reserve also took action to increase the reserves of commercial banks by raising the maximum interest rates payable on time deposits. The discount rate was lowered twice, down to 5.5 per cent. These monetary actions failed to influence the economy significantly.

Fiscal policy was on the passive side. Defense expenditures were reduced by $3 billion, and other expenditures were increased by $18 billion, but the increases were forced by the slowdown in economic activity. Thus, Social Security and welfare services rose by $10.3 billion alone. Of course, tax receipts fell, and the budget was thrown into a deficit of some $12 billion. Still the administration resisted new or enlarged spending programs but permitted an expansionary policy largely through the operation of the built-in stabilizers and increased Social Security payments.

The fall in GNP would not have caused much alarm (which it did) had it not been accompanied by some troubling trends in other areas. For despite the sluggish economy, prices continued to increase and so did the unemployment rate.

The implicit price index rose by 7.0 points for the year and was still increasing as the year closed. The CPI rose by 6.5 points (over 5.9 per cent), and the WPI rose by 3.9 points (3.7 per cent), although both growth rates seemed to be moderating in the second half of the year. The rise in prices was not really explained by the CEA, but often past inflationary periods were blamed for the continuation. President Nixon, despite pledges to the contrary, established a form of jawboning now euphemistically called inflation alerts and instructed the CEA to warn of price and wage increases that were deemed to contribute to the inflationary pressures.

Along with the slumping economy and rising prices, the unemployment rate began to creep up and by July had reached 5.0 per cent and by year's end had reached 6.1 per cent. As sales declined and wages rose, employers reduced the work force, not prices. The administration feared that any attack on unemployment would only make the inflation worse. Moreover, the capacity utilization rate declined further and by the last quarter stood at less than 75 per cent. The trade-off between prices and employment became all too obvious.

The stock market tumbled in May and remained in the doldrums for some time. The inflationary psychology spread, and everyone reacted to protect his interests against further inflation. Meanwhile, the war continued—now spread into Cambodia and Laos—causing much unrest, particularly among the young. Economic events cannot be divorced from these disrupting influences.

Still the Nixon administration blamed the economic conditions on the movement from a wartime to a peacetime economy and the inflation on the inherited pressures from previous administrations. It refused to alter its policies for meeting the problems but instead predicted that the economy would improve in 1971 without any drastic action. A deficit of $15 billion (national income accounts basis) was proposed in the federal budget, with a further decline in defense expenditures.

The National Bureau of Economic Research recognized the end of the long upswing that had begun in February 1961. It declared that November 1969 would be acknowledged tentatively as the date of the peak and that November 1970 would be the new trough. This would again make the recession a short one, but as can be seen from the above discussion, the location of these turning points is somewhat arbitrary in most cases and particularly difficult in cases like this one.

Finally, there was a tax change that did not emanate from the administration, which largely opposed it. This was the Tax Reform Act of 1969, which took effect in 1970. The administration believed it to be antibusiness and discouraging to investment and pledged to remedy its damaging effects as soon as possible. Most of the originally proposed reforms were watered down by Congress as the tax bill went through the political process. The main provisions of the bill that emerged were as follows:

1. Removal of the investment tax credit
2. Reduction in depletion allowances
3. Restriction on the use of accelerated depreciation
4. Provision for a minimum tax of 10 per cent of the amount of tax preferences received and a maximum tax of 50 per cent of earned income
5. Imposition of a tax on private foundations' investment income and on their undistributed income
6. An increase in the capital gains tax for large gains and the elimination of banks' and trust companies' use of capital gains on securities
7. Increased personal exemptions and standard deduction amounts
8. Reduction in the tax rates of single individuals and heads of households (the only rate reductions)
9. A new provision for a low-income allowance, giving larger amounts of tax-free income, with the benefit vanishing for incomes over the poverty level

As the year 1971 began, the administration hoped its economic policies would halt the inflationary process and bring the unemployment rate down to 4.5 per cent by the middle of 1972. It promised to be flexible in its policies to attempt to reach these goals.

In the first quarter of 1971 money GNP increased by 3.6 per cent (over 15 per cent at annual rates) and real GNP increased by 2.2 per cent (9 per cent at annual rates) over the last quarter of 1970. The rate of price increases declined in the implicit price index and the CPI, although they continued to increase in the WPI. Capacity utilization was up and the unemployment rate fell slightly. Monetary policy became easier via a faster growth in the money supply. Interest rates began to fall. Net exports rose, as did government expenditures. As yet, there were no dismaying signs in the economy.

In the next two quarters, during the spring and summer of 1971, money GNP fell to an annual growth rate of around 7.2 per cent and real GNP fell to 3.2 per cent annual rate of increase. Despite tax reductions, consumption did not rebound and investment demand was sluggish, although the administration promised to revise depreciation guidelines. Most of all, the foreign trade sector virtually collapsed as imports rose, until by the third quarter the net export balance stood at $1.1, and in the fourth quarter plunged into a deficit of $2.2 billion at annual rates.

Although there was some improvement in the rate of price increases, mainly in the CPI, prices were still rising at over 5 per cent per year. The price behavior of the previous quarter was not sustained, and although a 5 per cent annual price increase can hardly be called hyperinflation, it was a long way from the administration's idea of price stability.

The unemployment rate failed to fall and still hovered around 6 per cent, and the rate of capacity utilization remained very low, at around 74 per cent.

Monetary policy during this period was meant to be more restrictive, as the Federal Reserve was not able to control the growth in the supply of money in the first quarter and moved to reduce the growth rate. The Federal Reserve was again unsuccessful, and the money supply had grown at the annual rate of over 10 per cent to June and by over 16 per cent in the broader definition of the money supply. Discount rates, which had been declining, were reversed in July to the level of 5 per cent. Still, interest rates *rose* as the Federal Reserve attempted to control the growth of the money supply by attempting to influence the federal funds rate (the interest rate on loans *among banks*). The process is complex and little understood—suffice it to say that the Federal Reserve was unable to control the money supply and did not foresee the nation's changing monetary habits or portfolio adjustments.

There appeared to be little expectation that the administration's goals would be achieved if its policies were continued. Therefore, on August 15th, President Nixon, regarded as an economic conservative despite his assurances that he was a Keynesian, announced a change in policy so drastic that it stunned the economy and surprised the whole world. He renounced the free market in favor of direct government controls, a course of action recommended only by outsiders like J. K. Galbraith and other dissenters from Adam Smith's world. The reversal was sudden and apparently secret, for Paul McCracken (chairman of the CEA) had written a somewhat acrimonious piece for the *Washington Post* in which he ridiculed Professor Galbraith and attacked the use of wage and price controls.[21]

President Nixon's program was dubbed the "New Economic Policy" and consisted of the following features:[22]

1. A ninety-day freeze on prices, wages, and rents, with the possibility of continuing mandatory controls after the freeze
2. A tax package to stimulate the economy and, hopefully, employment
   a. A job development credit—a tax credit of 10 per cent in the first year and 5 per cent thereafter for new investment (Congress passed a flat 7 per cent investment tax credit.)[23]
   b. Repeal of the 7 per cent excise tax on automobiles (Congress approved, and also repealed the 10 per cent excise tax on light trucks.)
   c. Timing changes in the individual income tax for scheduled increases in personal exemptions and in the standard deduction (Congress slightly altered the amounts.)
   d. A temporary surcharge of 10 per cent on dutiable imports (No congressional action required)
   e. Establishment of the Domestic International Sales Corporation (DISC) to permit exporters to defer taxes payable on exports to match the tax system on exports used abroad (Congress modified the proposal.)

---

[21] Paul McCracken, "Galbraith and Price-Wage Controls," *Washington Post,* July 28, 1971.

[22] For details of the new economic policy, see *Economic Report of the President* (1972).

[23] Congressional action came with the passage of the Revenue Act of 1971, signed into law on December 10, 1971.

3. Cancellation of contemplated expenditure programs (revenue sharing, welfare reform) or reductions in planned expenditures (federal pay raise, foreign aid) (Congress restored the federal pay raise.)
4. Suspension of the convertibility of the dollar into gold and other reserve assets (No congressional action required)

Looking at these proposals and remembering the developments in the economy, it is difficult to escape the judgment that the balance-of-payments and trade problems really forced these drastic measures. Although this was vehemently denied, price stability and unemployment concerns seemed to play a secondary role.

Whatever the impetus for them, the proposals surprised and overwhelmed everyone, and it was not long before every shade of opinion was heard: conservatives criticized it as anticapitalist—a sellout by a conservative president to radical elements, and so on; liberals went around seeking arguments of the type that the president had gone too far, had usurped power, and so on; radicals saw the demise of capitalism and the fall of the United States economy.

One of the initial criticisms can be dispelled rather quickly—the usurpation of power—for Congress had given the president the power to impose wage and price controls in the Economic Stabilization Act of 1970. Indeed, the power was thrust upon Nixon, who had denied its necessity. The president also had the power to make these decisions with regard to international trade.

It soon became apparent that the initial ninety-day freeze would be followed by another period of some kind of mandatory controls. Accordingly, the initial freeze came to be called Phase I and its successor, Phase II. It seems better to deal with these plans as if they could be separated into the two distinct phases. Obviously, one must be careful about judgments, since the policies of the freeze and the expectations of more controls probably influenced the actions of many economic units. Indeed, uncertainty and confusion were widespread during this entire period, and any arbitrary division into phases can only be justified by simplicity in presentation.

PHASE I

The ninety-day freeze provided as a general policy that the rate of payment during this period could not exceed the rate in effect during the base period, which was the previous month—July 16 to August 14, 1971. The basic rule applied to wages, prices, and rents but *not* to interest rates, profits, or dividends. Exemptions to the freeze were few—raw agricultural products (the main one), export prices, welfare payments, workmen's compensation, and pay increases for promotions or to meet legal requirements.

It would be difficult to characterize the response of the public to these events. For many, controls were welcome, and there was a feeling that something was being done about inflation. Parts of all segments of the society—including labor and business—held these sentiments, and there was some hope for the future and a sense of relief. Others, of course, including many economists, denounced the controls as unnecessary, useless, undemocratic, and wasteful. The Internal Revenue System, which carried out spot checks, found a very high degree of compliance with the rules, and the Office of Emergency Preparedness, which handled most of the administration of the program, had remarkably few violators to prosecute. No one expected the program to work perfectly anyway.

The effect of the freeze on various sectors is interesting. According to the Quarterly Survey of Consumer Attitudes by the University of Michigan, most consumers felt the action by the administration was a good thing, but their buying attitudes did not show improvement. They still feared inflation, unemployment, and new controls over the economy. Apparently, the economic situation was so bad in the last year that they were "turned off" and their confidence in the government and the economy was so low that the "good" news had little effect. The rate of consumption spending fell in the last quarter of 1971, particularly for consumer durables, which would reflect the uncertainty most clearly. This might have been foreseen, for the controls were double-edged in that wages were being controlled as well as prices.

For investment, the only real incentive was the investment tax credit. But manufacturing firms were operating at 74 per cent of capacity and demand was sluggish. What need was there for more investment spending? Accordingly, many critics of the tax break saw the investment tax credit as increasing only profits, not jobs as originally intended. Firms that were replacing capital goods or that had planned new investment spending anyway would now reap the extra profits, but little capital spending was initiated in this period, tax credit or not. Investment did increase but not the type that would provide for additional employment.

The international trade measures designed to improve the terms of trade did produce a fall in imports, but exports fell drastically and net exports went from +$1.1 billion in the third quarter to −$2.2 billion in the fourth quarter.

Government expenditures increased rapidly in the fourth quarter as national defense expenditures rose and agricultural price supports called for larger outlays.

The result of these effects was an increase in money GNP from the third to fourth quarters of over $20 billion, or 8.0 per cent at annual rates; the increase in real GNP was $12 billion, or 6.6 per cent at annual rates. By mid-November the freeze was over and Phase II had begun. Prices could, therefore, rise (within limits) towards the end of the quarter. Thus, the implicit price index showed a modest increase in the fourth quarter of 0.5 points, or an increase of less than 2 per cent per year. Both the consumer price index and the wholesale price index showed similar increases in December after holding stable during the freeze. These price increases were expected by the administration as adjustments and corrections were made throughout the economic system.

Unemployment, however, did not decline, and the rate stood at 6 per cent at year's end. The administration blamed this on the increase in the labor force and a change in its composition. The capacity utilization rate remained stable at the low 74 per cent. Corporate profits rebounded in the fourth quarter, providing fuel to the heated argument that the whole program was weighted to benefit business more than, or at the expense of, other groups.

Monetary policy was mixed in this period, as the Federal Reserve wished to aid the administration's policies but was concerned over the rapid rise in the money stock that was the outcome of earlier actions. Therefore, the discount rate was reduced in November and December to 4.5 per cent. The growth in the stock of money (currency plus demand deposits) turned negative in September, and for October and November it did not grow at all. Interest rates declined slightly. It was clear that fiscal actions were more dramatic in this period.

PHASE II

The price freeze ended on November 13th, and for weeks it was clear that a new program would follow the freeze. The freeze had been used for immediate ends, and no one expected or desired it to be extended. After much speculation and endless debate the president presented his plans for Phase II of the new economic policy on October 7th.[24]

The goal of the post-freeze controls was to stabilize the economy at a rate of price increase in the 2 to 3 per cent range. To achieve this goal a new administrative hierarchy was established. Throughout the development of this system there was a deliberate attempt to keep it simple and avoid the large bureaucratic administration common to systems of direct control.

Accordingly, there were three main agencies created to administer the program: (1) the Cost of Living Council—the final source of power and coordinator of all programs; (2) a Price Commission to rule on cases involving prices and rents; and (3) a Pay Board to rule on wages, salaries, and fringe benefits.

The general guidelines developed by the Price Commission were appropriate mainly to the larger firms and provided for price increases to reflect cost increases or to preserve customary markups, but no increases in *profit margins* were permitted. The Pay Board announced its guidelines in November—the initial wage increase, subject to review by the board, was set at 5.5 per cent annually. Needless to say, these general guidelines were qualified and amended many times; much confusion over the rules and interpretations of them existed for some time, but this eventually gave way to acquiescence.

This brief outline of the first attempt by the United States to institute wage and price controls during peacetime is sufficient to show the radical departure from orthodox prescriptions for an ailing economy. As might be expected, criticism came from all quarters; yet, by and large, these drastic measures were received by the general public with remarkable equanimity. Some control over the economy was welcome, even if the outcome was uncertain. Apparently, strong measures are acceptable if the situation is grave or felt to be getting out of hand—a lesson that should be emphasized to the more doctrinaire schools of thought. Businessmen were wary, while organized labor castigated the entire program as antilabor and probusiness and threatened to wreck the entire plan.

Among economists, Galbraith, of course, must have felt repaid for his many years of proselytizing for wage and price controls. However, the CEA was visibly uncomfortable with direct controls and continually stressed their temporary nature. Some, like Sidney Weintraub, felt that a better incomes policy should have been devised, since the administration of Phase II would elevate into prominence trivial problems and thus allow politicians to avoid the larger issues of the day—war, pollution, justice, health care, and so on.[25] Milton Friedman felt that no type of incomes policy is justified, particularly when the economy is hardly at the crisis stage.[26] Friedman was particularly concerned with moral issues: as people attempt to circumvent the law, they learn disrespect for it. Since the controls probably would not work anyway, he said, the costs of misallocation of resources and the loss of freedom are not worth the benefits. No doubt a poll among economists

---

[24] Without dwelling on the point, it is clear that presenting Phase II at this date may have caused many plans to be altered, postponed, shelved, and so on, which may have restricted the effectiveness of the freeze (and beyond), which still had a month to run. The overlapping of Phases I and II in this manner may preclude an adequate judgment of the freeze period not only for effectiveness but also for degree of compliance.

[25] Sidney Weintraub, "The Lurking Dangers of Phase Two" (Op-Ed Page), *New York Times*, November 13, 1971, p. 33.

[26] Milton Friedman, "Morality and Controls I and II" (Op-Ed Page), *New York Times*, October 28, 1971, p. 41, and October 29, 1971, p. 41.

would have revealed every kind of opinion from one extreme to the other, but most economists in the Western tradition would probably have preferred free market forces to controls.

Needless to say, all the developments that occurred in the economy cannot be ascribed only to direct controls. In late 1971 the president announced his trip to China, which he undertook in February 1972, followed by his trip to the Soviet Union in May. Trade talks were important at both meetings. The war had intensified; the harbor at Haiphong had been mined, and the great powers were meeting. Meanwhile, the presidential campaign was beginning and political considerations would enter into every policy and every speech. Against this background, let us review the economic developments of this period.

The Record of Controls

The CEA forecast an increase of 9.5 per cent in GNP in 1972, a $100 billion increase. Real GNP forecasts were for a 6.0 per cent increase, and thus prices were expected to rise by about 3.25 per cent (and by the end of the year in the 2 to 3 per cent range). All sectors were to grow in demand, with the federal budget showing a deficit (national income accounts basis) of $36 billion and providing a stimulating fiscal policy.

Preliminary estimates for 1972 indicate that money GNP will be about $1,155 billion, or a 9.4 per cent increase over 1971; real GNP will be about 6.1 per cent over the previous year. The implicit price index rose by slightly over 3.0 per cent for the year, while the CPI increased by approximately 3.4 per cent and the WPI by approximately 6.5 per cent. As the year ended, most people were willing to concede that the controls had worked to a large extent, even though the price changes had exceeded planned amounts.

The unemployment rate fell from 6.0 per cent at the beginning of the year to 5.1 per cent at year's end. The fall in the unemployment rate was gradual and paralleled the gradual increase in the rate of capacity utilization, which rose from 75 per cent to approximately 80 per cent.

These improvements in the domestic economy were not matched by significant improvements in foreign trade, since estimates of net exports reveal large deficits continued in 1972. Thus, the foreign trade initiatives of the program appeared to be insufficient to reverse past trends.

Monetary Policy

The Federal Reserve reduced the margin requirements to 65 per cent from 80 per cent during the stock market slump in the spring of 1970. In December 1971 the margin requirement was reduced still further, to 55 per cent on stock. These moves were obviously designed to stimulate a shaky stock market during two disturbing periods—the enlargement of the war into Laos and Cambodia and the uncertainty of Phase II. Whether these measures were justified cannot be judged here. In any case, the margin requirement was increased back to 65 per cent in November 1972.

Discount rates and reserve requirements were not changed during 1972. Monetary policy was then directed primarily to control over monetary aggregates. Towards the end of 1971 the monetary authorities expressed their plan to aid the administration in its efforts to control the economy. They pursued a policy of easy money, as the stock of money grew at a rate of over 8 per cent during 1972.

Interest rates fell slightly but were soon up again to the rates comparable to the last half of 1971 and were still climbing at year's end. With a low discount rate, banks borrowed heavily from the Federal Reserve and the money supply increased accordingly. There was pressure on the Federal Reserve to raise the discount rate. Time deposits continued to grow at a rapid rate—over 12 per cent at annual rates—and the broader money stock definition grew by close to 12 per cent.

International Measures

The trade situation, as noted earlier, had deteriorated rapidly in recent years. The United States was having trouble with both merchandise balances and capital outflow. In 1971 the situation reached a crisis stage; confidence in the dollar collapsed and foreign holders of dollars began rushing to the Treasury to convert them to gold or other reserve assets or foreign currencies.

The dollar was so weakened that on August 15th President Nixon suspended convertibility of the dollar into gold or reserve assets. The dollar, in effect, was allowed to float against other major currencies. This dramatic move was aimed at forcing a realignment of exchange rates, which put the United States at a disadvantage, since the dollar had clearly been overvalued for many years. Therefore, exports were difficult to make while imports enjoyed a price advantage. The suspension of convertibility was meant to shock the international monetary centers into adopting reforms and revisions of international financial arrangements.

In addition, the United States imposed a surcharge of 10 per cent on goods imported into the country. The tax was not applied to all goods but to those where reciprocal trade agreements had previously reduced the duty (about half of United States imports). The administration cleverly maneuvered around this protectionist policy, finally admitting the temporary nature of the tax pending changes in the other areas of trade. The coercion caused many outcries from abroad, since other nations felt unjustly accused of being the cause of the United States troubles.

To underscore the point, the president also announced a 10 per cent reduction in foreign aid—a move designed to force other nations to bear their fair share of the burden of defense.

Finally, the plan called for the aiding of export firms in their taxation, as previously noted. Also, the investment tax credit applied only to domestically produced machinery and equipment as long as the surcharge was in effect.

After much confusion and consternation, representatives of the major nations of the world met in Washington, where the so-called Smithsonian Agreement was reached on December 18th. The agreement provided for the following:

1. A devaluation of the dollar against gold. The price of gold in terms of the dollar was to rise by 8 per cent, to $38.00 per ounce. The devaluation required approval of Congress, which after some chauvinistic speeches finally approved the increase in the price of gold.
2. A proposal was made to the IMF that exchange rates be permitted to vary by ±2.25 per cent against the previous range of ±1.0 per cent.
3. The United States received pledges from other nations to reduce trade barriers and discriminations against United States goods. Also, more funds would be provided for defense by these countries. In return, the United States removed the 10 per cent surcharge on imports.
4. Commitments were made by the major nations to work toward revisions and reforms of the international monetary system.

These moves should have improved the trade position of the United States, because imports became more expensive and our exports had a better chance in world markets. The results, however, were discouraging as the trade balance registered a $6 billion deficit and net exports (on a national income basis) recorded a $4.6 deficit.

Summary

The results of Phase II are mixed, and it may be too early to make final judgments. Debate over the effects of the direct controls began to accelerate at the end of the year in anticipation of the presidential request for authority to extend the controls beyond the expiration date of April 1973. In January 1973 President Nixon characteristically surprised nearly everyone and announced that Phase II would be supplanted by Phase III; this unexpected move changed the debate and, even more important, changed the expectations of economic units, possibly in a way that may preclude accurate judgments of Phase II.

PHASE III

The announcement of Phase III came as a shock, since it was not clear that the battle over inflation had been won. Phase III removed mandatory controls and moved toward voluntary compliance with the guidelines set in Phase II. The administration asked for authority to continue direct controls, and this authority was to act as a threat to business and labor and ensure self-restraint. Rent controls were eliminated and profit margins were permitted to increase if a firm's price increases did not exceed 1.5 per cent. Wage guidelines were to be carried over from Phase II. Only controls over food processing and retailing, construction and health care were to remain intact.

To administer the program, the Pay Board and the Price Commission were abolished and all powers were entrusted to the Cost of Living Council. The goal of Phase III was to reduce inflation to 2.5 per cent or less by the end of 1973 and to accomplish this end by dismantling the restrictive bureaucracy and relying on voluntary restraint.

What made this sudden reversal so unexpected were the recent developments in the economy: unemployment was falling and capacity utilization was increasing, and this combination usually results in price pressures; wholesale prices rose in December 1972 at the highest rate in over twenty years—20.1 per cent at annual rates; food prices (uncontrolled) continued to show increases. Ironically, when unemployment was increasing, capacity utilization was low, and the rate of price increases was decreasing, controls were imposed; when these trends were reversed, controls were removed.

The Record of Phase III

Before turning to the initial impact of Phase III on the economy, it is necessary to reiterate that economic decisions cannot be divorced from other noneconomic events. For example, consider the opposite expectations likely to be generated by two important events occurring in the same period: the war in Southeast Asia was sharply curtailed and the prisoners of war returned, and the Watergate scandal broke into the daily headlines. How these events influenced economic matters will never be known, of course, but it is likely that the optimistic expectations of peace would vie with the feelings of distrust for government and politicians. Moreover, these are only two events of the period, so that the record of the first part of 1973 must be examined rather provisionally.

Aggregate demand spurted in the first quarter of 1973, increasing at an annual rate of over 15 per cent (8.6 per cent in real terms). Personal consumption expenditures increased sharply and government expenditures also increased moderately, while investment remained relatively stable. The rapid rise in GNP caused considerable dismay, for it was accompanied by similar price advances. The implicit price index rose at over a 6 per cent annual rate; the CPI rose at a 9 per cent annual rate; and the WPI rose at a 22 per cent annual rate. Much of the increase in prices could be traced to food prices (never fully controlled), which rose 30 per cent at the consumer level and 60 per cent at the wholesale level. Still, other prices were advancing as well, and the need for cooling-off the economy was voiced by the CEA. A tax increase became a possibility even though President Nixon had campaigned on a pledge of no tax increases. However, the unemployment rate continued at approximately 5 per cent, and the familiar problem of rising prices and high unemployment rates (stagflation) was again apparent.

In the fiscal policy area, the Nixon administration budgets for the ensuing years registered a reduction in nondefense programs, mainly in social welfare, and many programs were cut entirely. Monetary policy moved toward tightness, as the Federal Reserve increased the discount rate to 5.5 per cent and the money stock grew at an annual rate of over 3 per cent. Demand deposits were falling while time deposits continued to increase, so that the broader monetary aggregate, M_2, increased at an annual rate of nearly 6 per cent.

As part of the attempt to correct for trade imbalances, the dollar was again devalued in mid-February 1973. Whether this action will be beneficial or not is too soon to tell, but booming farm exports and capital inflows were favorable signs.

In summary, Phase III removed the lid on suppressed inflation (some say too soon) and the movement to more voluntary controls together with uncertainty and conflicting expectations resulted in the continuation of past trends—rising prices, demand pressures accompanied by considerable unemployment, and balance-of-payment concerns. By the second quarter of 1973 it was apparent to all that Phase III had failed. During that period all prices had risen: consumer prices at an annual rate of 9 per cent, wholesale prices at an annual rate of 23 per cent, and the implicit price index at an annual rate of 15 per cent. Food prices particularly continued their upward spiral as grain shortages developed while demand continued to be strong. Still, the unemployment rate and the capacity utilization rate remained at the levels of the beginning of the period. Accordingly, in mid-June 1973, President Nixon announced the second price freeze, this time for only sixty days, on all prices. Other factor rewards were not frozen, since they more or less conformed to Phase II standards.

THE SECOND FREEZE

The second price freeze was greeted with considerably less enthusiasm than the earlier one. Business hostility toward the move combined with the inevitable projections to Phase IV, which was sure to follow, resulted in more grumbling and less cooperation. The failure of voluntary controls created much uncertainty over what was in store in Phase IV, which proved to be very similar to Phase II.

In other areas, the administration imposed export controls on grains and soybeans in the attempt to control food prices; however, federal expenditures continued to increase, and no change in taxes was proposed. The Federal Reserve began to move toward monetary stringency as it increased the discount rate to 7.5 per cent—an historical high. Uncertainty and pessimism were pervasive.

Criticism
of
Macroeconomic
Theory
and
Policy

Up to this point, we have examined the fundamentals of generally accepted macroeconomic
theory. To be sure, no economist would accept all
of the discussion in its present form; many would
wish to make amendments and qualifications. Still,
the area of agreement would probably exceed the
area of disagreement.

There are, however, sharp dissenters from traditional theory, who have claimed to see a different
economic reality from the one portrayed in the
traditional view. They see the economy responding
to different forces, operating with different motivations, and provoking different
institutional reactions. Even when they accept some sections of orthodox theory,
they are apt to use them in somewhat modified form to fit into their models. It is
appropriate now to bring in these views, so that they may be considered and
weighed. As is often the case, critical views can help hone one's own knowledge of,
and appreciation for, ideas previously held, which may have been vague or un-
justifiably certain. Naturally, every dissenting voice cannot be discussed here. We
must choose, and the basis upon which we do so is *influence*. If an economist's
ideas have influenced many others and have persuaded them to think out and act
upon new positions, his views deserve inclusion. The choice is an arbitrary one, and
only the more important and widely respected views of recognized leaders will be
discussed explicitly.

It would also be appropriate to attempt a critique of past macroeconomic
policies. To some extent, criticisms have been inserted throughout the discussion of
policy actions, but these need elaboration. Furthermore, critics of traditional
macroeconomic theory will also be critics of past policies; their models likely call
for different actions with respect to past economic conditions.

We begin by evaluating past policies, making criticisms with the traditional
macroeconomic model in mind. It will only be necessary to summarize the criti-

cisms already mentioned in previous discussions. Several new criticisms, however, deserve deeper analysis both for their own sake and because they lead us into the criticisms of the traditional model as a whole. Then we turn to the different models and compare them with the traditional one.

Past Macroeconomic Policies

In the review of postwar policies it was clear that political considerations often outweighed economic ones. While this may not be surprising, it does make the evaluation of policy actions difficult. Whether or not economists have explained their thinking adequately or offered sound advice, political realities have often hampered the adoption of logical policy measures. Nevertheless, some additional judgments must be made and, with the benefit of hindsight, some conclusions ventured.

The record of deliberate fiscal and monetary policy for the postwar period is not particularly good. It is fair to say that prior to the tax cut of 1964 little in the way of genuine fiscal policy, free of other considerations, was even contemplated by policy makers. Keynesian thought was slow to gain acceptance, and even "proper" fiscal action was undertaken primarily to reach other goals. Fortunately, the built-in stabilizers act independently of politics; otherwise the swings in the economy might have been wider.

Similar conclusions apply to monetary policy for the same time period. Monetary policy was often perverse, based as it was on erroneous forecasts or on pessimistic, only slightly justified, expectations. At times, monetary policy was basically correct but too timid, and at other times the pursuit of other goals (say, in foreign trade) just happened to coincide with the proper domestic policy.

Looking back over the first half of the period under review, it appears as if macroeconomic policies were basically ineffectual. On the whole, monetary policy had the edge over fiscal policy in effort if not in results. In the early 1960s a wider role for government intervention was discussed and became more tolerable, and more sophisticated views of the part that monetary and fiscal policies could play were heard. Both the Kennedy and Johnson administrations raised the level of discussion and understanding of macroeconomic policy and the new guided capitalism concept. Any real appraisal of macroeconomic policy must begin with this era. If we look over the shoulders of the chairmen of the CEA, Walter Heller and Arthur Okun, we can through their writings gain some insight into what policies were considered and what gains were made in policy awareness.

Both men tend to downgrade monetary policy. This may be a denial of the importance of monetary policy or a natural result of the independence of the Federal Reserve from the executive branch. For whatever reasons, monetary policy is not considered as extensively as fiscal policy. For Heller, the possibilities for fiscal policy were greatly enhanced by such developments as the tax cut proposal and its eventual enactment, which proved that the economy could be influenced and which essentially destroyed the older notions of balanced budgets and fears of public debt; the investment tax credit as a device to stimulate spending; manpower training and development programs; the wage-price guideposts; the monetary twist; and other government programs to stimulate research, technological progress, and regional development programs. Without question, these initiatives helped to elevate the public discussion of fiscal policies. The results of these policies are less clear.

Consider the lag between the tax cut proposal and enactment; the uncertain results of the wage-price guideposts and the monetary twist; the disappointing results of manpower training programs and regional development schemes. In short, intellectual advances may have been made but perhaps not demonstrable economic ones. Much of the failure of fiscal policy from the mid-1960s on is attributed to the Vietnam War, and Heller wistfully speculates on what might have been without it.[1]

One gets the same feeling from reading Okun on this period.[2] The budget was underestimated because of the Vietnam build-up; the tax increase was delayed; the investment tax credit was on again, off again; and in general, defense expenditures played havoc with budgets, inflation, and nondefense programs. In addition, economic forecasting is recognized as inadequate, yet proper policies depend on it.

What emerges, then, is a rather defensive stance for the inadequacy of fiscal policy (primarily). The CEA was aware of the proper policies, but political realities seemed to overrule economic considerations. Yet, it is open to question whether the policies proposed would have been adequate regardless of political interference. Some of the problems that plagued the United States economy had their beginnings a decade or so earlier and seem to recede in some periods and to reappear in others, interacting in some complex way within a changing economic structure. Recall the problems of inflation and unemployment; price rigidity as demand fluctuates; recent high unemployment levels in fairly booming periods; the emergence of excess capacity; the balance-of-payments difficulties; and in related areas, the merger movement and the changing structure of the economy, which may be partly responsible for the other problems.

These problems relate to the stabilization goal. What about the problems that would remain for the United States even if the economy were stabilized: the distribution of income; economic growth; economic security; and urban, ecological, and other problems?

In short, traditional fiscal policy may well be both insufficient and ineffectual in meeting the deep-seated problems of the United States economy. At least, the traditional weapons have proved incomplete even in meeting the goal of stabilization. Some of the reasons for this have already been suggested and others will be added later.

It is important to note that economists as a rule have been reluctant to admit the shortcomings of fiscal policy. They quite naturally point to political obstacles that obstruct or delay the functioning of the policies. And the preceding charge is more serious—that even at best, fiscal policy is only partially successful at times and ineffectual in other periods. Perhaps the plausibility of this charge is evidenced by the drastic and untraditional fiscal policy action of wage and price controls taken by a basically conservative Republican administration. It is a clear signal that all other measures were not sufficient, and thus this essentially anticapitalist move was dictated not by ideology or principle but by pragmatism and impulse. It was a strange move, and the acquiescence of the public attests to the fact that the traditional methods had been found wanting in effectiveness.

It has often been stated that monetary policy is more flexible than fiscal policy and that monetary actions can be more quickly adapted to changing conditions.

[1] Walter Heller, *New Dimensions of Political Economy* (New York: W. W. Norton, 1967).

[2] Arthur Okun, *The Political Economy of Prosperity* (New York: W. W. Norton, 1970).

In general, there is some truth to this observation. Yet the past record of monetary policy is not outstanding. In the early years it took a subordinate position with respect to the Treasury's operations and to fiscal policy when it existed. In the latter part of the 1960s monetary policy was forced to accept the leading position, if not the only one, in the attempt to stabilize the economy. It was bound to fail—too much was asked of it. Monetary policy is not capable of bearing the entire burden of managing the economy.

Problems with Monetary and Fiscal Policies

As noted earlier, one of the major shortcomings of macroeconomic policy is the failure to use it—the error of omission. But even when used, these policies are not very effective. We review some problems in summary form here, since many have been mentioned in other portions of the text.

There are, first, *timing problems*—all kinds of lags in both monetary and fiscal policy. Estimates of the lag in monetary policy run from a few months to a few years, and the lags in fiscal policy are well documented and run at least as long. With fiscal policy, there is the additional timing problem caused by the inflexibility of expenditures programs. A related problem is the lack of symmetry in combatting a recession versus an inflation. In recessionary periods fiscal actions become easy to push through Congress, while during inflationary periods the fiscal actions required are difficult to enact. For monetary policy, it is somewhat the reverse, because in recessionary periods an easy money policy is passive, and if the public does not wish to avail itself of easy credit, not much can be done. However, in inflationary periods a tight money policy can alter economic plans and force some painful choices. Both monetary and fiscal policy become ineffective in combatting cost push inflation and may well make matters worse, and timing problems may mask the underlying difficulty.

Recall, also, the differential impact of monetary and fiscal policy. For monetary policy, for instance, the link between the rate of interest and the level of investment appears to be weak, especially for the larger firms. Tight money policies, therefore, are made at the expense of small firms and the construction industry. In recessions fiscal policy easily expands for all areas of the budget, but in inflationary periods cuts are made mainly in social, nondefense programs.

There are also *institutional constraints*. The monetary authorities have little control over other financial institutions, and policies may be blunted by their existence. The institutional arrangements of the Federal Reserve System themselves cause friction from time to time. Fiscal policy depends on the unwieldy budgetary process. In addition, the budget is crowded with items that are contractual and cannot be altered.

These are some of the limitations on deliberate macroeconomic policy. They are well known and recognized problems, which need not be elaborated further. There have, of course, been many suggestions for overcoming these problems and improving the effectiveness of policy. These too were given earlier. Regardless of their merits, these suggested improvements are aimed at making the traditional policy-making process run more smoothly and respond more quickly. They are not directed at the issues that will occupy us for the remainder of this chapter: social problems, either created by, or by-products of, traditional macroeconomic policies; and criticisms of the traditional policies.

Social Problems

The social consequences of macroeconomic policies are seldom considered except for an occasional superficial recognition. The discussion over the application of monetary and fiscal policies can become very abstract indeed, and the arguments are made on logical grounds. Of course, abstract reasoning is necessary to present the situation and to analyze solutions, but one should also consider these policies in the light of their effects on the society and the elements that compose it. It is to this issue that we now turn before embarking on the more penetrating criticisms of the economic system and policies designed to control it that are made by some dissenting economists.

A poorly functioning economy leaves many of its resources unemployed. The waste is often enormous. There is the tendency to be concerned primarily over the unemployed labor force, but idle equipment is equally wasteful. We will consider both.

Many would agree that an unemployment rate of 4 per cent, while somewhat arbitrary, is still the best that can be hoped for under the circumstances of the 1973 economy. Indeed, the CEA suggested that changes in the composition of the labor force would make even a slightly higher figure tolerable.[3] Still, in 1973 a 4 per cent unemployment rate means that 3.5 million people will be without work. The actual unemployment rate of close to 5.0 per cent means that 4.5 million workers are out of work. Who are these unemployed people? The rate of unemployment for teenagers aged 16–19 is about three times as great as for the civilian labor force; the rate for nonwhite workers is two times that for white workers; and the rate for blue-collar workers is two times that of the white-collar worker. Thus, the unemployed come from the most disadvantaged groups in the society. To speak of one unemployment rate or another as being tolerable is to condemn millions of workers to lives of misery and frustration. The loss of dignity alone in this work-oriented society is sufficient punishment, not to speak of loss of income. Now, some unemployment is unavoidable, and the so-called frictional unemployment of men between jobs is to be expected (and even desirable) in a dynamic economy where men are free to change jobs. Perhaps 1 or 2 per cent of the unemployment rate can be so classified, but no one is sure. It is unemployment due to insufficient demand or to structural or technological causes that is of concern to policy makers. How much of the unemployment rate can be attributed to each cause can only be estimated, and no such attempt will be made here. Two things do stand out, however, from past experience. First, high levels of demand drive the unemployment rate down, thus negating some of the structural or technological arguments. Second and more important, the method of estimating the unemployment rates tends to underestimate the real volume of unemployment. Briefly, if workers, tired of seeking work and not finding it, drop out of the labor market, they are not actively seeking work and are not counted as unemployed. Similarly, part-time workers are excluded under certain circumstances, and of course, the underemployed are not considered at all. In general, the true unemployment rate is estimated to be about double that officially estimated.[4] Most of the uncounted unemployed would probably come from the nonwhite and other disadvantaged groups.

---

[3] *Economic Report of the President* (1972), p. 114.

[4] See Kenneth Strand and Thomas Dernburg, "Cyclical Variation in Civilian Labor Force Participation," *Review of Economics and Statistics* 46 (November 1964): 378–391.

The potential unrest and alienation from the society and the system responsible for their plight hardly need elaboration. Idleness, frustration, and the loss of dignity are associated with crime, drugs, and militancy. In human terms, to speak of a trade-off between unemployment and price increases appears as a cruel joke to those who have been traded, or are being considered for trading, in the name of price stability. What care they for orderly markets and stable securities exchanges or for the falling value of real wealth?

Discarded by the private sector, they look to government for help. Gone are the days when men could always return to the land and become at least partially self-sufficient. No crops grow in city streets, and the other handicraft skills have vanished in an economic system that demands specialization. The unemployed have found some help in unemployment compensation, welfare plans, job training programs, and other poverty programs. They have also found promises, and their expectations were raised, as were those of the working poor. Yet most of these programs were hastily conceived, poorly funded, and of little real lasting benefit. The welfare programs were demeaning and also ill-conceived, penalizing instead of rewarding work effort.

There is no need to review the awkward attempts by government to alleviate the problems of the disadvantaged. What concerns us is that monetary and fiscal policies, when they worked, did so at the expense of the poor. The poor were manipulated to achieve the goals of monetary and fiscal policy.

Consider monetary policy. In periods of easy money and credit the poor and the unemployed do not benefit directly. They remain poor risks and are forced into seeking loans from unscrupulous lenders or finance companies that charge high interest rates. Buying on credit involves exorbitant carrying charges and sometimes swift repossession. Other groups are encouraged to borrow at advantageous terms. To the extent that firms borrow and expand to create jobs, the policy appears rational, except that the link from low interest rates to job creation is not strong or even certain. When inflation threatens, interest rates rise, including the ones the poor pay, and more important, so do mortgage rates, which boost the housing costs. Meanwhile, monetary policy often means that bank profits—and bank branches—grow. The boom in bank construction is very visible to all. Similarly, high interest rates benefit bondholders, who are not among the disadvantaged. Interest rates rise on state and local bonds as well, and the interest from these is tax-free. Since large firms, union workers, and other groups are not seriously hurt, anti-inflationary policies hurt the poor disproportionately.

Consider now some of the effects of fiscal policy. In recessionary periods welfare and poverty programs are proposed, debated, and sometimes enacted. Often these are ill-conceived and ill-directed. In most cases they are meagerly funded as well. Still, they represent some concern for those left behind. When inflation threatens, however, these programs are slashed or eliminated. So too are programs to aid education—Head Start, remedial classes, and even school lunch programs are attacked. Nondefense spending in general is reduced while defense spending continues. Yet even defense expenditures no longer provide jobs for the unskilled, because weapons systems become increasingly sophisticated and technical. And as to farm subsidies, it is not the low-income farmer who benefits but those who do not need them.

Helping those who do not require help is also an effect of the taxation side of fiscal policy. The tax code is replete with loopholes, deductions, and special sections that benefit the higher-income groups. Tax reform is always strongly resisted. Thus, the progressive income tax turns out to be a proportional one, with most of the tax revenue being derived from the first tax bracket. Here, of course, the lower-income groups are penalized, since they cannot avail themselves of the loopholes and exclusions.

When taxes are altered to meet some fiscal policy goal, the poor are often affected more than others if the change involves a change in the first tax bracket or if, as in 1966, a surcharge is imposed. The unemployed may also be adversely affected, because they lose the exemptions and deductions to which they would have been entitled had they had income.[5]

On the other hand, the investment tax credit in the face of excess capacity appears to be simply a tax reduction. Depreciation liberalization, deferred taxes on exports, depletion allowances, and so on, seem to help business increase profits in the expectation that jobs will be created, and so on. But many feel that better results would be obtained by public spending programs designed to help the unemployed and underemployed directly rather than by subsidizing business to do it indirectly. These are just some of the ways that tax changes affect income groups; the list is not complete.

To make matters worse, in recent years macroeconomic policies have had little, if any, effect on the unemployment rate. This means that the disadvantaged are being subjected only to the detrimental effects of monetary and fiscal policies and receiving little in the way of benefits. The social consequences of ineffective policy measures have been slighted, although the failures were recognized.

Thus, wage and price controls were instituted in 1971. But even here, profits, dividends, and interest rewards were not controlled although wages were. Wages are easier to control, but the uneven system created strains. The poor sought exemptions and received some modest concessions only after lengthy discussion and only for those below the minimum wage. Meanwhile, food products were exempt, and the poor again felt discriminated against. Many large firms freely admitted that the wage-price controls had barely affected them, and their profits rebounded strongly.[6] Again, price stability meant basically wage stability, and the lower-income groups bore the brunt of the policy.

The same is true for policies to combat the problems in the international trade area. The poor and the unemployed do not cause balance-of-payment problems—they consume little in the way of imported goods. The exceptions, however, are singled out for direct policies. Low-income groups do consume low-cost imported textiles, clothing, and shoes. Buying these low-priced items, the poor can at least avoid the stigma of looking poor. Yet the cries for protection against these imports sent politicians looking for ways to limit them. The trade problems caused by the actions of firms, speculators, multinational corporations, and the government itself were given scant attention. Protectionism would also come at the expense of those at the bottom of the income scale.

---

[5] This is, of course, a major argument for the negative income tax. A related problem is the method of financing Social Security: by a regressive payroll tax. There are many instances when a household may be exempt from income taxes but still pay the payroll tax; or the payroll tax exceeds their income-tax liability. As benefits rise, Congress invariably increases the rates of taxation along with them, while working on provisions to exempt low-income groups from income taxation.

[6] See the interviews with the heads of some major corporations in Michael G. Jensen, "Impact of Controls: Business as Usual," *New York Times*, July 9, 1972, section 3, p. 1.

Unemployment wastes human resources; idle capacity wastes capital resources. The concern for unemployed men is understandably greater than the concern for unemployed machines, but both represent the failure of the economic system to use its scarce resources efficiently. As revealed previously, the United States economy has been characterized by excess capacity for some time. While it is difficult to measure capacity use and therefore all estimates are approximate, the existence of idle plant and equipment is not denied.[7] Idle plants (and idle men) clearly result in a loss of output from which the entire society suffers. They represent a major weakness of the free enterprise system and a problem that has plagued economists since the beginning of the discipline. Indeed, some believe that this excess capacity is one of the major manifestations of the underlying structural changes that have occurred in the economy.

The existence of excess capacity makes monetary and fiscal policies designed to influence investment spending much less effective. Low interest rates, investment tax credits, accelerated depreciation allowances, and all other policies to influence investment spending are of little avail when excess capacity already exists. Why build more plants and equipment when those in existence are not being used? As demand increases, this excess capacity will be utilized first before additional capital stock is acquired. Fiscal or monetary policy must be much stronger and perhaps sustained longer than would be the case if the economy were operating closer to capacity. And, of course, fewer jobs are created by policies that simply put idle machines to work. This and other lags can make fiscal and monetary policies much less powerful and their effects less certain.

Some Thoughts About the Applicability and Future of Macroeconomic Policy

In the remainder of this chapter and in the following chapters we examine the view that the structure of the United States economy (and other advanced economies) has changed enough to make traditional monetary and fiscal policies obsolete. The usual monetary and fiscal policy weapons may no longer be effective —they lack both power and timeliness.

Other more effective tools must be developed, or the structure of the economy must be changed or modified. This judgment comes at a time when the traditional tools are just being accepted by politicians. We may well have learned the lessons of Keynes when it is too late. The world he described (Marx, too, of course) no longer exists. It is not inappropriate, then, to ask in the light of this whether or not we have been expecting too much of the traditional monetary and fiscal policies. They either do not work effectively or must be pushed to great length to work at all.

Some may be led to conclude that other forms of macroeconomic policy, which were always available, should now be given more attention and used more extensively. Antitrust policies, for instance, can be used with greater vigor to dismantle centers of market power. It must be granted that there is greater scope for antitrust policies than has been utilized in the past. Market power allowed to grow unchecked will severely reduce the efficacy of monetary and fiscal policies as eco-

[7] All estimates in this text are taken from those published by the Federal Reserve in its monthly bulletin. These estimates are based on the work of Frank de Leeuw and others. For a description of the data and the statistical procedure, see F. de Leeuw, F. E. Hopkins, and M. D. Sherman, "A Revised Index of Manufacturing Capacity," *Federal Reserve Bulletin* 52 (November 1966): 1605–1615.

nomic units insulate themselves from both the regulation of the marketplace and the influence of government actions. Past experience leaves little hope that sudden reversals of past antitrust policies are imminent. They may even be too late. For instance, what would really be accomplished if General Motors were broken up into five distinct firms? Or if the AFL-CIO were broken up into smaller units? The merger movement, the drive for diversification, and the trend toward conglomeration have gone on too long now, and power has become entrenched as the number of viable firms shrinks.

Still, stronger application of antitrust policy could hold the line and stop the continuation of past trends. But such a policy requires a commitment, and so far, this has been absent, despite the rhetoric to the contrary. Perhaps new special-interest groups, like those created by Ralph Nader, can force action where none was contemplated. Nader has already accomplished much, and his work only serves to remind us of what government officials failed to do or, in many cases, failed to consider doing. The need for action is clear; the evidence has been accumulated, and the rest is up to elected and appointed government officials.

Another tool of macroeconomic policy that could be used more wisely is the concentration of government expenditures in areas where they will have the most favorable impact. Public expenditures could be undertaken with a view toward helping regions of the country that are in the worst economic distress—much like the emergency programs. Many expenditures are now made on the basis of congressional status, logrolling, and so on, rather than on real economic need. Furthermore, expenditures could be better matched with the development of regions according to long-range plans. Much could be done to facilitate regional growth and development by deliberate planning and pumppriming, as the economic situation dictates.

Other kinds of programs could be developed to replace defense expenditures if they diminish. Revenue sharing extensions, guaranteed incomes, health plans, recreational development, government as the employer of last resort, labor exchanges—all could be utilized to bolster demand and dampen the business cycle and lessen the need for fiscal and monetary actions.

Similarly, the tax code could be revised to eliminate many of the special-interest provisions and to eliminate the tax shelters used by some industries and individuals. In many cases these tax concessions represent nothing more than back-door spending—the granting of subsidies to various groups. Public expenditure to benefit specific groups is resisted at least, but tax concessions that amount to the same thing are only seldom rejected.

Yet it is not clear how these actions would necessarily improve the working of macroeconomic policy. More rational government expenditures and more equitable taxes are clearly desirable and easily justified on numerous grounds. It is doubtful, however, whether such changes will affect the basic economic structure, which appears to be the cause of many economic problems. Such policies may diminish the need to exert economic power by those who possess it, but when the situation warrants, the power is again revived. In fact, a case will be made later for this response by power holders to past efforts at economic control by traditional macroeconomic policies. In effect, the power lies dormant at times and is exercised at other times, and this rule of action depends upon the economic situation. Its operation can seriously impair our ability to evaluate the public policies actually pursued.

In short, some proposals to make the economy run more smoothly would no doubt be useful and desirable. They have much to commend them on moral and social grounds as well, but the question here is whether or not they would improve the operation of the traditional approach to manipulation of the economy. The question must remain an open one, for evidence is lacking either way. In what follows, however, it is assumed that such changes would result only in marginal improvements in the conduct of ordinary monetary and fiscal policies. The assumption is based on the premise that real economic power would be left relatively untouched by the new or revised programs suggested here.

Criticism of Traditional Macroeconomic Theory and Policy

We wish now to differentiate sharply between the mainstream type of criticism implied in modest departures from generally accepted macroeconomic analysis and criticism that is more fundamental. Some economists would disavow marginal adjustments and piecework revision and would require a greater departure from traditional thought. There is, of course, a kind of spectrum of criticism going from slight modifications to complete rejection of macroeconomic analysis, but we need not represent every shade of difference here. Instead, the spectrum is broken up into three units: a criticism of "Keynesian" economics from the conservative viewpoint; a view from the liberal position; and an analysis from the left, representing a form of rejection. Their position will become clear in the course of the discussion, but in general, they view the economic system from different perspectives, and while their works are based upon the United States economy, it is clear that their analyses extend to economic systems in general. In the course of the discussion the centrist position will also be introduced to furnish a standard for comparison. Economics being what it is, we are forced to chop up the spectrum of belief in this artificial way.

THE CRITIQUE OF MILTON FRIEDMAN

Perhaps the most severe criticism of the Keynesian model is to be found in the work of Milton Friedman and the so-called Chicago School. Over the years an attitude has developed at the University of Chicago best expressed currently by Milton Friedman.[8] It will be necessary to present much of this thought in summary only, and the focus will be on the monetarist contribution to economic analysis. The major thrust of Friedman's attack on the Keynesian model is found in the disagreement over the role of money in the economy. The money stock played a secondary part in the Keynesian model, and if Keynes realized the importance of money, some of his followers did not. Recall that Keynes and his followers emphasize the role of fiscal policy. Friedman reintroduces the stock of money as a primary

---

[8] Besides his works previously cited, his views can be obtained from *Capitalism and Freedom* (Chicago: University of Chicago Press, 1962); and (with Walter Heller), *Monetary Versus Fiscal Policy: A Dialogue* (New York: W. W. Norton, 1969). Also see his contribution to the panel topic at the annual AEA meetings in December 1971, "Have Monetary Policies Failed?" *American Economic Review* 62 (May 1972): 11–18. The general topic, very useful for our discussion, was "Have Fiscal and/or Monetary Policies Failed?" In subsequent pages of the same issue (pp. 19–23) John G. Gurley is critical of the whole purpose of macroeconomic policy, and (pp. 24–38) Arthur Okun answers essentially "not exactly" to the question; his response represents what might be expected from the central, mainstream viewpoint.

variable—the prime mover of the economic system. In his statistical work Friedman finds that the stock of money and changes in it are correlated with price changes and the business cycle. If this is true, it follows that control of the stock of money is needed to control the price level and the volume of economic activity.

Most economists now agree to varying extents with this conclusion. However, Friedman went much further and denied the influence of fiscal policy as a means of controlling economic activity. Only money is important, he seems to assert or his followers do. If fiscal policy is irrelevant, then monetary policy must do the job of stabilization, and the proper monetary policy is to control the stock of money and permit it to grow at some predetermined rate—the real growth rate of national output—in order to avoid the swings of the business cycle. This spells the end of discretionary monetary and fiscal policy. How does he reach these conclusions?

Looking back, Friedman finds that past forecasts of economic activity, and monetary policies based on them, were often wrong. Furthermore, the policies, even when correct, were timid and subject to long and uncertain lags. He feels it is better to have rules for the monetary authorities to follow. Much of the foundation for his analysis comes from the classical economists' model and particularly from the quantity theory of money. In addition, he retains a firm belief in the tenets of capitalism and the free market system, and here also he accepts traditional neoclassical microeconomic theory and the behavior of the economic units (as was the case with Keynes). In short, he is the intellectual heir of classical economics, and he has built upon this model within the Keynesian framework.

Recall the crude quantity theory of money, where the stock of money, M, determined the price level, P, with the velocity, V, and the volume of transactions, T, both held constant. V depended upon institutional factors and T on the full employment of resources. The modern quantity theory restates the proposition, so that the stock of money determines money income, with V still constant.

There has been much discussion of the proper measurement of the stock of money, M, and several variations have emerged. (There is no need to enter into that lengthy debate.) Moreover, it is held by monetarists that the stock of money and the rate of interest are unrelated (as opposed to Keynes's liquidity preference theory), and that altering the stock of money has no direct effect on the rate of interest (or else the constancy of V must be abandoned).

It would appear that such a simple and straightforward theory could be easily tested and judged. Friedman has done extensive research and has concluded that with suitable lags the stock of money has played the role he assigns to it and has explained all price level changes and swings in economic activity.[9] His followers, particularly at the Federal Reserve Bank of St. Louis, have also been busy and have claimed to show not only that Friedman is correct about the stock of money but that he is also correct when he asserts the futility of fiscal policy.[10] We have come a long way from the view that money does not matter to the view that money matters a great deal to the view held by some that only money matters. According to Friedman, changes in government expenditures and taxes have no discernible effect on the economy, and hence the multiplier is nonexistent. Gone, too, are such fiscal policy devices as the investment tax credit and accelerated depreciation allowances.

[9] Milton Friedman and Anna J. Schwartz, *A Monetary History of the United States, 1867–1960* (Princeton, N. J.: Princeton University Press, 1963).

[10] Michael W. Keran, "Monetary and Fiscal Influences on Economic Activity—The Historical Evidence," Federal Reserve Bank of St. Louis, *Review* 51 (November 1969): 5–24.

The argument is clear—control the stock of money and you control the economy; let the velocity of money predict the multiplier to which the level of national income will reach, since its relation with money is more stable than other relationships. Moreover, control the stock of money by determining in advance how fast it should increase, and give the monetary authorities a rule to follow.

Friedman's analysis is not without critics. Many now accept his contention that money was underemphasized in the Keynesian model. But economists like Tobin and Samuelson are puzzled over the mechanisms that would make only money matter.[11] It is not clear how M or ΔM causes a change in national product. Nor is it clear what happened to cost push inflation, since Friedman's analysis permits only demand pull. Naturally, Friedman's microeconomic theory prohibits cost push inflation, competition being powerful enough to forestall the use of any market power.

Still, how does a change in M affect Y? The ΔM cannot affect the rate of interest and in this way affect other variables and eventually income; that was ruled out. The statistical evidence merely shows that there is some association between M and Y, but causation is not automatically established.[12] It would appear that more general acceptance of the monetarist view will have to await a better theoretical description of the monetary mechanisms as well as more convincing empirical evidence.

In summary, Friedman's theory of the role of the money supply in the economic model is not convincing to many; the proposition cannot be discarded but neither can it be accepted. His concentration on monetary policy, and particularly on the automatic growth in the stock of money, is clearly a departure from the more traditional view, which assigns a larger role to fiscal policy and discretionary actions. Who is wise enough to determine the rules by which the monetary authorities are to be guided? As Samuelson put it, "For when men set up a definitive mechanism which is to run forever after by itself, that involves a single act of discretion which transcends both in its arrogance and its capacity for potential harm any repeated acts of foolish discretion that can be imagined."[13] It has been suggested that such a rule would be broken as soon as it was felt that some discretionary action would be preferable. Also, serious questions have been raised over whether or not the Federal Reserve is capable of controlling the money supply so precisely.

It is suggested that anyone wishing to know more of Friedman's work would do well to supplement this summary with readings from his very readable works. It would be well to start with *Capitalism and Freedom* to get some idea of his philosophical beliefs and then to trace their beliefs through his economic writings, thus partly disproving his claim to having produced a value-free, positive economics. Friedman has assumed the intellectual mantle of Henry Simons and Frank Knight of the University of Chicago. There would be many economists who would subscribe to their vision of the economic system.

[11] Their comments on the monetarist approach can be found in many places. For some succinct statements, see their contributions to a symposium held by the Federal Reserve Bank of Boston in June 1969 and published by the bank in *Controlling Monetary Aggregates* (1969).

[12] Furthermore, to take a complex economic structure with endogenous and exogenous variables (determined within and outside the system) interacting in complicated ways and reduce the economic structure to a single equation model is to make sweeping assumptions. To select one variable for the monetary sphere and one for fiscal policy and then run regressions to see which is more important is an interesting exercise but hardly a valid procedure and certainly not conclusive.

[13] Paul A. Samuelson, "The Folly of Monetary Rules," in *The Battle Against Unemployment*, ed. Arthur M. Okun (New York: W. W. Norton, 1965), pp. 201–202.

Moving towards the center, we find a greater number of economists. Representatives of this middle position have already been cited in the references to Walter Heller and Arthur Okun, Paul Samuelson and, indeed, all the past members of the Council of Economic Advisors. In general, they would be comfortable with economic theory as presented in this book and, while admitting difficulties and gaps in our knowledge, would still maintain that the economy can be managed with the tools in our possession. There is no need to review the position of these mainstream economists.[14]

THE VISION OF J. K. GALBRAITH

Moving farther to the left, one finds economists who are critical of macroeconomic (and microeconomic) theory or policies or both. Of course, all economists are critical of some aspects of theory and some aspects of policy, but the criticisms taken up here are much more fundamental and seriously question major portions of the mainstream thought and methodology. Included among these economists are Kenneth Boulding, Robert Heilbronner, Joan Robinson, Gunnar Myrdal, and perhaps best known, John Kenneth Galbraith.

Galbraith's main contribution can be found in his three most widely acclaimed books, but in his many works there are connecting threads and overlapping themes.[15] Throughout his work the importance of the corporation in the modern economy is stressed, particularly the large corporation. With size came power, and the exercise or containment of this power preoccupied Galbraith as he attempted to measure its impact on the economic system. He finds the traditional analysis of firms' behavior to be inapplicable to the most important segment of the economy, that dominated by large corporations. Indeed, most of microeconomics theory is rejected as obsolete.

Therefore, one major idea that permeates his work is that the market system is no longer reliable as the means of allocating resources rationally, which is to say that the relation between the expression of individual wants and the production to satisfy those wants has broken down, the whole process having been reversed. Production comes first, and the individual is persuaded to want the products through advertising. This system is basically irrational and leads to the overproduction of private goods, many of the frivolous variety, the underproduction of public goods, and the despoliation of our resources and environment. Much of this view is now commonly accepted, but the notion of production for its own sake contained in *The Affluent Society* merits serious reflection by those who are concerned over the composition of our national output.

The idea of production being propelled by irrational forces is carried over into his vision of the modern industrial state. He has little sympathy for those who would carry over the microeconomic theory of the nineteenth century into the industrial society of the twentieth. Neither does he have much faith in traditional distinctions among economic systems so readily condensed into "isms."

It is probably fair to state that according to Galbraith only intellectuals are inspired by ideology; the economy is driven by technological needs and realities.

---

[14] For a penetrating analysis of the sociology of intellectual beliefs and change, see Harry Johnson, "The Keynesian Revolution and the Monetarists' Counter-Revolution," *American Economic Review* 61 (May 1971): 1–14.

[15] The three books are *American Capitalism* (1952); *The Affluent Society* (1958); and *The New Industrial State* (1967), all published by Houghton Mifflin Company.

Modern technology requires size, power, and control. As a result, control over the large corporations has shifted to organized intelligence—the technocrats—the salesmen, engineers, production managers, and all those others whose skills a large corporation can assemble under one roof. The owners, and even the directors, of the corporation are forced to relinquish control by the highly technical nature of the firms' operations. Gone too is the simplistic assumption that firms maximize profits; since these profits do not accrue to managers, new goals have become more important. The new goals are autonomy and survival of the firm, sufficient growth to satisfy all concerned, and the freedom and ability to make use of changing technology. These new goals require control over the forces of the marketplace lest these forces require the sacrifice of these goals, and they require extensive planning. The better the control, the easier the planning; uncertainty is eschewed.

To meet these goals and to plan adequately requires power, and that is what the giant corporation must have. To assure its autonomy and growth and its planning ability, the giant corporation sets about to control the marketplaces it enters: the financial market by bypassing both its own stockholders and the money market in its needs for funds—profit retention does that; the product market by controlling and stabilizing the prices at which it buys and sells; the product market by assuring the demand for its production through advertising and the subverting of consumer sovereignty; the labor market by influencing the educational system so that the supply of technocrats is assured. Most important for our purposes, the large corporation has insulated itself from government control as well, and in fact has manipulated government to the point where the state acts on behalf of it.

Antitrust laws do not work or are inapplicable to these industrial giants. The laws either protect existing power (by preventing new mergers, and so on) or are inappropriate, since the state is largely responsible for their creation or existence of these corporations (regulated industries or the national defense firms). Furthermore, the goals of the corporation and those of society appear to be identical: production, growth, technological virtuosity and supremacy. This is no accident but a logical outcome of the motivational drives of the technocrats.

In any event, the state appears to guarantee the operation of the system, since its actions designed to benefit the economy as a whole inevitably benefit these firms in their attempts to protect their interests and reach their goals. Thus, the firms have an interest in keeping the demand (and price) for their outputs as high and stable as possible in order to plan efficiently. This goal is entirely consistent with the state's attempt to keep aggregate demand high by keeping the economy near the full employment level.

Monetary and fiscal policies then become handmaidens of the private planners in large corporations. In this state there is private planning, not state planning; there has been a transfer of functions and the surrender of power and control. Moreover, the alleged hostility between government and business has obviously faded, and government intervention into the economic system is no longer decried except by ideologues.

In fact, these large firms now look to government for research and development funds to subsidize new technology and for special arrangements for the use of government facilities, and so on. The state's aid to education nicely ensures a steady supply of highly trained technicians, who can step into posts specific to the firms' requirements and who are carefully moulded to fit in psychologically. All of government's growth policies—investment in both real and human capital—mesh well with the needs of this new industrial complex.

This vision of the evolving industrial economy is not without its critics, of course. There are those who dismiss it entirely—mainly those who maintain their belief in market forces. Others, however, agree to some extent but balk at accepting certain parts of the description. Walter Adams, for instance, might agree with much of the prior analysis, but he does not agree with the cause.[16] Adams holds that

. . . industrial concentration is not the inevitable outgrowth of economic and technical forces, nor the product of spontaneous generation or natural selection. In this era of big government, concentration is often the result of unwise, man-made, discriminating, privilege-creating governmental action. Defense contracts, R and D support, patent policy, tax privileges, stockpiling arrangements, tariffs, and quotas, subsidies, etc., have far from a neutral effect on our industrial structure.[17]

In another vein, Robert Solow contends that Galbraith's treatment of the large corporation is not all that new, and while admitting that the corporation has not been included in formal economic theory too successfully, he feels the traditional model of profit-maximizing behavior can still be useful.[18] Solow is willing, of course, to accept the existence of market imperfections. He suggests that much of economic activity is still performed in areas where size is not so great as to permit the kind of behavior postulated for the giants. He also questions the ability of these giants to plan with such impunity from market forces. Despite internal financing, many funds still come from capital markets, with consequent outside influence. On the product side, Solow maintains that no firm can advertise to the extent that its revenues become reliable and demand for its products predictable. He argues the traditional case that most of advertising is self-defeating and cancelling as firms compete for the market. If so, the expenditures are wasteful and do not serve the planning function as Galbraith contends.

In brief, Solow guardedly defends the traditional view of the economic structure. Galbraith's reply to these and other criticisms cannot be summarized neatly and should be read by those interested in the art of controversy. For our purposes, it is more useful to resume discussion of the structure he described.

Galbraith was content to describe the current economic structure as he saw it, and he had little to say about possible remedies for the corporate state or further directions it might take. The only restraining force he saw was in the scientific-educational establishment, but he offered little grounds for optimism that the institutional trends toward the industrial state would be reversed.

How does Galbraith's description of the economic system affect the theory and, more important, the policy of macroeconomics? Clearly, it turns traditional analysis on end, for monetary and fiscal policy—the state's actions—are seen to benefit the industrial system, and in fact, the state becomes subservient to the needs of the industrial system. It becomes difficult to tell where the public sector ends and the private sector begins—they seem to merge. Keeping employment and aggregate demand high helps society but helps even more the giant firms that dominate it.

[16] Walter Adams, "The Military-Industrial Complex and the New Industrial State," *American Economic Review* 58 (May 1968): 652–665.

[17] Ibid., p. 653.

[18] Robert M. Solow, "The New Industrial State, or Son of Affluence," *The Public Interest* 9 (Fall 1967): 100–108. In the same issue is J. K. Galbraith's "A Review of a Review," pp. 109–118, and Solow's "A Rejoinder," pp. 118–119.

For these firms to plan, it is necessary for demand to be high and prices stable—uncertainty is for the competitive model, not for these firms.

Therefore, one should expect to find more and more of the larger firms supporting governmental attempts to manage the economy. According to Galbraith, this has occurred, and government spending, particularly in defense, has been supported, or at least not resisted, by the large firms and organized labor as well. Also, direct price and wage controls might be received with much less fuss now, since stable prices facilitate planning. We have already seen that this expectation has been fulfilled. In brief, the new industrial state, the new alliance of government and big business, discards the old rationale for monetary and fiscal policies and calls for a reexamination of the location of power in the economic system. Institutional changes have outrun both our view of the economic structure and our methods for altering the economic system. Monetary and fiscal policies—macroeconomic policies in general—will have to be reexamined to determine their effects on the economic system and its structure and to reevaluate the benefits received by sectors, groups, industries, and so on, by the operation of such policies.

THE INSIGHTS OF BARAN AND SWEEZY

Moving farther leftward, one might expect to find more radical solutions to the problems of the mixed advanced economy. Certainly, there are many who completely reject the capitalist model as it has evolved in the United States. Some of these rejections are based largely on emotion and others on careful analysis and long study of the movement of economic systems. It is not our purpose to dismiss arguments based on emotion, but in order to parallel previous analysis, we will consider only one of the more reasoned criticisms here. For critiques of a theory, like the theory itself, should lend themselves to testing against reality.

One of the best works to meet these requirements and to allow continuity with the foregoing criticisms is Paul A. Baran's and Paul M. Sweezy's *Monopoly Capital*.[19]

In this book, as in Galbraith's analysis, the giant corporation dominates the economic system and sets the tone for the entire society. Again, it is seen as insulating itself from market forces and from the stockholders who own it. But unlike Galbraith's technocrats, the managers of these corporations come from the propertied class. The corporation still needs technically trained men, but they do not control the firm. The managers—"company men," they call them—still pursue the old goals of the capitalist class—high (maximum) profits and capital accumulation. The other goals, such as growth, strength, or size, may be pursued but are subservient to and served by profit. Thus, it is again not technological forces that determine the economic structure but the old motivations of early capitalism in new forms. Moreover, while these firms attempt to avoid risks, *they do not plan,* at least not as in Galbraith's model.

Of course, there are other differences between the two models, both of substance and nuance, but these are not important for our purposes. Let us begin with their similarities and see where significant differences occur. Both models throw out large portions of traditional microeconomic theory and substitute models in which

[19] (New York: Monthly Review Press, 1966). Among their other works, the most influential have been Paul M. Sweezy, *The Theory of Capitalist Development* (New York: Monthly Review Press, 1942); and Paul A. Baran, *The Political Economy of Growth* (New York: Monthly Review Press, 1957).

the giant corporation dominates the economic system and the society within which it operates by overwhelming everyone and everything subject to its influence.

Baran and Sweezy believe that the best way to evaluate the functioning of an economic system is to examine what it does with its economic surplus—the difference between what the system produces and the real costs of producing it. Their concept of an economic surplus extends Marx's notion of surplus value, which was equal to profits plus interest plus rents, to include the costs of distribution (all forms of selling expenses); the output of the finance, insurance, real estate, and legal services industries; and the entire public sector. According to Baran and Sweezy,

The size of the surplus is an index of productivity and wealth, of how much freedom a society has to accomplish whatever goals it may set for itself. The composition of the surplus shows how it uses that freedom: how much it invests in expanding its productive capacity, how much it consumes in various forms, how much it wastes and in what ways.[20]

Since these large firms maximize profits largely by reducing costs, the profit margins and hence the surplus tend to grow over time. How does the United States use its surplus?

Capitalist consumption expenditures can be expected to rise absolutely but decline as a proportion of rising income and as a proportion of the rising surplus. Thus, private capitalist consumption cannot be expected to absorb the economic surplus.

Investment expenditures similarly cannot absorb the surplus, for investment outlets are not large and numerous enough; either there will be excess capacity as a normal state of affairs or investment spending can be financed out of depreciation charges. The influence of technological change on investment is uncertain, while innovational investment is sharply controlled by the giant firms, which no longer must submit to competitive pressures but can introduce changes when they find them desirable.

It follows that the surplus must then be wasted—in the sales effort and service industries and in militarism and imperialism. Unable to employ this surplus productively, the system is forced to absorb it in distribution costs, advertising, market research, and all kinds of activities that facilitate the sale and exchange of goods and employ many people in these essentially unproductive tasks.

Monopoly capitalism is also characterized by persistent excess capacity; output and employment tend to be less than the potential. The managers of large corporations were quick to recognize (although not openly) the lesson of Keynes's policy of government compensatory spending. Government fiscal policy increases aggregate demand and the surplus as well and helps to keep the system intact. Taxes are shifted by the corporation, and hence there is little resistance to their imposition; workers or low-income groups tolerate the higher taxes because of the output and employment effects of government spending. Without the public sector resources would be idle; and this means that the public sector does not absorb the surplus either but in fact creates additional surplus by its fiscal policy actions.

The trouble with government fiscal policy is that over time and as a consequence of many factors the proportion of the budget devoted to nondefense expenditures has stabilized, and the ruling class structure, resisting further inroads on its privi-

---

[20] *Monopoly Capital*, pp. 9–10.

leged position but still needing large government expenditures, turned to defense spending to absorb the surplus. In addition, monopoly capitalism looked abroad for investment outlets, and the new imperialism was strengthened. With nondefense expenditures lagging behind as the economy grew, something had to be found to absorb the growing economic surplus, and these two areas could absorb many of the resources that otherwise would be idle. The output of these sectors does not add to the supply of goods that must be sold, but their activities do generate income. Baran and Sweezy could not see any substitutes for these sectors—space activities and reordered priorities are suggested—and they were led to the conclusion that only the breaking up of monopoly capitalism could be effective as a remedy for the irrationality of the system:

In the most advanced capitalist country a large part of the population lives in abysmal poverty while in the underdeveloped countries hundreds of millions suffer from disease and starvation because there is no mechanism for effecting an exchange of what they could produce for what they so desperately need. Insistence on the inviolability of equivalent exchange when what is to be exchanged costs nothing, strict economizing of resources when a large proportion of them goes to waste—these are obviously the very denial of the rationality which the concept of value and the principle of *quid pro quo* originally expressed.[21]

For Baran and Sweezy, socialism represents a more rational system, and they hoped that the demonstrated success of it as a system in other countries would convince the United States population to move toward it and away from the system of monopoly capitalism. For our purposes, it is necessary to reiterate that government macroeconomic policies merely maintain the system of monopoly capitalism, which Baran and Sweezy consider irrational. The economy and the government are dominated by the ruling class, which has managed to have its interests served by the exercise of the power it has obtained. Adherence to this view of the economy would make disputes over the acceptable rate of unemployment, the velocity of money, the full employment surplus, and so on, appear to be trivial and misguided efforts that merely conceal the real functioning of an economy such as the United States version of monopoly capitalism.

Before leaving the subject, it might be interesting to compare the role of education in the models of Galbraith and Baran and Sweezy. Recall that Galbraith held out some hope that the scientific-educational sector might help turn the trend toward the corporate state around. For Baran and Sweezy, the educational system serves the needs of the moneyed oligarchs. They have fine private schools and can resist aid to public education, and the resulting inequality in education merely strengthens class distinctions and blocks upward mobility (aside from token advances to meet the equal opportunity requirement). Not much optimism to be found here with regard to the educational establishment, even less than in Galbraith's almost wistful suggestion. Galbraith would probably reject the notion that socialism provides a viable alternative; in his model the needs of technology and planning tend to make "isms" obsolete.

These selected critics of the traditional macroeconomic model and policies have provided us with some insight into different perspectives of the economic system. It is now time to examine how the orthodox model developed earlier should be modified, if at all, as a result of these criticisms. This we will do in the next chapter.

[21] Ibid., p. 338.

Macroeconomic Analysis Reconsidered

In our study we have progressed from an introduction of more or less traditional macroeconomic theory through the discussion of its applicability in the formation of policy to the examination of some critiques. It is now appropriate to reconsider the traditional theory in the light of these criticisms. Aware now of the content of macroeconomics, we are in a better position to reexamine the model and to amend it if possible.

The Question of Assumptions

In the construction of a theory some assumptions must be made in order to limit the boundaries of permissible variations. In chapter 3 we surveyed the need for, and the role of, assumptions for theory in general and for macroeconomic theory in particular. It is clear that the assumptions made determine to a large extent the mechanisms of the model and the extent to which the model is realistic and practical. Well-constructed models may be irrelevant, and relevant models may be inelegant. What matters finally is the usefulness of the model to help us explain and understand reality. A road map is not reality, but using it, we move from one place to another.

If the critics of traditional macroeconomic theory are correct, the economic system, the reality, has changed too much for orthodox theory to be relevant. In reconsidering macroeconomic analysis, it is appropriate to begin by reexamining the assumptions we made in order to ascertain how much of the failure of the theory is due to them.

In the following discussion we are concerned only with the *major* assumptions—those that materially affect the model—and not with those assumptions made for pedagogical or expositional purposes, such as a constant *MPC* or "the" interest rate. The latter are simplifying assumptions that can be relaxed easily enough if desired.

This is not so for the major assumptions. Consider one of the more crucial ones—the assumption of *pure competition*. Nearly all of macroeconomic theory rests upon this microeconomic foundation; writers from Smith to Marx to Keynes all included it as part of their analyses. Recall that the assumption generally applies to *all* markets—labor, money, and product markets. Its main elements are

1. Many buyers and many sellers acting independently
2. Free entry into and out of all markets
3. Homogeneous goods, labor, and so on

Perfect competition requires a few more attributes, although these seldom are made explicit and are often used in a confusing way:

4. The existence of perfect knowledge for everyone in the marketplace
5. Complete mobility of resources
6. No transportation costs; no geographical limitations

In many discussions the terms *pure competition* and *perfect competition* are used loosely or interchangeably, but perfect competition is a much more rigorous and confining concept. A cursory look at the list of items reveals that the assumption of either concept is responsible for a large part of the criticisms reviewed in the previous chapter. Although Milton Friedman does not attack the theory on this score, for Galbraith and for Baran and Sweezy (and many others, of course), it is the giant corporation and market power that upsets the traditional analysis. In fact, most of microeconomic theory is questioned by them, including the analysis of imperfect competition when it is admitted. We have already seen how the rejection of competition led the critics into unorthodox views of the structure of the United States economy. Let us see how the assumption affects the working of the original model in order to appreciate the degree to which the assumption of competition is required.

Competition and the Macroeconomic Model

Traditional microeconomic theory has always been dominated by the vision of an entrepreneur pursuing some goal single-mindedly. All these entrepreneurs respond to market forces more or less predictably, so that the general tendency is toward equilibrium in all markets. Uncertainty is kept at a minimum, and expectations, whenever admitted, are always of the stabilizing kind; when acted upon, they reinforce the automatic tendencies toward market equilibrium. A good deal of the analysis is thus made static and more than a little dogmatic.

Important for our purposes is the model that makes these atomistic competitors respond and react to market forces in a predictable manner; change the market conditions, and adjustments to the changes can be forecast, at least for the direction of the response. The atomistic competitors are amenable to manipulation because their market responses are *flexible. Prices, output, employment, and so on, must be flexible,* free to move in upward and downward directions in response to market signals. Only in this way is it unambiguously correct to speak of a market equilibrium, or for our purposes, the general equilibrium condition. It is important that there be no restraints to interfere with market adjustments.

It could be expected that in the first instance excess demand would cause prices to rise and excess supply would cause them to fall. As firms respond to their industry demand and supply conditions, so industries would respond to aggregate demand and supply; the aggregation process is made feasible by the predictability of response. So, too, an aggregate production function is made theoretically possible. In fact, the high degree of aggregation necessary in macroeconomic models is facilitated by the assumption of competition in all markets.

Thus, we have an aggregate production function, and if we add another assumption common to the competitive model—diminishing returns—we are able to trace some change through the system. An increase in labor input, for instance, will probably reduce the productivity of labor, which in turn will increase costs; the increase in costs, if the output is to be supplied, must lead to an increase in price, because profits are to be maximized. The upward-sloping aggregate supply curve is assured. It follows that an increase in aggregate demand will lead to an increase in the price level, and if the economy is operating at full employment, the result is certain, even with the quantity theory. Only at extremely low levels of output is some doubt permitted and changes in the price level made debatable.

The macroeconomic models in part II are replete with cases of this kind, where many assumptions are included, some explicit and others implicit, but in any case permitting the mechanisms of the model to work toward some end result. It is not our purpose to review the models to point out examples, nor is it necessary to belabor the point. We must, however, question the conclusions to decide how many of them rest largely on the critical assumptions of the model. In order to make some judgments, it is probably best to construct a new model that does not make the customary assumptions. In this way, the foundations of the traditional model will be more clearly perceived. First, however, we digress briefly on methodology.

A Comment on Methodology

In the previous section the requirements for a competitive model were enumerated. They are quite stringent. Moreover, the economic prerequisites are accompanied by assumptions concerning people's behavior in the marketplace as determined by some basic motivations; the motivations, in turn, seem to be largely derived from economic needs. Not only are economic rewards elevated to a high place in human concerns, but they must be maximized or the costs minimized. The rewards—the goals—must themselves be severely limited; otherwise economic analysis becomes extremely difficult and complex. Market behavior is surely oversimplified here in the quest for rigorous theoretical formation.

The confining demands of the competitive model and the unsophisticated behavioral assumptions have not gone unnoticed. Many have pointed out the unreality of this market structure, and most economists would admit that real markets do not resemble closely the picture projected by the theoretical model. The question is, on what grounds can this theoretical model continue to be used when more and more economists find it no longer applicable to significant segments of advanced economies? According to many, the competitive market never did exist to any great extent and probably never will, and thus it may seem strange to build elaborate models on such a foundation.

The justification for the continued use of the pure competition assumption can be found in any microeconomic textbook and can be divided into three parts: (1) the rigorous nature of this assumption permits logical analysis—it is a good starting place from which the consequences of the model can be derived; (2) the use of the competition assumption provides a norm or standard by which to measure departures from the ideal; and (3) enough segments of the market are competitive, or enough firms behave *as if* they were competitive, to make the model sufficiently valid.[1]

Statement (3), that competition or near competition exists in many markets, is challenged by all those who contend that the competitive model is completely inapplicable to markets that really count in quantitative terms.

Citing the competitive model as a norm or standard has much to recommend it as a justification for the model's continued use. Even here, the justification rests on the conclusion, itself based on many assumptions, that the competitive market is the ideal, all departures from it diminishing society's welfare. Nevertheless, let us grant this rationale, for it does not affect the discussion that follows.

For our purposes, it is statement (1) that causes methodological problems: the use of the competitive model as a starting point for logical economic analysis. Presumably, once the model of pure or perfect competition has been analyzed and its principles, consequences, relations, and so on, have been uncovered, the results can always be modified to take account of any imperfections that are found to exist. We study the pure case first and then allow for impurities,[2] although this procedure may in fact be responsible as much for deceiving as for illuminating.

Under pure competition the firm, and the single entrepreneur who controls it, respond to market stimuli in predetermined ways. The behavior of the firm is predictable only because its options for actions are limited, because its maneuverability is circumscribed. Furthermore, it acts with certain knowledge, and the consequences of its actions are fully anticipated. In brief, the firm *learns* to respond to market situations (or is eliminated) because it knows what to expect from its limited actions. Thus constrained, it makes decisions and is not surprised by the results. It has been conditioned to behave in the prescribed manner.

For instance, a purely competitive firm that unilaterally raises its price will soon learn that this type of behavior is proscribed by the market; the loss of sales and the reactions of its competitors would be readily observed, and such unilateral actions are not likely to be repeated. Thus, the firm is controlled by the market, and its freedom to act is restricted. Failure to obey the rules of the game means certain expulsion from the market. The firm is also not free to pay resources what it wants to pay them, to differentiate its product, to influence the demand for its output, to block the spread of technological innovations, and so on. The firm is forced to conform to goals it does not set and to policies it would prefer to upset. The free market is tightly controlled, and if it works as it is supposed to, there is no need to interfere with it.

Given all this, the competitive model can be worked out and all the response mechanisms spelled out and built into the model. Change one variable and the consequences of that change can readily be traced through the system. All is known in this world, and the results of the analysis show that the competitive market is ideal with respect to efficiency and even justice. Of course, if the competitive

---

[1] See, for instance, Richard H. Leftwich, *The Price System and Resource Allocation*, 3d ed. (New York: Holt, Rinehart and Winston, 1966), pp. 24–25.

[2] Interestingly, the analogies given to support this procedure all come from the natural sciences, for instance, the frictionless state versus the friction of the real work. Ibid.

market is ideal, then any departure from it results in a loss of efficiency and the suboptimal use of resources: price is higher, output lower, and so on, under imperfect competition. The case for competition is closed.

Here is the danger: it is not appropriate to admit that imperfect competition exists and may be widespread and then measure the consequences by simply modifying the conclusions of the competitive model. *It is necessary to go back to the beginning and start the analysis with imperfect competition to understand the effects of imperfect markets.* There is no reason to expect imperfect competitors to be constrained in their actions in the same way as pure competitors, and their behavior, responses, goals, visions, expectations, and so on, may be completely at odds with those of pure competitors. Thus, their actions may seriously affect the working of the market economy, and the results of those actions may well be far different from those predicted by the modified competitive model. If we admit right at the beginning of the analysis the possibility of different behavior, then there is no reason why we should expect the same results as if we had started with pure competition and simply modified the results at the end of the analysis.

Take, for example, the simple case of a change in demand. In a competitive market a change in demand will have predictable results, but the same change in demand in an imperfect market may well have indeterminate results; a price and/or an output change can be expected in a competitive market, but in an imperfect market not even these predictions can be made with assurance. To modify the results of the competitive market simply will not do. In fact, indetermination reappears again and again for various changes in an imperfect market, and it often supplants the certainty of the competitive model. Aggregation becomes impossible, and to speak of an industry response is not always permissible.

Now, if we admit that large and growing segments of advanced economies involve imperfect competition, then we must also admit that responses to market changes and disturbances are likely to be unpredictable and indeterminate in advance (a priori). The predictable reactions of a purely competitive market are gone, and so is our ability to forecast market behavior accurately. If this is true for one market or industry, then assuming these industries occupy a strategic position in the economic structure, the effects of deliberate market disturbances may be unpredictable. This makes monetary and fiscal policies—those deliberate market disturbances—far less reliable in influencing the economy in the manner intended.

The point of this digression is to challenge the notion that macroeconomic models based on the competitive microeconomic model can easily be modified and the results altered at the very end of the analysis. It is not sufficient to admit imperfect competition into the picture after all the decisions, goals, expectations, and so on, have been reached earlier for a different set of controls and influences. On the contrary, imperfect competition must be introduced at the outset and the behavior appropriate to it incorporated into the entire analysis from start to finish. Unfortunately, mathematical expression and precise analysis are made impossible by this revision of method. The exposition of the model must become verbal for the most part.

This chapter and the next will explore such an impressionistic model and suggest its implications for macroeconomic theory and policy. The discussion, of necessity, must be suggestive rather than definitive, sketchy rather than complete. Still, much can be gained by the attempt, however amorphous the model. First, however, we will look at some of the potential deficiencies of the purely competitive model as the basis for a macroeconomic model.

The Competitive Microeconomic Model in Macroeconomic Models

There is no doubt that the assumption of pure competition played a pivotal role in the development of economic analysis. It both permitted and facilitated deductive reasoning in economic models and encouraged the development of the necessary tools of analysis. Yet the uncritical acceptance of its tenets, or rather, the unquestioning application of it for methodological purposes, seems to have excluded from the analysis the very elements that might have changed the results as indicated in the previous section. If one takes the premises of pure competition and applies deductive logic, the consequences of the model can easily be derived. But the premises themselves may preclude the asking of questions that do not follow from the premises. In short, the overwhelming attraction of this completely consistent and comprehensive model has inhibited the introduction into economic analysis of a changing and evolving economic structure.

It is not our purpose to examine all facets of the competitive model to seek out those parts that might be vulnerable either as premises or as deductions. We need only identify some of the major assumptions associated with the competitive model that could materially affect the analysis. These are presented here without undue elaboration; they will be recognized from previous allusions and will become instrumental in the formation of a different model.

The following items, without regard to order, are explicitly or implicitly parts of the competitive model:

1. The competitive mechanisms *deny the existence of excess capacity,* at least in the long run. All firms build the optimum plant for some output level (obtained by still more assumptions).
2. All firms (hence industries, economy) are subject to *diminishing returns.* This is the normal condition, which stems largely from the notion that firms are relatively small.
3. The model requires and assumes either that *perfect market knowledge exists or, more generally, that expectations are always stabilizing.* Uncertainty for economic units is either eliminated or, if a factor, not allowed to upset the market by leading to perverse actions.
4. *Firms and industries produce only one product,* and production methods are similar.
5. *All economic units have single-minded goals, which they pursue to the limits:* the entrepreneur maximizes profits; the wage earner maximizes his wage rate, and so on.
6. With these assumptions, all behavior, production functions, cost curves, and so on, are similar and lend themselves to *aggregation* to the industry level and then somewhat less confidently to the economy as a whole.
7. *The consumer is sovereign and guides production.*

It is easy to see how these elements of the competitive model might cause some difficulties. Reverse them or eliminate them and the model is no longer as self-contained and comprehensive as it was. To these factors we must add a few more, which most versions of the model fail to consider:

8. *Institutional changes* in the economic structure are frequently ignored. Particularly, the *corporation is ignored* and with it the possible different behavioral patterns and goals.
9. Of course, the model denies the existence of economic power, but in doing so, it precludes any consideration of the impact on the economy of an existing *inequality in the distribution of income and wealth.*
10. Since market forces are self-regulating, there is no need for outside intervention, that is, government intervention. If no external influences are needed, then political realities and institutions are ignored or underestimated. Hence, there is *no adequate theory of the public sector* and no intergovernmental problems.
11. Finally, little, if any, notice is given to the *social consequences* of the economic system or to economic policies in general.

These factors, together with the explicit conditions (large numbers, free entry, and homogeneous inputs and outputs), clearly restrict economic analysis. Of course, these points have all been recognized and debated. Critics have frequently pointed to the shortcomings of the pure competition model. Even defenders of the applicability of the model have acknowledged some of these problem areas. *But even those who use the competitive model wisely still rely upon modifications of the results to take these points into consideration.* The problems are not assumed away, but neither are they allowed to affect the analysis in a significant way.

Naturally, out of the criticisms of the competitive model, models of imperfect competition were developed. They have certainly not proved to be as powerful as the model of pure competition, and they remain crude by comparison. The competitive model strongly influences the models of imperfect competition, for even when imperfect models are used, many of the assumptions of the competitive model are carried over, sometimes uncritically. The same motivations are found, along with diminishing returns, similar production methods, cost curves, and so on. The result is one more manifestation that the competitive model has been modified in deference to reality and that some inefficiences—excess capacity and suboptimal resource use—have been allowed to develop.

Even so, the models of imperfect competition have not been integrated into the macroeconomic models. A glance at the problems should be sufficient to indicate why. It is difficult, if not impossible, to aggregate when motivations differ and adjustment responses are not uniform. Thus, the competitive model is used as the microeconomic basis for macroeconomic models, and the results are modified at the end of the analysis by introducing market realities.

Before we attempt to change the methodology, perhaps it would be wise to pause and examine the structure of the United States (or any other advanced) economy. In the process a deeper appreciation for the preceding criticisms may be gained, and the justification for a new model may become apparent.

The Structure of United States Industry

If, as is often contended, the changing structure of the United States economy has reduced the power of traditional economic theory to explain it, then it is necessary to examine that economic structure, however briefly, to evaluate the

TABLE 16.1

NUMBER OF FIRMS, BUSINESS RECEIPTS, AND NET PROFIT BY
TYPE OF ORGANIZATION, 1968

Business Form	Number of Businesses	Per Cent	Business Receipts (Millions)	Per Cent	Net Profit	Per Cent
Proprietorships	9,211,613	78.9	$ 222,105	13.0	$ 31,871	24.7
Partnerships	917,500	7.9	80,532	4.7	11,405	8.8
Corporations	1,541,637	13.2	1,403,500	82.3	85,962	66.5
Total	11,670,750	100.0	$1,706,187	100.0	$129,238	100.0

Source: Internal Revenue Service, *Statistics of Income, 1968, U.S. Business Tax Returns.*

claim. In this section some inspection of the United States economy is provided for that reason.

First, critics cite the emergence and dominance of the corporate form of business entity as evidence that the economic theory designed to explain the firm's behavior is obsolete. The entrepreneur of old has been largely superseded by institutions that do not and cannot tolerate individual domination. Let us look briefly at the composition of United States industry. Table 16.1 shows the number of firms, the business receipts, and net profit found in the three broad types of business entities in 1968.

It is clear that the number of sole proprietorships far exceeds the number of partnerships and corporations. Nearly 79 per cent of all firms were proprietorships. However, in terms of volume the corporate form of entity is most important, accounting for some 82 per cent of all business receipts and 67 per cent of all net profit. The corporate sector carries more weight. The explanation for these numbers is to be found in the fact that of the 9.2 million proprietorships, 7.0 million (over 75 per cent) had business receipts of less than $25,000, and only 0.03 million firms had business receipts in excess of $500,000. Furthermore, of the 9.2 million proprietorships, 7.2 million are found in agriculture, retail trade, and services, and only 0.2 million in manufacturing.

As for growth, in the two decades from 1939 to 1959, sole proprietorships grew by approximately 768 per cent, partnerships by 250 per cent, and corporations by 129 per cent; from 1959 to 1968 the changes are 0.01 per cent for proprietorships, −3.3 per cent for partnerships, and 43.6 per cent for corporations.

These summary data have already indicated the trends we sought: the corporate form of business entity is very important in the structure of United States industry, and it appears to be growing and thus can be expected to be even more important in the future. These trends are even more apparent for the manufacturing sector of the economy. Additional evidence of the importance of the corporate sector is quickly obtained by looking at GNP data. Over 55 per cent of GNP originates in the corporate sector.

Rearranging the tax data of Table 16.1, we can get some idea of the distribution of strength *within* the corporate sector. Table 16.2 shows the distribution of firms according to business receipts.

This table clearly shows the unequal distribution of size and strength within the corporate sector: 28.2 per cent of all corporations had business receipts of $25,000

TABLE 16.2
CORPORATIONS ARRANGED BY BUSINESS RECEIPTS, 1968

Business Receipts	Number of Firms	Per Cent of Firms	Per Cent of Business Receipts
$25,000 and under	435,314*	28.2	0.2
$100,000 and under	806,070	52.3	1.4
$500,000 and under	1,267,509	82.2	8.6
$1,000,000 and under	1,389,961	90.2	14.5
$5,000,000 and under	1,513,399	98.2	31.2
$5,000,000 and over	1,541,637	100.0	100.0

* Firms that reported total receipts rather than business receipts are assumed to fall into this class.
Source: See Table 16.1.

or less, and these firms accounted for only 0.2 per cent of all corporate business receipts; 90.2 per cent of all corporations accounted for only 14.5 per cent of receipts, and 98.2 per cent of all corporations accounted for only close to one third of business receipts. The last line of Table 16.2 is really revealing: *1.8 per cent of all corporations accounted for 68.8 per cent of business receipts,* and these firms each had receipts over $5 million. Out of over 1.5 million corporations, this amount of economic activity was carried out by only 28,000 firms, mainly in manufacturing and wholesale and retail trade. Thus, there are many small firms within the corporate sector coexisting with some very large firms.

A better grasp of the significance of the size of the larger corporations can be obtained by examining *The Fortune Directory* of the largest corporations in the United States. Table 16.3 presents the data for the 500 largest industrial corporations in the upper half and for the 50 largest companies in other areas in the lower half. The data for these other sectors are presented primarily for informational purposes, and we will look mainly at the industrial corporations.

Just a glance at Table 16.3 reveals some awesome economic facts: the top 500 industrial corporations had sales of over $500 billion (half a trillion dollars!) and had assets of nearly that size; they had net income of over $23 billion and employed over 14 million people. Putting these facts in perspective, "the 500 now account for 66 per cent of the sales of all United States industrial companies, 75 per cent of their total profits, and 75 per cent of all their employees."[3] Surely, this represents an enormous concentration of economic activity and strength and signals the possession of market power by these corporations.

Even within the top 500, it is obvious that there is a wide range of sizes, for the top 50 (see Table 16.3) account for nearly half of the totals for the group; furthermore, the top 200 corporations account for about 80 per cent of the totals and the top 300 for nearly 90 per cent. The economic structure is dominated at the top by comparatively few corporations, concentrated in comparatively few major industries. Looking over the list, auto companies, oil companies, electric companies, and communications companies take up the top positions. It hardly seems necessary to

[3] *Fortune* 85 (May 1972): 188.

TABLE 16.3
SALES, ASSETS, NET INCOME, AND EMPLOYEES OF LARGE FIRMS RANKED BY SALES OR ASSETS, 1971 (MILLIONS OF DOLLARS)

Firms Arrayed by Sales	Sales		Assets		Net Income		Employees	
	Amount	Per Cent	Amount	Per Cent	Amount	Per Cent	Number	Per Cent
Industrial Corporations								
500 Largest	502,898	100.0	455,567	100.0	23,412	100.0	14,324,890	100.0
Top 50	236,920	47.1	218,985	48.1	12,987	55.5	5,957,369	41.6
Top 100	315,180	62.7	292,442	64.2	16,311	69.7	8,428,939	58.8
Top 200	402,543	80.0	368,579	80.9	19,473	83.2	11,055,550	77.2
Top 300	450,274	89.5	411,367	90.3	21,484	91.8	12,543,205	87.6
Top 400	481,399	95.7	436,674	95.6	22,593	96.5	13,623,759	95.1
Commercial Banking Companies								
50 Largest*			313,665		1,977		384,727	
Life Insurance Companies								
50 Largest*			182,949		671		459,501	
Diversified Financial Companies								
50 Largest*			98,828		1,969		360,088	
Retailing Companies								
50 Largest	80,449		34,338		1,742		2,356,995	
Transportation Companies								
50 Largest†	24,700		45,412		352		894,342	
Utilities								
50 Largest*	48,628		154,191		5,846		1,414,290	
Total 800 Companies			1,284,950		35,968		20,194,833	

* Ranked by Assets
† Ranked by Operating Revenues

Source: Adapted from material originally appearing in *The Fortune Directory* © 1972 Time Inc.

385

justify further any statements about the concentration of power in the United States industrial structure. Still, it might be enlightening to imagine, as did Heilbroner,[4] what would happen to the United States economy if some catastrophe obliterated just 150 firms. Of course, the answer is the total collapse of the United States economy. Actually, it is not necessary to select 150 firms, for a much smaller number would accomplish the same result. The elimination of the top 50, 25, or even 10, would suffice; the interdependent relationships within the economy would guarantee that.

Furthermore, the concentration of economic activity appears to be growing. As one indication, the real growth of the top 500 in terms of sales is apparently greater than the growth of GNP in recent years, according to the *Fortune* magazine analysis.[5] As another indication, mergers within the 500 group continue to occur, although diminishing somewhat after 1971. The Federal Trade Commission noted: "In unprecedented fashion the current merger movement is centralizing and consolidating corporate control and decision-making among a relatively few vast companies."[6] Noting the growing trend of multiproduct and conglomerate corporations through mergers, the report warned of the consequences for competition and stated, "these interrelated developments pose a serious threat to America's democratic and social institutions by creating a degree of centralized private decision-making that is incompatible with a free enterprise system, a system relying upon market forces to discipline private economic power."[7]

Finally, as a result of ordinary growth, mergers, tax subsidies, and many other factors, a number of industries are dominated by only a few firms. The percentage of the industries' sales accounted for by a small number of firms—"the concentration ratio"—is quite large for several United States industries. Only a handful of firms dominate some industries, including some of the major ones.[8] There are difficulties, of course, in defining an industry and in measuring the impact on markets, but for our purposes, it is only necessary to establish that the structure of the economy is considerably different from the theoretical model of pure competition. The preceding discussion should be sufficient to demonstrate that claim.

The Effects of Market Structure

Recall that many economists either deny the existence of extensive market power or question the applicability of that power. The data in the previous section were supplied in order to show the existence of potential market power. The doubt that this power can be used effectively is more serious. It is not always easy to observe the use of market power, even when abuses of that power are involved. Neither is it easy to observe the real differences among markets as they diverge from the competitive model, particularly over time. In brief, even if market imperfections are

---

[4] Robert L. Heilbroner, *The Limits of American Capitalism* (New York: Harper & Row, 1967), (Torchbook ed.), p. 11.

[5] See chart in *Fortune* (May 1972): 185.

[6] Staff report of the FTC, *Economic Report on Corporate Mergers*, submitted as part of the Hearings Before the Subcommittee on Antitrust and Monopoly of the Committee on the Judiciary. U.S. Senate. 91st Congress (Washington, D.C.: Government Printing Office, 1968), p. 3.

[7] Ibid., p. 5.

[8] For the actual data, see report of the Subcommittee on Antitrust and Monopoly. Committee on the Judiciary. U.S. Senate. 89th Congress (Washington, D.C.: Government Printing Office, 1966), part I.

admitted, it does not follow that the effects of market power are directly observable or measurable. Just how, when, and if market power is applied to different market situations is seldom easily inferred. If students of industrial organization cannot separate the effects of market structure upon economic performance, then students of macroeconomics are left with an uncertain or indeterminate microeconomic foundation.

Consider one part of the problem to illustrate the nature of the issue: does market structure affect *macroeconomic* stability? Which is likely to lead to greater macroeconomic stability—a largely competitive economy or an economy that contains widespread imperfect markets? A simple question, but not easy to answer. Generally, if competitive markets can be expected to react quickly to changing market conditions, then sudden shifts in output, employment, and price, and other adjustments, will be more disruptive to the economy than the "stickiness" and inflexibility of imperfect markets. Less rapid adjustments to market conditions generally associated with imperfect competition can thus be conducive to overall market stability. Of course, this conclusion depends upon the forms of imperfect competition; upon how extensive the imperfections are in the economy, in which sectors, and so on; upon government interference; and upon many other factors. *Much, of course, depends upon the behavioral assumptions made for imperfect competitors and their goals and institutional structures.* Thus, conclusions about macroeconomic stability rest ultimately on the firms' behavior and institutional makeup, and we must return to the discussion of the previous chapter.

Pending further empirical research, the only way out of this dilemma is to pose additional hypotheses and begin the theoretical discussion anew in the hope that some clarification will result. It is preferable to have an incomplete answer to a question than never to have posed the question at all.

Towards a Different Model

Let us begin by taking superficial but unconventional looks at the United States economy in the light of the foregoing reexamination of it. At this stage, the analysis need not be rigorous or precise. Indeed, it is not the purpose of this chapter to spell out a fully specified model but to suggest some of the implications of a different conception of an advanced economy. The closer to reality a model becomes, the more precision must be sacrificed.

INSTITUTIONAL BACKGROUND

We begin with some institutional considerations that are necessary for the analysis.

1. The model recognizes or assumes that widespread imperfect competition exists in *key markets* in the economy. In these the corporation is the dominant form of business enterprise and the market structure can be characterized as oligopolistic.

The behavior of these corporations is much less predictable than conventional theory postulates. Here, we would like to emphasize some points:

a. Market power is assumed to exist but need not be exercised continuously. That is, market power can be exercised in some time periods or for some market situations and held in abeyance for others. This conduct makes it difficult to observe and measure market power in action.

b. Collusion among firms is not necessary, since close contact, however casual, is routine and lack of market information is no real barrier.

c. These large corporations, which dominate the key industries, need not desire technological advances or efficiency as a major goal. Friendly competition is standard, and stimulating competition is irksome and must come from other sources.

d. In the exercise of market power or friendly competition the rules of the game change and shift over time, sometimes in response to public reactions.

2. The model recognizes or assumes that the rest of the economy is characterized by some variant of the monopolistic competition market structure. Whether classified by industry, region, or other characteristics, these firms are not quantitatively important, particularly in the key industries. More important, they are not influential—*they follow rather than lead economic events and developments.* The market structure of pure competition is ruled out as unrealistic for any industry in advanced capitalism.

3. The model assumes that public control over the economic structure is insignificant and ineffective. Governmental concern over the economic structure has been sporadic at best and rather impotent in most cases. The lack of leadership, funds, and purpose has led to a high degree of tolerance for business practices, and much has been accepted in the name of the vague "national interest." Whatever activity does exist is in the federal sector, while states and localities appear helpless. (Analogous to the private sector, the federal government has the power and will to lead, as the oligopolists do, while states and localities surrender power and are forced to follow, as the smaller firms do.)

4. Until the recent consumer movement, which is still small, the general public was passive. Perhaps consumers recognized their lack of power or felt they were helpless, but more than likely their resentment was mixed with awe. Public toleration of business was fostered by a sense of long-run benefits rather than short-run costs. In any event, little power is assumed to inhere in the personal sector for reversing economic trends in market structure.

5. Organized labor is assumed to be passive at best with regard to market structure and may even be regarded as a defender of the status quo. Despite protestations to the contrary, the labor movement has lost its zeal and ideological motivations, and the exercise of market power by business is not as upsetting if the benefits are shared. To protect jobs, labor has become an ally rather than an adversary of large firms, since it advocates protectionism and backs the defense establishment, and so on. In brief, little in the way of change can be expected from organized labor (at least in the United States)—neither challenge to the existing economic structure nor resistance to trends that perpetuate it.

6. The model also includes, from the outset, the foreign trade sector. As with the competitive model, it is no longer legitimate to work with a closed economy and then alter the results to account for foreign trade. While foreign trade is a small part of GNP, its importance for domestic policies and international politics is enormous. The rise of the multinational corporation, the increase of direct and indirect investment abroad, charges of United States imperialism, trade-financing woes, and so on, all attest to the growing importance of the trade sector. For our purposes, it is assumed that large corporations consider foreign markets in making

routine decisions and thus have additional options as domestic economic conditions change. These firms are not restricted entirely by domestic concerns but can take actions in other markets, where the economic climate may be far different. In brief, the foreign sector is no longer relegated to residual sales efforts or secondary market development concerns. Foreign markets can be used as outlets for excess goods and can provide a safety valve for the export of capital; excess capacity at home can be partly offset by investing abroad, thus using up accumulated funds, or remedied by increasing sales abroad. It follows that production, sales, promotional efforts, and other decisions by the firm are influenced by, and in turn influence, foreign markets; and that this growing trend must be incorporated into any model of an advanced economy.

These brief but sweeping generalizations of some far-reaching institutional changes could no doubt be elaborated at some length, but this is not the place for such an attempt. The outline is enough to suggest, however, that no one model may ever be sufficient again to capture the dynamic influences of rapid institutional change.

A FRAGMENTED MICROECONOMIC MODEL

Concentrating mainly on the business sector, let us build a rather eclectic model of the large firm and the economy. There is no serious claim to originality here, but some small contribution may be realized in its construction and application. Building a model was thought to be preferable to using an adaptation of other models.[9]

OLIGOPOLISTIC KEY INDUSTRIES

Firms in key industries (metals, automobiles, petroleum, machinery, and so on) are assumed to be organized as corporations and characterized by the oligopolistic market structure. Furthermore, these industries are highly concentrated, with a few firms dominating the markets. While these industries may include medium and even small firms, the latter are assumed either to be not significantly different in behavior from the large ones or to be followers of the major decisions of the larger ones. They hide under the umbrella of the large firms, or some maverick behavior is tolerated by the large firms, which do not feel seriously threatened—all in the name of friendly competition to mask real market power. Thus, the large firms' behavior must be the center of attention.

Before turning to their pricing and output policies, some institutional background is necessary. First, these oligopolistic firms, run by hired managers, are not as rational in their operations as past economic theory postulated. Nor do they pursue single-mindedly one simple goal in the unswerving manner assumed in most microeconomic models. Their goals may change in response to current market conditions and to revisions in vague long-run plans. In the end, their goals may well be interdependent anyway, so that emphasizing one now and another later may give false impressions of rationality or irrationality. More important, the long-run goals and

---

[9] For those interested, several models have been developed that differ from the traditional model. In addition to those already cited, there are the following: the "capacity" model of J. Steindl, *Maturity and Stagnation in American Capitalism* (Oxford: Basil Blackwell, 1952); the "target rate of return" model of Otto Eckstein and Gary Fromm, "The Price Equation," *American Economic Review* 58 (December 1968): 1159–1183; the "sales maximization" model of W. J. Baumol, *Business Behavior, Value and Growth*, rev. ed. (New York: Harcourt, Brace and World, 1959); and many others.

plans (growth, self-preservation, public image, and so on) may frequently conflict with short-run goals (profit and sales increases). Obviously, plans are revised in the light of actual experience, so that rationality requires shifting goals and not the stubborn, irrational pursuit of one goal regardless of experience. While single-goal models are thus deficient, it is not easy to construct a model with shifting or multiple goals. It is difficult to build one theoretically, and appeals to empirical findings for help will be futile; for if the preceding behavior is reasonable, then the shifting goals and time period interactions can never be really observed or measured.

By assumption, then, the large firms have multiple and shifting goals depending on economic conditions. If we concentrate on the immediate short run, either profits or sales would be the likely variables of control. Let us arbitrarily assume that the firm will seek a level of profits, after taxes, that will be sufficient to facilitate the achievement of other simultaneous goals and long-run goals as well. Profits need not be maximized if a lesser return would not sacrifice the attainment of other goals. Presumably, the firm knows how much profit is necessary to reach these other goals, but we must not be surprised to find the amount somewhat vague (as the goals may be). In addition, firms may accept less than this target profit level if it is felt to be a temporary condition or if another goal shifts into the prominent position. As vague and imprecise as this hypothesis is, it will have to stand; otherwise a rigid maximization hypothesis must be accepted.

Second, it is assumed that these large firms do possess market power, defined simply as control over their markets. Many actions taken in the past have now resulted in these giant corporations, and their sheer size and power has insulated them from the vagaries of the marketplace. Recall, however, that this is potential market power and need not be exercised continuously or even consistently. These firms will use their might when required, and at other times, the market power will remain dormant. Much depends upon the market situation and public concern. Those who study imperfections of the marketplace and who attempt to observe or measure the exercise of market power completely miss this point: power is used selectively, not continuously.

Third, traditional limitations on the exercise of market power have been eroded. Any real competition must now come from outside the system, which means from foreign sources in an open economy. Galbraith's principle of countervailing power, in which market power is limited by the large firms buying and selling to each other, has also been diminished in importance as these firms have merged, diversified, and acquired potential competitors or former suppliers. Conglomeration and diversification have ensured supplies and spread the risks over many product lines —to the extent that industry classification becomes a game. Still, market power does shift over time as demand conditions change. Substitute products disrupt the comfortable competition, and advertising campaigns are successful in wooing away customers. These are temporary disruptions, and the firm is goaded to react, all of which gives the appearance of intense competitive effort, but the market returns to the quasistability until the next flurry. (Remember, these firms are in the key industries with essential products.) Less certain are the effects of geography on competition, but these possibilities are ignored here.

Fourth, if market power is significant enough, there is no need for these firms to stress the goal of efficiency, the traditional driving force. A good deal of inefficiency can be covered up, because the firm has some control over those market conditions that might penalize inefficiency, particularly price and the risk of insufficient funds. Planned obsolescence and marketing practices also help, of course.

Neither are these firms driven toward maximizing productivity and pushing ever outward the frontiers of technological advance. Galbraith's notion of technological virtuosity as a goal of the firm need not be discarded as long as it is postulated that the firm is not compelled to seek it but can be satisfied by the myth that it is efficient and technologically superior. These firms do have the resources to employ the latest techniques, but they need not develop them or introduce them speedily.

Perhaps enough has been said to convey a substantial impression of the kind of firm and behavior that we must consider. Without pursuing all the details or ramifications of these issues, it is time to turn to the short-run pricing and output decisions of the firm.

PRICING AND OUTPUT DECISIONS

Prices are determined by a markup over standard costs and are high enough to provide for the level or amount of the targeted profits. Output decisions are based on estimated sales volume. These statements require some additional explanation.

The sequences leading to these decisions are as follows. First, the firms calculate the standard cost of their products. The standard cost is calculated for the normal or typical operating rate with some notion of capacity ever present. The level of normal capacity will vary from industry to industry, but it is assumed that for these large firms an operating rate of 75 to 80 per cent is considered normal.[10] Thus, excess capacity is regarded as routine and perhaps even as essential. The firms may deliberately build in excess capacity in anticipation of further demand increases and thus be prepared to increase output and protect their market shares. In addition, a multiplant firm may be adjusting its scale of operations to keep costs constant or to meet geographical competition; excess capacity may be the result.

The standard cost concept reflects the belief that costs of production are fairly constant. The constant cost idea is also a product of, as well as a cause of, the lack of concern for efficiency; some of the variable costs (for instance, skilled labor) are regarded as overhead items and do not vary with output. Another reason for the belief in constant costs is the fact that many costs of production cannot be allocated precisely by the cost accountant to specific processes or products—particularly in multiproduct plants. Therefore, arbitrary assignment of costs is necessary, and these allocations tend to keep costs in a fairly constant range, relatively speaking. Standard costs do change but only in response to major changes in the data, for instance, a major hourly wage adjustment. Still, standard costs remain in effect for long periods of time, and since prices are based on the standard cost, they too remain inflexible for similar periods. (These are quoted prices, not actual transaction prices.) However, prices are not as inflexible as the standard costs and can rise or fall long before the standards are revised; the cost accountant must then perform the extra task of analyzing actual results and explaining the data more thoroughly.

Note that no attempt is made to maximize profits, even though some break-even exercises may be conducted. Firms may come close to maximizing profits, but they

---

[10] A dramatic example is provided by the steel industry. Estes Kefauver has written: "For the steel industry as a whole and specifically for the largest producer, U.S. Steel, when the production rate approaches 33 per cent of capacity, operations are profitable." *In a Few Hands: Monopoly Power in America* (Baltimore: Penguin Books, 1965), p. 110.

do not feel compelled to do so. Note also that actual costs determine the amount of profit but are not relevant to output decisions, no matter what the shape of the cost curves. Standard costs are regarded as constant costs, and this cost curve is horizontal.

How is the output level determined, then? Output is determined by sales estimates and other marketing data. Errors in estimates mean inventory changes (not necessarily price changes), and in the case of underestimates, excess capacity ensures that more output is available without delay. Inventory build-ups are protected as well as possible by not altering the style or quality of the product until the inventories are depleted (a form of planned obsolescence). Still, mistakes are made, but past profit accumulation helps to offset them; severe mistakes are remedied primarily by employment layoffs of the most dispensable workers and perhaps in the end by price discounts (or special terms) from catalog or list prices.

Of course, price competition is kept to a minimum, even when price discounts are necessary. Either costs are similar or, more likely, some variation of price leadership is at work, with all firms charging similar or identical prices. The more inefficient firms simply get less profit and must lower their goals accordingly. There could be some impetus to greater efficiency in this case.

Firms do not compete by changing prices for another reason—once set, the price variable can be ignored in favor of giving more attention to the sales volume. It is also true that most firms have a tendency to underestimate the elasticity of demand for their products. The reduction in price is regarded as not worth the risk of rocking the boat. Even if sales did increase somewhat as prices fell, it would not be worth possible retaliation from the rest of the industry. The smaller the firm, the greater the danger. The kinked demand curve model is a special case of this kind of oligopolistic behavior.

THE REMAINING BUSINESS SECTOR

In an advanced economy there are many industries besides the key industries. Some of the former can be characterized as oligopolistic (for instance, the cigarette industry), while others come much closer to the competitive model (for example, the apparel industry). Thus, it is assuming a lot to lump this wide range of market structures into a single sector. This separate unit (industries other than key ones) must also embrace agriculture, mining, contracting, and the service industries. We have thus aggregated a wide array of products, business forms, and market conditions. For our purposes, this is defensible, but it must always be kept in mind that this type of aggregation has severe limitations and is justified only by expediency.

The rationale for this arbitrary division of the economy into two sectors is to reflect quantitative importance and influence. The key industries are obviously quantitatively important but are also the leaders in the economy. The remaining businesses essentially follow economic events but do not initiate them; they react and respond to economic conditions but do not create them.

Thus, the market structure of the industries in the residual business sector is somewhat irrelevant. For in a macroeconomic sense, if they are quantitatively unimportant and relatively uninfluential, then the market structure is downgraded in importance.

Let us assume, then, that the remaining industries can be classified as monopolistically competitive, and that the traditional model that describes the behavior of firms in monopolistically competitive industries is adequate for our purposes. The model is vague enough anyway, so that all we need add to it is more market power and more goals to the usual profit maximization. What remains is that the firms in these industries behave like miniature oligopolies but with considerably less power and considerably less area for maneuver and manipulation (and, of course, influence).

THE GOVERNMENT SECTOR

For numerous reasons, it is an almost hopeless task to construct a theory of government behavior. All too often, government actions have been erratic, unpredictable, and baffling—at least as far as economic actions are concerned. Economists long have considered the public sector as exogenous to the explanatory model. No doubt this is expedient, and we are forced to make the same assumption. This means that we will assume that government behaves as it has in the past. As we explore the working of the model later, we can inject the "proper" government action along with the actions likely to be taken, using past history as a guide.

THE HOUSEHOLD SECTOR

The traditional theory of household consumption should also be questioned. Recall that the family unit acts so as to maximize utility subject to an income constraint, given prices and preferences. Consumption preferences and tastes are formed independently of any other consumer unit; goods are divisible; and so on. The theory is elegant but describes the behavior of only a small fraction of households. Some microeconomic concept akin to the relative income hypothesis is needed to capture the essence of more characteristic behavior.

For our model, the rejection of the traditional view of household microeconomic behavior is not that serious, since it never had a significant impact on macroeconomic analysis anyway. Without constructing a new theory it is sufficient here to indicate a few simple changes and proceed to the macroeconomic level.

We assume that income continues to be the best independent variable to explain consumption, but advertising outlays should be added as an important variable as well. The relation between advertising and consumption is direct; that is, the more advertising at any level of income, the more consumption at that level of income; if advertising outlays fall, consumption falls.

The remainder of the consumption function can be carried over as is, with all of the former difficulties included. One further observation will complicate matters somewhat: in periods of extreme uncertainty, consumption will fall (and saving rise), and advertising may prove less effective as well. What constitutes extreme uncertainty is not clear, nor can such periods or events be predicted.

THE LABOR SECTOR

Organized labor is assumed to act primarily as an economic institution. It attempts to obtain a high reward for its members and, despite its official announcements, makes the expansion of jobs and employment a secondary goal.[11] This pursuit of a high reward is made possible by governmental programs to aid the unemployed, who could have been made unemployed by the pressure of labor for

[11] For a discussion of possible union objectives and behavior, see J. Dunlop, *Wage Determination Under Trade Unions* (New York: Macmillan, 1944).

higher rewards. Some of the moral sting of the relentless pursuit for higher returns *for those employed* is removed as public action relieves the situation of those made unemployed as a consequence.

The ideological part of the labor movement in the United States has receded far into the background, and labor wishes to share in the rewards of the capitalist system, not to overturn it—Marx was wrong. As a consequence, organized labor acts so as to keep intact its share of the national income but not especially to increase that share. Thus, when profits rise, labor wants to share in the increase, and when profits fall, it resists wage decreases (for those employed) and may even attempt to protect some jobs.

It is important to note that most of the key industries have been organized, so that even if only one third of the labor force is unionized, its strength and numbers are concentrated in the most important sector of the economy. Just as the key industries can be expected to lead the economic activity of the nation, so organized labor in these industries can be expected to set the pace for the rest of the labor force. Their union contracts become the ones to emulate, and pattern bargaining contracts result.

Thus, in the nonunionized sector we can expect to find the attempt to secure similar gains and similar terms as those secured by major unions in major industries. Naturally, there will be a time lag, perhaps a considerable one, before the gains actually show up in nonunionized industries. These trends are well known and frequently observed. It is necessary to point out, however, that we are still involved in a considerable degree of aggregation and have brought together a wide assortment of nonunion occupations and industries—from waitresses to physicians to corporation presidents. Therefore, it is probably better to break up the nonunion sector into two general segments: first, those who can protect their rewards easily, such as professional people; and second, those who are so weak (unskilled nonunionized labor) that they suffer in the short run, and even in the long run may fall behind more powerful labor groups. Such a division, although arbitrary, might help in disclosing the unequal impact of economic fluctuations on the labor force.[12]

THE FOREIGN TRADE SECTOR

More and more attention is being given to foreign market development by domestic corporations. Decisions regarding foreign markets are made in conjunction with, not apart from, domestic concerns. Accordingly, exports of either goods or capital will have to be given greater consideration. In the past, exports have been treated as exogenous and have been ignored. It is now necessary to consider the economic conditions of foreign economies explicitly and to introduce conditions of trade as forcing some decisions. Comparative costs, international finance developments, trading blocs, and so on, have all altered the traditional views of foreign trade and commerce. In our model these factors can only be briefly mentioned, but their importance should not be underestimated.

As with exports, imports have been made to depend primarily on relative prices

---

[12] It is also interesting to note that the *productivity* of organized labor is readily observed and measured while the productivity of nonunionized labor is not. This is because more productivity data are available for manufacturing industries than for service industries. This fact should be remembered when the discussion turns to the productivity of labor. Rewards based on productivity data must inevitably fail to reflect accurately the economic contribution of the labor input. To explore this further would take us far afield, but the warning is worth heeding whenever productivity is the issue.

and income. These variables have been and continue to be important explanatory factors. For the United States economy the income variables help explain much of the observed rise in imports over the last decades.

The price variable, however, may have lost its strong influence, particularly for consumer goods. Growing affluence in the United States has meant less price elasticity for many imported goods. Not much reduction in demand can be expected from a rise in the price of Scotch whisky, foreign sports cars, or many other imports such as low-priced apparel and shoes. Price is not unimportant, but it is becoming less important. Thus, attempts to influence the volume of trade by changing the relative prices of goods—say by devaluation—are likely to be much less effective than in the past. The insensitivity to price is partly the result of unique goods available only from abroad, but increasingly in the past several decades it is also due to the superior design of foreign goods and the lead taken by foreign firms in introducing new products. The devaluations of the dollar in 1971 and 1973 have not reversed the balance-of-payments problem or in the short run even seriously affected it.

In our model some account must be given of these developments. Of necessity, the analysis must be suggestive at best, but wherever possible, these changes will be acknowledged. In this way some of the changing directions of foreign trade can be indicated.

It seems preferable to leave intact all other institutions and practices found in the usual models rather than to attempt a wholesale revision of all parts. It is better to concentrate attention on the major departures rather than to get bogged down in endless details. With this eclectic and impressionistic model, we can now begin to examine what effects these changes have on the conclusions reached earlier. How significant are the changes for both theory and policy, and what direction should further analysis take?

The Impressionistic Model in Operation

Let us use the model in the Keynesian tradition and put the emphasis on aggregate demand. The effects of changes in aggregate demand can best be understood by varying the level of demand at various operating levels of the economy. This is the most direct approach and should provide us with some insights into the eclectic model in operation. We wish to observe some effects of market structure on the economic system and the development and application of market power. By sacrificing precision and by observing an economy over time, we hope to gain insights into social and political consequences as well as economic ones. Based loosely on, but not limited to, the United States experience, this historical approach should permit the model to uncover some of the major problems of an advanced economic system in which market power has been allowed to develop.

The Depressed Economy

In a severely depressed economy output and employment levels are quite low relative to the potential levels. The impressionistic model would portray the economic conditions by sector as follows.

THE BUSINESS SECTOR

If the economy had been operating at a higher level in the not too distant past, we can expect that most firms and industries would find themselves with considerable excess capacity. The profit position of all firms is likely to be weak, with the larger firms in a better position, since their break-even points are calculated at a low rate of operation. Depending on the industry and the product, some large firms may be making small profits, while others are barely breaking even. Still other firms may be losing money but existing on past accumulation. In the remainder of the business sector the smaller firms have suffered enormously, since many of them have failed, leaving only the most efficient and financially prudent ones in operation.

In both cases, no net investment is likely to be forthcoming either from existing firms or from new entrants into the industries. Even gross investment is minimal, since firms may decide not to replace equipment as it wears out or deteriorates through idleness. Market expansion efforts are also likely to be minimal both in domestic and foreign markets. Firms are not likely to be venturesome and will avoid risks.

THE LABOR SECTOR

The power of the labor movement would be seriously compromised by the large amount of unemployment, the absence of the strike weapon, and the profit position of firms. Membership in labor unions may be stable or possibly growing in these circumstances, and there may even be renewed ideological interests; but in the end the real bargaining power is greatly restricted. In all likelihood, there will be an attempt to protect the jobs of those employed and to increase the number of employed rather than a policy of wage maximization. Naturally, the unskilled, the uneducated, and the handicapped bear a disproportionate share of the burden of unemployment. Firms can afford to discriminate in a loose labor market.

THE HOUSEHOLD SECTOR

With massive unemployment and falling incomes, we might expect that households would consume a larger fraction of their disposable incomes than formerly (APC rises). There would eventually be a tendency to consume more necessities, perhaps, as income fell, but in any case, saving would fall and could even turn negative.

Great insecurity would be manifested by little job changing and widespread uncertainty and fear. If income had fallen steadily over a period of time, expectations would probably be for continued declines, but if the fall in income had been erratic, expectations would be confused and mixed. Expectations of this kind do not lead to new initiatives or encourage the business sector to step up operations.

THE FOREIGN TRADE SECTOR

With income falling, imports are likely to fall also. Much depends upon the economic conditions existing in the economies of trading partners. Worldwide depression may leave relative prices unchanged, making imports vary with those goods that are (real) income elastic. Prices may not fall by the same amount in all countries, however, and the change in real income may result in changed levels of imports. Without examining this in detail, little can be stated with certainty, but most likely imports would fall in an economy like the United States, which is relatively self-sufficient in food-stuffs and other basic goods (at least at low consumption levels).

Similar problems occur in the discussion of exports. Exports need not fall; it depends upon relative prices and other economic conditions as well as on the type of goods being exported. Only a detailed examination of exports would reveal the situation. It may be easier to assume that exports will not increase as firms retrench, avoid risks, and play it safe. The more widespread the depression, the more prevalent this attitude.

With these observations in mind, it is possible to make the guarded assumption that the volume of trade may well remain stable or diminish slightly for an economy resembling that of the United States. This conclusion would not follow for other advanced economies where trade may be more crucial.

THE PUBLIC SECTOR

Naturally, as national income falls, so do the tax receipts of the public sector. However, many expenditure programs are unrelated to the current economic condition and long-term commitments have already been made. Thus, a budgetary deficit is to be expected, even without new spending programs, but the pressure for increased government expenditures would make such a result fairly certain. Humanitarian programs of relief payments, food distribution, additional unemployment compensation, and so on, would be demanded—without reference to fiscal policy. All levels of government would feel the pressure for action, but the federal government would receive most of it as well as most of the blame for the economic predicament.

MACROECONOMIC POLICY

Let us assume that the public sector responds to the crisis. In the latter half of the twentieth century no government in an advanced economy can afford to ignore the economic plight at depression levels, regardless of professed ideology. The "proper" policy is the expansion of the public sector via increased expenditure programs on public works, transfer payment schemes, direct purchases of goods and services, expansion of public payrolls, and so on. These actions may well occur even in the absence of planned fiscal policy measures as humanitarian concerns replace the ideological ones.

As postulated, no other sector of demand is likely to respond and turn the economic situation around, and of course, no other sector need respond to demands of what is in the national interest. If anything is to be done in reversing the economic situation in relatively short order, the public sector would have to assume that responsibility. As government expenditures increase, income would rise, probably by some multiple. As income increases, consumption would increase as well; the more direct the government program (transfer payments), the greater the increase in both.

The accelerator effect of changing consumption expenditures is *not* likely to work in influencing corresponding investment expenditures. Excess capacity is too great at low levels of output, and any increase in demand can be met by putting previously idle plants in operation. Therefore, the accelerator does not work effectively at this level of output, making continued public effort necessary to keep the expansion going.

Increases in employment can be expected as firms utilize their existing plant, and the demand for labor increases slowly as well. The expansion of employment would probably work against the pressures for wage increases of those employed, and wage demands are thus mitigated.

Similarly, price increases would be absent or minimal as economic activity increased. First, because increasing output may result in small but positive increases in profit as break-even points are further exceeded; second, pressures for price increases would be tempered by the uncertainty over the extent of the economic recovery; and third, by the lack of pressure from the cost side, particularly for wages.

All of this analysis would appear to validate the insight of Keynes: increases in aggregate demand at low levels of output would increase output and employment while leaving prices and wages relatively stable. Furthermore, the accelerator would be inoperative, at least in this short-run period, and finally, the public sector must take the responsibility for the economic recovery. Public action is required when private motivation is lacking. The traditional Keynesian model would appear to describe these conclusions adequately, and the revised model does not significantly affect the results or the analysis.

The increase in government expenditures will require deficit spending, since tax receipts are low and inadequate. The question becomes how to finance the deficit, particularly with the aim of achieving the maximum expansion from the spending programs. Resort to the money printing press or the sale of bonds directly to the Federal Reserve would increase the money supply and would permit full expansion, since there is no offset to the expansionary effects of the deficit budget in the form of reduced demand deposits or reduced commercial bank reserves.

The possibility that the full expansionary effect of the budget deficit will not be realized comes when the government borrows from the general public or from commercial banks. In the former case, the bonds are paid for by drawing down demand deposits, and in the latter case, by a reduction in reserves, and the growth of the money supply is restricted.

Recall, however, that the purchase of bonds in either case is likely to come out of idle funds, and these idle funds are now made active, and hence the overall result is still likely to be expansionary. Presumably, the financial community has grown used to the lower interest rate as the norm and becomes willing to release idle funds for bonds, or optimistic expectations follow from government initiatives. If interest rates are forced upwards by large-scale borrowing by government, investment spending is not adversely affected, since investment is not interest-elastic for existing firms, and consumption loans and mortgage loans are likely to continue without reduction. In conclusion, it appears likely that the overall effect of the deficit budget is expansionary without any serious limitations being posed by the method of financing. As long as the analysis is conducted along traditional lines (the new monetarism included), it continues to confirm the results of the earlier model, but still there is the sense that something has been omitted, and habits of thought must be discarded if new insights are to be obtained.

With the breakdown of competition, it is no longer sufficient to speak of broad groups or sectors as though they were homogeneous. Consider the following question, inappropriate in the pure competition model: as employment increases, *who gets the jobs and who is left behind?* Obviously, the skilled, the educated, the talented get the jobs first (the same groups retained their employment in the downswing), and the unskilled, the uneducated, and the handicapped remain unemployed. Social Darwinism, the natural selection process, operates and in the process creates groups or classes of people differentiated by ability or influence and, more particularly, by income. Some men are given or earn social status and prestige while others are made to feel inferior and are denied the dignity of working in a work-oriented society.

The gains in increased employment opportunities are diminished by the creation of antagonistic groups, which could lead to social conflicts at some later date. In this movement the unequal income distribution is created in the working force, and the inequality is not likely to be remedied quickly, even if the unemployed find jobs. Wage differentials become embedded, and the hierarchy within the labor sector becomes assured. These are important developments for the society, since they are likely to be carried forward over long periods—even when the economy recovers fully. Market imperfections are bound to be created to protect these conditions, so that the marketplace is prevented from balancing out or cancelling such advantages in a normal way and the preferred positions are perpetuated.

The social problems created or exacerbated in a depressed economy are not confined to the labor force. True, the frustration, the despair, the sense of hopelessness in the face of economic forces not understood, the sense of impotence, and so on, are long-lived scars on the labor force, driving it to conservative positions and making security a prime motivation. It may also be possible that some form of natural selection may operate in the business sector as well. The weak, inefficient, marginal firms could be driven out in a slump period, and only those firms with sufficient resources survive. The remaining firms are in a preferred position when recovery begins, since they have managed to secure stable shares of their respective markets. Their marketing organizations would attempt to reach long-run agreements, to create positive identification with the firms' products through trade names and advertising, and in general, to foster any arrangement with suppliers or customers that would assure a stable share of the market over time.

Along with the buying and selling arrangements, the surviving firm gains a preferred position through its better financial condition—it survived partly for this reason and is likely to benefit from this fact as well as from its superior position when economic conditions improve. Naturally, the larger, more diversified corporations are better able to withstand the downswing, and these firms emerge in an even more powerful position in the upswing. These firms are to be found in the key industry categories, so that it follows that these giant corporations gain even more protection from market forces. Barriers to entry are quickly erected to preserve and consolidate the immunity.

To sum up, the breakdown of economic prosperity such as postulated here has some economic and social effects that are far-reaching and long-lasting. These effects subvert the tenets of capitalism and help push the economy away from the pure model. Even if the analysis began with purely competitive markets, similar conclusions would result: some economic units emerge in a preferred position relative to others, and institutions and protective behavior will soon follow to assure the perpetuation of that strength. The fact that our analysis began with the recognition of market power does not change the conclusions. However, by introducing market imperfections into the analysis from the start, we are not blinded to the fact that imperfections are generated by the operation of the economy. Thus, while the economic analysis is not materially affected at this stage, the market structure will become an important factor in later stages of economic growth and development.

Also there is the unspecified, but nevertheless real, beginning of reliance upon government, particularly central government, as an institution financially responsible for economic stability. Few seriously question the death of laissez-faire capitalism anymore, but few have traced the implications of this development for the motivations and plans of the corporate business sector. How and to what extent does governmental economic intervention enter as an input into private corporate decisions?

The Economy in Recovery

Working with a severely depressed economy is not likely to yield many insights beyond the implications for market structure, income distribution, and the growth of government revealed in the previous section. No doubt, further examination of the depressed economy would be interesting, but to keep the analysis brief, more would be gained by moving to a discussion of the recovering economy. Moderate recessions are more likely to occur than major depressions, and these are more in need of examination.

THE LABOR SECTOR

Let us assume that economic recovery proceeds from the government impetus, and let us examine the effects of the expansionary period on various sectors. As the economic expansion proceeds, more and more workers gain employment; the fuller the recovery, the greater the gain in employment. There is now pressure on the union to move away from the single-minded goal of employment maximization to the goal of increasing the wage share of income. There are two reasons for the switch in goal emphasis: first, as recovery proceeds, corporate profits rise quickly and the wage share falls; and as employment grows at the lower end of the wage scale, there is pressure from those already employed to establish, protect, and maintain wage differentials. A hierarchy of wage scales develops as the skilled and trained members of the labor force demand recognition for their status by seeking higher wages—higher wages being their main way to distinguish themselves from the less skilled and to demonstrate their superiority.

Without competition in the labor market, these actions and goals become both feasible and realistic. The demand for higher wages and the desire for recognition in the form of wage differentials is sought first by organized labor. Located in key industries in which profits can be expected to grow early in the recovery, organized labor has both the opportunity and the incentive to react to the changing conditions. Collective bargaining demands can be expected to reflect these changed attitudes in the next contract negotiation.

In other areas of the economy the recovery does not proceed so quickly, and profits do not respond so rapidly. In these probably more competitive areas, labor is not in a position to demand higher wages, and the goal of increasing employment is not substantially supplanted. The labor force engaged in services, trade, retail, and so on, as well as in manufacturing in the more competitive industries like textiles and apparel is likely to find its wage scales falling behind those of organized labor. Furthermore, employment is more likely to grow in these areas, where the skill level is not as great and where wages remain relatively stable, preventing cost rises. The wage differentials sought by organized labor are fostered by these conditions.

Consider now the unemployed. As recovery proceeds, they fall even further behind. Wage differentials widen the gap between the employed and the unemployed, the skilled and the unskilled. Even ignoring possible price increases, as we have done so far, the unemployed find themselves in a deteriorating position economically and in a degrading position socially. As employment increases, those who remain in the unemployed ranks are subject to suspicion and even a measure of contempt. Firms can discriminate in their hiring practices as long as the quality of the remaining labor force is not a factor. The history of ethnic and racial discrimination illustrates the point. Still, the economic and social consequences of being at the bottom of the labor force and the accompanying feelings of bewilderment, confusion, resentment, and impotence in the face of forces they do not understand and over which they have no control are deeply embedded, and the scars do not disappear, especially as prosperity unfolds for others.

THE HOUSEHOLD SECTOR

As the recovery proceeds, households can be expected to revert to previous consumption patterns. Income increases, uncertainty diminishes, advertising increases, credit becomes more available, and so on, and these factors encourage consumption. To the extent that expectations of continuing recovery and prosperity are formed, these consumption patterns become implanted in household behavior, and the whole process of consumption by habit and emulation is established. The process may take some time as past debts are settled and new habits are formed, but once begun, it continues quite routinely. Naturally, for the unemployed, consumption patterns do not change radically, and the emulation of the consumption patterns of others can only occur in some vicarious manner.

THE BUSINESS SECTOR

At the outset of the recovery some or all of these trends and changing conditions may go unrecognized or be underestimated by the business sector, but as the recovery continues, expectations are revised and the changing behavior of other economic units is recognized as an integral part of revised expectations of future developments. It is reasonable to expect that the increase in demand generated by initial government spending will not be spread out evenly over the whole economy. Indeed, the first reaction of the business sector to the observed change in aggregate demand is likely to be one of caution, and the result is likely to be the acceptance of inventory depletion to meet the growing demand for output. Only after expectations have been revised to reflect optimism will there be any increase in employment and output; the lag in response could be lengthy, depending upon the speed and vigor of the recovery.

Assuming the recovery is reasonably steady and assured, the lag in reaction may be counted in quarters, and finally output and eventually employment will be increased. Whatever the distribution of demand over the economy, it is probable that a large part of the increase will be in the demand for the output of raw material industries, particularly for those materials used as inputs in the production of consumer goods. A large part of this demand for output will occur in the metals industries, petroleum, paper, rubber, and other industries that supply the needed inputs. In most of these industries large firms dominate, and the market structure is oligopolistic; these are some of the key industries described in the previous chapter.

A plausible sequence of events that occurs as the result of the increase in demand would be as follows: since the break-even points were set at low levels of capacity utilization (particularly for metals), prices need not rise immediately, but even with prices constant, profits are likely to rise as output levels grow. Now, after a further lag, during which the recovery proceeds and employment grows, organized labor in these industries will react to the improved conditions. In the next contract negotiation labor is bound to view rising profits as the rationale for higher wage demands. The productivity of labor may actually be falling, since new workers may be less efficient than those already employed, but even so, in recovery periods such arguments do not deter union leaders from pressing for more.

In any case, costs are almost sure to rise as the wage increase is granted. Industry-wide collective bargaining is probable, leading to little restraint by the firms, since costs rise for all. Increasing costs mean lower profits; hence the firms' goal of maintaining a target rate of return is in jeopardy. Without much delay prices are likely to be increased to protect profit margins, with the blame for the price hike being passed on to labor's demand for higher wages. It is possible that in some cases the price increase may be postponed until the price lists and catalogs can be revised; in other instances, a uniform markup over previous prices would suffice and would be implemented immediately. Since standard costs are not revised immediately, the price increase in either case must be an estimated increase needed to restore profit margins. Further price changes may prove necessary as costs are revised for rising output levels and productivity changes.

Capital expansion and investment spending need not be immediate concerns at the start of the recovery and even after it has proceeded for some time. At this stage it is assumed that sufficient excess capacity existed prior to the upswing and that major investment spending is not required. Still, the prudent firm will be making plans for expansion and evaluating various projects while it has the opportunity to make long-range plans. For the present, the firms' major goal remains the short-run target rate of profit, but the goal is subject to change over the course of the recovery.

Without too much of a lag, the recovery will spread to the industries that produce consumer goods. As employment and income increase, the essential needs will be quickly satisfied and consumption expenditures will be directed toward consumer durables and other "nonessential" goods and services. The demand for automobiles, television sets, entertainment items, and so on, will increase, as will the demand for services from professional people generally. Of course, the increase in demand will vary directly with advertising expenditures and easy credit policies. Credit will be discussed later; advertising expenditures, being pro-cyclical, can be expected to increase along with economic activity.

Once again, the further increase in demand and the effects of the increase will not be registered equally across the economy. Before very long the increase in consumption will be met by giant, oligopolistic firms in concentrated industries—from food products to meat processing to record companies to automobiles. With the conglomerate movement, an automobile, a refrigerator, and a television set may all be purchased from a single company. The same holds true for financial institutions, insurance companies, utilities, and so on—seemingly unconnected transactions are interconnected in the background.

As a consequence of operating at higher capacity levels and of dealing in consumer goods generally, the increase in demand is likely to lead to a quicker increase in price in these industries than for raw material producers. The break-even point may be calculated at a higher output level, so that as costs increase, prices will increase more directly. It is probable, also, that firms in some of the industries, particularly consumer durables, are likely to exercise some market power here and attempt to regain some profits lost in the recessionary period; that is, the short-run goal of increasing profits will become the dominant one.

To increase profits, sales must be increased, and hence advertising expenditures will soon rise, increasing costs but erecting a barrier to entry as well. This tactic may be successful in increasing sales for the firm or it may not, but one consequence of the increased sales effort may be to control smaller rivals in the field who do not have the advertising budget and other resources of the giant corporation. If the market share of the giant is increased, it may well come at the expense of the smaller rival. The smaller rival, to protect sales, may keep prices constant or increase them less, but this means smaller profit and less future growth.[1] This also is the exercise of market power by the leading firms. In short, there is a scramble for market shares of a growing market, and in the process there is an opportunity for the giant corporation to pursue another goal—that of survival by squeezing out its smaller rivals via the sales effort. A large firm could, of course, keep prices constant as costs rise to accomplish the same thing, but such a policy might appear too obvious. In any event, this struggle continues as the expansion of the economy proceeds and will help to explain the trend toward concentration as the economy approaches full employment.

Increasing prices and rising profits will not go unnoticed by labor in these industries, and demands for higher wages can be expected to follow as soon as possible. Labor is organized in most of these industries, and collective bargaining will emphasize the growing share of profits and the fact that wages are falling behind. Indeed, organized labor in consumer durables (for instance, automobiles) can be expected to push for even larger shares, and the terms of these contracts, if granted, become the pattern for all to emulate. If the firms have rosy expectations, the wage demands are likely to be granted and recovered in higher prices. If expectations are less optimistic, some resistance can be expected. Extreme uncertainty or *unrelated motivations* may cause complete resistance. For instance, the giant firms can use the ensuing strike to eliminate unwanted employees, remove executive positions, reduce unwanted inventory before introducing new models, eliminate more vulnerable firms in the industry, and so on. Much can be blamed on the labor force and its demands, and the large firms will exploit such situations when they choose to do so.

Let us assume that expectations are sufficiently optimistic to permit the firms to meet most of the terms of these key contracts. No doubt, prices will rise whether or not justified and by an amount equal to, or greater than, the additional wage costs. Again, the squeeze is on the smaller firm to the extent that it is less efficient. Still, the higher price protects it from annihilation but may still restrict its ability to expand as the market expands.

The increases in wages or better working conditions gained by workers in these remaining concentrated industries further widen and reinforce the gap between them and the rest of the labor force and the unemployed. Even in the same industry the wage contracts may exhibit wide variations, contributing to the hierarchy of the wage scale.[2] Other members of the labor force will share in the rewards of growing prosperity, and these increases are frequently overlooked. In general, professional people will benefit along with organized labor. Physicians, dentists, lawyers will

---

[1] For more of this analysis, see J. Steindl, *Maturity and Stagnation in American Capitalism* (Oxford: Basil Blackwell, 1952), pp. 40–55.

[2] It is clear that one form of Schultze's demand shift model could be initiated here, since firms and industries that are not expanding as rapidly as others may be forced to pay higher wages to employees, who base their demands on provisions of key contracts earned in other industries. If prices increase accordingly, inflation must result.

begin to protect their relative incomes, and later, architects, bankers, brokers, and so on, will follow their lead. The changing consumption patterns facilitate these actions as more medical care is sought (postponed in bad times) and more specialized services are needed in many other areas as well. Naturally, not all the professions share immediately in the benefits—teachers, public servants, salaried white-collar workers may well fall behind, creating still another hierarchy of rewards, based to a large extent on market power.

Increased demand in the more competitive industries has different effects from those where market power is prevalent. In the first place, the lack of market power itself means that less arbitrary actions in price setting and wage determination are permitted. In the second place, there is no great scramble over market shares. Competitive advertising exists, but market shares are not altered significantly even when these expenditures are stepped up. Economists have frequently pointed to the cancelling effect of these advertising efforts, but our analysis restricts the self-cancelling effects to these monopolistic competitors.

Prices, then, are apt to be more stable in these industries as demand increases. This can be traced largely to the lack of pressure from the cost side, particularly with labor costs. Since many of these industries are labor-intensive—services, trade, finance, and so on—labor costs are important. Yet employment in these industries can expand without disrupting wage demands. Jobs in these industries are filled by the less skilled and less trained, who themselves lack market power, being unrepresented by formal organizations. Furthermore, women make up a large part of this labor force, and they have traditionally been discriminated against in wage and salary rates. The supplemental nature of their contribution to the family income often acts as a barrier to higher wages. Further wage moderation is the natural result of the increase in the labor force as more and more women enter the labor force during periods of economic expansion.

In addition, discrimination against other ethnic and racial groups also means that wages will be held down in these industries. The unskilled and the powerless enter the employment ranks at the bottom and perhaps after some time lag. This is true even if they are employed by the large firms, and it is particularly apparent when they are employed in the smaller firms in trade or manufacturing.

In general, we can conclude that employment increases in the competitive industries at a greater rate than do wages. The result is the greater stability of prices in these competitive sectors than in other sectors.

With stable costs and prices, profit margins remain stable as well. Temporarily, the firms in these industries are content with this condition, since they have to fear possible new entrants should profit margins increase rapidly. Entry into these industries is relatively easy in many cases, so that stable rewards forestall potential competitors.

We should recall here that this sector embraces a number of industries, widely divergent, so that these generalities cannot be expected to be applicable to each in the same degree. The construction industry, which is characterized by market power on the side of organized labor, is obviously an exception. Another is agriculture, where increasing prosperity may accelerate the movement *away* from the industry. Agriculture, however, is so intertwined with short-run political considerations that it is best treated as a special case in every way.

The stability of prices and wages in this subsector runs counter to the usual economic analysis following an increase in demand. Naturally, such stability cannot last forever, but it is plausible to assume that for an unspecified time at least the increase in demand will be met by output at stable prices. If this is so, then these firms lose ground to the larger firms in the more concentrated industries. The smaller firms' profits do not grow as quickly, limiting their growth potential and financial independence. Their employees similarly fall behind in the wage race, and their participation in the growth of prosperity is limited; the generally rising price level reduces their real incomes even as some gain employment. The benefits of economic growth are not shared equally throughout the economic system.

THE PUBLIC SECTOR

In the public sector, if the past is any guide, the most likely response to the changed economic climate would be one of passivity; it would not wish to dampen expansion, nor would it push expansion along once it has begun. Once expansion is underway, government appears to draw back and keep its hands off, leaving the job of stabilization to the automatic stabilizers. Thus, programs begun for humanitarian purposes now languish for want of real support, although unmet social needs are still evident.

Of course, taxes continue to increase throughout this period, and government expenditures are likely to keep pace with them. It is easy to adhere to the balanced budget philosophy when increased expenditures are called for; politicians can always find ways to spend funds. But even balanced budgets are likely to be expansionary, so that government actions unintentionally facilitate the recovery. The alleged frugality of government spending allows politicians to boast without risk as the economy rebounds despite their actions.

In other areas of macroeconomic policy the same passive behavior can be expected. As shown earlier, the entire economic structure changes slowly throughout the recovery period up to this point: large firms become larger, unions gain strength, and smaller firms fall behind their larger rivals everywhere. All these trends appear early in the economic upswing and will be strengthened and accelerated as the recovery proceeds. In short, the entire economic structure is shifting and adjusting, and there is an accompanying shift in potential market power, which need not be exercised fully or at all in this period.

Changes in market structure at this stage are subtle, so that they are easily tolerated. Even for obvious abuses, antitrust policy would probably be used sparingly and ineffectively. The Justice Department lacks the zeal to upset improving economic conditions and probably the tools to fight the type of changes in market structure occurring in this period. Later, when the power becomes obvious to all, so will the impotence of antitrust laws and policy, but it will be too late.

Monetary policy is likely to be passive or, rather, accommodating during this period of upswing. To facilitate the recovery, interest rates would be kept low and credit policy in general made easy. This policy calls for a low discount rate and a moderate money stock growth via the purchase of government bonds. Monetary policy is unlikely to be aggressive in pushing the recovery, and in fact, the financing of the expansion may well come largely from an increase in the velocity of money as previously idle funds are activated.

The policy of maintaining low interest rates is not likely to affect investment spending materially, since excess capacity still exists and expectations of the future of the economy override in importance the cost of credit. There would be more consumer loans and mortgages, but these also are not likely to be as affected by the cost of credit as they are by its availability. Public borrowing—particularly by state and local governments—may be encouraged by low interest rates, thus adding to the recovery and working in the same direction as federal fiscal policy. Similarly, utilities and the construction industries may be borrowers in this period.

THE FOREIGN TRADE SECTOR

Little can be said with assurance about the foreign trade sector, since so much depends upon economic conditions abroad. If the major economies of the world are experiencing similar economic conditions, not much expansion of exports can be expected from "lower" domestic prices. Furthermore, to expand exports, domestic firms would have to commit some resources in market development abroad, but as long as the domestic market is far from saturated, they would prefer not to risk anything and concentrate on the domestic market. At higher levels of economic activity this conclusion might have to be qualified.

Imports, too, should not experience any sudden increase, again depending upon economic conditions elsewhere. Changes in imports will have to await a more substantial recovery. It follows that no radical changes in the foreign trade sector can be predicted, and therefore, domestic monetary and fiscal policy can proceed without the fear of upsetting trade or international finances and commercial policies.

CONCLUSION

In conclusion, in this intermediate range of an economy in recovery we still find the price level beginning to rise, with increasing output and some indications of bottleneck inflation becoming apparent. Again, by stretching the traditional model a bit, these tendencies do emerge. What the traditional model omits and what the present model uncovers is market power, which changes as a result of increased economic activity; that power is reinforced and used even in the early stages of economic recovery. The shifts in market structure are indicated, as is the potential for future abuses. The power struggle is carried over into the labor sector, where a hierarchy of wage distribution is developed.

In brief, the entire economic structure is strained in the upswing, and the resulting shifts pave the way for possible economic instability and erosion of the free market system. Changes in the economic structure are also translated into changes in the social and political structures. Economic power potentially controls political power as well, and the concentration of economic power poses a threat to political freedom and responsive government. As for the social structure, the perennial conflict between the haves and have-nots, between the favored and the forgotten, is initiated or reinforced in the economy in recovery. For now, potential problems and strife can only be called possible, because market power need not be used extensively here, and the dislocations in the economic structure are subtle and blurred by the overall improvement in economic conditions.

The Economy Approaching Full Employment

In the following sections we continue to trace the economic system through its recovery period toward full employment. We continue to assume that the recovery proceeds without interruption, so that the consequences of an expanding economy on the economic system can be discussed free of complications. In general, this procedure merely reflects the historical record of most advanced economies over the last few decades, but of course, it cannot be justified by this fact alone, and later the cycle will be reintroduced.

THE LABOR SECTOR

The trends witnessed in the earlier recovery stage continue as employment continues to increase. The tendency for wage differentials to appear and become permanent is actually made worse by new entrants to the employed ranks in the service trades. The increase in aggregate demand puts a strain on output until the labor bottleneck and shortages finally force the employment of that part of the labor force previously rejected; the young, blacks, Spanish-speaking people, and women are given employment. These groups enter the employed ranks at the bottom in low-paying, unskilled jobs.

Their entrance, however, is viewed as a threat to those already employed—particularly those just above them—for they might prove to be superior workers. Moreover, the status of those previously employed is reduced now that more are in that category. Also, as will be examined presently, the rising price level generally makes the wage earner feel less secure, because he vaguely feels worse off. Finally, the blue-collar worker, particularly, feels threatened by automation, feels degraded by the menial tasks he must perform in this age of science and education, and feels bitterness at all those who fail to perceive his plight—the students, the intellectuals, the corporations, the government. His discontent is manifested in a number of ways —sabotage of output, racism, the move toward political conservatism, and more to our purpose, the demand for higher and higher wages and fringe benefits to compensate him for his unsatisfying position. Without upward mobility, only more money will do.

Another offshoot of labor unrest can be found in the greater use of the strike weapon as an outlet for hostility. Union funds, which have grown in the recovery, offer security, and more militant spokesmen are heard when jobs are no longer scarce. No doubt, labor wants to share in the prosperity, but much more than labor's share is at stake in contract negotiations.

THE BUSINESS SECTOR

In the business sector expectations of continued recovery have been confirmed, and much of the uncertainty has been reduced by the prolonged improvement in economic conditions. As a consequence, some shift in goal emphasis can be expected, and in general, long-run concerns receive more attention. Prosperity reduces the risks of management, and industrial leaders all begin to look good, since their actions appear to be inspired; when times are good, managers appear to be very talented people.

In the *key industries* the pressure for higher wages is accelerated, as mentioned earlier, and the result is reflected in cost increases. Wage demands are not resisted as much in periods of prosperity as they would be in depressions. Rosy expectations break down the will of employers to resist labor's demands. Standard costs have now been revised, incorporating the latest productivity and other operating data, so that wage increases can be appended rather easily. At the same time, price increases can be announced without fear of retaliation by rivals. The price increase can amount to more or less than the wage settlement, but it will be certain, perhaps after a short time lag.

Firms grant wage increases and increase prices accordingly as a routine matter, mainly because their goals have shifted from short-run profit concerns to long-run goals of growth and security. Adequate target profits are necessary to attain the latter but they are no longer a preoccupation of managers, who widen their horizons. Now the sheer scale of operations and the sense of power are sufficient motivations for managers to push for growth and technological innovation. This not only results in the power and prestige but satisfies stockholders that their leaders are dynamic men with vision and foresight. Managers earn security for themselves as they reach out in new directions; when the economy is buoyant, so are its leaders.

Although profits need not be maximized, they are still high and are mostly retained by the large corporations. Obviously, this practice frees them from financial markets and from such controls as lenders usually exercise in making monetary arrangements. Stockholders are powerless in these large corporations but are mollified by stable dividends. The practice of retaining a large share of profits is justified by management as being necessary to meet dynamic conditions and growth potentials; stockholders acquiesce in the practice, since accumulated earnings increase the market price of their shares, and future capital gains possibilities replace the immediate gains of dividends.

The continued increase in aggregate demand would eventually put pressure on the existing plant to produce the output desired. Excess capacity is gradually worked off, but costs increase, particularly when operating rates exceed optimal levels. The pressure on capacity is joined with favorable expectations to permit some variation of the accelerator to become operative. The firms now have the means and the incentive to spend on new capital goods. The technological advances and new developments in capital goods had been accounted for by capital stock projects already planned, priced, and possibly approved, awaiting the proper time for undertaking them. Thus, there need not be any great lag between accumulating funds and spending them. Planning new investment projects is a continuous activity.

Out of these favorable conditions, capital accumulation proceeds, paid for largely out of surplus funds and depreciation provisions. Aggregate demand is increased, the multiplier activated, and the level of income increased as well. Additions to capital stock take place as soon as excess capacity is used up or technological developments make existing equipment obsolete. At this later stage, however, more and more firms find themselves in this position, and there occurs what might be called a capital goods boom. Capital goods industries (key industries) are affected early as new orders flow in, and later the expansionary phase spreads to other sectors—from key industries to the other business sectors.

If we assume that the new capital goods are more productive, embodying the latest technological advances, several consequences may follow from the increased investment spending. With improved capital stock, output potential increases, and as potential supply changes, new decisions and problems have to be met over the labor input and sales promotion.

If the capital-output ratio (K/Y) falls, there would be a tendency to substitute capital for labor in the production process. The same output can be obtained with less labor input, and thus labor's fears of being replaced (particularly the unskilled) have some basis. Perhaps less capital *and* less labor are needed in some industries. In either case, we might expect the new investment to lead to cost reductions from the levels incurred when the firms were pressing on capacity. Less capital may be required in the operation, but more critically, the productivity of labor may be increased now that it has better capital stock with which to work. If costs are pushed down to near former levels, profits will rise (since prices had risen earlier). If profits are rising, there will be even more incentive to increase output, but this tendency transfers the problem to the sales department, which must now find outlets for the increased production. Profit margins increase at first, but as its productivity increases, labor demands higher wages, and to restore the original profit margin, prices must rise to cover the increased costs. Thus, over time the sales department is confronted by two problems—how to increase sales when prices are stable and when they are rising.

Again the goals shift, to sales promotion and growth. If total industry sales are increasing with prosperity, there will be a scramble for market shares; each firm will want to share in the growth of the market or increase its share if possible. In near monopolistic industries this is no problem, but in oligopolistic industries some confrontations between large and small rivals can be expected. Two general possibilities appear almost immediately: the larger firms could keep prices relatively stable and indulge in nonprice competition via increased sales effort by advertising campaigns and quality differentiations. Taking advantage of economies of scale, the larger firms could increase their shares by advertising; they have the funds to finance the advertising campaign and can afford to forgo temporary high profits while they attempt to capture a larger market share. Competition via quality changes (with P constant) can also accomplish similar results.

The profits of the smaller rivals are reduced and their resources strained if they attempt to match these actions; if they do not, however, they face the loss of market shares. They are squeezed and their position is apt to deteriorate even further. If prices are allowed to rise by the larger firms, the position of the smaller firms is improved, but they still face the superior sales efforts of their larger rivals. Much depends upon antitrust actions, of course, but it appears likely that the smaller firms will fall behind and become more dependent on their larger rivals. Their growth potential is reduced and their financial resources are strained, and they may survive only as followers and in a stagnant condition.

However, the increases in sales efforts soon begin to reduce the profits previously expected from the accumulation of capital and cost reductions via economies of scale. A new trade-off appears. The sales effort required to sell the additional output acts as a limiting factor to the rate of capital accumulation. Falling profits limit both the incentive and the finances for continued capital accumulation. The brake on capital accumulation limits the growth of the industry and probably acts to increase prices as costs rise, thus ensuring the survival of the sounder smaller rivals. They remain marginal firms, however, and somewhat helpless.

The larger firms would acquire more control over their markets by taking over or merging with the smaller firms in the industry. In this way, the scramble for market shares is avoided and declining profits need not be tolerated. With lax antitrust efforts, these acquisitions have taken place regularly, and for good reasons, as shown here; control over markets is easier to achieve by direct action than by the indirect methods of fighting over market shares, even when the market is growing. Some growth in concentration can be expected from this source.

Still another method of increasing sales without indulging in internecine battles is to expand the sales efforts in foreign markets. No limitations on price or profits need be accepted if sales outlets can be found in which to sell surplus production.

If the domestic market is not growing fast enough to absorb the higher output levels, foreign markets can be a safety valve. Much of the expansion of foreign markets, traditionally avoided by United States firms, can be traced to the capital accumulation outrunning the growth of the domestic market. If, as has been the case in recent years, the international financial considerations (surplus dollars abroad) affect relative interest rates, wage rates, and the availability of funds, then another method of expanding sales is to accumulate capital abroad and produce directly for foreign markets. The trend toward multinational corporations is understandable with this analysis, but this institution is a source of potential trouble for both the country of origin and the country in which the capital is located.

Another outlet for surplus funds can be found in diversification to spread the risks over product lines and industries. The conglomerate movement puts under one roof various economic activities, so that resources are not all committed to one industry and hence limited by the growth of the market for that industry. Spreading the risk and avoiding growth limitations may not always be the rationale for the establishment of a conglomerate, but the effect is the same whatever the reason. These conglomerates go a long way in removing themselves from market influences of all kinds. Their tremendous resources permit nearly any action contemplated, from the elimination of competition to the manipulation of stock prices.

THE REMAINING BUSINESS SECTOR

Increases in price of the basic or raw materials industries represent cost increases to other industries that use their outputs as inputs. Price increases spread and become more general. However, unlike pure demand pull, prices could rise significantly long before production bumps against capacity output.

Prices in the remaining business sector also rise after some time lag; the lag itself is determined by market conditions and can vary from product to product and from industry to industry. Some pressure will come from the cost side as labor seeks catch-up wage increases. Having fallen behind in real income, labor feels free to press for more now that employment has expanded sufficiently so that the unemployed pool no longer acts as a restraint. Wage increases may also be granted to forestall unionization or to retain key personnel now that labor has become relatively scarce. As we have seen, this movement from the bottom impels the top of the hierarchy to preserve the same distribution of wages.

Again, self-employed professionals are able to keep pace with economic conditions more readily than are those in other areas of the service industries. Many of the unskilled in service areas might still find themselves classified as "working poor," who find that prosperity affects them only marginally. In fact, though wages rise, they may well fall farther behind, but since they are employed, there is no great loss of dignity or stigma attached to their condition. They are simply forgotten.

In general, the more competitive industries can be expected to follow the lead of the major industries. They expand their facilities after a time and increase their sales efforts to increase profits. In some industries prices and profits could rise rather rapidly while wages lag behind. The sector is too heterogeneous to generalize much; suffice it to say that demand pull forces are at work in this sector.

In agriculture the migration out of farming probably would continue, and many people from rural areas would relocate in the larger cities. They enter the employment ranks, if at all, at the bottom and remain there. The construction industry would be booming, of course, since business and the household sector will be demanding plants and homes. Prices would rise in the construction industries, as would the wages of the skilled craftsmen—plumbers, carpenters, masons, electricians, and so on. The demand for these skills and the restrictions of entry erected by these trades would guarantee that.

In summary, forces set in motion by actions of the major industries sweep through these secondary sectors, and they respond to these conditions. Rising expectations and demand pull forces, generated earlier, filter down to other firms and industries, which react to them. Feelings of optimism are contagious, and spending is stepped up.

THE HOUSEHOLD SECTOR

Expectations are buoyant in the household sector, since personal income and employment are rising steadily. Barring any shocks from outside to create extreme uncertainty (threat of war, say), consumption expenditures can be expected to rise with changing income. The rise in consumption would be spread out over all commodities, but particularly important would be the increase in consumer durables and housing. This trend assumes that credit is available on not too stringent terms, and as a result, private debt would rise with increasing prosperity.

The routine tendency for consumption to increase (in absolute terms) with rising income is reinforced by the stepped-up advertising and sales promotions of firms attempting to increase sales and market shares. Consumers are induced via advertising to consume an ever-widening array of goods and services; little, if any, production is directed by the expression of wants by the consumer exercising his "sovereignty." No institutional mechanism exists through which consumers could express their desires and direct the use of society's resources accordingly. Producers are under too much pressure to utilize capacity to tolerate consumer fickleness; so that whatever remains of consumer sovereignty is weak and imperfect and likely to operate only over long periods.

What happens to consumption as a result of the rising price level? The rising price level is not sufficient in itself to curtail consumption expenditures. When people hold expectations of continued price increases, they are not likely to reduce expenditures. In addition, they would probably hold expectations of continued income increases as well. Only if prices (or incomes) are expected to fall would any moderating influence be felt on consumption.

A rising price level is not without consequences. Anyone whose wages fall behind the rate of price increase obviously loses real income. Those whose wages keep pace, however, are not seriously affected. Everyone is likely to protect past consumption patterns, so that rising prices will affect saving more than consumption. There may be some effect on the composition of consumption as rising prices are reflected in changing *relative* prices. Consumers may end up spending more on some items and less on others, for example, more on durables than on nondurables.

The control of markets must include consumer markets as well, and to this end advertising campaigns and sales promotion techniques are developed and employed. The notion that the household sector is powerless and is manipulated is scarcely a new idea, but it must be included as an integral part of the larger model. Galbraith is one of the few who has done so in a consistent manner.

THE FOREIGN TRADE SECTOR

As the national income increases, the economy tends to increase imports, both consumer goods and raw materials. Thus, the earlier trends are continued, and the imports may well exhibit little price sensitivity if the goods are unique or necessary in the production of output. Depending on price level and income changes abroad, exports could continue to decline as domestic conditions improved. Again, the superior products available elsewhere discourage exports. More important, trading partners could develop the production of goods that were previously imported but that have increased greatly in price.

Exports are also discouraged by rising transportation costs and the development of formal trading blocs, which establish tariff and other trade barriers. In part, these trade problems help to explain the rise of the multinational corporation, which seeks to avoid trade restrictions by producing and selling abroad; this eliminates transportation costs as well. As we have seen, the large corporations create excess capacity and must seek markets for their output. Cost differentials, tax considerations, trade restrictions, and so on, make it preferable to produce and sell abroad rather than to export domestic production. Thus, these multinational corporations are located in *developed* economies and constitute a new form of economic imperialism, for the host country inevitably loses some control over its economy. Operating decisions of the firm are made in home offices in another country, making economic planning and manipulation of the economy extremely difficult.[3] Of course, the multinational corporation brings benefits as well and the continual balancing of pros and cons becomes a public issue in the host country.

Multinational corporations cause balance-of-payments problems in the short run as they export capital, which may or may not be self-correcting as the income flows back. In the longer run their existence and growth could have some really profound effects: the erosion of the distinction between the nation and its economic system, since foreigners have some control over the economy; the problems that could result from confrontations between the firms and host country; the question of allegiance in times of conflict or strife; the future of economic nationalism, and so forth.

These effects are sometimes registered in the balance of payments. The trade balance (goods and services) can be expected to decline with the increase in imports and in price relatives. The capital flows may also cause a problem for the prosperous economy. Aside from the direct investment of the multinational corporation and other long-term capital flows, the balance of payments can be worsened by short-term capital flows.

Thus, if domestic interest rates are kept low to promote economic expansion, short-term capital may flow out, and if interest rates are kept high to discourage spending and inflation, the economic expansion may suffer. Monetary policy must consider this dilemma; no longer can domestic considerations alone determine interest rate policy.[4]

THE PUBLIC SECTOR

If we continue to assume that public economic policy is passive and fairly unresponsive to changing economic conditions, then the prosperous stage of the upswing presents some interesting problems. Rational economic policy has not become a routine aspect of governmental operations, so that the economy is pushed along by automatic tendencies rather than by deliberate policy. Thus, the automatic

[3] For a discussion of these problems, see J. J. Servan-Schreiber, *The American Challenge* (New York: Atheneum, 1968).

[4] This discussion is not intended to describe the balance-of-payments problems of the United States in recent years, although some of this section is clearly relevant to that situation.

stabilizers continue to increase tax receipts as the national income grows, and unless offset by increased expenditures, fiscal drag will slow the expansion before full employment is reached. In fact, the economy can be turned around by the absence of deliberate fiscal policy, and the downswing initiated.

The actual response of the public sector to these developments is uncertain. No stabilization efforts can be expected from the state and local levels of government; any action must come from the federal level. Even at the federal level politics and philosophy will often weigh more than economic consequences. Tax reductions that occur at the proper time (always politically attractive) could stimulate further expansion. Tax reductions reduce the public sector's command over resources to spend on public goods and return funds to the private sector for private disposal— either higher consumption or private investment.

If tax reductions are considered, they may not accomplish the goal of stimulating the economy, since they are likely to be accompanied by demands to reduce government expenditures at the same time (which is philosophically consistent with tax cuts). A budget deficit is avoided, the private sector favored, and public power reduced by such a plan. Despite increasing prosperity, further spending on new or old government programs is resisted, particularly in the nondefense area of the budget. National defense expenditures generally are not seriously affected by economy moves, but social and international programs are. In short, there is the opposite public response to redress the potential evils of the rise of power in other sectors.

Of course, if government expenditures were increased while taxes began to stabilize or fall, the budgetary influence would continue to be expansionary. Such a policy could well overheat the economy over time to the extent that higher taxes would be necessary to reduce some private spending. Otherwise inflation is sure to follow (as in the United States in the mid-1960s). Tax increases are much more difficult to propose and are likely to be too little and too late. Inflation may well be easier to accept than policies that might halt the expansion and cause unemployment.

Actual policies depend upon the goals of the administration and ultimately upon which of the mutually exclusive goals it wishes to emphasize. For the sake of argument, let us assume that the administration prefers to accept inflation, as long as it is "moderate," over possible recession and unemployment. Therefore, its budget continues to be expansionary. Later we can examine the consequences of a reversal of priorities, once price stability becomes the major goal. For the present, any concern over inflation is confined to verbal denunciations.

Looking over the past record, the fears of inflation have generally been registered by the monetary side of macroeconomic policy. It is also true that monetary policy has been given the major assignment of stabilization in the same period. Some assessment of the weaknesses of such an approach has already been given, so that we can turn directly to some comments on alternative approaches.

Generally, monetary policy would probably be accommodating as the economic expansion proceeded. There would always be the fear of halting the expansion prematurely by any restraining action. Thus, both the money supply and the velocity of money could increase without undue concern. Deficit budgets might account for the increase in the money supply, and Federal Reserve actions in the bond market could keep the interest rates low. Such easy money and credit policies are effortlessly followed as long as the expansion proceeds steadily and moderately, but the faster the rate of increase, the less willing the monetary authorities would become to permit the effects of the booming economy.

In the first place, low interest rates may not significantly affect domestic spending after a while but may start short-term capital outflows. Before full employment is reached, therefore, balance-of-payments problems may well reverse the trend of monetary policy. In the second place, monetary authorities are likely to be particularly sensitive to price level rises, since price stability directly affects the value of the currency and the orderliness of financial markets. These responsibilities rest with the monetary authorities, and they are likely to scrutinize price developments more carefully than the Treasury. The balancing of further expansion against adverse price changes and balance-of-payments problems represents a dilemma for the monetary authorities, and no easy solution is possible. In the past, the goal of price stability has been emphasized more than economic expansion and full employment.

Let us assume that the economic expansion continued to the point where all of the price trends noted were increasing the price level at 4 to 5 per cent per year and that the employment trends noted had resulted in a similar percentage of the labor force (4 to 5 per cent) being unemployed. The existence of market power in all areas has resulted in structural problems that create inflationary tendencies before full employment is reached; the unskilled, the uneducated—those at the bottom—could not be absorbed in the economic expansion up to this point.

The familiar trade-off is evident, and the question of which goal to pursue now perplexes policy makers. Many would argue that in the past the goal of price stability won out too easily over full employment, even when the rate of inflation was less than suggested here.

MACROECONOMIC POLICY AS THE ECONOMY
NEARS FULL EMPLOYMENT

The apparent trade-off dilemma may well be irrelevant, for if monetary and fiscal policies could not be used to reach the goals anyway, then the trade-off is merely academic. Rather than posing alternatives, it merely describes an impasse in policy choices and suggests the difficulty of "fine-tuning" an economy.

Taking fiscal policy first, continued increases in spending are likely to have less and less effect on increasing employment. If the increases in expenditures go for social welfare purposes, they do not create jobs but keep the unemployed at some bare minimum subsistence level. Similarly with health programs—no great job increase can be expected. With regard to public housing, the government is in competition for scarce construction resources with the private sector and its housing needs. If it spends on job training programs, it lacks the institutional mechanisms to do much good, and the training is likely to be second-rate and for jobs which are dead-end or low-paying ones, subject to being automated out of existence in the future. The skills in demand (plumbing, carpentry, and so on) are in areas jealously guarded by strong labor unions. Union barriers prevent useful job training, and discrimination of all kinds aggravates the problem. The unemployables are not reached by such training programs, and prosperity may well increase the labor force, since more young people, women, and so on, are likely to participate more fully.

Government spending on public works has fallen off, because of its relative inflexibility when economic conditions change. Other job- and income-creating projects, like roadbuilding and reforestation, are not viable programs in the 1970s, and the leaf-raking kind of jobs are strongly resisted by everyone as wasteful and degrading.

Much of government spending has no potential for job creation: interest payments, pensions, veterans' payments, agricultural subsidies, foreign aid, and so on. Direct increases in public employment are resisted as bureaucracy-building and wasteful, and rational plans for government as an employer of last resort (*not* a traditional approach) have barely received any attention.

More to the point, increases in government spending for job creation and social welfare are likely to be resisted by conservative elements, who fear the centralization of power and prefer tax reductions. In the past, they have been successful in keeping social welfare programs, poverty programs, and employment and educational programs to a minimal level and hence have rendered them ineffective.

There remains spending on national defense, which has increased steadily and which represents a large portion of the budget. However, further increases are not likely to affect the employment of those at the bottom. Defense (and space) expenditures now are for such sophisticated equipment and research that only the highly skilled and highly educated will be affected.

Tax reductions also may be of little use. For those without incomes, a reduction in taxes is irrelevant, and since negative income taxes and guaranteed incomes (again, *not* traditional remedies) are not seriously considered in this context, the tax side appears ineffectual.

The tax structure itself contains much rigidity, and tax privileges and tax shelters are entrenched. To date, the middle- and high-income groups who avail themselves of tax privileges have won out over reform efforts. Without any redistribution of the tax burden, any reduction in taxes is likely to find its way into saving rather than consumption and therefore to limit the employment opportunities that might have been expected. Reducing taxes of low-income groups may only result in their buying higher-quality goods via emulation without necessarily creating jobs.

Tax reductions for the business sector may not stimulate investment (and hence employment) but only succeed in increasing profits. If firms have excess capacity, no new investment is likely. Excess capacity is probable, particularly in those firms that had anticipated or planned for further sales growth. This could be true of many of the large corporations.

Smaller corporations that did not build in excess capacity may respond favorably to tax reductions, depending upon their expectations. If they fear an abatement of the expansion, they may well retire past debt, or the like, rather than acquire new capital stock. If they retain their optimism, they may expand operations, but employment changes may not be great. Service industries may expand, but *new* entrants into the labor force, particularly women, will take these new and rather low-paying jobs.

In summary, traditional fiscal policy approaches may not be sufficient to reach the goal of full employment once the economy has reached the trade-off stage of development. Even when price stability is sacrificed, efforts to reach full employment are either resisted or are too limited in scope and operation.

Monetary policy may prove no more useful than fiscal policy at this level of output. Manipulation of the interest rate to stimulate or discourage private spending has other results as well. Low interest rates may stimulate capital outflows rather than domestic investment. The interest rate may be irrelevant for the investment decisions of large corporations. Smaller firms and the construction industry may benefit, but again the employment effects may be weak. Conversely, high interest rates may not curtail investment spending of the large firms but may cripple the smaller firm and the housing market. The flight of capital may be stopped, and such funds may well bid up the prices of domestic instruments or may be used in other nonemployment-creating ways. Thus, the interest rate as a tool of policy has lost much of its former power. The rise of the multinational corporation has hastened the decline of the influence of monetary policy, for firms can flee from domestic policy to areas where the monetary climate, availability of funds, interest rates, and so on, are more favorable. Again, the large firms have this additional option open to them.

The manipulation of the money supply, according to the monetarists, will affect the level of money income, but the consequences for changes in employment are unclear at best. Reductions in the money supply may help combat inflation to some extent, but changes in the velocity of money can offset some of the effect. In previous discussions the monetarist view was criticized for being vague as to the mechanisms through which changes in the money were supposed to affect economic activity. The failure to make this clear means that it is difficult to assess the merit of the argument in discussions of this type.

The only conclusion that is justified is that monetary as well as fiscal policy tools are insufficient and inadequate to manipulate the economy the closer that economy approaches full employment. Additional tools, applied in the traditional manner, may have some marginal benefits, but are unlikely to permit the policy makers to reach either the goal of full employment or price stability, and certainly not both. If either monetary or fiscal policy or both are applied to the pursuit of either goal, the policies will have to be used with such strength that they are likely to do more harm than good to the economy. The push towards the attainment of one goal could cripple the economy as it adjusts to the policy.

A do-nothing policy or a long-run policy of gradualism—small adjustments over long periods—is unlikely to be acceptable or workable. The latter effort of gradual adjustments was adopted by the Nixon administration until the policy became an obvious failure and was replaced by wage and price controls. Let us discuss this period further in order to focus on the economic system's reaction to the adoption of one goal. Then by permitting the economy to decline, we will get some insight into the advanced economy in recession.

MONETARY AND FISCAL POLICIES IN OPERATION

Assume that the primary goal becomes that of price stability. There are some good reasons for the choice. First, monetary policy is easier to implement than fiscal policy, with less of a time lag and other institutional delays. Second, price stability is favored by powerful special-interest groups. Recall that wealthholders may be hurt by rising prices, as are creditors generally, so that the financial community may have a strong interest in maintaining price stability. Third, there is the concern over inflationary psychology, which, once started, appears to spread throughout the economy; it is difficult to stop or to reverse.

If monetary policy is relied upon to stabilize prices, the effects on the economy will be selective, as previously indicated. The large corporations are virtually untouched by the tight money policy, while smaller firms and selected industries may suffer. The banking and financial sector enjoys the benefits; the borrowers complain of the lack of funds and high interest rates. If the policy is to be effective, however, somebody must be hurt by it and forced to alter his plans. If monetary policy is used alone, the "wrong" people and the "wrong" sectors are hurt. Those who possess market power, from the large corporation to the local doctor, are not seriously affected despite their complaints to the contrary.

Thus, there is little constraint on those who do have some control over the price of their output and over other market conditions (as well as foreign market options). The price and wage pressures, observed earlier in the upswing, continue, since nothing has been done to change the condition from which the pressures and demands originate. Inflation can continue while some sectors are retrenching and some additional unemployment begins to appear.

More than likely, there will be increased pressure to reduce government expenditures. The failure of monetary policy will eventually become evident to all, and fiscal policy will be reactivated. It may then be recalled that public spending contributed to the inflation in the first place. Rising expenditures meant large budget deficits, which were financed by borrowing, which tended to increase the money supply, and both monetary and fiscal policies of public activity helped to create the inflation and economic conditions they are now asked to reverse.

Once again, the "wrong" programs and the "wrong" people become easy targets. For social welfare, poverty, education, and health programs are likely to become the scapegoats for inflation and be sacrificed to achieve price stability. To reduce expenditures in these areas not only aggravates the economic and social condition of those at the bottom but fails to attack the real sources of inflation and thus proves ineffective as well as inhumane.

In brief, the call for reduced government expenditures, if heeded, will probably result in affecting those who are the most vulnerable and least able to protect themselves; those responsible for the economic conditions are unaffected or can protect themselves by alternative means. The same result is probable from the tax side of fiscal policy. The tax concessions made to key industries (depletion allowances, farming provisions) or individuals (capital gains, numerous loopholes) will probably continue, while general tax concessions—the investment tax credit or liberal depreciation allowances—are debated as the economic condition deteriorates. Any tax imposed to combat inflation is also likely to come at the expense of those at the bottom in the form of an easily administered income tax surcharge of a flat rate or increases in sales and other taxes at the local levels of government.

Thus, as a practical matter, fiscal policy applied with the past as a guide is not likely to curb inflation or to affect those responsible for it. In fact, it would probably affect those who are the least responsible, the least powerful, and the least secure. Perhaps some moderation of price increases may be the result as uncertainty over future actions is created, but this is obtained at the cost of a small increase in unemployment. Again, those who did not share in the economic growth and prosperity are generally the ones who are discriminated against by the operation of fiscal policy as well as monetary policy.

The Economy in Recession Again

Our purpose is not to build a model of the business cycle or even to describe one in detail. Rather we wish to study the consequences of the changing economic structure and institutions, along with some of the social and political effects. Accordingly, we will trace some of these effects by assuming that the economy falls into a recession caused by the trends outlined in the previous section. That is, if price stability is elevated to the primary goal, monetary policy becomes tight, and when it fails to achieve price stability, government expenditures are reduced. The fall in aggregate demand from the public sector causes much uncertainty in the private sector, so that investment spending is curtailed and perhaps some consumption expenditures as well. Prices still rise and unemployment grows, and macroeconomic policy is judged ineffective by some, while others call for more of the same policies, hoping they will work eventually. This is the economic situation as the economy slowly sinks into a recession.

THE ECONOMIC SITUATION

In the classical model a reduction in demand would result in falling prices and eventually falling wages. Flexible prices and wages would result in a period of deflation, but full employment would be maintained. Flexible prices may have some redistribution effects, but the economy would settle down and adjust to the changed conditions—at least over time.

The simple Keynesian model, which includes rigid and inflexible prices and wages, would conclude that unemployment would follow the fall in aggregate demand, and this may well be the result even if prices and wages are flexible. Still, the Keynesian model intimates that full employment can be reached with the proper macroeconomic policy.

Such complacency does not follow from our model. The large corporations would react to falling demand by reducing employment, not prices; organized labor would react by acquiescing in the employment reductions, not by accepting wage cuts. Since costs do not fall materially, standard costs do not change, standard markups over costs do not change, and hence prices do not change.

Since the price is determined with large amounts of excess capacity, profits may fall, since less capacity is utilized now, but profit margins over costs do not fall. The falling absolute profits may make capital accumulation slightly more difficult and hinder growth, but in a recessionary period such goals are made subordinate to the protection of an adequate profit to satisfy short-run concerns. If the recession continues over several time periods, some selective price reductions may be made to favored customers.

Inflexible prices are not new, nor are the wage rigidities that help make them so. Money wage reductions are ruled out by organized labor, which prefers to protect the wages of those who remain employed. Unemployment is inevitable in these industries—the major ones—in which institutional rigidities prevent adjustments that could ameliorate the condition.

Of course, the larger firms in these industries can withstand the deterioration of economic conditions better than their smaller rivals. Their superior financial condition gives them options to overcome the current situation or to make the most of it. They may find the time opportune to acquire smaller firms, diversify further, follow through on other merger plans, modernize plants, and build for the future. They could also pursue foreign expansion more seriously. Finally, in bad times, they could lobby for better treatment by the public sector—for tariff and trade restrictions, for tax concessions, for antitrust immunities, and for all kinds of special considerations. This may also be a good time to write off past mistakes by taking losses in bad times, when everyone expects setbacks anyway. Executives who are carried in boom times may also find themselves unnecessary when the situation is reversed. In general, however, skilled or specialized labor is retained as long as possible. Small firms fall behind or are eliminated; medium-sized firms are caught in the middle, but inflexible prices shield them from failure. The tendency toward uniform prices helps to guarantee the survival of firms, but relative positions within the industry may be affected.

The unemployed spill over into the more competitive industries and to the service sector generally. Wages are already comparatively low in this area, and the influx of unemployed does nothing to improve the situation. If wages are depressed further, prices can remain fairly stable. However, wages could also be rising in this sector if workers are still in the catch-up phase (as against organized labor) of wage demands. Prices may actually rise in the recession, with little or no gain in employment.

Again, in the service sector those who deal in professional services can protect themselves. The price of medical services, dental care, and the like, can rise without much difficulty, while other professionals, teachers and government workers, are trying to catch up with the prior losses in real income. All of this is familiar by now: prices rise eventually, even in a recession. Furthermore, price increases, however small, can begin to accumulate into a wage-price spiral as workers scramble to protect their real incomes.

Both unemployment and the price level can increase at the same time, contrary to the either/or trade-off analysis. They both creep upwards, and there is nothing done by the private sector to halt the process. Simultaneously, inflationary psychology is in evidence, along with growing uneasiness, uncertainty, and pessimism. Under these conditions economic units pursuing their own self-interest cannot be expected to take actions that might relieve the pressures in the short run or to make anything but tentative plans for the long run. There will be no voluntary wage and price reductions, no forgoing of the drive to catch up by those who fall behind, and no moderation of policies by those who insist on keeping ahead.

In the public sector the automatic stabilizers are activated, and transfer payments to households proceed routinely. The recession, however, has reduced tax receipts, so that deficits can be expected. The increased government expenditures add to the inflationary pressures, for these expenditures create incomes without creating jobs; the demand side is increased but not the supply side. Increases in other areas of public expenditures would be generally resisted as inflationary; if any increases did occur, they would be in areas that do not create jobs for the unemployed and hence aggravate the situation (defense spending, subsidies, highway construction, and so on). More than likely, there would be pressure to reduce public spending, particularly on the federal bureaucracy, so that the salaries and numbers of public employees would be reduced amidst an accompanying fanfare. Public spending is not seriously affected, because there are fixed obligations (debt) or a fixed philosophy (national defense).

Tax increases are never popular and are even more resisted in recessionary periods. To be justified, tax increases would have to be weighted against upper- and middle-income groups and involve some redistribution of the tax burden. However, since the major portion of tax receipts comes from the first few tax brackets, not much can be expected of tax increases; tax privileges, concessions, and loopholes will be protected, so that any tax increase would have to be enacted at the expense of social justice.

Tax reductions to increase aggregate demand, and hopefully employment, may have some positive effects but at the risk of aggravating the inflation still further. Questions of goals and priorities will be raised, and debates over which is the greater evil, unemployment or inflation, will ensue. The unemployed are powerless, but financial interests are not; therefore, the policies are weighted toward price stability.

Fiscal policy appears useless, hampered as it is by inflexibility and institutional realities. The problem is made even more difficult by the rise in activity of state and local governments, whose problems are far removed from fiscal policy concerns and whose actions may actually lead to the worsening of the economic condition. Even if utilized, fiscal policy is not likely to work, either in creating jobs or reducing inflation, unless it is carried to such extremes that economic chaos will result. The days of "fine-tuning" are over—the changing economic structure and institutional realities have seen to that.

Monetary policy fares no better; to be effective it must be carried to extremes and even then works mainly on selected markets, crippling them while leaving the real sources of power unaffected. Price stability exacts a high cost of its own in terms of unemployment and uncertainty. Traditional approaches are not very effective in this new situation of rising prices *and* unemployment.

Through all this runs the curious ambivalence of many who find themselves benefiting from the economic situation, especially the rising price level. They cannot explain it theoretically or by past experience and thus continue to call for price stability. The old slogans help them to convince themselves that all is not topsy-turvy. Those who manage to keep ahead of the price level changes—those who may in fact cause the increases—benefit from their superior positions—national defense contractors, organized labor in key industries, corporation presidents who can boast of rising money profits and sales, government officials who seize the power that increasing taxes confer.

The poor, the unemployed, and all those who fall behind face a rather cruel dilemma. If they favor price stability to protect their meager money incomes, they may worsen the condition of their unfortunate unemployed numbers, but if they favor employment schemes to improve their lot, they may be asked to pay for these via higher taxes. The frustration and disillusionment that result cannot be overcome by transfer payments, for the futility of government actions is clearly seen from below and is viewed with cynicism as special-interest groups continue to prosper. The household sector, always relatively powerless, finds that it cannot win in this economic situation, nor can it look to government for help. The mood is one of sullenness.

In the foreign trade sector the domestic situation of rising prices worsens the balance of trade, while rising unemployment forestalls some actions that might have improved it. The cries for protection will be mixed with those for free trade: protection from lower prices abroad, free trade for low-cost imports for the poor. Once again, domestic economic policies cannot be pursued in isolation, for their effects would aggravate the balance-of-payments problems. The ineffectiveness of monetary and fiscal policies for domestic purposes is exaggerated by foreign trade constraints.

Future Trends and Suggested Correctives

It is likely that the trends toward the concentration of power will continue slowly but steadily, and if so, the traditional use of monetary and fiscal policy weapons of another era are likely to become more ineffective. The traditional policy tools are not well suited to the changing economic conditions brought on by structural imbalances. It is, therefore, appropriate to ask what alternatives are available and what are their consequences.

It is possible, but not immediately probable, that the entire concept of active federal intervention in the economic system may be scrapped. In its place, greater reliance upon state and local governments to solve economic problems may be substituted, with the federal government relegated to managing the international situation and the larger affairs of state. Decentralization of power and wealth through revenue sharing may result from the failure of the central government to solve the difficult economic problems. If this trend develops the problems of economic power would get worse, for the control over economic forces would be scattered among fifty states and numerous localities. At present, of course, the discarding of federal intervention is not seriously being considered, but the signs of frustration are clear and the increasing governmental role is becoming evident.

More than likely, economic events will prevent the redistribution of public power and control. For if indirect measures are doomed to failure, then more direct methods must be attempted, and these are better administered at the federal level. Some form of direct controls over prices and wages may well be forced upon us and become a permanent feature of advanced capitalism. No longer an emergency or wartime measure, controls may be necessary to curb the excesses of economic power. The extent and form of such controls over the economy can vary, but some controls may be required. The controls can be economywide, cover selected sectors and industries, or resemble an incomes policy that is more relaxed. It is not necessary to spell out the administrative details or to examine the merits of various plans, to point out that the free market, long subject to erosion, may no longer be reliable now that market power has developed to throw its previous mechanisms off balance.

In addition to market controls, more rational, long-term government planning may also be required of advanced capitalist systems. Mere reaction to economic events is not sufficient, but control over these events is necessary. Planning, even of the informal type, is preferable to unpredictable responses and short-term institutional and political restraints. Some vision, some courageous leadership, and some ordering of priorities are required to achieve economic and social order.

As part of long-term planning, some consideration must be given to an alternative to controls: nationalization. It might be possible to achieve control by nationalizing key industries (basic raw materials, metals, transportation, drug, construction, health, and so on) and imposing a milder incomes policy on the remainder of the economy. Galbraith has suggested nationalizing the national defense industry also, and others may have alternative choices in mind. One way to deal with market power is to usurp it and control it by placing it in the hands of the public sector. It is true that the power may corrupt those who usurp it or that great efficiency may not result from the transfer, but those who advocate nationalization prefer the power to be concentrated in more rather than in fewer hands. Selective nationalization (and the threat of more) can be effective in redirecting market power, so that its abuses can be curtailed and subordinated to the public will.

Some might argue that antitrust policy could accomplish the same result with less damage to the tenets of capitalism. But such a policy would not get at the roots of market power and could result in a loss of efficiency if economies of scale were sacrificed. Economies of scale may require size to make use of available technology, and so forth. Antitrust actions may well be too late in many industries and, if used at all, may well protect market power by preserving the existing market structure. In some cases, the threat of antitrust actions may help prevent concentration, but if the past is any guide, this negative sanction is easily avoided. Still, antitrust policies may help and can be used in conjunction with other remedies; used alone, however, they are likely to be ineffective or do more harm than good. Extending the antitrust laws to organized labor is open to similar criticism. Compulsory collective bargaining schemes appear to be a circuitous route to achieve indirectly what direct controls or an incomes policy would accomplish far more easily.

In the international area new monetary arrangements may be required to facilitate trade and to avoid the periodic breakdown of international monetary relations. Balance-of-payments difficulties need new solutions to ensure that domestic economic policies can achieve employment stability. New international rules of the game may be required in short-run difficulties and will certainly be needed to deal with the multinational corporation. Indeed, the problems raised by the multinational corporation may force such institutional changes and speed up the monetary reforms so needed by world trade. Until then, international trade will cause domestic problems for governments and periodic crises for international financial and political relations.

Finally, a few remarks must be made to point out another result of market power and a contribution to the attainment of that power: the unequal distribution of income and wealth. The unequal distribution of income and wealth clearly permits the concentration of economic power in a few hands and perpetuates that power. Economic power carries with it political power, and democratic processes are threatened. The power is perpetuated by its use in obtaining special treatment from the subverted government—in taxes, expenditures, contracts, subsidies, and trade restrictions. Democratic principles are compromised in a government that is subservient to powerful business interests. The society is threatened as the gap between the haves and the have-nots widens. The conflict of interests increases for men who govern but who are asked for special consideration by certain powerful groups; public officials own stock in these companies, represent them through their law firms, rely upon them for campaign funds, and so on. Obviously, much more than economic stability is involved here, but this curiously appears to be forgotten by those who object to the loss of economic freedom that they maintain follows from interference with the free market.

In fact, free markets are largely confined to those markets that affect the poor and disadvantaged. Unskilled labor markets are free, as is the market for migrant farm workers. The social consequences of these free markets are well known. The effects of racial, age, or sex discrimination upon the opportunity for upward mobility are also familiar. The lack of opportunity is frequently manifested in the unequal distribution of income. How much of the real or latent social unrest can be traced to this source? This subject cannot be pursued here, for it is too large. Suffice it to say that market power, so prevalent and so accepted, has far-reaching consequences not only on the economic system but on the political and social systems as well. A handful of men, the leaders of the top corporations, have an enormous amount of power, and their decisions affect the lives of millions of people. It is appropriate to ask to what extent these large firms can be considered "private."

Economic
Growth

Until very recently the desirability of economic growth was never seriously questioned, nor did it appear to be a subject open to value judgments. However, at least for advanced economies, the need for further growth has become the subject of much recent debate. A growing awareness that the Earth's resources are limited, and the environmental crisis in general, have·enlivened a previously routine topic and generated much interesting discussion. The resource crisis is real and is a genuine cause for concern. Before turning to these issues, however, we must gain some understanding of how an economy grows and of the problems connected with growth. Later we can ask why, or if, growth is necessary for advanced economies—for underdeveloped economies, the question may be irrelevant if not presumptuous.

We first describe briefly the evolution of growth theory and trace its development to the standard post-Keynesian model of economic growth. Then we consider the growth models, using our impressionistic model. Finally, the issue of growth versus no growth is examined more fully.

The Classical Economists

The classical economists had many insights into the process of economic growth; they correctly included many of the long-run variables—population, income distribution, capital accumulation, productivity, education, and so on. Although the handling of these variables in the development process was not always consistent, the classical economists did manage to formulate logical models, so that once the confusion is swept away, a grand schema emerges and a rather lofty view of the growth process becomes discernible.

Despite or perhaps because of the already evident early stages of the Industrial Revolution, their vision of the future was remarkably pessimistic.[1] Adam Smith in *The Wealth of Nations* incorporated population as an endogenous variable—both influencing and being influenced by the growth process. In the early stages of economic growth the demand for labor is high and wages are bid up. The result is an increase in population, which is at first beneficial, since a greater division of labor,

[1] For this and many other perspectives of classical economic thought, see Joseph A. Schumpeter, *History of Economic Analysis* (Oxford: Oxford University Press, 1954).

and thus increased output, is made possible. As we will see, this condition cannot continue indefinitely, and in the long run wages will fall to subsistence wages (physical subsistence in some interpretations, cultural subsistence later). Meanwhile, capital is accumulated via the process of saving by the capitalist, who advances his saving to laborers while the capital good is under construction. It is the thrift—parsimony—of the capitalist that makes capital accumulation possible. Note, however, that this type of reasoning led to the conclusion that saving immediately was matched by an equal amount of investment—a conclusion so universally accepted that it lasted really until Keynes questioned it.

Smith foresaw growth problems in that the rising population would keep wages and consumption low and capitalists' rewards low as well, for their saving of previous years was now invested in capital stock, where the yields had fallen. Thus, laborers and capitalists alike find their income shares falling, while the landowners' shares would be rising (although Smith's analysis of rent is deficient, if not misleading).

The pessimism of Malthus is well known. His essay on population, written in reaction against the prevailing optimistic mood, attempted to describe the "laws" of population growth and agricultural output. There was no mistaking the message: population tends to grow at a geometric rate, while food output grows at an arithmetic rate. As population growth exceeds food production growth, human suffering increases, and the remedy could only be to reduce population. The positive "checks" to population growth were plague, famine, war, disease—that is, misery. The other preventive "checks"—moral restraint (late marriages, abstinence) or vice (prostitution, promiscuity)—could not be relied upon or were distasteful morally.

This is a dismal picture, for it suggests that whenever real wages or living standards rise above some subsistence level, population expands until the checks reduce the population down to the subsistence level again. Unless people limit the growth of population, they are apparently doomed to live in poverty. Malthus' principles were very influential, but they were not particularly original or well founded. The identification of Malthus with the population variable has shifted the attention away from his contribution in other areas of economics. His ideas of saving and investment, the possibility of a general glut of all goods (contrary to Say's Law), and his notion of aggregate demand were modern in tone and prompted Keynes to label him a precursor. Keynes wrote approvingly of him in the attempt to call attention to his contributions.[2]

Ricardo, building on these ideas and those of other forerunners, and adding his rent theory and his emphasis on distribution, constructed a model that was powerful in imagination and deduction and extremely influential. Whether or not people agreed with the formulation or conclusions of his model, they could not ignore them; all who worked in the discipline had to take them into account. The model's deductive logic and precise expression became the standard for economic analysis, which still persists long after the model itself has been discarded.

Ricardo accepted and modified some of the ideas of Smith and Malthus and built a dynamic model of economic change and development that can be summarized in outline form as follows: in the early stages of development the rate of return on capital goods is high, so that capitalists accumulate by saving and advancing funds to laborers during the production period. The demand for labor is high

---

[2] His essay on Malthus appears in *Essays in Biography* (New York: Horizon Press, 1951), pp. 81–124.

and wages are bid up, and as we know, wages above the subsistence level lead to increases in population. A larger population puts pressure on the available food supply, so that more and more inferior land must be cultivated to feed the growing numbers. Rent appears on the more fertile land, and rents increase as the use of inferior land increases. The reward to landowners thus rises as development proceeds.

Capitalists, however, run into diminishing returns, and the rate of profit falls steadily. Population expands and forces wages down to a minimum. Only the landowners' share continues to increase as more marginal land is cultivated and rents steadily rise. Soon capitalists have no further incentive to accumulate. Population growth ceases, and everyone lives on the brink of subsistence except the landlords, who presumably spend their growing income shares on luxuries, imports, and the good life.

The economy will have reached the stationary state, and little hope is held out for further progress. For the early classical economists, the stationary state was an unfortunate condition forced on the economy by these dynamic forces, which appeared to be beyond human intervention and manipulation. No wonder economics was branded as the dismal science when the ultimate result of economic development was gloomily forecast as a condition wherein most of the population would be living at the subsistence level (now defined as culturally determined) and dominated by forces they could not control. Economic stagnation was not pleasant to contemplate.

In retrospect, it is easy to point out the errors in this broad model: technological change is omitted; the population variable is too simple and mechanical; the industrial and agricultural revolutions were not perceived; and in general, the whole model is too mechanical—no one learns from experience, no one forms expectations and acts on them, and so on. It is not our purpose to criticize these ideas fully.

However, two important areas of concern for the world in the 1970s do appear in these early attempts to explain economic development: population and the stationary state. Once again, population growth appears to be pressing on the supply of natural resources, and continued population growth threatens survival of human life as it is now known. The population variable regains a prominent position after having been gradually downgraded following classical thought.

Consider also the stationary state as an economic condition. In the hands of the early classical writer the stationary state signaled economic stagnation and represented a deplorable condition. In the hands of John Stuart Mill the stationary state becomes quite something else. Some maintain that he came to hold a more optimistic view of population control, while others say his evolutionary thought was influenced by his late flirtation with socialism. At any rate, this is what he wrote:

I cannot, therefore, regard the stationary state of capital and wealth with the unaffected aversion so generally manifested towards it by political economists of the old school. I am inclined to believe that it would be, on the whole, a very considerable improvement on our present condition. I confess I am not charmed with the ideal of life held out by those who think that the normal state of human beings is that of struggling to get on; that the trampling, crushing, elbowing, and treading on each other's heels, which form the existing type of social life, are the most desirable lot of human kind, or anything but the disagreeable symptoms of one of the phases of industrial progress . . . that the life of the whole of one sex is devoted to dollar-hunting, and of the other to breeding dollar-hunters. This is not a kind of social perfection which philanthropists to come will feel any very eager desire to assist in realizing. Most fitting, indeed, is it, that while riches are power, and to grow as rich as possible the universal object of ambition, the path to its attainment should be open to all, without favor or partiality. But the best state for human nature is that in which, while no one is poor, no one desires to be richer, nor has any reason to fear being thrust back, by the efforts of others to push themselves forward.[3]

Mill apparently found solace in the stationary state, and rather than deplore its arrival, he seemed to welcome it as a relief from competitive capitalism. Actually, the stationary state meant something different for Mill than for Ricardo. Loosely interpreted, Mill's view would have stressed population control while permitting a low rate of growth and technological change.

Marx also dissented from the classical economists' forecast of economic development. Long before the stationary state was reached, he said, the increasing misery of the laborer would revolutionize the whole system. For Marx, the very success of capitalism would drive it to limits from which it would inevitably fail. Marx's model was also expressed in terms of class and income-group conflicts. The capitalist in his exploitation of labor is driven to accumulate more capital, but more capital means falling profit rates. Since labor is the sole source of value, the capitalist exploits labor by paying it less than the exchange value of the output, thus extracting a surplus. To gain more profit, the capitalist utilizes the surplus to acquire more capital, but the process of accumulation contains contradictions: to extract a surplus, labor must be employed, but the substitution of capital for labor in the capital accumulation process reduces the surplus and profit rates fall anyway; in addition, the unemployed labor pool grows, keeping wages down and population growth low as well.

As capital accumulation proceeds, the smaller firms are squeezed out and are taken over by the larger ones seeking to survive through efficiency, and the concentration of capital in a few hands is the result. Class conflicts are more sharply delineated, and eventually the increasing misery of the workers prompts them to revolt and expropriate the means of production.

Again, it is not necessary to spell out the details of the model or to criticize it fully. For our purposes, it is sufficient to note that Marx built a model of an economic system in evolutionary change—in an historical context—and showed the social consequences of class conflicts. Right or wrong, he was the first economist to recognize the effects of economic development upon the society. As Schumpeter put it:

I wish only to insist on the greatness of the conception and on the fact that Marxist analysis is the only genuinely evolutionary economic theory that the period produced. Neither its assumptions nor its techniques are above serious objections—though, partly, because it has been left unfinished. But the grand vision of an immanent evolution of the economic process—that, working somehow through accumulation, somehow destroys the economy as well as the society of competitive capitalism and somehow produces an untenable social situation that will somehow give birth to another type of social organization—remains after the most vigorous criticism has done its worst. It is this fact, and this fact alone, that constitutes Marx's claim to greatness as an economic analyst.[4]

---

[3] John Stuart Mill, *The Principles of Political Economy* (originally published 1848; reprinted New York: D. Appleton, 1872), vol. II, p. 336.

[4] Schumpeter, *History of Economic Analysis*, p. 441. Of course, Marx's contributions to sociology and history, and so on, are not discussed in the text.

The Stationary State—Economic Stagnation

The concept of the stationary state has a long and interesting history in economic analysis. For some, the stationary state represented only a convenient methodological device. Loosely interpreted, such an economy was in full equilibrium, with net investment being zero and the stock of capital being fixed. In such an equilibrium condition the real forces at work in the economy and the distribution of output can be examined, free from the complication of growth, the business cycle, changing levels of capital stock and potential output fluctuations.[5]

Other economists, like those mentioned, saw the stationary state as a very real condition that the economy would approach with economic development. Aside from John Stuart Mill, economists viewed the stationary state with misgivings, since their models predicted some dire consequences. The stationary state is transformed from a theoretical concept to a possible real state, and in the transformation economic stagnation is made the central issue.

If we jump in time to the twentieth century, we find the idea in the hands of Keynes, who visualized capital stock in such abundance that the rate of return from capital would fall to a very low figure, which "would mean the euthanasia of the rentier, and, consequently, the euthanasia of the cumulative oppressive power of the capitalist to exploit the scarcity value of capital."[6] As the rentier disappears, the state will have to undertake the task of capital accumulation by socializing investment, if full employment is to be reached. Keynes's prediction was indeed premature, since he failed to consider the growth of the economy, which would require more capital stock and hence forestall the decline in the marginal efficiency of capital.

Alvin Hansen took up the idea of secular stagnation and attributed it largely to the *lack* of population growth, contrary to earlier analyses.[7] The decline in the rate of population growth meant inadequate outlets for investment. In addition, there were no more frontiers to develop. The decline in investment opportunities was made worse by the fact that new inventions and new techniques were essentially of the capital-widening or the capital-saving kind. Dramatic new innovations calling for large increases in capital stock were not contemplated. Furthermore, new techniques required less capital per unit of output. As investment outlets dried up, the question was what to do with the excess saving in the form of retained earnings, out of which investment is largely financed.

Of course, Hansen was misled by short-run demographic factors and was overly pessimistic concerning the nature of innovations that required more capital stock and whole new industries. Still he, like Keynes before him, was pointing to the tendency of advanced capitalism to produce more savings than are required by the declining investment outlets. In the past, colonialism or trade helped to forestall any real crisis.

The same lack of investment outlets and excess saving led Baran and Sweezy to conclude that other areas would have to use the surplus.[8] Thus, the surplus is

[5] For example, see the work of J. B. Clark, *The Distribution of Wealth* (New York: Macmillan, 1900).

[6] J. M. Keynes, *The General Theory of Employment, Interest, and Money* (New York: Harcourt, Brace, 1936), p. 376. Chapter 24 of *The General Theory* is recommended reading in its entirety.

[7] See his presidential address to the AEA, "Economic Progress and Declining Population Growth," *American Economic Review* 29 (March 1939): 1–15; reprinted in *Readings in Business Cycle Theory*, ed. G. Haberler (Homewood, Ill.: Richard D. Irwin, 1951).

[8] Paul A. Baran and Paul M. Sweezy, *Monopoly Capital* (New York: Monthly Review Press, 1966).

absorbed by national defense and the sales efforts, but such rescuing efforts merely transform the economy into the irrational system described earlier. Magdoff describes the new imperialism as advanced economy capital seeks outlets in other countries.[9] Steindl sees economic stagnation as being the result of the system of monopoly capital, where market structure concentrates power and resources.[10]

Indeed, many others have written on the stationary state and economic stagnation, but there is no need to identify every trace of this early concept. Our purpose in discussing it at all was to prepare the ground for the later discussion of the growth versus no growth controversy. The other variables in this discussion also have a modern ring and thus will fit into later discussion, too: population concerns, imperialism, and economic concentration. Thus, the stationary state, an old concept, is revived as a controversy over goals—a controversy that is made more intricate by the accompanying concept of economic stagnation. Finally, the issue of income distribution must be considered in the context of growth versus no growth, and so the methodological stationary state also has not lost its relevance.

Post-Keynesian Growth Theory

To trace the development of growth theory up to the present would be interesting but would take us far afield. Even Keynes made some observations on economic development, as suggested earlier, but for the most part he was concerned with short-run economic fluctuations. Yet the logical extension of his model appeared to be in the long-run implications of his analysis. Immediately following World War II this direction was followed by one of his students, Sir Roy Harrod, and thereafter the long run once again gained the attention of economic theorists. The focus on economic growth and development continued throughout the 1950s and into the 1960s, when, as we have seen, it became a political issue as well. The sociology of this economic issue would itself be an interesting topic, but we are concerned here only with the theoretical development.

THE HARROD–DOMAR MODEL

As often happens in the history of the discipline, several men may be working with similar ideas at the same time—the marginalists, for instance. With respect to growth theory, Sir Roy Harrod and Evsey D. Domar were developing the theory along similar lines—hence their names are linked to identify their common approach and similar analyses.[11]

The essential features of this type of growth model can best be brought out by using Domar's model. His model very clearly illustrates the dual character of investment spending: on the one hand, investment is a sector of aggregate *demand* (as in foregoing models), and on the other hand, net investment adds to the productive capacity of the economy and thus increases potential aggregate *supply* as well. The dual nature of investment presents a problem for an economy that wishes to grow at a steady rate. For investment in this period will create additional

---

[9] Harry Magdoff, *The Age of Imperialism* (New York: Monthly Review Press, 1969).

[10] J. Steindl, *Maturity and Stagnation in American Capitalism* (Oxford: Basil Blackwell, 1952).

[11] Sir Roy's final model can be found in his book *Towards a Dynamic Analysis* (London: Macmillan and Co., 1948), and Domar's model in "Expansion and Employment" and "The Problem of Capital Accumulation," *American Economic Review* 37 (March 1947): 34–55 and 38 (December 1948): 77–94. Both of these are reprinted in E. D. Domar, *Essays in the Theory of Economic Growth* (New York: Oxford University Press, 1957).

output in the next period. Some of this additional output will be taken by the household sector in the form of consumption expenditures. However, since the *MPC* is less than 1, additional investment is necessary to buy the remaining output. If investment expenditures are insufficient, income will fall and idle capacity will develop. Obviously, with idle capacity, economic growth is much more difficult to maintain, as the business sector becomes discouraged. In Domar's model consumption is passive and investment is the driving force—the Keynesian influence.

If investment grows at too fast a rate, inflation will develop, since aggregate demand will exceed the productive capacity of the economy. The growth of productive capacity is determined by the productivity of the new investment, and if investment demand exceeds the ability of investment to produce additional output, inflation will result as the attempt to bid for the available resources proceeds. Again, steady economic growth is made difficult by the limitation of resources.

This type of growth model (owing largely to its simplicity) results in what has been called the razor's edge—any movement away from the correct amount of investment sends the economy into secular stagnation or inflation. This follows from the conditions of the model: if investment is too little, idle capacity will develop, but the business sector will conclude, paradoxically, that it has invested too much; if investment is too large, inflation will develop, but the business sector will conclude that it has not invested enough. This paradox creates the motivations for next period's investment plans, but these plans will only succeed in moving the economy away from the path of steady equilibrium growth.

Domar was not particularly pessimistic about the ability of the economy to utilize the growing capacity (his main concern) as long as aggregate demand grew by the appropriate amount. Thus the question: what is the appropriate rate of growth of aggregate demand (that is, investment) necessary to utilize the growing productive capacity that results from continued capital accumulation?

The Model

It is a simple matter to derive the required rate of growth of investment demand once the dual nature of investment spending is realized. The long-run consumption function is assumed to be a proportional one, so that the saving (or unconsumed output) function is also proportional and is written,

$$(18.1) \qquad S = \alpha Y; \qquad \frac{S}{Y} = \frac{\Delta S}{\Delta Y} = \alpha.$$

Equation (18.1) merely states in symbolic form the long-run saving function, which passes through the origin, making $\overline{APS} = \overline{MPS} \; (= \alpha)$.

The net addition to potential productive capacity is measured in the dollar value of potential output and expressed as

$$(18.2) \qquad Y = \sigma K; \qquad \frac{Y}{K} = \frac{\Delta Y}{\Delta K} = \sigma.$$

Equation (18.2) states that output varies proportionally with capital stock, the factor of proportionality being σ, the productivity of capital. If $\sigma = 0.3$, then a stock of capital of $600 is capable of producing an output, Y, of $200. Equation (18.2) also states that additions to capital stock (ΔK) are equivalent in productivity with previously existing capital stock. This assumes that technology is held constant.

With equations (18.1) and (18.2), the required rate of growth of investment is seen to be a constant equal to

(18.3)
$$\frac{\Delta I}{I} = \alpha\sigma.$$

This constant rate, $\alpha\sigma$, of investment demand is derived as follows. Since $\Delta K = I$ by definition, I can be substituted for ΔK in equation (18.2) to give

(18.4)
$$\frac{\Delta Y}{I} = \sigma \quad \text{or} \quad \Delta Y_s = \sigma I,$$

which shows the growth of potential supply, ΔY_s, the growth in productive capacity.

On the demand side, a growing economy must equate $\Delta S/\Delta Y$ and $\Delta I/\Delta Y$ as a *moving* equilibrium condition, so that

(18.5)
$$\frac{\Delta S}{\Delta Y} = \frac{\Delta I}{\Delta Y} = \alpha$$

from equation (18.1), or quite simply,

(18.5)′
$$\Delta Y_d = \frac{\Delta I}{\alpha},$$

which shows the growth on the demand side by the change in investment spending. Note that equation (18.5)′ is nothing more than the simple multiplier.

For balanced equilibrium growth, $\Delta Y_s = \Delta Y_d$, period by period; by substitution into this equilibrium condition, equations (18.4) and (18.5)′ become

$$\sigma I = \frac{\Delta I}{\alpha},$$

and rearranging gives

(18.6)
$$\frac{\Delta I}{I} = \alpha\sigma.$$

Equation (18.6) is the expression for the required rate of growth of investment that will result in balanced growth, with neither idle capacity (secular stagnation) nor secular inflation. Note that the required rate depends on the propensity to save and on the productivity of capital. The higher the propensity to save, the higher the required rate of investment growth, since investment must increase to absorb the rising amount of unconsumed output. Similarly, the higher the productivity of capital, σ, the higher the required rate of investment growth, since more output would be (potentially) produced and again investment must increase to absorb the rising output levels.

Before examining the model in greater detail, a clearer conception of how it works may be given by a numerical example. Let us assume that $\alpha = 0.2$ and $\sigma = 0.3$, so that the required rate of growth of investment is 6 per cent, which is the growth rate of income as well. If we assume an initial equilibrium condition in the first period, we can examine the consequences of various rates of growth of investment.

In case 1 of Table 18.1 the equilibrium growth rate is maintained, since the required rate of investment is 6 per cent per period. In column (2) the level of capital stock is shown, which when multiplied by the productivity of capital stock

TABLE 18.1
NUMERICAL ILLUSTRATION OF GROWTH PROCESS

(1) Period	(2) Capital Stock (K)	(3) Potential Capacity Output ($Y_s = \sigma K$)	(4) Actual Output ($Y = C + I$)	(5) Consumption (C)	(6) Investment (I)
Case 1. Investment Grows at Required Rate: 6 Per Cent ($\alpha\sigma = 0.2 \times 0.3$)					
1	500	150	150	120	30
2	530	159	159	127.2	31.8
3	561.8	168.54	168.54	134.832	33.708
4	595.508	178.6524	178.6524	142.92192	35.73048
5	631.23848, and so on				
Case 2. Investment Grows at Slower than Required Rate: 5 Per Cent (< 6 Per Cent)					
1	500	150	150	120	30
2	530	159	157.5	126	31.5
3	561.5	168.45	165.375	132.300	33.075
4	594.575, and so on				
Case 3. Investment Grows at Faster than Required Rate: 7 Per Cent (> 6 Per Cent)					
1	500	150	150	120	30
2	530	159	160.50	128.40	32.10
3	562.1	168.63	171.735	137.388	34.347
4	596.447, and so on				
Case 4. Investment Grows by a Constant Amount: 30 Per Period					
1	500	150	150	120	30
2	530	159	150	120	30
3	560	168	150	120	30
4	590, and so on				

(0.3) results in the productive capacity of the economy given in column (3). The level of aggregate demand $(C + I)$ is given in column (4). Column (5) shows consumption demand from the consumption function $C = 0.8Y$, and column (6) is investment demand, which is determined by making various assumptions.

For case 1, the balanced growth rate, the initial capital stock level of 500 in period 1 results in output of 150, which is all purchased back by consumption of 120 and investment of 30. In period 2 the investment of period 1, 30, is added to the previous level of capital stock to give the new level of 530. This higher level of capital stock, 530 multiplied by 0.3, the productivity of capital, gives the new potential output of the economy as 159. On the demand side, I has grown by 6 per cent, to 31.8, which when multiplied by 5 (the simple multiplier), gives the level of aggregate demand of 159, which is equal to aggregate supply. Finally, consumption is determined to be 127.2 from the consumption function. As long as I grows by the required rate of 6 per cent per period, the equilibrium growth of output will be matched by the growth of demand, and the economy will progress steadily at the same rate. Investment demand increases each period by just the proper amount to absorb the increase in productive capacity.

In case 2 the growth rate of investment demand is smaller than required—5 per cent. Starting at the same initial output, period 1 shows the economy in short-run equilibrium. In period 2, however, I grows by only 5 per cent, to 31.5. It is clear now that the model only includes autonomous investment, for it is considered an exogenous variable. The higher level of I, 31.5, is again subject to the simple multiplier of 5, so that aggregate demand increases to 157.5 and consumption, which is always passive, increases to 126 ($157.5 \times MPC$ of 0.8). Last period's investment of 30 is added to the previous level of capital stock for a total of 530, which when multiplied by the productivity of capital gives the potential output level of 159. It is clear that productive capacity is not being utilized, since potential output is greater than actual output. The idle capacity is created by investment demand growing too slowly—but again note the seeming paradox, for it will appear that too much has been invested. This interpretation is a natural one in the face of excess capacity. In period 3 it would not be unreasonable to expect investment to fall still further; in our model the same rate of growth of I is maintained, however, but in either case the growth of productive capacity still is greater than the growth of demand. The continuation of this process would lead to secular stagnation.

For the sake of completeness, cases 3 and 4 are included. In case 3, I grows at a faster rate than required, so that the demand side grows faster than the supply side. The result, of course, is inflation, which will continue as long as investment demand exceeds that required amount which is just sufficient to absorb the added capacity. Note the paradox again, for it will appear as if not enough had been invested. The productive capacity is too small, relative to the demand for output.

Finally, if investment increases by a constant amount, the level of aggregate demand will remain constant, as was learned in the short-run equilibrium analysis. Productive capacity, however, grows period by period as new investment is added to the level of capital stock, so that once again potential output outruns aggregate demand period after period. Case 4 shows these circumstances. It is now evident what was assumed away in short-run income determination analysis—the addition to capital stock and productive capacity [Columns (2) and (3)] were ignored; investment as a sector of demand only was considered.

Some Comments on Domar's Model

It is clear that Domar's model is a product of the Keynesian analysis. As such, it is more applicable to advanced economies than to underdeveloped ones. Indeed, its very simplicity limits its direct application to any economy. Nevertheless, the model does serve as a starting point in the analysis of economic growth and does capture some of the salient features of the growth process in advanced capitalist economies.

Beyond the simple insights, however, the model is restricted by the assumptions made. It assumes full employment and, in fact, makes no explicit mention of the labor force, thus tacitly assuming that the labor force (and population?) grow at the required rate to prevent unemployment. In addition, technology is held constant and all investment is reduced to the autonomous variety. The underlying production function assumes that capital and labor are used in fixed proportions, so that no substitution is permitted between capital and labor. (The isoquants are right angles.) In fact, the model is somewhat one-sided; the demand side is clearly developed, but the supply side and the productivity of capital are left vague.

Of course, the simple model given here has been refined and modified by Domar in his other works on economic growth and by others who have scrutinized the mechanisms of his model. The use of the simple model is limited to its contribution to the theory of economic growth. It is of little practical importance for policy makers in advanced economies and is of even less use in underdeveloped economies. Most growth models developed for Western advanced economies simply cannot be thrown into use willy-nilly in other, different economies. The economic structure, religion, traditions, customs, political systems, social conditions, cultures of other countries may be so different as to make the simple growth models appear naive when applied to their economic systems. This may appear obvious, but mistakes have been made in the past and some strange advice given to developing economies.

Harrod's growth model takes us essentially along the same path and reaches similar conclusions. This is not to suggest that they are identical models, for there are many differences. In the end, however, little would be gained by examining the Harrod model in detail, for the essential features have been suggested in discussing the Domar model.[12]

NEOCLASSICAL GROWTH MODELS

Not long after the insights of the Harrod-Domar type of model had become commonly accepted, new growth models appeared, which as a group are referred to as neoclassical. Some of these models were inspired by the rigid assumptions of the Harrod-Domar model, and others sought additions and refinements to the simple model. In either case, the analysis became highly mathematical and the interpretations became much more complex. Therefore, in keeping with the un-sophisticated mathematical techniques used in this book, only a few suggestions will be offered to indicate the nature and content of these models.

The neoclassical model begins with an enlarged aggregate production function that includes technology as a separate factor:

$$(18.7) \qquad\qquad Y = f(A, K, N).$$

---

[12] Harrod actually proposed three growth rates—the actual one; the natural growth rate, which the fully employed labor force, population change, and technological advance permit; and the warranted growth rate, which is the rate consistent with investors' and savers' motives. Thus, Harrod brings more elements into the growth process, including the accelerator for investment outlays. The Harrod and Domar models are similar mainly in the formal sense.

The type of technological change envisioned, however, is neutral in that it increased the productivity of both labor and capital and left the rate of substitution between them unaffected. Moreover, like the Harrod-Domar model, the simple neoclassical model assumed constant returns to scale, so that an equal increment of capital and labor would result in the same increment in output.

Unlike in the Harrod-Domar model, however, factors need not be used in fixed proportions, but substitutions can be undertaken or output increased by the addition of one factor to the fixed amount of the other factor; of course, diminishing returns are assumed in the latter case.

These elements of the model appear to improve upon those of the Harrod-Domar model. Additional assumptions, however, again return the model to one of formal theory and reduce its applicability. Perfect competition is assumed in all markets, and generally, factors receive the value of their marginal products.[13] Now, with these assumptions (along with diminishing returns, factor substitutability, and so on), the basic model asks the question of how the economy will grow and what contributions to growth are made by labor, capital, and technological change.

If in equation (18.7) technological change is absent, then output will vary according to factor inputs alone. But capital and labor contribute differently to the production process, and it is this factor that prohibits the simple conclusions of the Harrod-Domar model. For with factor substitution permitted and diminishing returns assumed, the growth process is much more difficult and complex.

Capital contributes to the production process (and is paid accordingly by assumption) an amount equal to the marginal product of capital times the amount of capital, which for small changes can be written,

$$(18.8) \qquad \Delta Y = MP_K(\Delta K), \qquad \text{with } \bar{N}.$$

For labor, the same idea is given by

$$(18.9) \qquad \Delta Y = MP_N(\Delta N) \qquad \text{with } \bar{K}.$$

For changes in both factors, it follows that

$$(18.10) \qquad \Delta Y = MP_K(\Delta K) + MP_N(\Delta N).$$

From the assumptions of constant returns to scale, it follows from (18.10) that *equal* increments of K and N (say 5 per cent) will result in an equal increment of Y (also 5 per cent). For the growth of output, equation (18.10) can be written,

$$(18.11) \qquad \frac{\Delta Y}{Y} = \frac{MP_K}{Y}\left(\frac{\Delta K}{K}\right) + \frac{MP_N}{Y}\left(\frac{\Delta N}{N}\right)$$

after dividing by Y on the left and by its equivalent, K and N, on the right side. The expressions MP_K/Y and MP_N/Y in (18.11) show how output changes with respect to the change in inputs—capital and labor, respectively. These terms measure the elasticity of output of factor inputs.[14] If we substitute a for the

---

[13] See, for instance, R. M. Solow, "A Contribution to the Theory of Economic Growth," *Quarterly Journal of Economics* 70 (February 1956): 65–94; and especially "Technical Changes and the Aggregate Production Function," *Review of Economics and Statistics* 39 (August 1957): 312–320.

[14] For those interested in the mathematics, the neoclassical production function written as

$$(1) \qquad Y = Y(N, K)$$

can be expressed according to Euler's theorem as

$$(2) \qquad Y = \frac{\partial Y}{\partial N}(N) + \frac{\partial Y}{\partial K}(K)$$

elasticity of output with respect to capital, then $1 - a$ would measure the labor input complement.

Equation (18.11) becomes

(18.12)
$$\frac{\Delta Y}{Y} = a\left(\frac{\Delta K}{K}\right) + (1 - a)\left(\frac{\Delta N}{N}\right).$$

If $a = 0.15$, this means that owners of capital receive 15 per cent of the income, which is equal to the value of the marginal product of capital, or what is the same thing, that a 1 per cent rise in capital stock would increase the national output by 0.15 per cent. Obviously, labor is the complement $1 - a$ to these magnitudes, with the identical interpretation. The assumption of constant returns to scale is easily seen from equation (18.12), since if the capital and labor input both increase by 5 per cent, the rate of growth of output will be 5 per cent:

$$\frac{\Delta Y}{Y} = 0.15(0.05) + 0.85(0.05),$$

$$= 5\%.$$

However, if labor and capital do not grow at the same rate (why should they?), then the growth rate is affected. Thus, if capital grows by a rate of 5 per cent and labor by 8 per cent,

$$\frac{\Delta Y}{Y} = 0.15(0.05) + 0.85(0.08),$$

$$= 0.0075 + 0.068,$$

$$= \text{approximately } 7\tfrac{1}{2}\%.$$

---

where partial derivatives are the respective marginal products. With the assumption of constant returns to scale, the differential of the production function gives

(3)
$$dY = \frac{\partial Y}{\partial N}(dN) + \frac{\partial Y}{\partial K}(dK).$$

Now, dividing both sides of (3) by Y and multiplying and dividing the terms on the right-hand side by K and N gives

(4)
$$\frac{dY}{Y} = \frac{\partial Y}{\partial N}\left(\frac{dN}{N}\right)\left(\frac{N}{Y}\right) + \frac{\partial Y}{\partial K}\left(\frac{dK}{K}\right)\left(\frac{K}{Y}\right).$$

But

$$\frac{\partial Y}{\partial N}\left(\frac{N}{Y}\right) = \frac{\partial(\log Y)}{\partial(\log N)}$$

is the elasticity of output with respect to N, and

$$\frac{\partial Y}{\partial K}\left(\frac{K}{Y}\right) = \frac{\partial(\log Y)}{\partial(\log K)}$$

is the elasticity of output with respect to K.

Expression (4) can be written

(5)
$$\frac{dY}{Y} = \frac{\partial(\log Y)}{\partial(\log N)}\left(\frac{dN}{N}\right) + \frac{\partial(\log Y)}{\partial(\log K)}\left(\frac{dK}{K}\right).$$

If we substitute

$$\frac{\partial(\log Y)}{\partial(\log N)} = 1 - a \quad \text{and} \quad \frac{\partial(\log Y)}{\partial(\log K)} = a$$

then (5) becomes

(6)
$$\frac{dY}{Y} = 1 - a\left(\frac{dN}{N}\right) + a\left(\frac{dK}{K}\right),$$

as in the text, and the interpretation of (6) is the same as that given above. For more details, see J. E. Meade, *A Neoclassical Theory of Economic Growth* (New York: Oxford University Press, 1961).

Now, if the numbers are reversed,

$$\frac{\Delta Y}{Y} = 0.15(0.08) + 0.85(0.05)$$

$$= \text{approximately } 5\tfrac{1}{2}\%.$$

It is now clear that explicit recognition of output elasticities affects the growth rate. In the Harrod-Domar model with its right-angled isoquants output would grow by the lesser factor input growth, as in the preceding by 5 per cent. The additional labor or capital adds nothing to the output and is wasted. Indeed, the possibility of factor substitution in the neoclassical model permits the possibility of stagnation or unemployment as capital grows faster than labor, or vice versa.

Thus, the neoclassical model brings out the interdependence of α and σ in the Domar model. In the Domar model σ was constant, so that growth was limited to the growth in inputs; technology was constant. If α increased, growth was made possible via greater capital accumulation. Since both capital and labor growth contributed equally to the growth of output, the increases in capital would increase output equally. If $\alpha = 0.10$ and $\sigma = 0.3$, then the growth rate would be 3 per cent. If saving increased to 0.15, the growth rate could increase to 4.5 per cent.

With the recognition that the contribution of capital to output is less than the one-for-one ratio, growth is made more difficult; if $a = 0.15$, the rate of growth is no longer the simple 4.5 per cent but is now only something like 3.8 per cent (3 per cent plus change in growth rate). Furthermore, additions to capital could reduce the productivity of capital by the assumption of diminishing returns, making growth still more difficult. Thus, α and σ become even more interdependent and cannot be considered to be data capable of manipulation without repercussions.

The simple growth path is blocked by complications. Further refinements and complexities can be introduced by incorporating technological change into the analysis directly, but enough has been suggested to permit the extension of the model without specific discussion. For although the neoclassical model makes its contribution over the simple Harrod-Domar model, it makes additional assumptions in the process, which detract from its applicability. Perfect competition, the marginal productivity theory, constant returns to scale, and so on, all force the model to be formally correct and straightforward but limited in practical analysis, even for advanced economies. For underdeveloped economies, such assumptions are even less realistic, so that policy makers will not be significantly aided by the formal neoclassical model.

The Relevance of Growth Theory

ADVANCED ECONOMIES

It is clear that the Harrod-Domar model and the neoclassical model are concerned with the growth of an advanced economy. Many institutional factors are assumed to exist that permit the rather abstract analysis of growth to be conducted free of disturbances from the political, social, cultural, and other institutional factors. Even without these potential disturbances, the models are still extremely abstract and rigid if strictly interpreted.

Additions, refinements, and other alterations to the basic models soon followed their publication, and the literature on economic growth expanded phenomenally.

The theory was advanced and the analysis made more sophisticated by the break-down of the economy for sectoral growth, the inclusion of agriculture, the inclusion of technological change, and so on.[15]

Little work has been done, however, in the area of the effects on economic growth of market structure, the concentration of power and economic activity, and the movement toward conglomeration and diversification. Highly aggregated models are bound to underestimate the impact on economic growth of market structure and changes in the structure. Only a few suggestions about its possible influence are included here, and more will be discussed later in the section on growth problems.[16]

As long as capital formation is in private hands, it is relevant to inquire into the motivations for capital accumulation. If as the models indicate, investment plays a crucial role in the growth process, then who is responsible for making investment decisions is also a pertinent question. The circumstances surrounding investment spending and capital accumulation decisions are all relevant and must be considered in the analysis of economic growth.

In the United States economy the top 500 corporations accounted for about one half of the net investment in 1971. Recall that growth is only one of the goals of the corporation, and a new element is introduced into the growth analysis of the advanced economy. For if there is excess capacity, there will be a reduction in new capital formation. But this excess capacity could be the result of market power, which came about through changes in the market structure. The exercise of market power resulted in the availability of funds in the form of retained earnings; these funds, if spent on investment projects, could have been wasted by the overestimation of future demand and the building of excess capacity. The available internal funds permit more risk taking and require less justification for their use, since little external control is exercised. If past capital accumulation cannot be utilized, there is no real incentive to accumulate more.

The funds, however, might still be used but in a manner not conducive to the growth of the economy: the large firms could swallow up the smaller ones; the movement toward conglomeration and diversification is made more attractive, and there is always the outlet in direct investment in foreign economies. None of these avenues is particularly encouraging for economic growth.

Furthermore, the existence of market power frees the larger firms from having to spend on research and development, and new techniques that could influence growth are not forthcoming. The firms could actually hinder growth by not utilizing available knowledge but postponing the introduction of new technology until the old capital stock is worn out. Thus, even if they discover new techniques through research or if they buy up inventions from external sources, they may not be impelled by market forces to employ them.

The profits flow to established firms with power, so that expansion of these firms in selected industries is permitted, or the growth in certain areas of the economy or in certain product lines is made possible by the continued generation of funds. The accumulation of funds need not flow to those firms and industries that are

---

[15] The literature on growth is too extensive for a detailed review. Some additional sources are, however, provided in the reference section at the end of the book for those who wish to pursue the topic.

[16] For estimates on the sources of growth in the past, see Edward F. Denison, *The Sources of Economic Growth in the United States*. Supplementary Paper No. 13 (New York: Committee for Economic Development, 1962).

dynamic and innovative and that might be expected to contribute extensively to economic growth. The funds may instead flow to stable industries with declining markets and uninspired managers who are made complacent by their firms' market power (for example, the steel industry).

What was suggested for capital formation can be extended to labor's contribution to the growth process. Management of these larger firms becomes routine and uninspired because of technocrats whose imaginations are dulled by the lack of competition. Down through the ranks, the jobs are made routine and uninteresting while the individuals in them wonder about their contribution to the firm; the decision-making process is far removed and impersonal, and individuals make no effort to improve the performance of their tasks, as Adam Smith suggested would be the case when division of labor became widespread.

Organized labor also has become comfortable, losing its drive and becoming less productive because of its complacency and resentment, since labor is demeaned in the age of the highly trained and skilled specialists. A labor force that feels detached from the productive effort is hardly conducive to economic growth, nor are the trends toward greater absenteeism, sabotage, loss of pride in work, and similar attitudinal changes. Many have written on the dehumanizing work performed in many productive processes, and large corporations with their extensive techniques are merely pushing forward the general trend of reducing work to monotonous and routine operations.

This latter development leads to the final element in the growth process to be included here: technological change. Organized labor could react to changes in technology that reduce the number of jobs or result in the dehumanizing process. Labor could attempt to forestall the introduction of labor-saving capital goods and has done so in the past. The attempt, however, is likely to prove only a holding or stalling action, and eventually the new equipment is installed. Meanwhile, however, economic growth is also hampered by such actions.

The reduction of work to boring and routine tasks has not received much attention from leaders in the labor movement. Social philosophers have noted the apparent discontent of workers as registered in absenteeism, sabotage, and the like. Often, too, the demand for higher wages is symptomatic of frustration and loss of pride and dignity in one's occupation. No elaboration is required to note that these actions do not contribute toward the necessary conditions for economic growth.

The effect of market structure on technological change is a matter of considerable controversy. The question is whether large firms, with their available funds and research departments, really account for major technological advances or whether the smaller, more dynamic firms do.[17] Galbraith in *American Capitalism* claimed that the costs of research were such that only larger firms could afford it and would have the resources to utilize the technological advances, once these were made. This conclusion is questionable, and evidence does not suggest it to be a realistic outcome of the institutionalizing of research. Large firms, in fact, may get bogged down in the bureaucracy of research departments, where only safe or conservative research is permitted to be undertaken.

The importance of the issue is seen in the increase in the federal budget for research and development expenditures. The federal government already spends nearly $18 billion on R & D, but most of these activities are defense-related and not directed toward achieving greater economic growth. However, the impact on

[17] For a discussion of this topic, see F. M. Scherer, *Industrial Market Structures and Economic Performance* (Chicago: Rand McNally, 1970), ch. 15.

technological change of governmental activities is understated by simply referring to dollar expenditures. The amount of economic activity directed toward national defense also means that many scientists are engaged in developing defense and space technology. In these areas technological advance increases rapidly, making the obsolescence of weapons, and so on, a continuous problem. But the brains used for these purposes are obviously not being exploited for research into industrial techniques and innovations that might improve the growth potential or solve the problems plaguing the advanced economies: housing, health care, transportation, pollution control, and so on. Indeed, scientists have specialized in areas required by defense and space research, so that any slowdown in these areas results in unemployment among these specialists. The concentration and specialization of talent has had some far-reaching consequences on many facets of economic development and growth, but no measure will ever be capable of gauging the extent of them. This is still another example of the problems that result from the economy devoting an enormous amount of its resources to war and defense; to reverse the direction of the economy can cause serious problems, for the system cannot easily rebound from these long-lived distortions. The economy cannot easily adjust to meet changing economic conditions—either in the short run or the long run.

UNDERDEVELOPED ECONOMIES

The standard growth models must be greatly modified if they are to be made applicable to underdeveloped economies. Otherwise, they offer little in the way of policy advice that can be used by an economy struggling to develop. In fact, it may be preferable to build the growth models to meet the special circumstances of particular countries than to rely upon a few general models.

Nations differ too much in their natural resources, cultures, political systems, traditions, and so on, to permit ready-made models of economic development. Models developed for advanced economies assume many of these factors away or consider them of secondary importance. Yet economic factors may play a secondary role in these countries and be subordinate to political and social considerations. It is easy to grasp how political instability may hinder economic growth, but not so apparent is the way in which cultural attitudes may affect development. In some societies success, particularly business success, is not a worthy achievement nor is the taking of risk for profit deemed acceptable. Socially acceptable behavior may prohibit growth by limiting the kinds of activity that merit approval, and these activities may be governed more by tradition than by a desire to amass more material wealth.

Growth models that fail to consider noneconomic factors in the society may have only limited use for most of the underdeveloped world. It should be clear that taking a few variables of the growth process and superimposing them on a different culture with different institutions in the hopes of understanding economic development is likely to prove little more than an academic exercise. Moreover, these models may not even be a worthwhile place to begin the analysis of economic development: for most underdeveloped regions, a truly interdisciplinary approach is required, and the best starting point may well be in noneconomic fields.[18]

[18] For a more extensive treatment of the applicability of the preceding growth models to underdeveloped economies, see K. K. Kurihara, *The Keynesian Theory of Economic Development* (New York: Columbia University Press, 1959). For some examples of noneconomic factors inhibiting economic development, see Margaret Mead (ed.), *Cultural Patterns and Technical Change* (New York: UNESCO and New American Library, 1955).

Some Selected Problems in Economic Growth

THE GROWTH VERSUS NO GROWTH CONTROVERSY

As we have seen, the desire for, and justification of, economic growth has a rather interesting intellectual history. Early economic thinkers saw the need for growth and also the possible problems once the economy had developed; if they favored growth, it was mainly because the day of reckoning was always far off. John Stuart Mill saw mainly the problems as the economy had already "taken off" into sustained growth. As development proceeded, the long-run problems gave way to short-run cyclical concerns of the first half of the twentieth century. Following World War II, economic growth again became a major concern, but this time the emphasis was somewhat shorter in duration, and soon doubts about the desirability of economic growth were being heard. Now the ambiguities of economic growth were being made explicit, and finally, growth was openly questioned, not as an intellectual concern but as a policy matter. For the first time a genuine discussion of the problems of economic growth was extended to many areas of the society, and the controversy over growth versus no growth commanded the attention of scientists, laymen, politicians, and economists alike. The arguments are practical ones, as we will see, and not steeped in philosophy, but Mill probably would have enjoyed participating in the discussion.

Advocates of the no growth policy do not rely particularly on philosophical arguments to present their case. Value systems and their origins are not among the foremost concerns of those who would limit growth. Environmental and ecological concerns are responsible for the questioning of the need for further economic growth. In the production of more and more goods, natural resources are being used up at an alarming rate, and sources of energy are being strained by the production of nonessential goods and services demanded by the affluent economies. The planet is being despoiled by pollution of the air and waters as man burns up his energy supplies in the quest for more and more goods. These concerns are well known now, and the problems of production are clear for all to contemplate. The forecasts of scientists, both reasoned and hysterical, have made most people aware of the issues at stake, even if they have failed to communicate the necessity for immediate action.

Meanwhile, the less developed economies continue to send their resources to the advanced economies, thereby assuring themselves of continued growth problems while permitting the already advanced economies to indulge themselves in nonessential production. The gap between the haves and the have-nots appears to widen and poses a continual threat of world unrest born out of frustration and resentment.

Concurrently with environmental and ecological concerns population problems are also debated. Limiting the growth of population is one of the goals of those who see the planet threatened by the environmental damage brought about by the need to produce more for more people. The population pressures are worldwide, but those living in advanced economies have a special obligation, since they are using up most of the natural resources.

The arguments are stated in terms of survival, for the present trends cannot continue much longer without endangering man as a species. The issues are indeed grave, and although much discussion has ensued, the need for action has never been taken completely seriously. Perhaps the failure to understand the value systems is partly responsible for the apathy. For intellectual concern is easily generated, but no one knows how to channel this concern into action. How do we persuade people to reject their old values and be receptive to new ones; how do we convince the affluent to give up the gadgets, from which they derive individual and immediate gratification, to consume goods more in the public interest? It is clear that all the objective information that has been supplied concerning the scarcity of resources, the environmental crisis, and so on, has not affected individuals in their daily lives, and only a reversal of values could be effective if these problems are to be solved or even dealt with.

Of course, these forecasts elicited reactions from all sides and from all elements in the society. Often admitting the existence of these problems, critics questioned their seriousness and accused the environmentalists of hysteria. Naturally, the arguments focus on data and forecasts, and conflicting information results mainly in confusion. The debates did, however, take the discussion away from the philosophical issues and permit everyone to postpone whatever consideration he might have given to the immediate problems. The debate continues, but the sense of urgency is gone.

Some of the critics of the survival thesis look to changes in technology to bail the world out of its environmental and ecological troubles. Technological change has served us well in the past, they say, and there is no need to question man's ingenuity in the future. Hysteria does not help, innovations do, and given the need, solutions will follow. There is still time, and now that the problems are generally recognized, creative minds in science can be expected to rise to the challenge. The faith in technology is still strong enough to overcome emotional responses, confusion, and fear.

It is not within the scope of this book to delve into a critical analysis of these positions and to evaluate the evidence presented. Indeed, economists need not be convinced of the scarcity of resources and concern for the rational use of them.

However, faith in technology and doubt about the urgency of the concerns or their seriousness are not the only points raised by those who object to the prognoses of the environmentalists. In many ways, the additional issues they raise pose more dilemmas than those revealed by the environmentalists and bring the matter closer to more economic concerns: how much growth is enough, and who is to decide when and how to limit it?

WHO BENEFITS FROM GROWTH?

Ultimately, the costs of economic growth must be weighed against the benefits. Therefore, before any limitation of growth can be considered, it is imperative that some attention be given to the effects of growth upon the society and, indeed, the world.

It is not surprising to find that the pleas to curtail economic growth come from the well-educated and more affluent members of the society. The standard of living for these people is already quite high, so that limiting the additional production of goods and services involves no sacrifice. Their material wealth is quite extensive and includes all of the gadgets that the advanced economy can produce. Naturally, there are many concerned people who do not fit this description, but nevertheless, they have the means to acquire these goods whenever they desire. At least they have an option, a choice among living standards.

The poor do not have any options, and few among them wish to remain poor; given a choice, most would prefer a higher living standard. The notion of poverty being ennobling is, not surprisingly, an observation made by those who are not poor. Most probably, the poor wish to consume the same array of products that is available to the other members of society. Given the means, they too would consume the electric can opener and the stereo components. Why not? Their tastes are formed by the same sources as are those of the affluent—television, magazines, newspapers, and so on. The poor are made quite aware of the number and variety of goods available to others. Thus, unsatisfied wants, created by the affluent, mount up, and the discontent and frustration mount along with them. In the summer riots of the 1960s the stores looted first were appliance stores, where the modern gadgets are located—TV sets, radios, musical instruments, and so on—the things the poor were taught to want but to which they were denied access.

To limit growth, then, may involve asking the poor to remain relatively poor forever. Limiting production not only curtails the supply of goods but precludes the possibility of falling prices as output expands and markets become saturated. Why should the distribution of wealth remain frozen? Does not economic growth provide the possibility of upward mobility?

How about job creation—does not economic growth provide for a growing number of jobs? If not more jobs, does not growth permit more social programs and welfare schemes to become acceptable out of the society's growing affluence?

The answers to these questions are by no means self-evident. Perhaps the jobs created cannot be filled by the poor and unskilled but only by the highly trained. The unskilled jobs may well be automated out of existence. If so, then economic growth cannot be justified on job-creating grounds unless extensive training programs are inaugurated and increasing amounts spent on education. Otherwise, upward mobility will be merely a slogan.

As for growth channeling more funds into social programs, that is also open to serious question. There is still strong resistance to welfare plans, health and housing schemes, family assistance plans, and so on. The humanitarian impulse is not enlarged by economic growth even if the economy becomes more able to meet the demands of the less advantaged.

In brief, it is not at all clear that the poor benefit from economic growth, but it is equally possible that limiting economic growth will preclude their participation in the benefits from further growth. On balance, it would appear that the poor would object to limiting economic growth, with some justification, unless they can be assured of a greater share of the products from the existing productive capacity.

The same questions occur when limitations on growth are proposed to the less developed economies. Again, it is arrogant of the affluent economies to propose a no growth policy for underdeveloped countries. People in these societies are living on the brink of subsistence now—why should they agree to close off the avenue by which their lot may be improved? The underdeveloped economies are not responsible for bringing the world to its present stage of environmental crisis—they have not consumed the bulk of the planet's resources nor polluted its air and waters. Indeed, they have supplied the resources to advanced economies, which have squandered them. How can they be asked to sacrifice more—have they not been exploited enough?

THE DISTRIBUTION OF INCOME AND WEALTH

The foregoing problems can ultimately be traced to the great inequalities of wealth and income that exist within society and among economies. The facts are obvious, but their importance for the growth versus no growth controversy is not.

If economic growth is limited, the productive capacity of the economy is limited, which means the size of the national income pie is *fixed*. How will the shares of a *fixed* national output be distributed? There must ensue a squabble over how to divide up the given output. It is no longer a question of how to share in the benefits of economic growth, nor is it possible to mollify the poor by holding out the hope of future gains. Nor will it be possible to limit inflation by a growing output. All kinds of pressures will be placed on the economic system by a fixed output.

However, with output fixed, we might learn what kind of people we are. For with output fixed, it will no longer be possible to ignore the unequal distribution of income and wealth. The nation's attention will be directed at how past gains were shared by the society, and we will be forced to observe the inequalities that currently exist and have existed for some time. The contest between the haves and the have-nots will make us face the situation directly, and the outcome would reveal the moral fiber of the society. These struggles and possible political and social upheavals would extend beyond any one economic society to encompass all of the world communities. It is not clear that the advocates of a no growth policy have recognized the consequences of their proposal. If further growth means more irrational production but less well-being, more gadgets but less satisfaction, more income but fewer jobs, more goods but less of a world to enjoy them in, and more for some but less for others, then any attempt to limit growth will be welcomed by many and fought by just as many, and in the end, a revolution of some sort—of ideas, institutions, economic and political systems—may be inevitable.

Appendix A
Income Determination Models Including Induced Investment

This appendix presents the income determination models with induced investment. The models are not explained at length, and it is hoped that the reader can supply his own explanation. The presentation of the models follows the procedure used throughout, so that a minimum of effort should be required to comprehend them.

Model 1. Focus on Induced Investment

(A.1) $$Y = C + I + G$$
(A.2) $$C = C_a + c(Y - T)$$
(A.3) $$I = I_a + dY$$
(A.4) $$G = \overline{G}_a$$
(A.5) $$T = \overline{T}_a.$$

Substituting (A.2), (A.3), and (A.4) into (A.1) gives the equilibrium level of income:

(A.6) $$Y = \frac{1}{1 - c - d}(C_a - cT + I_a + G_a).$$

This model is substantially like that given in the text with government added. Again, we have the supermultiplier,

$$\frac{1}{1 - c - d} > \frac{1}{1 - c}.$$

Model 2. Induced Investment plus Transfer Payments and the Foreign Trade Sector

(A.7) $$Y = C + I + G + (X - M)$$
(A.8) $$C = C_a + c(Y - T + R)$$
(A.9) $$I = I_a + dY$$

(A.10)	$G = \overline{G}$
(A.11)	$T = \overline{T}$
(A.12)	$R = \overline{R}$
(A.13)	$X = \overline{X}$
(A.14)	$M = M_a + mY.$

Substituting (A.8) through (A.14) into (A.7) to obtain the equilibrium level of income gives

$$(A.15) \quad Y = \frac{1}{1 - c - d + m}(C_a - cT + cR + I_a + G + X - M_a).$$

The supermultiplier is reduced now that we have included induced imports, an additional spending leakage. Now as income rises, imports increase also, and less is spent on domestic production.

Model 3. Induced Investment with Income Taxes Added

(A.16)	$Y = C + I + G + (X - M)$
(A.17)	$C = C_a + c(Y - T_a - tY + R)$
(A.18)	$I = I_a + dY$
(A.19)	$G = \overline{G}$
(A.20)	$T = T_a + tY$
(A.21)	$R = \overline{R}$
(A.22)	$X = \overline{X}$
(A.23)	$M = M_a + mY.$

Substituting (A.17) through (A.23) into (A.16) to obtain the equilibrium level of incomes gives

$$(A.24)\ Y = \frac{1}{1 - c - d + m + ct}(C_a - cT_a + cR + I_a + G + X - M_a).$$

Again the multiplier is reduced as taxes increase with income, an additional leakage. The multiplier has become a complex expression and is no longer easily grasped or, more important, easily calculated from real world data; too many things change at once for ready calculation. The concept remains correct, but the magnitude of the multiplier is far less than the textbook or classroom examples.

Appendix B
The Interaction of the Multiplier and the Accelerator

In the course of examining the accelerator theory of investment, the instability made possible by investment spending was alluded to several times. The reader may be interested in the nature and causes of this instability and the limits of investment fluctuations.

Recall that any change in one of the components of aggregate demand produces a multiplier effect upon the level of income. The size of the multiplier is largely determined by the *MPC*. If income increases, induced investment occurs via the accelerator principle determined by the size of v, the capital-output *ratio*. The dynamic possibilities as these two relations interact are the sources of the instability mentioned. Consider what the process of interaction would be like. Suppose autonomous investment increased. This would lead to an increase in Y by some multiple; as Y increased, induced I would increase, further increasing Y, and as Y continued to rise, C would increase, further increasing Y and I, and so on. The interaction causes the system to feed on itself; whether or not the movement eventually stops or reaches a new equilibrium depends upon the values of c and v, but this is easier seen in model form.

The Multiplier-Accelerator Model[1]

$$\text{(B.1)} \qquad Y_t = C_t + I_t$$
$$\text{(B.2)} \qquad C_t = C_a + c(Y_{t-1})$$
$$\text{(B.3)} \qquad I_t = I_t + v(Y_{t-1} - Y_{t-2}).$$

---

[1] The original model of the multiplier-accelerator was given by P. A. Samuelson, "Interaction Between the Multiplier Analysis and the Principle of Acceleration," *Review of Economics and Statistics* 21 (May 1939): 75–78. In this original model consumption was used instead of Y in the accelerator expression, and the lags were different. The use of Y in the accelerator permits investment spending also to influence further investment spending.

This model is dynamic and requires time for the interaction to occur, and thus the subscript t is necessary, as in previous dynamic models. Consumption is made a function of last period's income, and investment is made a function of autonomous I plus the induced part, which is a function of the change in income of the previous period. The lag in consumption has already been discussed, while the lag in investment allows delays of all kinds—decision making, order to delivery, and so on. These are simple lags, which are more suggestive of reality than unlagged responses.

Substituting (B.2) and (B.3) into (B.1) for the level of income gives

(B.4) $$Y_t = C_a + cY_{t-1} + I_t + v(Y_{t-1} - Y_{t-2}).$$

The static solution to (B.4), which yields the equilibrium level of income, would be the usual

(B.5) $$Y = C_a + cY + I,$$

because by definition of an equilibrium, $Y_t = Y_{t-1} = Y_{t-2} = Y_{t-n}$, and therefore all the lags disappear and the accelerator becomes zero. Therefore, equation (B.4) shows the path of the disequilibrium system as it moves toward or away from the equilibrium level.

Whether or not the system moves to a new equilibrium or away from a possible equilibrium depends upon the values of c and v. Professor Samuelson worked out the various combinations of c and v and showed the paths the system would take with them. Figure B.1 shows the combinations of c and v, and Figure B.2 shows the resulting paths.

Combinations of c and v that lie in the regions A and B take the system to a new equilibrium; in A (combinations of c and low values of v) the system moves smoothly; in B (combinations of c with higher v's) the system converges to a new equilibrium but by a damped cyclical route with the cyclical amplitudes diminishing over time. As the combinations of c and v get larger, the system tends to explode,

FIGURE B.1
COMBINATIONS OF c AND v FOR DYNAMIC PATHS

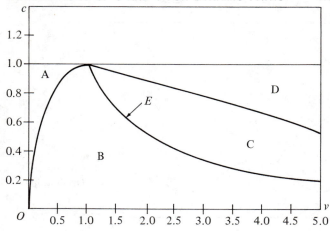

and the path is away from an equilibrium level of income. In C the path is cyclical, with the amplitudes increasing; in D the explosion is more direct. In the E region the values along the line E in Figure B.1, the combinations of c and v would lead to continuous cyclical oscillations of constant amplitude (a sine curve), and the equilibrium level of income is never reached.

FIGURE B.2
DYNAMIC PATHS OF THE SYSTEM

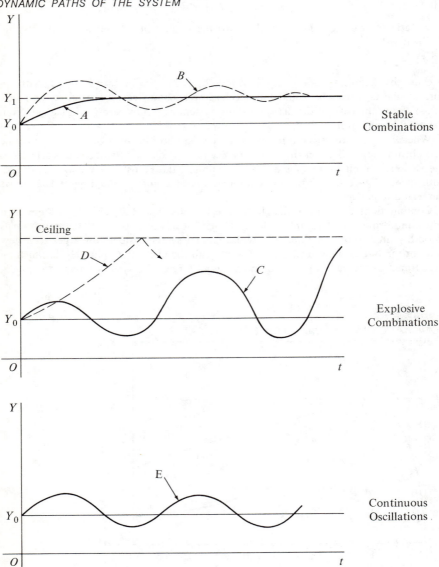

The model can be criticized along the same lines as the accelerator theory was in chapter 9, since it carries over all the assumptions made there. The same can be said of the multiplier part, which is here adapted without qualifications. The model does bring out, however, the instability of investment and presents a prime component in the explanation of the business cycle.

The model of J. R. Hicks, which uses this analysis, is probably the most widely known.[2] Without entering into a discussion of his model, we can use some of his ideas to reexamine the explosive cases shown by regions C and D. Obviously, an economy cannot continue to experience a rising income and output or a falling income and output. There must be a "ceiling" and a "floor."

The ceiling is given by the full employment of resources, beyond which it is impossible for real output to increase further. Once the ceiling is approached, the decline in the *rate of change* of output will turn the economy around. The floor is caused by the fact that gross investment cannot fall below zero (while positive I_a continues), and eventually replacement investment will provide the impetus for income growth. Thus, there are limits to the cycle of income and output caused by these boundaries.

[2] J. R. Hicks, *A Contribution to the Theory of the Trade Cycle* (Oxford: Oxford University Press, 1940).

Appendix C

The measurement of the velocity of money is a very complicated matter, and a thorough discussion of the problem is better left to other sources. However, some empirical evidence is necessary to illustrate the problem of the changing velocity of money as it affects monetary policy. In this appendix one can get some idea of the magnitude of the change and how it changes over time and over the course of the business cycle.[1]

For our purposes, the velocity of money is defined with reference to income and is computed from

$$V_y = \frac{\text{GNP}}{\text{Private Money Supply}}.$$

FIGURE C.1

INCOME AND TRANSACTIONS VELOCITY, 1919–1968

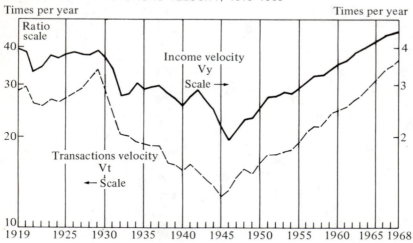

Source: Garvy and Blyn, p. 48. Based on data from the Board of Governors of the Federal Reserve System; United States Department of Commerce; and E. Oliver and A. J. Schwartz, *Currency Held by the Public, the Banks, and the Treasury Monthly, December 1917–December 1944,* Technical Paper No. 4 (National Bureau of Economic Research, 1947).

[1] The discussion of the velocity of money in this appendix and the table and figure are adapted in whole or in part from George Garvy and Martin R. Blyn, *The Velocity of Money* (New York: Federal Reserve Bank of New York, 1969).

Private money supply excludes Treasury cash. Figure C.1 shows how income velocity has varied over the past fifty years. Note also the rising trend in the post-war era. Several other measures of velocity (with different definitions) also exhibit the same tendencies.[2] The transaction velocity of money, shown in Figure C.1, is one of these, but transaction measures include many duplications.

Table C.1 shows how income velocity changes with respect to the business cycle. The determination of cycle peaks and troughs is made by the National Bureau of Economic Research in its business cycle studies.

[2] Ibid., p. 51. The interested student should consult this work to gain an appreciation of this entire subject.

TABLE C.1
CYCLICAL CHANGES IN GROSS NATIONAL PRODUCT, MONEY SUPPLY, AND INCOME VELOCITY, 1946–1968

Percentage Changes Between Troughs and Peaks

Cyclical Phase	GNP (1)	GNP Adjusted* (2)	Money Supply† (3)	Money Supply‡ (4)	Income Velocity (Y_1) (5)	Income Velocity (Y_2) (6)
1946 I –1948 IV (expansion)§	+ 34	+ 40	+ 6	+ 6	+ 26	+ 32
1948 IV–1949 IV (contraction)	− 3	− 4	− 1	0	− 3	− 3
1949 IV–1953 II (expansion)	+ 44	+ 32	+ 16	+ 15	+ 24	+ 14
1953 II –1954 III (contraction)	− 1	+ 3	+ 2	+ 3	− 2	+ 1
1954 III–1957 III (expansion)	+ 22	+ 24	+ 5	+ 4	+ 17	+ 19
1957 III–1958 II (contraction)	− 2	− 3	0	+ 1	− 2	− 3
1958 II –1960 II (expansion)	+ 15	+ 17	+ 2	+ 2	+ 13	+ 15
1960 II –1961 I (contraction)	0	− 1	+ 1	0	− 1	+ 2
1961 I –1968 IV (continuing expansion)	+ 76	+ 75	+ 35	+ 35	+ 30	+ 29
Entire Period, 1946 I–1968 IV	**+ 352**	**+ 351**	**+ 83**	**+ 83**	**+ 149**	**+ 147**

Source: Garvy and Blyn, p. 61.

Cyclical phases shown between peaks and troughs, . . . are based on seasonally adjusted series except for column (4).

* GNP minus federal government purchases of goods and services. Because of lack of monthly GNP figures, analysis on a monthly basis is not feasible.

† Daily average series of private demand deposits plus currency.

‡ Column (3) plus United States government demand deposits (not seasonally adjusted).

§ Instead of the 1945-IV trough, for which GNP data are not available, the expansion is measured from the first quarter of 1946. Money supply for 1946-I is estimated from the end-of-month rather than from the daily averages series.

As is evident from the table, the income velocity varies with the business cycle, rising in expansionary periods and falling during contractionary periods. Also, changes in income velocity are much greater during expansions than during contractions. Income velocity has increased from +13 per cent to +30 per cent, while falling by a few percentage points during contractions.

Note also the inclusion of a different definition of money and the resulting different measure of income velocity (Y_2). The same conclusions hold using these definitions. Over the entire period GNP increased by over 350 per cent and the income velocity increased by almost 150 per cent. The assumption of a stable velocity is suspect at best, and at worst it becomes untenable.

Additional References

Introduction

Robbins, Lionel. *An Essay on the Nature and Significance of Economic Science.* London: Macmillan and Co., 1952.

Chapter 1

The official source for national income data is U.S. Department of Commerce, Bureau of Economic Analysis, Social and Economic Statistics Administration. Specific sources are as follows:

1. The national income data appear monthly in the *Survey of Current Business;* the July issue of the *Survey* contains the official accounts and detailed extensions.
2. For definitions, concepts, problems, see *National Income: A Supplement to the Survey of Current Business, 1954; and U.S. Income and Output: A Supplement to the Survey of Current Business, 1958.*
3. For more recent changes of concepts, see *Survey of Current Business,* August 1965, and for data revisions, *The National Income and Product Accounts, 1929–1965, Statistical Tables* (1966).

Chapter 3

Allen, R. G. D. *Mathematical Analysis for Economists.* London: Macmillan and Co., reprinted 1960.
Samuelson, Paul A. *Foundations of Economic Analysis.* Cambridge: Harvard University Press, 1961.

Chapter 4

Goodwin, Richard M. "The Multiplier." In *The New Economics,* ed. S. E. Harris. New York: Knopf, 1947, pp. 482–499.
Haberler, Gottfried. "Mr. Keynes' Theory of the 'Multiplier': A Methodological Criticism." In *Readings in Business Cycle Theory.* Homewood, Ill.: Richard D. Irwin, 1951.
Hansen, Alvin H. *A Guide to Keynes.* New York: McGraw-Hill, 1953.

Chapter 5

Lerner, Abba P. *The Economics of Control*. New York: Macmillan, 1944.

Smithies, Arthur, and J. Keith Butlers (eds.). *Readings in Fiscal Policy*. Homewood, Ill.: Richard D. Irwin, 1955.

Chapter 6

Ellis, Howard S., and Lloyd A. Metzler. *Readings in the Theory of International Trade*. Philadelphia: Blakiston, 1950.

Kindleberger, Charles P. *International Economics*. 4th ed. Homewood, Ill.: Richard D. Irwin, 1968.

Chapter 7

Bronfenbrenner, Martin, and Franklyn D. Holzman. "Survey of Inflation Theory." *American Economic Review* 53 (September 1963): 593–661.

Council of Economic Advisors. "The Employment Act: Twenty Years of Policy Experience." In *Economic Report of the President* (1966), pp. 170–186.

Hansen, Alvin H. *Economic Issues of the 1960's*. New York: McGraw-Hill, 1960.

Mansfield, Edwin. *The Economics of Technical Change*. New York: W. W. Norton, 1968.

Chapter 8

Evans, Michael K. *Macroeconomic Activity, Theory, Forecasting, and Control*. New York: Harper & Row, 1969.

Federal Reserve Bank of Boston. *Consumer Spending and Monetary Policy: The Linkages*. Conference Series No. 5. June 1971.

Katona, George. *The Powerful Consumer*. New York: McGraw-Hill, 1960.

——. *Psychological Analysis of Economic Behavior*. New York: McGraw-Hill, 1951.

—— and Eva Mueller. *Consumer Response to Income Increases*. Washington, D.C.: Brookings Institution, 1968.

Veblen, Thorsten. *The Theory of the Leisure Class*. Modern Library ed. New York: Random House, 1934.

Chapter 9

Bowman, Mary Jean (ed.). *Expectations, Uncertainty and Business Behavior*. New York: Social Science Research Council, 1958.

Duesenberry, James S. *Business Cycles and Economic Growth*. New York: McGraw-Hill, 1958.

Fisher, Irving. *The Theory of Interest*. New York: Macmillan, 1930.

Hicks, J. R. *A Contribution to the Theory of the Trade Cycle*. Oxford: Oxford University Press, 1940.

Samuelson, Paul A. "Interaction Between the Multiplier Analysis and the Principle of Acceleration." *Review of Economics and Statistics* 21 (May 1939): 75–78.

Chapter 10

Bronfenbrenner, Martin. "Some Fundamentals in Liquidity Theory." *Quarterly Journal of Economics* 59 (May 1945): 405–426.

Cochrane, James L. *Macroeconomics Before Keynes.* Glenview, Illinois: Scott, Foresman, 1970.

Friedman, Milton. *Studies in the Quantity Theory of Money.* Chicago: University of Chicago Press, 1956.

Lekachman, Robert. *A History of Economic Ideas.* New York: Harper, 1959.

Modigliani, Franco. "Liquidity Preference and the Theory of Interest and Money," *Econometrica* 12 (January 1944): 45–88.

Ritter, Lawrence S. "The Role of Money in Keynesian Theory." In *Banking and Monetary Studies,* ed. Dean Carson. Homewood, Ill.: Richard D. Irwin, 1963, pp. 134–150.

Chapter 11

Klein, Lawrence R. *The Keynesian Revolution.* 2d ed. New York: Macmillan, 1966.

Tobin, James. "Money Wage Rates and Employment." In *The New Economics,* ed. S. E. Harris. New York: Knopf, pp. 572–587.

Chapter 12

Ball, R. J. *Inflation and the Theory of Money.* Chicago: Aldine Publishing Co., 1965.

Dernburg, Thomas F., and Duncan M. McDougall. *Macroeconomics.* New York: McGraw-Hill, 1959.

Kuh, Edwin. "A Productivity Theory of Wage Levels—An Alternative to the Phillips Curve." *Review of Economic Studies* 34 (October 1967): 333–360.

Perry, George L. *Unemployment, Money Wages, and Inflation,* Cambridge, Mass.: M. I. T. Press, 1966.

Phelps, Edmund S. "Money-Wage Dynamics and Labor-Market Equilibrium." *Journal of Political Economy* 76 (July–August 1968): 678–711.

Sheahan, John. *The Wage-Price Guideposts.* Washington, D.C.: Brookings Institution, 1967.

Chapter 13

Domar, Evsey D. "The Burden of the Debt and the National Income." *American Economic Review* 34 (December 1944): 798–827.

Guttentag, Jack M. "The Short Cycle in Residential Construction." *American Economic Review* 51 (June 1961): 275–298.

Lutz, Friedrich A., and Lloyd W. Mints (eds.). *Readings in Monetary Theory.* Homewood, Ill.: Richard D. Irwin, 1951.

Ott, David J., and A. F. Ott. *Federal Budget Policy.* Rev. ed. Washington: Brookings Institution, 1969.

Smithies, Arthur, and J. Keith Butlers (eds.). *Readings in Fiscal Policy.* Homewood, Ill.: Richard D. Irwin, 1955.

Teigen, Ronald L. "The Effectiveness of Public Works as a Stabilization Device." In *Readings in Money, National Income, and Stabilization Policies,* ed. W. L. Smith and R. L. Teigen. Homewood, Ill.: Richard D. Irwin, 1965, pp. 302–308.

Chapter 14

Galbraith, J. K. *A Theory of Price Control.* Cambridge, Mass.: Harvard University Press, 1952.
Triffin, Robert. *Our International Monetary System.* New York: Random House, 1968.

DATA SOURCES

Survey of Current Business; Federal Reserve Bulletin; Economic Report of the President; and Federal Reserve Bank of St. Louis, *Monetary Trends, U.S. Financial Data,* and other statistical reports.

Chapter 15

Anderson, L., and G. Jordan. "Monetary and Fiscal Actions: A Test of Their Relative Importance in Economic Stabilization." Federal Reserve Bank of St. Louis, *Review* 50 (November 1968): 11–24.
————. "Monetary and Fiscal Actions: A Test of Their Relative Importance in Economic Stabilization—Reply." Federal Reserve Bank of St. Louis, *Review* 51 (April 1969): 12–16.
Kaldor, N. "The New Monetarism." *Lloyds Bank Review* 97 (July 1970): 1–18.
Tobin, James. "The Monetary Interpretation of History." *American Economic Review* 55 (June 1965): 464–485.
Ulmer, Melville J. *The Welfare State.* Boston: Houghton Mifflin, 1969.

Chapter 16

Berle, Adolf A., and Gardiner C. Means. *The Modern Corporation and Private Property.* Rev. ed. New York: Harcourt, Brace and World, 1967.
Heilbroner, Robert L. (ed.). *Economic Means and Social Ends.* Englewood Cliffs, N.J.: Prentice-Hall, 1969.
Myrdal, Gunnar. *Challenge to Affluence.* New York: Vintage Books, 1962.
Robinson, Joan. *Economics: An Awkward Corner.* New York: Pantheon Books, 1967.
Scherer, F. M. *Industrial Market Structure and Economic Performance.* Chicago: Rand McNally, 1970.
Shubik, Martin. "A Curmudgeon's Guide to Microeconomics." *Journal of Economic Literature* 8 (June 1970): 405–434.

Chapter 17

Dahl, Robert A., and Charles E. Lindblom. *Politics, Economics and Welfare.* New York: Harper & Row, 1953.
Kindleberger, Charles P. *American Business Abroad: Six Lectures on Direct Investment.* New Haven: Yale University Press, 1969.

Robinson, Joan. *Economic Philosophy*. Chicago: Aldine Publishing Co., 1962.
Tobin, James. "Inflation and Unemployment." *American Economic Review* 62 (March 1972): 1–18.

Chapter 18

Fanon, Frantz. *The Wretched of the Earth*. New York: Grove Press, 1968.
Knorr, Klaus, and William J. Baumol (eds.). *What Price Economic Growth*. Englewood Cliffs, N.J.: Prentice-Hall, 1961.
Kuznetts, Simon. *Modern Economic Growth*. New Haven: Yale University Press, 1966.
Myrdal, Gunnar. *Rich Lands and Poor: The Road to World Prosperity*. New York: Harper, 1957.
————. *Asian Drama: An Inquiry into the Poverty of Nations*. New York: Twentieth Century Fund, 1968.
Phelps, Edmund S. "The Golden Rule of Accumulation." *American Economic Review* 51 (September 1961): 638–643.
———— (ed.). *The Goal of Economic Growth*. New York: W. W. Norton, 1962.
Shepard, Paul, and Daniel McKinley (eds.). *The Subversive Science*. Boston: Houghton Mifflin, 1969.

Index